Time Out New York

Penguin Books

PENGUIN BOOKS

Published by the Penguin Group
Penguin Books Ltd, 27 Wrights Lane, London W8 5TZ, England
Penguin Books USA Inc., 375 Hudson Street, New York, New York 10014, USA
Penguin Books Australia Ltd, Ringwood, Victoria, Australia
Penguin Books Canada Ltd, 10 Alcorn Avenue, Toronto, Ontario, Canada M4V 3B2
Penguin Books (NZ) Ltd, 182-190 Wairau Road, Auckland 10, New Zealand

Penguin Books Ltd, Registered Offices: Harmondsworth, Middlesex, England

First published 1990
Second edition 1992
Third edition 1994
Fourth edition 1996
Fifth edition 1997
Sixth edition 1998
Seventh edition 1999
Eighth edition 2000
10 9 8 7 6 5 4 3 2 1

Color reprographics by Intercontinental Graphics Inc., New York, New York, USA
Printed and bound by Cayfosa-Quebecor, Ctra. de Caldes, Km 3 08 130 Sta, Perpètua de Mogoda, Barcelona, Spain

---

The future is now New York is the self-proclaimed millennium capital of the world.

NYC
2000
NYC 200
WAY

Edited and designed by
Time Out New York Guides
627 Broadway, seventh floor
New York, NY 10012
Tel: 212-539-4444
Fax: 212-253-1174
E-mail: guides@timeoutny.com,
newyorkguide@timeout.com

Editor Shawn Dahl
Art Director Amy Struck
Associate Editor Lesa Griffith **Managing Editor** Aimee Szparaga
Guides Assistant Christopher Bollen
Copy Editors Ian Landau; Tom Gogola, Jay Hodges, Robert Legault, Chiedo Nkwocha
Research Becki Heller, Adele Kudish
Index Camille Cauti

With
Time Out New York
E-mail: letters@timeoutny.com
Internet: www.timeoutny.com

President/Editor-in-Chief Cyndi Stivers
Editor Joe Angio **Design Director** Ron de la Peña
Production Director Sarah Day **Technology Director** Shambo Pfaff
Production Manager Carl Kelsch **Digital Operator** Ryan Dunlavey

Publisher Alison Tocci **Advertising Director** Anne Perton
Senior Advertising Account Managers Dan Kenefick, Jim Lally, Tony Monteleone
Advertising Account Managers Tamyra d'Ippolito, Julie Fisher, Frances Grant, Ridwana Lloyd-Bey
North American Guides Advertising Director Liz Howell
Advertising Production Manager Tom Oesau **Advertising Designers** Michael DeSimone, Kurt Purdy
Assistant to the Publisher Claudia Pedala

Marketing Director Marisa Guillen Fariña
North American Guides Publicity and Promotions Associate Lu Chekowsky

Financial Director Daniel P. Reilly

For
Time Out Guides Ltd
Universal House
251 Tottenham Court Road
London W1P 0AB
Tel: 44 (0)20 7813 3000
Fax: 44 (0)20 7813 6001
E-mail: guides@timeout.com
Internet: www.timeout.com

Editorial Director Peter Fiennes **Series Editors** Ruth Jarvis, Caroline Taverne **Art Director** John Oakey

Group Advertising Director Lesley Gill **Sales Director** Mark Phillips

Publisher Tony Elliott **Managing Director** Mike Hardwick **Financial Director** Kevin Ellis
Marketing Director Gillian Auld **General Manager** Nichola Coulthard **Production Manager** Mark Lamond

Chapters in this guide were written, researched or updated by:
History Benjamin Chertoff **Soar Subjects** Ian Landau **Architecture** Shawn Dahl **Tour New York** Christopher Bollen; *Your own kind* Katya Rogers, *Name cropping* Aimee Szparaga **Downtown** Lesa Griffith, Aimee Szparaga; *Walk like a musician* Damion Sammarco **Midtown** Christopher Bollen, Lesa Griffith; *Public spectacle* Katya Rogers **Uptown** Christopher Bollen, Lesa Griffith; *Movin' on up* Ian Landau **Outer Boroughs** Lesa Griffith; *To die for* Jem Aswad, *Gorillas in the midst* Julien Gorbach **Accommodations** Paula Szuchman **Bars** and **Restaurants** adapted from *Time Out New York Eating & Drinking 2000; Manhattan transfers* Adam Rapoport, *Learning to share* Salma Abdelnour **Shopping & Services** Kristina Richards (Fashion, Health & Beauty), Emily Stone (Objects of Desire); *Sex (shopping) in the city* William Van Meter, *Meat street manifesto* Emily Stone **New York by Season** Ian Landau **Art Galleries** Saul Anton **Books & Poetry** Christopher Bollen, Daphne Uviller **Cabaret & Comedy** Greg Emmanuel (Comedy), H. Scott Jolley (Cabaret) **Clubs** Adam Goldstone, Bruce Tantum **Film & TV** Lesa Griffith **Gay & Lesbian** Les Simpson **Kids' Stuff** Barbara Aria **Museums** Saul Anton (Art museums), Billie Cohen (Non-art museums); *Space is the place* Billie Cohen **Music** Smith Galtney (Pop), Susan Jackson (Classical), Gail O'Hara (Music editor), K. Leander Williams (Jazz), Mike Wolf (Rock); *From Jamaica with love* Margeaux Watson **Sports & Fitness** Lesa Griffith **Theater & Dance** Gia Kourlas (Dance), Jason Zinoman (Theater) **Trips Out of Town** Lesa Griffith **Directory** Christopher Bollen

Cover and inside photographs by Anna Kirtiklis
Additional photographs courtesy of Library of Congress, 5, 6, 12, 13, 15; New York Historical Society, 7, 14; William Henry Jackson/Library of Congress, 11; Ger Burgman, 16; Skidmore, Owings & Merrill/Pixel by Pixel, 19; David Heald/Guggenheim, 20, 287; Circle Line, 28; United States Post Office, 54; Christie's Images Ltd., 57; Wildlife Conservation Society/Dennis De Mello, 85; Queens Museum of Art, 86; Michael Moran, 87; Kay Wheeler, 88; Algonquin Hotel, 93; Artie's Delicatessen, 144; Katayone Adeli, 172; Joan Marcus–Marc Bryan-Brown/Disney, 215; NYC & Company–the New York Convention and Visitors Bureau, 218, 222; Amy Struck, 219; Guy Meyer Jr., 220; PaceWildenstein, 236; James Rudnick, 244; Mother, 251; Ryan Thomas/Twilo, 256; Toby Wales/BAM, 259; Virginia Sherwood/ABC, 261; Les Simpson, 268, 271; Brooklyn Botanic Garden, 275; Jason Green/New York Botanical Garden, 283; Alys Tomlinson, 297; Knitting Factory, 307; Don Perdue, 316; Nathaniel S. Butler, 323; Bob Coglianese, 324; Hermann and Clarchen Baus, 335; Richard Mitchell, 337; Paul Kolnik, 339; Lois Greenfield, 345; Ken Friedman, 348; Patti Courville, 353; Hunter Mountain, 355; John Hill/Tiger Hill Studios, 356.

Maps by J.S. Graphics, 17 Beadles Lane, Old Oxted, Surrey RH8 9JG, U.K.; maps on pages 407–411 reproduced by kind permission of the Metropolitan Transportation Authority.

Contents

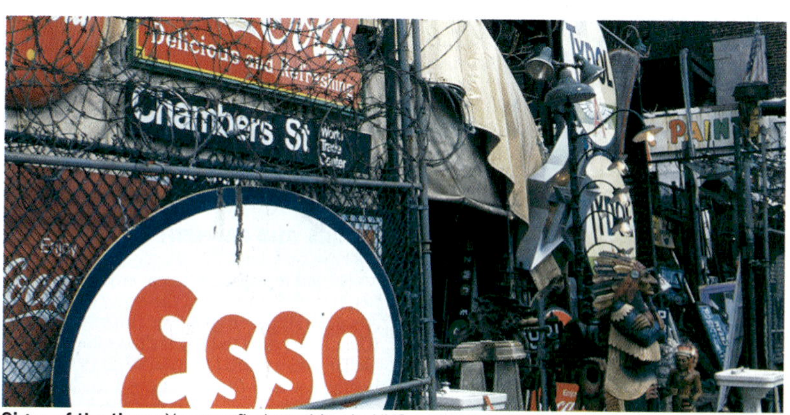

Signs of the times You can find anything in NYC—including vintage ads on Houston Street.

Introduction

New York City's lifeblood surges through the arteries and veins of its avenues and streets. Energy pumps continuously through Wall Street, Times Square, Williamsburg in Brooklyn, even the Fresh Kills landfill on Staten Island. Effort spent in one area is regenerated in another. Keeping up with the pulse can be exhilarating—and exhausting.

Chances are, you'll feel like you've gotten a good workout (mentally *and* physically) after spending some time in the city that never sleeps. Although the subways are great for covering distances, people tend to walk everywhere. You can traipse up and down Museum Mile, ducking into the area's art institutions for a quick look around; the next day, you might wander Soho's streets, loaded down with shopping bags. Or maybe you're hooked on nightlife: first, you'll check out an avant-garde dance performance and then head to a club to make your own moves. Well, the *Time Out New York Guide* will give you the full story on things to do like these (and, of course, many more).

We've done most of the legwork for you; the hard part will be fitting in everything you want to do in one visit. We think the view from the Empire State Building is amazing. But don't be mad at yourself if you don't get all the way to the 102nd floor—thousands of New Yorkers never make it, either, choosing instead to spend a free weekend afternoon wandering places like the Brooklyn Botanic Garden.

Our best advice: Go ahead, indulge yourself. Get your heart pounding for whatever it desires and have some fun in NYC 24-seven.—*Shawn Dahl, Editor*

ABOUT THE TIME OUT CITY GUIDES

The *Time Out New York Guide* is one of an expanding series of *Time Out* City Guides produced by the people behind London and New York's successful weekly listings magazines. Our guides are written and updated by resident experts who strive to provide all the most up-to-date information you'll need to explore the city, whether you're a local or first-time visitor.

This eighth edition of the *Time Out New York Guide* has been thoroughly updated by the staff of *Time Out New York* magazine. *TONY* has been "the obsessive guide to impulsive entertainment" for all inhabitants of the city (and a few passers-through) for five years. Our writers aim to provide you with inside tips for taking on the world's most exciting city—and winning. Some chapters have been rewritten from scratch; all have been thoroughly revised, and new feature boxes have been added. This edition includes, for the first time, street maps of Brooklyn and Queens to go with the complete street maps of Manhattan; a New York City subway map, covering all five boroughs, is also included.

► There is an online version of this guide, as well as weekly events listings for many other international cities, at **www.timeout.com.**
► The website for *Time Out New York,* the weekly listings magazine, is at **www.timeoutny.com.**

THE LOWDOWN ON THE LISTINGS

While navigating this guide and the city, there are a few facts you should know. Addresses, telephone numbers, transportation directions, opening times, admission prices and credit card information are all included in our listings. We've given up-to-date details on facilities, services and events, all checked and correct at press time. However, owners and managers can—and often do—change their policies. It's always best to call and check the when, where and how much.

Throughout the book, you'll find bold-faced items (sights or restaurants, for example) for which we give the detailed listings information within that chapter or in one that is cross-referenced. For your convenience, we've included cross-reference boxes throughout (they're outlined in red, like the one at left).

PRICES AND PAYMENT

We have noted whether places such as shops, hotels and restaurants accept credit cards or not, but have only listed the major cards: American Express (**AmEx**), Diners Club (**DC**), Discover (**Disc**), JCB Credit Cards (**JCB**), MasterCard (**MC**) and Visa (**V**). Some businesses will also accept other cards. Virtually all shops, restaurants and attractions will accept U.S.-dollar travelers'

View finder Catch a glimpse of Manhattan as you fly into the city—via helicopter, that is.

checks issued by a major financial institution (such as American Express).

The prices we've listed should be treated as guidelines, not gospel. Fluctuating exchange rates and inflation can cause prices—especially in stores and restaurants—to change overnight. While every effort has been made to ensure the accuracy of this guide, the publishers cannot accept responsibility for any errors it may contain. If you find things altered beyond recognition, ask why—and then write to let us know. Our goal is to furnish the most accurate information available, so we always want to know if you've been badly treated or overcharged.

TELEPHONE NUMBERS

All telephone numbers in this guide are written as dialed within the United States. Manhattan's area codes are 212 and 646; Brooklyn, Queens, the Bronx and Staten Island's are 718 and 347; generally (but not always), 917 is reserved for cellular phones and pagers. If you are calling a number from within the same area code, then dial the seven-digit phone number only. If the area codes differ, you must dial 1, then the area code and the seven-digit phone number (from abroad, leave off the 1). Phone numbers beginning with 800, 877 and 888 are free of charge when called from anywhere in the U.S. When numbers are listed as letters (e.g. 800-AIR-RIDE) for easy recall, dial the corresponding numbers on the telephone keypad.

ESSENTIAL INFORMATION

For all the practical information you might need for visiting the city—including visa and customs procedures, access for people with disabilities, emergency telephone numbers, a list of helpful websites and how to use the subway system—turn to the **Directory** chapter at the back of this guide. It starts on *page 359.*

THE LAY OF THE LAND

We've included cross streets in all of our addresses, so you can find your way more easily. And there's a series of fully-indexed **color street maps,** a map of the surrounding metropolitan area and subway and bus maps at the back of the guide, starting on *page 391.* The very last page is **Key Sights**—a quick list of those places you've heard about; the directions are given so you can quickly get started on your sightseeing.

LET US KNOW WHAT YOU THINK

We hope you enjoy the *Time Out New York Guide,* and we'd like to know what you think of it. We welcome tips on places that you believe we should include in future editions and appreciate your criticism of our choices. There's a reader's reply card at the back of this book. Or please e-mail us at newyorkguide@timeout.com.

A note about our advertisers

We would like to emphasize that no establishment has been included in this guide because it has advertised in any of our publications, and no payment of any kind has influenced any review. The opinions given in this book are those of *Time Out* writers and entirely independent.

TOWER HAS

Perspective

Feature box

Wrinkle-free Steel-frame construction allowed buildings like the 20-story Flatiron to rise to new heights.

History

Retrace the first wobbly steps of a city now known for its confident pace

THE PROSPECTORS

Before Manhattan ever lured wide-eyed visitors with awesome skyscrapers and street-corner spectacles—in fact, long before it was even called Manhattan—this lush, forested region offered the finest natural harbor on the East Coast. The island itself was well protected from the elements and strategically located along a vast river—in short, it was the greatest trading post Mother Nature ever created. New York became a natural destination for immigrants seeking their fortunes, and at every stage in the region's history, the buzzword was commerce.

The first starry-eyed European to get a glimpse of the island was not Christopher Columbus but Giovanni da Verrazano, a Florentine sailing under the French flag and searching for the fabled Northwest Passage to China. In 1524, he took refuge from a storm in what is now New York Harbor; later, he took a small boat into the Upper Bay, where he was greeted by the local Native Americans. Today, Verrazano is remembered by the graceful bridge that links Staten Island with Brooklyn and bears his name.

It would be 85 years before the next European arrived. Henry Hudson, who was employed by the Dutch East India Company, was also looking for the Northwest Passage. He sailed up the river later named for him as far as Fort Orange (today the state capital, Albany). Hudson's logbook relates that he encountered "friendly and polite people who had an abundance of provisions, skins, and furs of martens and foxes, and many other commodities, such as birds and fruit, even white and red grapes, and they traded amicably with the peoples."

LET'S MAKE A DEAL

In 1613, four years after Hudson's journey, a trading post—the beginning of a Dutch settlement—was established at Fort Orange. In 1621, Holland granted the Dutch West India

It's a stretch The Brooklyn Bridge (above) was the world's longest suspension bridge in 1883.

Company a long-term trade and governing monopoly over New Netherland (and elsewhere). Soon the first Dutch settlers, about 30 families, arrived in the area. By 1626, when the first director-general (or governor), Peter Minuit, took power, 300 Europeans lived on the tip of a certain 13-mile-long island called Manahatta.

In an exchange now regarded as the best real-estate bargain in human history, Minuit gave a Munsee Indian chief a few trinkets and blankets (which scholars have revalued from the famous $24 to a still bargain-basement $600) and got him to sign an incomprehensible document. Minuit then assumed the deal was sealed; the Dutch had bought themselves all of Manhattan Island. Of course, like all of the best real-estate deals, this one was a bit of a scam: The Native Americans had very different ideas about property and could not conceive of owning land, let alone in perpetuity.

It also turned out to be a shakedown. Once the Europeans had moved in, they wouldn't budge. The Dutch settlement tried to tax native hunters and keep them from owning firearms, and enforced harsh penalties for petty crimes. It was only a matter of time before a bloody war between the Dutch and the Native Americans broke out in the 1640s. It lasted two and a half years. Guess who won?

Europeans allowed little trace of New York's original inhabitants to remain, apart from various Munsee place names, such as Canarsie (grassy place), Rockaway (sandy place), Maspeth (bad water place) and Matinecock (at the lookout point).

PEG-LEG PETE

After the colonists massacred more than 100 Indians in 1643, the Dutch West India Company hired Peter Stuyvesant to keep the peace. Stuyvesant's right leg had been shattered by a cannonball—hence his nickname, Peg-Leg Pete. He ordered a defensive ditch and wall (today's Wall Street) to be built along the northern end of what by now was called New Amsterdam, and the muddy streets were paved with cobblestones. A commercial infrastructure was established (banks, brokers' offices, wharves), and chandlers and taverns soon lined the booming waterfront. Manhattan's capitalist culture was born.

And so was its first locally administered government. Stuyvesant founded a municipal assembly, and he encouraged the education of the colony's children. In his 17 years as governor, the settlement doubled in size. The town grew more cosmopolitan, expanding to include English, French, Portuguese and Scandinavian settlers, and the area's first African slaves. Both English and Dutch were spoken.

But old Peg-Leg was a little too authoritarian. His intolerance of Jewish refugees and Quaker leader John Bowne provoked scoldings from his bosses at the Dutch West India Company, who forced Stuyvesant to make the new settlement a haven for religious freedom.

THE BRITISH ARE COMING!

Perhaps the Dutch West India Company tried to expand its colony too quickly. By 1661, less than four decades after the Dutch had settled the place, New Amsterdam was nearly bankrupt. When four British warships sailed into the harbor one day in August 1664, the population abandoned the fortifications Stuyvesant had built and welcomed Captain Richard Nicolls and his crew. New Amsterdam was renamed after the British king's brother, the Duke of York.

By 1700, New York's population had reached about 20,000. The colony was a big moneymaker for the British, but it was hardly what you would call a stable concern. In 1683, to cut administrative costs, the British had tried to consolidate New York, New Jersey and New England into a single dominion. The colonies rebelled, and after 21 months of battle, ten men were hanged for treason. In the 1730s, John Peter Zenger's *New York Weekly Journal* provoked gasps by accusing British governor William Cosby's administration of corruption. Zenger's trial on libel charges resulted in a landmark decision: The newspaper publisher was acquitted because, as his lawyer argued, the truth cannot be libelous.

The Zenger verdict sowed the seeds for the First Amendment to the Constitution, which

I, Stuy Governor Peter "Peg-Leg Pete" Stuyvesant ruled with a strong arm.

established the principle of freedom of the press. This was just the beginning of trouble for the British.

REVOLUTION—AND THE BATTLE FOR NEW YORK

In British-run outposts in Virginia, Philadelphia and Boston, great thinkers such as Thomas Jefferson, Benjamin Franklin and John Adams spread the ideals of fair and democratic government. The merchants of New York, meanwhile, felt the pinch from their British bosses, who imposed more and higher taxes on their colonial possessions to pay off debts accumulated in colonial wars against France.

The colonies declared independence on July 4, 1776, but the British weren't about to give up New York—because of its economic importance and because of its strategic position on the Hudson River. That summer, British commander Lord Howe sailed 200 ships into New York Harbor and occupied the town. New Yorkers vented their fury by toppling a gilded equestrian statue of George III that stood on Bowling Green.

The war's first major battle took place in Brooklyn and in Long Island. It was a complete disaster for the Americans, led by George Washington, who retreated to New Jersey. (While preparing his army, Washington slept at what is now called the Morris-Jumel Mansion in Washington Heights; *see chapter* **Uptown**.) On September 11, 1776, Benjamin Franklin met Lord Howe in Staten Island's Billop Manor House (now known as the Conference House), but he refused Howe's offer to make all colonists full-fledged British subjects. "America cannot return to the domination of Great Britain," said Franklin, demanding independence.

Life in occupied New York was pretty grim. The town was teeming with British soldiers and loyalists fleeing the American army. Fires destroyed much of the city, and many inhabitants died of starvation. When the

The wonder years

A timeline of key events in New York history

1524 Giovanni da Verrazano is the first European to visit what is now Manhattan.
1609 Henry Hudson sails into New York Harbor.
1624 The Dutch found New Amsterdam.
1626 First governor Peter Minuit arrives and "buys" Manhattan from the Indians. New Amsterdam's population: 300.
1643 Peter Stuyvesant is made governor.
1661 The Dutch colony nearly goes bankrupt.
1662 Quaker John Bowne's struggle wins the people of New Amsterdam the right to religious freedom.
1664 The British invade. New Amsterdam is renamed New York.
1733 John Peter Zenger's *New York Weekly Journal* establishes the right to free speech.
1754 King's College (which will become Columbia University) is founded.
1776 The Declaration of Independence is adopted. The Revolutionary War rages; the British occupy New York.
1783 The defeated British army leaves New York.
1785–90 New York serves as the new nation's capital.
1811 The Commissioners' Plan lays out the grid system that determines the pattern of the city's future growth.
1812–14 America fights another war with Britain. New York is isolated from international trade.
1837 Financial panic ruins all but three city banks.
1843 Immigrants flood into the city.
1851 *The New York Times* is first published.
1857 Frederick Law Olmsted and Calvert Vaux lay out Central Park.
1859 Cooper Union, the first American school open to all—regardless of race, religion or gender—is established.
1860 Abraham Lincoln is elected president.
1861 The Civil War erupts.
1863 Conscription causes riots in New York.
1865 The Union wins, and slavery is abolished.
1870 The Metropolitan Museum of Art is founded.
1872 Organized labor strikes for an eight-hour workday.
1883 The Brooklyn Bridge is completed.
1886 The Statue of Liberty is unveiled.
1890 Photojournalist Jacob Riis publishes *How the Other Half Lives*, spurring new housing regulations.
1895 The New York Public Library is founded.
1898 New York City—comprising Manhattan, Brooklyn, Queens, Staten Island and the

Crown finally surrendered in 1783, bitter British forces in New York greased the city's flagpole in an attempt to make it harder for the revolutionaries to raise the banner of the new republic.

But the war was won. On December 4, Washington joined his officers for an emotional farewell dinner at Fraunces Tavern on Pearl Street (now the Fraunces Tavern Museum; *see chapter* **Museums**), where the general declared his retirement. That didn't last long: On April 23, 1789, in the Old Federal Hall (on the same site as the present one, on Wall Street), he took the oath of office as the first president of the United States of America, and New York became the capital city.

THE FIRST U.S. CAPITAL

Before the revolution, Alexander Hamilton, a young immigrant from the Caribbean island of Nevis, was studying at King's College (now Columbia University) and hobnobbing with colonial high society. Hamilton had married into a powerful merchant family after serving under Washington in the war. In 1784, he took advantage of New York's newfound status as the nation's capital to push for the founding of the nation's first bank—much to the horror of Thomas Jefferson, who envisioned a simple, agrarian economy.

Meanwhile, Jefferson insisted that the nation's capital be moved to a new city built on mosquito-infested swampland next to his beloved Virginia. But Hamilton, who had become the first U.S. Treasury Secretary, had already secured New York's control over the new nation's money. The city's business boomed, merchants grew richer, and the port prospered. With its financial clout secured, New York no longer needed to be the political capital.

CROWD CONTROL

By 1800, more than 60,000 people lived in what is now lower Manhattan. Rents were high, and

Bronx—is incorporated, creating the world's second-largest city.
1902 The world's first skyscraper—the Fuller Building (later known as the Flatiron)—is built.
1907 Metered taxicabs are introduced.
1911 The Triangle Shirtwaist factory fire sparks the introduction of workplace-safety regulations.
1917 America enters WWI.
1920 Women win the right to vote. Prohibition is enacted; speakeasies open throughout the city.
1929 The Wall Street stock-market crash on October 29 plunges the nation into the Great Depression. The Museum of Modern Art opens nine days after the crash.
1930s Franklin D. Roosevelt's New Deal funds massive public-works projects. The Empire State Building, the Chrysler Building and Rockefeller Center are built.
1939 Corona Park, Queens, hosts the World's Fair.
1941 America enters WWII.
1946 The United Nations is established in New York.
1947 Brooklyn Dodger Jackie Robinson breaks the color barrier in major league baseball.
1959 The Guggenheim Museum opens.
1962 Lincoln Center opens.
1965 The entire city endures a 25-hour power blackout.
1968 A student sit-in shuts down Columbia University.
1970 The World Trade Center is completed.
1975 The city almost goes bankrupt.
1977 Another citywide blackout. More than 3,000 people are arrested for looting, rioting and arson.
1978 Mayor Ed Koch presides over an economic turnaround.
1987 Another Wall Street crash.
1990 David Dinkins is elected as the city's first black mayor.
1991 The city's budget deficit hits a record high.
1993 Terrorists bomb the World Trade Center. Rudolph Giuliani is elected as the city's first Republican mayor in 28 years.
1997 A new wave of immigration peaks. The Dow Jones average tops 7,000. The murder rate hits a 30-year low. Disney arrives on 42nd Street.
1998 New York City falls to 37th on the list of the most dangerous urban centers in America.
1999 The Dow hits 10,000. The city budget surplus hits a record high. The city mourns the death of John F. Kennedy Jr. Unarmed immigrant Amadou Diallo is shot at 41 times and killed by police, who are acquitted of any wrongdoing in February 2000, causing a public outcry.
2000 First Lady Hillary Rodham Clinton runs for U.S. Senate from New York. New York City's population: 7.5 million.

housing demands were great, although development had been scattershot The government decided the city needed a more orderly way to sell and develop land. A group of city officials, called the Commissioners, came up with a solution: the famous "grid" street system of 1811. It ignored all the existing roads—with the exception of Broadway, which ran the length of Manhattan Island, following an old Indian trail—and organized New York into a rectangular grid with wide, numbered avenues running north to south and streets running river to river.

When the 362-mile Erie Canal opened in 1825—linking New York to the Midwest via the Hudson River and the Great Lakes—the port city became even more vital to the young country. Along with the new railroads, this trade route facilitated the making of many fortunes, and New York's merchants and traders flourished.

THE ABOLITIONISTS

Today, the African-American Burial Ground near City Hall in lower Manhattan preserves the chilling memory of a time when New York was second only to Charleston, South Carolina, as a slave-trade port. As late as the 1700s, such prominent local families as the Van Cortlandts and Beekmans increased their fortunes by dealing in human beings.

But as northern commercial cities became less reliant on manual labor, dependence on slavery waned—and the abolition movement bloomed. When New York State abolished slavery in 1827, the city celebrated with two days of fireworks and parades. As the South remained defiant, the abolition movement grew stronger in Boston and New York.

In New York, the cause was kept alive in the columns of Horace Greeley's *Tribune* newspaper and in the sermons of Henry Ward Beecher, pastor of the Plymouth Church of the Pilgrims on Orange Street in Brooklyn. The brother of Harriet Beecher Stowe (who wrote *Uncle Tom's Cabin*) once shocked his congregation by auctioning a slave from his pulpit and using the proceeds to buy back her freedom.

NEW YORK AND THE CIVIL WAR

Preservation of the Union was the hot issue of the 1860 presidential campaign. Abraham Lincoln wavered in his position on slavery—until one fateful trip to New York that year, when he addressed a meeting in the Great Hall of Cooper Union (the first American school open to all, regardless of race, religion or gender). In his speech, Lincoln declared, "Neither let us be slandered from our duty by false accusations against us, nor frightened from it by menaces of destruction to the government nor of dungeons to ourselves. Let us have faith that right makes might, and in that faith let us, to the end, dare to do our duty as we understand it."

The newly formed Republican Party moved to make Lincoln its presidential candidate. The Southern states promptly seceded from the Union and became the Confederate States of America. The Civil War had begun.

WHITE RIOT

When Lincoln started a military draft in 1863, the streets of New York erupted in rioting. Although New York sided with the Union against the Confederacy, there was considerable sympathy for the South, particularly among poor Irish and German immigrants, who feared that they would lose jobs to freed slaves.

For three days, New York raged. African-Americans were assaulted in the streets; Horace Greeley's office was attacked twice; Brooks Brothers was looted. When the smoke cleared, 100 were dead and 1,000 injured. The violence came to an end only when Union troops returning from victory at Gettysburg subdued the city. The Draft Riots remain the single worst civilian uprising in American history—beyond Watts, beyond Crown Heights, beyond Rodney King.

But apart from the 1863 riots, New York emerged from the Civil War unscathed. The city had not seen any actual fighting—and it had prospered as the financial center of the North. As immigration soared, so did the bank balances of New York's upper-class captains of industry.

HIGH FINANCE

Jay Gould made enormous profits in the stock market during the Civil War by having the outcome of military engagements secretly cabled to him and trading on the results before they became public knowledge. Gould, together with another master swindler, Jim Fisk, seduced shipping magnate Cornelius Vanderbilt into buying vast quantities of Erie Railroad bonds before the bottom dropped out of the market. (Vanderbilt had the resources to sit out the crisis and the grace to call Gould "the smartest man in America.") Vanderbilt, Andrew Carnegie and banker J.P. Morgan consolidated their fortunes by controlling the railroads. John D. Rockefeller made his money in oil; by 1879, he owned 95 percent of the refineries in the United States.

All of these men—each in his own way representing a 19th-century blend of capitalist

Silence of the lambs Central Park's Sheep Meadow got its name from its grazing population.

genius and robber baron—erected glorious mansions in New York. Their homes now house some of the city's art collections, and their legacies are as apparent on Wall Street as they are along Fifth Avenue. Swindles, panics and frequent market collapses were cyclical events in the late 19th century, but New York's millionaires weathered the crises, built major cultural institutions and virtually created high society.

The 1800s saw the birth of the Metropolitan Museum of Art (now the largest art museum in the western world), the Astor Library (now the Public Theater), the American Museum of Natural History, the New York Historical Society and the Metropolitan Opera. Carnegie gave Carnegie Hall to New York, even though the devoted Pittsburgher never really mingled much among New York's rich (his Fifth Avenue mansion is now the Cooper-Hewitt National Design Museum). Six years after the New York Public Library was created in 1895, Carnegie donated $5.2 million to establish branch libraries. The nucleus of the library consists of the combined collections of John Jacob Astor, Samuel Jones Tilden and James Lenox (*see chapters* **Museums** *and* **Music**).

MAJOR CAPITAL IMPROVEMENTS

The wealthy also started moving uptown. By 1850, the mansions along Fifth Avenue had indoor plumbing, central heating and a reliable water supply—secured by the 1842 construction of the Croton Reservoir system. In 1857, Frederick Law Olmsted and Calvert Vaux welcomed crowds to Central Park, the nation's first landscaped public green space. A daring combination of formal gardens and vast, rolling hills, the park remains the city's great civilizing force, offsetting the oppressive grid and bringing an oasis of sanity into the heart of Manhattan (*see chapter* **Uptown**).

Nineteenth-century New York also witnessed the advent of many industrial marvels. In 1807, Robert Fulton started the world's first steamboat service on Cortlandt Street. Samuel Morse founded his telegraph company in the 1840s. By the 1860s, Isaac Merritt Singer was producing 13,000 sewing machines a year here. In the late 1800s, Thomas Edison formed the world's first electric company in New York, which still carries his name, Consolidated Edison; in 1882, 800 new electric street lamps turned New York into the city that never sleeps.

Another extraordinary achievement of the time was the Brooklyn Bridge (1869–83), the longest suspension bridge in the world at the time and the first to use steel cable (*see chapter* **The Outer Boroughs**). Designed by John A. Roebling (who died in an on-site accident before construction began) and completed by his son, Washington, the bridge opened up the independent city of Brooklyn—and helped pave the way for its merger with New York.

The Met set Uptown money created the Metropolitan Museum of Art on Fifth Avenue in 1870.

POLITICAL MACHINATIONS

The 1898 consolidation of all five boroughs into the City of New York assured New York's 20th-century transition to a crucial world-class force: It became the planet's second-largest city (London was biggest). But this happened only after several false starts. Local bosses wouldn't give up their power, and most of the town had been mired in corruption. William M. "Boss" Tweed, the young leader of a Democratic Party faction called Tammany Hall (named after a famous Indian chief), turned city government into a lucrative operation: As commissioner of public works, he collected large payoffs from companies receiving city contracts. Tweed and his ring are estimated to have misappropriated $30 million to $200 million from various building projects, including the Tweed Courthouse (52 Chambers St). They distributed enough of that money in political bribes to keep a lot of influential mouths shut.

The likes of Tweed ultimately ran up against Theodore Roosevelt, a different kind of New York big shot. The future president drew his power not so much from his wealth and class as from the sheer force of his personality (and his ability to work the media). As a state assemblyman in the 1880s, Roosevelt turned the town on its ear, accusing capitalist Jay Gould of corrupting a judge. Although Gould was exonerated, Roosevelt earned his reputation as a fighter of corruption. And as president of the city's police board in the 1890s, he made friends with news reporters and led a temperance movement—two things that could never be pulled off simultaneously today. (*See chapter* **Midtown** for information on the Theodore Roosevelt museum.)

COMING TO AMERICA

"Give me your tired, your poor, your huddled masses yearning to breathe free," entreats Emma Lazarus's "The New Colossus," inscribed at the base of Frédéric Auguste Bartholdi's 1886 Statue of Liberty—one of the first sights seen by newcomers to the U.S. as they approached by sea.

The first great waves of immigrants started arriving in America well before the Civil War; the twin ports of welcome were Boston and New York. An influx of Irish surged after the 1843 potato famine, and German liberals arrived after their failed 1848 revolution. The 1880s saw the advent of southern Italians and large numbers of immigrants from the old Russian empire—Ukrainians, Poles, Romanians and Lithuanians, many of them Jews. Chinese laborers, who had been brought to America to do backbreaking work on the railroads in California, moved east to New York in droves to escape a violent anti-Chinese movement on the West Coast.

From 1855 to 1890, the immigration center at Castle Clinton in Battery Park processed 8 million people. The Ellis Island center, built in 1892, served the same purpose for roughly the same length of time and handled twice that number. With the introduction of a quota system in 1921, the intake slowed; Ellis Island was closed in 1932 (*see chapters* **Downtown** *and* **Museums** for information on the Ellis Island Immigration Museum and the Statue of Liberty).

HOW THE OTHER HALF LIVES

New immigrants usually ended up in the grim, crowded tenements of the Lower East Side. By 1879, the first of a series of housing laws was passed to improve conditions for the poor, and in 1886, New York established its first settlement house for the underprivileged, at 146 Forsyth Street. In 1890, writer and photographer Jacob Riis published *How the Other Half Lives,* an exposé of sweatshops and squalor in the ghetto; the uptown populace was horrified. The settlement-house movement and the temperance drive would preoccupy New York's philanthropic circles through the Depression.

The frenetic growth of the city's industries created appalling health-and-safety conditions. Child labor was common. "Nearly any hour on the East Side of New York City you can see them—pallid boy or spindling girl—their faces dulled, their backs bent under a heavy load of garments piled on head and shoulders, the muscles of the whole frame in a long strain," wrote poet Edwin Markham in 1907. In 1872, 100,000 workers went on strike for three months until they won the right to an eight-hour workday.

But it took the horror of the 1911 fire at the Triangle Shirtwaist factory (23–29 Washington Pl) in Greenwich Village to stir politicians to action. The fire killed 146 women—because the proprietors had locked the doors to the fire escapes to keep the workers at their sewing machines. The state legislature passed more than 50 health-and-safety measures within months of the fire.

THE SUBWAY

If, while staring at a subway map, you wonder why there is no easy connection between such natural depots as Grand Central and Penn Station, it is because those terminals were at one time run by different private rail companies. The original names of the subways—the IRT (Interborough Rapid Transit), BMT (Brooklyn-Manhattan Transit Corporation) and IND (Independent Subway System)—are still preserved in old subway signage. Many lifelong New Yorkers still use these names to refer to various routes.

The 656-mile subway system, an astounding network of civic arteries that today serves 4 million passengers a day, became the 20th century's largest single factor in the growth of the city. The first of the three companies started excavation in 1900, but by the 1940s, the system had been consolidated and hasn't changed much since.

The subway also holds a unique place in the city's imagination: It offers the perfect metaphor for New Yorkers' fast, crowded lives lived among strangers. Most famously, the Duke Ellington Band's signature song, written by Billy Strayhorn, implored its listeners to "Take the 'A' Train," noting, "that's the quickest way to get to Harlem." Subway culture permeates New York life. Tin Pan Alley's songwriters composed such popular ditties as "Rapid Transit Gallop" and "The Subway Glide," and new words and phrases, like "rush hour," entered the language.

NEW YORK STORIES

Since the 19th century, New York has consistently sprouted its own artistic and literary movements. Following the seminal

Fantasy island In 1905, Coney Island was home to three extravagant amusement parks.

figures of New York letters—people like satirist Washington Irving and Gothic storyteller Edgar Allan Poe, a transplanted Southerner—were Brooklyn poet Walt Whitman and novelists Edith Wharton and Mark Twain. Wharton became an astute critic of old New York society; her most memorable novels, *The Age of Innocence* among them, are detailed renderings of New York life at the turn of the century. Samuel Clemens, a.k.a. Mark Twain, moved in and out of New York (mostly Greenwich Village) during his most prolific period, when he published *The Adventures of Tom Sawyer, Life on the Mississippi* and *Huckleberry Finn.*

By the turn of the century, a strain of social activity was evident in New York literature. Lincoln Steffens (the political muckraker), Stephen Crane (*Maggie: a Girl of the Streets*), Theodore Dreiser (*Sister Carrie*) and O. Henry all pricked the city's conscience with style and fervor.

THE JAZZ AGE

Once World War I had thrust America onto center stage as a world power, New York benefited from wartime commerce. The Roaring '20s brought looser morals (women voting and dancing the Charleston!), just as Prohibition provoked a bootleg-liquor culture. Speakeasies fueled the general Jazz Age wildness and made many a gangster's fortune. Even Mayor Jimmie Walker went nightclubbing at a casino located in Central Park.

At Harlem's Cotton Club, Lena Horne, Josephine Baker and Duke Ellington played for white audiences enjoying what poet Langston Hughes called "that Negro vogue" (*see chapter* **Uptown**). On Broadway, the Barrymore family—Ethel, John and Lionel (Drew's forebears)—were treading the boards between movies. Over at the New Amsterdam Theater on West 42nd Street, the high-kicking Ziegfeld Follies dancers were opening for such entertainers as W.C. Fields, Fanny Brice and Marion Davies.

New York also saw the birth of the film industry: D.W. Griffith's early films were shot in Manhattan, and the Marx Brothers made movies in Astoria. In 1926, hundreds of thousands of New Yorkers flooded the streets to mourn the death of matinee idol Rudolph Valentino.

RADIO DAYS

After the 1929 stock-market crash, when Americans stopped going out and turned instead to their radios for entertainment, New York

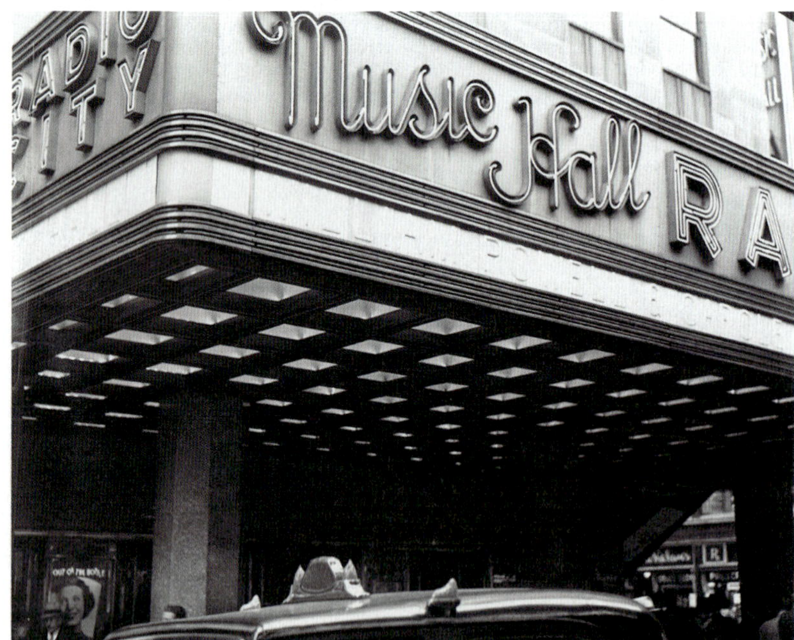

Hall of fame Once the largest theater in the U.S., Radio City still dazzles audiences.

Read all about it Free for all, the New York Public Library became the city's epicenter of knowledge.

became the airwaves' talent pool. Unemployed vaudeville players such as George Burns and Gracie Allen became stars, as did Jack Benny and Fred Allen. The careers of artists as disparate as Bing Crosby and Arturo Toscanini were launched on New York radio. Italian immigrant Enrico Caruso became one of the first worldwide recording stars here. The Art Deco masterpiece Radio City Music Hall became the industry's great Depression-era palace.

And as theatrical productions were tailored for the airwaves, some of the most acclaimed stage directors made their names in radio. In 1938, Orson Welles and John Houseman, who both had already shaken up Broadway with an all-African-American stage version of *Macbeth,* shocked America with their radio adaptation of H.G. Wells's *War of the Worlds.*

LA GUARDIA, FDR AND THE POWER BROKER

The first skyscrapers (including the Woolworth Building) were erected at the turn of the last century, but the 1920s saw a second boom in buildings: The Chrysler and Empire State Buildings and Rockefeller Center were all built by the 1930s. Art Deco design dominated these projects (*see chapter* **Architecture**).

In 1932, with the Depression in full swing, the city elected a stocky, short-tempered young congressman, Fiorello La Guardia, as mayor. Boosted by former New York governor Franklin D. Roosevelt's election as president, La Guardia imposed austerity programs that, surprisingly, won wide support. FDR's New Deal, meanwhile, re-employed the jobless on public-works programs and allocated federal funds to roads, housing and parks.

Enter Robert Moses, the city's master builder. As the head of a complex web of governmental authorities and commissions, Moses employed thousands of New Yorkers to build huge public parks (including Long Island's Jones Beach) and recreation centers; he also mowed down entire neighborhoods to construct bridges (including the Verrazano-Narrows) and expressways that invited urban sprawl. No one since Dutch colonizer Peter Minuit had left a greater stamp on the city. Before his influence faded in the 1960s, Moses erected such indelible New York landmarks as Lincoln Center, Shea Stadium and the Flushing World's Fair Grounds.

BUILDING BETTER ARTISTS

The Federal Works Progress Administration (WPA) also made money available to New York's actors, writers, artists and musicians. And as the Nazis terrorized the intelligentsia in Europe, the city became the favored refuge. Architects Ludwig Mies van der Rohe and Walter Gropius (the former director of the influential Bauhaus school of design) and composer Arnold Schoenberg were among those who moved to New York from Germany, along with many visual artists.

Arshile Gorky, Piet Mondrian, Hans Hofmann and Willem de Kooning were among the painters welcomed by the fledgling Museum of Modern Art, founded in 1929 by three collectors. By the '50s, MoMA had fully embraced a generation of painters known as the New York School. Critics such as Clement Greenberg hailed Abstract Expressionism as the next step in painting. Jackson Pollock, Lee Krasner, Willem and Elaine de Kooning, Robert Motherwell and Mark Rothko became the stars of a gallery scene that, for the first time, topped that of Paris.

When a young man named Andrew Warhola decided to leave Pittsburgh to become an artist, it was no surprise that he chose to come to New York. Dropping the last letter of his name, Warhol used commercial silk-screening techniques to fuse the city's ad culture and art world until the two could barely be distinguished. At the peak of the 1960s Pop Art movement, some critics argued that painting had reached its final destination in New York.

MEDIA CENTRAL

The 1920s literary scene was dominated by Ernest Hemingway and his friend F. Scott Fitzgerald, whose *The Great Gatsby* portrayed a dark side of the 1920s. They worked with editor Maxwell Perkins at Scribner's publishing house, along with Thomas Wolfe, who constructed enormous semiautobiographical mosaics of small-town life. In the '20s, such literary luminaries as Dorothy Parker, Robert Benchley, George S. Kaufman and Alexander Woollcott

Punk palace In the mid-'70s, the Ramones and Talking Heads got their start at CBGB.

gathered regularly at the famous Round Table at the Algonquin Hotel (*see chapter* **Books & Poetry**). Royals of stage and screen like Douglas Fairbanks, Tallulah Bankhead and various Marx Brothers would show up to pay their respects. Much of the modern New York concept of sophistication and wit took shape in the alcoholic banter of this glamorous clan.

By World War II, the city's socialist scene—divided over the support some showed for Stalin—inspired the work of a generation of intellectuals, including Norman Podhoretz, Irving Howe, Lionel and Diana Trilling, and William F. Buckley Jr. At the same time, a counterculture sprang up: Jack Kerouac and Allen Ginsberg attended Columbia in the '40s, giving rise to the Beats of the '50s. Throughout the century, Greenwich Village was the lab for alternative culture, from '20s Bolshevism to the '60s New York School of poets (John Ashbery and Kenneth Koch among them).

ENCORES AND HOME RUNS

In the theater, George and Ira Gershwin, Irving Berlin, Cole Porter, Richard Rodgers and Oscar Hammerstein II codified and modified the Broadway musical, adding plots and characters to the traditional follies format. Eugene O'Neill revolutionized American drama in the '20s, only to have it revolutionized again by Tennessee Williams a generation later. By mid-century, the Group Theater had fully imported Stanislavski acting techniques to America, launching the careers of Actors Studio founder Lee Strasberg, director Elia Kazan and the young stage actor Marlon Brando.

Theater—especially on Broadway—became big business in New York. The Shubert brothers started a national 100-theater empire here in the 1910s. In mid-century, David Merrick pushed such modern musicals as *Gypsy*. By the '60s, Joseph Papp's Public Theater was bringing Shakespeare to the masses with free performances in Central Park that continue to this day.

Meanwhile, in the outer boroughs, baseball generated a lot of excitement. The New York Yankees played against either the NY Dodgers or the NY Giants in 13 World Series ("subway series" to New Yorkers) between 1921 and 1956. The unbeatable Yankees—Babe Ruth, Lou Gehrig, Joe DiMaggio and later Mickey Mantle—provided as many thrills as any Broadway show. Jackie Robinson integrated baseball in Brooklyn in 1947; when the Dodgers left town a decade later, the borough was devastated (the Giants left the same year).

THE INTERNATIONAL CITY

The affluence of the 1950s allowed many families to head for the suburbs: Towns sprang up around new highways, and roughly a million children and grandchildren of European immigrants—mostly Irish, Italian and Jewish—moved to them. Their places in the city were taken by a new wave of immigrants—a million

Puerto Ricans and African-Americans, most of the latter relocating from the South.

Meanwhile, the United Nations, the international organization supporting global peace and security, established its headquarters overlooking the East River in Manhattan on land donated by John D. Rockefeller (*see chapter* **Midtown**).

By the mid-1970s, poverty, prejudice and an increase in street crime had cast a shadow of fear across the city. Many white New Yorkers in working- and middle-class neighborhoods grew disenchanted with the city and its ability to provide safe streets or effective schools and fled to the suburbs in large numbers. To make matters worse, by 1975 the city was all but bankrupt. With a growing population on welfare and a declining tax base, the city resorted to heavy municipal borrowing.

Culturally, New York remained a mecca for music and nightlife. The Brill Building gave Carole King, Neil Diamond and Burt Bacharach their starts, and Bob Dylan rose to fame in the Village. In the mid-'70s, CBGB, on the Bowery, launched Blondie, the Ramones and Talking Heads, while midtown's Studio 54 blended disco, drugs and Hollywood glamour into a potent, if short-lived, cocktail.

BOOM AND BUST

New York climbed out of its fiscal crisis under Mayor Edward Koch, a onetime liberal from Greenwich Village who wangled state and federal help to ride the 1980s boom in construction and finance. The '80s and early '90s were the best and worst of times for New York: A new art scene and booming Wall Street takeover culture brought money back downtown, fueling the revitalization of the East Village, Soho and Tribeca. But the AIDS and crack epidemics hit the city hard, as did racial politics. David Dinkins became New York's first African-American mayor in 1989. His tenure, however, was marred by racial tensions—incidents in Crown Heights, Brooklyn, and Washington Heights polarized the people of those neighborhoods as well as the entire city.

Dinkins was succeeded in 1994 by Rudolph Giuliani, a tough Italian-American lawyer who had entered the political limelight as a fearless federal prosecutor. Crime rates plunged in the late '90s, thanks in part to the mayor's relentless crackdown on petty crime. While racism and, perhaps most acutely, police brutality remain troublesome in New York, the continued growth of the culture and high-tech industries, combined with 1960s-level crime figures, have brightened New York's reputation.

THE 21ST CENTURY

New York's economy is stronger now than it has ever been, and its effects ripple down every avenue, street and alley. They say it's hard to throw a stone without hitting a Starbucks; the same goes for Barnes & Noble and so many other businesses surfing a prosperous wave powered by people spending lots of money. Giuliani projected a city-budget surplus of more than $2 billion for 2000. One result has been cuts in taxes—including the elimination of sales tax on clothing items with price tags under $110. New public projects include the $15 million Flushing Meadows Pool and the $98 million Hudson River Park.

On the other hand, real-estate prices have risen beyond affordability for many New Yorkers: The average purchase price of an apartment rose 21 percent between 1998 and 1999; contrast that with a meager 2 percent average annual inflation rate. Formerly dangerous neighborhoods like Harlem and Alphabet City are now sought-after areas where one-bedroom rentals can go for $2,000 a month. But the gentrification has led to a displaced class of working homeless, whose earning power can't keep up with real-estate values.

Even so, New York remains ground zero for cultural progress and innovation. Its trailblazing residents are forging ahead into the 21st century with groundbreaking art, literature, music, films and fashion. New York may not be the capital of the U.S., but it is the capital of the world.

Hizzoner's house New York's mayoral residence, Gracie Mansion, will have a new occupant in 2002.

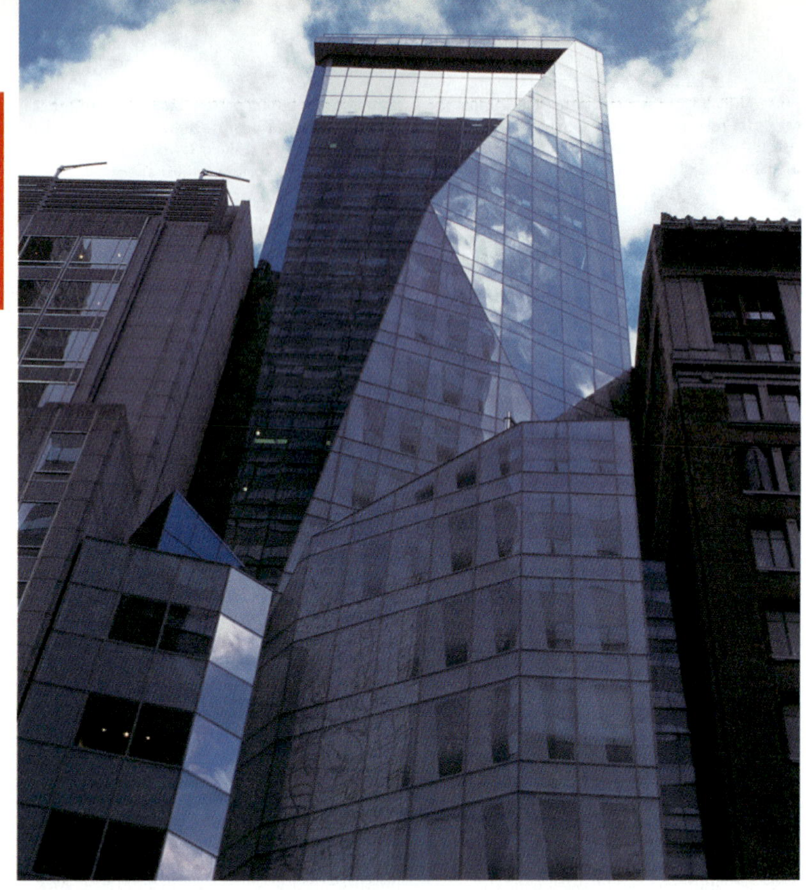

Soar Subjects

With the arrival of the LVMH tower, the city's freeze on bold design seems to be thawing

In June of 1999, the influential *New York Times* architecture critic Herbert Muschamp turned his discriminating eye toward the new **LVMH Tower,** then nearing completion at 19 East 57th Street, between Madison and Fifth Avenues. Awed by the 23-story tower's dramatic folded planes of glass, Muschamp declared it "one of two new Manhattan buildings that rise from the level of real estate to the plane of architecture" (the other building being the **Austrian Cultural Institute,** five blocks south at 11 East 52nd Street, between Madison and Fifth Avenues).

Muschamp's giddy joy is understandable. For the past several decades, it has been a vexing paradox that while New York nurtures artistic achievement, this spirit of creativity has rarely extended to the city's built environment. With the arrival of the LVMH Tower, however, the

LVMH in the sky with diamonds The future of New York City's architecture looks bright.

city's freeze on bold new urban-design projects seems to be thawing. Indeed, thanks to a surging economy that has filled private developers' and the city's coffers with cash, architects, urban planners and, of course, the mayor are all dreaming up large-scale projects that could dramatically alter the city landscape in years to come.

Recent project proposals cover almost every part of town and range in size from unfathomably large to modest. One of the most heralded is a plan to build a glamorous new **Penn Station** in the Central Post Office across Eighth Avenue from the station's current site—a proposal that carries a lot of emotional weight, since the destruction of the original station, in 1965, shocked the public and led to the creation of the city's Landmarks Preservation Commission.

Another project raising aesthetes' hopes (and naysayers' eyebrows) is the **Guggenheim Museum**'s plan to build a downtown outpost along six piers on the East River at the foot of Wall Street. In spring 2000, the Gugg revealed the proposed design, by controversial architect Frank Gehry. If built—and that's a big if—the museum's eye-popping outline would rival his much-praised Guggenheim in Bilbao, Spain.

Back to the future The proposed design for the new Penn Station honors the past.

Other ideas floated recently include a sports stadium on the far west side of Manhattan (a plan aggressively championed by Mayor Rudolph Giuliani); a complete reconstruction of Staten Island's **St. George Ferry Terminal**; a Hollywood-on-the-East-River complex of movie and television sound stages at the Brooklyn Navy Yard; and a hotel and cultural center—replete with art-house movie theater, restaurants and a bookstore—at Astor Place in the East Village, to be designed by international architectural phenom Rem Koolhaas.

Architects, urban planners and, of course, the mayor are all dreaming up large-scale projects that could dramatically alter the city landscape.

"I think the excitement over the Frank Gehry announcement and the excitement over the LVMH building augur well [for the city]," says Kent Barwick, president of the Municipal Art Society, one of the city's oldest and most respected urban-design and preservation advocacy groups. "I think there's a group of architects from around the world who are increasingly interested in building in New York, and clients who are willing to give them a chance. For a long time, you could say that New York was just a safe bet—that rather unimaginative developers hired rather unimaginative architects to build predictable and high-profit enterprises."

Which of the above projects will come to fruition and which will never get past the blueprint phase? It's anybody's guess. Gone are the days when a planner like Robert Moses possessed the unchecked power to foist public works on the city in a quasi-imperial manner. (During the mid-20th century, in his dual role as chairman of the Triborough Bridge and Tunnel Authority and City Parks Commissioner, Moses presided over the construction of the Cross Bronx Expressway, the Triborough Bridge, Shea Stadium, Orchard Beach and countless other projects). These days, major construction

▶ For historical architecture sights, see chapter **Architecture.**
▶ To find out more about New York's political past, see chapter **History.**

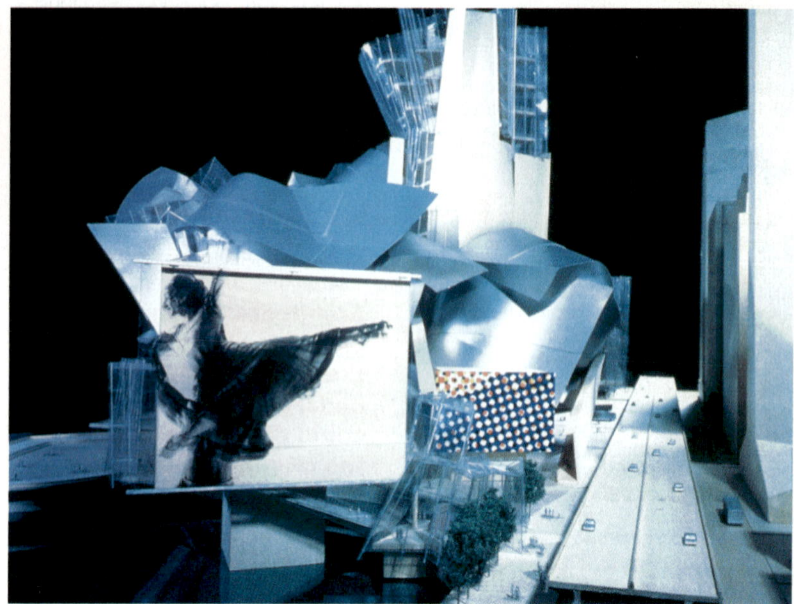

Hari-Gehry Frank Gehry's design for the Guggenheim might never get built. But it should be!

proposals face a battery of reviews and political hurdles, and often pit developers against the residents of the communities in which they're trying to build.

Two recent examples of how grand ideas can run into trouble are developer David Walentas's plan to dramatically alter the waterfront in the Dumbo section of Brooklyn and Donald Trump's plans to erect the world's tallest apartment building, on the east side of Manhattan, near the United Nations headquarters. Walentas fought 20 years for his plan, which would have brought a hotel, a movie theater and a shopping mall to the area between the Manhattan and Brooklyn Bridges. He was forced to scale back his aims when the city—which, along with the state, owns the waterfront land—decided to expand a proposed Brooklyn Bridge Park.

But there was no stopping the Donald. **Trump's World Tower,** at First Avenue and 47th Street, has all its permits secured and is under construction, although that hasn't prevented neighbors of the building—including retired news anchor Walter Cronkite and a number of business titans—from trying to get the courts to reduce the building's height from its planned 70 stories. Trump's antagonists say the World Tower's size is out of scale with the rest of the neighborhood and that it will cast long gloomy shadows for blocks (plus, it will diminish the nearby U.N. building's sleek stature).

Even if Trump is able to crush his foes, it is unlikely that the New York skyline will ever contend with a building like his World Tower again. Largely because of the zoning loopholes Trump exploited, the City Planning Commission has proposed major changes to the laws. If the new legislation is adopted, height limits will govern skyscraper construction in every part of town except the midtown and downtown central business districts.

The new laws also scrap the "tower-in-the-park" style of building, which allowed developers to construct taller buildings in exchange for providing public space (usually uninviting) at street level. Announcing the proposed changes in December 1999, City Planning Commission Chairman Joseph Rose said they were designed to create an "intelligible zoning ordinance that respects neighborhood context, while also assuring that New York City is able to develop much needed housing and commercial space."

Of course, if the economy takes a turn for the worse and depletes investors' cash reserves, all the grand projects dancing in developers' heads—and all the changed zoning laws—won't matter very much.

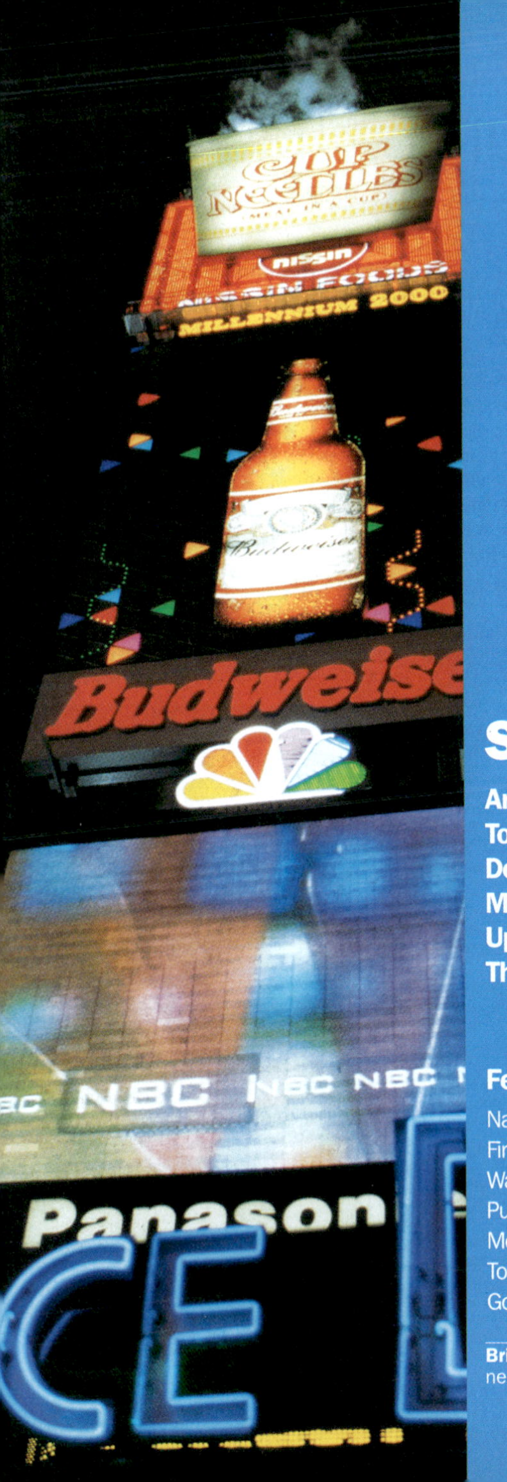

Sightseeing

Feature boxes

Bright lights, big city Times Square's neon advertising is a sight to see.

Architecture

Even on this island of mammoth towers, some buildings just stand out

O. Henry once said of New York, "It'll be a great place if they finish it." In fact, it is the constant construction that has made the city an architectural wonderland. Here are a few highlights of New York's architectural styles, including the year construction was completed.

▶ Anyone with a strong interest in the architecture of the city might want to visit the Urban Center (see chapter **Museums**).
▶ Other chapters to help you plan your architecture sightseeing: **Tour New York, Further Reading,** and the **Sightseeing** section. See also **Soar Subjects,** page 18.

Dutch Colonial

The style imported by New York's first European settlers (1626–64) generally features wood-frame buildings with tile roofs, stepped gables and stone stoops.

Pieter Claesen Wyckoff House Museum

Circa 1652. 5902 Clarendon Rd at Ralph Ave, East Flatbush, Brooklyn (718-629-5400). Travel: 2, 5 to Newkirk Ave, then B7, B8 or B78 bus to Clarendon Rd. Times vary; call for details.
Possibly the oldest building in New York State, Pieter Claesen Wyckoff's farmhouse was built on land bought in 1636 from the Canarsie Indians.

Bowne House

1661. 37-01 Bowne St between 37th and 38th Aves, Flushing, Queens (718-359-0528). Subway: 7 to Main St–Flushing. Tue, Sat, Sun 2:30–4:30pm. $2.
Nine generations of the family descended from John Bowne—a fighter for religious freedom—lived here until it was turned into a museum in 1945. Only part of the house is original.

Dyckman Farmhouse Museum

Circa 1785. See chapter **Uptown.**
This home was rebuilt in the 18th century; however, it is based on the original structure's style.

British influence

Much building went on while the British controlled the city (1664–1783), though little of it remains; however, the Georgian style then in vogue can be seen in these structures.

Historic Richmond Town

Circa 1670–1860. See chapter **Outer Boroughs, Staten Island.**
Several buildings of different styles were moved here from various sites on Staten Island and restored.

Morris-Jumel Mansion

1765. See chapter **Uptown.**
This Palladianesque mansion was built for a British colonel. The wooden building features a sweeping portico.

Van Cortlandt House Museum

1748. Van Cortlandt Park, Broadway at 242nd St, Riverdale, Bronx (718-543-3344). Subway: 1, 9 to 242nd St–Van Cortlandt Park. Tue–Fri 10am–3pm; Sat, Sun 11am–4pm. $2, under 12 free. Cash only.
This two-and-a-half-story stone manor house features classic Georgian touches: It's almost square, with dormer windows poking out of the top floor. The interior retains most of the period's architectural features.

The Federal period

As a new country, the United States developed its own version of the Georgian style, called Federal, which was favored in the city through the late 1800s. Tenement and brownstone residences were built by the thousands during this period.

City Hall

1803–12. City Hall Park between Broadway and Park Row (Mayor's office: 212-788-3000). Subway: J, M, Z to Chambers St; 2, 3 to Park Pl; 4, 5, 6 to Brooklyn Bridge–City Hall. Closed to public. Call two weeks in advance for group tours only.

Column what you will Soho's landmarked cast-iron buildings are here to stay.

The Mayor's headquarters is a neoclassical specimen that combines the Federal style with French Renaissance influences. The interior is pure American Georgian.

Charlton-King-Vandam Historic District

Circa 1820s. 9–43 and 20–42 Charlton St, 11–49 and 16–54 King St, 9–29 Vandam St, 43–51 MacDougal St. Subway: 1, 9 to Houston St.

In addition to having the largest concentration of Federal-style houses in New York, this area includes fine examples of Greek Revival, Italianate and late-19th-century domestic architecture.

Beaux Arts

Probably the best known (and loved) era of New York architecture came with the Gilded Age of the early 1900s. A careful appropriation of European Renaissance forms, Beaux Arts design was incredibly successful at creating imposing yet uplifting public buildings. In response to the destruction of the original Pennsylvania Station (designed by McKim, Mead & White, the city's most important architectural firm at the time) in 1965, only 54 years after it was built, the city's Landmarks Preservation Commission was instituted. Thankfully, many beautiful buildings remain.

New York Public Library

1902–1911. See chapters **Midtown** *and* **Museums.**

The epitome of Beaux Arts, the library was designed by the firm Carrère & Hastings, which also designed the **Frick** mansion (now a museum) and **Grand Army Plaza** in Manhattan.

General Post Office

1913. See chapter **Directory.**

McKim, Mead & White designed the General Post Office to complement the original Penn Station. Other evidence of the firm's taste for the French and Italian Renaissance: the **Municipal Building** (circa 1914, 1 Centre St at Chambers St), the **University Club** (circa 1899, 1 W 54th St at Fifth Ave), the **Metropolitan Club** (circa 1894, 1 E 60th St at Fifth Ave) and the **Morgan Library** (*see chapter* **Museums**).

Grand Central Terminal

1913. See chapter **Midtown.**

Warren & Wetmore designed the majestic soaring (and now restored) Grand Central Terminal, as well as the ornate building behind it—the **Helmsley Building** (circa 1929, 230 Park Ave between 45th and 46th Sts).

Cast iron

New technology allowed buildings to be constructed quickly from cheap precast materials (*see chapter* **Downtown, Soho**).

Haughwout Building

1857. 488–492 Broadway at Broome St. Subway: J, M, Z, N, R, 6 to Canal St.

Located in Soho, this "Parthenon of cast-iron architecture" is so called for its elegant proportions and beautiful detail (*see photo, page 22*). Other fine cast-iron examples include the **Cary Building** (*105–107 Chambers St at Church St*); **72–76 Greene Street,** known as "the King of Greene Street"; and **28–30 Greene Street,** "the Queen." Also explore the district known as Ladies' Mile (Broadway between Union and Madison Squares) to see many other examples.

85 Leonard St

1860–61. See chapter **Downtown.**

This is the only extant structure known to have been designed by James Bogardus, the self-described "inventor of cast-iron buildings."

Skyscrapers

They're what New York is famous for: the tallest buildings in the world (well, many of them were at some point). For further exploration, visit the Skyscraper Museum (*see chapter* **Museums**).

Flatiron Building

1902. 175 Fifth Ave between 22nd and 23rd Sts. Subway: N, R to 23rd St.

The Flatiron was one of the earliest buildings to use an interior steel cage for support. Its exterior echoes the traditional Beaux Arts facades of the time. *See chapter* **Midtown.**

Woolworth Building

1913. 233 Broadway between Park Pl and Barclay St. Subway: N, R to City Hall; 2, 3 to Park Pl.

Architect Cass Gilbert designed this monument of wealth as a kind of Gothic cathedral, complete with gargoyles. It was the world's tallest edifice until the Chrysler Building came along.

The Chrysler Building

1930. 405 Lexington Ave at 42nd St. Subway: S, 4, 5, 6, 7 to 42nd St–Grand Central.

At 1,046 feet, this was the tallest skyscraper in the world (just beating 40 Wall St) until the Empire State Building was finished. *See chapter* **Midtown.**

The Empire State Building

1931. See chapter **Midtown** *for listing.*

A 102-story Art Deco tower of limestone and granite with thin vertical strips of nickel that glint when they catch the sun, the Empire State was the work of William F. Lamb, who was told to "make it big." Built in only 18 months, it soon became the world's favorite building, as well as its tallest. Other important Art Deco works include **Rockefeller Center** (*see chapter* **Midtown**), the monochrome tower of the **Fuller Building** (1929, 45 E 57th St at Madison Ave) and the twin copper crowns of the **Waldorf-**

Absolut Mies van der Rohe The Seagram Building epitomizes the International Style.

Astoria Hotel (1931, 301 Park Ave between 49th and 50th Sts). Raymond Hood's **News Building** (1930, 220 E 42nd St between Second and Third Aves) is a soaring skyscraper of white brick piers with black and reddish-brown spandrels (as seen in the *Superman* films).

McGraw-Hill

Circa 1931. 330 W 42nd St between Eighth and Ninth Aves. Subway: A, C, E to 42nd St–Port Authority.

Architect Raymond Hood didn't intend to build a modern structure, but in the end his design—with shimmering blue-green terra-cotta and ribbons of double-hung windows—is a perfect blend of Art Deco and International styles. The "jolly green giant" has recently been cleaned and repaired.

Glass boxes

After the Art Deco era of skyscraper construction (and once the Depression ended), a Modernist and International Style emerged.

United Nations Secretariat

1950. See chapter **Midtown.**

The main building of the UN is a perfectly proportioned single rectangle (its face is designed to the "golden ratio" of the Greeks), and the design incorporates New York's first walls made entirely of glass.

Lever House

1952. 390 Park Ave between 53rd and 54th Sts. Subway: E, F to Lexington Ave; 6 to 51st St.

Designed by the firm Skidmore, Owings & Merrill, this narrow steel and greenish glass skyscraper rises out of its broad mezzanine lobby, which seemingly floats above the street, its supporting columns set back from the perimeter. It is currently undergoing a restoration.

Seagram Building

1958. 375 Park Ave between 52nd and 53rd Sts. Subway: E, F to Lexington Ave; 6 to 51st St. See chapter **Midtown.**

Ludwig Mies van der Rohe designed this bronze-and-bronze-glass office tower with Philip Johnson. The 38 stories occupy only 52 percent of the site, resulting in a plaza that gratifyingly stretches out to the broad boulevard of Park Avenue.

Other postwar standouts

Solomon R. Guggenheim Museum

1952. See chapter **Museums** *for listing.*

As his crowning achievement, America's most celebrated architect, Frank Lloyd Wright, designed a conical museum that's wondrous inside and out.

TWA Terminal A

1962. John F. Kennedy International Airport, Terminal A. See chapter **Directory.**

Eero Saarinen's design was controversial for years after the terminal's opening, but is now landmarked. The *AIA Guide to New York* says it's "soaring, sinuous, surreal and…well worth a visit."

World Trade Center

1972–73. 1 and 2 World Trade Center between Church and West Sts and Liberty and Vesey Sts. See chapter **Downtown.**

At 1,350 feet tall, the 110-story twin towers of 1 and 2 World Trade Center dominate the lower Manhattan skyline. A plaza, a hotel, an underground mall and five other office buildings complete the WTC complex.

Citicorp Center

1978. 599 Lexington Ave between 53rd and 54th Sts. Subway: E, F to Lexington Ave; 6 to 51st St.

Constructed of aluminum and glass, Citicorp Center's angled roof adds a unique silhouette to Manhattan's skyline.

Sony Building

1984. 550 Madison Ave between 55th and 56th Sts. Subway: E, F to Fifth Ave. See chapter **Midtown.**

With this building, Philip Johnson (a former proponent of the International Style) changed the face of architecture in New York from Modern glass to Postmodern stone. He designed this pink granite office tower (notorious for its ornamental "Chippendale" top) for AT&T. In 1991, Sony moved in and enclosed the public plaza on the ground floor.

Tour New York

Get a crash course on the real Gotham with guided tours that suit all interests

The masterpiece of diversity that is New York City offers an equally varied assortment of tours to show off its many faces. Gaze at the towering silver spires by boat, glide through the Central Park greenery by bicycle, experience the thrills and frustrations of a midtown traffic jam by bus, or explore the nooks and crannies of a Chinese apothecary on foot. It's your choice: Through a telescope, microscope or kaleidoscope, New York will meet and amaze you at every level.

▶ For more information on the various walking tours of New York, see the Around Town section of ***Time Out New York.***

▶ Self-guided tours of Manhattan are detailed in **Public spectacle,** page 56, and **Walk like a musician,** page 36.

▶ If you're interested in following the paths of your favorite writers, check out the literary walking tours in chapter **Books & Poetry.**

Sightseeing

By bicycle

Central Park Bicycle Tours

Tours meet outside 2 Columbus Circle, 59th St and Broadway (212-541-8759). Subway: A, C, B, D, 1, 9 to 59th St–Columbus Circle. Apr–Dec 10am, 1pm and 4pm. Jan–Mar by appointment only. $30, under 15 $20. Includes bicycle rental fee.

This leisurely two-hour bicycle tour visits the John Lennon memorial at Strawberry Fields, the Belvedere Castle, the Shakespeare Garden and many other Central Park sights. There are plenty of opportunities to rest when the guide stops to talk and when the tour breaks for refreshments. Call in advance to reserve either the English- or Spanish-language tour. For more biking options in the city, see chapter **Sports & Fitness.**

By boat

Bateaux New York

Pier 62, Chelsea Piers, 23rd St at the West Side Hwy (212-352-2022; www.bateauxnewyork.com). Subway:

Sky scraping The Liberty chopper offers a bird's-eye view of the Empire State Building.

C, E to 23rd St. Dinner cruise 7–10pm, $100–$115; brunch cruise Sat, Sun noon–2pm, $60.
Eat a meal against a skyline backdrop while traveling in a glass-covered vessel. The à la carte menu was created by the chef at Veritas (*see chapter* **Restaurants, American creative**). After dinner, you can shake it to Broadway, jazz and blues tunes on a hardwood dance floor.

Chelsea Screamer

Pier 62, Chelsea Piers, 23rd St and the West Side Hwy (212-924-6262). Subway: C, E to 23rd St. May–Oct Mon–Fri approximately one tour every two hours; Sat, Sun one tour per hour. $15, under 12 $10. Reservations not required; call for exact cruising times.
This narrated speedboat cruise takes you past the Statue of Liberty, Ellis Island, the *Intrepid*, the Brooklyn Bridge and, of course, Manhattan's skyscrapers. This is not for the mild-mannered—the bright yellow-and-blue boats really do "scream" along in the river.

Circle Line

Pier 83, 42nd St at Twelfth Ave (212-563-3200; www.circleline.com). Subway: A, C, E to 42nd St–Port Authority. Three-hour tour $22, seniors $19, under 12 $12; two-hour tour $18, seniors $16, under 12 $10; evening cruise $18, seniors $16, under 12 $10; speedboat $15, children $10.
Circle Line's three-hour circumnavigation of Manhattan is one of the best and cheapest ways to get a glimpse of the whole city. Watch midtown's urban jungle turn into dense forests at the tip of the island, and keep an eye out for Columbia University's rowing teams practicing in their sculls. A two-hour cruise sticks to mid- and lower Manhattan (the "harbor lights" version sails year-round at sunset). For a superquick adventure tour (April–September only), there's a 30-minute ride on a speedboat called the *Beast*. Call or check website for departure schedules.
Other location: *Pier 16, South Street Seaport, Water St to the East River (212-630-8888). Subway: A, C to Fulton St; J, M, Z, 2, 3, 4, 5 to Broadway–Nassau. Mid-Mar–Dec. One-hour cruise $12, seniors $10, children $7; speedboat $15, children $10. Jun–Sept. Two-hour evening music cruises; call for performance schedule.*

The Petrel

North Cove Marina, Battery Park City (877-693-6131). Subway: E to World Trade Ctr; 1, 9 to Cortlandt St. May–Oct. Call for charter rates and times.
A 70-foot yawl designed by Sparkman and Stephens, the *Petrel* is built of teak and mahogany. It was launched in 1938 as a racing yacht, and the owners still pride themselves on using a sail as much as possible. This is a New York favorite, so you'll need to book one week in advance. The boat sails between May and October and winters in Martha's Vineyard.

Name cropping

When neighborhoods change, the names never stay the same

In a city that's constantly reinventing itself, it's not surprising that Manhattan's many neighborhoods follow suit. Soho, for example, wasn't always a stylish hub. In fact, developers in the late 1950s dubbed the area "hell's hundred acres," in reaction to the neighborhood's commercial slums. But artists in search of maximum space and minimum rent moved in, converting warehouses into work studios. By 1968, the Artists Association (now known as the Soho Alliance) was formed to fight for tenants' rights. When the group needed a name that reflected the neighborhood, someone noticed an abbreviation on a city planning map: "So. Houston." London's Soho was booming at the time, and a lightbulb went on. The city's first neighborhood acronym was born.

These days, local realtors are trying to rename areas of the city to up their appeal to potential buyers and renters. Sure, it's still the same sketchy area, but the wishful implication is that it *could* be the next Soho.

Here's a list of Manhattan's neighborhood nicknames. Some you use all the time; others—we're sure—you've never heard of. Your next visit to the Big Apple may include a trip to the famed eateries of Boho or Mepa's many galleries. In any case, you'll know exactly where you're going.

The Old

Soho All the world is fabulous South of Houston.
Tribeca Robert DeNiro and Miramax rule the Triangle below Canal Street, which extends north of Chambers Street, between Broadway and the Hudson River.
Noho North of Houston Street—below 8th Street and between Third Avenue and Mercer Street—is home to *Time Out New York*.

Staten Island Ferry

South St at the foot of Whitehall St (718-727-2508). Subway: N, R to Whitehall St; 1, 9 to South Ferry; 4, 5 to Bowling Green. Free.
The poor man's Circle Line is actually just as much fun, provided you bring the one you love. No-cost (and unguided) panoramas of Manhattan and the Statue of Liberty turn a trip on this commuter barge into a romantic sojourn when the sun goes down. When you get to Staten Island, it may not be as scenic, but it has a nice personality. Boats depart South Ferry at Battery Park every half hour, 24 hours a day.

NY Waterway

Pier 78, 38th St at West Side Highway (800-533-3779; www.nywaterway.com). Subway: A, C, E to 42nd St–Port Authority. $19, children $9, seniors $16. Call for seasonal schedule.
For a concise, scenic overview of downtown, take this guided 90-minute cruise. What these tours lack in refinement, they make up for in Manhattan-centric neighborhood history. The close-up view of Lady Liberty is particularly worth the ride. In 2000, NY Waterway added a two-hour version, which voyages north as well. The company also runs a commuter ferry service and offers free buses to and from midtown. From May to November, twilight cruises are available, as well as sightseeing tours up the Hudson. **Other location:** *Pier 17, South Street Seaport, South St at Beekman St (800-533-3779).*

Bus tours

Gray Line

Port Authority Bus Terminal, Eighth Ave at 42nd St (212-397-2600; www.graylinenewyork.com). Subway: A, C, E to 42nd St–Port Authority. 9am–8pm, $22–$56. AmEx, Disc, JCB, MC, V.
Gray Line offers more than 20 bus tours around the city, from a basic two-hour ride to the monster nine-hour "Manhattan Comprehensive," which includes a three-course lunch. Call for prices and tour destinations. **Other location:** *Times Square Visitors' Center, Broadway between 46th and 47th Sts (212-768-1560).*

Hassidic Tours

Tour bus departs from 42nd St at Fifth Ave (800-838-8687; www.jewishtours.com). Subway: B, D, F, Q to 42nd St; 7 to Fifth Ave. Sun 9:30am–1:30pm. $36. Reservations required.
New York City is home to a large Jewish community. Hassidic Jews conduct these excursions and introduce their way of life to the general population. You will travel to Brooklyn to visit a synagogue, witness a Torah scroll being written, have lunch at a kosher deli and explore a Hassidic library. The tours include some walking, and there's time to shop for Jewish gifts and delectables.

New York Apple Tours

800-876-9868. Tours begin at New York Apple Tours' Visitors Information Center (777 Eighth Ave between

The New

Considered jokes a few years ago, these names are now etched in the New York lexicon.
Nolita The area North of Little Italy, below Houston Street and from Broadway to the Bowery, is Martin Scorsese's old turf.
Dumbo You'll find artists, not elephants, Down Under the Manhattan Bridge Overpass.
Nomad Wander the neighborhood North of Madison Square Park (between 23rd and 34th Streets) for some of the city's best food.

The Tried

Still in the experimental phase, these are names realtors are trying to push.
Socha *We* thought the area South of Chambers Street was the Financial District.
Soca South of Canal is not to be confused with Tribeca or Socha.
Lolita Isn't lower Little Italy Chinatown? (But Lolita *is* a pretty name.)
Mepa The Meatpacking District will never sound pretty…or clever.
Sobro Isn't it easy enough to say South Bronx? Though this one has some flava.
Weche The area west of Chelsea could use a name—just not *this* one.
Loho The Lower East Side below Houston Street (above Canal Street, between Forsyth and Clinton Streets) will always be the Lower East Side to us.
Loma Gee, all this time residents have simply said "the Flatiron District" when referring to the area below Madison Square Park.
Lobro Dude, that's the area of lower Broadway south of Canal Street.

The Untrue

Leave it to locals to come up with their own personal (and witty) acronyms for the city's nooks and crannies.
Sunnyside Up or Down (or 7-UP/7-DOWN) The area of Sunnyside, Queens, above or below the 7 train.
No BS The area of Brooklyn north of Bedford-Stuyvesant ain't to be messed with.
Aslic This optional name for Astoria and Long Island City is best used outside of Queens.
Pig-Stuy The area below Murray Hill, above the East Village and west of Gramercy Park—near the Police Academy and Stuyvesant Town.
Woho The wild, wild West of Soho.
Trinoca It's Triangle north of Canal Street, not a swine parasite.

A three-hour tour Get a river view of Manhattan on the Circle Line.

47th and 48th Sts), the Plaza Hotel (Fifth Ave at 59th St) and the Empire State Building (34th St at Fifth Ave). Starting at 9am, buses continuously follow a 65-stop route. $25–$78. AmEx, DC, Disc, JCB, MC, V.
These double-decker buses are a hit with out-of-towners—although Manhattanites think of them as a nuisance and a health hazard. NYAT pleaded guilty in September 1999 to avoiding EPA emissions and DOT safety standards. At press time, the city was trying to revoke the company's tour license, stepping up the process in May 2000, after one of the buses fatally struck a pedestrian. If Apple Tours can clean up its act, don't hesitate to take a guided tour uptown or downtown, or combine the two for a daylong ride around Manhattan in open-top, red-and-yellow double-deckers. Typically the on-board commentary lacks interesting information, so think of the ride as a scenic means to get to key sights. Once you have a ticket, you can get on and off at any point along the route. (On the combined tour, you can spread your sightseeing over two days.) Buses are frequent enough to make this practical.

By helicopter

Liberty Helicopter Tours

VIP Heliport, West Side Hwy at 30th St (212-967-4550, recorded info 212-465-8905). Subway: A, C, E, 1, 2, 3, 9 to 34th St–Penn Station. 9am–9pm, $53–$160. AmEx, MC, V.
The Liberty choppers are larger than most, which makes for a fairly smooth ride. There are 10 to 40 rides a day, depending on the weather. Reservations are unnecessary, and several tours are offered. Even the shortest ride is long enough to get a good close-up view of the Statue of Liberty, Ellis Island and the World Trade Center.

By foot—walking and other tours

Adventure on a Shoestring

212-265-2663. Sat, Sun. $5. Call for current tours, meeting locations, times and reservations.
Adventure on a Shoestring's motto is "Exploring the world within our reach…within our means," and founder Howard Goldberg is undyingly faithful to "real" New York and to the tour's $5 price tag (which hasn't gone up in 30 years). Tours like "Colorful Chinatown," "Hell's Kitchen Hike" and "Haunted Greenwich Village" explore New York, neighborhood by charming neighborhood. The 90-minute tours often conclude with a group lunch and useful handouts.

Big Apple Greeter

1 Centre St at Chambers St, 20th floor (212-669-8159; fax 212-669-3685; www.bigapplegreeter.org). Subway: 4, 5, 6 to Brooklyn Bridge–City Hall. Mon–Fri 9:30am–5pm; recorded information at other times. Free.
If you don't feel like letting one of the many tour companies herd you along the New York–by– numbers trail, or if you'd simply prefer to have a knowledgeable and enthusiastic friend to accompany you as you discover the city, put in a call to Big Apple Greeter. Since 1992, this immensely successful program has been introducing visitors to one of 500 carefully chosen volunteer "greeters" and giving them a chance to see New York beyond the well-trod tourist traps. Go visit Vinny's mom in Bensonhurst, have Renata show you around the hidden treasures of Polish Greenpoint, or let Carmine take you to the parks in the South Bronx where hip-hop was invented. The service is completely free and can also be tailored to visitors with disabilities. Write, call or fax the office at least ten days in advance to book yourself a New York friend.

Big Onion Walking Tours

212-439-1090; www.bigonion.com. Tours are scheduled every weekend and holiday. Thu–Sun from Memorial Day to Labor Day. Most are $10, students and seniors $8.
This business, founded by Columbia University doctoral candidates in history, puts together astoundingly informative tours of New York's historic districts and ethnic neighborhoods. Private tours are also available.

Destination Downtown

Tour meets at Alexander Hamilton U.S. Custom House, 1 Bowling Green between State and Whitehall Sts (212-606-4064). Subway: N, R to Whitehall St; 4, 5 to Bowling Green. Thu noon. Free.
The site of New York's first settlement and the epicenter of modern world finance is Wall Street. Explore the neighborhood's historic wealth on a free 90-minute tour hosted by the Alliance for Downtown New York and Big Onion Walking Tours. The guides and routes change each week. Usual destinations include the New York Stock Exchange, Federal Hall, Trinity Church and Dutch archeological sites.

Foods of New York Walking and Tasting Tours

Tour meets on Seventh Ave South at Bleecker St (732-636-4650; www.foodsofny.com). Subway: 1, 9 to

Christopher St–Sheridan Sq. Tue–Sun 11:30am–2pm. $25 (all food included). Reservations required.
These entertaining tours, which started in 1998, take the mystery out of where to eat in New York. Your food-savvy guide walks you through some of Greenwich Village's most famous eating establishments and specialty food shops—Rocco's Bakery, Joe's Pizza and the restaurant row of Cornelia Street are typical destinations. Be sure to go with an empty stomach; you'll sample at least seven different foods along the way.

Grand Central Partnership

Tour meets at Philip Morris Building, 120 Park Ave at 42nd St (212-883-2468). Subway: S, 4, 5, 6, 7 to 42nd St–Grand Central. Fri 12:30pm. Free.
If you want a comprehensive look at the splendors of the restored Grand Central, check out this weekly tour, which covers both the terminal and its neighborhood with an emphasis on social history and architecture.

Harlem Spirituals

690 Eighth Ave between 43rd and 44th Sts (212-391-0900). Subway: A, C, E to 42nd St–Port Authority. 8am–7pm; book at least one day in advance. $15–$80. AmEx, MC, V.
Sunday-morning gospel tours take in Sugar Hill, Hamilton Grange and the Morris-Jumel Mansion, as well as a service at a Baptist church. Gospel tours (Sun, Wed and Fri) stop by the Schomburg Center for Research in Black Culture and visit a Baptist church choir. Lounge at cabarets on the evening "Soul Food and Jazz" tours (Mon, Thu, Sat). Historical tours (Thu) include lunch.

Joyce Gold History Tours of New York

212-242-5762; www.nyctours.com. Mar–Dec Sat, Sun 1pm. Jan, Feb private tours by appointment. Call for current tours and meeting locations. $12.
Joyce Gold, a history professor at New York University and a Manhattan expert, has been conducting these informative two- to three-hour weekend tours for more than 15 years. Her talks focus on neighborhood evolutions and cultural movements, and she can customize walks to address the special interests of any group.

The Late Great Pennsylvania Tour

Tour meets at tourist information booth in Penn Station, Seventh Ave at 31st St (212-719-3434). Subway: A, C, E, 1, 2, 3, 9 to 34th St–Penn Station. Fourth Mon of the month, 12:30pm. Free.
The 34th Street Partnership hosts a 90-minute tour through America's busiest rail station. Get an earful of the building's history (complete with ghost story)

The nature of New York The Union Square Greenmarket is a fresh destination for a tour.

and an eyeful of the artifacts that have remained through its many transformations.

Lauren's Walking Tours

718-204-5133, 917-405-8856; www.lonedaughter.com. $15–$30. Call for schedule and meeting locations.

Lauren Hertel offers some intriguing approaches to experiencing the city. Her "Singles Series," open only to the unattached, explores the sights of Greenwich Village or Harlem by night and promises to "combine history with social life." The "Ethnic Enclaves Series" provides a three-hour eating-and-walking expedition to such neighborhoods as Cuban Union City, NJ. Hertel also hosts a "Sunday Harlem Gospel" tour in German and a late-night bike ride through Manhattan.

Mainly Manhattan Tours

212-755-6199. Sat noon; Fri, Sun 1pm. $10.

Anita Baron, a born-and-bred New Yorker and former Big Apple Greeter, conducts three tours every weekend. "West Side Story" includes Lincoln Center, Hotel des Artistes, the Dakota and Zabar's food market. "Greenwich Village: New York's Left Bank" visits the homes of famous literary residents Mark Twain, Edith Wharton and e.e. cummings. "42nd Street: Off, Off, Off Broadway" takes in the East River, the United Nations, Bryant Park and the surrounding architecture. Call for information on more tours, dates and times.

Municipal Art Society Tours

457 Madison Ave between 50th and 51st Sts (212-935-3960, recorded information 212-439-1049; www.mas.org). Subway: E, F to Fifth Ave; 6 to 51st St. Call for times, location and schedule.

The society organizes some very informative tours, including hikes around Harlem, the Upper West Side, Greenwich Village and Brooklyn Heights. It also offers a free tour of Grand Central Terminal on Wednesdays at 12:30pm and private tours by appointment.

New York City Cultural Walking Tours

212-979-2388; www.nycwalk.com. Private tours $25 per hour for a group of four or more, $15 per hour for a group of three or fewer. Public tours Sun 2pm. $10.

Alfred Pommer's tours explore New York's neighborhoods—Murray Hill, Gramercy Park, Soho, Little Italy—through history, architecture, pictures and stories. Private tours can be scheduled. Call for meeting locations of public tours.

New York Curmudgeon Tours

212-629-8813. Sun 10am, $15. Call for meeting locations.

Bill Walters, a seasoned theater professional, guides you past many of New York's famous Broadway theaters, from those in Times Square to the Ed Sullivan. He combines an insider's personal experience with historical tidbits to bring the city's famed entertainment scene to life.

NYC Discovery Tours

212-465-3331. Sat, Sun $12. Call for schedule and meeting locations.

These two-hour weekend walking tours come in three New York varieties: neighborhood tours (Soho to Central Park), theme tours (art history to bar history) and biography tours (George Washington to Marilyn Monroe). The company offers an extensive selection year-round, and private tours are available by appointment.

Radical Walking Tours

718-492-0069. Two weekend tours a month at 1pm. $10. Call for dates and meeting locations. No reservations required.

Bruce Kayton's 15 different tours emphasize left-wing history and include tales of Yippie leader Abbie Hoffman, Bob Dylan's folkie days, Margaret Sanger and the birth-control movement, and the Black Panthers. Follow Kayton for a glimpse back at more idealistic, pre–IPO crazed New York.

Street Smarts N.Y.

212-969-8262. Sat, Sun 2–4pm, 6–8pm. $10. Call for meeting locations. No reservations required.

New York City has a thriving ghost population, and Street Smarts offers a tour that visits several bars, streets and hotels that are infamously haunted. Other Street Smarts tours include a gaslight-era pub crawl, "glorious" Gramercy Park and an adults-only tour of the Bowery called "Dandies, Dudes and Shady Ladies."

Talk-a-Walk

30 Waterside Plaza, New York, NY 10010 (212-686-0356; fax 212-689-3538).

This mail-order service offers a choice of four 85-minute audiocassette tours ($9.95 each). Each tour package contains directions, a street map and commentary for a two- to four-hour walk. You can fax your address to the number above to receive a free three-page brochure.

Tours with the 92nd Street Y

1395 Lexington Ave at 92nd St (212-996-1100; www.92ndsty.org). Subway: 4, 5, 6 to 86th St. Call for schedule. Prices vary and reservations required.

The 92nd Street Y offers an impressive array of walking tours, day trips and weekend excursions, including everything from "The Famous Chelsea Hotel" to "Maple Tapping and Herbal Lunch, Native American–Style." Walking tours are usually on Sundays.

Urban Park Rangers

212-360-2774 (9am–5pm). Places and times vary. Free.

A division of the New York City Department of Parks (*888-NY-PARKS; www.nycparks.org*), the Rangers organize pleasant walks and talks in all city parks. Subjects and activities covered include fishing, wildlife, bird-watching and Native American history. The Around Town section of *Time Out New York* lists tour locations and schedules every week.

Find your kind

To fly with your favorite flock, it's important to know where it nests

Here's a ready reference guide for birds who hope to find matching feathers (*see section* **Necessities** *for listings*).

If you like the looks of...	Go to...
Girls in cowboy hats and tiny agnès b. tanks or boys in dark denim with bed-head hair	Balthazar, Canteen, or any street corner on Prince Street from Mott to Thompson Streets.
The *Friend*ly dress-down Friday crew, à la Monica, Phoebe, Chandler, Ross, Rachel and Joey	Drip Café, EJ's Luncheonette for brunch and Prohibition on Saturday night
Anyone dressed like an extra from *Swingers*	Torch, Lansky Lounge, Supper Club
The new "suit," just out of college, with a hungry Platinum card	Bryant Park Grill for after-work mating rituals, Brooks Brothers for shirt shopping
The D & G set—sheathed in black threads from head to toe	Lunch at the Royalton's 44 for Anna Wintour sightings, Pastis for early-evening snacks, Moomba for late-night rubbernecking
English lads and their birds	The ultimate football match at Nevada Smith's on Third Avenue, followed by a Sunday roast at Tea & Sympathy
International backpackers	Anything free—like Hotel 17's rooftop parties, Monday-night movies in Bryant Park and concerts at SummerStage in Central Park
Earnest suffering artists—paint-splattered jeans (him) and Lisa Loeb specs (her) de rigueur	Max & Roebling on Williamsburg's Bedford Avenue for essential retro tchotchkes, L-Cafe, Sweetwater Tavern
Gawky fresh-faced models with a portfolio in one hand and a subway map in the other	The Coffee Shop, Veruka or Lot 61
Skate punks with pink-and-blue hair and huge flared jeans	Astor Place, Washington Square Park, Union Square, during school hours
Duck boot–wearing New Englanders (who never actually muddy their feet)	Friend of a Farmer restaurant, Union Square Greenmarket, the Crate & Barrel shop (*60th St at Madison Ave*)
The buppie and the beautiful	Clementine, Mekka, Monday night at Cheetah
Muscle queens, old queens and plain old gay guys 'n' gals	The Cock for the young'uns, Bar d'O for the middle aged, Juniorverse at Twilo for all
Goateed wanna-be DJs with the latest copy of *The Flyer;* chicks with "I'm the DJ's girlfriend" attitude	Temple Records, Organic Grooves, Pearl River Mart and Kmart
The espresso-croissant–nouvelle-vague crowd	Jules Bistro, Casimir, Café Gitane, the sidewalk tables at Café Colonial
The aspiring producer, with an iBook under one and a model on the other	Odeon, Nobu, Bubby's and the Screening Room
The kegger crowd—big bangs and tight stonewashed jeans on her; a flannel shirt and backward baseball cap on him	McSorley's for the breakfast pint, Boxers for lunchtime boozing, Webster Hall till dawn and Yankee Stadium for the game, dude

Downtown

A dash of grit, a bit of glam, a helping of financial acumen and a heap of creative ambition season the streets of lower Manhattan

Because New York City grew northward from the area now known as Battery Park, the richest and most diverse concentration of neighborhoods and people is below 14th Street. Here, the crooked streets (most of which have names, not numbers) are made for walking. Wander for hours through the architectural wonderland of the Financial District and Civic Center, through the trendy art-lined streets of Soho and the vivid ethnic enclaves of the Lower East Side, and on to the punk playground of the East Village and the café community of Greenwich Village.

Battery Park

You'll be most conscious of being on an island at the southern tip of Manhattan. The Atlantic breeze blows in over New York Harbor, along the same route taken by the hope-filled millions who arrived here by sea. Trace their journey past the golden torch of the **Statue of Liberty** and through the immigration and quarantine center of **Ellis Island** (now a must-see museum), on to the statue-dotted promenade of Battery Park. Today, few steamships chug in; instead, the harbor is filled in summer with Jet Ski daredevils who jump the wakes left by motorboats and dodge the occasional sailboat. Seagulls perch on the promenade railing, squawking at fishermen, whose lines might snag a shad or a striped bass (although state health department officials recommend not eating these fish more than once a month). The promenade is also a stage for numerous performers, who entertain people waiting to be ferried to the Statue of Liberty and Ellis Island. The park itself frequently plays host to international touring events such as the **Cirque du Soleil** (*see chapter* **Kids' Stuff**). Free outdoor music is often a summer-evening feature here as well. **Castle Clinton,** situated

Harboring peace Spend some quiet time in Battery Park, on the lip of New York Harbor.

inside the park, was built during the Napoleonic wars to defend the city against the British, who had just been overthrown. The castle has been a theater and an aquarium in its day, but now serves as a visitors' center, with historical displays, a bookstore and ticket-purchase center for those seeking admission to the Statue of Liberty and Ellis Island.

Whether or not you join the crowds of tourists heading for Lady Liberty, you can go around the shore to the east and catch the famous—and free—**Staten Island Ferry** for a surprisingly romantic ride that offers an unparalleled view of the downtown skyline and, of course, a look at the iconic statue (*see chapter* **Tour New York**). The ferry's historic terminal was destroyed by fire in 1991, and its replacement has not yet been built. But next door is the beautiful **Battery Maritime Building** (*11 South St between Broad and Whitehall Sts*), a terminal for the many ferry services between Manhattan and Brooklyn in the years before the Brooklyn Bridge was built. The restaurant **American Park at the Battery** (*212-809-5508*) also sits at the eastern end of the Battery Park promenade; although its surf-and-turf menu is expensive, the outdoor patio overlooking the harbor is a prime spot to sip a cocktail. To the west is the restored **Pier A** (*22 Battery Place at West St*), Manhattan's last Victorian pier shed; it's now home to fine-dining establishments and historic vessels. When it's not undergoing some form of construction, the pier makes for a scenic stroll.

North of Battery Park is the triangle of **Bowling Green,** the city's oldest extant park and home to the beautiful 1907 Beaux Arts **U.S. Custom House,** which is now the fascinating **National Museum of the American Indian.** Sculptor Arturo DiModica's muscular bronze bull, which represents the snorting power of Wall Street, is nearby, as is the **Shrine of Elizabeth Ann Seton**—a strange, curved Federal-style building dedicated to the first American-born saint. Also in the vicinity is the **Fraunces Tavern Museum** (*see chapter* **Museums**), a restoration of the alehouse where George Washington celebrated his victory over the British. There, you can peruse the relics of revolution-era New York displayed in the many period rooms.

Battery Park

Between State St and Whitehall St and Battery Pl. Subway: 1, 9 to South Ferry; 4, 5 to Bowling Green.

Even though the park faces New York Harbor, the seagulls and folks fishing for bluefish and striped bass are sure signs of the Atlantic's proximity (just beyond the Verrazano-Narrows Bridge). The harbor itself is gorgeous, and one of the most peaceful experiences you can have in the entire city is to sit on a bench and look out onto the Statue of Liberty, Ellis Island, Staten Island and all the boats bobbing on the water.

The Statue of Liberty & Ellis Island Immigration Museum

212-363-3200; www.nps.gov/stli. Travel: N, R to Whitehall St; 1, 9 to South Ferry; 4, 5 to Bowling Green, then take Statue of Liberty Ferry, departing every half hour from Gangway 4 or 5 in Battery Park at the southern tip of Manhattan. 9am–5pm; 3:30pm last trip out. Extended hours Jul–Aug. $7, seniors $6, children 3–17 $3, under 3 free. Purchase tickets at Castle Clinton in Battery Park.

"A big girl who is obviously going to have a baby," wrote James Agate about the Statue of Liberty. "The birth of a nation, I suppose." Get up close to this most symbolic New York structure by visiting the island it stands on (as 5.5 million people did in 1999). Frédéric Auguste Bartholdi's statue was a gift from the people of France (the framework—which can be seen only if you go inside the statue—was designed by Gustave Eiffel), but it took the Americans years to collect enough money to give Liberty her pedestal. The statue stands 111 feet 6 inches toe-to-crown; there can be an excruciating wait to climb the 154 steps to the observation deck, so go early. On Ellis Island you can walk through the restored buildings dedicated to the millions of immigrants who passed through there. Ponder the ghostly personal belongings that people left behind in their hurry to become part of a new nation. It's an arresting and moving museum (*see chapter* **Museums**).

Shrine of Elizabeth Ann Seton

7 State St between Pearl and Whitehall Sts (212-269-6865). Subway: N, R to Whitehall St. 7am–5pm. Free.

Wall Street

Since the city's earliest days as a fur-trading post, wheeling and dealing has been New York's prime pastime and commerce the backbone of its prosperity. **Wall Street** (or just "the Street," if you want to sound like a local) is the thoroughfare synonymous with the world's greatest capitalist gambling den.

Wall Street itself is actually less than a mile long; it took its name from a small wooden defensive wall the Dutch built in 1653 to mark the northern limit of New Amsterdam. In the days before telecommunications, financial institutions established their headquarters here to be near the action. This was where corporate America made its first audacious architectural assertions; there are many great buildings here built by grand old banks and businesses.

Notable ones include the old **Merchants Exchange** at 55 Wall Street (now the **Regent Wall Street**; *see chapter* **Accommodations**), with its huge Ionic columns, giant doors and,

Settle down Luis Sanguino's *The Immigrants* is one of the many reasons to visit Battery Park.

inside, a rotunda that holds 3,000 people; the **Equitable Building** (*120 Broadway between Pine and Cedar Sts*), whose greedy use of vertical space helped instigate the zoning laws governing skyscrapers (stand across the street from the building to get a decent view); and **40 Wall Street** (now owned by real-estate tycoon Donald Trump), which in 1929 went head-to-head with the Chrysler Building in a battle for the mantle of "world's tallest building." (The Empire State Building beat them both a year later.) At the western end of Wall Street is the Gothic spire of **Trinity Church.** Once the island's tallest structure, it is now dwarfed by neighboring skyscrapers. Stop in and see brokers praying that the market stays bullish, or stroll through the adjacent cemetery, where cracked and faded tombstones mark the final resting places of dozens of past city dwellers, including signers of the Declaration of Independence and the U.S. Constitution.

A block east is the **Federal Hall National Memorial**, a Greek Revival shrine to American inaugural history—sort of. This is the spot where Washington was sworn in as the country's first president on April 30, 1789. The original building was demolished in 1812.

Across the street is the **New York Stock Exchange**. The visitors' center here is an excellent resource for those clueless about the workings of financial trading, and you can look out over the trading floor in action. (For a sense of Wall Street's influence through the years, check out the **Museum of American Financial History.**) The exchange is computerized these days, so except for crashes and panics, it's none too exciting as a spectator sport (for the "Buy! Buy! Buy!" action you've seen in the movies, head over to the **New York Mercantile Exchange**; *see page 37*). Far more fun is people-watching on the street outside the NYSE—an endless pageant of power, with besuited brokers marching up and down Broad Street, glowing with the confidence instilled by unprecedented market gains.

The **Federal Reserve Bank,** a block north on Liberty Street, is an imposing Florentine Renaissance–style building. It holds the nation's largest store of gold—just over 9,000 tons (you might have seen Jeremy Irons clean it out in *Die Hard 3*)—in a vault five stories below street level.

As you'd expect, the Wall Street area is fairly deserted after the end of the business day. But there is something relaxing about the empty streets during off-hours, and a stroll through the area, especially on weekends, can be a pleasant alternative to seeing it in full hustle-and-bustle mode. Otherwise, the time to visit is around midday, when the suits emerge for hurried lunches. Join them in stopping for a burger at the ultimate **McDonald's** (*160 Broadway between Wall and Dey Sts*). By some quirk of individualism, it boasts uniformed doormen, a stock ticker, a special dessert menu and a Liberace-style pianist.

Federal Hall National Memorial

26 Wall St at Nassau St (212-825-6888). Subway: 2, 3, 4, 5 to Wall St. Mon–Fri 9am–5pm. Free.

Federal Reserve Bank

33 Liberty St between William and Nassau Sts (212-720-6130; www.ny.frb.org). Subway: 2, 3, 4, 5 to Wall St. By appointment only. Free.

The free one-hour tours through the bank must be arranged at least two weeks in advance; tickets are sent by mail.

Museum of American Financial History

28 Broadway at Beaver St (212-908-4110). Subway: 4, 5 to Bowling Green. Tue–Sat 10am–4pm. $2 donation.

This tiny museum and gift shop is located on the ground floor of the Standard Oil building, the original site of John D. Rockefeller's office. Walking tours are every Friday at 10am.

New York Stock Exchange

20 Broad St at Wall St (212-656-5168). Subway: J, M, Z to Broad St; 2, 3, 4, 5 to Wall St. Mon–Fri 9am–4:30pm. Free.

A gallery overlooks the trading floor, and there are lots of multimedia exhibits.

Trinity Church Museum

Broadway at Wall St (212-602-0872; www.trinitywallstreet.org). Subway: N, R to Rector St; 4, 5 to Wall St. Mon–Fri 9–11:45am, 1–3:45pm; Sat 10am–3:45pm; Sun 1–3:45pm; closed during concerts. Free.

The small museum inside Trinity Church chronicles the parish's past and the role it played in New York's history.

World Trade Center and Battery Park City

The area along lower Manhattan's west coast contains grand developments that combine vast amounts of square footage with new public plazas, restaurants and shopping areas. Concerted efforts have been made to inject a little cultural life into these spaces, and plenty of street performers work the area during the summer months—though the general atmosphere is defined by an all-work-and-no-play sensibility.

Opened in 1970 and formally dedicated in 1973, the **World Trade Center** is actually seven buildings, though to most visitors it means the famous twin towers, which look like two huge silver sticks of butter floating above the downtown skyline. Tower 2 contains the famous observation deck; on good days you can walk outside and ponder the crazies who have suction-climbed the walls, parachuted off the top floor or walked a tightrope between the two towers. It's the city's tallest structure, and for a short time in the '70s (until Chicago's Sears Tower was completed), it also held the world height record. Fine dining in the clouds is available at **Windows on the World** and **Wild Blue** (*see chapter* **Restaurants** *for review*), or you can medicate your vertigo with a drink at the **Greatest Bar on Earth** (*see chapter* **Bars**). Redecorated in 1999, the bar has a sleek, modern look—a refreshing contrast to the '70s decor of the WTC 2 lobby (which showcases a rather scruffy wool-and-hemp tapestry by Spanish artist Joan Miró). In the mezzanine plaza, you can pick up discounted tickets to a Broadway show at the TKTS outlet (*see chapter* **Directory, Tickets**).

A massive underground mall with 123 shops lies below the Trade Center complex.

Death becomes her Take in the beauty of the Trinity Church Museum cemetery.

Gap, Banana Republic, the Limited and Borders have outlets here, and there are also hair salons, cosmetics stores and tons of inexpensive eating establishments. Nearby, at 22 Cortlandt Street, is **Century 21,** a huge store that sells designer clothes at sometimes massive discounts (*see chapter* **Shopping & Services**). Covered pedestrian bridges over West Street lead to the **World Financial Center** and the rest of **Battery Park City,** a 92-acre project built on landfill created by the earth moved for the WTC's foundations. The World Financial Center, completed in 1988, is the ultimate expression of the city-within-a-city concept. Architect Cesar Pelli's four glass-and-granite postmodern office towers—each crowned with a geometric form—surround an upscale retail area, a marina where water taxis to New Jersey dock and a series of plazas with terraced restaurants. The glass-roofed **Winter Garden,** filled with indoor palm trees, is a popular venue for concerts and other entertainment, most of which are free (*see chapter* **Music, Summer venues**).

The most impressive aspects of Battery Park City, however, are the esplanade and park, which run north and south from the Financial Center along the Hudson River. In addition to offering spectacular, romantic views of the sunset behind **Colgate Center** (look for the huge Colgate sign/clock) and Jersey City, New Jersey, across the river, the esplanade is a paradise for joggers, in-line skaters and bikers—although just walking it is plenty of fun, too. On summer weekends, when you can see a lot of skin, the packed and sweaty scene can get pretty aggro with two-wheelers, six-wheelers and no-wheelers jostling for position. The northern end of the park (officially called **Nelson A. Rockefeller Park**) features the large North Lawn, which becomes a surrogate beach in summer. Sunbathers, kite flyers and soccer players all vie for a patch of grass. Basketball and handball courts, concrete tables with chess and backgammon boards painted on them, and playgrounds with swings round out the recreational options available on the esplanade. Tennis courts and baseball fields are nearby, just off West Street at Murray Street. The park ends

Walk like a musician

Keep in step with New York's most notorious rock stars

New York has long been associated with rock & roll and often credited with creating such distinct genres as rap, new wave and punk rock. Unfortunately, much of the city's rock & roll lore has fallen into the dustbin of history. Many past hot spots, such as the original **Max's Kansas City** (once at 213 Park Avenue South) and **Danceteria** (formerly on 21st Street between Fifth and Sixth Avenues), have disappeared, only to be replaced by frozen-yogurt stands and the like. But the downtown music scene is not one to be obliterated (figuratively speaking), and despite the recent war on sex and drugs, the city still attracts and churns out a steady lineup of talented rockers, whose paths to success can be traced in a single afternoon.

To begin the tour, make your way to 8th Street at Sixth Avenue. Among the myriad shoe stores is **Electric Lady Studios** (*52 W 8th St, 212-677-4700*), formerly owned by **Jimi Hendrix** and consequently immortalized by his album *Electric Ladyland*. The place is still going strong today, with such artists as **Weezer, Santana, Mary J. Blige, D'Angelo** and **Van Halen** recording there recently.

Resume your trek by heading east until you come to Astor Place, where 8th Street becomes **St. Marks Place** (the stuff **Lou Reed** songs are made of), home base for dwindling ranks of crusty punk rockers. Marching onward past Second Avenue, you'll find that dingy record stores give way to residential townhouses (and the occasional boutique, café and 'shroom dealer). Stop at 96 and 98 St. Marks Place, between First Avenue and Avenue A, to view the cover subjects of **Led Zeppelin**'s 1975 double album *Physical Graffiti*; they're also the stoop in the **Rolling Stones**' "Waiting on a Friend" video.

Right next door is the tiny, one-room **Mojo Guitar Shop** (*102 St. Marks Place, 212-260-7751*), where **Dee Dee Ramone** and **Iggy Pop** once got into a fight over a Danelectro Silvertone. Proprietor Chris Cush bills the altercation as "the Punk Meets the Godfather." As for the Danelectro, well, Iggy got it. He tried to give it to Dee Dee, but Dee Dee wouldn't take it, claiming it had bad

at Chambers Street but links up with piers to the north that are slowly being claimed for public use and will eventually become the **Hudson River Park.** The southern end of the park links Battery Park City with Battery Park. At this intersection, you'll find the inventively designed **South Cove** area, **Robert F. Wagner Jr. Park** (with an observation deck that offers fabulous views of the harbor and the Verrazano-Narrows Bridge) and New York City's Holocaust museum, the **Museum of Jewish Heritage.** The entire park area is peppered with fine art, most notably Tom Otterness's whimsical sculptural installation *The Real World Behind the North Lawn*. The park also hosts outdoor cultural events during the warmer months.

The residential area of Battery Park City is home to, among others, wealthy Wall Streeters, whose high rents go toward subsidizing public housing elsewhere in the city. To outsiders, the community feels cut off from the rest of Manhattan (it literally lies west of West Street), and because it's so new (some buildings are still under construction), it lacks the kind of distinction that makes New York so unique.

Lower Manhattan Cultural Council

212-432-0900; www.lmcconline.org

An arts information service for artists and the public, the LMCC offers information on cultural events happening in and around lower Manhattan.

New York Mercantile Exchange

1 North End Ave at Vesey St (212-299-2499). Subway: A, C to Chambers St; E to World Trade Ctr; N, R, 1, 9 to Cortlandt St. Mon–Fri 9am–5pm. Free.

Watch from the visitors' galleries as the real drama of the trading floor unfolds. Here, manic figures in color-coded blazers scream and shout as they buy and sell billions in oil, gas, electric power and gold commodities. The Exchange also houses a museum that traces the roller-coaster history of this American tradition. The trading-floor action ends in the early afternoon, so come early.

World Financial Center & Winter Garden

West St to the Hudson River, Vesey St to Albany St (212-945-0505; www.worldfinancialcenter.com). Subway: N, R, 1, 9 to Cortlandt St. Free.

Phone for information about the many free arts events, which range from concerts to flower shows.

Sightseeing

vibes. Good or bad, the vibe of this store continues to satisfy such talent as **Jon Spencer,** who visits the shop in search of rare and vintage guitars.

St. Marks Place runs into **Tompkins Square Park** at Avenue A. The park is considered the heart of the East Village, and is an urban playground for the members of **Luscious Jackson,** who occasionally shoot hoops on the Tompkins Square court. The area around the park holds a lot of rock & roll significance, too—especially for the **Beastie Boys,** whose *Pollywog Stew* EP was recorded at **171-A** (which is both the name and address of the recording studio that has also been used by the members of the hardcore band the **Bad Brains**).

At the corner of 7th Street and Avenue A is **Niagara** (*112 Ave A, 212-420-9517*). Though the bar has gone through many incarnations, it was one of the first venues the Beastie Boys ever played. A whirl down 7th Street between Avenues B and C will take you to the building that was once home to scenester and music manager **Janet Billig** (*224 E 7th St*). In the salad days of indie rock, Janet's floor was the home-away-from-home for many a nascent superstar, including members of **Nirvana, Pearl Jam, Mudhoney, Hole, Soundgarden, Babes in Toyland** and **Smashing Pumpkins.** And it was on one of these visits that Nirvana played their first New York City gig at a little haunt called the **Pyramid Club** (*101 Ave A between 6th and 7th Sts, 212-473-7184*), located just a few steps back to A on the west side of the avenue between 6th and 7th Streets.

X-small Little 99 Rivington was once Paul's Boutique, à la the Beastie Boys.

A quick left on 6th Street brings you to **Wonder Bar** (*505 E 6th St between Aves A and B, 212-777-9105*), formerly known as the **Chameleon,** where on open-mike nights budding talents played, such as the then-unknown **Beck,** who was living in NYC at the time. Turn around and walk west again past Avenue A to **A-1 Record Shop** (*439 E 6th St between First Ave and Ave A, 212-473-2870*), where **Premier, Moby** and **Fatboy Slim** come seeking the hottest beats.

Sightseeing

World Trade Center

Church St to West St between Liberty and Vesey Sts (212-323-2340, groups 212-323-2350). Subway: C, E to World Trade Ctr; N, R, 1, 9 to Cortlandt St. Observation deck in World Trade Center Tower 2 open 9:30am–9:30pm; Jun–Aug 9:30am–11:30pm; rooftop promenade open weather permitting. $13, students 13–17 or student ID $11, seniors $9.50, children 6–12 $6.50, under 6 free. MC, V.

The WTC's rooftop promenade is the world's highest open-air observation platform. Even from the bottom looking up, the view is enough to make your head spin. Ascend to the 110th floor, and you'll really feel the vertigo. The scariest thing is that there's another tower of roughly equal size only a stone's throw away. First thing in the morning is the best time to avoid a wait, which can take up to a half hour.

The Seaport

While New York's importance as a port has diminished, the city's fortune rolled in on the salt water that crashes around its natural harbor. The city was perfectly situated for trade with Europe—with goods from middle America arriving via the Erie Canal and Hudson River. And because New York was the point of entry for millions of immigrants, its character was formed primarily by the waves of humanity that arrived at its docks.

The **South Street Seaport** is the best place to see this seafaring heritage. Redeveloped in the mid-1980s, the Seaport is an area of reclaimed and renovated buildings converted to shops, restaurants, bars and a museum. It's not an area that New Yorkers often visit, though it is rich in history. The shopping area of Pier 17 is little more than a picturesque tourist trap of a mall by day and a postwork yuppie watering hole by night, but the other piers are crowded with antique vessels. The **Seaport Museum**—detailing New York's maritime history—is fascinating (*see chapter* **Museums**). The museum is located within the restored 19th-century buildings at Schermerhorn Row (*2–18 Fulton St, 91–92 South St and 189–195 Front St*), which were constructed on landfill in 1812. The Seaport's public spaces are a favorite with street performers; there are outdoor concerts in

Walk like a musician (continued)

Schlepp back to Avenue A and head two blocks down to **East 4th Street,** between Avenues A and B, the very block **Madonna** called home early in her career. Just steps away on 3rd Street at Avenue D are the **Lilian Wald Houses,** the projects in which **Scott Weiland** was busted for buying heroin—the bust that sent him to jail.

Return to A, continue south to Rivington Street (*Ave A turns into Essex St below Houston St*). A left here will take you to **ABC No Rio** (*156 Rivington St between Clinton and Suffolk Sts, 212-254-3697*). Part art collective, part rock club, this eclectic commune was the seat of the anti-folk scene and the site of Beck's first gigs.

Backtrack again, heading west on Rivington Street, to the very street corner that graced the cover of the Beastie Boys album *Paul's Boutique.* It's now occupied by the hip yet humble **Rivington 99 Café** (*99 Rivington St at Ludlow St, 212-358-1191*), which pays homage to the Boys with a commemorative album cover displayed on the wall. Continuing on your westerly path, you'll eventually reach the Bowery. Make a right and head north. Past the welfare hotels and flophouses, and just north of Houston Street, you'll find the birthplace of punk rock—**CBGB-OMFUG** (*315 Bowery at Bleecker, 212-677-0455*), which stands for "Country, Blue Grass, Blues and Other Music For Uplifting Gourmandizers." The **Ramones, Blondie,** the **Talking Heads,** the **Dead Boys, Television** and even the Beastie Boys won their first fans here. Angst-ridden guitar rockers still play here nightly.

Conclude your walking tour by taking in a show and sucking back a few brews. Amid rockers downing cheap spirits, loud music and gritty decor, you'll feel like a sole survivor. As such, you're entitled to snooze like the best of them. For that, you must bid farewell to downtown, and make your way northwest. A 15-minute cab ride (haven't you earned it?) up Third Avenue and left on 23rd Street will bring you to New York's premier rock & roll resort, the **Chelsea Hotel** (*222 W 23rd St between Seventh and Eighth Aves, 212-243-3700*). Built in 1884, it's been home to countless artists, poets and musicians—including **Bob Dylan** and **Leonard Cohen**—but you probably know it as the place where **Sid Vicious** of the **Sex Pistols** stabbed and killed his girlfriend, **Nancy Spungen.**

Now *that's* a real rock-star ending.

the summer. At 11 Fulton Street, the **Fulton Market** building (with gourmet food stalls and seafood restaurants that spill out onto the cobbled streets in summer) is a great place for slurping oysters while watching people stroll by. The surrounding streets are filled with upscale brand-name shops such as J. Crew and Abercrombie & Fitch. If you enter the Seaport area from Water Street, the first thing you'll notice is the whitewashed ***Titanic* Memorial Lighthouse,** originally erected the year after the great ship went down and moved to its current location in 1976. The area offers fine views of the **Brooklyn Bridge** (*see chapter* **The Outer Boroughs**). The smell on South Street is a clear sign that the Fulton Fish Market, America's largest, is here too, though the fish is trucked in and out by land. The thriving market may relocate to the Bronx.

Fulton Fish Market

South St at Fulton St (212-487-8476). Subway: A, C to Broadway–Nassau; J, M, Z, 2, 3, 4, 5 to Fulton St. 9am–3pm. Tours Apr–Oct on first and third Thursday of the month, 6am. $10, reservations required. AmEx, MC, V.

South Street Seaport

Water St to the East River, between John St and Peck Slip (for info about shops and special events, call 212-SEA-PORT). Subway: A, C to Broadway–Nassau; J, M, Z, 2, 3, 4, 5 to Fulton St.

Civic Center

The business of running New York takes place among the many grand buildings of the **Civic Center.** Originally, this was the city's focal point (the park in front is the swath of land upon which the Declaration of Independence was read to Washington's army in 1776). When **City Hall** was built in 1812, its architects were so confident the city would grow no farther north, they didn't bother to put any marble on its northern side. The building, a beautiful blend of Federal form and French Renaissance details, is unfortunately closed to the public (except for scheduled group tours; *see chapter* **Architecture**). **City Hall Park,** which got a $30 million renovation in 1999, has a new granite time wheel that displays the park's history through the ages. For years, the steps of City Hall and the park have been the site of press conferences and political protests. Under Mayor Rudolph Giuliani, the steps were closed to such activity, although civil libertarians successfully defied the ban in April 2000. The much larger **Municipal Building,** which faces City Hall and reflects it architecturally, is home to other civic offices, including the marriage bureau, which can churn out newlyweds at remarkable speed. **Park Row,** east of the park and now lined with cafés and electronics shops, once held the offices of 19 daily papers and was known as Newspaper Row. It was also the site of Phineas T. Barnum's sensationalist American Museum, which burned down in 1865.

Facing the park from the west is Cass Gilbert's famous **Woolworth Building,** a vertically elongated Gothic cathedral of an office building that has been called "the Mozart of Skyscrapers" (*see chapter* **Architecture**). Its beautifully detailed lobby is open to the public during business hours. Two blocks down Broadway is **St. Paul's Chapel** (*between Fulton and Vesey Sts*), an oasis of peace modeled on London's St. Martin-in-the-Fields, and one of the few buildings left from the century of British rule (it dates to 1766). The houses of crime and punishment are also located in the Civic Center, around Foley Square—once a pond and later the site of one of the city's most notorious slums, Five Points. Here, you'll find the **New York County Courthouse** (*60 Centre St*), a hexagonal neoclassical building with a beautiful interior rotunda featuring a mural called *Law Through the Ages*. Next door is the **United States Courthouse** (*40 Centre St*), a golden pyramid-topped tower above a Corinthian temple. Back next to City Hall is the old New York County Courthouse, more popularly known as the **Tweed Courthouse,** a symbol of the runaway corruption of mid-19th-century city government. Boss Tweed, leader of the political machine Tammany Hall, pocketed $10 million of the building's huge $14 million cost. But $4 million in the late 19th century still got the city a beautiful building. Its Italianate detailing may be symbolic of immense greed, but it *is* of the highest quality. The **Criminal Courts Building,** at 100 Centre Street, is by far the most intimidating of them all. Great slabs of granite give it an awesome presence, emphasized by the huge looming towers that guard the entrance. This Kafkaesque home of justice has been known since its creation as "the Tombs," a reference not only to its architecture but to the deathly conditions of the city jail it once contained.

All of these courts are open to the public weekdays from 9am to 5pm, though only some of the courtrooms allow visitors. Your best bet for a little courtroom drama is the Criminal Courts, where if you can't slip into a trial, you can at least observe hallways full of seedy-looking lawyers and the criminals they represent. Or, for a twist on predinner theater, check out Arraignment Court (*Sun–Wed 5pm–1am; Thu–Sat 5–9pm*).

A major archaeological site, the **African Burial Ground,** is located on Duane Street between Broadway and Lafayette Street. The ground is a remnant of a five-and-a-half-acre cemetery, closed in 1794, where 20,000 African men, women and children were buried. The site was unearthed during construction of a federal office building in 1991 and was designated a National Historic Landmark.

City Hall Park

Between Broadway and Park Row and Chambers St. Subway: J, M, Z to Chambers St; 2, 3 to Park Pl; 4, 5, 6 to Brooklyn Bridge–City Hall.

City Hall, at the northern end of the park, contains the mayor's office and the legislative chambers of the City Council, and is thus ringed with news vans waiting for the mayor to appear. Of course, the pretty landscaping and abundant benches also make it a popular lunchtime spot for area office workers.

St. Paul's Chapel

211 Broadway between Fulton and Vesey Sts (212-602-0874). Subway: A, C to Broadway–Nassau St; J, M, Z, 2, 3, 4, 5 to Fulton St. Sun–Fri 9am–3pm.

Chinatown

Chinatown used to be the largest Chinese-immigrant community in the western hemisphere, but in recent years many of the area's residents have moved to other Chinese enclaves in Brooklyn and Queens or to other cities. Still, Manhattan's Chinatown is impressive, and the neighborhood is a bracing change from the sanitized Chinatowns in San Francisco and London. More than 150,000 Chinese live in its many tenements and high-rise buildings, and many of them work in this concentrated and very self-sufficient area. New immigrants arrive daily, and some residents almost never leave. Not much English is spoken on its busy streets—which get even wilder during the Chinese New Year festivities in January or February, and around the 4th of July, when it is the city's best source of (illegal) fireworks. The posters in shop windows advertising Chinese movies highlight the area's cultural cohesion. You could almost be in Hong Kong's Wan Chai district.

Food is everywhere. The markets on **Canal Street** sell some of the best fish, fruits and vegetables in the city. There are countless restaurants; Mott Street—from Worth Street right up to Kenmare Street—is lined with Cantonese and Szechuan places, as is East Broadway. And vendors sell wonderful snacks, such as bags of little sweet egg pancakes. Worth a visit, too, is the **Chinatown Ice Cream Factory** (*65 Bayard St between Mott and Elizabeth Sts, 212-608-4170*), whose flavor options run from fresh lychee sorbet to green-tea ice cream. Canal Street is also (in)famous as a source of blank cassette tapes and counterfeit designer items; vendors hawk everything from fake Rolexes to the cheapest "brand name" running shoes. It's a bargain-hunter's paradise. Push past the doors of any of the area's gift shops and you'll be rewarded with all manner of

Canvas the area Seafaring vessels like this sailboat fill the South Street Seaport docks.

Vendor splendor Toys abound in Chinatown.

unique, inexpensive one-of-a-kind Chinese imported goods, from teacups and good-luck charms to kitschy pop-culture paraphernalia. One of the best shops is the bilevel **Pearl River Mart,** at the corner of Canal Street and Broadway, which is filled with imported food, dresses, traditional musical instruments and videos (*see chapter* **Shopping & Services**).

A statue of the Chinese philosopher marks **Confucius Plaza** at the corner of Bowery and Division Streets. On Bayard Street is the **Wall of Democracy,** where political writings about events in Beijing are posted. On weekends, **Columbus Park** at Bayard and Mulberry Streets is the hangout of choice for elderly men and women wishing to get in a game of mah-jongg, while younger folks practice martial arts. The place is jam-packed with families taking a break from shopping; you may even catch an all-Asian volleyball tournament. Immediately upon entering the open doors of the **Eastern States Buddhist Temple of America,** you'll notice the glitter of hundreds of Buddhas and the smell of incense. A much larger Buddhist temple, **Mahayana Temple Buddhist Association,** is near the entrance to the Manhattan Bridge.

For a different taste of Chinatown culture, there's the noisy **Chinatown Fair,** an amusement arcade that featured a live tic-tac-toe–playing chicken in a glass box up until January 1998, when it was replaced by a wooden bird. The **Music Palace Movie Theater,** at 93 Bowery at Hester Street, features strictly Chinese films with English subtitles. Finally, although gentrification has not really invaded Chinatown, the **Double Happiness** bar (*see chapter* **Bars**) could start the trend—downtown clubbers have made it a popular watering hole.

Moving east, Chinatown stretches across the lower end of **Sara Delano Roosevelt Park,** where kids play spirited games of basketball and handball. City officials closed a market of tin-roofed food stalls in the park in 1998, and political activists continue to agitate for its reopening. Across Forsyth Street, Chinatown runs through what is more commonly called the Lower East Side. This area has fewer restaurants and shops than the western end but is quickly becoming prime property.

Chinatown Fair

8 Mott St at Canal St. Subway: J, M, Z, N, R, 6 to Canal St.

Eastern States Buddhist Temple of America

64B Mott St between Canal and Bayard Sts (212-966-6229). Subway: J, M, Z, N, R, 6 to Canal St. 9am–7pm.

Mahayana Temple Buddhist Association

133 Canal St at Bowery, No. 33 (212-925-8787). Subway: B, D, Q to Grand St; J, M, Z, N, R, 6 to Canal St. 8am–6pm.

Lower East Side

The Lower East Side tells the story of New York's immigrants: One generation makes good and moves to the suburbs, leaving space for the next wave of hopefuls. It is busy and densely populated, a patchwork of strong ethnic communities, and great for dining and exploration. Today, Lower East Side residents are largely Asian and Latino, though the area is more famous for its earlier settlers, most notably Jews from Eastern Europe. It was here that mass tenement housing was built to accommodate the 19th-century influx of immigrants (including many Irish, German, Polish and Hungarian families). Unsanitary, overcrowded buildings forced the introduction of building codes. To appreciate the conditions in which the mass of immigrants lived, take a look at the **Lower East Side Tenement Museum** (*see chapter* **Museums**).

Between 1870 and 1920, hundreds of synagogues and religious schools were established here. Yiddish newspapers were published, and associations for social reform and cultural studies flourished, along with vaudeville and Yiddish theaters. (The Marx Brothers, Jimmy Durante, Eddie Cantor and George and Ira Gershwin were just a few of the entertainers who lived in the area.) Now, however, only 10 to 15 percent of the population is Jewish; the **Eldridge Street Synagogue** finds it hard to round up the ten adult males required to conduct a service.

Puerto Ricans and Dominicans began to move to the Lower East Side after World War II. Bodegas, or corner groceries, abound, with their brightly colored awnings. Many restaurants serve Puerto Rican standards, such as rice and beans with fried plantains. In the summer, the streets throb with the sounds of salsa and merengue as the residents hang out slurping ices, drinking beer and playing dominoes.

Beginning in the 1980s, those who could be described as the latest immigrants started to move to the area: young artists, musicians and other rebels, attracted by the area's low rents. The bars, boutiques and music venues that cater to this crowd initially sprouted on Ludlow Street, essentially creating an extension of the East Village. Now, they're spreading like dandelions to the surrounding streets. Stanton and Orchard Streets, in particular, have sprouted clubs and restaurants such as **Arlene Grocery** and **Baby Jupiter.** Then there's **Tonic,** on Norfolk Street, and the **Bowery Ballroom,** a popular music venue on Delancey Street between Bowery and Chrystie Street (*see chapters* **Bars** *and* **Music**). Recently, many small boutiques have opened next door to the clubs—or within them, in the case of the indie-lit **Incommunicado** bookstore and press (*212-473-9530*) inside Tonic.

The Lower East Side has always been a haven for political radicals, and this tradition lives on at **ABC No Rio,** a squat at 156 Rivington Street between Clinton and Suffolk Streets that also houses a gallery and performance space.

Despite the few trendy shops that have cropped up along the block, Orchard Street below Stanton is the heart of the **Orchard Street Bargain District**, a row of stores selling utilitarian goods; this is the place for cheap luggage, sportswear, hats and T-shirts. Some remnants of the neighborhood's Jewish roots remain. The shabby **Sammy's Roumanian** is only for those with strong stomachs—hearty servings of Eastern European fare are served with a jug of chicken fat and a bottle of vodka—but it's one of the most famous of the Lower East Side eateries. If you prefer "lighter" food, **Katz's Deli** sells some of the best pastrami in New York and the orgasms are pretty good, too, if Meg Ryan's performance in *When Harry Met Sally…* is any indication (the famous "I'll have what she's having" scene was filmed there). **Ratner's,** a kosher dairy restaurant, is a New York institution that also perfectly illustrates the collision between old and new Lower East Side: Its back room, **Lansky Lounge,** is a swinging club named for the infamous mobster Meyer Lansky, a former area resident. **Guss' Pickles,** at 35 Essex Street between Hester and Grand Sts, is another Lower East Side landmark.

Eldridge Street Synagogue

12 Eldridge St between Canal and Division Sts (212-219-0888). Subway: F to East Broadway. Sun 11am–4pm.

This beautifully decorated (and now restored) building was the pride of the Jewish congregation that

Cut and dried Veggies, roots and herbs are sold by the scoopful in Chinatown.

once filled it. Tours are at 11:30am and 2:30pm on Tuesdays and Thursdays.

First Shearith Israel Graveyard

55–57 St. James Pl between Oliver and James Sts. Subway: B, D, Q to Grand St.
The burial ground of the oldest Jewish community in the United States—Spanish and Portuguese Jews who escaped the Inquisition—contains gravestones dating from 1683.

Israel Israelowitz Tours

718-951-707; www.jewishdestinations.com/oscar.htm.
Call for details of guided tours of the Lower East Side and lecture programs.

Sammy's Roumanian

157 Chrystie St at Delancey St (212-673-0330). Subway: B, D, Q to Grand St. Mon–Fri 3–10pm, Sat, Sun 3pm–midnight.
The place to go for authentic Jewish soul food and spirits.

Shapiro's Winery

124 Rivington St between Essex and Norfolk Sts (212-674-4404). Subway: F to Delancey St; J, M, Z to Essex St. Tours on the hour, Sun 11am–5pm. Free.
Shapiro's has been making kosher wine ("so thick you can cut it with a knife") since 1899. The wine tours include tastings.

Little Italy

Another neighborhood that has undergone tremendous change in the past several decades is Little Italy—once a vivid pocket of ethnicity, with all the sights and sounds of the mother country. It's shrinking, though, as Chinatown encroaches, Italian families flee to the suburbs, and stylish boutiques move in. These days, the neighborhood hardly resembles the insular community portrayed in Martin Scorsese's *Mean Streets*. All that's really left of the Italian community that has existed here since the mid-19th century are the cafés and restaurants on Mulberry Street, between Canal and Houston Streets, and short sections of cross streets. But ethnic pride is still going strong. Italian-Americans flood in from Queens and Brooklyn to show their love for the old neighborhood during the **Feast of San Gennaro** in September (*see chapter* **New York by Season**). In summer, Italian films are shown outside in the **De Salvio Playground** at Spring and Mulberry Streets.

Naturally, Little Italy is caught up in the lore of the American Mafia, and there are a few sights related to this aspect of the community. Celebrity don John Gotti ran much of his operation from a social club at 247 Mulberry Street (*between Prince and Spring Sts*); in a twist of fate that sums up the changes happening in the neighborhood, it is now an upscale boutique. Mobster Joey Gallo was shot to death in 1972 while eating with his family at **Umberto's Clam House,** which has since relocated around the corner (to *386 Broome Street at Mulberry Street)*. The Italian eateries here are mostly pricey, ostentatious grill-and-pasta houses that locals avoid. Still, it's worth your while to enjoy a dessert and coffee at one of the many small cafés lining the streets (*see chapter* **Restaurants**). For a drink, head straight to **Mare Chiaro** (*176½ Mulberry St between Broome and Grand Sts*), a dive that was once a favorite haunt of Frank Sinatra's back in the day and is now a destination for young revelers.

The neighborhood is, not surprisingly, home to great food stores (specializing in strong cheeses, excellent wines, spicy meats, freshly made pasta and the like). For that truly unique gift, **Forzano Italian Imports** (*128 Mulberry St at Hester St*), is the best place in New York for papal souvenirs, ghastly Italian pop music and soccer memorabilia. Two buildings of note here are **St. Patrick's Old Cathedral** (*260–264 Prince St at Mulberry St*), which was once the premier Catholic church of New York but was demoted when the Fifth Avenue cathedral was consecrated, and the former **Police Headquarters Building** (*240 Centre St between Grand and Broom Sts*), which was converted into much sought-after co-op apartments in 1988. The very hip northern end of the neighborhood, which lies just to the east of Soho, is now known as Nolita. Mott and Elizabeth Streets—between Houston and Prince Streets in particular—host an array of small kitschy art and gift shops and expensive artisanal (jewelry and glass) boutiques. The area also has some good restaurants and funky boutiques (*see chapter* **Shopping & Services**).

Soho

Soho is designer New York, in every sense. Walk around its cobbled streets, among the elegant cast-iron buildings, boutiques and bistros, and you'll find yourself sharing the sidewalks with the beautiful people of young, moneyed, fashionable NYC. The bars and cafés are full of these trendsetters, while the shop windows display the work of the latest arrivals in the world of fashion. The area's art galleries, though still plentiful, have been vacating their converted lofts to move to cheaper (and now cutting-edge) neighborhoods like Dumbo in Brooklyn and far west Chelsea.

Soho (south of Houston Street) was earmarked for destruction during the 1960s, but the area was saved by the many artists who

Booze cruise Hipsters from all over the city head to Ludlow Street for its many bars.

inhabited its (then) low-rent former warehouse spaces. They protested the demolition of these beautiful buildings, whose cast-iron frames prefigured the technology of the skyscraper. Two examples of cast-iron architecture at its best are **109 Prince Street** (*at the corner of Greene Street*), which now houses a Replay clothing store, and **95 Greene Street.** As loft living became fashionable and the buildings were renovated for residential use, landlords were quick to sniff the profits of gentrification. Several upscale hotels, including the **Mercer** and the **SoHo Grand,** have opened in the area, and the names on the shop windows read like a who's who of fashion: CK, Louis Vuitton, Vivienne Tam, Vivienne Westwood, agnès b., Anna Sui and Helmut Lang are just a few of the designers who have opened boutiques (*see chapters* **Shopping & Services** *and* **Accommodations**). Surprisingly, plenty of sweatshops remain here, especially near Canal Street—though, increasingly, the buildings also house such businesses as graphic design studios, magazines and record labels. There has also been a noticeable influx of large chain stores: Starbucks, Old Navy, Pottery Barn, J. Crew and Banana Republic have all put down roots, prompting locals to mutter darkly about the "malling of Soho."

West Broadway, the main thoroughfare of Soho, is lined with chain stores, pricey shops and art galleries. On the weekend, you're as likely to hear French, German and Italian as you are English, due to the huge number of European tourists attracted by the fine shopping. Four blocks east, on Broadway, the **Guggenheim Museum** has a branch that exhibits both temporary shows and selections from the museum's permanent collection. Other galleries and museums specializing in lesser-known artists are located on Broadway. **The New Museum of Contemporary Art** often exhibits controversial works; the neighboring **Museum for African Art** is also worth a look. Just off Broadway on Spring Street is the **Fire Museum,** a small building housing a collection of gleaming antique engines dating back to the 1700s.

West of West Broadway, tenement- and townhouse-lined streets contain remnants of the Italian community that dominated this area. Elderly men and women walk along Sullivan Street up to the **Shrine Church of St. Anthony of Padua,** which was founded by the Franciscan Friars in 1866. The church also supports a nearby convent and rectory. Some businesses that predate Soho's gentrification are still thriving, including **Joe's Dairy** at 156 Sullivan Street, **Pino's Prime Meat Market** at 149 Sullivan Street and **Vesuvio Bakery** at 160 Prince Street.

▶ To further explore Soho's art scene, see chapters **Museums** and **Art Galleries.**
▶ Learn more about Soho and other downtown building designs in chapter **Architecture.**

Tribeca

Tribeca (triangle below Canal Street) today is a textbook example of the process of gentrification in lower Manhattan. It's very much as Soho was 15 or 20 years ago: Some parts are deserted and abandoned—the cobbles dusty and untrodden, and the cast-iron architecture chipped and unpainted—while other pockets throb with arriviste energy. Unlike Soho, however, the rich and famous have been the pioneers here: Harvey Keitel, MTV Chairman Tom Freston and many other local and national celebrities live in the area. In particular, this is a hotbed of trendy restaurants, including **Nobu, Layla** and **Danube** (*see chapter* **Restaurants**). A number of bars have established themselves as well, especially near the corner of North Moore Street and West Broadway, and clubs such as the **Knitting Factory** (*see chapter* **Music**) are expanding the cultural offerings. The buildings here are generally larger than those in Soho and, particularly toward the river, are mostly warehouses (many have been recently converted to condos). However, there is some fine smaller-scale cast-iron architecture along White Street and the parallel thoroughfares (*see chapter* **Architecture**), including **85 Leonard Street,** the only remaining cast-iron building attributable to James Bogardus, the developer of the cast-iron building method. On

Shutter to think Detailed old buildings like this one line the quaint streets of the West Village.

Harrison Street is a row of well-preserved Federal-style townhouses.

As in Soho, art is a prominent industry here, and there are several galleries representing the more cutting-edge (read: hit-or-miss) talents. Salons, furniture stores, spas and other businesses that cater to the upscale residents of the neighborhood are also entrenched.

Tribeca is also the unofficial headquarters of New York's film industry. Robert De Niro's **Tribeca Film Center** houses screening rooms and production offices (*375 Greenwich St at Franklin St*) in the old Martinson Coffee Building. His **Tribeca Grill** (*212-941-3900*) is on the ground floor. Also in the Film Center are the Queens-bred brothers Bob and Harvey Weinstein and the main offices of their company, **Miramax.** The **Screening Room** (*see chapter* **Film & TV**) shows art-house films in an upstairs theater and serves gourmet food in its elegant dining room.

West Village

Most of the West Village, roughly the area between Seventh Avenue and the Hudson River, is filled with quaint tree-lined streets and historic townhouses. It was historically a middle-class neighborhood, but today many of the city's media power elite live here; they fill its bistros and bars that line Bleecker Street and Hudson Street, the area's main thoroughfares. The northwest corner of this area is known as the **Meatpacking District,** a nod to the many area businesses that sell quality veal and other meats. In recent years, clubs have taken advantage of the large spaces available here, and now partyers share the empty nighttime streets with transsexual prostitutes. Restaurants have staked a claim as well: The always-bustling **Florent**, a 24-hour French diner, has been here for years. Newer arrivals such as **Pastis** and **Markt** lure a sleek celeb-studded crowd (*see chapter* **Restaurants, Chic**). As with any burgeoning neighborhood, the Meatpacking District has sprouted several new shops (*see* **Meat street manifesto,** *page 168*).

Farther south and west of Hudson Street are quaint cobblestone streets. At Bethune and Washington Streets is **Westbeth,** a block-long building formerly owned by Bell Telephone (it's where the vacuum tube and the transistor were invented); the 1900 structure was converted to lofts for artists in 1965. Around the corner on Bank Street is the **Westbeth Theatre Center Music Hall,** which often has fine rock shows (*see chapter* **Music**). A development of luxury condos along Washington Street—outside the historic landmarked district—has sparked claims that the neighborhood's charm is slowly diminishing. On Hudson Street, between Perry and 11th Streets, is the famous **White Horse Tavern,** where poet Dylan Thomas spent the better part of the 1940s. Earlier in the century, John Steinbeck and John Dos Passos passed the time at **Chumley's,** a Prohibition-era speakeasy, still unmarked at 86 Bedford Street (*see chapter* **Bars**). On and just off Seventh Avenue South are numerous jazz and cabaret clubs, including the **Village Vanguard** and **Small's** (*see chapter* **Music**).

The West Village is also a renowned gay area, with many famous bars, including the **Stonewall** on Christopher Street. Originally the Stonewall Inn, this bar was the scene of the 1969 Stonewall Rebellion, which marked the birth of the gay-liberation movement. There are as many same-sex couples strolling along Christopher Street as straight ones, and plenty of shops, bars and restaurants that are out and proud.

> ▶ More information on downtown nightlife can be found in chapters **Bars** and **Music.**
> ▶ A complete review of Stonewall and other gay establishments can be found in chapter **Gay & Lesbian.**

Greenwich Village

The middle section of "the Village" has been the scene of some serious hanging out throughout its history. Stretching from 14th Street down to Houston Street, and from Broadway west to Seventh Avenue South, Greenwich Village's leafy streets lined with townhouses, theaters, coffeehouses, and tiny bars and clubs have witnessed and inspired bohemian lifestyles for almost a century. It's a place for idle wandering, for people-watching from sidewalk cafés, for candlelit dining in secret restaurants, or for hopping between bars and cabaret venues. The Village gets overcrowded in summer, and it has lost some of its quaintness as the retail center of lower Broadway has spread west, but much of what attracted creative types to New York still exists. The jazz generation lives on in smoky clubs (*see chapter* **Music**). Sip a fresh roast in honor of the Beats—Jack Kerouac, Allen Ginsberg and their ilk—as you sit in the coffee shops they frequented. Kerouac's favorite was **Le Figaro Café,** at the corner of MacDougal and Bleecker Streets.

The hippies, who tuned out in **Washington Square,** are still there in spirit, and often in person: The park hums with musicians and street artists (although the once-ubiquitous pot dealers have largely become victims of strict policing). Chess hustlers and students from **New York University** join in, along with today's new generation of hangers-out: hip-hop kids who drive down to West 4th Street in their booming Jeeps and Generation Y skaters/ravers who clatter around the fountain and the base of the **Washington Square Arch** (a miniature Arc de Triomphe built in 1892 in honor of George Washington).

The Village first became fashionable in the 1830s, when elegant townhouses were built around Washington Square. Most of these are now owned by NYU. The university dominates this section of the Village, and many of the large apartment complexes on or near the square serve as dormitories. Literary figures including Henry James, Mark Twain, Herman Melville and Edith Wharton lived on or near the square. In 1871, the growing artistic community founded the **Salmagundi Club,** America's oldest artists' club, which is still extant, and now situated above Washington Square on Fifth Avenue (No. 47). And although it has moved from its original location at the corner of 8th Street, the **Cedar Tavern** on University Place (*between 11th and 12th Sts*) is worth a visit. It's where the leading figures of Abstract Expressionism discussed how best to throw paint: Jackson Pollock, Franz Kline and Larry Rivers drank here in the 1950s.

Eighth Street, now a long procession of punky boutiques, shoe shops, piercing parlors and cheap jewelry vendors, was the closest New York got to San Francisco's Haight Street; Jimi Hendrix's **Electric Lady Studios**—yes, he was the owner— are still here at No. 52 (*see* **Walk like a musician,** *page 36*); Bob Dylan lived at and owned 94 MacDougal Street through much of the '60s, performing in Washington Square Park and at clubs such as **Cafe Wha?** Once the stamping ground of Beat poets and hipster jazz musicians, the area around **Bleecker Street** (*between La Guardia Pl and Sixth Ave*) is now a dingy stretch of poster shops, cheap ethnic restaurants and a number of music venues that showcase local talent and cover bands for the college crowd. The famed Village Gate jazz club used to be at the corner of Thompson and Bleecker Streets; it is now a CVS pharmacy.

In the triangle formed by 10th Street, Sixth Avenue and Greenwich Avenue, you'll see the neo-Gothic Victorian **Jefferson Market Courthouse;** once voted America's fifth most beautiful building, it's now a library. Across the street is **Balducci's** (*see chapter* **Shopping &**

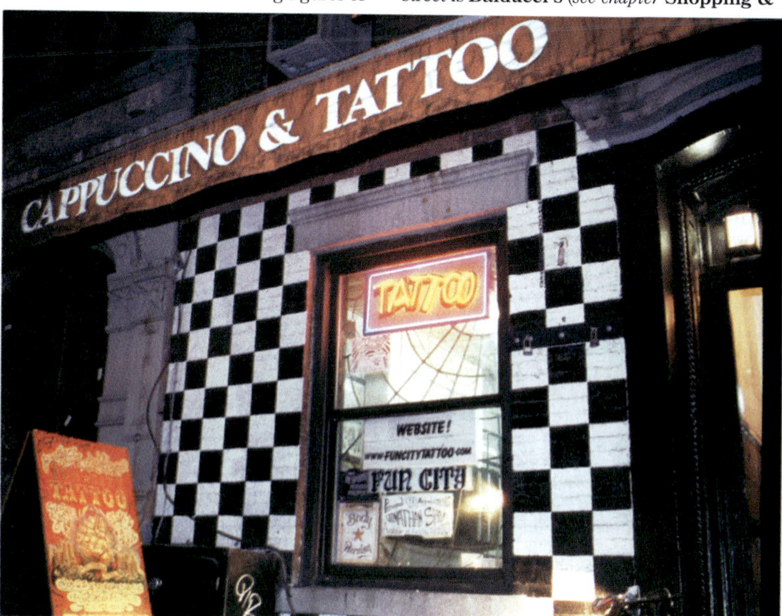

Ink spot Get something brewed and tattooed at the popular Fun City in the East Village.

Services), one of the finest food stores in the city, and down Sixth Avenue at 4th Street, you stumble on "the Cage," outdoor basketball courts where you can witness hot hoops action (*see chapter* **Sports & Fitness**).

Jefferson Market Courthouse

425 Sixth Ave between 9th and 10th Sts (212-243-4334). Subway: A, C, E, B, D, F, Q to W 4th St. Library open Mon, Thu 10am–6pm; Tue, Fri noon–6pm; Wed noon–8pm; Sat 10am–5pm. Free.

Salmagundi Club

47 Fifth Ave at 12th St (212-255-7740). Subway: L, N, R, 4, 5, 6 to 14th St–Union Sq. Open for exhibitions only; phone for details. Free.

Now the home of a series of artistic and historical societies, the club's fine 19th-century interior is still elegant.

Washington Square Park

Between Waverly Pl and 4th St, and MacDougal St and Fifth Ave. Subway: A, C, E, B, D, F, Q to W 4th St.

Located smack in the middle of bustling Greenwich Village, Washington Square Park is the city's most famous park below 14th Street. Drug dealers once plied their trade in every corner of the park; nowadays, musicians ring the park's middle section, and street performers work around (and even in) the fountain, while the southwest corner is home to a community of die-hard chess players. The best thing to do here is find somewhere to park yourself and indulge in the best people-watching just about anywhere on earth.

East Village

Far scruffier than its western counterpart, the East Village has a long history as a countercultural mecca. Originally considered part of the Lower East Side, the neighborhood first took off in the 1960s, when throngs of writers, artists and musicians moved in and turned it into ground zero for the '60s cultural revolution. Many famous clubs and coffeehouses were established, including the Fillmore East rock club on Second Avenue between 6th and 7th Streets (now demolished), and the Dom, where the Velvet Underground was a regular headliner, at 23 St. Marks Place (now a community center). In the '70s, the neighborhood took a dive, as drugs and crime became prevalent—but that didn't stop many artists and punk rockers from living here. In the early '80s, area galleries were among the first to display the work of hot young artists Jean-Michel Basquiat and Keith Haring.

Today, the area east of Broadway between 14th and Houston Streets is no longer quite so edgy, though remnants of its spirited past live on. Now, you'll find a generally amiable population of punks, yuppies, hippies, homeboys, homeless and trustafarians—would-be bohos who live off trust funds. This motley crew has crowded into the area's tenements—along with older residents, mostly survivors from various waves of immigration.They support the area's funky, cheap clothes stores (check for quality before forking over any cash), record shops, bargain restaurants, grungy bars and punky clubs.

St. Marks Place (essentially 8th Street between Lafayette Street and Avenue A), lined with bars squeezed into tiny basements and stores overflowing onto the sidewalks, is the main drag (in more ways than one). It's packed until the wee hours with crowds browsing for bargains in T-shirt shops, record stores and bookshops. The more interesting places are to the east, and you'll find cafés and great little shops of all kinds on and around Avenue A between 6th and 10th Streets. Since tattooing became legal in New York City in 1997 (it had been banned since 1961), a number of parlors have opened up, including the now famous **Fun City,** at 94 St. Marks Place between First Avenue and Avenue A, whose awning advertises CAPPUCCINO & TATTOO.

Astor Place, with its revolving cube sculpture, is always swarming with young skateboarders. It is also the site of Peter Cooper's recently refurbished **Cooper Union,** the city's first free educational institute, opened in 1859; it's now a design and engineering college (and still free). The area bustles with youthful energy; there are even plans to build a European-designed hotel and screening room in the parking lot across the

Bauble and weave FInd cheap jewelry and trinkets along St. Marks Place.

street from Cooper. In the 19th century, Astor Place marked the boundary between the ghettos to the east and some of the city's most fashionable homes, such as **Colonnade Row,** on Lafayette Street. Facing these was the distinguished Astor Public Library, now the **Joseph Papp Public Theater,** a haven for first-run American plays and producer of the **New York Shakespeare Festival** (*see chapter* **Theater & Dance**) as well as a trendy nightspot called **Joe's Pub** (*see chapter* **Cabaret & Comedy**). In the '60s, Papp rescued the library from demolition and got it declared a landmark.

East of Lafayette Street on the Bowery are several missionary organizations that cater to the downtrodden who still make the Bowery the Bowery. In recent years, a few restaurants have also set up shop here. At 315 Bowery is the hallowed **CBGB-OMFUG** club, the birthplace of American punk. CB's still packs in guitar bands, both new and used (*see chapter* **Music** *and* **Walk like a musician,** *page 36*). Many other local bars and clubs successfully apply the formula of cheap beer and loud music, including the **Continental, Brownies** and the **Mercury Lounge.**

East 7th Street is a Ukrainian stronghold; the focal point is the Byzantine-looking **St. George's Ukrainian Catholic Church,** built in 1977 but looking considerably older. Across the street there is often a long line of beefy fraternity types waiting to enter **McSorley's Old Ale House,** the oldest pub in the city (or so it claims); it still serves just one kind of beer—its own brew (*see chapter* **Bars**). There is good one-of-a-kind shopping in the boutiques of young designers and vintage clothing dealers that dot 7th, 8th and 9th Streets between Second Avenue and Avenue A.

On 6th Street, between First and Second Avenues, is **Little India** (one of several in New York). Here roughly two dozen Indian restaurants sit side by side, the long-running joke being that they all share a single kitchen. And if you're wondering about the inordinate number of burly men on Harleys on 3rd Street between First and Second Avenues, it's because the New York chapter of the **Hell's Angels** is headquartered here.

Avenues A through D, an area known as **Alphabet City,** run parallel to the East River. Here, a largely Latino population (Avenue C is known as "Loisaida Ave," the phonetic spelling of "Lower East Side" when pronounced with a Spanish accent) is slowly being overtaken by counterculture arrivistes. Two interesting churches on 4th Street are built in the Spanish-colonial style: **San Isidro y San Leandro,** at No. 345 between Avenues C and D, and **Iglesia Pentecostal Camino Damasco,** at No. 289 between Avenues B and C. The neighborhood's long, rocky romance with heroin continues (Stone Temple Pilot frontman Scott Weiland was busted here in 1998 during a sweep of housing projects on Avenue D); consequently, venturing much farther east than Avenue B can be dodgy at night. Alphabet City is not without its attractions, though: **The Nuyorican Poets Café** (*see chapter* **Books & Poetry**), a stronghold in the recent resurgence of espresso-drinking beatniks, is famous for its slams, in which performance poets do battle before a score-keeping audience. **Tompkins Square Park,** now well maintained and landscaped, has historically been the site of demonstrations and rioting. The last uprising was in 1991, after the controversial decision to evict the park's squatters and renovate it to suit the tastes of the area's increasingly affluent residents. Political dissent lives on at **Blackout Books,** an anarchist bookshop at 50 Avenue B between 3rd and 4th Streets. North of Tompkins Square, around First Avenue and 11th Street, are remnants of earlier communities: good Italian cheese shops, Polish restaurants, discount fabric shops and two great Italian patisseries. Visit **De Robertis** (*176 First Ave at 11th St, 212-674-7138*) for delicious cakes and **Veniero's Pasticceria** (*342 11th St at First Ave, 212-674-7264*) for wonderful minipastries and butter biscuits.

St. Mark's Church in-the-Bowery

131 E 10th St at Second Ave (212-674-6377). Subway: 6 to Astor Pl. Mon–Fri 10am–6pm.

St. Mark's was built in 1799 on the site of Peter Stuyvesant's farm. Stuyvesant, one of New York's first governors, is buried here, along with many of his descendants. The church is now home to several arts groups (it was where the wedding and funeral took place in the film *The Group*). Call for details of the performances here.

Tompkins Square Park

Between 7th and 10th Sts and Aves A and B. Subway: 6 to Astor Pl.

The community park of the East Village, Tompkins Square is one of the liveliest places in the entire city. Here, drum circles, Latino musicians, acoustic-guitar–wielding hippie types, punk squatters, dogs, the neighborhood's yuppie residents and the homeless mix and mingle and sit on the grass under huge old trees. In summer, the park's southern end is often the site of musical performances, while the north is the province of basketball, hockey and handball enthusiasts.

Midtown

The heart of the city beats 24 hours a day to the rhythm of corporate America, plus there's plenty of culture here, too

Midtown, roughly 14th to 59th Streets, is the city's engine room, powered by the hundreds of thousands of commuters who pour in each day. During working hours, the area is all business. The towering office buildings are home to huge international corporations, well-known book and magazine publishers, record companies and advertising agencies. Garment manufacturers have long clustered in the area on and around Seventh ("Fashion") Avenue. Midtown is also where you'll find most of the city's large hotels (and the legions of tourists and traveling execs who occupy them), the department stores and classy retailers of Fifth Avenue and Rockefeller Center, and landmarks such as the Empire State Building, St. Patrick's Cathedral and Carnegie Hall. By night, locals and visitors gravitate to the *Blade Runner*–like voltage of Times Square to see movies and Broadway shows, to eat in the numerous restaurants or to do some late-night shopping for music and home electronics.

Flatiron District

Running along Sixth Avenue from 14th to 23rd Streets and bounded on the east by Park Avenue South, the Flatiron District is on the edge of downtown in more ways than geographically. It's now known as a style enclave and a hotbed of new-media businesses.

As Broadway cuts diagonally through Manhattan, it inspires a public square wherever it intersects an avenue. Two such places, **Union Square** at 14th Street and **Madison Square** at 23rd, once marked the limits of a ritzy 19th-century shopping district known as **Ladies' Mile.** Extending along Broadway and west to Sixth Avenue, this collection of huge retail palaces (Macy's first store was on Sixth between 13th and 14th Streets) attracted the "carriage trade"—wealthy ladies buying the latest fashions and household goods from all over the world. By 1914, most of the department stores had moved farther north, leaving behind the proud cast-iron buildings that had housed them. Today, the area has reclaimed much of its cachet as a shopping destination. The upscale home-design store **ABC Carpet & Home** is in a beautiful old building at the corner of 19th Street and Broadway. **Paul Smith** and **Emporio Armani** showcase the season's latest designs on Fifth Avenue (*see chapter* **Shopping & Services**), while Sixth Avenue is dotted with such large chain stores as **Old Navy** and **Bed, Bath & Beyond**.

Union Square is named after neither the Union of the Civil War nor the lively labor rallies that once took place here, but simply for the union of Broadway and Bowery Lane (now Fourth Avenue). From the 1920s until the early 1960s, it had a reputation as a political hot spot, a favorite location for rabble-rousing oratory. These days, while protesters sometimes start marches here en route to City Hall (as after the Amadou Diallo trial in February 2000), the gentrified square is best known as home to the **Union Square Greenmarket**—an excellent farmers' market. The streets leading from it are chock-full of restaurants, including one of the city's best:

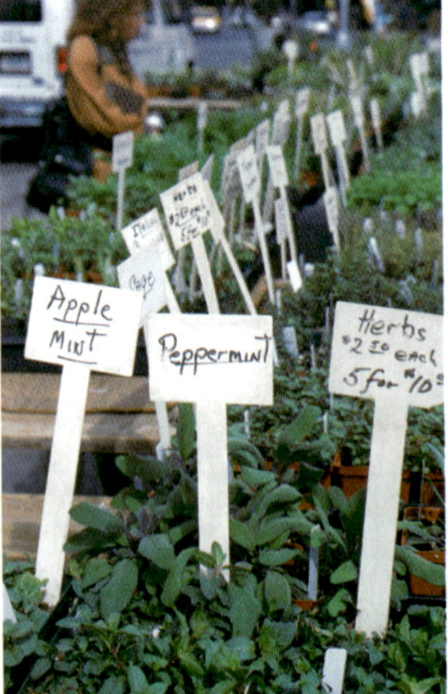

Urban herbs New Yorkers get their greens at the Union Square Greenmarket.

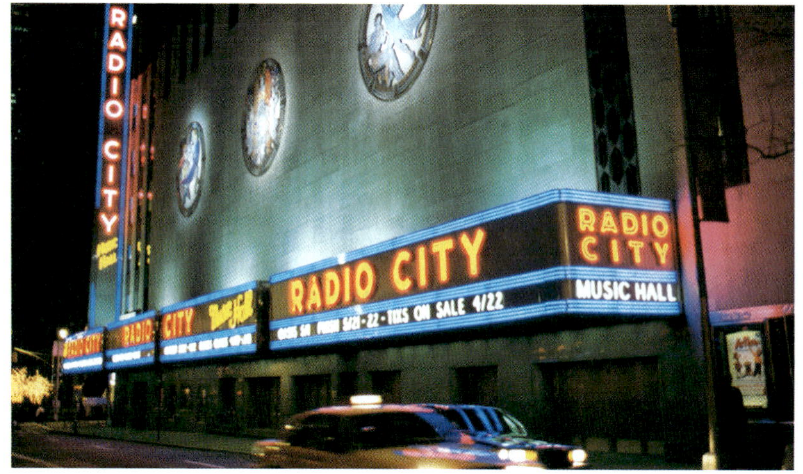

Deco delight Renovated in 1999, Radio City Music Hall glitters anew.

Union Square Cafe. The park is also a popular meeting place. In the summer months, the large outdoor **Luna Park** bar beckons daytime cocktailers, while skateboarders practice wild stunts on the steps and railings of the square's southern edge. West of the **Virgin Megastore** and 14-screen movieplex, which are located at the southern tip of the square, 14th Street is a down-market retail bonanza of cheap goods.

At the northern end of the neighborhood, the Renaissance palazzo **Flatiron Building**—originally named the Fuller Building, after its first owners—is famous for its triangular shape and for being the world's first steel-frame skyscraper. It's just south of Madison Square—the intersection of 23rd Street, Broadway and Fifth Avenue. The Flatiron gives its name to the neighborhood, an area dotted with boutiques, bookshops, photo studios and labs, not to mention wandering models. But with big Internet-related companies such as iVillage.com colonizing lofts in buildings on Broadway and Fifth Avenue since the early '90s, the area has a new nickname: **Silicon Alley.**

► See chapter **Shopping & Services** for more information on midtown shopping.
► To discover midtown's free public-art attractions, see **Public spectacle,** page 54.
► Learn more about the area's bar scene in chapter **Bars.**
► For an in-depth look at area skyscrapers, see chapter **Architecture.**

Madison Square (*23rd St to 26th St between Fifth and Madison Aves*) is also rich in history. It was the site of P.T. Barnum's Hippodrome and the original Madison Square Garden, as well as the scene of prize fights, one famous society murder and lavish entertainment. After years of neglect, the statue-filled park is finally getting a face-lift, and the area bordering the park's east side is now a hot spot. For years, it was notable only for the presence of such imposing buildings as the gold-topped **Metropolitan Life Insurance Company,** the **New York Life Insurance Company** and the **Appellate Court,** but two upscale restaurants, **11 Madison Park** and **Tabla,** along with the slick gym **Duomo,** have injected a shot of chic into this once-staid area (*see chapters* **Restaurants** *and* **Sports & Fitness**).

Union Square Greenmarket

North end of Union Square, 17th St between Union Sq East and Broadway (212-477-3220). Subway: L, N, R, 4, 5, 6 to 14th St–Union Sq. Mon, Wed, Fri, Sat 7am–6pm.

Gramercy Park

To enter Gramercy Park, a tranquil and gated square at the bottom of Lexington Avenue between 20th and 21st Streets, you need a key, something possessed only by those who live in the beautiful townhouses and apartment buildings that surround it—or who stay at the **Gramercy Park Hotel** (*see chapter* **Accommodations**). Anyone, however, can

Stocked market A former Nabisco factory, Chelsea Market is now packed with gourmet food purveyors.

enjoy the charm of the neighboring district, between Third and Park Avenues. Gramercy Park was developed in the 1830s, copying the concept of a London square. **The Players,** at 16 Gramercy Park, is housed in a building that was bought by Edwin Booth, brother of Abraham Lincoln's assassin, John Wilkes Booth, and the foremost actor of his day. Booth had it remodeled as a club for theater professionals. (Winston Churchill and Mark Twain were also members.) At No. 15 is the **National Arts Club,** whose members have often donated impressive works in lieu of annual dues. Its bar houses perhaps the only original Tiffany stained-glass ceiling left in New York City.

Irving Place, leading south from the park to 14th Street, is named after Washington Irving, who didn't actually live on this street (his nephew did). It does have a literary past, though: **Pete's Tavern,** which insists that it (not McSorley's) is the oldest bar in town, was where wit O. Henry wrote "The Gift of the Magi." Near the corner of 15th Street is **Irving Plaza,** a popular midsize rock venue that hosts many big-name acts (*see chapter* **Music**). East of Irving Place, at the corner of 17th Street and Park Avenue South, is the last headquarters of the once all-powerful Tammany Hall political machine. Built in 1929, the building now houses the **Union Square Theater** and the **New York Film Academy.**

West of Gramercy Park is the **Theodore Roosevelt Birthplace,** now a small museum. The low, fortresslike **69th Regiment Armory** (*Lexington Ave at 25th St*), now used by the New York National Guard, was the site of the sensational 1913 Armory Show, which introduced Americans to the modern forms of Cubism, Fauvism, the precocious Marcel Duchamp and other artistic outrages.

National Arts Club

15 Gramercy Park South between Park Ave South and Irving Pl (212-475-3424). Subway: 6 to 23rd St. Open for exhibitions only.

Theodore Roosevelt Birthplace

28 E 20th St between Broadway and Park Ave South (212-260-1616). Subway: 6 to 23rd St. Wed–Sun 9am–5pm. $2, children under 17 free. Cash only.
The president's actual birthplace was demolished in 1916 but has since been fully reconstructed, complete with period furniture and a trophy room.

Kips Bay and Murray Hill

Running from 23rd to 42nd Streets between Park Avenue (and Park Ave South) and the East River, this area is dominated by two things: large apartment buildings and hospitals. The southern portion, known as **Kips Bay** (after Jacobus Kip, whose 17th-century farm used to occupy the area), is populated mainly by young professionals. Though the area has its own historical past (Herman Melville wrote *Billy Budd* at 104 E 26th St), it was, until recently, considered a nondescript neighborhood. But the slightly below-market rents and explosion of restaurants on nearby Park Avenue South have attracted a fashionable set that includes designer John Bartlett, not to mention a new name: Nomad (No͟rth of Ma͟dison Square Park, *see* **Name cropping,** *page 26*). Third Avenue is the main thoroughfare, and it's dotted with ethnic restaurants representing a variety of mainly Eastern cuisines, including Afghan, Turkish and Tibetan. One exception to the otherwise sleepy tone of the neighborhood is the **Rodeo Bar,** on Third Avenue at 27th Street, a Texas-style restaurant and roadhouse that offers live roots music (*see chapter* **Music: Popular music**). Lexington Avenue between 27th and 30th Streets is called **Curry Hill,** due to the swath of Indian restaurants and grocery stores offering inexpensive food, spices and imported goods (*see chapter* **Restaurants, Indian**). Other than a recently developed complex with a multiplex movie theater (*see chapter* **Film & TV**), a bookstore and several large chain stores at 30th Street, Second Avenue is primarily home to a collection of pubs and small, undistinguished restaurants. First Avenue is hospital row: **New York University Medical Center,** the city-run **Bellevue Hospital** and the city's Chief Medical Examiner's office are all here.

Between 30th and 40th Streets is **Murray Hill.** Townhouses of the rich and powerful were once clustered here around Park and Madison Avenues. While it's still a fashionable neighborhood, only a few streets retain the elegance that once made it such a tony address. **Sniffen Court,** at 150–158 East 36th Street, is an unspoiled row of carriage houses located within spitting distance of the Queens-Midtown Tunnel's ceaseless traffic.

The charming Italianate **Morgan Library** (*Madison Ave between 36th and 37th Sts*) is the reason most visitors are drawn to the area. Two elegant buildings (once the home and personal library of John Pierpont Morgan), linked by a modern glass cloister, house the silver and copper collections, manuscripts, books and prints owned by the famous banker, mostly gathered during his travels in Europe (*see chapter* **Museums**).

Chelsea

Chelsea is the region between 14th and 30th Streets west of Sixth Avenue. It is populated mostly by young professionals and has become a hub of New York gay life (*see chapter* **Gay & Lesbian**). You'll find all the trappings of an urban residential neighborhood on the upswing: countless stores (some dull) and a generous number of bars and fine restaurants, mostly clustered on Eighth Avenue. Chelsea's western warehouse district, currently housing some large dance clubs, is being developed for residential use. Pioneering galleries, like the **Dia Center for the Arts** at the west end of 22nd Street, have dragged the art crowd westward, and the whole area has become a thriving gallery district (*see chapter* **Art Galleries, Nonprofit spaces**).

Cushman Row (*406–418 W 20th St between Ninth and Tenth Aves*), in the **Chelsea Historic District,** is a good example of how Chelsea looked when it was developed in the mid-1800s—a grandeur that was destroyed 30 years later when noisy elevated railways came to dominate the area and steal the sunlight. Just north, occupying the entire block between Ninth and Tenth Avenues and 20th and 21st Streets, is the **General Theological Seminary**; its garden is a sublime retreat. On Tenth Avenue, the flashing lights of the **Empire Diner** (a 1929 chrome Art Deco beauty) attract pre- and postclubbers. In recent years, the diner has been joined by a number of other hip eating establishments, including the taxi garage–turned–hot spot **Lot 61** (*see chapter* **Bars**).

Private property Only the buildings bordering Gramercy Park have the entrance key.

Sixth Avenue around 27th Street can seem like a tropical forest at times—the pavement disappears beneath the palm leaves, decorative grasses and colorful blooms of Chelsea's **flower district.** The garment industry has a presence here as well. Sixth Avenue in the mid-20s is also full of antiques showrooms, which sell everything from old posters to classic furniture, and an excellent flea market operates year-round on weekends in an empty parking lot on 25th Street (*see chapter* **Shopping & Services**).

On 23rd Street, between Seventh and Eighth Avenues, is the **Chelsea Hotel,** where many famous people checked in—some of whom never checked out, like Sid Vicious's girlfriend Nancy Spungen. It's worth a peek for its weird artwork and ghoulish guests, and a drink at the lavish lounge **Serena** in the basement (*see chapters* **Accommodations** *and* **Bars**). On Eighth Avenue, you'll find the **Joyce,** a stunning renovated Art Moderne cinema that's a mecca for dance lovers, and on 19th Street, the wonderful **Bessie Schönberg Theater,** where poets recite and mimes do…well, whatever mimes do. Farther toward the river on 19th Street is the **Kitchen,** the experimental arts center with a penchant for video (*see chapter* **Theater & Dance**).

On Ninth Avenue, a former Nabisco plant (where the first Oreo cookie was made in 1912) has been renovated and turned into the **Chelsea Market.** The block-long building is actually a conglomeration of 17 structures built between the 1890s and the 1930s. An upscale food arcade on the ground floor offers meat and fish, wine, tempting cheesecakes and imported Italian foods, among other things. But the building has also become a media center, with the Food Network taping shows in a glassed-in street-level kitchen and studio, and companies such as Oxygen Media and New York 1 News installed in offices on the floors above.

The perfect barometer of the high-pressure real-estate market is at 601 W 26th Street at Eleventh Avenue. Until 1999, the 1930s **Starrett-Lehigh Building**—acclaimed as a masterpiece of the International Style—was a neglected $6-a-square-foot industrial loft and warehouse. Today, Martha Stewart Living Omnimedia, Hugo Boss and ScreamingMedia pay more than $30 a square foot for raw space.

After you've hit some of the art galleries that have colonized the area, keep heading west along 22nd Street to watch a peaceful sunset over the **Hudson River Piers.** These were originally the terminals for the world's grand ocean liners (the *Titanic* was scheduled to dock here). Most are in a state of disrepair, though development has transformed the four between 17th and 23rd Streets into a

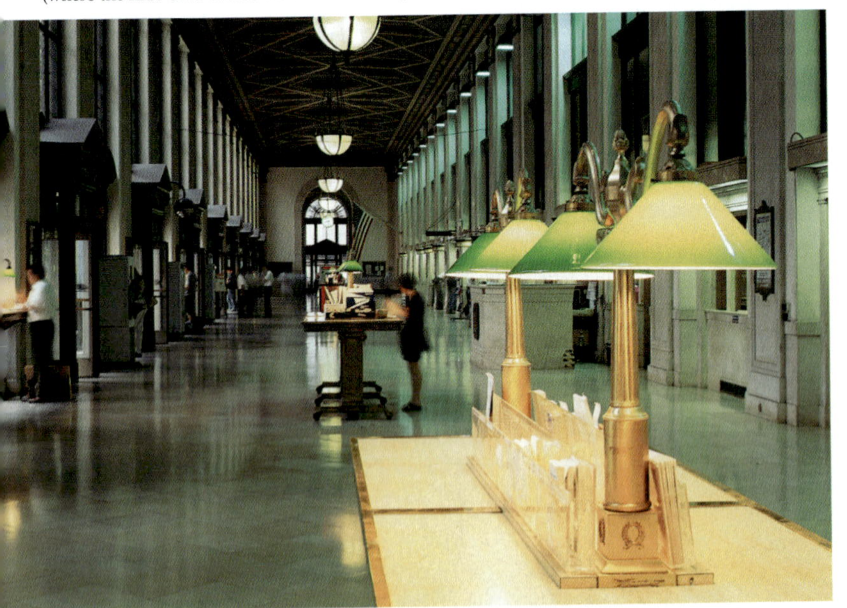

Letter-perfect The General Post Office on Eighth Avenue is a Beaux Arts gem.

dramatic-looking sports center and TV studio complex called **Chelsea Piers** (*see chapter* **Sports & Fitness**).

Chelsea Historic District

Between Ninth and Tenth Aves from 20th to 22nd Sts. Subway: C, E to 23rd St.

Chelsea Market

75 Ninth Ave between 15th and 16th Sts. Subway: A, C, E to 14th St; L to Eighth Ave. Mon–Sat 8am–7pm; Sun 10am–6pm.

General Theological Seminary

175 Ninth Ave between 20th and 21st Sts (212-243-5150). Subway: C, E to 23rd St. Mon–Fri noon–3pm; Sat 11am–3pm. Free.

You can walk through the grounds of the seminary (when open) or take a guided tour in summer (call for details).

Herald Square and the Garment District

Seventh Avenue in the 30s has a stylish moniker: Fashion Avenue. Streets here are permanently gridlocked by delivery trucks. The surrounding area is the **Garment District,** where midtown office buildings stand amid the buzzing activity of a huge manufacturing industry that's been centered here for a century. Shabby clothing and fabric stores line the streets (especially 38th and 39th Streets), but there are intriguing shops selling exclusively lace, buttons or Lycra swimsuits. Most are wholesale only, although some sell to the public. At Seventh Avenue and 27th Street is the **Fashion Institute of Technology,** a state university where aspiring Calvin Kleins and Norma Kamalis (both former students) dream up the fashions of tomorrow. FIT's gallery features excellent exhibitions that are open to the public (*see chapter* **Museums**).

Macy's will most definitely cater to your needs and desires, though you can usually find the same items cheaper elsewhere. Plunked at the corner of Broadway and 34th Street, and stretching all the way to Seventh Avenue, Macy's still impresses as the biggest department store in the world (*see chapter* **Shopping & Services**). **Manhattan Mall,** down a block, is a phenomenally ugly building, a kind of neon-and-chrome Jell-O mold. This is American mall-shopping at its best, though, and most of the big chain stores have outlets here. **Herald Square,** this retail wonderland's home, is named after a long-gone newspaper. The southern part is known as **Greeley Square,** after the owner of the *Herald*'s rival, the *Tribune,* a paper for which Karl Marx wrote a regular column. *Life* magazine was based around the corner on 31st Street, and its cherubic mascot can still be seen over the entrance of what is now the **Herald Square Hotel.** East of Greeley Square, mostly on 32nd Street, is a bustling district of Korean shops and restaurants. Worth avoiding only a few years ago, the squares now offer welcoming bistro chairs and rest areas for weary pedestrians looking to take a break.

The giant doughnut of a building one block west is the famous sports and entertainment arena **Madison Square Garden** (*see chapters* **Music: Popular music** *and* **Sports & Fitness**). It occupies the site of the old Pennsylvania Station—the McKim, Mead & White architectural masterpiece that was tragically destroyed by 1960s planners, an act that brought about the creation of the Landmarks Preservation Commission. The railroad terminal, its name shortened to **Penn Station,** as if in shame (although it is the country's busiest station, serving some 600,000 people daily) lies beneath the Garden. But in an amazing turn of events, a $486 million project is in the works to move Penn Station back home, so to speak. The **General Post Office** (*see chapter* **Directory**), designed by the same architects in 1913 to complement the old station, still stands across Eighth Avenue. The Beaux Arts colonnade, occupying two city blocks, is getting a dramatic restoration—architect David Childs (of Skidmore, Owings & Merrill) has reinvented the building as a new Pennsylvania Station, with a soaring glass-and-nickel–trussed skylight covering the main 33rd Street entrance and the hall's ticketing and check-in counters. Service for Amtrak and proposed rail links to Newark, La Guardia and JFK airports will be housed here (along with post office operations). The current Penn Station, which will be upgraded and linked to the Post Office building, will continue to house New Jersey Transit, the Long Island Railroad and subways (*see chapter* **Soar Subjects**).

Herald Square

Junction of Broadway and Sixth Ave at 34th St. Subway: B, D, F, Q, N, R to 34th St–Herald Sq.

General Post Office

421 Eighth Ave between 31st and 33rd Sts (212-967-8585). Subway: A, C, E to 34th St–Penn Station. Open 24 hours. Free.

To see how New York really keeps running, take the self-guided tour of Manhattan's largest post office, displaying postal artifacts and Depression-era murals. As the building that never sleeps, it's a microcosm of New York. Window 45 gives round-the-clock info. Go on Tax Day, April 15, when the place is jammed with tardy filers right up to the midnight hour.

Broadway and Times Square

The Times Square night is illuminated not by the moon and stars but by acres of glaring neon. An enormous television screen high above makes the place feel like some giant's brashly lit living room. Waves of people flood the streets as the blockbuster theaters disgorge their audiences. This bustling core of entertainment and tourism is often called "the Crossroads of the World," and few places represent the collective power and noisy optimism of New York as well as **Times Square.**

Originally called Long Acre Square, Times Square was renamed after *The New York Times* moved to the site in the early 1900s, announcing its arrival with a spectacular New Year's Eve fireworks display. Around its building, 1 Times Square, the *Times* erected the world's first moving sign, on which the paper posted election returns in 1928. The *Times* is now on 43rd Street, but the sign (a new, improved one) and New Year's Eve celebrations remain at the original locale. Times Square is really just an elongated intersection, where Broadway crosses Seventh Avenue. That's why the Theater District is known as **Broadway** (*see chapter* **Theater & Dance**). It's home to 30 or so grand stages used for dramatic productions, plus 30 more that are movie theaters or nightclubs. The peep shows—what's left of Times Square's once-famous sex trade—are now relegated to Eighth Avenue.

This transformation began in earnest in 1990, when the city condemned most of the properties along **42nd Street** between Seventh and Eighth Avenues (a.k.a. "the Deuce"). A few years later, the city changed its zoning laws, specifically making it harder for adult-entertainment establishments to continue operating legally. The few remaining video supermarkets now sell kung fu films next to skin flicks (thanks to a city ordinance that requires 40 percent of their stock to be nonpornographic), and the live peep shows of yore are virtually nonexistent. Times Square's XXX days were officially numbered when the Walt Disney Company moved in and renovated the historic **New Amsterdam Theatre,** lair of the long-running musical *The Lion King.*

Public spectacle

Get an eyeful of midtown's art-laden lobbies on this walking tour

You're in midtown. You've shopped till you're ready to drop and next on the to-do list is to hit the museums. But MoMA's and the Whitney's lines are around the block, and the Met is just too big. If you're looking for a quick—and free—art fix, many of midtown's skyscrapers house secret stashes of work by some of the world's biggest names. Here's a quick tour of the highlights.

Start at **Rockefeller Center.** Planned in 1929, the center's 19 buildings each have a mural, along with sculpture, mosaics, metalwork and enamels. To unify the elements, the designers used the theme "New Frontiers and the March of Civilization," a motif exemplified by Jose Maria Sert's sepia-toned mural in the entrance of the GE Building at **30 Rockefeller Plaza** (*49th St between Fifth and Sixth Aves*). Abraham Lincoln stands tall as the *Man of Action*; the seated Ralph Waldo Emerson is the *Man of Thought*. Rockefeller Center, representing modern America, looms in the background. This mural replaced a 1933 work by Diego Rivera, which was deemed too pro-communist by John D. Rockefeller—a conflict depicted in the 1999 film *Cradle Will Rock*. Above the entrance is another Sert mural, *Time*, depicting past, present and future. The trompe l'oeil figures seem to shift their weight as you walk around the lobby.

Across 49th Street in **20 Rockefeller Plaza,** Christie's new auction house continues the public-art tradition with Sol LeWitt's site-specific 1999 mural *Wall Drawing #896 Colors/Curves*. Visible from the street behind a 200-foot-high glass facade, the mural's simple geometric shapes and flat areas of color cover all four walls of the soaring entryway. LeWitt, a conceptualist and minimalist, redefines notions of line and color; alternating broad bands of primary colors give form to the undulating shapes.

No Rockefeller Center work of art is more recognizable than New York sculptor Paul Manship's iconic 1934 gold leaf–covered *Prometheus*, which overlooks ice skaters (or diners, depending on the season) in the sunken area of the plaza.

For American art, head to the lobby at **1290 Sixth Avenue** (*between 51st and 52nd Sts*), where you can see Thomas Hart

Other corporations followed. Times Square is now undeniably safer and less grimy than it was in the '70s and '80s. To see how much things have changed, stop by **Show World** (*Eighth Ave between 42nd and 43rd Sts*), a former porn emporium that now sells tourist trinkets and hosts short (nonporn) film series and Off-Off Broadway (fully clothed) performances.

The streets west of Seventh Avenue are dotted with dozens of eating establishments catering primarily to theatergoers. West 46th Street between Eighth and Ninth Avenues—**Restaurant Row**—has an almost unbroken string of them.

As you'd expect, office buildings in the area are filled with entertainment companies: recording studios, theatrical management companies, record labels, screening rooms and so on. **The Brill Building** (*1619 Broadway at 49th St*) has the richest history, having long been the headquarters of music publishers and arrangers. The strip it's on is known as **Tin Pan Alley** (though the original Tin Pan Alley was West 28th Street). Such luminaries as Cole Porter, George Gershwin, Rodgers and Hart, Lieber and Stoller, and Phil Spector produced their hits here. Visiting rock royalty and aspiring musicians drool over the selection of new and vintage guitars and countless other instruments in a string of shops on 48th Street, just off Seventh Avenue.

At the southwestern end of the square is the headquarters of **MTV** (*44th St and Broadway*), which often sends camera crews into the streets to tape various segments (*see chapter* **Film & TV**). Especially during warmer months, crowds of screeching teens congregate under the windows of the network's second-floor studio, hoping for a wave from visiting celebrities inside.

Across the street from MTV, at 4 Times Square, is the swanky new glass home of magazine-publishing giant **Condé Nast**—the first office tower to be built in Manhattan since the late-'80s recession. During construction, the building was the site of several major mishaps; one woman was killed and the area was closed for several days when a scaffold crashed to the street. On the plus side, the structure's skin features tiny sunlight-

Benton's colorful nine-panel mural *America Today* (1931). The work was commissioned by the New School for Social Research, where it was on view until the Equitable Group acquired it in 1984.

Across the street is the **PaineWebber Art Gallery** (*1285 Sixth Ave between 51st and 52nd Sts*), which opened in 1985 in the lobby of the company's headquarters. Each year sees four or five short-term exhibitions (on loan from other cultural institutions); past shows have included the history of the bicycle and images from science.

Go through the exterior courtyard passageway that links the PaineWebber Building to the **Equitable Center** (*787 Seventh Ave between 51st and 52nd Sts*), where you can see another of Sol LeWitt's "Wall Drawings," along with the work of famous bunny sculptor Barry Flanagan. In the Equitable Center's main entrance is Roy Lichtenstein's three-story-high *Mural with Blue Brushstroke*, a compendium of the Pop artist's signature images. The **AXA Gallery** (formerly the Equitable Gallery) is in the same building; it sponsers multimedia exhibits.

End your tour with a breath of fresh air: Outside the **Credit Lyonnais** building (*1301 Sixth Ave between 51st and 52nd Sts*) is a three-part green-patina bronze of Venus de Milo–like figures by art superstar Jim Dine.

Mural, mural on the wall Christie's lobby art is the newest in Rockefeller Center.

Sightseeing

capturing cells that generate some of the energy needed for the building's day-to-day operations. Also found here is the **Nasdaq MarketSite.** Opened in March 2000, the multimedia "electronic stock market" spot dominates Times Square with its eight-story-tall, 9,800 square-foot cylindrical video screen.

Make a brief detour uptown on Seventh Avenue, just south of Central Park, for a glimpse of the great classical-music landmark **Carnegie Hall** (*see chapter* **Music**). Across the street is the ever-popular **Carnegie Deli**, one of the city's most famous sandwich shops (*see chapter* **Restaurants, Delis**).

Nightlife in the square is dominated by the theaters and theme restaurants; however, for a genuinely quirky experience, check out the **Siberia Bar,** a hole-in-the-wall vodka lover's paradise in the 50th Street station of the downtown 1 and 9 subway (*see chapter* **Bars**).

West of Times Square, past the curious steel spiral of the Port Authority Bus Terminal on Eighth Avenue and the knotted entrance to the Lincoln Tunnel, is an area known as **Hell's Kitchen.** During the 19th century, an impoverished Irish community lived here, amid gangs and crime. Following the Irish were Greeks, Puerto Ricans, Dominicans and other ethnic groups. It remained rough-and-tumble (and provided the backdrop for the popular musical *West Side Story*) through the 1970s, and in an effort to attract the forces of gentrification, the neighborhood renamed itself Clinton, after **De Witt Clinton Park** on Eleventh Avenue between 52nd and 54th Streets. Today, crime has receded, and Clinton's pretty, tree-lined streets and neat red brick apartment houses are filled with a diverse group of old-timers, actors and professionals of all racial backgrounds.

Ninth Avenue is the area's main drag, and in recent years it has sprouted many new, inexpensive restaurants and bars catering to a young crowd. There's also a small Cuban district around Tenth Avenue in the mid-40s, an otherwise rather desolate stretch of the city.

On 50th Street between Eighth and Ninth Avenues is **Worldwide Plaza,** a massive commercial and residential development. It houses **Cineplex Odeon Worldwide Encore,** a second-run movie theater that charges only $4 per ticket (*see chapter* **Film & TV**).

South of 42nd Street, the main attraction is the **Jacob K. Javits Convention Center,** on Eleventh Avenue between 34th and 39th Streets; this enormous structure hosts conventions and trade shows. Finally, along the Hudson River piers, you'll find the **Circle Line** terminal on Pier 83, at 42nd Street (*see chapter* **Tour New York**). At the end of 46th Street is the aircraft carrier ***Intrepid,*** which features the **Sea-Air-Space Museum** (*see chapter* **Museums**).

Nasdaq MarketSite

4 Times Sq, Broadway at 43rd St (877-627-3271). Subway: N, R, S, 1, 2, 3, 9, 7 to 42nd St–Times Sq. Mon–Thu 9am–8pm, Fri 9am–10pm, Sat 10am–10pm, Sun 10am–8pm. $7, reservations required.

New York City's Official Visitor Information Center

810 Seventh Ave at 53rd St (212-484-1222; www.nycvisit.com). Subway: B, D, E to Seventh Ave; N, R to 57th St; 1, 9 to 50th St. Mon–Fri 8:30am–6pm; Sat, Sun 9am–5pm.

Part of New York's effort to define itself as a welcoming tourist destination, this new visitors' center has an information desk, hundreds of brochures and maps, and an ATM.

Show World

669 Eighth Ave between 42nd and 43rd Sts (212-247-6643). Subway: N, R, S, 1, 2, 3, 9, 7 to 42nd St–Times Sq. 24 hours.

Times Square

42nd St at Broadway. Times Square Visitors' Center, 1560 Broadway between 46th and 47th Sts, entrance on Seventh Ave (212-768-1560). Subway: N, R, S, 1, 2, 3, 9, 7 to 42nd St–Times Sq.

Fifth Avenue

This majestic thoroughfare is New York's Main Street, the route of the city's many parades and marches. It runs through a region of chic department stores and past some of the most famous buildings and public spaces.

The **Empire State Building** is at 34th Street. Although it's visible from much of the city (and lit up at night in various colors, according to the season or holiday), only at the corner of 34th Street and Fifth Avenue can you marvel at its height from top to bottom. In 1931, it was the champ: the world's tallest building at 1,250 feet (1,472, or 448 meters, including the transmitter). It's still arguably the best of Manhattan's heights. Why? Location, location, location: The observatory is in the dead center of midtown and offers brilliant views in every direction. After a 1997 shooting incident, airport-style metal detectors were installed, but the building is still impossibly romantic, so don't forget to pack a loved one for the ascent to the 102nd floor.

Impassive stone lions guard the steps of the **New York Public Library** at 41st Street. This beautiful Beaux Arts building provides an astonishing escape from the noise outside. The **Rose Main Reading Room,** on the library's top floor, reopened in 1998 after a $15 million renovation. The attention to detail the restorers lavished on the room is sure impressive: leaf blowers were used to clean the sunken-paneled ceiling; the 18 bronze chandeliers were polished and outfitted with 1,620 new lightbulbs; the 23-foot-long tables and matching oak chairs were completely refinished. Behind the library is **Bryant Park,** an elegant lawn often filled in the warm months with lunching office workers that brags a dizzying schedule of free entertainment (*see chapter* **New York by Season, Summer**).

On 44th Street between Fifth and Sixth Avenues is the famous **Algonquin Hotel,** where scathing wit Dorothy Parker held court at Alexander Woollcott's Round Table (*see chapter* **Accommodations**). The city's diamond trade is conducted along the 47th Street strip known as **Diamond Row.** In front of glittering window displays, you'll see Orthodox Jewish traders, precious gems in their pockets, doing business in the street. Near here (*231 E 47th St between Broadway and Eighth Ave,* but since demolished) was where **Andy Warhol's Factory** enjoyed some of its 15 minutes of fame.

Walk off Fifth Avenue into **Rockefeller Center** (*48th–51st Sts*), and you'll understand why this masterful use of public space is so lavishly praised (*see* **Public spectacle,** *page 56*). As you stroll down the Channel Gardens, the stately Art Deco **GE Building** gradually appears over you. The sunken plaza in the middle of the center is the site of a restaurant in the summer and the famous ice-skating rink in winter (when the equally renowned Rockefeller Center Christmas tree perches above it). Gathered around the plaza's perimeter are the **International Building** and its companions. The **NBC** television network's glass-walled ground-level studio (home of its *Today* program) at the southwest corner draws a weekday-morning crowd. When taping ends, the same crowd—along with thousands of other pedestrians—makes its way to the many chain stores thriving above and below Rockefeller Center. Over on Sixth Avenue is **Radio City Music Hall,** the world's largest cinema when it was built in 1932. The Art Deco jewel was treated to a seven-month, $70 million restoration in 1999. It's a stellar example of the benefits of historic preservation.

Across Fifth Avenue from Rockefeller Center's sweeping straight lines is

I see him! Teenyboppers camp outside MTV for a glimpse of the latest boy band.

St. Patrick's Cathedral, a beautiful Gothic Revival structure that's the largest Catholic cathedral in the United States.

One more bit of culture before you shop: In the 1920s, 52nd Street was "Swing Street," a row of speakeasies and jazz clubs. All that's left is the **'21' Club** (at No. 21), long a power-lunch spot (*see chapter* **Restaurants, Landmarks**). This street also contains the **Museum of Television & Radio. The Museum of Modern Art** is on 53rd Street, as is the **American Craft Museum** (*see chapter* **Museums**).

The blocks of Fifth Avenue between Rockefeller Center and Central Park house expensive retail palaces that sell everything from Rolex watches to gourmet chocolate. Along the stretch between **Saks Fifth Avenue** (*50th St*) and **Bergdorf Goodman** (*58th St*), the rents are among the highest in the world, and you'll find such names as Cartier, Chanel, Gucci and Tiffany (*see chapter* **Shopping & Services**), along with the first U.S. outpost of Swedish clothing giant H&M, the merchandising outlets of Warner Bros. and Disney, as well as the National Basketball Association's official store. The pinnacle of this malling trend is the soaring brass spine of **Trump Tower** (*725 Fifth Ave at 56th St*), the Donald's ostentatious pink-marble shopping emporium.

Fifth Avenue is crowned by **Grand Army Plaza,** at 59th Street. A statue of General Sherman presides over public space, with the elegant chateau, **Plaza Hotel** to the west (one of the ritziest places in town since Edwardian times) and the famous **FAO Schwarz** toy store at ground level to the east.

Empire State Building

350 Fifth Ave between 33rd and 34th Sts (212-736-3100; www.esbnyc.com). Subway: B, D, F, Q, N, R to 34th St–Herald Sq; 6 to 33rd St. Observatories open 9:30am–11:30pm; last tickets sold at 11:25pm. $7, children under 12 and senior, $4. Cash only.

Visit it before seeing anything else to get the lay of the land. Expect to wait in line at the second stage (86th floor), where a second elevator takes you to the giddy heights of floor 102. If you're a fan of virtual-reality rides, the Empire State houses two amusing big-screen flight simulators (though both are useless as actual tours): **New York Skyride** (*10am–10pm; $11.50, children and seniors $8.50*).

NBC

30 Rockefeller Plaza, 49th St between Fifth and Sixth Aves (212-664-3700). Subway: B, D, F, Q to 47–50th Sts–Rockefeller Ctr. Tours Mon–Sat 8:30am–5:30pm, Sun 9:30–4:30pm. $17.50, seniors and children $15. Children under six not admitted.

Gaze through the *Today* show's studio window with hordes of onlookers between 48th and 49th Streets.

New York Public Library

Fifth Ave between 40th and 42nd Sts (212-930-0830). Subway: B, D, F, Q to 42nd St; 7 to Fifth Ave. Mon, Thu, Fri, Sat 10am–6pm; Tue, Wed 11am–7:30pm. Some sections closed Mondays.

Radio City Music Hall

Sixth Ave between 50th and 51st Sts (212-247-4777). Subway: B, D, F, Q to 47–50th Sts–Rockefeller Ctr. Tours Mon–Sat 10am–5pm, Sun 11am–5pm. $15, children under 12 $9.

Rockefeller Center

48th to 51st Sts between Fifth and Sixth Aves (212-632-3975). Subway: B, D, F, Q to 47–50th Sts–Rockefeller Ctr. Free.

Self-guided tours are available at the **GE Building,** 30 Rockefeller Plaza (the north–south street between Fifth and Sixth Aves).

St. Patrick's Cathedral

Fifth Ave between 50th and 51st Sts (212-753-2261; www.stpatrickscathedral.org). Subway: B, D, F, Q to 47–50th Sts–Rockefeller Ctr; E, F to Fifth Ave. Free. Sun–Fri 7am–8:45pm; Sat 8am–8:45pm. Tours given Mon–Fri 9–11am and 1:30–4:30pm. Call for tour dates and times. Services Mon–Fri 7, 7:30, 8, 8:30am, noon, 12:30, 1, 5:30pm; Sat 8, 8:30am, noon, 12:30, 5:30pm; Sun 7, 8, 9, 10:15am, noon, 1, 4, 5:30pm.

Midtown East

Sometimes on New Year's Eve, you can waltz in the great hall of **Grand Central Terminal,** just as the enchanted commuters did in *The Fisher King*. This 1913 Beaux Arts station, renovated in 1998, is the city's most spectacular point of arrival (though the constellations of the winter zodiac that adorn the ceiling of the main concourse are backward—a mistake made by the original artist). Thanks to the renovation, the terminal has itself become a destination, with upscale restaurants and bars such as **Michael Jordan's** eponymous steak house (*see chapter* **Restaurants**), star chef Charlie Palmer's **Métrazur** (*east balcony of Grand Central Terminal, 212-687-4600*) and the sophisticated cocktail lounge **Campbell Apartment** (*see chapter* **Bars**). There's even the Euro-style food hall **Grand Central Market,** selling gourmet goodies from New York and around the world. The station stands at the junction of 42nd Street and Park Avenue, the latter rising on a cast-iron bridge and literally running around the terminal.

East 42nd Street also offers much architectural distinction, including the spectacular hall of the former **Bowery Savings Bank** (at No. 110, now a special-events space owned by the Cipriani restaurant family) and the Art Deco detail of the **Chanin**

Building (No. 122). Built in 1930, the gleaming chrome **Chrysler Building** (at the corner of Lexington Avenue) pays homage to the automobile. Architect William van Alen outfitted the base of the main tower with brickwork cars, complete with chrome hubcaps and radiator caps enlarged to vast proportions and projected out over the edge as gargoyles. The building's needle-sharp stainless-steel spire was added to the original plans so that it would be taller than 40 Wall Street, which was under construction at the same time. **The News Building** (No. 220), another Art Deco gem, was immortalized in the *Superman* films and still houses a giant globe in its lobby, although its namesake, the *Daily News* tabloid newspaper, no longer has offices there.

The street ends at **Tudor City,** a pioneering 1925 residential development that's a high-rise version of Hampton Court in England. North of here is the area of **Turtle Bay,** though you won't see too many turtles in the East River these days. This neighborhood is dominated by the **United Nations** and its famous glass-walled Secretariat building. Although you don't need your passport, you are leaving U.S. soil when you enter the UN complex—this is an international zone. Optimistic peacemongering sculptures dot the grounds, and the **Peace Gardens** along the East River bloom with delicate roses. Threatening that peace, however, is Donald Trump's 72-story **Trump World Tower,** which is going up just a few blocks north of the UN, on First Avenue between 47th and 48th Streets. When completed, it will be the world's tallest residential building. Several high-powered area residents, including the venerated news anchor Walter Cronkite, formed a coalition to stop him, to no avail (*see chapter* **Soar Subjects**).

Rising behind Grand Central, the **Met Life** (formerly Pan Am) building was once the world's largest office tower. Its most celebrated tenants are the peregrine falcons that nest on the roof, living on a diet of pigeons they kill in midair. Next to the Met Life tower is the **Helmsley Building.** Built by Warren & Wetmore, the architects of Grand Central, the building features glittering gold detail that's a fitting punctuation to the vista looking down Park Avenue.

On Park Avenue itself, amid the many blocks of international corporate headquarters, is the **Waldorf-Astoria Hotel** (*see chapter* **Accommodations**). The famed hotel was originally located on Fifth Avenue but was demolished in 1929 to make way for the Empire State Building and was rebuilt here in 1931. Ninety-minute tours are given on Fridays and Sundays at 9am (contact the concierge at 212-872-4790). Many of the city's most famous revolutionary International Style office buildings are located here as well (*see chapter* **Architecture**). Built in 1952, **Lever House** (*390 Park Ave between 53rd and 54th Sts*) was the first glass box on Park. The 1958 **Seagram Building** (*375 Park Ave between 52nd and 53rd Sts*), designed by Ludwig Mies van der Rohe and others, is a stunning bronze-and-glass structure that also contains the landmarked, Philip Johnson–designed **Four Seasons** restaurant (*see chapter* **Restaurants**). On 56th Street is Johnson's **Sony Building,** with its distinctive postmodern Chippendale crown. Inside, you'll find Sony's public arcade and **Wonder Technology Lab,** offering hands-on displays of innovative technology (*see chapter* **Kids' Stuff**).

The newest addition to this cluster of stellar architecture is the **LVMH Tower,** 19 East 57th Street between Fifth and Madison Avenues (*see chapter* **Soar Subjects**). Designed by Christian de Portzamparc, the youngest architect to be awarded the Nobel of architecture, the Pritzker Prize, the U.S. headquarters for the French luxury-goods company is a reworked vision of Art Deco. It has already spearheaded a new (and long-awaited) wave of world-class buildings in the city.

One new project that's taking advantage of what already exists is the **Bridgemarket** complex (*First Ave at 59th St*), which opened at the end of 1999 in what was once a farmers' market under the Queensboro Bridge. The renovated space is now the site of a **Terence Conran Shop** (*see chapter* **Shopping & Services**) and the restaurant **Guastavino's,** named after the gracefully curved Guastavino-tiled ceilings. Spanish architect Rafael Guastavino Y Moreno's legacy can be seen throughout the city in places such as the **Oyster Bar** at Grand Central Terminal and the **Registry Room** at Ellis Island (*see chapters* **Restaurants** *and* **Downtown**).

Grand Central Terminal

42nd to 44th Sts between Vanderbilt and Lexington Aves. Subway: S, 4, 5, 6, 7 to 42nd St–Grand Central.

United Nations Headquarters

First Ave at 46th St (212-963-7713). Subway: S, 4, 5, 6, 7 to 42nd St–Grand Central. 9:15am–4:45pm. Free. Guided tours every half-hour. $7.50, children under 5 not permitted.

Uptown

Once a bucolic getaway for 17th-century New Yorkers, uptown is now the city's cash-and-culture cache—and still the place for a mini escape

Central Park's glorious green space, which is bigger than the principality of Monaco, will always dominate Manhattan life between 59th and 110th Streets. The neighborhoods on either side are quite different. The east is rich and respectable, full of old-guard fashion boutiques and museums; the west is more intellectual, revolving around the academia of Columbia University and the music and performance of Lincoln Center.

Central Park

As natural as it may seem, this vast 843-acre park is as prefab as Manhattan's street grid; everything except the rock is man-made. It took 20 years for journalist and landscape architect Frederick Law Olmsted and architect Calvert Vaux to create their masterpiece. It was long believed that the land on which the park was built had been nothing more than a swamp when construction began in 1840, but it's now clear that some 600 free blacks and Irish and German immigrants occupied an area known as Seneca Village, located in what is now the West 80s.

The Byzantine **Bethesda Fountain and Terrace,** at the center of the 72nd Street Transverse Road, is the park's most popular meeting place. Just south is the **Mall,** site of an impromptu roller-disco rink (with not-to-be-missed costumes and acrobatics), in-line skating paths and volleyball courts.

To the east, on a mound behind the Naumburg Bandshell, is the site of the **Central Park SummerStage** and its impressive series of free concerts and spoken-word performances (*see chapters* **New York by Season** *and* **Music**). To the west is the **Sheep Meadow**—yes, sheep actually grazed here up until the 1930s (*see photograph, page 11*). You may see kites, Frisbees or soccer balls zoom past, but most people are here to work on their tans. If you get hungry, repair to glitzy **Tavern on the Green** (*see chapter* **Restaurants, Landmark**), or wolf down a hot dog at the adjacent snack bar. South of Sheep Meadow, kids line up for a ride on the **Carousel.** You can jump on, too, for a buck.

West of Bethesda Terrace, near the 72nd Street entrance, is peaceful **Strawberry Fields.** This is where John Lennon, who lived and died nearby, is remembered. You can rent a boat, gondola or bicycle at the **Loeb Boathouse** (*see* **Be a spokes person,** *page 326*) on the **Lake,** crossed by the elegant **Bow Bridge.** For sailing on a smaller scale, head east to the **Conservatory Water,** where enthusiasts race model sailboats. The wild **Ramble** area is known for bird-watching by day and anonymous, mostly gay, rendezvous at night (for the adventurous only).

Farther uptown is **Belvedere Castle,** which houses the **Henry Luce Nature Observatory**; the **Delacorte Theater,** where the New York Shakespeare Festival mounts plays during the summer; and the **Great Lawn,** where concerts and other events are held. The **Reservoir,** above 86th Street, was renamed in honor of Jacqueline Kennedy Onassis, who used to jog around it. North of the sports fields and tennis courts, the park is wilder and wooded. Kids fish the **Harlem Meer** at the northeastern corner and people stop to smell the roses in the beautiful, formal **Conservatory Garden** (*Fifth Ave at 105th St*). *See chapter* **Kids' Stuff** to learn more about fun park activities for children.

The Carousel

Mid-park at 64th St (212-879-0244). Apr–Oct 10:30am–6pm; Nov–Mar 10:30am–5pm; closed on extremely cold days. $1 per ride, $5 for six rides.

The park's first carousel, which was powered by a horse and a blind mule, opened in 1871. Today's carousel was installed in 1951. The horses are all hand-carved.

Central Park Zoo/Wildlife Center

See chapter **Kids' Stuff.**

Charles A. Dana Discovery Center

Enter at Fifth Ave at 110th St (212-860-1370). Subway: 6 to 110th St. May–Sept Tue–Sun 10am–5pm; Oct–Apr Tue–Sun 10am–4pm. Free.

Stop in for weekend family workshops, cultural exhibits and outdoor performances on the plaza.

The Dairy

Mid-park at 64th St (212-794-6564). Apr–Sept Tue–Sun 11am–5pm; Oct–Mar Tue–Sun 11am–4pm. Free.

Built in 1870 to show city kids where milk comes from, the Dairy is now the park's information center, with an interactive exhibit and history video.

Henry Luce Nature Observatory

Belvedere Castle, mid-park at 79th St (212-772-0210). Subway: B, C to 81st St; 6 to 77th St. Apr 1–Sept 1 Tue–Sun 10am–5pm; Sept 2–Mar 31 Tue–Sun 10am–4pm. Free.

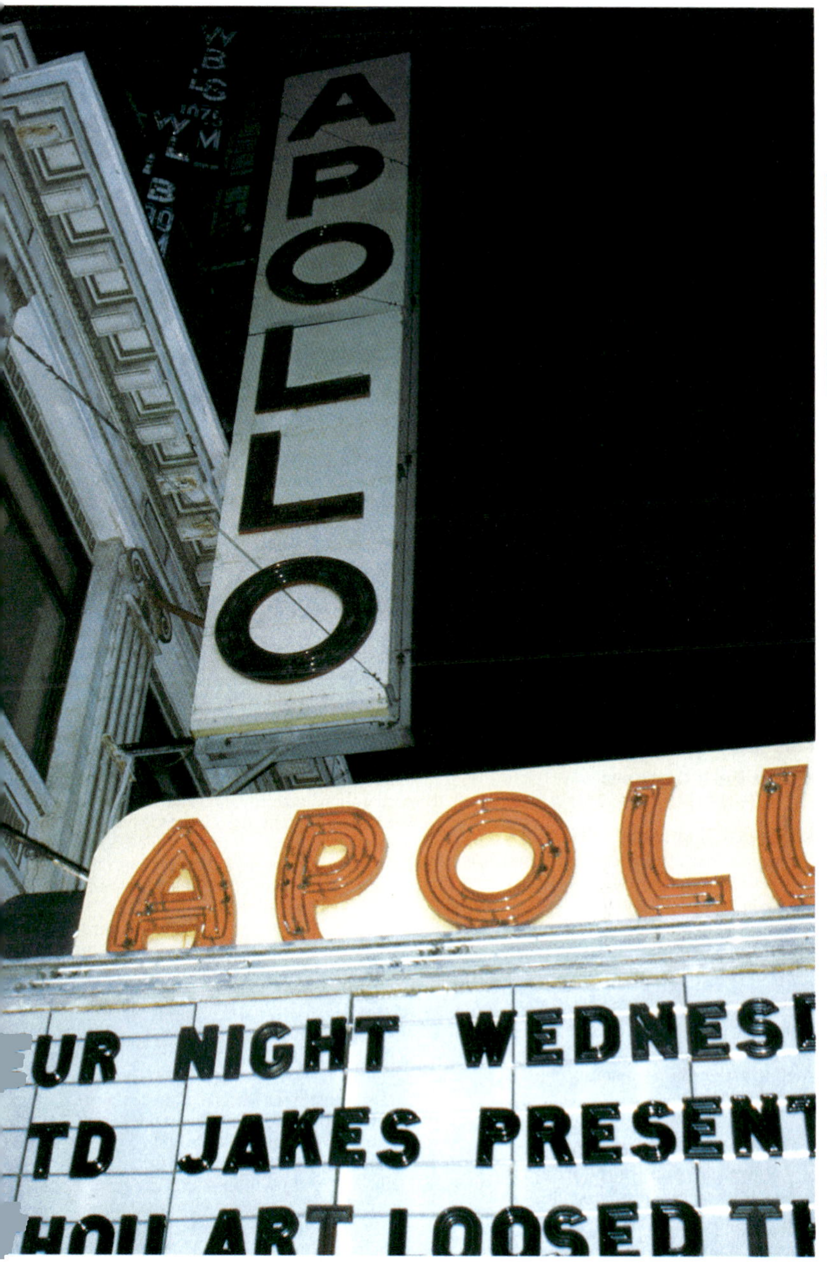

It's showtime! The biggest names in hip-hop and R&B play Harlem's Apollo Theater.

Tram spotting Catch a magnificent view of the city from the Roosevelt Island Tram.

Enjoy the hands-on "Woods and Water" exhibit that surveys the park's variety of plants and animals. Or pick up a birdwatching kit that includes binoculars, maps and bird-identification guides. Learn to bird on ranger-led walks that start at the Castle and head into the Ramble every Sunday at 9am.

Loeb Boathouse

The Lake, enter at Fifth Ave at E 74th St (212-517-4723). Subway: 6 to 77th St. Mar–Nov 9am–dusk. Call for seasonal restaurant hours. Boat rental: $10 per hour plus $30 deposit; $30 per half hour for chauffeured gondola, only at night. Cash only.
Rent a rowboat, ride a gondola or sit down for a romantic lunch at the waterside café.

Urban Park Rangers

888-NY-PARKS or 212-360-2774. 9am–5pm.

Wollman Memorial Rink

Wollman is Manhattan's best (and busiest) open-air rink, and it's impossibly romantic at night, when the city lights tower over the park's lovely canopy (*see chapter* **Sports & Fitness** *for listings*).

Upper East Side

Once Central Park opened in 1859, New York society felt ready to move north. By the mid-1800s, the rich had built mansions along Fifth Avenue, and by the beginning of the 20th century, the super-rich had warmed to the (at first outrageous) idea of living in apartment buildings, provided they were near the park. Many grand examples of these were built along Park Avenue and the cross streets between Park and Fifth Avenues.

The Upper East Side, especially the avenues hugging Central Park, is where much of New York's wealth and power are concentrated. The high-society residents of the mansions, townhouses and luxury apartment buildings of Fifth, Madison and Park Avenues between 59th and 96th Streets include elderly ladies-who-lunch as well as young trust-funders who spend their (ample) spare change in Madison Avenue's chichi boutiques. Meanwhile, the rich heads of corporations take advantage of tax write-offs to fund cultural institutions here; the results of these philanthropic gestures, made over the past 100 years, are the art collections, museums and cultural institutions that attract visitors to the area referred to as **Museum Mile.**

Museum Mile is a promotional organization, rather than a geographical description, but since most of the member museums line Fifth Avenue, it is an apt name (*see chapter* **New York by Season, Summer**). The **Metropolitan Museum of Art,** set just inside Central Park on Fifth between 80th and 84th Streets, is the grandest of them all. A sunset drink in the Met's rooftop sculpture garden is a chance to check out not only Central Park's vistas but also the city's singles scene in action. Walking north from the steps of the Met, you reach the spiral design of Frank Lloyd Wright's **Guggenheim Museum** at 88th Street; the **National Academy of Design** at 89th; the **Cooper-Hewitt Museum,** the Smithsonian Institution's design collection set

► For more information on the museums in this section, see chapter **Museums.**
► Check out chapter **Art Galleries** for additional listings on uptown dealers.
► For stellar stores on the Upper East Side, see chapter **Shopping & Services.**

in Andrew Carnegie's mansion, at 91st; the **Jewish Museum** at 92nd; and, at 94th, the **International Center of Photography,** which displays everything from late-19th-century photography to contemporary works. ICP will be moving at the end of 2001, when the building's new owner converts it to a private residence.

The brick fortress facade at 94th Street and Madison Avenue is all that's left of the old **Squadron A Armory.** Just off Fifth Avenue at 97th Street are the onion domes and rich ornamentation of the **Russian Orthodox Cathedral of St. Nicholas.** A little farther north are two excellent (and seldom crowded) collections: the **Museum of the City of New York** and **El Museo del Barrio,** at 103rd and 104th Streets, respectively.

There's another museum cluster in the 70s: The **Frick Collection** faces the park at 70th Street. At Madison and 75th Street is the **Whitney Museum of American Art,** home of the (often controversial) Whitney Biennial.

The area's wealth has also been used to found societies promoting the languages and cultures of foreign lands. Nelson Rockefeller's **Asia Society** is on Park Avenue at 70th Street (though it is closed for renovations until fall 2001; the temporary site is at 502 Park Ave at 59th St). Nearby are the **China Institute in America** and the **Americas Society,** which is dedicated to the nations of South and Central America. On Fifth Avenue is the **Ukrainian Institute** at 79th St and the **Goethe-Institut/German Cultural Center** at 83rd St.

Since the 1950s, **Madison Avenue** has symbolized the advertising industry (even though only a couple of agencies have actually had offices on the street). Now it's synonymous with ultra-luxe shopping. The world's best couturiers—**Yves Saint Laurent, Givenchy, Giorgio Armani,** et al.—all have boutiques here. Thriftier shoppers might prefer to head to **Bloomingdale's,** that frantic, glitzy supermarket of fashion (*see chapter* **Shopping & Services**). Commercial art galleries also abound here, including **M. Knoedler & Co. Inc.** and **Gagosian** (*see chapter* **Art Galleries**). Established artists such as Frank Stella prefer to show here rather than downtown in the Soho or Chelsea circuses. For a quick bite during your Madison Avenue stroll, stop in at **E.A.T. Cafe** (*between 80th and 81st Sts, 212-772-0022*), a take-out food emporium and restaurant serving owner Eli Zabar's signature breads, and salads that would make any dieter happily swoon. The prices might make them faint: an egg-salad sandwich costs $10.

At 66th Street and Park Avenue is the **Seventh Regiment Armory,** the interiors of which were designed by Louis Comfort Tiffany, assisted by a young Stanford White. It houses the Winter Antiques show, among other events (*see chapter* **New York by Season**).

The aura is less grand from **Lexington Avenue** to the East River, but the history is just as glamorous. The **Mount Vernon Hotel Museum** (*61st St at First Ave*), one of only eight 18th-century houses left in the city, was built as a coach house in 1799 and in the 1820s became a country inn. For an evening of laughs nearby, check out **Chicago City Limits** (*First Ave at 61st St*), New York's longest-running improvisational comedy venue (*see chapter* **Cabaret & Comedy**). Kim Novak, Montgomery Clift, Tallulah Bankhead and Eleanor Roosevelt all lived a little bit farther west, on the tree-lined streets of brownstones known as the **Treadwell Farm Historic District,** on 61st and 62nd Streets between Second and Third Avenues.

The central building of **Rockefeller University**—from 64th to 68th Streets on a bluff overlooking FDR Drive—is listed as a national historic landmark. Its Founder's Hall dates from 1906, five years after the medical-research institute was established. Look out for the President's House and the domed Caspary Auditorium. The next few blocks of **York Avenue** are dominated by medical institutions, including the New York Hospital/Cornell Medical Center, into which the city's oldest hospital was incorporated.

Rockefeller University

1230 York Ave between 63rd and 68th Sts (212-327-8000). Subway: 6 to 68th St–Hunter College.
Founder's Hall is open to groups by appointment only.

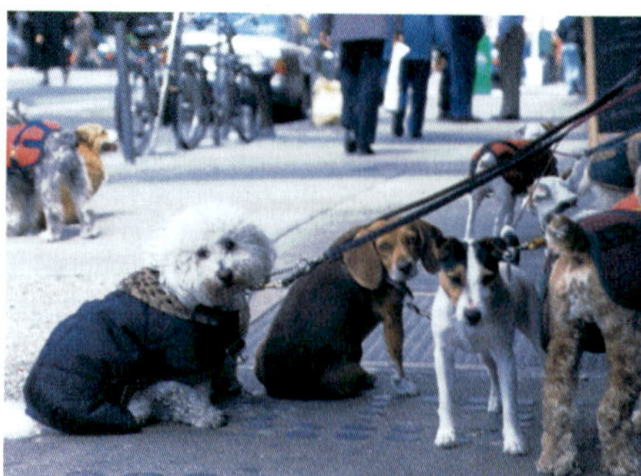

My name is Phideaux Pups on the Upper East Side have their own dog walkers.

Mira! Mira! El Museo del Bario will capture your attention with its Latino exhibits.

Seventh Regiment Armory

643 Park Ave at 66th St (212-452-3067). Subway: 6 to 68th St–Hunter College. By appointment only.

Yorkville

The east and northeast parts of the Upper East Side are residential, mostly yuppie-filled neighborhoods. There are countless restaurants and bars here, including the rip-roaring **Elaine's** (*see chapter* **Restaurants**) and the tropical **Penang** (*1596 Second Ave at 83rd St, 212-585-3838*), which serves Malaysian food. There are tons of cozy neighborhood Italian and Chinese restaurants, and 86th Street, the main thoroughfare, is lined with all the chain stores you could need, from Barnes & Noble to HMV.

The area extending from the 70s to 96th Street east of Lexington Avenue has been known historically as **Yorkville,** once a predominantly German neighborhood and quaint riverside hamlet. In the last decades of the 19th century, East 86th Street became the Hauptstrasse, filled with German restaurants, beer gardens and pastry, grocery, butcher and clothing shops. Tensions flared when World War II broke out, as Nazis and anti-Nazis clashed in the streets; a Nazi newspaper was even published here. While the German influence has waned, the European legacy includes **Schaller & Weber** (*Second Ave between 85th and 86th Sts, 212-879-3047*), a homey grocery that has been selling 75 different varieties of German sausage and cold cuts since it opened in 1937. Another must-see is the **Elk Candy Company** (*1628 Second Ave between 84th and 85th Sts, 212-585-2303*), which moved to a brand-new shop in 1997 but still sells 60 kinds of marzipan candies.

On East End Avenue at 86th Street is the **Henderson Place Historic District,** where two dozen handsome Queen Anne row houses, commissioned by fur dealer John C. Henderson, stand, their turrets, double stoops and slate roofs intact; the block looks much as it did in 1882. Across the street is **Gracie Mansion,** New York's official mayoral residence since 1942 and the only Federal-style mansion in Manhattan still used as a home. The house, built in 1799 by Scottish merchant Archibald Gracie, is the focal point of tranquil **Carl Schurz Park,** named in honor of the German immigrant, senator and newspaper editor. Linger here for spectacular views of the fast-moving East River. The park's long promenade, the **John H. Finley Walk,** is one of the most beautiful spots in the city (especially in the early morning and at dusk). During the Revolutionary War, George Washington built a battery on this strategic site.

The **92nd Street Y** (*Lexington Ave at 92nd St*) offers the city's most extensive walking-tour program, as well as concerts and lectures (*see chapters* **Tour New York** *and* **Books & Poetry**). While you're in the neighborhood, be sure to stroll by the wood-frame home at 160 East 92nd Street between Lexington and Third Aves. Built in the mid-1800s, the house has retained its historic shutters and Corinthian-columned front porch. The founders of *The New Republic* housed their staff here in the early 1900s, and it was jewelry designer Jean Schlumberger's home for three decades before he died in 1987.

Gracie Mansion

Carl Schurz Park, 88th St at East End Ave (212-570-4751). Subway: 4, 5, 6 to 86th St. March–November tours by appointment only. Call for details.
The tour takes you through the mayor's living room, a guest suite and smaller bedrooms.

Roosevelt Island

Roosevelt Island, a submarine-shaped East River isle, was called Minnehanonck ("island place") by the Indians who sold it to the Dutch (who made a vast creative leap and renamed it Hog's Island). The Dutch farmed it, as did Englishman Robert Blackwell, who moved there in 1686. His family's old clapboard farmhouse is in **Blackwell Park,** adjacent to Main Street (the one and only commercial street, on which you can find several restaurants). In the 1800s, a lunatic asylum, a smallpox hospital, prisons and workhouses were built on what was by that point known as Welfare Island. On the southern tip are the weathered neo-Gothic ruins of the **Smallpox Hospital** and the burned-out shell of **City Hospital.** The **Octagon Tower,** at the island's northern end, is the remaining core of the former New York City Lunatic Asylum. Charles Dickens visited during the 1840s and was disturbed by its "lounging, listless, madhouse air." In an early feat of investigative journalism, reporter Nellie Bly feigned insanity and had herself committed to the asylum for ten days in 1887, then wrote a shocking exposé of the conditions in this "human rat trap."

Roosevelt Island has been a perfectly sane residential community since the state began planning its development in 1971 (people started moving into apartments in 1975). Take the red cable cars that cross the East River from Manhattan for some of the best vistas of the city (embark at Second Avenue and 60th Street). The trams have starred in a host of films, including *City Slickers.* You can also take the Q train for a less scenic (but faster) ride. When you arrive, you'll have to ride three escalators up the equivalent of ten stories to get out of the subway stop, one of the deepest in the metropolitan area. The riverfront promenades afford fabulous panoramas of the skyline and the East River. Wander down the **Meditation Steps** for river views, or take one of the riverside walks around the island.

Roosevelt Island Operating Corporation

591 Main St (212-832-4540). Mon–Fri 9am–5pm. Call for details of events and free maps of the island.

Upper West Side

The Upper West Side is a fairly affluent residential area packed with movie theaters, bars and restaurants that's also home to dozens of celebrities, including Jerry Seinfeld, a proud West Sider who owns a multimillion-dollar apartment overlooking Central Park. Historically, its residents have been thought of as intellectually and politically liberal. European immigrants were attracted here in the late 19th century by the building boom sparked by Central Park, as well as by Columbia University's new site to the north.

The Upper West Side begins at **Columbus Circle**—a rare rotary in a city of right angles—where Broadway meets 59th Street, Eighth Avenue, Central Park South and Central Park West. To the south, across from a 700-ton statue of Christopher Columbus, is 2 Columbus Circle, an odd, almost windowless building that once housed the NYC Convention and Visitors Bureau. Built as a modern-art gallery by Huntington Hartford in 1964, its future is uncertain as the circle undergoes a massive redevelopment. Donald Trump already has his imprint on the north side of the circle with his megapricey **Trump International Hotel and Tower,** which features the acclaimed restaurant **Jean Georges** (*see chapter* **Restaurants**). To the west, on the former site of the New York Coliseum, which was torn down in 2000, the $1.6 billion Columbus Center is going up. It will house the headquarters of AOL/Time Warner, an auditorium for Jazz at Lincoln Center, a Mandarin Oriental Hotel and shops.

On Broadway at 68th Street, the popular 12-screen (plus a huge 3-D IMAX facility) **Sony Lincoln Square Cinema** is an example of a multiplex done right (*see chapter* **Film & TV**). It's not unusual to see folks striding around this area in evening dress; that's because they're going to **Lincoln Center,** a complex of concert halls and auditoriums that's the heart of classical music in the city. Its buildings are linked by sweeping public plazas and populated by sensitive-looking musical types or, in the summer, amateur dancers who gather in the plaza to dance alfresco at Midsummer Night Swing (*see chapter* **New York by Season**).

The uptown lowdown Low Library looms over Columbia's Ivy League campus.

Sightseeing

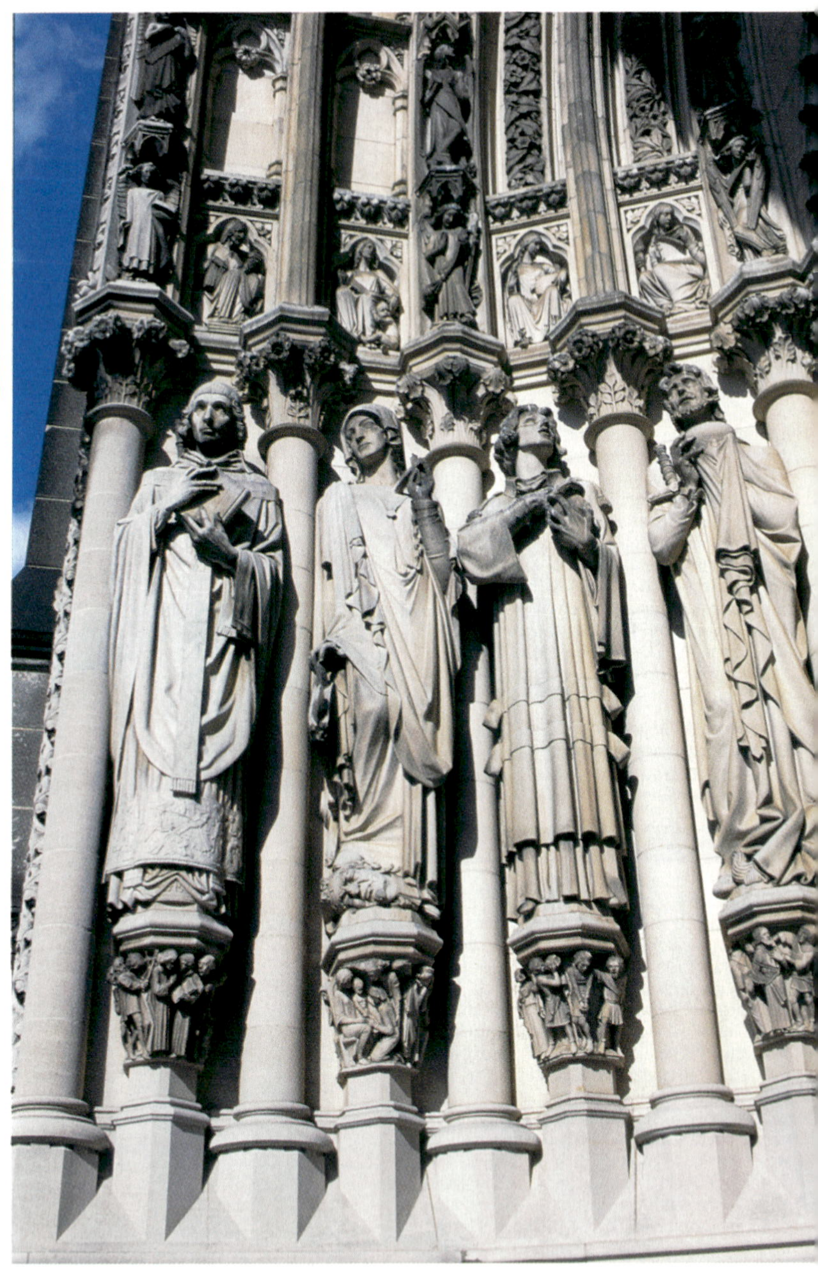

Psalm pilots Poetry, both sacred and secular, can be heard at St. John the Divine.

From Lincoln Center Plaza, you can see a small-scale Statue of Liberty replica atop a building on West 64th Street. Up Broadway, at 2 Lincoln Square, is the small but fascinating **Museum of American Folk Art.**

It took longer for the West Side to become a fashionable residential area than it did Fifth Avenue, but once the park was built, Central Park West promptly filled up with luxury apartment buildings. After well-off New Yorkers had adjusted to the idea of living in "French flats," as they called them, apartment living became almost desirable.

The Art Deco building at 55 Central Park West at 66th Street is best remembered for its role in *Ghostbusters.* The **Dakota,** on 72nd Street, is most famous these days as the building outside which John Lennon was murdered. It was one of New York's first great apartment buildings and the one that first accelerated the westward drift. (When it was completed in 1884, skeptical New Yorkers commented that it was so far away from the center of town that it might as well be in the Dakotas.) Yoko Ono and other famous residents can be seen popping in and out. The massive, twin-towered **San Remo** at 74th Street dates from 1930 and is so exclusive that even Madonna had to settle for the waiting list and ended up buying an apartment farther south on Central Park West.

The **New York Historical Society,** the oldest museum in the city, is at 77th Street. Across the street, the **American Museum of Natural History** attracts visitors with its IMAX theater (which shows Oscar-winning documentary nature films) and permanent rain forest exhibit, as well as with such standbys as stuffed and mounted creatures, dinosaur skeletons and ethnological collections (*see chapter* **Museums**). The recent opening of the museum's $210-million spherical **Rose Center for Earth and Space**, which includes the retooled Hayden Planetarium, has brought hordes of visitors (*see* **Space is the place,** *page 288*).

Columbus and Amsterdam, the next avenues west from Central Park West, experienced a renaissance when Lincoln Center was built in the '60s. The neighborhood has long been gentrified and is now full of restaurants, gourmet food shops and boutiques, though a few of the old inhabitants and shops remain. A popular Sunday outing is still the Columbus Avenue stroll, which usually starts at the **Flea Market** (*77th St and Columbus Ave, see chapter* **Shopping & Services**) and continues either up or down Columbus. If you head south, be sure to stop at **Pug Bros. Popcorn** (*265 Columbus Ave between 72nd and 73rd Sts, 212-595-4780*) for a bag of crispy caramel corn handmade in old-fashioned copper kettles, and for an iced cappuccino in the back garden at **Café La Fortuna** (*69 W 71st St between Columbus Ave and Central Park West, 212-724-5846*), a neighborhood favorite for more than 70 years.

On Broadway, the **72nd Street subway station** is notable for its Art Nouveau entrance, and notorious for its crowded, narrow platforms. It's on Sherman Square, named after the general. The opposite triangle, at the intersection of 73rd Street and Broadway, is **Verdi Square.** It's a fitting name: Along with Arturo Toscanini and Igor Stravinsky, Enrico Caruso lived in the nearby **Ansonia Hotel** (*Broadway between 73rd and 74th Sts*) and kept other inhabitants entertained and awake with renditions of his favorite arias. The Ansonia, a vast Beaux Arts apartment building with exquisite detailing, was also the location for the 1992 thriller *Single White Female.* Bette

Torah de force The Jewish Museum honors the artworks and history of the Jewish people.

Midler got her break at the long-gone Continental Baths, a gay spa and cabaret that occupied the Ansonia's lower floors in the 1970s. This was also where star DJs Frankie Knuckles and Larry Levan honed their skills.

The **Beacon Theater,** on Broadway at 75th Street, was once a fabulous movie palace and is now a concert venue. The interior is a designated landmark. Across the street the gourmet markets **Fairway** and **Citarella** vie for shoppers. Fairway is known citywide for its bountiful and reasonably priced produce, and Citarella is renowned for its seafood and meat departments. A few blocks north are the **Children's Museum of Manhattan; H&H Bagels,** the city's largest purveyor of this New York staple; the enormous **Zabar's** (*Broadway between 80th and 81st Sts, 212-787-2000*), supplier of more than 250 types of cheese, hand-sliced smoked fish, prepared foods and more (*see chapter* **Shopping & Services**); and the nearby **Barney Greengrass—The Sturgeon King** (*541 Amsterdam Ave between 86th and 87th Sts, 212-724-4707*), an old-time cafeteria-style restaurant with a to-die-for smoked-salmon–and–bagel platter.

Just west of Broadway, on the north side of 94th Street, is the 1920s **Pomander Walk,** a quaint row of townhouses built around a courtyard. Sadly, it's now overshadowed by a new high-rise going up atop **Symphony Space** (*see chapter* **Music**), which features repertory film series and eclectic musical programs, including the famous Wall-to-Wall concerts. Nearby is the **Claremont Riding Academy** (*see chapter* **Sports & Fitness**), where you can rent horses (they live upstairs!) to ride in Central Park.

Riverside Park, an undulating stretch of riverbank, lies between Riverside Drive and the banks of the Hudson River, from 72nd to 145th Streets. Once as fashionable an address as Park Avenue and similarly lined with opulent private houses, Riverside Drive was largely rebuilt in the 1930s with luxury apartment buildings. You may see luxury yachts berthed at the **79th Street Boat Basin,** along with a few houseboats and a café in the adjacent park (open in the summer). Farther north and overlooking the park at 89th

Movin' on up

Upper Manhattan takes off as Harlem experiences its second renaissance

Not too long ago, the idea of venturing to Harlem to sightsee was one that many visitors to New York found tempting but daunting. Yes, Harlem was one of the most famous urban areas in the world—the geographic and spiritual capital of black America—but the combined long-term effects of poverty, crime and neglect had cast a pall over the neighborhood. Today, all of that has begun to change. After losing 30 percent of its population in the 1970s, Harlem is now attracting new residents for the first time in 50 years. Thanks to a surging economy, a sharp drop in crime and large investments by the city, state and federal government, a second Harlem Renaissance is under way, one characterized by both commercial and cultural development.

Nowhere is Harlem's new face more visible than along **125th Street,** traditionally the neighborhood's main commercial thoroughfare. Although the street had a depressed and desperate feel just a few years ago, today it's bustling and much of the recent development has provided long-needed basic services to the neighborhood. In the summer of 1999, for instance, a large **Pathmark** opened at 125th Street and Lexington Avenue in East Harlem. A few blocks to the west, at 125th and Lenox, Harlemites now grab lattes at **Starbucks**. Still farther west, at 125th and Frederick Douglass Boulevard, is the new **Harlem USA** mall, which contains retail giants Old Navy, Modell's, HMV, the Disney Store and a multiplex movie theater. Not only have these developments brought jobs, they've spurred newcomers to move to the neighborhood. In a welcome trend, many middle-class blacks—as well as people of other races—have taken advantage of Harlem's comparatively low real-estate prices and become homeowners in the area.

Tourists, too, have benefited from this second renaissance. Dozens of walking tours prowl the neighborhood throughout the week, allowing visitors to soak up Harlem's rich history. The neighborhood is also reclaiming its mantle as an entertainment mecca. Smoky jazz bars recall the days when bebop giants Thelonious Monk and

Street and Riverside Drive is the **Soldiers' and Sailors' Monument** to the Civil War dead.

Soldiers' and Sailors' Monument
Riverside Dr at 89th St. Subway: 1, 9 to 86th St.
The 1902 monument was designed by French sculptor Paul DuBoy and architects Charles and Arthur Stoughton.

Morningside Heights

The area sandwiched between Morningside Park and the Hudson River from 110th to 125th Streets is **Morningside Heights,** a neighborhood dominated by **Columbia University.** One of the oldest universities in the U.S., Columbia was chartered in 1754 as King's College (the name changed after the Revolutionary War). It moved to its current location in 1897. Thanks to its large student presence and that of its sister school, **Barnard College,** the surrounding area has an academic feel, with bookshops and cafés along Broadway and quiet, leafy streets toward the west overlooking Riverside Park.

Miss Mamie's Spoonbread Too (*366 W 110th St at Columbus Ave, 212-865-6744*) is the place for gumbo and banana pudding, as well as Monday-night live piano sing-alongs. **Nacho Mama's** (*2893 Broadway between 112th and 113th Sts, 212-665-2800*) is loved for its burritos; **Tom's Restaurant** (*2880 Broadway at 112th St, 212-864-6137*), made famous because the *Seinfeld* gang practically lived there, packs them in for brunch; and the **West End** (*2911 Broadway between 113th and 114th Sts, 212-662-8830*) is notable for its $6 pitchers and the fact that it was the hangout for many a Beat poet. For dessert, follow your nose to **Mondel Chocolates** (*2913 Broadway at 114th St, 212-864-2111*), sating students' sweet teeth since 1944.

The neighborhood has two immense houses of worship (*see chapter* **Directory, Religion**), the **Cathedral of St. John the Divine** (the largest in the U.S.) and **Riverside Church,** built with Rockefeller money and containing the world's largest carillon. Ride to the top of the 21-story steel-frame tower for views across the Hudson. Look down on **Grant's Tomb** in

You can have it mall Harlem USA is one of the new hot spots in the neighborhood.

Dizzy Gillespie ruled Harlem's stages. Among the stops: **Showman's** (*125th St at Eighth Ave, 212-864-8941*); **St. Nick's Pub** (*St. Nicholas Ave at 149th St, 212-283-9728*); and the **Lenox Lounge** on Lenox Avenue (Malcolm X Blvd) between 124th and 125th Streets, once a fave hangout of Billie Holiday and Malcolm X. Back on 125th Street, plans are afoot to renovate the famed **Apollo Theater** (*212-531-5305*). Three other legendary Harlem entertainment spots are also to be refurbished in the future: **Minton's Playhouse** (*Cecil Hotel, 206–210 W 118th St between St. Nicholas and Seventh Aves*), **Small's Paradise** (*135th St at Adam Clayton Powell Jr. Blvd*) and the **Renaissance Ballroom** (*Adam Clayton Powell Jr. Blvd at 147th St*).

Obviously, problems persist in Harlem. Years of neglect will not be erased overnight. But without a doubt, the neighborhood is well on its way to reclaiming its status as an economically and culturally vital area of the city.

Riverside Park at 122nd Street, burial site of Ulysses S. Grant, the Civil War general and U.S. president. Behind the mausoleum is a folk-art garden of multicolored mosaic benches, created by about 3,000 volunteers, many of them neighborhood children, in a 1970s project launched by Chilean-born artist Pedro Silva to discourage vandalism.

The hammering and chiseling at the Cathedral of St. John the Divine will continue well into this century. Construction began in 1892 in Romanesque style, was stopped for a Gothic Revival redesign in 1911 and didn't begin again until 1941. Then, after another pause for fund-raising, work resumed in earnest in the 1990s. When the towers and great crossing are completed, this will be one of the world's largest churches and the closest thing New York will have to rival the grandeur of Paris's Notre Dame. In addition to Sunday services, the cathedral also hosts concerts, tours and, on occasion, memorial services for the rich and/or famous. Be sure to check out Pop artist Keith Haring's altarpiece and, in season, the cathedral's rose and herb gardens.

Across the street at the **Hungarian Pastry Shop** (*1030 Amsterdam Ave between 110th and 111th Sts, 212-866-4230*), academic types arrive with books and laptops and work feverishly over cups of coffee (free refills) and croissants. Others flirt, sketch and chat away the day in this European-style coffeehouse. Next door is **V&T Pizzeria** (*1024 Amsterdam Ave, 212-663-1708*), where students order some of the best pizza in the city. After hours, students and locals head to the **1020** bar (*1020 Amsterdam Ave at 110th St, 212-961-9224*) and **Soha** (as in "South of Harlem," *see chapter* **Bars**), a funkily decorated club offering live jazz without a cover or drink minimum.

Cathedral of St. John the Divine

1047 Amsterdam Ave at 112th St (212-316-7490; www.stjohndivine.org). Subway: B, C, 1, 9 to 110th St–Cathedral Pkwy. Mon–Sat 7am–6pm; Sun 7am–8:30pm. Services: Mon–Sat 8, 8:30am, 12:15, 5:30pm; Sun 8, 9, 9:30 (Spanish), 11am, 7pm.

Columbia University

Between Broadway and Amsterdam Ave and 114th to 120th Sts (212-854-1754). Enter Barnard College at Broadway, just north of 116th St (212-854-5262). Subway: 1, 9 to 116th St–Columbia University.

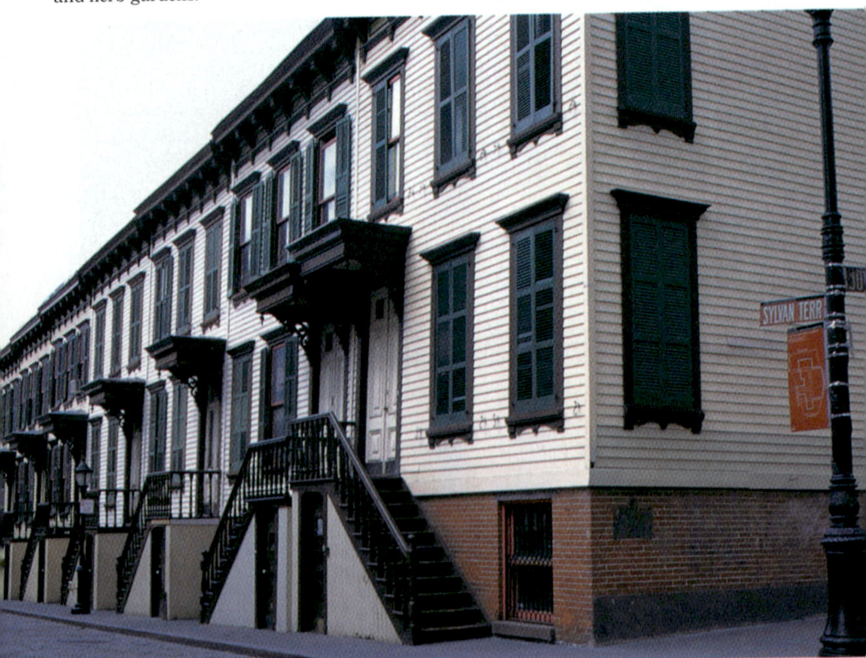

Wooden it be nice A slice of Old New York, Sylvan Terrace is a row of wood-framed homes.

General Grant National Memorial

Riverside Dr at 122nd St (212-666-1640). Subway: 1, 9 to 125th St. 9am–5pm. Free.
This memorial is more commonly known as Grant's Tomb, because Ulysses S. Grant is buried here with his wife, Julia.

Riverside Church

Riverside Dr at 122nd St (212-870-6700). Subway: 1, 9 to 125th St. 9am–4pm.

Harlem

Harlem is shaking its reputation as a dangerous place (*see* **Movin' on up,** *page 70*). Sure, some parts are run-down, and if you're white, be prepared to stand out in the crowd. But no one should hesitate to visit this historic area. Its institutions and streets are named after great liberators, teachers and orators, and there are constant reminders of proud Afrocentric culture, from Francophone Africans selling trinkets to Jeeps vibrating with hip-hop street politics.

Harlem was originally composed of country estates, but when the subways arrived at the turn of the century, the area was developed for middle-class New Yorkers. When the white bourgeoisie failed to fill the grandiose townhouses, speculators reluctantly rented them to African-Americans. The area's population doubled during the 1920s and '30s, a growth that coincided with the cultural explosion known as the Harlem Renaissance. The poets, writers, artists and musicians living in this bohemian republic helped usher in the Jazz Age.

The neighborhood's soundtrack is now provided by the rap and reggae of the younger generation, as well as by the salsa and merengue of the Cubans and Dominicans who have joined the Latino population of **Spanish Harlem,** or El Barrio ("the neighborhood"), the section east of Fifth Avenue and above 96th Street. Treat your senses to the colorful fruits, vegetables, spices and meats at **La Marqueta,** Park Avenue's multistore food emporium located between 110th and 116th Streets. **El Museo del Barrio,** Spanish Harlem's community museum, is on Fifth Avenue at 104th Street (*see chapter* **Museums**).

The **Graffiti Hall of Fame,** on 106th Street between Park and Madison Avenues, is actually just a schoolyard, but here you'll see the large-scale work of old-school graffiti artists—you may even bump into someone completing a piece. There are also several *casitas,* Puerto Rican "little houses," which function as communal hangouts and create a slice of island life amid the high-rise projects. An especially beautiful one is on 110th Street between Lexington and Third Avenues.

Call to prayer Masjid Malcolm Shabazz in Harlem is named for its founder.

At 116th Street and Lenox Avenue (Malcolm X Blvd) is **Masjid Malcolm Shabazz,** the silver-domed mosque of the late Malcolm X's ministry. Opposite this is the market where street vendors who once lined 125th Street now hawk T-shirts, tapes and (purportedly) African souvenirs. **Sisters Cuisine** (*1931 Madison Ave at 124th St, 212-410-3000*) balances Guyanese food with such Caribbean favorites as Jamaican jerk chicken and curried goat. Just north is the **Lenox Lounge,** where Malcolm X's early career as a hustler began and where you can still hear jazz (*see chapter* **Music**). A couple of blocks north is **Sylvia's** (*328 Lenox Ave between 126th and 127th Sts, 212-996-0660*), famous for its soul-food gospel brunch, and at 138th Street is the **Abyssinian Baptist Church,** containing a small museum dedicated to Adam Clayton Powell Jr., the first black member of New York's City Council and Harlem's congressman from the 1940s through the 1960s. Just below 125th Street, on Fifth Avenue, is **Marcus Garvey Park.** It's at the center of a historic district of elegant brownstones; some of the most beautiful are open to the public several times a year. Call the Mt. Morris Park Community Association (*212-369-4241*) for details.

The **Studio Museum in Harlem** (*see chapter* **Museums**) presents exhibitions focusing on the area and its artists, while at the **Schomburg Center for Research in Black Culture,** part of the New York Public Library system, Harlem's rich history lives on. As the largest research collection devoted to African-American culture, the center's archives include audio and visual recordings of outstanding black musicians and speeches that explore the political messages of leaders like Marcus Garvey and Jesse Jackson.

Harlem's main commercial drag is 125th Street, and the **Apollo Theater** (located between Adam Clayton Powell Jr. and Frederick Douglass Blvds) is its focus. For four decades after it began presenting live shows in the 1930s, the Apollo was the world's most celebrated venue for black music. It's had its ups and downs in the last 30 years or so but continues to present live music (*see chapter* **Music**). Tours of the theater are given daily (*call 212-531-5337 for details*). The Theresa Towers office complex, at 125th Street and Adam Clayton Powell Jr. Boulevard, was formerly the **Hotel Theresa.** Fidel Castro stayed here during a 1960 visit to the United Nations, and his visitors included Nikita Khrushchev and Gamal Abdel Nasser.

Farther west on 125th Street is another black music landmark. **The Cotton Club,** originally located on 142nd Street, was the neighborhood's premier nightclub from the 1920s to '50s. Dubbed the Aristocrat of Harlem, the club launched such entertainment royalty as Duke Ellington, Cab Calloway and Dorthy Dandrige but is now more a showcase for live blues and jazz.

The area between 125th and 155th Streets west of St. Nicholas Avenue is known as **Hamilton Heights,** after Alexander Hamilton, who had a farm here at **Hamilton Grange.** The Federal-style home, designed by the same architect who designed City Hall, may be moved to nearby **St. Nicholas Park** within the next few years. This is a gentrified part of Harlem, where you'll find the neo-Gothic City College, the City University of New York's northernmost outpost. On the City College campus, check out the **Croton Gatehouse** (dubbed the "Pump Station" by locals) at Convent Avenue at 135th Street. In the 1880s, the Gatehouse played an important role in bringing water from the Croton Reservoir to New York City.

While you're in the area, tour **Strivers' Row** (*Adam Clayton Powell Jr. Blvd between 138th and 139th Sts*), a strip of magnificent neo-Georgian houses developed in 1891 by David H. King (who also constructed the original Madison Square Garden). In the 1920s, such prominent members of the black community as Eubie Blake and W. C. Handy lived here, and you can still see signs on the gates that read WALK YOUR HORSES.

Stop for a bite at **Londel's Supper Club** (*2620 Frederick Douglass Blvd between 139th and 140th Sts, 212-234-6114*), owned by Londel Davis, a police-officer–turned–restaurateur who serves some of the best blackened catfish in town. Or try a chicken-and-waffles combo at the **Sugar Shack** (*2611 Frederick Douglass Blvd at 139th St, 212-491-4422*). The area hops at night, especially at the legendary **St. Nick's Pub** (*773 St. Nicholas Ave at 149th St,212-283-9728*), where purists

Washington shlepped here The war general stopped at the Morris-Jumel Mansion in 1776.

can hear live old-school jazz and jam sessions every night except Tuesday.

A little farther north, on Broadway at 155th Street, is **Audubon Terrace.** This double cluster of Beaux Arts buildings, part of artist John James Audubon's former estate, houses an unusual group of museums: the **Hispanic Society of America,** the **American Numismatic Society** and the **American Academy of Arts and Letters** (*see chapter* **Museums**).

Abyssinian Baptist Church

132 W 138th St between Adam Clayton Powell Jr. Blvd and Lenox Ave (212-862-7474). Subway: 2, 3 to 135th St. 9am–5pm. Services: Sun 9, 11am.

The Abyssinian is celebrated for its history and its gospel choir. Go a half-hour early on Sunday to be assured of a seat, probably in the balcony and next to a fellow tourist.

The Cotton Club

656 W 125th St at Riverside Dr (212-663-7980; www.cottonclub-newyork.com). Subway: 1, 9 to 125th St. Mon, Wed–Fri 8pm–4am; Sat, Sun noon–midnight. $32, includes buffet. MC, V.

The club hosts a variety of live music including blues and jazz every Friday and Saturday night. Music begins a half-hour after doors open.

Hamilton Grange

Convent Ave at 141st St (212-283-5154). Subway: A, C, B, D, 1, 9 to 145th St. Fri–Sun 9am–5pm.

Schomburg Center for Research in Black Culture

515 Malcolm X Blvd at 135th St (212-491-2200; www.nypl.org/research/sc). Subway: 2, 3 to 135th St. Mon–Wed noon–8pm; Thu–Sat 10am–6pm; Sun 1–5pm by appointment only. Free.

Washington Heights

The area from 155th Street to the northern tip of Manhattan is called **Washington Heights.** A growing number of artists and young families are moving to the area, attracted by Art Deco buildings, spacious streets and low rents. Here, the island shrinks in width, and the parks on either side culminate in the wilderness and forest of **Inwood Hill Park.** Some believe the famous 1626 transaction between Peter Minuit and the Munsee Indians for the purchase of a strip of land called Manahatta took place here. The 196-acre refuge contains the island's last remnant of primeval forest. Largely due to the efforts of landscape architect Frederick Law Olmsted, the area was not leveled in the 1800s—the house-size glacier-deposited boulders were probably a factor, too. Today, with a little imagination, you can hike through this mossy forest and see a bit of the beautiful land the Munsees called home.

High Bridge (*Amsterdam Ave at 177th St*) will give you an idea of how Old New York got its water supply. This aqueduct carried water across the Harlem River from the Croton Reservoir in Westchester County to Manhattan. The central piers were replaced in the 1920s to accomodate passing ships.

The main building of **Yeshiva University** (*186th St at Amsterdam Ave*) is one of the strangest in New York, a Byzantine orange-brick structure decorated with turrets and minarets. Equally surprising is the **Cloisters,** at the northern edge of flower-filled Fort Tryon Park. A reconstructed monastery incorporating several original medieval cloisters that the Rockefellers shipped over from Europe, it might have been custom-designed for romantic picnics. Actually, it houses the Metropolitan Museum's medieval collections—illuminated manuscripts, priceless tapestries and sculpture. It also offers incredible views of the New Jersey Palisades and the Hudson River (*see chapter* **Museums**).

The neighborhood also has two significant American historic sites. **Dyckman House,** a Dutch farmhouse with a high-shouldered gambrel roof and flared eaves, built around 1783, is the oldest surviving home in Manhattan and something of a lonely sight on busy Broadway (*at 204th St*). In 1915, when the house was threatened with demolition, the Dyckman family's descendants purchased it and filled it with heirlooms. **Morris-Jumel Mansion** (*Edgecombe Ave at 160th St*) was where George Washington planned for the battle of Harlem Heights in 1776, after the British colonel Roger Morris moved out. The handsome 18th-century Palladian villa also has some fantastic views. Cross the street to see **Sylvan Terrace,** between 160th and 162nd Streets, which has the largest continuous strip of old wooden houses in Manhattan (*see chapter* **Architecture**).

Dyckman Farmhouse Museum

4881 Broadway at 204th St (212-304-9422). Subway: A to Dyckman St. Tue–Sun 11am–4pm. Free.

Inwood Hill Park

Entrance on 207th St and Seaman Ave (212-304-2365). Subway: A, 1, 9 to 207th St.

Morris-Jumel Mansion

65 Jumel Terrace (which runs from Edgecombe Ave to St. Nicholas Ave) between 160th and 162nd Sts (212-923-8008). Subway: A, C to 163rd St. Wed–Sun 10am–4pm. $3, students and seniors $2. MC, V.

Built in 1765, the mansion is Manhattan's only surviving pre-revolutionary house. Now surrounded by brownstones, it originally sat on a 160-acre estate that stretched from river to river.

An eye for an eye The Brooklyn Museum of Art raised its profile when it successfully fended off critics of "Sensation," its controversial show of young British artists.

The Outer Boroughs

Don't forget, New York City is made up of five boroughs—walk over a bridge, hop on a ferry or ride the subway and say ciao, Manhattan!

The population of New York City—counting all five boroughs—hovers around 7.5 million, and fewer than 2 million of those people live in Manhattan. But the population of Manhattan swells to around 10 million during the day. So if you feel you're spending too much time looking at the back of the head of the person in front of you in line, or if you've had enough of the crowded stores, escape the throng by hopping on a train or a boat to see where most New Yorkers live.

The four "outer boroughs" of NYC—Brooklyn, the Bronx, Queens and Staten Island—developed at a slower pace and on a smaller scale than Manhattan. In each, you'll find good food, interesting architecture, splendid views, places to bike and walk, and you'll get a taste of how people make living in the city work (and working in the city livable).

Brooklyn

Even though Manhattan is not connected to it by land, the best way to get to Brooklyn is to walk 1,595.5 feet across its namesake bridge. The 1883 completion of the **Brooklyn Bridge** transformed Brooklyn from a spacious suburb that still contained areas of farmland into a bustling city. Stroll or bike across the pedestrian walkway at the center of the bridge for spectacular views of lower Manhattan, the Statue of Liberty and New York Harbor as it opens at the Verrazano-Narrows Bridge. To the north, you'll see a series of bridges linking Manhattan to other parts of Brooklyn and Queens, as well as the jewel-like tops of the Empire State and Chrysler Buildings. The bridge itself is an exciting piece of engineering and architecture. As you walk along it, you'll see plaques detailing the story of its construction.

The **Anchorage** of the bridge, a cathedral-like structure with ceilings up to four stories high, holds up the Brooklyn side (the Manhattan side has one, too, but it's not open to visitors). In summer the Anchorage is the site of art exhibits and concerts (*see chapter* **Music, Summer venues**), and it's a great place to cool off after a walk across the bridge.

Also under the bridge, but at the water's edge, is **Fulton Landing,** a pier jutting into the East River at Old Fulton and Water Streets. It's a prime spot for taking photos of the Manhattan skyline. To the right is the expensive **River Café** (*see chapter* **Restaurants, American creative**) and to the left is **Bargemusic,** a refurbished barge where you can listen to chamber-music concerts (*see chapter* **Music, Classical & Opera**).

South of the bridge is the **Brooklyn Heights Esplanade,** a pedestrian-only perch overlooking the East River that runs from Cranberry Street to Remsen Street, with its main entrance at the foot of Montague Street. This walkway offers spectacular views of Manhattan and the bridges. Benches are plentiful; it's a good place to sit and observe other tourists, lunching locals and skating kids. Stroll through Brooklyn Heights to see well-preserved Federal-style and Greek Revival brownstones. Middagh, Cranberry, Willow, Orange, Pineapple and Montague are some of the prettiest streets. Restaurants are plentiful on Montague Street. Also in the Heights, on Orange Street, is the dignified **Plymouth Church of the Pilgrims,** founded by famous abolitionist Henry Ward Beecher.

The waterfront below Brooklyn Heights, from the Manhattan Bridge to Atlantic Avenue, will be undergoing a drastic change. During the next few years, this little-used stretch of piers will be converted into an 80-acre public park that will include open space, recreation facilities and commercial activities.

Brooklyn was incorporated into New York City in 1898; the remains of its days as a separate municipality still exist in the somewhat fragmented downtown. **Borough Hall** (*209 Joralemon St at Fulton St*), built in 1851, is at the center. Its renovation in the early 1990s won the Municipal Art Society's top prize for restoration of a public structure. Borough Hall is linked to the **New York County Supreme Court** by a vast plaza, where farmers from the tristate area sell fresh produce on Fridays and Saturdays. Nearby is the massive **General Post Office** (*271 Cadman Plaza East between Tillary and Johnson Sts*).

The primary business district is across the way in the recently built **Metrotech Center.** A commons provides a shady place to rest between Metrotech and **Polytechnic University,** the second oldest science-and engineering school in the country. At the easternmost edge of the commons is **Wunsch Student Center** (*311 Bridge St*). Long before it became part of the Poly campus, the 1846 Greek Revival structure was the home of the Bridge Street African Wesleyan Methodist Church, which met there until the congregation moved to Bedford-Stuyvesant in 1938.

Farther east, at the very edge of downtown, is the **Brooklyn Academy of Music** (locals call it "BAM"). At this venue, one of the city's oldest, brand-new/cutting-edge theater, music and performance art that's too hot for Manhattan can find a space. The Brooklyn Philharmonic is the orchestra in residence, and the Next Wave Festival draws audiences from all over the metropolitan area for its contemporary and emerging-artists programs (*see chapters* **Music** *and* **Theater & Dance**). The latest addition is the four-screen **BAM Rose Cinema** (*see chapter* **Film & TV**).

North of downtown is the arty enclave **Williamsburg.** Since rents for Manhattan loft spaces are beyond the reach of all but a lucky few, the active machine of artistic creation has packed its paint and clay and moved across the river to this postindustrial neighborhood. While the artists' migration began well over a decade ago, only in recent years has gentrification followed: Some of the city's hottest restaurants and bars, mostly clustered around the L train's Bedford Avenue subway stop, serve the new bohemian population and attract Manhattanites, too (*see chapters* **Restaurants** *and* **Bars**).

Williamsburg is also one of New York's more curious multiculti amalgams. To the south, Broadway divides a noisy, vibrant Latino neighborhood from a quiet, ordered community of Hasidic Jews. Williamsburg's northern half is shared by Polish and Italian blue-collar residents, who originally worked the East River docks. Manufacturing still occurs here, but many of the old factory buildings continue to be converted into lofts and artists' studios. Not surprisingly, the neighborhood also houses several art galleries, such as **Pierogi 2000** (*see chapter* **Art Galleries**), and on some weekends area artists hold group exhibitions in their studios or organize sprawling, almost carnival-style street fairs. Check the free neighborhood weekly, *Waterfront Week,* for details.

▶ For info on the Smith Street restaurant boomlet, see **Manhattan transfers,** page 146.

▶ See also chapter **Museums.**

▶ A **Brooklyn map** is on pages 404 to 405.

Brooklyn is full of all-day diversions. The **Brooklyn Museum of Art,** originally planned to be the largest museum in the world, is a good place to start. Although it was never finished, it's still enormous and contains more than 1.5 million artifacts. In 1999, the museum made headlines with "Sensation," a (to some) controversial show of British artists (*see chapter* **Museums**). The **Brooklyn Botanic Garden,** right next door, has one of the world's largest collections of bonsai trees. In the spring, the **Cherry Blossom Esplanade** trees, bursting with pink, dazzle visitors; the **Cranford Rose Garden** is at its best in June, when its 1,200 varieties bloom. Look for the roses named for Diana, Princess of Wales, Cary Grant, Audrey Hepburn and Julie Andrews (who stopped by to see her namesake blooms). Year-round, plant lovers can stroll the gardens as well as the indoor, climate-controlled **Steinhardt Pavilion.**

Brooklyn's 526-acre heart of green, **Prospect Park,** is just south of the museum and the garden. Although it's smaller than Central Park, it's calmer and more rural—a wonderful place to bird-watch or rent a pedal-boat from the boathouse. Frederick Law Olmsted and Calvert Vaux (designers of Central Park) wanted Prospect Park to be enjoyed on horseback. While it is possible to rent horses at nearby **Kensington Stables,** biking is the next best thing (*see chapter* **Sports & Fitness**). Pedal alongside in-line skaters and runners, past Frisbee-catching dogs and picnicking families scattered in the park's meadows. At the southern and eastern ends of the park, West Indian drummers set up every Sunday during the summer; feel free to join the circle of dancers. You might even be offered an ice-cold sorrel. Children of all ages enjoy riding the hand-carved horses, goats and lions on the park's carousel. At the **Prospect Park Wildlife Center,** near the intersection of Empire Boulevard and Flatbush Avenue, visitors can learn about animals in their natural habitat. In the summer, a series of outdoor concerts and events are scheduled for the Celebrate Brooklyn! festival (*see chapter* **New York by Season**). In the southwestern part of the park is the **Quaker Friends Cemetery,** where actor Montgomery Clift found his final place in the sun. The wooded area is closed to the public, but you might linger outside the chain-link fence and pay your respects.

Beyond Prospect Park, great bike rides abound. Leave the park and get onto the bike path on Ocean Parkway, a wonderful roadway that cuts through the center of Brooklyn. You'll see old men playing chess and women gossiping about the neighborhood news. You

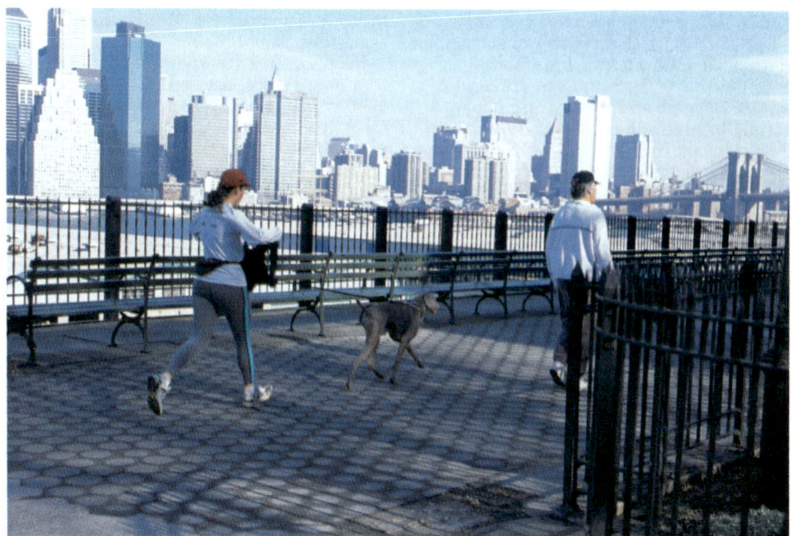

City escape Get a different perspective of Manhattan from the Brooklyn Heights Esplanade.

can take the parkway all the way to Coney Island, or, for a spectacular ride underneath the Verrazano-Narrows Bridge, cut across Avenue P to 72nd Street and head west to the Shore Parkway path.

Architecture buffs might try a tour through Victorian **Flatbush,** just south of Prospect Park. The homes are extravagant, and no two are alike (the turn-of-the-century developer wouldn't allow it). In early spring, the Flatbush Development Corporation sponsors a tour of mansions that were inhabited by the city's elite, including reporter Nellie Bly, silent-film star Mary Pickford and the philanthropic Guggenheims.

As you explore Brooklyn, pay attention to the unique character of each neighborhood. More than 90 ethnic groups proudly fly the colors of their homeland. **Fort Greene,** near downtown, is Brooklyn's bohemian center, with an increasingly multiethnic population of successful creative types: Spike Lee, Chris Rock, Rosie Perez and Branford Marsalis have all called this neighborhood home.

Bedford-Stuyvesant, just east of Fort Greene, is predominantly African-American. Stroll the streets to see the stately brownstones, or join the Brownstoners of Bedford-Stuyvesant House Tour to get a more intimate view. Also in the area, the **Concord Baptist Church of Christ** allows you to experience some old-time religion alongside one of the largest black congregations in the U.S. The fabulous gospel music here will convince you that the devil doesn't have dibs on all the best tunes.

On the border between Bed-Stuy and Crown Heights, **Weeksville** is a row of four houses that were once a part of the larger Weeksville community, the first free black settlement in New York. One of the houses is now a museum; the pair of leg irons on view are a grim reminder of bleaker days.

Crown Heights and **Flatbush** are primarily West Indian. Calypso and soca music blare out of windows and doors. Every block has at least one carry-out place where you can get spicy jerk chicken or meat patties. Try **Sybil's** (*2210 Church Ave at Flatbush Ave, 718-469-9049*), a brightly lit cafeteria-style Caribbean restaurant. Service is friendly, and the staff will help you choose between the *escabèche* and the akee. The best day to be in the neighborhood is Labor Day in September, when most residents, who have spent a good part of the year preparing, turn out for the West Indian Day Carnival and Parade (*see chapter* **New York by Season**). More than two million people watch the resplendent revelers make their way up Eastern Parkway to a thumping Caribbean beat.

Carroll Gardens is a quiet, charming Little Italy. Although it's fun just to walk through Carroll Park, where grandmothers watch kids run about and old men play boccie, it's even better to stroll on Court Street and stop in the shops for a taste of Italy. Buy a prosciutto loaf from the **Caputo Bakery**

(*329 Court St between Sackett and Union Sts, 718-875-6871*), pick up freshly made buffalo mozzarella at **Caputo's Fine Foods** (*460 Court St between 3rd and 4th Sts, 718-855-8852*), grab an aged sopressato from **Esposito and Sons** (*357 Court St between President and Union Sts, 718-875-6863*), and then settle down in the park. Carroll Gardens is also a hotbed of restaurants both old, like **Marco Polo** (*345 Court St at Union St, 718-852-5015*), and new (*see* **Manhattan transfers,** *page 146*).

Brighton Beach is known as "Little Odessa" because of its large population of Russian immigrants—you'll feel as if you've landed somewhere in Eastern Europe. If you get an irresistible yen for caviar, vodka and smoked sausage, this is the place to go. You can wander the aisles of **M&I International** (*249 Brighton Beach Ave between Brighton 1st and Brighton*

Sightseeing

To die for

Beauty springs eternal at Brooklyn's Green-Wood Cemetery

A century ago, Brooklyn's stunning Green-Wood Cemetery vied with Niagara Falls as New York state's greatest tourist attraction. Now, most people don't even know it's there. Located ten blocks south of Prospect Park, Green-Wood is flanked by a power station, a subway yard, Fort Hamilton Parkway and evidently the best streets in Brooklyn for stripping cars. It's easy to reach but difficult to get around (no bikes or blades allowed), and even with the beautifully detailed $3 map for sale at the gate, you're usually lost.

But isolation, inaccessibility and 160 years of meticulous maintenance have sealed it like a time capsule, and five minutes past the dazzling, 106-foot-tall gates, you're in an E.L. Doctorow novel. You don't have to be a necromancer or a Goth to be mesmerized by Green-Wood—until they invent a time machine, it's the closest you'll get to the 19th century.

One of America's first two major cemeteries, Green-Wood is set on 478 acres of a steep, glacier-sculpted hill—across which George Washington's troops hauled ass during the Battle of Long Island. The cemetery welcomed its first long-term resident in 1838 (there are about 600,000 today) and rapidly became the Pastis of the afterlife for New York's Victorian high society. Today it's New York's Père Lachaise: The gravesites of the city's most famous and infamous residents are scattered throughout the cemetery. People who shaped New York, such as politico William "Boss" Tweed and architect Stanford White, share Green-Wood with international names like Louis Tiffany, P.T. Barnum, Mae West, Leonard Bernstein and Jean-Michel Basquiat.

Originally conceived for public relaxation as well as everlasting rest, Green-Wood was attracting a half-million visitors a year by 1865, and the death-obsessed Victorians played to the crowds. Architecturally, the cemetery's structures rival and frequently resemble the most dazzling buildings in nearby Park Slope. The older areas are an obstacle course of mausoleums, monuments, columns, obelisks, arches, benches, boughs, gates, winged orbs and even (no lie) baseball equipment, along with a stadium's worth of statues, angels, cherubs and gargoyles. Some even seem to be jostling each other, vying for eternal social status, but far more convey heartfelt love, dignity and grief (the large number of children's graves is a sobering reflection on Victorian times).

The countless exotic trees and bushes are a living arboreal museum (dazzling in the spring and fall); the greenery attracts an orgy of birds. The plant life blankets the hill with a quiet rarely found anywhere else in the city. There are also four ponds, a fountain and a year-round gaggle of geese.

Beauty is to be found in every corner of Green-Wood, but the following 15-minute stroll is a good start: Walk along Battle Avenue from the main gates to Battle Path for a 30-mile-long view across the harbor. Then head briefly back down Battle Avenue and turn left onto Fern Avenue for sweeping Manhattan views.

Green-Wood Cemetery
25th St at Fifth Ave, Sunset Park, Brooklyn (718-768-7300; www.green-wood.com). Subway: N, R to 25th St. Mon–Sun 8am–4pm. Walking tours available through John Cashman's Walking Tours (718-469-5277) and Big Onion Walking Tours (see chapter **Tour New York***). Call for prices and hours.*

2nd Sts), a huge Russian deli and grocery, or make a reservation at one of the local nightclubs. Dress is formal, food and vodka plentiful, and dancing goes on until the wee hours.

Brooklyn has the largest population of observant Jews outside Israel, and to get a better understanding of their rituals and beliefs, you can go to the heart of that community in **Borough Park.** Take a Hassidic Discovery tour (*see chapter* **Tour New York**) or just wander the streets grazing on the great food. On Fridays before sundown, the streets are at a fever pitch just before the Sabbath (*Shabbes*) begins; on Saturdays, the neighborhood appears to be abandoned.

Arabs have made part of **Atlantic Avenue** their own, on the border between Brooklyn Heights and Cobble Hill. The epicenter is most certainly **Sahadi Importing Company** (*187 Atlantic Ave between Court and Clinton Sts*), which carries every imaginable Mediterranean delicacy. In fact, stop in at any of the restaurants along the strip, and you'll find a savory souvenir of your trip to Brooklyn.

Coney Island (which is not an actual island) is a destination in itself. It was once home to the most extravagant amusement parks in the world; its distinguishing symbol is an abandoned ride, the 250-foot Parachute Jump. In 1911 and then again in 1944, apocalyptic fires destroyed the wooden structures at two of the funfairs; the third, Steeplechase Park, closed in 1964. Nowadays, despite a thriving (but much less extravagant) collection of rides, sideshows and other spangly things, the greatest attraction is the air of decayed grandeur. If you are a thrill-ride seeker, you can't miss the Cyclone, a 74-year-old wooden roller coaster at **Astroland Amusement Park.** The ride lasts only 90 seconds, but the initial drop is nearly vertical, and the dozen or so cars clatter along the 3,000 feet of track at speeds of up to 60 miles per hour. It's rated as one of the top ten roller-coaster experiences in the world.

After your ride, grab a **Nathan's Famous** hot dog (*1310 Surf Ave at Stillwell Ave*), get a gander at the rather tame **Coney Island Sideshows by the Seashore** and walk out to the beach or stroll along the boardwalk, perhaps as far as the **Aquarium for Wildlife Conservation** (*see chapter* **Kids' Stuff**), where you can marvel at the famous beluga whales.

Coney Island is a gathering place for teenagers, senior citizens and oddball improvisational performers. It is becoming more precious as Times Square and Greenwich Village give way to the gentrifying forces of the Gap and Disney. On any given day—winter or summer—you can find a show: Perhaps it's the Puerto Rican man who does a passionate salsa dance to recorded music with a blow-up doll or the guy who calls himself Lizard Man because he parades around with a foot-long lizard perched on his head.

Post it Those desperately seeking something in Williamsburg can find it on a neighborhood notice board.

Aquarium for Wildlife Conservation

Surf Ave at W 8th St (718-265-FISH). Subway: D, F to W 8th St–NY Aquarium. 10am–6pm. Winter hours 10am–4:30pm. $8.75, children and seniors $4.50.

Brooklyn Botanic Garden

900 Washington Ave between Eastern Pkwy and Empire Blvd (718-623-7200). Subway: A to Franklin Ave, then S to Botanic Garden; 2, 3 to Eastern Pkwy–Brooklyn Museum. Oct–Mar Tue–Fri 8am–4:30pm; Sat, Sun, holidays 10am–4:30pm. Apr–Sept Tue–Fri 8am–6pm; Sat, Sun 10am–6pm. $3, students and seniors $1.50, children under 16 free. Sat 10am–noon, Tue free. Cash only.

Brooklyn Bridge

Subway: J, M, Z to Chambers St; 4, 5, 6 to Brooklyn Bridge–City Hall.

New York has many bridges, but none as beautiful or famous as the Brooklyn Bridge. The twin Gothic arches of its towers are a grand gateway, no matter which way you are heading. The span took more than 600 men some 16 years to build; when completed in 1883, it was the world's largest suspension bridge and the first to be constructed of steel. Engineer John A. Roebling was one of 20 men who died on the project—before construction even started. His son stayed on the job until he was struck by

Transglobal express Ride the 7 train through Queens' ethnic neighborhoods.

caisson disease (the bends), and then with his wife's help supervised construction from the window of his Brooklyn apartment. "All that trouble just to get to Brooklyn!" was the vaudevillian quip of the time. The walkway is great for an afternoon stroll; for incredible views, take the A or C train to High Street, and walk back to Manhattan.

Brooklyn Heights Esplanade

On the East River between Remsen and Cranberry Sts. Subway: 2, 3 to Clark St, then walk down Clark St toward the river.

Brooklyn Information and Culture

718-855-7882; www.brooklynx.org

This organization, also known as BRIC, provides information about Brooklyn. To get the quarterly calendar of Brooklyn events, *Meet Me in Brooklyn,* call BRIC then dial extension 42 (the Brooklyn Tourism Council).

Concord Baptist Church of Christ

833 Marcy Ave between Putnam and Madison Aves (718-622-1818). Subway: A, C to Nostrand Ave. Call for times of services.

Coney Island Sideshows by the Seashore/Coney Island USA

1208 Surf Ave at W 12th St (718-372-5159; www.coneyisland.com). Subway: B, D, F, N to Coney Island–Stillwell Ave. Mid-Jun–late Sept Fri–Mon 2pm–midnight. Oct–mid-Jun Sat, Sun 2pm–midnight. $5, children under 12 $3.

Plymouth Church of the Pilgrims

75 Higgs St between Orange and Cranberry Sts (718-624-4743). Subway: A, C, to High St; 2, 3 to Clark St.

The church gives free tours on Sunday at 12:15pm after its service.

Prospect Park

Flatbush Ave at Grand Army Plaza (events hot line 718-965-8999, Leffert's Homestead 718-965-6505, Prospect Park Wildlife Center 718-399-7339; www.prospectpark.org). Subway: 2, 3 to Grand Army Plaza. Carousel at Flatbush Ave and Empire Blvd (718-282-7789). Subway: D, Q to Prospect Park.

Weeksville Society Hunterfly Road Houses

1698–1708 Bergen St between Rochester and Buffalo Aves (718-756-5250). Subway: A, C to Utica Ave.

Queens

Queens is called the Borough of Homes. No other borough has as many single-family homes, and nearly every building boom in the last century was led by developers in Queens. On a drive through the borough's neighborhoods, you'll see almost every style of American housing, from single-family detached, townhouse and bungalow to co-op condominium and duplex.

The quantity of available, affordable housing has made Queens a mecca for immigrants—a full third of Queens residents are foreign-born. The borough was also the city's manufacturing capital, and though New York no longer supports much heavy industry, what little remains is mostly in Queens. Much of the borough's unused industrial space has been converted into artists' lofts.

Queens developed as a series of small towns whose names remain as neighborhood appellations, including Forest Hills, Flushing, Bayside and Kew Gardens. Residents will say that they are from Flushing, for example, rather than from Queens.

Because of its patchwork development, Queens is difficult to navigate. While the other boroughs have discernible patterns to them, Queens is a maze. Arm yourself with a good map and be prepared to enjoy wherever the roads take you.

Queens has long been a cradle for jazz talent. Louis Armstrong lived at 34-56 107th Street in Corona. The house, which will hold the **Louis Armstrong Archives,** is currently undergoing renovation and will eventually be open to the public. Satchmo is one of almost 100 jazz musicians from the 1930s, '40s and '50s who lived in Queens. Those who were from the South found the space and greenery they were accustomed to, and for others, like Count Basie, Fats Waller and Ella Fitzgerald, Queens offered a quiet, dignified retreat: a house, a yard and a driveway—the American Dream. Renowned jazz bassist Milt Hinton still lives here, in the St. Albans area. **Flushing Town Hall** sponsors a Queens Jazz Trail tour. You can follow a guide or pick up a map there and go on your own improvisational pilgrimage.

At every turn, there is evidence that the immigrants who have come to Queens from around the world have made the borough their own. The signs of many stores on **Main Street** in **Flushing** are in Chinese. **Jackson Heights** is perfumed with curry and other spices used by the local Indian residents. Come to these neighborhoods to see how these people have made their mark on the culture—and to eat.

The 7 train, which becomes elevated in Queens, is also known as the **International Express,** because just about every stop in Queens takes you into a different ethnic community. In 2000, the train line got some attention when Atlanta Braves baseball player John Rocker made derisive, racist comments about the riders on the 7, which goes to Shea Stadium. His words outraged the city, which proudly defended its diversity.

Stop at 74th Street–Broadway in Jackson Heights, and you'll be struck by the glittering red, blue and green saris and jewels worn by many residents, not to mention the fresh fruits displayed by grocers along the street. Check out the **Sari Palace** at 37-07 74th Street for Indian clothing and jewelry. Experience mehndi, the intricate henna design usually painted on the hands and arms of brides, at the **Gulzar Beauty Salon** at 74-01 Roosevelt Avenue or the **Menka Beauty Salon** at 37-56 74th Street. Spend hours going through the menu at **Shaheen** at 72-09 Broadway, **Jackson Diner** at 37-03 74th Street, **Delhi Palace** at 37-33 74th Street or **Shaheen's Palace** at 73-10 37th Street.

Elmhurst is just down the pike, at the 82nd Street–Jackson Heights or 90th Street–Elmhurst Avenue stop. Here you'll find Mexicans from Oaxaca, Puebla and Guerrero, who flooded the area in the late 1980s. Colombians and Ecuadoreans are also beginning to create a presence. For a great place to eat, try **Amancer**

Queens for a day Glittering jewels illuminate New York's most diverse borough.

Rancheros at 85-09 Roosevelt Avenue or **Taco Mexico** at 88-12 Roosevelt Avenue. To make a full day of your trip, call the **Queens Council on the Arts** to find out when festivals or parades are happening.

Newly arrived Asian immigrants have made **Flushing** their home; it's also where most of Queen's historic houses are located. Main Street in Flushing (the last stop on the 7 train) is dotted with Chinese and Korean restaurants and food stores. Street vendors sell Toho, a creamy tofu custard with honey and rosewater syrup.

The **Friends' Meeting House,** built in 1694 by religious activist John Bowne, is still used as a Quaker meeting place, making it the oldest house of worship in continuous use in the United States. Next door is **Kingsland House,** a mid-18th-century farmhouse that's also the headquarters of the **Queens Historical Society.** You can also visit **Bowne House,** which dates back to 1661 (*see chapter* **Architecture**).

Long Island City, the neighborhood closest to Manhattan, is home to **P.S. 1,** a former public school converted into a nonprofit gallery and studio space (*see chapter* **Museums**); it merged with the Museum of Modern Art in 1999. P.S. 1 attracts artists from around the world with open workshops, multimedia galleries, several large permanent works and controversial, censor-taunting exhibitions. MoMA is also planning to open an additional temporary space in 2002, to exhibit works while it expands its Manhattan location. Nearby, the rather unkempt riverside **Socrates Sculpture Garden** contains large-scale sculptures by both well- and lesser-known artists, and hosts occasional concerts and video presentations. Just down the road is the **Isamu Noguchi Garden Museum,** Noguchi's great self-designed sculpture studios, where more than 300 of his works are displayed in 12 galleries (*see chapter* **Museums**).

Sprawling **Astoria,** adjacent to Long Island City, is known for its outstanding Greek and Eastern European restaurants and markets. There's some sightseeing to be done, too. Long before Hollywood was movieland, there was Astoria. W.C. Fields, Rudolph Valentino, Gloria Swanson and the Marx Brothers all made films

Gorillas in the midst

Go *megillah* over the gorillas at the Bronx Zoo's new rain-forest home for the great apes

A trail runs through a humid forest and into the hollowed-out center of a gargantuan fake ceibu tree. Another great tree looms over the tunnel's entrance, its massive buttress roots typical of those found in the Congo's Ituri Forest. But this scene isn't in the heart of Africa; it's in the middle of the Bronx.

Opened in 1999, the $43-million "Congo Gorilla Forest" is the most ambitious project in the Bronx Zoo's 102-year history. The 6.5-acre re-creation of Congo's wilds took four years to build and consists of some 20,000 plants of 400 varieties, numerous waterfalls and 30,000 square feet of rock outcroppings. It also features two troops of endangered lowland gorillas.

"This is theater, in many ways," says project manager Lee Ehmke. "We're doing something that's got a beginning, a middle and an end. There's a built-in sense of mystery and drama."

If this is theater, it's even wilder than *The Lion King.* Visitors follow the trail (separated from the forest by almost invisible wire netting) as it snakes past a stand of trees in which black-and-white colobus monkeys play. Then it's on to the Okapi Forest, where Congo's elusive giraffe relative—which wasn't even known outside the country until 1901—shares space with DeBrazza's and Wolf's monkeys and red river hogs. Blue-cheeked, red-nosed mandrills socialize in an adjacent enclosure.

Next is an indoor gallery filled with birds, fish, amphibians and reptiles, as well as interactive displays about rain forest ecosystems. Visitors then watch a seven-minute film—narrated by Glenn Close—on rain-forest preservation projects. When the film finishes, the movie screen lifts and the curtain parts to reveal a panoramic view of the lowland gorillas.

The Bronx Zoo, which opened the nation's first gorilla exhibit in the 1950s, currently has one troop of nine and another of ten. One of the original reasons for creating "Congo" was to upgrade the gorillas' living conditions—they were previously housed in the cramped Gorilla House. The view of the apes from inside the building is wonderful,

at **Kaufman Astoria Studios,** which opened in 1917. Filming still goes on; the Children's Television Workshop—producers of *Sesame Street*—and the Lifetime Network are based here (*see chapter* **Film & TV**), as is the **American Museum of the Moving Image** (*see chapter* **Museums**). At the northernmost end of Astoria is the **Steinway** piano factory, where some of the best pianos in the world are still (mostly) hand-crafted.

Of course, you'll find plenty of places to eat Greek; the neighborhood has been attracting Greek immigrants since the 1920s. Try any of the restaurants along 31st Street (*see chapter* **Restaurants, Greek**), or pick up some bread, feta and olives for a picnic.

At the heart of Queens: **Flushing Meadows–Corona Park,** a huge complex that contains **Shea Stadium,** home of the New York Mets, and the **United States National Tennis Center,** where the U.S. Open is played every August (*see chapter* **Sports & Fitness**).

The 1939 and 1964 World's Fairs were held in **Corona Park** (then known as Flushing Meadow Park), and some incredible abandoned structures are still standing, including the huge stainless-steel Unisphere globe, now a restored landmark. Outside the curved concrete structure of the **New York Hall of Science,** you can marvel at cast-off pieces of space rockets. A leftover 1939 World's Fair pavilion is the home of the **Queens Museum,** where the main attraction is a 1:12,000 scale model of New York City made for the 1964 fair (*see chapters* **Museums** *and* **Kids' Stuff**).

Today, **Corona Park** is the scene of weekend picnics and hotly contested soccer matches between teams of European- and South American–born locals, not to mention the annual Hong Kong Dragon Boat Races (*see chapter* **New York by Season, Summer**). You can rent bikes at the Passerelle Ramp and the Meadow Lake Boathouse from May to October.

Enjoy more open space at the **Queens County Farm Museum** in edge-of-borough **Floral Park.** The farm, which dates to 1772, features exhibits on the city's agricultural history.

Near Kennedy Airport, the tidal wetlands of the **Jamaica Bay Wildlife Refuge** are prime spots for bird-watching, especially in May and September. Bring your binoculars and spot both birds and planes. **Kennedy Airport** is itself a sight to behold. The curvy, modern Terminal 5 is headquarters of TWA. Designed by architect Eero Saarinen, the terminal is one of New York's landmarked buildings (*see chapter* **Architecture**).

If you're a bit of a gambler, one of the best bargains in New York City is a day at **Aqueduct** racetrack, site of the winter-spring Thoroughbred racing season. Seats cost from $1 to $3 (no kidding!), compared with $50 to $80 at other tracks. Most races are grade II stakes, but the grade I Wood Memorial, a Kentucky Derby test run, is held in April (*see chapter* **Sports & Fitness**).

but it's nothing compared to the one from the Gorilla Encounter tunnel, which runs through the apes' enclosure. The glass-encased walkway is two feet below ground level, so the animals can climb over the top of the tunnel with the help of a tree.

At the final stop, the Conservation Choices Pavilion, touch-screens allow visitors to select which zoo-sponsored rain-forest conservation program will receive their $3 admission fee. *See page 89 for listing.*

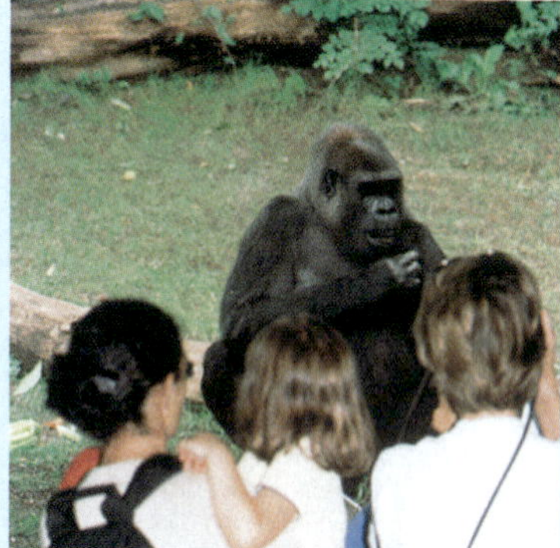

Gorilla, interrupted The Bronx Zoo's simian residents are going ape over their new home.

American Museum of the Moving Image

35th Ave at 36th St (718-784-0077; www.ammi.org). Subway: G, R to Steinway St. Tue–Fri noon–5pm; Sat, Sun 11am–6pm.

In addition to special exhibits, classic films are shown on a regular basis (*see chapters* **Film & TV** *and* **Museums**).

Steinway Piano Factory

Steinway Pl between 19th Ave and 38th St (718-721-2600). Subway: N to Ditmars Blvd.

Free factory tours were suspended for renovations during 2000. Call to see if they have resumed.

▶ A **Queens street map** is on page 403.
▶ See also chapter **Sports & Fitness**.

Little Big Apple Get a giant's-eye view of New York at the Queens Museum.

Corona Park

Between Northern Blvd and Jewel Ave. Subway: 7 to Willets Pt–Shea Stadium.

Flushing Town Hall

137-35 Northern Blvd (718-463-7700). Subway: 7 to Main St–Flushing. Mon–Fri 9am–5pm; Sat, Sun noon–5pm.

Jamaica Bay Wildlife Refuge

Cross Bay Blvd at Broad Channel (718-318-4340). Subway: A to Broad Channel. 8:30am–5pm. Free.
The wildlife refuge is part of a local network of important ecological sites administered by the National Parks Service. You can spot pairs of breeding osprey, a fish-eating hawk that has rebounded from the brink of extinction. Migratory species, including the long-legged curlew sandpiper, can be seen in spring and early fall. Guided walks, lectures and all sorts of nature-centered activities are available.

Louis Armstrong Archives

Queens College, 6530 Kissena Blvd between Melbourne and Reeves Aves (718-997-3670). Travel: E, F to Parsons Blvd, then Q25 bus to Queens College.

Queens Council on the Arts

79-01 Park Ln South, Woodhaven (718-647-3377, info 718-291-ARTS; queenscouncilarts.org). Subway: J to 85th St–Forest Pkwy. Mon–Fri 9am–4:30pm.
This organization provides exhaustive details, updated daily, on all cultural events in the borough.

Queens County Farm Museum

73-50 Little Neck Pkwy, Floral Park (718-347-3276). Travel: E, F to Kew Gardens, then Q46 bus to Little Neck Pkwy. Mon–Fri 9am–5pm outdoor grounds only; Sat, Sun 10am–5pm tours of farmhouse and museum galleries. Voluntary donation.

Socrates Sculpture Park

Broadway at Vernon Blvd, Long Island City (718-956-1819). Subway: N to Broadway. 10am–sunset. Free.
Set in a vacant postindustrial lot on the East River, the park is dotted with pieces like the engagingly interactive *Sound Observatory*.

Friends' Meeting House

137-16 Northern Blvd between Main and Union Sts, Flushing (718-358-9636). Subway: 7 to Main St–Flushing. By appointment only.

Kingsland House/ Queens Historical Society/ Weeping Beech Park

143-35 37th Ave at Parsons Blvd, Flushing (718-939-0647). Subway: 7 to Main St–Flushing. Tue, Sat, Sun 2:30–4:30pm. $3. Cash only.
Built in 1785 by a wealthy Quaker, Kingsland House was moved to a site beside Bowne House. The Queens Historical Society now uses it for exhibitions detailing local history. Staffers can give you more information about the borough's historical sites.

The Bronx

The Bronx is so named because it once belonged to the family of Jonas Bronck, a Swede from the Netherlands who built his farm here in 1636. (People would say, "Let's go over to the Broncks'.") As Manhattan's rich were moving into baronial apartments on Fifth Avenue, a similar metamorphosis took place to the north. As a result, the Bronx contains some of the city's most important cultural landmarks, including the **Bronx Zoo,** the **New York Botanical Garden** and **Yankee Stadium.**

The **Grand Concourse,** a continuation of Madison Avenue, is the Bronx's main thoroughfare. It was built up in the 1920s and is now lined with grand Art Deco apartment buildings. The architecture was influenced by the two World's Fair Expositions in Paris, especially the 1925 show, which first unveiled Art Deco designs. You'll see gorgeous mosaics, decorative terra-cotta, etched glass and ironwork adorning the buildings along the street. It's worthwhile to walk around the area and even sneak a peek in a lobby or two. The **Bronx General Post Office** at 558 Grand Concourse is easy to overlook—the exterior is dull—but inside are wonderful murals painted by Ben Shahn as part of a WPA project in the 1930s. The grandest building on the Grand Concourse is the landmarked **Andrew Freedman Home,** a 1924 limestone palazzo between 166th and McClennan Streets. In his will, mysterious millionaire Freedman stipulated that the bulk of his $7 million be used to build a retirement home for wealthy people who had fallen on hard times. Today, it still houses the elderly—but financial ruin is no longer a residency requirement.

The rotunda of the **Hall of Fame of Great Americans,** modeled after Rome's Pantheon, is a site-specific monument. It was built on a precipice (at *Hall of Fame Terr and University Ave*) for sweeping views of Harlem, the Hudson Valley and the New Jersey Palisades across the Hudson River. This colonnade honors scholars, politicians, thinkers, educators and other great Americans. The hall and nearby buildings were all built by Stanford White (of McKim, Mead & White) for New York University's uptown campus, though they now house Bronx Community College. Several blocks north, at East Kingsbridge Road and Grand Concourse, is the small clapboard house where **Edgar Allan Poe** lived for a year until his sickly young wife died.

Near the foot of the concourse, at 161st Street, is **Yankee Stadium** (*see chapter* **Sports & Fitness**). Tours can be arranged through the Yankee office. You'll see the clubhouse, the dugout and the famous right-field fence, built low enough so that Babe Ruth could set his home-run records. The best way to get to the stadium is by boat: New York Waterways will carry you from New Jersey or Manhattan to the game and back aboard the *Yankee Clipper.* On the way to the game, enjoy spectacular views of the city's skyline (*see chapter* **Tour New York**).

Riverdale is perhaps the city's most beautiful neighborhood. It sits atop a hill overlooking the Hudson River, and its huge, rambling homes on narrow, winding streets have offered privacy to the famous and the obscure. Perhaps the most famous home, **Wave Hill,** is open to the public. Originally a Victorian country estate where exotic plants were cultivated, its illustrious past tenants include William Thackeray, Theodore Roosevelt, Mark Twain and Arturo Toscanini. The gardens are now a small, idyllic park with great views of the river. Concerts are presented during the summer.

For a completely different view of Bronx life, go to **Parkchester** and **Co-op City.** Each in its time was the largest housing complex ever built. Parkchester, in the East Bronx, is bordered by East Tremont Avenue, Purdy Street, McGraw Avenue and White Plains Road. Completed in the early 1940s, it was the first city-within-a-city. It has easy subway access to Manhattan and loads of shops and movie theaters. The designers included lots of pedestrian pathways and landscaping. In contrast, the behemoth Co-op City (35 towers of 35 stories each), in the North Bronx just east of the Hutchinson River Parkway, has malls, parks and schools, but no real community center. (This is where New York novelist and screenwriter Richard Price grew up, and it's the backdrop in his early books.) Both are extraordinary examples of American urban planning.

There are many colleges and universities in the Bronx, but **Fordham University,** a Jesuit institution founded in 1841, is the most prominent. Its small, Gothic-style campus is a wonderful shady place for a walk—and you can stick around for a rousing game of college basketball.

Art education Former public school P.S. 1 shows avant-garde installations.

In nearby **Belmont,** a mostly Italian-American neighborhood, the houses are small and plain, but the main street, **Arthur Avenue,** is lively and inviting (except on Sunday, when many residents attend mass or spend time at home with their families). The avenue is lined with shops offering every kind of Italian gastronomic delicacy. Stop, browse and have a bite at the **Arthur Avenue Retail Market** (*Arthur Ave at 185th St*), a European-style bazaar built in the 1940s by Mayor Fiorello La Guardia to get pushcarts off the street but still provide a place for immigrant merchants to work. Inside is **Mike's Deli** (*718-295-5033*), where handsome Italian men ply you with compliments and push Parmesan. The cappuccino is better than anything you'll find at Starbucks, and the restaurants offer great fare at reasonable prices.

Belmont is a perfect place to end up after visiting the **New York Botanical Garden** and the **Bronx Zoo.** The Botanical Garden is a lush, gorgeous place to wander and rest—even for a whole day! Its collection of plants is one of the best in the world. Visit the newly renovated **Enid A. Haupt Conservatory,** originally built in 1902.

The zoo opened in 1899 and was then considered rambling and spacious. It's still the largest urban zoo in the U.S., but it now seems a little cramped, compared with more modern zoos like San Diego's. Still, it's fun to wander along the banks of the Bronx River and see the animals. The newest addition—and a big hit—is the Congo Gorilla Forest (*see* **Gorillas in the midst,** *page 84*).

About 10 minutes from the zoo is New York's own little Lourdes. At **St. Lucy's Roman Catholic Church,** the line in front of an outdoor grotto is often 20 people long. The faithful believe that the water has healing powers—even though it comes from a tap. (The grotto was fed by a natural spring when it was built in 1939.) Incidentally, the church itself makes no claims about the water.

The Bronx is a great parks borough. Watching a game of cricket in 1,100-acre **Van Cortlandt Park** at Broadway and 249th Street will do a lot to dispel the rough-and-tumble image of "da Bronx." The **Van Cortlandt Mansion,** a fine example of pre-Revolutionary Georgian architecture, sits amid this vast expanse of green; it has been open to the public since 1897. It was built by Frederick Van Cortlandt in 1748 as the homestead of his wheat plantation (*see chapter* **Architecture**).

Much farther to the northeast, facing Long Island Sound, is **Pelham Bay Park,** which offers all sorts of diversions, including the man-made shoreline of **Orchard Beach.** Inside the park is the **Bartow-Pell Mansion,** a Federal manor set amid romantic formal gardens.

Perhaps the most unexpected part of the Bronx (or the entire city, really) is **City Island,** a mile and a half long and a half-mile wide island on Long Island Sound. Settled in 1685, it was originally a prosperous shipbuilding center with a busy fishing industry. Now, it offers New Yorkers a slice of New England–style maritime

Heart of glass Flora flourish year-round in the New York Botanical Garden conservatory.

recreation—it's packed with marinas, seafood restaurants and nautically themed bars. Join the crowds at **Johnny's Famous Reef Restaurant** (*2 City Island Ave at Belden's Point, 718-885-2086*) for steamed clams, slaw and a nice cold beer. If you're fishing for some nautical history, visit the **North Wind Undersea Institute.**

The majority of the Bronx's population these days is Latino. The palace at the center of Bronx nightlife is **Jimmy's Bronx Café** (*see chapter* **Restaurants, Latin American/Caribbean**). Jimmy Rodriguez opened the club in the '90s in an old car dealership off the Major Deegan Expressway at Fordham Road. The cuisine is Caribbean seafood, but the dancing on Friday and Saturday nights is what has made it a hit.

Bartow-Pell Mansion

895 Shore Rd North at Pelham Bay Park (718-885-1461). Travel: 6 to Pelham Bay Park, then W45 bus (ask driver to stop at the Bartow-Pell Mansion; bus does not run on Sun) or take a cab. Wed, Sat, Sun noon–4pm. $2.50, under 12 free.
The International Garden Club has administered this 1836 mansion since 1914; the grounds include formal gardens, a fountain and a carriage house and stable.

Bronx County Historical Society Museum

Valentine-Varian House, 3266 Bainbridge Ave between Van Cortlandt Ave and 208th St (718-881-8900). Subway: D to 205th St. Mon–Fri by appointment only; Sat 10am–4pm; Sun 1–5pm. $2.
This 1758 fieldstone farmhouse is a fine example of the pre-Revolutionary Federal style.

Bronx Zoo/Wildlife Conservation Society

Bronx River Pkwy at Fordham Rd (718-367-1010; www.wcs.org). Subway: 2, 5 to Bronx Park East. Apr–Oct Mon–Fri 10am–5pm; Sat, Sun, holidays 10am–5:30pm. Nov–Mar 10am–4:30pm. $7.75, children under 12 and seniors $4, Wednesday free. Cash only.
The pythons slither around a lush indoor tropical rain forest; the ponds brim with crocodiles. The elusive snow leopard wanders around the peaks of the "Himalayan Highlands,"and more than 30 species of rodentia coexist in the Mouse House. Birds, giraffes, lions and reptiles abound; the zoo is home to more than 6,000 creatures. Although it covers 265 acres, it's not too hard on the feet; there's a choice of trams and monorails. The newest attraction is "Congo Gorilla Forest" (*see* **Gorillas in the midst,** *page 84*).

City Island

Travel: 6 to Pelham Bay Park, then Bx29 bus to City Island. Call the City Island Chamber of Commerce (718-885-9100) for information about events and activities.

Corpus Christi Monastery

1230 Lafayette Ave at Baretto St (718-328-6996). Subway: 6 to Hunts Point. Morning prayer 6am, Mass 7:15am, evening prayer 4:50pm, night prayer 5–7pm; Sun Mass 8:15am.
Visit on Sunday morning for Mass or in the afternoon, when the cloistered Dominican nuns sing the office. Both services are music-filled, and the 1890 church is lit mostly by candles, exposing a mosaic floor and austere walls.

Edgar Allan Poe Cottage

Grand Concourse at East Kingsbridge Rd (718-881-8900). Subway: B, D, 4 to Kingsbridge Rd. Sat 10am–4pm, Sun 1–5pm. $2.
The cottage in Fordham Village where Poe once lived has been moved across the street and turned into a charming museum dedicated to his life.

North Wind Undersea Institute

610 City Island Ave, City Island (718-885-0701). Travel: 6 to Pelham Bay Park, then Bx29 bus to City Island. Mon–Fri noon–4pm; Sat noon–5pm. $3, $2 concessions. Cash only.
Among the attractions at this old maritime folk museum are whale bones, ancient diving gear and a 100-year-old tugboat.

New York Botanical Garden

200th St at Kazimiroff Blvd (718-817-8700). Travel: Metro North from Grand Central Terminal to New York Botanical Garden; B, D, 4 to Bedford Park Blvd, then Bx26 bus. Apr–Oct Tue–Sun and holidays 10am–6pm. Nov–Mar Tue–Sun 10am–4pm. $3, students and seniors $2, children $1, under 2 free. Wed 10am–6pm, Sat 10am–noon free. Ask about Garden Passport, which includes grounds, tram tour and adventure garden admission. Cash only.
Across the street from the zoo, you'll find a complex of grand glass houses, set among 250 acres of lush greenery that includes a 40-acre patch of virgin forest along the Bronx River.

Pelham Bay Park

718-430-1890. Subway: 6 to Pelham Bay Park.

St. Lucy's Roman Catholic Church

833 Mace Ave at Bronxwood Ave (718-882-0710). Subway: 2, 5 to Allerton Ave.

Wave Hill

West 249th St at Independence Ave (718-549-2055). Travel: Metro-North from Grand Central Terminal to Riverdale. Tue, Thu–Sun 9am–5:30pm; Wed 9:30am–dusk. $4, students and seniors $2. Tue, Sat before noon free. Cash only.
The 28-acre Wave Hill, with its formal European gardens, is now a venue for concerts, educational programs and exhibitions, including a sculpture garden featuring works by on-site artists.

Staten Island

Staten Island may be part of New York City, but it's fair to say that the borough has a love-hate relationship with the rest of the city—with the emphasis on hate. A move to secede from the city was approved by a healthy margin a few Election Days ago, and while Staten Island didn't actually break away, residents continue to argue that City Hall takes their taxes to pay for the other boroughs' problems and gives them nothing in return but garbage. (The infamous landfill at Fresh Kills is one of the world's largest man-made structures.) Driving through Staten Island's tree-lined suburbs and admiring its open spaces and vast parks, you can see why the generally well-to-do inhabitants of this borough are so eager to opt out of the pressing urban concerns of the rest of New York City.

Because of its strategic location, Staten Island was one of the first places in America to be settled. Giovanni da Verrazano discovered the Narrows—the body of water separating the island from Brooklyn—in 1524, and his name graces the bridge that connects the two boroughs today. (At 4,260 feet, or 1,311 meters, it's the world's second-longest suspension bridge.) Henry Hudson christened the island "Staaten Eylandt" (Dutch for *State's Island*) in 1609. In 1687, the Duke of York sponsored a sailing competition, with Staten Island as the prize. The Manhattan representatives won the race, and since then it has been governed from New York.

You reach the island from Manhattan via the **Staten Island Ferry.** The ride from Battery Park in lower Manhattan is free (*see chapter* **Tour New York**). You pass close to the **Statue of Liberty** before sailing into the St. George ferry terminal, which is slated for an $81 million reconstruction as part of a project that also includes the building of a minor-league baseball stadium for a New York Yankees farm team, shops and two museums.

The **Snug Harbor Cultural Center** was originally a maritime hospital and home for retired sailors. It comprises 28 buildings—grand examples of various periods of American architecture—in an 80-acre park. In 1976, the city took over the site and converted it into a cultural center, which now puts up exhibitions and hosts arts events. Near the lighthouse at the island's highest point is the **Jacques Marchais Museum of Tibetan Art,** a collection of art and cultural treasures from the Far East with an emphasis on all aspects of Tibetan prayer, meditation and healing (*see chapter* **Museums**). Its Buddhist temple is one of New York's more tranquil places.

Historic Richmond Town is a spacious collection of 29 restored buildings, some dating back to the 17th century. Many of the buildings have been moved here from elsewhere on the island. There's a courthouse, a general store, a bakery and a tinsmith, as well as private homes. During the Revolutionary War, Billop House (now **Conference House**) was where an unsuccessful peace conference took place between the Americans, led by Benjamin Franklin and John Adams, and England's Lord Howe. The building has been turned into a museum. Combine your visit here with a trip to nearby **Tottenville Beach.**

Staten Island's famous dead are a reflection of the borough's illustrious—and shadowy—past. In **Moravian Cemetery** (*at Richmond and Todt Hill Rds*) lie industrialist Commodore Cornelius Vanderbilt, Civil War hero Robert Gould Shaw and...Gambino crime family head Paul "Big Pauly" Castellano (remember Don Corleone's bucolic Staten Island estate in *The Godfather*?).

Conference House (Billop House)

7455 Hylan Blvd (718-984-2086). Travel: Staten Island Ferry, then S78 bus to Hylan Blvd at Craig Ave. Apr–Dec Fri–Sun 1–4pm. $2, seniors and children $1.

John Adams recalled that for the attempted peace conference at Billop House, Lord Howe had "prepared a large handsome room" and made it "not only wholesome but romantically elegant." Built circa 1680, this is the earliest manor house in New York City, and it has been restored to its former magnificence.

Historic Richmond Town

1441 Clarke Ave between Arthur Kill and Richmond Rds (718-351-1611). Travel: Staten Island Ferry, then S74 bus to Richmond Rd–Court Pl. Wed–Sun 1–5pm. Jul 4 to Labor Day Wed–Fri 10am–5pm. $4, seniors and students $2.50, under 6 free. Cash only.

Eight of the houses are open to the public, including Lake-Tysen House, a wooden Dutch Colonial farmhouse built around 1740 for a French Huguenot. Voorlezer's House is the oldest surviving elementary school in America. Actors in 18th-century garb lurk in the doorways; crafts workshops are never far away. It's as if you've left the city far behind.

Snug Harbor Cultural Center

1000 Richmond Terr (718-448-2500, 718-815-SNUG for tickets; www.snug-harbor.org). Travel: Staten Island Ferry, then Snug Harbor trolley or S40 bus. 8am–5pm. Tours Sat, Sun 2pm. $2 suggested donation for gallery.

Exhibitions of painting, sculpture and photography are held in the Newhouse Center. The Staten Island Botanical Garden is here, with tropical plants, orchids and a butterfly house. Opera, chamber groups and jazz musicians play in the 1892 Veterans' Memorial Hall, the city's second oldest music hall. The John A. Noble Collection showcases maritime history and art. Art Lab offers classes, and there's also a children's museum.

Staten Island Chamber of Commerce

130 Bay St between Victory Blvd and Slosson Terr (718-727-1900).

Call for details of cultural events and travel directions on Staten Island.

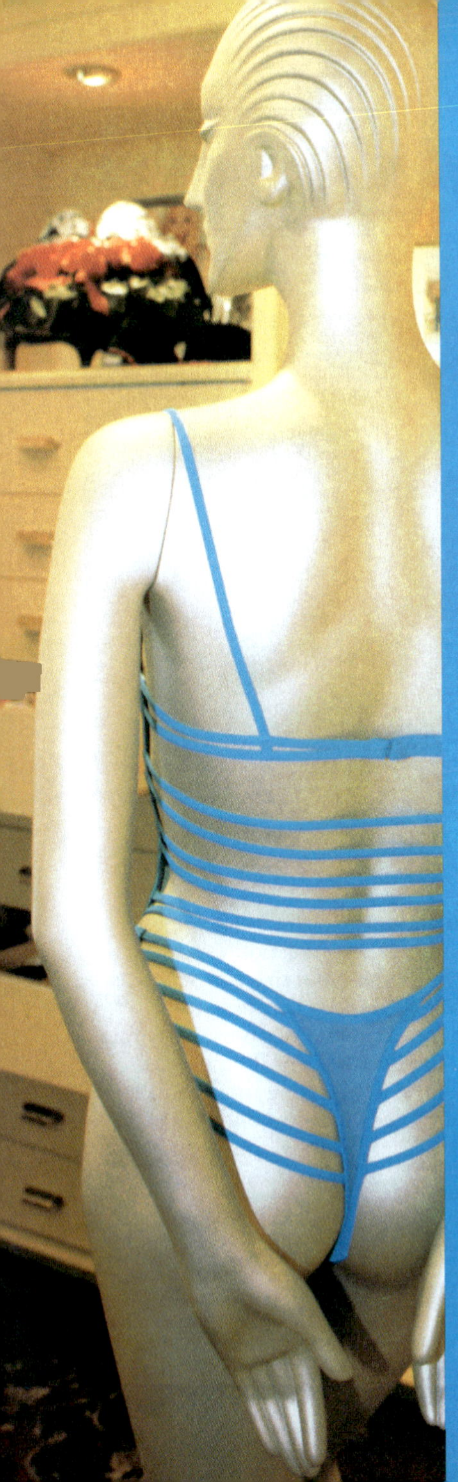

Necessities

Feature boxes

Just what you need New York offers plenty of things to spend your money on.

Accommodations

How to find a room of your own in a city of 7.5 million people

New York has 70,000 hotel rooms, with another 6,000 scheduled to open by 2002, so finding a place to stay should be easier than ever, right? But remember, this is the city that never sleeps. New York finished 1999 with an 82.4 percent occupancy rate, lower than the year before, but still astronomically high compared to a national average of less than 64 percent. And at $218 per night, the average room rate in NYC is also the highest in the country.

The good news is, Gotham's economic boom has left no neighborhood untouched. From high-tech Wall Street chains and Soho designer hotels to East Village bed-and-breakfasts—and even a new Hilton Garden Inn on Staten Island (slated to open in spring 2001)—hotels are popping up all over.

Each neighborhood attracts a different sort of hotel. New York has the greatest proportion of small chain and independent hotels of any big city in the country, with just under half of its properties unaffiliated with a national or international chain. Spearheaded by stylish boutique hotels such as Ian Schrager's Morgans (which opened in 1984), the indie-hotel movement is thriving. But whatever the type of lodging, hotels are pulling out all the stops to get the guests.

So don't despair. Look for introductory rates at new and newly renovated hotels (but don't be surprised if construction work is still going on in the room next to yours). Take advantage of designer-hotel one-upmanship and ask about package deals that include breakfast. Avoid overrun midtown and head toward lower Manhattan, where 1,500 new rooms have popped up since 1995. Go online, where hotel-reservation agencies offer deals even when everyone swears the city is booked solid. And if

Nights of the Round Table The Algonquin's lobby bar is a good place to relax with a drink.

Central
Park
HOSTEL

all else fails, make a friend quickly and ask about a spare bed.

One more caveat: Even though room taxes were rolled back to 13.25 percent a few years ago, they can still cause sticker shock for the uninitiated. There's also a $2-per-night occupancy tax. And ask in advance about unadvertised costs—like phone charges, minibars and faxes—or you might not find out about them until you check out.

Telephone tip: The toll-free 800, 877 and 888 numbers listed here work only within the U.S.

▶ For more accommodations listings, see chapter **Gay & Lesbian**.

▶ For more information contact the **Hotel Association of New York City,** 437 Madison Avenue, New York, NY 10022 (212-754-6700; www.hanyc.org).

▶ **NYC & Company–the Convention and Visitors Bureau** (800-NYC-VISIT) has a free booklet that includes listings of more than 140 hotels.

HOTEL RESERVATION AGENCIES

These companies book blocks of rooms in advance and thus can offer reduced rates. Discounts cover most price ranges, from economy upward; some agencies claim savings of up to 65 percent, although 20 percent is more likely. If you know where you'd like to stay, it's worth calling a few agencies before booking, in case the hotel is on their list. If you simply want the best deal, mention the part of town in which you'd like to stay (*see* **Hood advice,** *page 102*) and the rate you're willing to pay, and see what's available. The following agencies work with selected New York hotels and are free of charge. A few require payment for rooms by credit card or personal check ahead of time, but most let you pay directly at the hotel.

Accommodations Express

801 Asbury Ave, sixth floor, Ocean City, NJ 08226 (609-391-2100, 800-444-7666; www.accommodationsxpress.com).

Central Reservation Service

9010 SW 137th Ave, #116, Miami, FL 33186 (305-408-6100, 800-555-7555; fax 305-408-6111; www.reservation-services.com).

Hotel Reservations Network

8140 Walnut Hill Ln, suite 203, Dallas, TX 75231 (214-361-7311, 800-715-7666; fax 214-363-3978; www.hoteldiscount.com).

Express Hotel Reservations

3825 Iris Ave, Boulder, CO 80301 (303-440-8481, 800-407-3351; www.express-res.com).

Quikbook

381 Park Ave South, New York, NY 10016 (212-779-ROOM, 800-789-9887; fax 212-779-6120; www.quikbook.com).

STANDARD HOTEL SERVICES

All hotels have air-conditioning—a must in summer—unless otherwise noted. In the **Deluxe, Stylish, First-class, Business** and **Boutique** categories, all hotels have the following services and amenities: alarm clock, one or more bars, cable TV, concierge, conference facility, fax (in business center or in room), hair dryer, laundry, minibar, modem line, radio, one or more restaurants, room service and in-room safe (unless otherwise noted). Additional services are included at the end of each listing.

Most hotels in all categories have disabled access, nonsmoking rooms and an iron and ironing board in the room or on request. Call to confirm.

"Breakfast included" means continental breakfast, which can be as little as coffee and toast or as much as croissants, fresh orange juice and cappuccino.

While many hotels boast a "multilingual" staff, the term may be used loosely.

Deluxe

All hotels in this category have a business center and valet service.

The Carlyle Hotel

35 E 76th St between Madison and Park Aves (212-744-1600, 800-227-5737; fax 212-717-4682; www.dir-dd.com/the-carlyle.html). Subway: 6 to 77th St. Single/double $450–$595, suite $650–$2,250. AmEx, DC, MC, V.

The sumptuous Carlyle is one of New York's most luxurious hotels, featuring whirlpools in almost every bathroom. Ever since it opened in 1930, the hotel has attracted famous guests—especially those who want privacy. Service is so discreet that two members of the Beatles stayed here after the group split up without either knowing about the other. The Cafe Carlyle, a cozy cabaret with low lighting and rose-velvet banquettes, is a perpetual draw for its live musical acts, which include the gravel-voiced Bobby Short, who's been pleasing the Carlyle crowds for 31 years (*see chapter* **Cabaret & Comedy**). Across the hall is Bemelmans Bar, named for Ludwig Bemelmans, the creator of *Madeline*; it's lined with murals he painted in 1947, when he lived at the hotel.

Hotel services *Cellular phone rental. Currency exchange. 24-hour dry cleaning. Fitness center and spa. Video rental.* **Room services** *CD player. VCR.*

Four Seasons Hotel

57 E 57th St between Madison and Park Aves (212-758-5700, 800-332-3442; fax 212-758-5711;

Tap of luxury The Regent Wall Street is the first five-star Financial District hotel.

Necessities

www.fourseasons.com). Subway: N, R to Lexington Ave; 4, 5, 6 to 59th St. Single from $515, double from $565, suite from $1,200. AmEx, DC, JCB, MC, V.
Renowned architect I.M. Pei's sharp geometric design (in neutral cream and honey tones) is sleek and ultramodern, befitting this favorite haven of media moguls. The Art Deco–style rooms are among the largest in the city, with bathrooms made from Florentine marble and tubs that fill in just 60 seconds. Views of Manhattan from the higher floors are superb. Guests can unwind at Fifty Seven Fifty Seven, the hotel's ultrachic piano bar and restaurant, where power brokers gather nightly (*see chapter* **Restaurants, Celebrated chefs**).
Hotel services *Currency exchange. 24-hour dry cleaning. Fitness center and spa. Gift shop. Parking. Video rental.* **Room services** *Nintendo. VCR in suites, otherwise on request. Voice mail. Web TV.*

Le Parker Meridien

118 W 57th St between Sixth and Seventh Aves (212-245-5000, 800-543-4300; fax 212-708-7471; www.parkermeridien.com). Subway: N, R to 57th St. Single/double $210–$395, suite $210–$2,500. AmEx, DC, JCB, MC, V.
One of the big draws at this "Traditionally French, Decidedly New York" midtown classic is the rooftop pool. The award-winning breakfasts, complete with smoothie shots, red-berry–risotto oatmeal and Hudson Valley duck confit hash, are a close second. A new bar that has been decked out in primary colors makes an excellent third.
Hotel services *Cellular phone rental. Currency exchange. Fitness center and spa. Gift shop. Parking.* **Room services** *DVD player. Kitchenettes in some rooms. VCR. Voice mail.*

Millenium Hilton

55 Church St between Fulton and Dey Sts (212-693-2001, 800-HILTON; fax 212-571-2316; www.hilton.com/hotels/nycmlhh). Subway: N, R, 1, 9 to Cortlandt St. Single $455, double $505, suite $550–$2,000. AmEx, DC, Disc, JCB, MC, V.
This 58-story black-glass skyscraper, located next to the World Trade Center and a stone's throw from Wall Street, draws a large corporate clientele. The Millenium (the name is intentionally misspelled) has fax machines in each room and high-tech facilities, not to mention a rooftop swimming pool and solarium overlooking St. Paul's Church. The upper floors have splendid views of New York Harbor and the Brooklyn Bridge.
Hotel services *Currency exchange. Fitness center. Parking.* **Room services** *CD player and kitchenette in suites. VCR rental. Voice mail.*

The New York Palace

455 Madison Ave at 50th St (212-888-7000, 800-697-2522; fax 212-644-5750; www.newyorkpalace.com). Subway: E, F to Fifth Ave. Single/double from $440, tower room from $565, suite from $900. AmEx, DC, Disc, JCB, MC, V.
Every inch of the luxurious New York Palace was renovated in 1998. The room decor now ranges from traditional to Art Deco. The main hotel—once the Villard Houses, a cluster of mansions designed by Stanford White—is the home of Sirio Maccioni's acclaimed Le Cirque 2000, and the decor is something to see: Pre-Raphaelite murals combined with a circus motif. It's nearly impossible to get into, but guests in the tower don't have to worry—both Le Cirque and the nearby Sushisay will deliver straight to your room.
Hotel services *Currency exchange. 24-hour dry cleaning.* **Room services** *Dual-line phones. Fax/copier. Voice mail.*

The Pierre Hotel

2 E 61st St at Fifth Ave (212-838-8000, 800-PIERRE4; fax 212-758-1615; www.fourseasons.com). Subway: N, R to Fifth Ave. Single from $430, double from $480, suite from $695. AmEx, DC, Disc, JCB, MC, V.

The Pierre has been seducing guests since 1929 with its service and discreet, elegant atmosphere. If the rooms are out of your price range, you can always take afternoon tea in the magnificent rotunda. Front rooms overlook Central Park, and some of Madison Avenue's most famous stores are only a block away.
Hotel services *Beauty salon. Cellular phone rental. Currency exchange. 24-hour dry cleaning. Fitness center. Gift shop. Notary public. Parking. Theater desk.* **Room services** *CD player on request. In-room exercise equipment on request. VCR. Voice mail.*

The Plaza Hotel

768 Fifth Ave at 59th St (212-759-3000, 800-759-3000; fax 212-759-3167; www.fairmont.com). Subway: N, R to Fifth Ave. Single/double $335–$800, suite $800–$15,000. AmEx, Disc, DC, JCB, MC, V.
Perfectly located for a shopping spree, the 93-year-old Plaza Hotel is just a few minutes' walk from Fifth Avenue's most exclusive stores. It's also across the street from Central Park, with breathtaking views from the upper-floor rooms facing 59th Street. Although Ivana Trump no longer runs the place, her signature touches remain. Rooms and suites, renowned for their Baroque splendor, have been freshly renovated; 200 have their original marble fireplaces. If you're an architecture buff, ask for the Frank Lloyd Wright suite (number 223), done up with Wright reproductions. The architect lived here from 1953 to 1959 while the Guggenheim Museum was being built. Downstairs, the famous Palm Court has a delightful Tiffany ceiling. Also, stop in at Istana, a Mediterranean restaurant featuring a tapas afternoon tea, more than 30 types of olives and a sherry menu. Or better yet, unwind from a day of rigorous shopping at the new 8,000-square-foot spa.
Hotel services *Beauty salon. Currency exchange. 24-hour dry cleaning. Spa and fitness center. Ticket desk. Video rental.* **Room services** *Playstation. VCR on request. Voice mail.*

Trump International Hotel and Tower

1 Central Park West at Columbus Circle (212-299-1000, 888-448-7867; fax 212-299-1150). Subway: A, C, B, D, 1, 9 to 59th St–Columbus Circle. Double from $355, suite $500–$1,500 (call for weekend rates). AmEx, Disc, DC, JCB, MC, V.
The Donald's glass-and-steel skyscraper towers over Columbus Circle, just steps from Central Park. Inside, all is subdued elegance—from the small marble lobby to the 168 suites equipped with fax machines, Jacuzzis and floor-to-ceiling windows. Each guest is assigned a personal assistant to cater to his or her whims, and a chef will come to your room to cook on request. Better yet, head downstairs to Jean Georges, named for its four-star chef Jean-Georges Vongerichten, of Jo-Jo and Vong fame (*see chapter* **Restaurants, Celebrated chefs**).
Hotel services *Cellular phone rental. Fitness center. Personal attaché service.* **Room services** *CD player. Computer on request. Kitchenette. Telescope. VCR.*

The Waldorf-Astoria

301 Park Ave at 50th St (212-355-3000, 800-924-3673; fax 212-872-7272; www.hilton.com/hotels/nycwahh). Subway: E, F to Lexington Ave; 6 to 51st St. Single $255–$475, double $335–$375, suite $375–$1,700. AmEx, DC, Disc, JCB, MC, V.
The famous Waldorf salad made its debut in 1931 at the grand opening of what was then the world's largest hotel. Ever since, the Waldorf has been associated with New York's high society (former guests include Princess Grace, Cary Grant, Sophia Loren and a long list of U.S. presidents). In 1999, the grande dame of New York hotels wrapped up a $60 million renovation that restored the main lobby to its original Art Deco grandeur. The Peacock Alley restaurant's chef, Laurent Gras, gets rave reviews, and Oscar's is an American-style bistro.
Hotel services *Beauty salon. Fitness center with steam rooms. Parking.* **Room services** *Kitchenette in some suites. VCR on request. Voice mail.*

Stylish

The Dylan

52 E 41st St between Madison and Park Aves (212-338-0500; 800-314-3101; fax 212-338-0569; www.dylanhotel.com). Subway: S, 4, 5, 6, 7 to 42nd St–Grand Central. Single/double $295–$395, suite $650. AmEx, DC, Disc, MC, V.
Opened in spring 2000 in the former Chemists' Club building, the Dylan hotel makes good on its history. The once-crumbling 1903 Beaux Arts brick-and-limestone structure and its marble grand staircase, which spirals up three floors from the lobby, have been restored to the tune of $30 million. Fabrics in rooms and public spaces are soft and rich: velvet, suede, silk, mohair and chiffon. Don't miss dinner in the restaurant Rx, which retains the original six-foot-high stone fireplace of the former ballroom.
Hotel services *Business center. Fitness Center. Parking.* **Room services** *CD and DVD players. Voice mail.*

The Mansfield

12 W 44th St between Fifth and Sixth Aves (212-944-6050, 877-847-4444; fax 212-764-4477; www.mansfieldhotel.com). Subway: B, D, F, Q to 42nd St; 7 to Fifth Ave. Single/double from $235, suite from $395. AmEx, MC, V.
This small, stylish hotel, popular with the fashion industry, offers unique complimentary treats. The espresso and cappuccino flow freely all day, and some rooms have sound-therapy machines so you can listen to the ocean, a tropical forest or a running stream. Fashionistas love the minimalist decor; others may find it sparse and somber. Breakfast is included, and though there's no restaurant, the M Bar serves caviar and a light menu under a newly uncovered domed skylight. The Mansfield is part of the Boutique Hotels Group, which has four other properties in the city (the Roger Williams, the Wales, the Shoreham and the Franklin).

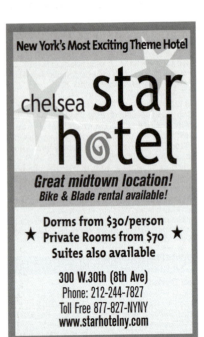

Hotel services *Cellular phone rental. Currency exchange. Access to nearby gym for $10. Video and CD library.* **Room services** *CD player. VCR. Voice mail.*

The Mercer

147 Mercer St at Prince St (212-966-6060, 888-918-6060; fax 212-965-3820). Subway: N, R to Prince St. Single from $370, double from $400, suite $1,050–$2,250. AmEx, DC, Disc, MC, V.

When entrepreneur Andre Balazs bought the site for the Mercer hotel, scenesters were thrilled...though they had to wait five years for its doors to open. The 75-room gem's location in the dead center of Soho gives it a leg up on its closest competitors, the four-year-old SoHo Grand and the new 60 Thompson. The straight-faced, black-clad staff quietly shows you to your chic room: Each features techno amenities, furniture made of exotic African woods and an oversize bathroom.

Hotel services *Free access to nearby gym. Lobby book-and-magazine library. Private stationery. Private meeting rooms. Video and CD library.* **Room services** *Cassette and CD player. Computer on request. Kitchenettes with microwave ovens. Three two-line telephones. Fireplace. VCR on request.*

Morgans

237 Madison Ave between 37th and 38th Sts (212-686-0300, 800-334-3408; fax 212-779-8352). Subway: S, 4, 5, 6, 7 to 42nd St–Grand Central. Single $280–$305, double $285–$375, suite $375–$400. AmEx, Disc, DC, JCB, MC, V.

The cozy, understated Morgans was the first non-nightclub venture by Studio 54 impresarios Ian Schrager and the late Steve Rubell. It's named in honor of J.P. Morgan, whose nearby library was converted into a museum (*see chapter* **Museums**) in 1924. The cavelike Morgans Bar remains a favorite late-night haunt of models and other trendy types, and the restaurant, Asia de Cuba, serves spicy Chino-Latino cuisine.

Hotel services *Cellular phone rental. Complimentary breakfast. Currency exchange. Free access to nearby gym.* **Room services** *DVD rental. Radio, CD player and VCR on request. Voice mail.*

On the Ave

2178 Broadway at 77th St (212-362-1100, 800-509-7598; fax 917-441-0295; www.stayinny.com). Subway: 1, 9 to 79th St. Single/double $125–$185, suite $205, penthouse suite $325. AmEx, DC, Disc, JCB, MC, V.

On the Ave brings some sorely needed style to the Upper West Side's stodgy hotel scene. Its most winning attractions are the canopied "floating beds," the sleek, industrial-style bathroom sinks and the two new rooftop penthouse suites. Original artwork and innovative touches, such as individual breakfast trays that can double as laptop desks, help enliven the minimalist decor. On the Ave lacks a bar and a restaurant, so patrons must be prepared to venture into the surrounding environs for food, drink and entertainment.

Hotel services *Complimentary breakfast. 24-hour dry cleaning.* **Room services** *Voice mail.*

Paramount

235 W 46th St between Broadway and Eighth Ave (212-764-5500, 800-225-7474; fax 212-575-4892). Subway: N, R to 49th St. Single $165–$450, double $205–$475, suite $325-$1,000. AmEx, DC, Disc, JCB, MC, V.

Designed by Philippe Starck and owned by Ian Schrager, the Paramount, like the Royalton (*see below*), is chic almost beyond belief. The cavernous, windowless lobby was inspired by the great transatlantic liners. A "weather mirror" near the elevator on each floor gives the daily forecast, and Vermeer's *Lacemaker* is silk-screened on the headboard of each bed. (There's also a Dean & DeLuca café, an espresso bar and the supertrendy Whiskey Bar). Beware when booking: Some rooms are as small as 9 feet by 10 feet, with barely enough room for a single twin bed.

Hotel services *Business center. Cellular phone rental. Fitness center. Magazine kiosk. Ticket desk. Valet. Video rental.* **Room services** *VCR. Voice mail.*

Royalton

44 W 44th St between Fifth and Sixth Aves (212-869-4400, 800-635-9013; fax 212-575-0012). Subway: B, D, F, Q to 42nd St; 7 to Fifth Ave. Standard $305–$355, superior $340–$400, deluxe $390–$440. AmEx, DC, MC, V.

Like the Paramount (*see above*), Ian Schrager's Royalton was designed by Philippe Starck, who knows how to style soothing hotel rooms. Leggy waitresses in satin minidresses serve fashionable young things in the dark vaultlike lobby, and the restaurant (called 44) has some of the most sought-after lunch tables in town. The rooms feature sleek slate fireplaces and round bathtubs. Discounted weekend rates are often available.

Hotel services *Currency exchange. 24-hour dry cleaning. Fitness center. Parking. Valet. Video rental.* **Room services** *Fax on request. VCR. Voice mail. Web TV.*

60 Thompson

60 Thompson St between Spring and Broome Sts (212-431-0400, 877-431-0400; fax 212-431-0200; www.60Thompson.com). Subway: C, E to Spring St. Single/double $335–$425, suite $500–$575, penthouse suite $1,500. AmEx, DC, Disc, MC, V.

This new Soho entrant has added 100 rooms to the neighborhood, and stands in stark contrast to the nearby Mercer and SoHo Grand. Since it's the tallest building around, the views from this dark-brick hotel—and its penthouse bar—extend from the surrounding low-rise apartment buildings all the way north to the Empire State Building. Guests enter through a shady outdoor garden café. Thomas O'Brien of Aero Studios designed the "Thompson Chair" (available for purchase) that's in each guest room, and the chrome faucets in the mosaic-tiled bathrooms. Fifties-style lamps complement floor-to-ceiling leather headboards and mahogany beds. Terraced suites are surprisingly quiet.

Hotel services *Business center. Cellular phone rental. 24-hour dry cleaning. Fitness center. Parking. Valet.*

Necessities

Video rental. **Room services** *CD player. Microwave ovens on request. VCR. Voice mail.*

SoHo Grand Hotel

310 West Broadway between Grand and Canal Sts (212-965-3000, 800-965-3000; fax 212-965-3244; www.sohogrand.com). Subway: A, C, E, 1, 9 to Canal St. Single $329–$379, double $349–$399, suite from $1,400. AmEx, DC, Disc, MC, V.

When it welcomed its first guests in 1996, this was Soho's first hotel to open since the 1800s. Architecturally, it's one of the city's most striking inns. The unusual design pays homage both to Soho's contemporary artistic community and to the area's past as a manufacturing district. A dramatic bottle-glass–and–cast-iron stairway leads up from street level to the elegant lobby and reception desk, where a monumental clock presides. Rooms are decorated in soothing grays and beiges, with photos from local galleries on the walls. Minibars are stocked with nonfat munchies. The Grand Bar (*see* **The best hotel bars,** *page 105*) and the Canal House restaurant are each worth a visit.

Hotel services *Business center. Fitness center. 24-hour dry cleaning.* **Room services** *CD player. VCR. Voice mail.*

The Time

224 W 49th St between Broadway and Eighth Ave (212-320-2900, 877-846-3692; fax 212-245-2305; www.timehotel.com). Subway: C, E, 1, 9 to 50th St; N, R to 49th St. Single/double from $279, suite $400–$1,100, penthouse suite $2,500–$5,000. AmEx, DC, Disc, JCB, MC, V.

Designer Adam D. Tihany says of this stylish Times Square hotel, "The idea is to truly experience a color—to see it, feel it, taste it, smell it and live it." This experience includes guest rooms entirely furnished in the primary color of your choice, complete with artfully placed food of that color (such as an apple) and a color-inspired scent and reading material. Sound like too much? You can always chill out in the hotel's neutral, subdued public spaces, or at Palladin, Jean-Louis Palladin's first restaurant in New York.

Hotel services *Business center. Cellular phone rental. Fitness center. Screening room. Shopping services.* **Room services** *CD player. VCR. Video rental. Voice mail. Web TV.*

Tribeca Grand Hotel

2 Sixth Ave between Church and White Sts (212-519-6600, 877-519-6600; fax 212-519-6700; www.tribecagrand.com). Subway: C, E to Canal St. Single/double $399–$549. Suites $649–$1,499. AmEx, DC, Disc, JCB, MC, V.

Opened in May 2000, just blocks away from its sister property, the SoHo Grand, the newest Grand is the first major hotel to open in the ultratrendy triangle below Canal. The much-anticipated Tribeca

Hood advice

Choose the New York neighborhood that suits your needs and desires

As the crime rate plummets and rents skyrocket, the dreaded G-word—gentrification—has been slowly gobbling up the city. Along with a proliferation of fusion restaurants, designer gyms and, yes, Starbucks, hotels are sprouting on every corner (*see* **Brooklyn lodgers,** *page 117*). Grouchy New Yorkers may grumble about having to share their home turf, but for travelers tired of Times Square, it's nice to be able to bunk elsewhere in the city. Here's a guide to choosing the right neighborhood for you.

FINANCIAL DISTRICT

Once solely the territory of traders and buyers, the historic Financial District now booms beyond quitting time. In 1995, the area had 2,000 hotel rooms; today there are nearly 3,500. In 2000, the former Merchants Exchange building reopened as the city's first **Regent Hotel** (*see page 107*). The new **Holiday Inn Wall Street** (*see page 107*) touts itself as the most wired hotel in the city, while the cozy 46-room **Wall Street Inn** (*see page 107*) takes a low-stress tactic, occupying a quiet street next to Goldman Sachs's headquarters. A new **Ritz-Carlton** (*800-241-3333*) and **Embassy Suites** (*800-362-2779*) are scheduled to open by the end of 2001. You know the neighborhood is heating up when the nonprofit Alliance for Downtown New York is considering giving the area a buzzname: SoCha, for South of Chambers Street (*see* **Name cropping,** *page 26*). Nightlife is still relatively quiet, but with the champagne bars of Tribeca within walking distance, you can be in the bubbly in no time.

TRIBECA/SOHO

The opening of the **Tribeca Grand** (*see above*) means you can finally unpack in this trendiest of trendy areas. If you're in search of hip bistros and bars, by all means check in. However, aside from a few shops and the artsy Screening Room movie theater (*see*

Grand might be hard to get into for a while. Once home to the late John F. Kennedy Jr., the neighborhood supports some of the city's best restaurants, many of them owned by Robert De Niro, a local. The hotel's plush 98-seat screening room will keep visiting filmmakers happy, and rooms live up to the most wired expectations. The somber, candlelit Church Bar and Lounge is the perfect spot for a nightcap.
Hotel services *Business center. Currency exchange. 24-hour dry cleaning. Fitness room. Screening room. Valet parking. Video and CD library.* **Room services** *CD player. Computer on request. Fax/printer/copier/scanner. Free local phone calls. Playstation. VCR. Voice mail. Web TV.*

W New York

541 Lexington Ave at 49th St (212-755-1200, 877-W-HOTELS; fax 212-644-0951; www.whotels.com). Subway: E, F to Lexington Ave; 6 to 51st St. Single/double $299–$389, suite $499–$1,100. AmEx, DC, Disc, JCB, MC, V.
Designed for the sophisticated executive and leisure traveler, the W New York offers just about every convenience. Rooms are attractive and soothing, with oversize desks, chaise longues and luxurious featherbeds. If the atmosphere isn't enough to calm frayed nerves, there's craniosacral massage at the alternative Away Spa, or organic teas at Heartbeat, the hotel's health-conscious restaurant. Expect the same suavity from W's two sister hotels, the Court and the Tuscany. Opening in November 2000 is W no. 4: W at Union Square, in the landmark 1911 Guardian Life building, a fine example of Renaissance Revival architecture.
Hotel services *Baby-sitting. Breakfast. Business services. Fitness center and spa. Nonsmoking rooms. Parking.* **Room services** *CD player. VCR.*
Other locations: *W New York–The Court, 130 E 39th St between Park and Lexington Aves (212-685-1100; fax 212-889-0287). W New York–The Tuscany, 120 E 39th St between Park and Lexington Aves (212-686-1600; fax 212-779-7822). W at Union Square, 201 Park Ave South at 17th St (877-W-HOTELS).*

First-class

Algonquin

59 W 44th St between Fifth and Sixth Aves (212-840-6800, 800-555-8000; fax 212-944-1618; www.camberleyhotels.com). Subway: B, D, F, Q to 42nd St; 7 to Fifth Ave. Single/double $259–$379, suite $309–$419. AmEx, DC, Disc, JCB, MC, V.
Arguably New York's most famous literary landmark, this was the place where Dorothy Parker, James Thurber and other literary lights of the 1920s and '30s gathered to gossip and match wits at the Oak Room's legendary Round Table. The rooms are on the small side but cheerful and charming, and the hallways now feature *New Yorker*–cartoon wallpaper.

chapter **Film & TV**), the neighborhood is still low on daytime activities.

Forever-fabulous Soho is your best bet, day and night. New hotels such as the **Mercer** (*see page 101*) and **60 Thompson** (*see page 101*), not to mention the **SoHo Grand** (*see page 102*), mean you have an adequate—though pricey—room selection. The Guggenheim's downtown extension, the Angelika Film Center, the Film Forum and an infinite number of affordable and upmarket Soho shops are all in the neighborhood, and Nolita (North of Little Italy) is just next door. You'll have no need to take the subway anywhere. But if you place a premium on personal space, beware: The sidewalks are wall-to-wall all weekend.

TIMES SQUARE/THEATER DISTRICT

This is still the neighborhood for the stereotypical "true New York experience," complete with neon lights, teeming crowds and the stars of Broadway. A half-dozen theme restaurants and the glitzy, new E-Walk, a vast entertainment palace, pound the final nails in the coffin of the once-infamous Times Square sex trade. That's not to say you won't have fun, and at the very least, your choice of dozens of different hotels, from the massive **Marriott Marquis** (*1535 Broadway between 45th and 46th Sts, 212-398-1900*) to the Art Deco and affordable **Hotel Edison** (*see page 114*).

UPPER EAST SIDE/ UPPER WEST SIDE

The two neighborhoods couldn't be more different in character, but the hotels all have four things in common: peace, quiet, Central Park and museums galore. If you're looking to "go local," stay uptown—chances are you'll feel like a resident, especially if you take a borrowed dog for a walk, thereby joining the thousands of other ritual pooch-paraders who characterize these family neighborhoods. You can walk to the Met, the Guggenheim and the Whitney on the East Side; Lincoln Center and the brand-new state-of-the-art Rose Center for Earth and Space on the West. And take your pick of lodgings: the **Phillips Club** (*see page 107*), the **Mayflower Hotel** (*see page 110*), the **Bentley** (*see page 106*), **Hosteling International** (*see page 116*), **On the Ave** (*see page 101*) and the **YMCA** (*see page 117*) are all good choices.

Don't miss Matilda, the house cat, who has her own miniature suite in a corner of the lobby. On Sunday and Monday evenings, there are readings by local authors (*see chapter* **Books & Poetry**); every other night is a cabaret.

Hotel services *Baby-sitting. Cellular phone rental. 24-hour fitness center. 24-hour dry cleaning.* **Room services** *Refrigerator in suites and on request. VCRs in suites. Voice mail.*

Barbizon Hotel

140 E 63rd St at Lexington Ave (212-838-5700, 800-223-1020; fax 212-223-3287). Subway: N, R, Q to Lexington Ave; 4, 5, 6 to 59th St. Single $185–$340, double $305–$375, suite from $365. AmEx, DC, Disc, MC, V.

The Barbizon was originally a hotel for emancipated women (whose parents could feel confident that their daughters were safe in its care). During its years as a women-only residence, guests included Grace Kelly, Sylvia Plath, Ali McGraw and Candice Bergen, and the rules stated that men could be entertained only in the lounge. The hotel recently completed a $40 million renovation, which included adding a branch of the local Equinox health club (free for guests) with a 60-by-24–foot pool and full spa. Children under 12 stay for free if sharing their parents' room.

Hotel services *Beauty salon. CD library. 24-hour dry cleaning. Fitness center. Valet.* **Room services** *CD player. Laptop. Minibar. Voice mail.*

Fitzpatrick Grand Central Hotel

141 E 44th St between Lexington and Third Aves (212-351-6800, 800-367-7701; fax: 212-818-1747; www.fitzpatrickhotels.com). Subway: S, 4, 5, 6, 7 to 42nd St–Grand Central. Single from $325, double from $355, suite from $395. AmEx, DC, Disc, MC, V.

You can't miss the fact that this family-run East Sider, and its sister property, the Fitzpatrick Manhattan, are New York's only Irish-owned lodgings: There are kelly-green carpets with a Book of Kells pattern in the lobbies…and a Liam Neeson penthouse suite (*see* **Extra! Extra!,** *page 112*). The hotel restaurants serve rashers, bangers, soda bread (what else?) and high tea. Just don't plan to go on St. Patrick's Day; you'll never get in.

Hotel services *Cellular phone rental. 24-hour dry cleaning. Free access to nearby gym. Valet.* **Room services** *Computer. DVD rental.*

Other location: *Fitzpatrick Manhattan, 687 Lexington Ave between 55th and 56th Sts (212-355-0100, 800-367-7701; fax 212-308-5166).*

Hotel Elysée

60 E 54th St between Madison and Park Aves (212-753-1066; fax 212-980-9278; members.aol.com/elysee99). Subway: E, F to Lexington Ave; 6 to 51st St. Single/double $265–$325, suite $425–$525. AmEx, DC, JCB, MC, V.

The Elysée has been restored to its original 1930s look, and it displays photographs of the likes of Joan Crawford and Marlene Dietrich gathered around a piano. This is a charming and discreet hotel with attentive staff. The quarters feature antique furniture and Italian-marble bathrooms; some rooms also have colored-glass conservatories and roof terraces. It's popular with publishers, so don't be surprised if you see a famous author enjoying the complimentary afternoon tea in the club room. You can also eat in the Monkey Bar next door, where a well-coiffed clientele dines on American cuisine. Rates include continental breakfast and evening wine and hors d'oeuvres.

Hotel services *Baby-sitting. Free access to nearby gym. Valet parking.* **Room services** *Kitchenette in suites. VCR. Voice mail.*

The Iroquois

49 W 44th St between Fifth and Sixth Aves (212-840-3080, 800-332-7220; fax 212-398-1754; www.slh.com). Subway: B, D, F, Q to 42nd St; 7 to Fifth Ave. Single/double $169–$375, suite $495–$950. AmEx, DC, Disc, JCB, MC, V.

The Iroquois, once a budget hostelry, has morphed into a full-service luxury hotel—guess the investors smelled money in the neighborhood. A mahogany-paneled library, marble-lined bathrooms and a lobby furnished in polished stone are just part of a $13 million renovation that did away with an archaic barbershop and a photographer's studio. The famous Algonquin sits directly across the street, but the only similarity is the Native American name. Breakfast included.

Hotel services *Cellular phone rental. 24-hour dry cleaning. Fitness center and spa. Video library. Parking. Valet.* **Room services** *CD player. VCR.*

The Kitano

66 Park Ave at 38th St (212-885-7000, 800-548-2666, fax 212-885-7100; www.kitano.com). Subway: S, 4, 5, 6, 7 to 42nd St–Grand Central. Superior $380, deluxe $395–$495, suite $600–$1,700. AmEx, DC, Disc, JCB, MC, V.

The Kitano has a serene Japanese aesthetic—warm mood lighting, mahogany paneling, polished stone floors, even complimentary green tea. It is also home to the Japanese restaurant Nadaman Hakubai and an authentic tatami suite. The views of surrounding Murray Hill are pleasant, and there are two large terraces for functions and parties. The Kitano is popular with businesspeople, but those who like to shake off that corporate feeling after a long day may have a hard time here—the sleek decor and neutral colors feel a bit like an office (albeit a high-rent one).

Hotel services *Computer rental. 24-hour dry cleaning. Gallery. Gift shop. Free access to nearby gym. Limousine service to Wall St.* **Room services** *VCR. Voice mail.*

The Mark

25 E 77th St between Fifth and Madison Aves (212-744-4300, 800-843-6275; fax 212-472-5714; www.themarkhotel.com). Subway: 6 to 77th St. Single from $420, double from $450, suite $650–$2,500. AmEx, DC, Disc, MC, V.

Towering potted palms and arched mirrors line the entranceway to this cheerful European-style Upper

East Sider. The marble lobby, decorated with 18th-century Piranesi prints and magnums of Veuve-Clicquot, is usually bustling with dressy international guests and white-gloved bellmen. Especially popular are Mark's Bar, a clubby hideaway with lots of dark green furnishings and polished wood, and the more elegant restaurant Mark's.

Hotel services *Currency exchange. 24-hour dry cleaning. Fitness center. Valet.* **Room services** *Fax. Kitchenette. Printer. VCR. Web TV.*

The Michelangelo

152 W 51st St between Sixth and Seventh Aves (212-765-1900, 800-237-0990; fax 212-581-7618; www.michelangelohotel.com). Subway: B, D, E to Seventh Ave; N, R to 49th St; 1, 9 to 50th St. Single/double $365–$435, suite $495–$1,300. AmEx, DC, Disc, JCB, MC, V.

Posh and very European, this charming little haven in the Theater District welcomes guests with a cozy lobby full of peach marble, oil paintings, giant potted palms and overstuffed couches in rose and salmon tones. The 178 sizable rooms are decorated in styles ranging from French country to Art Deco; each room includes two TVs (one in the bathroom), a fax machine, a terry-cloth robe and a giant tub. Complimentary breakfast includes espresso, cappuccino and Italian pastries.

The best Hotel bars

For old New York panache

Slink into the Carlyle's dark, sedate **Bemelmans Bar,** where some bartenders have been pouring drinks for 40 years. The bar's murals are by Ludwig Bemelmans, creator of the children's book *Madeleine*. *See page 95.*

For the ab fab

Try the SoHo Grand's bar—the **Grand Bar** (surprise!), It drips with attitude, but then, that's part of the fun. Beautiful waiters and an internationally fabulous crowd make it people-watching heaven (just don't be obvious). *See page 102.*

For a midtown drink

The W New York's **Oasis Bar** and **Whiskey Blue** (owned by Rande "Mr. Cindy Crawford" Gerber) are the hot spots. Calm as California, the Oasis is a nice weekday spot for a protein-smoothie boost. *See page 103.*

For seedy characters

Hide out at the **Gramercy Park Hotel Bar,** where regulars, rock stars and beat reporters take advantage of affordable drinks and good bar snacks. The place is exquisitely dark and dingy. *See page 109.*

To take your great aunt to

Wander into the Biedermeier-bedecked **Mark's Bar** in the Mark, which doubles as a cozy tearoom and attracts an older crowd. It's a good place for a post-museum drink. *See page 104.*

For the art of the deal

Sip a potent martini and discuss that latest IPO in the woody men's-club atmosphere of the Plaza's **Oak Bar.** Oversize windows look out onto Central Park. *See page 99.*

To be seen

44 at the Royalton, big with Condé Nast editors, still maintains that Ian Schrager appeal—with sleek young women and men lounging on plush couches after work. Insouciance is de rigueur. *See page 101.*

For guys named Jack

If that's your moniker, **Le Parker Meridien**'s recently refurbished **Jack's Bar** serves you for free from 8 to 10pm. A favorite with record execs. *See page 97.*

Good libations W New York's Oasis Bar is a cool midtown watering hole.

Necessities

Hotel services *Business center. 24-hour dry cleaning. 24-hour fitness center. Limousine service to Wall St (Mon–Fri). Valet.* **Room services** *CD player on request. Computer and printer on request. Complimentary shoe shine and newspaper. Voice mail.*

Roger Smith

501 Lexington Ave between 47th and 48th Sts (212-755-1400, 800-445-0277; fax 212-758-4061). Subway: E, F to Lexington Ave; 6 to 51st St. Single/double $169–$245, suite $225–$400. AmEx, DC, Disc, JCB, MC, V.

The hotel is owned by sculptor and painter James Knowles, and some of his work decorates the lobby. Many of the large rooms have been recently renovated, and each is uniquely furnished. Roger Smith is popular with touring bands, and there's often live jazz in the restaurant. Breakfast is included. The staff is helpful, and there's a library of videos for those who want to stay in for the night.

Hotel services *Valet parking. Valet. Video rental.* **Room services** *Coffeemaker. Kitchenettes with microwave ovens in suites. VCR in some rooms. Voice mail.*

The Warwick

65 W 54th St at Sixth Ave (212-247-2700, 800-223-4099; fax 212-713-1751; www.warwickhotels.com). Subway: B, Q to 57th St. Single/double $199–$305, double $255–$295, suite $335–$1,250. AmEx, DC, JCB, MC, V.

Built by William Randolph Hearst and patronized by Elvis and the Beatles in the 1950s and '60s, the Warwick is still polished and gleaming. It was once an apartment building, and the rooms are exceptionally large by midtown standards. Ask for a view of Sixth Avenue (double-glazing keeps out the noise). The top-floor "Suite of the Stars" has a wraparound balcony and was once the home of Cary Grant.

Hotel services *Baby-sitting. Business center. Cellular phone rental. Currency exchange. Fitness center. Parking. Theater desk.* **Room services** *Microwave on request. VCR on request. Voice mail.*

Heads up The recently opened Giraffe is an option on the newly cool Park Avenue South.

Business

Beekman Tower Hotel

3 Mitchell Pl, 49th St at First Ave (212-355-7300; fax 212-753-9366). Subway: E, F to Lexington Ave; 6 to 51st St. Studio suite from $335, one bedroom from $420, two bedroom from $685.

Built in 1928, the Beekman's distinctive tower is an Art Deco landmark. The charming hotel is a member of the family-owned Manhattan East Suites, the city's largest all-suite hotel group (it has eight other properties in the city; *call 800-ME-SUITE for more information*). Rooms include kitchenettes, and a grocery service is available, so the refrigerator can be stocked while you're out doing business. The Top of the Tower restaurant on the 26th floor has a terrace with panoramic views.

Hotel services *Fitness center. Weekly and monthly rates. Parking. Valet. 24-hour dry cleaning.* **Room services** *Kitchenette. Voice mail.*

The Benjamin

125 E 50th St at Lexington Ave (212-715-2500, 888-4-BENJAMIN; fax 212-465-3697; www.thebenjamin.com). Subway: E, F to Lexington Ave; 6 to 51st St. Superior from $320, deluxe from $350, suite $420–$775. AmEx, DC, Disc, JCB, MC, V.

Now occupying Emory Roth's famous city landmark the Hotel Beverly (which Georgia O'Keeffe used to paint from her apartment across the street), the Benjamin has reclaimed its historic heritage while modernizing into a fully equipped executive suite hotel with a high-tech communications system and other ammenities (*see* **Extra! Extra!**, *page 112*). The recent refurbishment has restored Roth's original details. In addition, noted chef Larry Forgione moved his popular restaurant An American Place (*see chapter* **Restaurants, Celebrated chefs**) to the hotel (the kitchen also provides the room service). And for the ecoconscious: The Benjamin is the only Ecotel-certified establishment in the city.

Hotel services *Business center. Fitness center and spa.* **Room services** *CD player in suites. Cordless phone. Fax/printer/copier. Kitchenette. VCR. Voice mail.*

The Bentley

500 E 62nd St at York Ave (212-644-6000, 800-545-4000; fax 212-751-7868; www.nychotels.net).

Subway: N, R, Q to Lexington Ave; 4, 5, 6 to 59th St. Single/double $99–$325, suite $205–$325. AmEx, DC, Disc, JCB, MC, V.

This slender, 21-story glass-and-steel hotel, located as far east as the Upper East Side goes, has unparalleled views of the East River and the Queensboro Bridge. Converted from an office building in 1998, the Bentley is an ideal getaway for tired execs: It has soundproof windows and blackout shades. The mahogany-paneled library has a complimentary cappuccino bar, and there's a new nearby spot for souvenir shopping: around the corner at designer Terence Conran's new shop at Bridgemarket (*see chapter* **Shopping, For the home**). Rates include breakfast (served in the 21st-floor Bentley Lounge, which has 360-degree views).

Hotel services *Business center. Gift shop. Parking. Spa. Ticket desk.* **Room services** *CD and DVD players. Nintendo. Voice mail.*

The Holiday Inn Wall Street

15 Gold St at Platt St (212-232-7700, 800-HOLIDAY; fax 212-425-0330; www.HolidayInnWSD.com). Subway: A, C to Broadway–Nassau St; J, M, Z, 2, 3, 4, 5 to Fulton Street. Single/double from $175, suite from $275. AmEx, DC, Disc, JCB, MC, V.

A little cheaper than its neighbors, this new Holiday Inn is good for the business exec who brings the family; it offers special weekend and children's rates, and suites with pull-down Murphy beds. If you book a single, however, expect one of the smallest rooms in the city—some are as narrow as 11 feet. Keeping up with the e-times, this Holiday Inn has automated check-in and check-out kiosks and "virtual office" rooms with high-speed Internet access, portable telephones, an eight-foot L-shaped desk, ergonomic office chair and unlimited office supplies.

Hotel services *Business center. Fitness center. Parking.* **Room services** *CD player. Playstation. Portable phones. Voice mail.*

The Phillips Club

155 W 66th St between Broadway and Amsterdam Ave (212-835-8800, 877-854-8800; fax 212-835-8850; www.phillipsclub.com). Subway: 1, 9 to 66th St. Suite $400–$1,000. AmEx, DC, Disc, JCB, MC, V.

Perhaps the chicest of New York's growing number of extended-stay hotels, the Phillips Club is located on the Upper West Side, across from Lincoln Center and two blocks from Central Park. Suites, ideal for business travelers who come often or for families who stay a while, all have fully equipped kitchens, and there's free access to the Reebok Club. And with the recent opening of a high-end Balducci's market on the ground floor, all the ingredients for a home-cooked meal are close at hand.

Hotel services *Business center. 24-hour dry cleaning. Parking. Valet.* **Room services** *VCR. Voice mail.*

The Regent Wall Street

55 Wall St between William and Hanover Sts (212-845-8600, 800-545-4000; fax 212-845-8601; www.regenthotels.com). Subway: 2, 3 to Wall St. Single/double $545–$750, suite $850–$1,600. AmEx, DC, Disc, JCB, MC, V.

The first five-star hotel in the Financial District, and the first hotel ever on Wall Street, the Regent opened in 2000 after an $80 million remodeling of the historic building it occupies. Built in 1842, 55 Wall Street was originally the Merchants' Exchange. From 1863 to 1899, it was the U.S. Customs House, and it was also the home of the National City Bank and a Citibank branch. The 12,000-square-foot ballroom, with 60-foot-high Corinthian columns, marble walls and an elliptical dome, was designated by the Landmarks Preservation Commission as one of the city's most important historic public spaces. But for all its grandeur, rooms at the Regent are exquisitely comfortable, offering great views, high ceilings, soaking tubs for two and all the business amenities your broker heart desires.

Hotel services *Business center. Fitness center and spa. Gift shop. Parking. Valet.* **Room services** *CD and DVD players. Voice mail.*

The Wall Street Inn

9 South William St at 85 Broad St (212-747-1500; fax 212-747-1900). Subway: 4, 5 to Bowling Green; 2, 3 to Wall St. Single/double $225–$450. Call for corporate and weekend rates. AmEx, DC, Disc, MC, V.

This 46-room hotel, tucked into the landmark warren of streets known as the Stone Street district, is the reincarnation of an old 1830 Lehman Brothers Bank building. Opened in 1999, the Wall Street Inn is an elegant boutiquelike option in an area dominated by chain-hotel giants. To reach beyond the financial-business types who make up 98 percent of the clientele, the hotel offers hefty discounts on weekends. Note that there's no restaurant or room service (although breakfast is included), but luckily the lower Manhattan restaurant scene is growing.

Hotel services *Business center. Fitness center. Video library.* **Room services** *VCR. Voice mail.*

Boutiques

Hotel Casablanca

147 W 43rd St between Sixth Ave and Broadway (212-869-1212, 800-922-7225; fax 212-391-7585; www.casablancahotel.com). Subway: N, R, S, 1, 2, 3, 9, 7 to 42nd St–Times Sq; B, D, F, Q to 42nd St. Single from $245, double from $265, suite from $375. AmEx, DC, JCB, MC, V.

This is a cozy 48-room hotel in the Theater District with a cheerful Moroccan-style lobby. Rick's Café (get it?) is on the second floor, serving free wine and cheese on weeknights. A rooftop bar is set to open by the end of 2000. Breakfast is included.

Hotel services *Business center. Cybercafé. Free access to nearby gym. 24-hour dry cleaning. Valet. Video library.* **Room services** *VCR. Voice mail.*

The Giraffe

365 Park Ave South at 26th St (212-685-7700, 877-296-0009; www.hotelgiraffe.com). Subway: 6 to 28th

St. Single/double from $325, suite $475–$995. AmEx, DC, JCB, MC, V.

Situated in the up-and-coming Rose Hill area between Murray Hill and the Flatiron District, this hotel, opened in 2000, is named after the owner's favorite animal (in case you were wondering). Built in the minimalist European Moderne style of the 1920s and '30s, the intimate 73-room Giraffe is the neighborhood's first upscale boutique accommodation. On weekday evenings, guests convene in the lobby for complimentary wine and cheese, while a pianist tickles the keys of a baby grand. For dinner, head downstairs to the Chinoiserie or to nearby Tabla, one of Danny Meyer's acclaimed restaurants (*see chapter* **Restaurants, Indian**).

Hotel services *Business center. Free access to nearby gym. Parking. 24-hour dry cleaning. Valet.* **Room services** *CD player. VCR. Video library. Voice mail.*

The Gorham New York

136 W 55th St between Sixth and Seventh Aves (212-245-1800, 800-735-0710; fax 212-582-8332; www.gorhamhotel.com). Subway: B, Q, N, R to 57th St; B, D, E to Seventh Ave. Single/double $189–$275, suite $219–$305, penthouse $475. AmEx, DC, JCB, MC, V.

The 120-room Gorham, opposite the City Center theater, has four clocks over the front desk showing the hour from Paris to Tokyo. The lobby's marble floors, maple walls and slightly worn oriental carpets contribute to the rather European ambience. Rooms, though not luxurious, have been recently redecorated in a contemporary style. The kitchenettes in each are a definite plus for families.

Hotel services *Baby-sitting. Fitness center. Parking. 24-hour dry cleaning.* **Room services** *Kitchenette. Nintendo. Voice mail.*

The Inn at Irving Place

56 Irving Pl between 17th and 18th Sts (212-533-4600, 800-685-1447; fax 212-533-4611; www.innatirving.com). Subway: L, N, R, 4, 5, 6 to 14th St–Union Sq. Rates $295–$475. AmEx, DC, JCB, MC, V.

For a bit of Victorian charm, book a room at this 19th-century townhouse near Gramercy Park. With only a dozen rooms, it's one of Manhattan's smallest inns and also one of its most romantic. Instead of a front desk, there's a parlor with a blazing fireplace and an antique cart serving punch and sherry. Some rooms are quite small, but each has a fireplace and a four-poster bed. The Madame Wollenska suite has a pretty window seat. The inn is also a model mecca and hideaway for chic Hollywood types. Rates include breakfast.

Hotel services *24-hour dry cleaning. Tearoom. Valet.* **Room services** *CD player. VCR.*

The Library

299 Madison Ave at 41st St (212-499-9099, 212-983-4500; fax 212-449-9099). Subway: S, 4, 5, 6, 7 to 42nd St–Grand Central. Single/double $245–$325. AmEx, DC, JCB, MC, V.

If you want to bone up on your French lit, you might want to check into the mahogany-rich Library, which is organized according to the Dewey decimal system—each floor is a category, such as math or science, and each room is a subject, like anthropology, and is stocked with relevant books. "You leave knowing more than when you arrived," says owner Henry Kallan, who also owns the Giraffe (*see page 107*). The 1912 terracotta and tapestry-brick building was treated to a $10 million renovation before it opened in mid-2000. Complimentary breakfast and evening wine and cheese are served on the living-room–like second floor. Kallan has started a commuter club for those who take the train at nearby Grand Central Terminal. For $500 a year, a member and his/her companion can use the hotel facilities, drop off shopping with the concierge and rent rooms at the corporate rate.

Hotel services *Baby-sitting. Free access to nearby gym. Parking. Ticket desk.* **Room services** *CD player. Kitchenettes in suites. VCR. Voice mail.*

The Lowell Hotel

28 E 63rd St between Madison and Park Aves (212-838-1400, 800-221-4444; fax 212-605-6808). Subway: N, R, Q to Lexington Ave; 4, 5, 6 to 59th St. Single from $325, double from $395, suite $665–$1,395. AmEx, DC, Disc, MC, V.

Renovated in 1997, the Lowell is a small, charming hotel in a landmark Art Deco building. Rooms feature Scandinavian comforters, Chinese porcelain and marble baths; there are even wood-burning fireplaces in the suites. The gym suite has lodged Madonna, Arnold Schwarzenegger and Michelle Pfeiffer, among others. Breakfast is included.

Hotel services *Baby-sitting. Currency exchange. Fitness center.* **Room services** *CD players in suites. DVD player on request. VCR. Voice mail.*

Comfortable

Unless otherwise indicated, all hotels in this category have a fax service, cable TV, 24-hour dry cleaning and a safe available at the front desk, and hair dryers in the room or on request.

Best Western Manhattan

17 W 32nd St between Fifth Ave and Broadway (212-736-1600, 800-567-7720; fax 212-790-2758). Subway: B, D, F, Q, N, R to 34th St–Herald Sq. Single/double $89–$329, suites $139–$429. AmEx, DC, Disc, JCB, MC, V.

This is a good-value hotel with a stylish Beaux Arts facade, a black-and-gray marble lobby and rooms inspired by different neighborhoods—choose between a floral Central Park look or a trendy Soho motif. The hotel is just a few blocks from Macy's and the Empire State Building, but the block is a bit seedy. Intrepid travelers will enjoy exploring the Korean shops and restaurants on 32nd Street (the hotel doesn't have its own restaurant); first-timers might want to opt for a more mainstream locale. There is no dry-cleaning service.

Hotel services *Fitness center. Laundry.* **Room services** *Modem line. Refrigerator. Voice mail.*

Chelsea Hotel

222 W 23rd St between Seventh and Eighth Aves (212-243-3700; fax 212-675-5531; www.chelseahotel.com). Subway: C, E, 1, 9 to 23rd St. Single from $135, double from $165, studio from $185, suite from $300. AmEx, JCB, MC, V.

The Chelsea has a reputation to uphold. Built in 1884, the famous redbrick building oozes history. In 1912, *Titanic* survivors stayed here for a few days; other former residents include Mark Twain, Dylan Thomas, O. Henry and Brendan Behan. No evidence remains of the hotel's most infamous association: the murder of Nancy Spungen by Sex Pistol Sid Vicious. The lobby doubles as an art gallery, showing work by past and present guests, and rooms are large, with high ceilings. Most rooms, but not all, have a private bathroom and air conditioner. The cocktail lounge Serena lures a sleek crowd to the basement (*see chapter* **Bars**).

Hotel services *Beauty salon. Concierge. Laundry. Restaurant.* **Room services** *Kitchenettes and refrigerators in some rooms. Modem line. Voice mail.*

Clarion Hotel Fifth Avenue

3 E 40th St between Fifth and Madison Aves (212-447-1500, 800-228-5151; fax 212-213-0972). Subway: B, D, F, Q to 42nd St; 7 to Fifth Ave. Single/double $159–$325. AmEx, DC, Disc, JCB, MC, V.

The rooms at the Clarion are newly renovated and a good value. Ask for room numbers that end in three to six (the higher the floor, the better) for a street view and lots of light; back rooms are darker and look directly into offices. The Clarion is a stone's throw from the New York Public Library, Bryant Park and Lord & Taylor. Ask about corporate and weekend rates.

Hotel services *Business services. Complimentary newspaper. Fax.* **Room services** *Modem line. Radio. Voice mail.*

Comfort Inn Manhattan

42 W 35th St between Fifth and Sixth Aves (212-947-0200, 800-228-5150; fax 212-594-3047; www.comfortinnmanhattan.com). Subway: B, D, F, Q, N, R to 34th St–Herald Sq. Single/double $129–$349. AmEx, DC, Disc, MC, V.

This small family-oriented hotel, around the corner from Macy's and the Empire State Building, got a $4.5 million renovation several years ago. Alex at the front desk is a hoot. A hotel fixture for more than a decade, he loves collecting bizarre English place names, so come prepared if you can. Rates include breakfast.

Hotel services *Ticket desk.* **Room services** *Radio. Refrigerator and microwave in some rooms. Voice mail.*

The Empire Hotel

44 W 63rd St between Broadway and Columbus Ave (212-265-7400, 888-822-3555; fax 212-245-3382). Subway: A, C, B, D, 1, 9 to 59th St–Columbus Circle. Single/double $180–$300, suite $300–$650. AmEx, DC, Disc, JCB, MC, V.

This hotel is located opposite Lincoln Center and next door to the eccentrically stylish Iridium restaurant and bar (*see chapter* **Music: Popular music**). The lobby is surprisingly baronial, with wood paneling and velvet drapes. The rooms are small—some almost closet-size—but tasteful, with plenty of chintz and floral prints.

Hotel services *Bar. Conference facility. Currency exchange. Gift shop. Restaurant. Theater/tour ticket desk. Video rental.* **Room services** *CD/cassette player. Minibar. Modem line. Refrigerator on request. Room service. Two-line phones. VCR. Voice mail.*

Excelsior Hotel

45 W 81st St between Central Park West and Columbus Ave (212-362-9200, 800-368-4575; fax 212-7580-3972). Subway: B, C to 81st St; 1, 9 to 79th St. Single/double $139–$199, suite $199–$259. AmEx, DC, Disc, MC, V.

On the Upper West Side, where hotels are scarce, the Excelsior offers a prime location just steps from Central Park and across the street from the American Museum of Natural History. The rooms are newly renovated but still affordable.

Hotel services *Cellular phone rental. Coffee shop. Conference facility. Fitness center. Library. Restaurant. Valet.* **Room services** *Modem line. Radio. Voice mail.*

Gramercy Park Hotel

2 Lexington Ave at 21st St (212-475-4320, 800-221-4083; fax 212-505-0535). Subway: 6 to 23rd St. Single $165, double $180, suite from $210. AmEx, DC, Disc, JCB, MC, V.

This hotel is in a surprisingly quiet location adjoining the small green oasis of Gramercy Park (to which only hotel guests and neighboring residents receive a key). Guests vary from business travelers to rock stars, and though its decor has seen better days, the piano bar is still a favorite local hangout for young media types and tipsy senior citizens alike (*see* **The best hotel bars,** *page 105*). There are no nonsmoking rooms.

Hotel services *Bar. Beauty salon. Conference facility. Laundry. Newsstand/ticket desk. Restaurant. Valet.* **Room services** *Room service. Voice mail.*

Hotel Beacon

2130 Broadway between 74th and 75th Sts (212-787-1100, 800-572-4969; fax 212-787-8119). Subway: 1, 2, 3, 9 to 72nd St. Single $185, double $205, suite $235. AmEx, DC, Disc, JCB, MC, V.

If you're looking for a break from the throngs of tourists clogging Times Square—or if you want to see how Gothamites really live—consider the Beacon. It's in a desirable residential neighborhood and only a short walk from Central Park, Lincoln Center and the famous Zabar's food market. The hotel has a cheerful black-and-white marble lobby and friendly staff. The hallways are a bit drab, and rooms vary in decor, but they are all clean and spacious. Since the Beacon is the tallest building in the

Ray of light Madonna lived in the Chelsea Star Hotel before she became a lucky star.

area, its windows let in light and offer views of the neighborhood (unlike many other hotels).
Hotel services *Laundry (self-service and valet).*
Room services *Kitchenette. Radio. Voice mail.*

Hotel Metro

45 W 35th St between Fifth and Sixth Aves (212-947-2500, 800-356-3870; fax 212-279-1310; www.hotelmetronyc.com). Subway: B, D, F, Q, N, R to 34th St–Herald Sq. Single/double $165–$250, suite from $250. AmEx, DC, MC, V.

It's not posh by any stretch of the imagination, but the Metro has good service and a convenient location near the Empire State Building. The lobby has a charming retro feel, though the halls are army-chic, with olive-drab doors and greenish-gray carpets. Rooms are small but neat and clean, and the roof terrace offers splendid views. The Metro Grill in the lobby specializes in Mediterranean and Italian food.
Hotel services *Complimentary breakfast. Fitness center. Restaurant. Rooftop terrace. Ticket desk.* **Room services** *Coffeemaker. Modem line. Refrigerator. Room service. Voice mail.*

Hotel Wellington

871 Seventh Ave at 55th St (212-247-3900, 800-652-1212; fax 212-581-1719; www.wellingtonhotel.com). Subway: B, D, E to Seventh Ave; N, R to 57th St. Single/double $155–$170, suite from $240. AmEx, DC, JCB, MC, V.

This hotel has some fetching old-fashioned touches (like a gold-domed ceiling with a chandelier), though it's a tad frayed around the edges. Still, it's close to Central Park, Broadway and the Museum of Modern Art.
Hotel services *Bar. Beauty salon. Restaurant. Valet.* **Room services** *Refrigerator in some rooms. Room service. Voice mail.*

The Lucerne

201 W 79th St between Amsterdam Ave and Broadway (212-875-1000, 800-492-8122; fax 212-721-1179; www.newyorkhotel.com). Subway: 1, 9 to 79th St. Single/double $160–$230, suite $190–$450.AmEx, DC, Disc, JCB, MC, V.

From the outside, the landmarked Lucerne, with its adorned entry columns and elaborate prewar facade, recalls the heyday of high-society New York. The rooftop patio has views of Central Park and the Hudson River, and if you're a performing-arts buff, you can haunt nearby Lincoln Center; or simply head to the downstairs jazz bar and grill. There's no dry-cleaning service. The Lucerne is part of the Empire Hotel Group and has six sister locations (for more information visit the website listed above).
Hotel services *Coffee shop. Concierge. Conference facility. Fitness center. Laundry. Parking.* **Room services** *Kitchenette and microwave in suites. Modem line. Radio. Voice mail.*

The Mayflower Hotel

15 Central Park West at 61st St (212-265-0060, 800-223-4164; fax 212-265-0227). Subway: A, C, B, D, 1, 9 to 59th St–Columbus Circle. Single $190–$230, double $210–$250, suite $260–$300. AmEx, DC, Disc, MC, V.

This haven for musicians faces Central Park and is just a few blocks from Lincoln Center. You can't argue with the spectacular park views from the front rooms, though the decor is getting a bit drab. The Conservatory, on the first floor, is still a nice spot for a light breakfast.
Hotel services *Bar. Conference facility. Fitness center. Restaurant.* **Room services** *Room service. VCR on request. Voice mail.*

Ramada Milford Plaza Hotel

270 W 45th St, entrance on Eighth Ave (212-869-3600, 800-2RAMADA; fax 212-944-8357; www.ramada.com). Subway: A, C, E to 42nd St–Port Authority. Single $129–$189, double $129–$199. AmEx, DC, Disc, JCB, MC, V.

The dismal shopping-mall lobby, with its fluorescent lighting and lack of decor, makes this enormous Theater District hotel anything but welcoming. Still, as the ads used to say, it is in the center of it all, close to the Broadway shows and Restaurant Row. There's very visible 24-hour security, and thanks to an influx of new upscale coffeehouses and shops, this stretch of Eighth Avenue is much more visitor-friendly than it was in years past. The hotel has a room devoted to international phone calls.

Hotel services *Bar. Concierge. Currency exchange. Fitness center. Gift shop. Laundry. Restaurant.* **Room services** *Modem line. Voice mail.*

The Roosevelt Hotel

45 E 45th St at Madison Ave (212-661-9600, 888-TEDDY-NY; fax 212-885-6162; www.theroosevelt hotel.com). Subway: S, 4, 5, 6, 7 to 42nd St–Grand Central. Single/double $169–$289, suite $350–$1,800. AmEx, DC, MC, V.

After a two-year, $65 million makeover, this historic charmer is back and better than ever. Built in 1924, the 1,040-room hotel was a haven for celebs and socialites in the Golden Age (Guy Lombardo did his first New Year's Eve "Auld Lang Syne" broadcast from here). Nostalgic grandeur remains in the bustling lobby, with its 27-foot fluted columns, lots of marble, huge sprays of fresh flowers—and, often, large groups of teen tourists on class trips. The Palm Room serves afternoon tea under a brilliant blue-sky mural; the Madison Club Cigar Bar serves cocktails in a clubby setting adorned with stained-glass windows.

Hotel services *Bar. Beauty salon. Business center. Conference facility. Concierge. Fitness center. Restaurant. Valet. Valet parking.* **Room services** *Kitchenette and VCR in suites. Modem line. Room service. Voice mail.*

Less than $150

Unless otherwise noted, hotels in this category provide cable TV, a fax machine at the front desk and hair dryers in the rooms or on request. Most do not have a bar, restaurant or laundry service.

Broadway Inn

264 W 46th St at Eighth Ave (212-997-9200, 800-826-6300; fax 212-768-2807; www.broadway inn.com). Subway: A, C, E to 42nd St–Port Authority. Single $95–$115, double $125–$210, suite $169–$295. AmEx, DC, Disc, MC, V.

In contrast to Times Square's megahotels (many of which have prices to match), this inn (a renovated single-room-occupancy) feels small and personal—think Off Broadway rather than Broadway. The small lobby has exposed-brick walls, ceiling fans, shelves loaded with books you can borrow and a hospitable front-desk staff. The 40 rather spartan guest rooms are clean and fairly priced. Be warned: The stairs are steep, and the inn has no elevator. Rates include continental breakfast.

Hotel services *Free access to nearby gym. Concierge. Safe.* **Room services** *Kitchenette in suites. Radio.*

Carlton Arms Hotel

160 E 25th St at Third Ave (212-679-0680). Subway: 6 to 23rd St. Single with shared bath $57–$63, with private bath $68–$75; double with shared bath $73–$80, with private bath $84–$92; triples $90–$111; quads $95–$117. MC, V.

The Carlton Arms is a cheerful, basic budget hotel popular with Europeans. The corridors are brightly decorated with murals of the city; each room has been painted by a different artist. The artwork is hit-or-miss, but fun. Check out the funky top-floor public bathroom with walls covered in toys, tickets, sunglasses and other tchotchkes. Discounts are offered for students and overseas guests. There is no air conditioning, cable TV or fax.

Hotel services *Café. Telephone in lobby.* **Room services** *Iron on request.*

The Chelsea Star Hotel

300 W 30th St at Eighth Ave (212-244-7827; fax 212-279-9018; www.starhotelny.com). Subway: A, C, E to 34th St–Penn Station. Dorm room from $25, private room with shared bathroom from $65, one-bedroom apartment from $135. MC, V.

It's gone from hot-sheets hotel to hostel and now to a theme hotel "perfect for all budgets." And the Chelsea Star Hotel certainly has a right to its name, considering that it was one of Madonna's first New York homes in its red-light days. Her room is small with a rather gritty view of Madison Square Garden, but you can spend the night in it for only $25. An aspect of '80s seediness still pervades this refurbished old dive, now under new management, but it's all a part of the experience. A roof deck, brick-lined dorm and common room make this one of the best deals in the city for hostelers and starstruck wanderers. One-bedroom apartments are available at discounted weekly and monthly rates.

Hotel services *Bicycle and in-line skate rental. Concierge. Common room. Internet access. Kitchenette. Safe.* **Room services** *Modem line in apartments. Linen.*

Cosmopolitan

95 West Broadway at Chambers St (212-566-1900, 888-895-9400; fax 212-566-6909; www.cosmo hotel.com). Subway: A, C, E, 1, 9 to Chambers St. Single $109, double $139. AmEx, DC, MC, V.

It's not luxurious by anyone's standards, but after years as a down-at-the-heels rooming house, this recently renovated little hotel does have rock-bottom rates and a primo location in Tribeca, an easy walk to Chinatown, Little Italy, the South Street Seaport and Soho.

Hotel services *Concierge. Discount parking. Safe.* **Room services** *Modem line. Voice mail.*

The Gershwin Hotel

7 E 27th St between Fifth and Madison Aves (212-545-8000; fax 212-684-5546). Subway: N, R, 6 to 28th St. $30 per person in four- to eight-bed dorms, $99–$169 for one to three people in private rooms ($12 more Thu–Sat). AmEx, MC, V.

The bohemian Gershwin offers extremely reasonable accommodations just off Fifth Avenue. It's popular with young student types who don't demand much from their lodgings. While the lobby pays homage to Pop Art with Lichtenstein and Warhol works, the rooms are spartan. Infrastructure problems mean you may find yourself with no hot water or with malfunctioning elevators. Administration can be uneven, so when booking be very specific about dates and be sure to reconfirm to avoid any mix-ups.

Hotel services *Bar. Conference facility. 24-hour dry cleaning. Gift shop. Lockers. Public telephones. Roof garden. Transportation desk.* **Room services** *Alarm clock. Modem line. TV in private rooms. Voice mail.*

Habitat Hotel

130 E 57th St at Lexington Ave (212-753-8841, 800-255-0482; fax 212-829-9605; www.stayinny.com). Subway: N, R to Lexington Ave; 4, 5, 6 to 59th St. Single with shared bath from $75, double with shared bath from $85, single/double with private bath from $105, penthouse studios from $285. AmEx, DC, Disc, MC, V.

In 1999, the Habitat Hotel had some well-publicized trouble taking over the rooms of what had become a dilapidated women's residence (about 20 tenants still legally remain). A $20 million overhaul has resulted in a fresh-looking "sophisticated budget" hotel with an urban feel. Each room has a sink and mirror, and black-and-white photos of the city grace

Necessities

Extra! Extra!

Where to find the city's best out-of-the-ordinary amenities, services and digs

SUITE TALK

If you've just won the lottery and feel like treating your five closest friends to an unforgettable weekend in the Big Apple, book the brand-new triplex penthouse at the **Time Hotel** (*see page 102*), inaugurated by Hillary Clinton in early 2000. It'll run you about $6,000 a night, but the glass-enclosed solarium and 360-degree views of Times Square seem almost worth the jaw-dropping rate.

The Liam Neeson penthouse suite at the **Fitzpatrick Grand Central** (*see page 104*) is *only* $2,000 a night, and it consists of two garden rooms, each with separate terraces overlooking the city. The room is furnished in sumptuous Irish fashion (yes, it has Waterford crystal chandeliers and Irish bed linens); the walls are adorned with autographed stills from the actor's famous films. Neeson has a ceremonial key to the suite.

The Alchemy Suite at the **Dylan Hotel** is a Gothic chamber built in 1932 to replicate a medieval alchemist's laboratory (*see page 99*). With its vaulted ceiling, slender columns and intricately designed stained-glass window depicting the original Chemists' Club, the suite beckons those who fancy the darker side of lodging.

EVERYTHING HAS A PRICE

At any of the city's three (soon to be four) **W** hotels (*see page 103*), just about everything in your room is for sale. (Queen-size featherbeds sell for $150, leather wastebaskets for $90 and silver-plated yo-yos engraved with the W logo for a mere $18.) And, if the custom-designed Thomas O'Brien chairs in the rooms at **60 Thompson** (*see page 101*) are a perfect fit, you can take one home (ask for the price).

THAT SPECIAL TOUCH

The Benjamin (*see page 106*) doesn't just have fabulous pillows, it has a whole menu of them (also for sale, $30–$65). Take your pick of 11 specialty headrests, from a jelly neckroll (with a removable gel core that can be heated or chilled) to a snore-reducing pillow that keeps the head away from the chest. Old-fashioned? All bedrooms have goose-down pillows.

At the **Tribeca Grand** (*see page 102*), you'll find a tray of coveted Kiehl's body-care products. If you discover that there's something you can't live without, you can purchase full-size containers to take home.

As for the **Trump International Hotel and Tower** (*see page 99*)—do you think those telescopes in the rooms are always pointed at heavenly bodies...in the sky? Hmm.

Even the bargain spot **Chelsea Star Hotel** (*see page 111*) has a unique amenity: It rents out bicycles and in-line skates so you can get a wheel look at the city.

the walls. Space is tight when you pull out the trundle (which makes the room a double) and the shared bathrooms are tiny, but overall the Habitat makes an ideal resting place for group and budget travelers. Breakfast included.

Hotel services *Laundry.* **Room services** *Alarm clock. Modem line. Radio. Refrigerator on request. Voice mail.*

The Herald Square Hotel

19 W 31st St between Fifth Ave and Broadway (212-279-4017, 800-727-1888; fax 212-643-9208; www.heraldsquarehotel.com). Subway: B, D, F, Q, N, R to 34th St–Herald Sq. Single with shared bath $60, with private bath $85; double $99–$120; triple $130; quad $140. AmEx, Disc, JCB, MC, V.

Herald Square Hotel was the original *Life* magazine building, and it retains its cherub-adorned entrance. All rooms were renovated in 1999, and most have private bathrooms; corridors are lined with framed *Life* illustrations. As the name suggests, it is near Macy's and the Empire State Building, and it's a good deal, so book well in advance. There are discounts for students.

Hotel services *Safe.* **Room services** *Modem line. Radio. Voice mail.*

Hotel 17

225 E 17th St between Second and Third Aves (212-475-2845; fax 212-677-8178; www.citysearch.com/nyc/hotel17). Subway: N, R, 4, 5, 6 to 14th St–Union Sq; L to Third Ave. Single from $50, double from $75, triple from $140, weekly rates from $305. Cash and traveler's checks only.

This is the ultimate dive hotel and one of the hippest places to stay if you're an artist, musician or model; everyone in the underground circuit knows the

Something's fishy The in-room Black Moors at SoHo Grand will keep you company.

ANIMAL MAGNETISM

Feeling lonely? If you're at the **SoHo Grand** (*see page 102*), you can request a pet goldfish to keep you company—vase included (these fish are too good for mere bowls). Choose from Black Moors or Calico Ryukins. If you travel with Fido, the hotel also has a full menu of cat and dog services and amenities, such as toys, toothbrush and toothpaste, pillows and vitamins.

In keeping with its new motto of "Uptown, not uptight," **Le Parker Meridien** (*see page 97*) has replaced traditional DO NOT DISTURB signs with GO AWAY and FUHGEDDABOUDIT, and it has the most liberal pet policy in the city. Recent guests include a koala bear and a cheetah—accompanied by the conservation ambassador from the Zoological Society of San Diego.

The **Mayflower Hotel** (*see page 110*) also allows pets, so long as they're friendly—i.e., no burly snarling pit bulls allowed.

FOOD FETISH

Chefs from the four-star Jean Georges restaurant at the **Trump International Hotel and Tower** (*see page 99*) will prepare a private French dinner in your suite's kitchen.

Guests of **60 Thompson** (*see page 101*) can charge their bills to their rooms at several nearby restaurants and shops.

The **Millenium Hilton** (*see page 97*) introduced a "Dealmakers' Delights" menu of updated favorites of last century's rich and powerful: William Waldorf Astor's Seafood Newburg, Nelson Rockefeller's Chicken Croquettes and Henry Clay Frick's Lobster Thermidor.

At the **Holiday Inn Wall Street** (*see page 107*), the "Beyond Room Service" staff will deliver meals from a variety of neighborhood restaurants. Choose from Chinese, Japanese, continental, Indian and a 24-hour delicatessen.

The Inn at Irving Place (*see page 108*) has an afternoon five-course tea in its cozy Victorian parlor, and it is one of the city's most popular. If you've got a jones for scones (and model watching), this is a civilized break (by reservation only).

place. Madonna posed here for a magazine shoot, and Woody Allen used the hotel in *Manhattan Murder Mystery*. The decor is classic shabby chic, with labyrinthine hallways leading to high-ceilinged rooms, filled with a hodgepodge of discarded dressers, gorgeous old fireplaces, velvet curtains and 1950s wallpaper. Don't be put off by the permanent NO VACANCY sign.
Hotel services *Air-conditioning in doubles and triples. Cellular phone rental. Laundry. Roof terrace.* **Room services** *Alarm clock. Cable TV in some rooms.*

Hotel Edison

228 W 47th St at Broadway (212-840-5000, 800-637-7070; fax 212-596-6850; www.edisonhotelnyc.com). Subway: N, R to 49th St; 1, 9 to 50th St. Single $130, double $145 ($15 for each extra person, four-person maximum), suite $165–$225. AmEx, DC, Disc, JCB, MC, V.
After a two-year renovation that started in 1998, the Edison looks decidedly spruced-up. The large, high-ceilinged Art Deco lobby is particularly colorful, and even the green-marble–lined corridors look good. Rooms are standard, but theater lovers won't find a more convenient location. The coffee shop, a.k.a. the Polish Tea Room, just off the lobby, is a longtime favorite of Broadway actors and their fans.
Hotel services *Bar. Beauty salon. Currency exchange. Restaurant. Safe. Travel/tour desk.* **Room services** *Radio. Voice mail.*

Hotel Grand Union

34 E 32nd St between Madison and Park Aves (212-683-5890; fax 212-689-7397). Subway: 6 to 33rd St. Double $126, triple $143, quad $174 (all taxes included). AmEx, Disc, MC, V.
There is certainly nothing fancy about the Hotel Grand Union, but you will find spacious rooms and clean, private bathrooms for the same price that similar hotels would charge for shared bathrooms. Many of the rooms have been renovated, and in the busy seasons they quickly fill with European and Japanese tourists, so reserve at least a month in advance. The helpful staff will book tours for you and provide useful New York advice.
Hotel services *Coffee shop. Safe.* **Room services**. *Modem line. Refrigerator. Room service. Voice mail.*

Howard Johnson

429 Park Ave South between 29th and 30th Sts (212-532-4860, 800-446-4656; fax 212-545-9727; www.bestnyhotels.com). Subway: N, R, 6 to 28th St. Single from $119, double from $129, suite from $149. AmEx, DC, Disc, JCB, MC, V.
Popular with Europeans, this hotel has good-value suites, a noteworthy staff, and a small breakfast bar. This once rather desolate stretch of Park Avenue South is now one of the city's hipper neighborhoods.
Hotel services *Laundry.* **Room services** *Minibar. Modem line. Radio.*

Larchmont Hotel

27 W 11th St between Fifth and Sixth Aves (212-989-9333; fax 212-989-9496). Subway: F to 14th St; L to Sixth Ave. Single $70–$80, double $90–$109. AmEx, DC, Disc, MC, V.
This attractive, affordable newcomer is housed in a renovated 1910 Beaux Arts building on a quiet side street. Guests enter through a hallway adjacent to the lobby, making the place feel more like a private apartment building. Some rooms are small, but all are cheerful and clean. Each is equipped with a washbasin and a robe and slippers, although none has a private bath. Rates include breakfast.
Hotel services *Concierge. Kitchenette on each floor. Safe.* **Room services** *Voice mail.*

Malibu Studios Hotel

2688 Broadway at 103rd St (212-222-2954, 800-647-2227; fax 212-678-6842; www.malibuhotelnyc.com). Subway: 1, 9 to 103rd St. Single/double with shared bath $49–$79, with private bath $89–$109; triple/quad with private bath $109–$145. Cash or traveler's checks only.
Rooms are tidy, and the Malibu has some surprising touches for a budget operation—even chocolates at check-in. Free passes to local nightclubs are often available. Far from the traditional tourist sights, this Upper West Sider offers visitors a chance to explore a primarily residential neighborhood that's near Riverside Park and not far from Columbia University. The area is generally safe, but it can get a bit dicey after dark. Rates include breakfast. No cable TV or hair dryer.
Hotel services *Concierge. Safe.* **Room services** *CD player and iron on request.*

The Marcel

201 E 24th St at Third Ave (212-696-3800; fax 212-696-0077; www.nycityhotels.net). Subway: 6 to 23rd St. Single/double $120–$165. Deluxe from $210. AmEx, DC, Disc, MC, V.
One of the few hotels in this bustling but undistinguished corner of the city, the 71-room Marcel is popular with fashion-industry types for its easy access to Park Avenue South, Gramercy, Flatiron, midtown and downtown. The sky-blue lobby is tiny but stylish, with sexily curved couches by Goodman Charlton. The compact rooms have nice design touches, such as oversize leather headboards (but avoid rooms facing Third Avenue—the traffic is loud). Although there's no restaurant, the plentiful dining options of Park Avenue South are a short walk away. Complimentary breakfast is served in your room or in the dark-wood Marcel Lounge (which features comedy and cabaret at night). Room service is available from the East Side Diner. The Marcel is part of the Amsterdam Hospitality Group, which has six other properties in the city (for more information visit the website listed above).
Hotel services *Safe. 24-hour dry cleaning. Video library.* **Room services** *Alarm clock. CD player. Dataport phones. Iron and board. Modem line. Nintendo. Radio. VCR. Voice Mail.*

Murray Hill Inn

143 E 30th St between Lexington and Third Aves (212-683-6900, 888-996-6376; fax 212-545-0103;

www.murrayhillinn.com). Subway: 6 to 28th St. Single from $75, double from $95. Cash or traveler's checks only.

Tucked away on a quiet, tree-lined street in midtown within walking distance of the Empire State Building and Grand Central Terminal, this 50-room inn offers good value for the price. Rooms are basic, but neat and clean. Some rooms have private baths; all have sinks. Discounted weekly rates available. Book well in advance.

Room services *Modem line.*

Other location *The Amsterdam Inn, 340 Amsterdam Ave at 76th St (212-579-7500; fax 212-579-6127; www.amsterdaminn.com).*

Off-Soho Suites Hotel

11 Rivington St between Bowery and Chrystie St (212-979-9808, 800-633-7646; fax 212-979-9651). Subway: B, D, Q to Grand St; F to Second Ave; J, M to Bowery. Suite with shared bath $97–$115, with private bath $179–$189. AmEx, MC, V.

Off-Soho is an excellent value for suite accommodations, but the Lower East Side location might not suit everyone. If you're into clubbing, bars and the Soho scene, this spot is perfect—but take a cab back at night. All suites are roomy, clean and bright, with fully equipped kitchens and polished wooden floors.

Hotel services *Café. Fitness room. Laundry. Parking. Safe.* **Room services** *Alarm clock. Microwave. Modem line. Refrigerator. Room service.*

Pickwick Arms

230 E 51st St between Second and Third Aves (212-355-0300, 800-742-5945; fax 212-755-5029). Subway: E, F to Lexington Ave; 6 to 51st St. Single with shared bath $70, with semiprivate bath $80, with private bath $100; double from $125. AmEx, DC, MC, V.

The rooms may be small at the Pickwick Arms, but they are clean. And although the hotel is in a reasonably quiet district, it's still near restaurants, movie theaters, Radio City Music Hall and the United Nations. Most of the rooms have private bathrooms, but some share an adjoining facility, while others share a bathroom down the hall.

Hotel services *Bar. Coffee shop. Safe.* **Room services** *Radio. Room service. Voice mail.*

Quality Hotel and Suites Midtown

59 W 46th St between Fifth and Sixth Aves (212-719-2300, 800-848-0020; fax 212-790-2760; www.hotelchoice.com). Subway: B, D, F, Q to 47–50th Sts–Rockefeller Ctr. Single from $139, double from $169, suite from $199. AmEx, DC, MC, V.

This convenient Theater District hotel, built in 1902 and refurbished in 1998, has somehow managed to hang on to its old-time prices. Breakfast included.

Hotel services *Barbershop. Beauty salon. Conference facility. 24-hour business center. 24-hour fitness center.* **Room services** *Safe. Radio.*

Riverside Towers Hotel

80 Riverside Dr at 80th St (212-877-5200, 800-724-3136; fax 212-873-1400). Subway: 1, 9 to 79th St. Single $90, double $100, suite $110. AmEx, DC, Disc, JCB, MC, V.

The Riverside offers a good rate for the Upper West Side, and it's the only hotel in Manhattan located on the Hudson River. The views are fine, and there's a quiet park across the street. Accommodations are basic; this is strictly a place to sleep. The wonderful Zabar's market is up the street on Broadway.

Hotel services *Laundry. Safe.* **Room services** *Hot plate. Modem line. Refrigerator.*

ThirtyThirty New York City

30 E 30th St between Madison Ave and Park Ave South (212-689-1900, fax 212-689-0023; www.3030nyc.com). Single/double from $125. Subway: 6 to 28th St. AmEx, DC, MC, V.

Formerly the rundown Martha Washington Hotel, a women's residence, the 250-room ThirtyThirty opened in mid-2000, joining its sister hotel the Habitat as a budget spot with style. The block is pretty dingy, populated mainly by rug merchants, but it's near Silicon Alley, the Flatiron District and midtown.

Hotel services *Dry cleaning. Laundry. Safe.* **Room services** *Refrigerator rental. Voice mail.*

Washington Square Hotel

103 Waverly Pl between Fifth and Sixth Aves (212-777-9515, 800-222-0418; fax 212-979-8373; www.wshotel.com). Subway: A, C, E, B, D, F, Q to W 4th St. Single $110–$125, double $125–$155, quad $155–$178. AmEx, MC, V.

Location, not luxury, is the key here. Bob Dylan and Joan Baez lived in this Greenwich Village hotel when they were street musicians singing for change in nearby Washington Square Park. Rooms are no-frills, and hallways are so narrow that you practically open your door into the room opposite. Rates include breakfast and Tuesday-night jazz at C3 (the bistro next door).

Hotel services *Fitness center.* **Room services** *Modem line. Voice mail.*

Westpark Hotel

308 W 58th St between Eighth and Ninth Aves (212-246-1440, 800-248-6440; fax 212-246-3131). Subway: A, C, B, D, 1, 9 to 59th St–Columbus Circle. Single from $135, $15 for additional person; suite from $195. AmEx, DC, MC, V.

Located near Columbus Circle for 50 years, the 90-room Westpark has seen better days, but the location and price make it a decent deal. The hotel will undergo a floor-by-floor renovation starting in November 2000, and the prices here reflect a discount. Try to get a room overlooking Central Park.

Hotel services *Complimentary breakfast. 24-hour dry cleaning. Free access to nearby gym.* **Room services** *VCR. Voice mail.*

The Wolcott Hotel

4 W 31st St between Fifth Ave and Broadway (212-268-2900; fax 212-563-0096; www.wolcott.com). Subway: B, D, F, Q, N, R to 34th St–Herald Sq. Single/double $99–$150, suite $109–$180. AmEx, JCB, MC, V.

The ornate gilded lobby comes as a surprise in this Garment District hotel, whose claims to fame include past guests Edith Wharton and *Titanic* survivor Washington Dodge. The rooms are on the small side, but inexpensive.

Hotel services *Concierge. Business center. Conference facility. Fitness center. Laundry.* **Room services** *Modem line. Nintendo. Safe. Voice mail.*

Wyndham Hotel

42 W 58th St between Fifth and Sixth Aves (212-753-3500, 800-257-1111; fax 212-754-5638). Subway: N, R to Fifth Ave; B, Q to 57th St. Single $130–$145, double $145–$160, suite $190–$365. AmEx, DC, Disc, MC, V.

Popular with actors and directors, the Wyndham has generous-sized rooms and suites with walk-in closets. The decor is a little worn, but homey. This is a good midtown location—you can walk to the Museum of Modern Art, Fifth Avenue shopping and many of the Broadway theaters—but it's low-priced, so book well ahead.

Hotel services *Bar. 24-hour dry cleaning Restaurant. Safe.* **Room services** *Refrigerator in suites. Voice mail.*

Hostels

Bed linens and towels are included in the room rate for the hostels listed here, unless otherwise noted.

Chelsea Center

313 W 29th St between Eighth and Ninth Aves (212-643-0214; fax 212-473-3945; chelcenter@aol.com). Subway: A, C, E to 34th St–Penn Station. $27 per person in dorm, including linen. Cash only.

The Chelsea Center is a small, welcoming hostel with clean bathrooms and a patio garden in the back. It has the feel of a shared student house. Since there's a limited number of beds in each dorm, book at least a week in advance. There's no curfew or air-conditioning, and the price includes continental breakfast. There is also an East Village location, for which bookings should be made through the Chelsea Center.

Hotel services *All rooms nonsmoking. Fax. Garden patio. Kitchen facilities. TV room.*

Hosteling International New York

891 Amsterdam Ave at 103rd St (212-932-2300; fax 212-932-2574; www.hinewyork.org). Subway: 1, 9 to 103rd St. $27 per person in dorm sleeping 10–12 people, $29 in dorm sleeping 6–8, $32 in room sleeping 4, $3 extra for nonmembers; family room $90, private room with bath $120. AmEx, DC, JCB, MC, V.

This 500-bed hostel was formerly a residence for elderly women. It was recently renovated and now includes a new coffee bar with CD jukebox. Rooms are basic, clean and air-conditioned; the staff is friendly; and there's a garden in the back. Peak-season rates (May to October) are slightly higher.

Hotel services *All rooms nonsmoking. Café. Cafeteria. Conference facility. Fax. Garden. Laundry. Lockers. Shuttles. Travel bureau. TV lounge and game room.*

International House

500 Riverside Dr at 125th St (212-316-8473, in summer 212-316-8436; fax 212-316-7182). Subway: 1, 9 to 125th St. Single $100, double/suite $125. MC, V.

This hostel is in a peaceful location, surrounded by college buildings and overlooking the small but well-tended Sakura Park. There's a subsidized cafeteria with main dishes for around $3 and a delightful living room and terrace overlooking the park. Only the suites have private bathrooms. Summer is by far the best time to book, since during the academic year, International House is filled with foreign graduate students and visiting scholars. Summer single rates drop to as low as $45. Be warned that though the area immediately around Columbia University is generally safe, you might not want too stroll to far afield after dark if you don't know the neighborhood.

Hotel services *Bar. Cafeteria. Conference facility. Currency exchange. Fax. Game room. Laundry. TV room.*

Jazz on the Park Hostel

36 W 106th St between Central Park West and Manhattan Ave (212-932-1600; fax 212-932-1700; www.jazzhostel.com). Subway: B, C to 103rd St. 4- to 14-bed dorm room $27–$29, 2-bed dorm room $44 (double occupancy). MC, V.

This hostel is next to Central Park, and not only does it occasionally have live jazz on the weekend, but the manager's name is Jazz—and he's congenial. He also has some revealing info on the spooky mansion next door. The basic rooms can be cramped (there's no storage space for luggage) and in winter the heating can be overkill, but the price is a bargain. Book in advance.

Hotel services *Bike and in-line skate rental (summer only). Café. Complimentary breakfast. Internet access. Laundry. Private lockers. TV room.*

Park View Hotel/Hostel

55 W 110th St (Central Park North) at Lenox Ave (212-369-3340; fax 212-369-3046; www.nycityhotels.net). Subway: 2, 3 to Central Park North–110th St. 4- to 6-bed dorm room $30, private room with shared bath $77. AmEx, MC, V.

This 400-bed converted apartment building was filled with Euro students and backpackers the minute it opened in February 2000. The mod orange-and-yellow lobby is a welcome change from the usual hostel dinginess. The rooms and bathrooms are just as colorful and clean, easily meeting the needs of super-budget travelers. Recent additions are a communal kitchen on each floor, a game room with pool table and a rooftop deck. Central Park is right across the street. Try and get a room overlooking the Harlem Meer. Note: there's no air-conditioning.

Hotel services *Bicycle and in-line skate rental. Fax. International pay phones. Internet access. Phone card machine.*

YMCA (Vanderbilt)

224 E 47th St between Second and Third Aves (212-756-9600; fax 212-752-0210; www.ymca.com). Subway: S, 4, 5, 6, 7 to 42nd St–Grand Central. Single $72, double $86, suite $138. AmEx, MC, V.

This cheerful YMCA's more expensive quarters have sinks, but rooms aren't very large; the beds barely fit into some of them. Book well in advance by writing to the reservations department and including a deposit for one night's rent. There are about 377 rooms, but only the suites have private baths.
Hotel services *All rooms nonsmoking. Fax. Laundry. Luggage room. Fitness facilities.* **Room services** *Cable TV. Voice mail.*

YMCA (West Side)

5 W 63rd St between Central Park West and Broadway (212-875-4100; fax 212-875-1334; www.ymca.com). Subway: A, C, B, D, 1, 9 to 59th St–Columbus Circle. Single $65, with bath $95; double $75, with bath $105. AmEx, MC, V.
A cavernous building close to Central Park and Lincoln Center, this Y has rooms that are simple and clean. Book well in advance. A deposit is required to hold a reservation. Most of the 540 rooms have shared bathrooms. Towels are not supplied.
Hotel services *Cafeteria. Fax. Laundry. Fitness facilities.* **Room services** *Cable TV. Voice mail.*

YMHA (de Hirsch Residence at the 92nd Street Y)

1395 Lexington Ave at 92nd St (212-415-5650, 800-858-4692; fax 212-415-5578). Subway: 6 to 96th St. Single $79, double $49 per person; two-month stays or longer, single with shared bath $895 monthly; double with shared bath $595–$725 monthly. AmEx, MC, V.
The Young Men's Hebrew Association is rather like its Christian counterpart, the YMCA, in that to stay there you don't have to be young, male or—in this case—Jewish. The dorm-style rooms are spacious

Necessities

Brooklyn lodgers

When there's no room at Manhattan's inns, take a look in Brooklyn

Brooklyn is no longer Manhattan's runty step-sibling. There's a newly booming art and restaurant scene, and Brooklyn's lodging options are slowly increasing. Here are three choices that cover the hotel spectrum.

New York Marriott Brooklyn

333 Adams St between Willoughby and Tillary Sts, Brooklyn Heights (718-246-7000, fax 718-246-0563; www.marriott.com). Subway: A, C, F to Jay St–Borough Hall; 2, 3, 4, 5 to Borough Hall. Single/double from $145, suites from $289. AmEx, DC, Disc, MC, V.
Opened in 1998 in the Metrotech area, the Marriott Brooklyn has had no problem filling up with business travelers and visitors. Boasting a 93 percent occupancy rate (compared to Manhattan's 82.4 percent average), the hotel plans to open a 280-room addition in 2002. The hotel is what you'd expect from a Marriott, with all the usual amenities, but its business center and inclusion of dataport phones in every room helped this one win the company's 1999 Hotel of the Year Award. Nearby is the landmark Gage & Tollner restaurant (*718-875-5181*); in-house is the Archives which displays local memorabilia and serves American food. A five-minute walk will take you to busy Montague Street and the sweeping view of Manhattan from the Brooklyn Heights Esplanade.

Angelique Bed & Breakfast

405 Union St between Smith and Hoyt Sts, Carroll Gardens (718-852-8406; www.sspoerri.com/abb). F, G to Carroll St. Single $60–$75, double $100–$125. MC, V.
Housed in an 1889 brownstone in charming Carroll Gardens, Angelique has four rooms done in cozy quasi-Victorian style. The Blue Room has a view of Manhattan. On a warm summer day, you can relax in the back garden or take the F train three stops to Prospect Park. And you can eat like a king (or queen)—the B-and-B is just around the corner from Smith Street, Brooklyn's new restaurant row (*see* **Manhattan transfers,** *page 146*).

Awesome Bed & Breakfast

136 Lawrence St, between Fulton and Willoughby Sts, Downtown Brooklyn (718-858-4859; www.placestostay.com). Subway: A, C, F to Jay St–Borough Hall; M, N, R to Lawrence St; 2, 3, 4, 5 to Borough Hall. Single/double $89–$109. MC, V.
One stop from Manhattan on the 4 or 5 train is this six-room home-away-from-home. It's a nondescript commercial brick building on the outside, but the inside brims with character. The theme rooms include "ancient Madagascar" and "Aurora Borealis," also known as the "groovy room"—complete with purple walls and lots of daisies. Nearby is Montague Street—Brooklyn Heights' main drag—and the Esplanade. The Awesome also has a Financial District location—a one-room suite in a loft with a Jacuzzi-size bath ($135). Breakfast is included.
Other location: *Nassau St at Fulton St (212-528-8492).*

and clean, with two desks and plenty of closet space. There are kitchen and dining facilities on each floor.

Hotel services *Fitness center. Laundry. Library. TV lounge. Refrigerator on request.*

Bed-and-breakfast

New York's bed-and-breakfast scene is deceptively large. There are thousands of beds available, but since there isn't a central B-and-B organization, rooms may be hard to find. Many of the B-and-Bs are unhosted, and breakfast is usually continental (if it's offered at all). The main difference from a hotel is the more personal ambience. Prices are not necessarily low, but B-and-Bs are a good way to feel less like a tourist and more like a New Yorker. Sales tax of 8.25 percent is added on hosted bed-and-breakfast rooms, but not on unhosted apartments if you're staying for more than seven days. It's always a good idea to ask about decor, location and amenities when booking and, if safety is a concern, whether the building has a 24-hour doorman. One caveat: Last-minute changes can be costly; some agencies charge guests for a night's stay if they cancel reservations less than ten days before arriving.

More B-and-Bs are listed in the chapter **Gay & Lesbian**—and they all welcome those from the straight world, too.

A Hospitality Company

580 Broadway, Suite 1009, New York, NY 10012 (212-965-1102; fax 212-965-1149; www.hospitalitycompany.com). Studio $99–$165, one-bedroom apartment $125–$195, two-bedroom apartment $175–$295. MC, V.

A Hospitality Company has more than 150 furnished apartments available for nightly, weekly or monthly stays, from East Village walk-ups to Murray Hill doorman buildings, and is popular among visiting artists (one opera diva requested a grand piano during her stay). Every place has cable TV, and many have VCRs and stereos. The nightly B-and-B rate includes continental breakfast.

All Around the Town

150 Fifth Ave, Suite 711, New York, NY 10011 (212-675-5600; fax 212-675-6366; aroundtown@worldnet.att.net). Studio $130–$175, one-bedroom apartment $150–$280. AmEx, DC, MC, V.

Accommodations can be arranged in most Manhattan neighborhoods. Furnished apartments, all unhosted, include continental breakfast. There is a three-night minimum; ask about reduced rates for monthly stays.

At Home in New York

P.O. Box 407, New York, NY 10185 (212-956-3125, please call only Mon–Fri 10am–5pm, 800-692-4262; fax 212-247-3294; athomeny@erols.com). Hosted single/double $70–$160, unhosted studio $115–$400. Cash only (though AmEx, Disc, MC, V can be used to guarantee rooms).

This agency (run from a private residence) has reasonably priced accommodations in about 300 properties; most are in Manhattan; a few are in Brooklyn, Queens and Staten Island. The minimum stay is two nights.

Bed & Breakfast (& Books)

35 W 92nd St, Apt 2C, New York, NY 10025 (212-865-8740 phone and fax, please call only Mon–Fri 10am–5pm). Hosted single $85–$110, hosted double $100–$130, unhosted studio $110–$160, unhosted one-bedroom from $160, unhosted two-bedroom apartment from $200. Cash or traveler's checks only (though AmEx, DC, Disc, MC, V can be used to guarantee rooms).

Several hosts in this organization are literary types—hence the bookish title. There are 40 hosted and unhosted rooms.

Bed and Breakfast in Manhattan

P.O. Box 533, New York, NY 10150 (212-472-2528; fax 212-988-9818). Hosted $90–$120, unhosted from $130. Cash only.

Each of this organization's 100 or so properties has been personally inspected by the owner, who also helps travelers select a bed-and-breakfast in the neighborhood best suited to their interests.

City Lights Bed and Breakfast

P.O. Box 20355, Cherokee Station, New York, NY 10021 (212-737-7049; fax 212-535-2755). Hosted single/double with private or shared bath $90–$130, unhosted single/double $130–$300, monthly hosted $1,200–$1,600, unhosted $2,000–$3,500. DC, MC, V.

This helpful agency lists 300 to 400 properties in Manhattan and Brooklyn. A two-night minimum stay and a 25 percent deposit are required.

West Village Reservations

Village Station, P.O. Box 347, New York, NY 10014-0347 (212-614-3034; fax 425-920-2384; toll-free fax within the U.K. 0845-127-4464; mail@westvillagebb.com; www.westvillagebb.com). Room $85–$150, studio apartment $120–$150, larger apartment from $185. AmEx, MC, V.

This reservation service has locations all over Manhattan, but primarily downtown. The B-and-B rooms are priced according to room size, number of guests and whether the bathroom is adjacent to the room (i.e., private) or shared with other guests. Hosts provide neighborhood information and continental breakfast. All apartments are private and completely furnished.

Bars

No matter what your poison is, New York City's got plenty of places where you can chug, sip, shoot or spill

There's no disputing that New York is a damn fine drinking town. In the past few years, a slew of bars have set up shop in the once run-down, but now trendy, Lower East Side. Upscale restaurants continue to open with drinking dens attached, but the brewhouse and cigar-bar fads are fading, and the Cosmopolitan—the early-'90s libation of choice—is now officially tired. (Ask instead for a new import like a pisco sour or baffle your bartender by requesting a Moscow mule.) The bars here should quench the thirst of any type of drinker, from the polite sipper to the happy-hour hooch hound.

▶ For more bar listings, see chapters **Cabaret & Comedy, Clubs, Gay & Lesbian** and **Music.**

▶ Also see our picks for **Best Hotel Bars,** page 105.

▶ If you want an even larger selection of bar reviews and listings, pick up ***Time Out New York Eating & Drinking 2001.***

Downtown

Angel

174 Orchard St between Stanton and Houston Sts (212-780-0313). Subway: F to Second Ave. Mon–Thu 6pm–3am; Fri, Sat 6pm–4am. Average drink: $5.50. MC, V.

Walking into Angel is like soaring into the big blue. High azure walls welcome you into this womblike anomaly—Angel (and its denizens) are supercool Lower East Side, but it's got a touchy-feely, how-ya-doin' *Cheers* vibe. While a DJ keeps the pulse going, couples smooch in a loft lounge. Be glad if bartender Chris is on duty—he mixes one mean *mojito.*

Baby Doll Lounge

34 White St at Church St (212-226-4870). Subway: A, C, E, N, R to Canal St; 1, 9 to Franklin St. Mon–Fri noon–4am. Average drink: $6. AmEx, MC, V.

The name gives this topless haven a slightly glamorous aura, but it's actually old-man-bar raw. Find a stool and enjoy the show, but be warned: It's not always pretty. The dancers (a loose term) range in age (from 21 to 45) and sex appeal. The front stage has a greasy pole for the girls who really go after tips. There

Under the influence The sultry mood at Sway will persuade you to stay all night.

isn't a cover or a minimum, but you must always have a drink in hand—and they ain't cheap.

Burp Castle

41 E 7th St between Second and Third Aves (212-982-4576). Subway: F to Second Ave; 6 to Astor Pl. Sun–Thu 4pm–1am; Fri, Sat 4pm–3am. Average drink: $5. AmEx, MC, V.

Never mind its absurd name; the cassock-clad bartenders and Brueghelesque murals combine to make Burp Castle one of the city's weirder theme bars, but they also illustrate the proud 900-year beer-brewing tradition of Belgian Trappist monks. Gregorian chants and Mozart's *Requiem* are popular tunes here. Famed for its massive selection (500 varieties, including Hoegaarden and La Chouffe on tap) and knowledgeable bartenders, Burp Castle is a beer nut's haven.

Chumley's

86 Bedford St at Barrow St (212-675-4449). Subway: 1, 9 to Christopher St–Sheridan Sq. Mon–Thu 5:30pm–midnight; Fri 5:30pm–2am; Sat 2pm–2am; Sun 2pm–midnight. Average drink: $5. Cash only.

Stay away from Chumley's on weekends unless you long for the glassy-eyed fraternity boys of your college years. Even on weeknights, the customers look a little too proud of themselves for having found the unmarked entrance, a remnant from its speakeasy past. The list of writers—from Frank McCourt to John Gunther—who have gathered here over the years is seemingly endless, and the walls are ringed with the dust jackets Lee Chumley asked early patrons to donate from their latest works.

Double Happiness

173 Mott St between Broome and Grand Sts (212-941-1282). Subway: B, D, Q to Grand St; J, M to Bowery; 6 to Spring St. Sun–Thu 6pm–3am; Fri, Sat 6pm–4am. Average drink: $7. MC, V.

Named for the Chinese character for marriage, this former mob-owned speakeasy melds Chinese decorative elements with a gangster vibe. The building's original stone- and brickwork is visible in the archways in the main room and in the stone walls behind the bar. But don't expect cool air down in this cavern. The place gets pretty sweaty when the 25-and-under little chicks pack in around midnight.

Fez

Inside Time Cafe, 380 Lafayette St between Great Jones and 4th Sts (212-533-2680). Subway: B, D, F, Q to Broadway–Lafayette St; 6 to Bleecker St. Sun–Thu 6pm–2am; Fri, Sat 6pm–4am. Average drink: $6. AmEx, MC, V.

With Time Cafe up front and music and performance downstairs, it's easy to forget that Fez is a pretty good bar for just sitting. The Moroccan-themed room (shiny copper tables, Islamic-patterned mosaics, portraits of real Middle Eastern divas) has low, plush couches to sink into. Sit back and absorb the exotic Berber texture with a Sahara Dreamcicle in hand.

Devil's advocate You can hear fiery beats at Hell in the Meatpacking District.

Good World Bar & Grill

3 Orchard St between Division and Canal Sts (212-925-9975). Subway: B, D, Q to Grand St; F to East Broadway. Mon–Fri 2pm–4am; Sat, Sun 10am–4am. Average drink: $4.50. AmEx, DC, Disc, MC, V.

New Yorkers face an eternal conundrum: They want to be where it's at, but once too many of their fellow scenesters find out about a place, it's no longer where it's at—it's where it *was* at. Which is why Good World has legs. Its location, in a former Chinese barber shop on a quiet block, has helped keep it on the frontier of cool. The place hums with energy. Take your pick from more than 60 beers, scan the menu of Swedish bar snacks, and worry later about how you're ever going to hail a cab home.

The Greatest Bar on Earth

1 World Trade Center, West St between Liberty and Vesey Sts, 107th floor (212-524-7000). Subway: E to World Trade Ctr; N, R, 1, 9 to Cortlandt St. Mon, Tue noon–2pm, 4:30pm–midnight; Wed–Sat noon–2pm, 4:30pm–2am; Sun 11am–3pm, 4:30–9pm. Average drink: $8. AmEx, DC, Disc, JCB, MC, V.

The rarefied setting and lineup of loungecore, Latin and funk DJs, along with middle-aged crooners and cover bands make this bar a magnet for visitors *and* residents. Order a sweet and fruity gin blossom or the house special WOW martini (with Blandy's Madeira). While it has peaked as a hot spot, the Greatest Bar on Earth is still fun, especially for the view on a clear night.

Guernica

25 Ave B between 2nd and 3rd Sts (212-674-0984). Subway: F to Second Ave. Sun–Wed 6pm–2:30am; Thu–Sat 6pm–3:30am. Average drink: $5. AmEx, DC, Disc, MC, V.

Guernica is both a lounge and a fully equipped restaurant, serving full- and small-portion dishes (the owners don't like the term "tapas") in the space made famous by the legendary after-hours hive Save the Robots. Guernica has the same proprietors as Ludlow Bar, and they've redone the room in a style that's downtown funk by way of Gaudí and Picasso. Patrons may venture downstairs for lounging and dancing (to DJ-spun tunes), though the owners prefer to think of the place as a restaurant-lounge that happens to have a cabaret license.

Halo

49 Grove St between Seventh Ave South and Bleecker St (212-243-8885). Subway: 1, 9 to Christopher St–Sheridan Sq. 7pm–3am. Average drink price: $8. AmEx, Disc, MC, V.

"Hello? Halo? Is anyone there?" Yes, someone *is* at this restaurant-lounge. More than one. And their names are usually seen in bold-face type. Jennifer Lopez had her birthday fete here; Matt Damon and Ben Affleck have partied here as well. Halo is just a couple blocks from Moomba—so expect a few stars to shuttle between the two. And hurry, before that clique goes *click* and hangs up on this place.

Hell

59 Gansevoort St between Greenwich and Washington Sts (212-727-1666). Subway: A, C, E to 14th St; L to Eighth Ave. Sat–Thu 7pm–4am; Fri 5pm–4am. Average drink: $6.50. AmEx, MC, V.

A lounge from the owners of the Chelsea coffee bar Big Cup, Hell has been around since 1996. It packs in a 50/50 gay-straight crowd on Thursday's House in Hell; Bastille Day and Wigstock are especially festive. DJs play a funky, soulful shake-your-booty blend, culled from as far back as the '50s, along with music from bands that don't even have record deals yet. Come have a dance with the devil.

Hogs & Heifers

859 Washington St at 13th St (212-929-0655). Subway: A, C, E to 14th St; L to Eighth Ave. 11am–4am. Average drink: $4.25. Cash only.

Theme park or trailer park, it's hard to tell, what with all the genuine rednecks and curious onlookers mingling in one weird demographic. It's almost too dark to see the National Rifle Association decal plastered on the front window. More than 100 bras hang on antlers over the bar, shed by customers (Julia Roberts among them) who decided that dancing on the bar would be fun. (Perhaps it's because the floor's usually so crowded?) Judging by the smell, beer is the popular drink. You're sure to witness jukebox dancing and impromptu stripping. Likelihood of scoring a date is extremely high, especially if you want to score with a hog or a heifer.

Other location: *Hogs & Heifers North, 1843 First Ave at 95th St (212-722-8635).*

Joe's Bar

520 E 6th St between Aves A and B (212-473-9093). Subway: F to Second Ave; 6 to Astor Pl. Noon–4am. Average drink: $3. Cash only.

Imagine a saloon in a faded Nashville hotel, where has-beens swap sob stories with never-weres, circa 1965. Floating in the murk that passes for air are the sounds of George Jones singing his guts out on

Dream house Pretend you're a robber baron at the Campbell Apartment in Grand Central.

the jukebox. Tattered Christmas ornaments that date back to Hank's (Williams, not Rollins) time hang from the pressed-tin ceiling. There's enough whiskey in the liquor cabinet to keep a hard-livin' boozer happy for a month. That's Joe's, except the place is the East Village and the time is now.

Joe's Pub

See chapters **Cabaret & Comedy** and **Music** for reviews.

Junno's

64 Downing St between Bedford St and Seventh Ave South (212-627-7995). Subway: 1, 9 to Houston St. Mon–Thu 5:30pm–2am; Fri, Sat 5:30pm–4am. Average drink: $5. AmEx, MC, V.

This West Village gem is brought to you courtesy of Junno Lee, known to cognoscenti as the onetime owner of a lively speakeasy on Sixth Avenue. His latest venture may be glossier and more legal, but it's no less swinging. The tiny space houses a bright blue bar and a restaurant serving gorgeous French- and Korean-inflected Japanese fare, with an emphasis on seafood. Grab yourself a cocktail and sip away into the wee hours. Depending on his mood, Lee may wheel out a karaoke machine—that's when the true merriment begins. MC Lee calls on each table to send up someone to sing from a 500-selection songbook. But you play by his rules: no more than one singer per song unless the number is a duet.

Magnum force Bubbly's the thing at Flute.

Lakeside Lounge

See chapter **Music: Popular music** for reviews.

Lansky Lounge

104 Norfolk St between Delancey and Rivington Sts (212-677-9489). Subway: F to Delancey St; J, M, Z to Essex St. Tue, Wed 8pm–2am; Thu 8pm–4am; Sat 9:30pm–4am. Average drink: $6. AmEx, MC, V.

If you can find it (down a set of stairs, through a dark alley, up more stairs), Lansky Lounge—probably the only New York bar closed on Friday—is the place for quirky late-night noshing and necking. Famous Jewish mobsters (including, of course, Meyer Lansky) glower from posters on the walls of the dark 1940s-style lounge. Loll in one of the black-and-red-vinyl booths, sip a martini and order from the all-kosher menu of Ratner's food. After 10pm, a DJ gets the place swinging.

Max Fish

178 Ludlow St between Houston and Stanton Sts (212-529-3959). Subway: F to Second Ave. 5:30pm–4am. Average drink: $3. Cash only.

Unless you enjoy hearing ear-busting music, waiting in line to order a drink and listening to the asshole at the next table blather about his dumb band, it's best to avoid most downtown bars between the hours of 9pm and 2am. By 2am, it's safe again. Max Fish, now ten years old, was a Ludlow Street pioneer, and it's still the paradigm of Lower East Side cool. As late-night scenes go, this place attracts an interesting crowd—musicians, artists, writers and a few drunken regulars—who come back to roost and have a nightcap (or three).

McSorley's Old Ale House

15 E 7th St between Second and Third Aves (212-473-9148). Subway: N, R to 8th St–NYU; 6 to Astor Pl. Mon–Sat 11am–1am; Sun 1pm–1am. Average drink: $3. Cash only.

Established in 1854, McSorley's is one of the city's oldest and dustiest taverns. Chug some beer, scarf some chili and watch men pee through the peekaboo bathroom door—but do it on a weekday, unless long lines of collegiate knuckleheads turn you on. This ancient saloon pays homage to everything virile, gallant, red of blood and stout of heart. Although women have been allowed in since 1970, McSorley's still has a frat-boy feel; the old ghosts—not to mention hordes of living, breathing, baseball-cap-wearing guys—still roam the sawdust-covered floors.

MercBar

151 Mercer St between Prince and Houston Sts (212-966-2727). Subway: N, R to Prince St; B, D, F, Q to Broadway–Lafayette St. Mon, Tue 5pm–2am; Wed–Sat 5pm–4am; Sun 6pm–2am. Average drink: $9. AmEx, Disc, MC, V.

MercBar has everything cold and lonely hunters dream about: lovely ladies, central heating and stiff drinks. It's also got Gauloise-smoking Europeans and inflated drink prices. This is definitely not the Adirondacks, but it's the most genuinely warm, woody, rough-hewn spot downtown has to offer. If the cowskin banquettes don't convince you, check out the antler wall in the back or the canoe suspended from the ceiling. In Manhattan, hunting season lasts all year.

Moomba

133 Seventh Ave South between 10th and Charles Sts (212-989-1414). Subway: 1, 9 to Christopher St–Sheridan Sq. 6pm–4am. Average drink: $8. AmEx, DC, MC, V.

If you can get past the velvet rope and scary doormen, Moomba's attentive staff will actually make you feel as though you belong in this celebrity supercollider. You're probably not coming here to eat at the restaurant, so climb up to the third floor to see and be seen in the sophisticated lounge. For the moment, at least, this is the point of convergence for sharp-dressed men with chiseled jaws (oh, and Donald Trump) and razor-thin women in sparkly dresses—and the cell phones that connect them to the real world. The dim lighting will keep you wondering late into the night whether that really *was* Stella McCartney hiding behind a cocktail.

North Star Pub

93 South St at Fulton St (212-509-6757). Subway: A, C, 2, 3, 4, 5 to Fulton St–Broadway Nassau; J, M, Z to Fulton St. 11:30am–midnight. Average drink: $5.25. AmEx, DC, Disc, MC, V.

Popular with homesick Brits and local Anglophiles, this waterfront pub is the genuine article (you can order imported Brit beer and HP sauce with which to drench your pub grub).

The Room

144 Sullivan St between Prince and Houston Sts (212-477-2102). Subway: C, E to Spring St. 5pm–4am. Average drink : $5. Cash only.

The Room is actually two rooms. The front is a narrow area, just wide enough to allow you to stand at the bar with a postcollegiate crowd. Choose from 60 international beers, such as Mave's Pear Cider and Red Tail Ale. The larger back room has well-worn chairs and couches and a clubhouse feel. The cozy, candlelit atmosphere is conducive to getting to know someone better. It's not very big, but that's part of the attraction.

Other location: *The Other Room, 143 Perry St between Greenwich and Washington Sts (212-645-9758).*

Sway

305 Spring St between Hudson and Greenwich Sts (212-620-5220). Subway: C, E to Spring St; 1, 9 to Canal St. 9pm–4am. Average drink: $7. AmEx, MC, V.

Press-shunning Sway is a swinging spot. It has a candlelit Moroccan interior, complete with low tables and couches, arched passageways and too-cool-for-school bartenders in leather pants, cowboy hats and tinted eyeglasses. If you do get past the picky doormen, the models and model wanna-bes inside will all seem less than impressed.

Swift Hibernian Lounge

34 E 4th St between Bowery and Lafayette St (212-260-3600). Subway: B, D, F, Q to Broadway–Lafayette St; 6 to Bleecker St. Noon–4am. Average drink: $4.50. AmEx, DC, Disc, MC, V.

While Swift probably gets its fair share of B-Bar turn-aways, this bit of Eire in Noho deserves better. The lounge's front room is braced by exposed brick, low wooden seating and murals of scenes from Jonathan Swift's work. A rickety bookshelf holds the satirist's complete oeuvre. At the bar, a well-chosen selection of beer (more than 80 bottled and 26 on tap) and vintage port reveal an attention to detail that ultimately manifests itself in the best pint of Guinness drawn in New York. When the going gets rough, steady yourself against the large tables, and take in even more murals of various Irish scenes, many of which involve (surprise!) the robust sipping of suds.

Swim

146 Orchard St between Rivington and Stanton Sts (212-673-0799). Subway: F to Second Ave. 5pm–4am. Average drink: $5. AmEx, MC, V.

Swim isn't the first Lower East Side bar to have a DIY design scheme, a DJ-driven soundtrack and reedy patrons. But it does distinguish itself in one way: It serves sushi. Climb to the second floor of this slim duplex to nosh on a spicy tuna roll ($5) at one of several blond-wood tables. Yes, you'll find a better raw-fish selection north of Houston, but at 2am, who wants to walk that far?

Temple Bar

332 Lafayette St between Houston and Bleecker Sts (212-925-4242). Subway: B, D, F, Q to Broadway–Lafayette St; 6 to Bleecker St. Mon–Thu 5pm–1am; Fri, Sat 5pm–2am; Sun 7pm–midnight. Average drink: $8. AmEx, DC, MC, V.

Dark and smart, Temple Bar is a flash of hotel-bar glamour on Lafayette Street, with attentive waitresses, drinks made in cocktail shakers and small snacks. The prices match the pretension level, but neither seems to deter the older generation of downtowners who frequent this dark-wood bar. From 5 to 8pm, a stylish crowd of tieless workers returns for good martinis and a plausible pick-up scene (both gay and straight).

Von Bar

3 Bleecker St between Elizabeth St and Bowery (212-473-3039). Subway: B, D, F, Q to Broadway–Lafayette St; 6 to Bleecker St. Sun–Thu 6pm–2am; Fri, Sat 6pm–4am. Average drink: $5. AmEx, MC, V.

You'd almost expect two walls lined with bookshelves and a rolling ladder here. On one of those shelves you'd probably find a copy of "Mi Ultima Respira" by Luis Buñuel, because this is exactly the type of place he'd frequent. Von serves only beer and wine, which simply adds to the comfortable, tranquil atmosphere. If you want to feel good all over, come at twilight or while it's snowing. If it happens to be both, be sure that the person you're with is someone you want to be with for a long time.

Welcome to the Johnsons

123 Rivington St between Essex and Norfolk Sts (212-420-9911). Subway: F to Delancey St; J, M, Z to Essex St. Mon–Fri 3pm–4am; Sat, Sun 1pm–4am. Average drink: $4. Cash only.

Anyone who's ever made out on a plastic-covered couch in a basement rec room will feel a twinge of nostalgia at Welcome to the Johnsons. Named for a hypothetical suburban family, the laid-back bar conjures up memories of a Van Halen–saturated youth with its fake wood paneling, basketball trophies, a Ms. Pac-Man machine and an avocado-green fridge.

White Horse Tavern

567 Hudson St at 11th St (212-989-3956). Subway: 1, 9 to Christopher St–Sheridan Sq. Sun–Thu 11am–2am; Fri, Sat 11am–4am. Average drink: $4.50. Cash only.

One night in 1953, Dylan Thomas announced, "I've had 18 straight whiskeys. I think that's the record," and passed out. He woke up the next day, went out for a few beers, checked into a hospital and died of alcohol poisoning. Thomas's final drink, like countless others before it, was served at the White Horse. When he drank here, the tavern was popular with sailors; after his death, writers and writers manqué began holding court at the big round tables. Now, notes the manager ruefully, the White Horse is more likely to be packed with frat boys on the make and yuppies with mere "writerly pretensions."

Necessities

Midtown

Campbell Apartment

Grand Central Terminal, off the West Balcony, 15 Vanderbilt Ave at 43rd St (212-953-0409). Subway: S, 4, 5, 6, 7 to 42nd St–Grand Central. 11:30am–1am. Average drink: $11. AmEx, DC, Disc, MC, V.

A magnet for the 6:16-to-Greenwich set, the Campbell Apartment is a loungey cigar-and-cognac retreat opened by Mark Grossich, founder of the Bar and Books chain of cocktail lounges. So why the name? From 1923 to 1941, this was the private office and salon of New York Central Railroad trustee John Campbell. Located in Grand Central's West Balcony, Campbell's intricate wood paneling, painted plaster ceiling, leaded glass windows and dramatic, carved-wood balcony (all designed to resemble the trappings of a 13th-century Florentine palazzo) have been fully restored. The bar serves vintage wines, champagnes, single-malt Scotches and fine cigars. In addition, there is "cocktail fare" and a "Taste of Grand Central" menu with appetizers from selected restaurants in the terminal.

Carnegie Bar and Books

156 W 56th St between Sixth and Seventh Aves (212-957-9676). Subway: B, Q, N, R to 57th St. Mon–Sat 4:30pm–1am; Sun 4:30pm–midnight. Average drink price: $8.50. AmEx, DC, MC, V.

This Bar and Books outpost is the warmest spot on a cold midtown block, with an inviting faux library and an angular, dramatic stairway. The room's attempted

Going underground Imbibe incognito at the Subway Inn on the Upper East Side.

old-club feel is betrayed by its newness, but a few drinks will get you past that. The only sensible thing to do is relax, order a pack of Dunhills and wonder at the expense-accounted folks' good behavior. Jacket or collared shirt and tie are required for men.

Flute

205 W 54th St between Seventh Ave and Broadway (212-265-5169). Subway: B, D, E to Seventh Ave. Mon–Wed 5pm–2am; Thu–Sat 5pm–3am. Average drink: $7. AmEx, DC, MC, V.

Despite Flute's location in the center of the flashy Theater District, this bar still conveys the aura of mystery it must have had when it was a notorious Prohibition-era speakeasy. The menu of sparkling wines ranges from a dry Californian Pacific Echo ($8 a glass) and the more honeyed and complex Charles Heidsieck 1995 ($16 a glass) to Krug Grande Cuvée Multi-Vintage—$190 for the bottle. Four pages of champagnes are followed by a heady list of cognacs, ports, sherries and single-malt Scotches.

The Ginger Man

11 E 36th St between Fifth and Madison Aves (212-532-3740). Subway: B, D, F, Q, N, R to 34th St–Herald Sq. Mon–Wed 11am–2am; Thu, Fri 11:30am–4am; Sat 12:30pm–4am; Sun 3pm–midnight. Average drink: $6. AmEx, DC, MC, V.

One of the best places to grab a cold pint in Murray Hill, the Ginger Man combines the feel of a down-to-earth pub with the elegance of one of the city's finer restaurants. Named after the boozy J.P. Donleavy novel, the bar features more than 150 types of beer (Lucifer Golden Ale, Ipswich Oatmeal Stout), and the Irish-oriented menu includes a hearty Guinness stew.

King Cole Bar

St. Regis Hotel, 2 E 55th St between Fifth and Madison Aves (212-339-6721). Subway: B, Q to 57th St; E, F, N, R to Fifth Ave. Mon–Thu 11:30am–1am; Fri, Sat 11:30am–2am; Sun noon–midnight. Average drink: $12. AmEx, DC, Disc, MC, V.

Paneled in rich mahogany and outfitted with cushy leather-upholstered chairs, the St. Regis's jewel-box–like bar is home to Maxfield Parrish's 1906 mural of Old King Cole and is also the reputed birthplace of the Bloody Mary ($14). Just as you would expect from the best hotel bars, King Cole transports you out of Manhattan but remains urbane enough to remind you that you could be nowhere else.

Landmark Tavern

626 Eleventh Ave at 46th St (212-757-8595). Subway: A, C, E to 42nd St–Port Authority. Noon–midnight. Average drink: $6. AmEx, DC, Disc, MC, V.

When the Landmark Tavern opened in 1868, it looked out on the Hudson River. These days, it fronts Eleventh Avenue; other than that, little has changed at this small pub. Customers still linger at the original long mahogany bar, ignoring their flushed faces reflected in its mirrors; and Franklin stoves still burn on cold winter nights. Take a seat in the dark rear dining room and stuff yourself with starchy grub, or make a meal of the Scotch-eggs appetizer—two hard-boiled eggs encased in sausage, then breaded, deep-fried and put under the broiler. It's the perfect accompaniment to a pint (or more) of Murphy's or to one of 70 single-malt Scotches.

Lot 61

550 W 21st St between Tenth and Eleventh Aves (212-243-6555). Subway: C, E to 23rd St. Mon 6pm–4am; Tue, Wed 6pm–2am; Thu–Sat 6pm–4am. Average drink: $12. AmEx, DC, MC, V.

A former truck garage–cum–club/restaurant, Lot 61 is a must-see hot spot—provided you get past the hulking doormen. Feeding off of West Chelsea's burgeoning art scene, Lot 61 attracts an art-gallery clientele—and it *looks* like a gallery, right down to its collection of commissioned works by big-name artists like Damien Hirst. Sliding scrims and funky furniture give depth to the warehouse-size space, while the menu of eclectic appetizers and (egads!) 61 martinis gives you something to talk about besides tonight's opening.

Oak Bar

The Plaza Hotel, 768 Fifth Ave at 59th St (212-546-5320). Subway: N, R to Fifth Ave. Mon–Sat 11am–2am; Sun noon–1am. Average drink: $11. AmEx, DC, Disc, JCB, MC, V.

The quintessential smoky tavern, the Oak Bar—and everything in it—simply encourages you to light up. Even the Everett Shinn murals, painted in muted tones, seem to look better through a curtain of smoke. As businessmen and their out-of-town clients puff away, inhale the transient vibe of hotel-bar patrons. There's no in-crowd, and best of all, there's no jukebox—just the low hum of conversation and clinking cocktail glasses.

The Pentop Bar and Terrace

Peninsula Hotel, 700 Fifth Ave at 55th St, 23rd floor (212-956-2888). Subway: E, F to Fifth Ave. Mon–Thu 5pm–midnight; Fri, Sat 5pm–1am. Average drink: $12. AmEx, DC, MC, V.

Unlike New York's superhigh bars—Rainbow Bar & Grill and Greatest Bar on Earth—the rooftop bar at the Peninsula Hotel is a mere 23 stories up. So instead of looking down on the city's buildings, you're walled in by them. Up here, you get a gander at some deluxe apartments in the sky and usually hard-to-see architectural details. The crowd is heavy on midtown execs and hotel guests, all of whom keep the waiters busy filling glasses and bowls of cheese-bread.

P.J. Clarke's

915 Third Ave at 55th St (212-759-1650). Subway: E, F to Lexington Ave; 6 to 51st St. Noon–4am. Average drink: $5. AmEx, DC, MC, V.

The atmosphere is the star at Clarke's and, along with the late kitchen hours, is the real reason for visiting this landmark, where a mix of young office yahoos, elderly gents, tourists—and the occasional literary lion—crowd the bar and drink Guinness on tap.

Rudy's Bar & Grill

627 Ninth Ave between 44th and 45th Sts (212-974-9169). Subway: A, C, E to 42nd St–Port Authority. 8am–4am. Average drink: $3. Cash only.

Into people-watching? You'll find a mélange of media folk, actors and career barflies packing this tiny, dingy dive. Now try to guess how many are subsisting on Rudy's free hot dogs and $2.25 drafts. The jukebox features an impressive collection of jazz discs, but you won't know it until the noisy after-work crowd goes home. Don't forget to take in Rudy's so-called beer garden; it's filled with plastic lawn furniture and clotheslines strung with laundry and lightbulbs.

Serena

See chapter **Clubs** for review.

Ow, he bit me! Crimson lighting gives the Stinger Club that bordello ambience.

Uptown

Dive Bar

732 Amsterdam Ave between 95th and 96th Sts (212-749-4358). Subway: 1, 2, 3, 9 to 96th St. Noon–4am. Average drink: $4. AmEx, DC, Disc, MC, V.

This is the consummate neighborhood hangout; too far from Columbia to be a college bar, too far from Amsterdam Avenue's lower strip to be a hellish pick-up joint. Swell barkeeps, tasty pub grub, lots of good beer, single-barrel bourbon and single-malt Scotch keep everyone happy and relaxed. Broadway Dive also has crotchety locals and an alt-rock jukebox. Dive 75 is the latest addition; the Art Deco bar was shipped in from Chicago, creating the illusion that the saloon has been here forever.

Other locations: *Broadway Dive, 2662 Broadway between 101st and 102nd Sts (212-865-2662); Dive 75, 101 W 75th St at Columbus Ave (212-362-7518).*

Necessities

Hogs & Heifers North

See **Hogs & Heifers,** page 121.

Lenox Lounge

See chapter **Music: Popular music** for review.

Soha

988 Amsterdam Ave between 108th and 109th Sts (212-678-0098). Subway: 1, 9 to 110th St–Cathedral Pkwy. 4pm–4am. Average drink: $4. AmEx, MC, V.

Finally, Columbia students and other Upper West Siders don't have to schlepp all the way downtown to go to a cool bar. (The name, by the way, stands for south of Harlem.) The mysterious black exterior conceals a chic Soho-style art house. But don't let the decor fool you—at heart, Soha is a homey neighborhood bar where you can gossip and shoot pool. Loungers are welcome to order in food (since the bar doesn't serve its own) while sipping Soha's libations.

Subway Inn

143 E 60th St between Lexington and Third Aves (212-223-8929). Subway: N, R to Lexington Ave; 4, 5, 6 to 59th St. 8am–4am. Average drink: $3. Cash only.

Hidden from plain sight on a busy NYC street, this dark sanctuary is completely removed from the surrounding Upper East Side scene. The bar's utility-grade name attracts exactly the crowd you'd expect: construction workers, Vietnam vets, businessmen grabbing a quick one and other thirsty souls who aren't exactly looking to see and be seen. Drop in and enjoy a cheap drink—before some developer with no sense of poetry sends in the wrecking crew.

Brooklyn

Black Betty

366 Metropolitan Ave at Havemeyer St, Williamsburg, Brooklyn (718-599-0243). Subway: L to Metropolitan Ave. Mon–Fri 5pm–4am; Sat, Sun 6:30pm–4am. Average drink: $4.50. AmEx, MC, V.

The young and shiftless flock to this South Williamsburg oasis for its generously poured libations, far-ranging beer selection, Middle Eastern decor and food, and real music-lover's jukebox. The space, which once housed mobster Jimmy Napoli's Hi-Way Lounge, provides a long-awaited alternative to the Northside nightlife that dominates Billyburg and an easy-to-reach alternative for bored Manhattanites. The kitchen is open from 6:30pm to midnight.

Galapagos

70 North 6th St between Wythe and Kent Aves, Williamsburg, Brooklyn (718-384-4586). Subway: L to Bedford Ave. 6pm–4am. Average drink: $5. Cash only.

Named for the islands Darwin made famous, Galapagos is an art performance/club space (and former mayonnaise factory) with a screening room and a reflecting pool. You enter via a spooky catwalk traversing an 800-square-foot antechamber that is flooded with water. There's even a submerged room visible beneath the apparently bottomless lake.

Great Lakes

284 Fifth Ave at 1st St, Park Slope, Brooklyn (718-499-3710). Subway: F to Fourth Ave–9th St; M, N, R to Union St. Mon–Fri 6pm–4am; Sat, Sun 1pm–4am. Average drink: $4. MC, V.

Spend enough nights dealing with bitchy hostesses, cocky bartenders and glamorama crowds, and you begin to crave a bar like Great Lakes. This sparsely decorated outpost evokes the simple feel of the Midwest, while attracting a loyal clientele that comes for the booze, conversation and live music.

Sparky's Ale House

481 Court St at Nelson St, Carroll Gardens, Brooklyn (718-624-5516). Subway: F, G to Carroll St. Mon–Fri 4pm–4am; Sat, Sun 2pm–4am. Average drink: $3.50. Cash only.

Tucked away in Carroll Gardens, Sparky's is a genuine neighborhood bar with an outstanding selection of beer. Although you can't buy spirits here, you can choose from about 30 taps and 100 bottles. The friendly bartenders don't bark when their laid-back customers arrive with dogs in tow, and regulars can join Sparky's Mug Club—members keep their own glass behind the bar. The jukebox is stocked with an above-average selection of rock & roll classics, and the back room offers more fun and games: pool, darts and Foosball.

The Stinger Club

241 Grand St between Driggs Ave and Roebling St, Williamsburg, Brooklyn (718-218-6662). Subway: L to Bedford Ave. Mon–Sat 5pm–4am; Sun 3pm–4am. Average drink: $4. Cash only.

Nestled on a quiet section of Grand Avenue, the Stinger Club may be the best new bar in Williamsburg. Catering to the area's fun-loving bohemians, it's as laid-back as it is artfully edgy. Red lighting abounds, giving the Stinger a bordellolike ambience, and diner-style booths allow the indie kids to get intimate. The bar's secret is its cheap pitchers of Brooklyn Lager (made by the neighborhood brewery). The suds soothe earaches induced by live performances of local rock bands.

Restaurants

New York City's global eating options, from foie gras to fou fou, will have you shouting "Feed me!"

Listen to New Yorkers talk about the restaurants they love, and you'll hear something more than just individual taste and habit, or civic pride. Like everything else in this city, dining out is part spectacle and sport, part protected solace. More than in most cities, restaurants are central to everyday life here. New Yorkers wear a good deal on their sleeves—mainly because they don't have room in their closets at home—and where you eat has a lot to do with how you like, or can afford, to live. everyone eats out occasionally; some people do it all the time. To satisfy this voracity there is, famously, all manner of eating to be done in New York; the renowned hot dog competes for attention with the rarefied talents of the best chefs on the planet. Papaya King for lunch; Daniel for dinner.

Newcomers immediately adopt restaurants as their own, while born-and-bred New Yorkers are forever updating their lists as tastes and neighborhoods change. The one rule to enjoyment is to embrace the vastness: the authentic Greek grill in Astoria; the intensely hip downtown spot, whose star will burn out before you have time to tell friends about it; and the midtown joint that somehow escaped the wrecking ball and is still serving steaks to old men who ate there when they were young. New York is a city of unparalleled contrasts, and the best way to experience it is to eat out.

It's as hard as ever to get a table in a restaurant that's hot, but it's also a good idea to call ahead and check to see if the place that was sizzling last week is still in business. To snare a table at one of the city's premier eateries, you'll often need to reserve weeks in advance (and then get a table at 5:30 or 10pm). Many smaller restaurants and bistros prefer to operate on a first-come, first-served basis, and you may have to wait at the bar. Book ahead, when possible, at all the restaurants listed in the **Celebrated chefs, Landmark restaurants** and **Chic** sections below (though it's smart to call any restaurant and inquire about reservations before you make a trip).

Toque of the town Powerhouse chef David Bouley specializes in Austrian cuisine at Danube.

Few New York restaurants add a service charge to the bill (unless your party is of eight or more), but it is customary to double the 8.25-percent sales tax as a tip. As with all financial transactions in NYC, restaurant customers complain vociferously if they feel that they're not getting a fair deal. Don't be afraid of offending your waiter by moaning, but *never* withhold a tip. Many small places accept cash only—ask before you sit down.

Prices below indicate the average cost of a main course at dinner, unless otherwise specified.

► For the latest restaurant reviews, see the Eat Out section of ***Time Out New York.***
► The new ***Time Out New York Eating & Drinking 2001*** is a guidebook with more than 2,000 reviews of restaurants and bars; it's on sale at newsstands and bookstores around the city.
► To find the best restaurants in a certain area of NYC, check out **Restaurants by neighborhood,** page 163.

Favorites

Celebrated chefs

An American Place

Benjamin Hotel, 565 Lexington Ave at 50th St (212-888-5650). Subway: E, F to Lexington Ave; 6 to 51st St. Mon–Fri 7–10:30am, 11:45am–3pm, 5:30–11pm; Sat, Sun 7:30–11am, 11:45am–3pm, 5–9:30pm. Average main course: $30. AmEx, DC, Disc, MC, V.

Somewhere, James Beard is smiling—well, right outside this open kitchen, actually. In an act of culinary feng shui, chef-proprietor Larry Forgione has hung a portrait of his mentor. Among Forgione's signature dishes: creamy, caramelized Hudson Valley foie gras (in a beach-plum glaze), cedar-planked salmon (with corn pudding, sweet peas and sorrel) and for dessert, warm banana Betty and seasonal fruit crisps. There's still plenty to remind you that Forgione was one of the first celebrity chefs in the country (and certainly in New York) to champion home-grown American cooking.

Aquavit

13 W 54th St between Fifth and Sixth Aves (212-307-7311). Subway: E, F to Fifth Ave. Noon–2:30pm, 5:30–10:15pm. Three-course prix fixe: $64. AmEx, DC, Disc, MC, V.

Situated in an imposing town house across the street from MoMA, Aquavit is the grandest of New York's Scandinavian restaurants. Chef Marcus Samuelsson puts a modern spin on Swedish food, raising it to the level of art. The result: layers of intense, fresh flavor. The roulade of lump crabmeat comes with chilled tomato soup and pea froth (a sauce that's whipped into a frenzy). The basic and more traditional dishes, such as a smorgasbord appetizer platter, are excellent. In fact, the entire menu is good, but it's also ever-evolving. You can get a $20 three-course prix-fixe lunch in the more informal café.

Babbo

110 Waverly Pl between MacDougal St and Sixth Ave (212-777-0303). Subway: A, C, E, B, D, F, Q to W 4th St. 5–11:30pm. Average main course: $18. AmEx, DC, MC, V.

Mario Batali's cooking at Babbo has been described as "aggressive Italian," but that doesn't begin to do justice to the attack-dog intensity and richness of dishes like beef-cheek ravioli, slathered with a gravy of crushed squab livers and black truffles, or the rat-a-tat ensemble of flavors in the lamb's-tongue salad. These dishes may seem heavy for a meal at 11pm (which is pretty much the only reservation slot you'll get if you don't call weeks in advance), but the huge portions are worth losing sleep over.

Daniel

60 E 65th St between Madison and Park Aves (212-288-0033). Subway: B, Q to Lexington Ave; 6 to 68th St–Hunter College. Mon–Sat noon–2:30pm, 5:45–11pm. Three-course prix fixe: $72. AmEx, DC, MC, V.

Over the years, hordes of exacting Upper East Siders, discerning celebrities and the occasional Texas oilman have come to worship at this temple of haute cuisine. But the restaurant never has, and never will be, about scene. It's about food. On those nights when chef Daniel Boulud is at the top of his game, he is the man you want cooking for you and your plutonium card. A native of Lyons, France, Boulud has an uncanny ability to elevate rustic, peasant ingredients to works of art: Braised pork belly emerges from the oven as a lacquered cube of crisp skin and lush fat; whole-roasted halibut first arrives in a copper display pan, and then returns as supple fillets glazed with a pearly tapioca sauce. The restaurant relocated to this $10 million space in 1999, but it lacks the energy of the original (smaller) Daniel. If that energy returns, you will have a hard time finding a better dining experience anywhere in the country. For a (slightly) more relaxed environment, try **Café Boulud** (*20 E 76th St between Fifth and Madison Aves, 212-772-2600*).

Danube

30 Hudson St at Duane St (212-791-3771). Subway: A, C, 1, 2, 3, 9 to Chambers St. Mon–Sat 11:30am–2:30pm, 5:30–11pm. Average main course: $29. AmEx, DC, MC, V.

Some restaurateurs like to spread their influence around town; David Bouley is sticking to just one block. The chef-restaurateur expanded Tribeca's renowned **Bouley Bakery** (*120 West Broadway at Duane St, 212-964-2525*) in spring 1999 and opened his much-anticipated Danube around the corner in

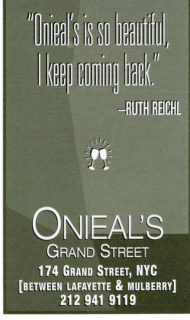

the fall. Plush and elaborately appointed, Danube showcases the food of Austria, a country whose culinary heritage has yet to make waves stateside. Dishes like roasted foie gras (with balsamic cherries) and beef cheeks (in a Zweigelt wine sauce with garlic-chive spaetzle) have awakened New Yorkers to this sleeper cuisine. Danube's decor is a nod to the gilded luxury of the Austro-Hungarian empire: The dining room is replete with violet suede banquettes, fringed lamp shades, patterned carpeting and enormous, glittering reproductions of Gustav Klimt paintings.

Felidia

243 E 58th St between Second and Third Aves (212-758-1479). Subway: N, R to Lexington Ave; 4, 5, 6 to 59th St. Mon–Thu noon–2:30pm, 5–11pm; Fri noon–2:30pm, 5–11:00pm; Sat 5–11:00pm. Average main course: $28. AmEx, DC, MC, V.

Regarded by many as New York's finest Italian restaurant, Felidia plays the part to the hilt. But don't expect fussy creations from chef-owner Lidia Bastianich. A native of Istria (a tiny region of Italy bordering Croatia and Slovenia), Bastianich cooks earthy, robust food that relies more on butter and olive oil than on tomato sauce. Service at Felidia tends to be on the stiff side, as does the crowd. But you didn't come here to be hip, just to eat well.

Fifty Seven Fifty Seven

Four Seasons Hotel, 57 E 57th St between Madison and Park Aves (212-758-5757). Subway: N, R to Fifth Ave; 4, 5, 6 to 59th St. Mon–Fri 7–11am, 11:30am–2pm, 6–10:30pm; Sat, Sun 7am–2pm, 6–10:30pm. Average main course: $30. Prix fixe: $52. AmEx, DC, Disc, MC, V.

This ultramodern, ultrachic bar and restaurant in the Four Seasons Hotel is the preferred watering hole of media mongers who gather nightly to discuss million-dollar deals and provide gossip for the tabloids. When it comes to the food (served by circumspect waiters), you get what you pay for, thanks to Susan Weaver's inventive cooking. (Have the $52 prix-fixe and you'll get a bit more than you pay for.) Among her appetizing creations: delicate sea scallops with creamy risotto, and aromatic guinea hen with chanterelles. The only downside: All those bleeping cell phones mar the elegance of I.M. Pei's Postmodern room.

Jean Georges

Trump International Hotel and Tower, 1 Central Park West at Columbus Circle (212-299-3900). Subway: A, C, B, D, 1, 9 to 59th St–Columbus Circle. Mon–Thu noon–3pm, 5:30–11pm; Fri noon–3pm, 5:30–11:30pm; Sat 5:30–11:30pm. Four-course prix fixe: $78. Seven-course prix fixe: $105. AmEx, DC, Disc, MC, V.

Just as Calvin Klein and Giorgio Armani encouraged the moneyed masses to ease up on the starched collars and cuff links, Jean Georges has let the restaurant world know that four-star elegance need not be defined by mahogany and chandeliers. This life-size bento box seduces with refined modernity: tidy alcoves, frosted-glass panels and checkerboard carpet. Megachef Jean-Georges Vongerichten complements this striking setting with cuisine that is utterly of the moment. If you can neither score a reservation nor afford a meal at Jean Georges, you do have options: Dine in the adjacent, more casual Nougatine Café, or try one of Vongerichten's other hot spots—**Mercer Kitchen** (*99 Prince St at Mercer St, 212-966-5454*), **Jo-Jo** (*160 E 64th St between Lexington and Third Aves, 212-223-5656*) or **Vong** (*200 E 54th St at Third Ave, 212-486-9592*).

Le Bernardin

155 W 51st St between Sixth and Seventh Aves (212-489-1515). Subway: B, D, F, Q to 47–50th Sts–Rockefeller Ctr; N, R to 49th St; 1, 9 to 50th St. Mon noon–2:30pm, 6–11pm; Tue–Thu noon–2:30pm, 5:30–11pm; Fri noon–2:30pm, 5:30–11:30pm; Sat 5:30–11:30pm. Three-course prix fixe: $75. Tasting menu: $120. AmEx, DC, Disc, MC, V.

Go for dinner at this midtown powerhouse, and you'll undoubtedly be treated like it needs your business, but rest assured—it doesn't. Le Bernardin is doing

The best Restaurants

For a food epiphany
Daniel, page 129

For a tête-à-tête
March (expensive), page 133, or
Pó (less expensive), page 152

To impress a client
Four Seasons, page 134

To be seen looking stylish
Pastis, page 138

For a hideaway lunch
Pearl Oyster Bar, page 155

For a Soho shopping break
Once Upon a Tart, page 161

To take kids
Two Boots Restaurant, page 152

To go with a large group
Carmine's, page 151, or
Jimmy's Bronx Cafe, page 154

To go after clubbing
Empire Diner, page 162, or
Florent (weekends only), page 137

To eat and smoke
Casimir, page 146

For brunch
Mesa Grill, page 133

To eat raw fish
Nobu or Next Door Nobu, page 133

Celebrity central It's the A-list crowd that makes Elaine's popular with locals.

just fine, even though it has about 250 seats to fill (twice) every night. It is perhaps the finest seafood restaurant in the country, and one of the best restaurants overall. This is why: Chef Eric Ripert's focus on deceptively simple preparation using the freshest ingredients has inspired many to follow his meticulous manner. Few, however, can match Ripert's creative flair (sprinkling osetra over Spanish mackerel tartare, spicing red snapper Chinese-style). He lets the clarity of flavors from the sea shine through.

March

405 E 58th St between First Ave and Sutton Pl (212-754-6272). Subway: N, R to Lexington Ave; 4, 5, 6 to 59th St. Mon–Sat 6–11pm; Sun 6–10:30pm. Four-course prix fixe: $68. Seven-course prix fixe: $93. AmEx, DC, Disc, JCB, MC, V.

Famous among foodies, March remains unknown to the populace at large. Candles in tiny tabletop lamps with silk lamp shades are the restaurant's only light, and the shadows set a romantic mood. Chef Wayne Nish offers four-course and seven-course prix-fixe menus, backed by a superb wine list; they're a smart way to sample March's vintages, since each course comes with a different preselected glass. If most of March's offerings sound familiar (seared bluefin tuna, braised veal), take one taste and they'll remind you why they've become standards in the first place.

Mesa Grill

102 Fifth Ave between 15th and 16th Sts (212-807-7400). Subway: N, R, L, 4, 5, 6 to 14th St–Union Sq. Mon–Fri noon–2:30pm, 5:30–10:30pm; Sat, Sun 11:30am–3pm, 5:30–11pm. Average main course: $26. AmEx, DC, Disc, MC, V.

A big-name chef, big-flavored food and a colorful room are the secrets to Mesa Grill's enduring buzz. Bobby Flay's nuevo Southwestern rethink seems to have turned everything on the plate smoky and jalapeño-studded. Even humble muffins, corn breads and salads carry a pungent chipotle or chili zing. There are many inventions on this menu, and they often turn out to have a clear flavor logic, like a roasted-garlic–goat-cheese tamale. The dining room tends to be crowded and clamorous, and there's often a wait even if you have a reservation. Consider it your chance to truly appreciate that first citrusy margarita of the evening.

Nobu

105 Hudson St at Franklin St (212-219-0500). Subway: 1, 9 to Franklin St. Mon–Fri 11:45am–2:15pm, 5:45–10:15pm; Sat, Sun 5:45–10:15pm. Omakase (chef's choice) dinner: $70 and up. AmEx, DC, MC, V.

Even though it's the most celebrated Japanese restaurant in America, Nobu is strangely casual. Chopsticks are wrapped in paper, the decor is more whimsical than elegant and, yes, that is Sean Penn in jeans and a T-shirt at the next table. That's not to say this restaurant offers common dining. Under the auspices of owners Drew Nieporent and Robert De Niro, Nobu Matsuhisa has unquestionably established himself as one of the most influential chefs, redefining Japanese cuisine. Look for South American and California influences (as in sublime slivers of fluke with chili paste, lime juice and fresh cilantro), and by all means, order the signature miso-marinated black cod. You'll no doubt need to order many more dishes; portions are modest, and all those not-so-expensive items add up quickly. Chances are, though, you won't mind. Service at Nobu is almost always excellent, and as the meal progresses, you'll realize that Japanese food rarely tastes this good anywhere else.

Other location: *Next Door Nobu, 105 Hudson St at Franklin St (212-334-4445).*

Landmark restaurants

'21'

21 W 52nd St between Fifth and Sixth Aves (212-582-7200). Subway: E, F to Fifth Ave; B, D, Q to 47–50th Sts–Rockefeller Ctr. Mon–Thu noon–2:30pm, 5:30–10:15pm; Fri noon–2:30pm, 5:30–11pm; Sat 5:30–11pm; Sun 5:30–10:15pm. Average main course: $35. AmEx, DC, Disc, JCB, MC, V.

The unofficial mess hall of capitalism has an up-to-the-minute chef in Erik Blauberg and a few nouveau infiltrators, such as Hawaiian snapper tartare with papaya and mango. But toys still hang from the low ceiling, and this hallowed haunt of old-boydom has retained the chicken hash and the famous burger the size and weight of a newborn. This former speakeasy's other traditions—the money chatter, orchestrated swank and cocktail-fueled cheer—remain, as redolent as the aroma of well-prepared sirloin.

Elaine's

1703 Second Ave between 88th and 89th Sts (212-534-8103). Subway: 4, 5, 6 to 86th St. 6pm–2am. Bar 6pm–2am. Average main course: $23. AmEx, DC, Disc, MC, V.

In business for nearly 40 years, Elaine's has never been known for its food, a mix of Italian and American standbys. But that hasn't stopped an A-list crowd,

Necessities

including Woody Allen and Barbra Streisand, from treating it like their own TV room. Which is almost what it looks like. If you've come to eat—and not just to throw back the whiskey and gab with gravel-voiced proprietress Elaine Kaufman—go for the brontosaurus-size veal chop, broiled to a crunchy state just this side of burnt, or a bowl of dependable pasta.

Four Seasons

99 E 52nd St between Park and Lexington Aves (212-754-9494). Subway: E, F to Lexington Ave; 6 to 51st St. Mon–Fri noon–2:15pm, 5–9:30pm; Sat 5–11:30pm. Average main course: $38. AmEx, DC, Disc, JCB, MC, V.

The only restaurant in Manhattan that's been granted official landmark status, the legendary Philip Johnson–designed Four Seasons plays host to power-lunching publishing execs by day and free-spending tourists at night. The tycoons gather in the manly Grill Room, amid plenty of leather and steel, while civilians repair to the Pool Room, home to an illuminated pool and a collection of seasonal trees. The continental cuisine is consistent, but that is not what draws the crowds: The Four Seasons's always gracious service and spectacular 41-year-old interior make this oasis of calm a perennial favorite.

The Oyster Bar and Restaurant

Grand Central Terminal, Lower Concourse, 42nd St at Park Ave (212-490-6650). Subway: S, 4, 5, 6, 7 to 42nd St–Grand Central. Mon–Fri 11:30am–9:30pm; Sat 11:30am–9:30pm. Average main course: $20. AmEx, DC, Disc, MC, V.

Since 1913, this Grand Central institution has been serving fine, simple seafood under vaulted tile ceilings. The Oyster Bar can be noisy and pricey, but no experience is more placid and dignified than stopping here after the early-dinner rush to be alone at the bar with a mug of pilsner and a plate of perfect half shells on ice. Much of the Oyster Bar's thunder has lately been stolen by megahyped newcomers to renovated Grand Central Station. But let's see who's still in business 50 years from now.

Learning to share

If you partake in New York's tasting-plate trend, you'll relish big flavor in little bites

Just as more and more restaurants are introducing prix-fixe–only menus, which force you to endure an onslaught of courses whether you want to or not, along comes a countertrend: the small-plate menu. Now some establishments have taken to offering *only* that. When you're in the mood to linger over a drink and all you want to eat are the olives in your martini and a few tasty morsels, these purveyors of *petit* dining are your best bet.

Grace (*114 Franklin St between West Broadway and Church St, 212-343-4200*) and the **Tasting Room** (*72 E 1st St between First and Second Aves, 212-358-7831*) were among the first eateries to devote their existence to satisfying the small but adventurous appetite. As you sip a Black Forest cocktail at Grace, snack on a mini sandwich of *raclette* and ham or a plate of mascarpone-polenta cakes with fennel-roasted beets. The Tasting Room's nibbles, designed to be savored alongside the large selection of wines by the glass, include citrus-cured scallops and lamb tartare.

At **Métrazur** (*Grand Central Terminal, East Balcony, 42nd St at Park Ave, 212-687-4600*), the "lounge plates" should be ordered in threes. Choose smoked trout, shaved ham with figs and parsley-dusted calamari, for instance, and call it a meal.

Before or after a Broadway show, drop by the Theater District's **Thalia** (*828 Eighth Ave at 50th St, 212-399-4444*) for savory snacks from the "Small Eats" menu, featuring dishes such as shrimp rolls with hot mustard, and leeks with arugula and hard-cooked eggs. Or pair an "edible martini" of olives or tuna tartare with a real martini.

Japanese cuisine offers a dizzying number of options for light dining. In the basement-level lounge at **Bond St** (*see page 136*), the small menu is divided into sashimi, rolls and appetizers. Skip the sashimi for more unusual options, such as the soft-shell crab roll served with wasabi sour cream or the fried lobster wontons.

At another Japanese-inspired gem, **Junno's** (*64 Downing St between Bedford and Varick Sts, 212-627-7995*), diners order cocktails (such as the tangy Mademoiselle) and share starters like tuna tataki (delicate slices of tuna steak in a gingered ponzu) or grilled baby squid in a spicy miso sauce.

The menu at **Blue Ribbon Bakery** (*see page 139*) offers diners pages of starterlike plates—cheeses, crostini, soups, salads, smoked fish and cured meats—from every point on the globe. In the same meal, you can sample hummus, escargots, and Baltic

Peter Luger

178 Broadway at Driggs Ave, Williamsburg, Brooklyn (718-387-7400). Subway: J, M, Z to Marcy Ave. Sun–Thu 11:30am–10pm; Fri, Sat 11:30am–11pm. Steak for two: $58. Cash only.

Pulled from a bank of infernal broilers, Peter Luger's massive porterhouses (the only cut this 112-year-old restaurant serves) emerge a crunchy dark brown, still tender pink on the inside. Dripping with fat and melted butter, this huge cut of beef is easily New York's (and perhaps the country's) best steak. You don't have much choice about dinner; the tough-guy waiters pretty much tell you what you're going to order, and dispense menus only to Luger virgins. The restaurant itself is painfully bright with worn wooden tables. If you're ready for a no-nonsense night of carnivorous indulgence, get yourself to Brooklyn.

Rainbow Grill

30 Rockefeller Plaza, 49th St between Fifth and Sixth Aves, 65th floor (212-632-5100). Subway B, D, F, Q to 47th–50th Sts–Rockefeller Ctr. Noon–3:30pm, 5:30–11:30pm. Rainbow Room Fri, some Saturdays 7pm–midnight. Average main course: $40. AmEx, MC, V.

After being shut down for more than a year (to much outcry from New Yorkers), the Rainbow Room was reopened by the Ciprianis of Harry's Bar fame. Now this timeless jewel at the top of 30 Rock serves Italian and international dishes in the Rainbow Grill (formerly the Promenade Bar). The Rainbow Room proper is open only on Friday (and sometimes Saturday). Dress to kill, and dance to big bands and mambo music while enjoying the restaurant's breathtaking view and Art Deco trappings.

Russian Tea Room

150 W 57th St between Sixth and Seventh Aves (212-974-2111). Subway: B, Q, N, R to 57th St. Mon–Fri 11:30am–3:30pm, 5pm–12:30am; Sat, Sun 10am–3:30pm, 5pm–12:30am. Average main course: $27. AmEx, DC, Disc, MC, V.

Great, meaty borscht and the kind of rye bread about which Jewish dads daydream are two reasons to

herring. Just beware of the basket of fresh breads delivered to your table—if you're not careful, you'll be too stuffed to move.

If, on the other hand, you want to build a meal around dough, head to the Bread Bar at the Indian-fusion restaurant **Tabla** (*see page 150*). Diners can choose a bread, such as a basket of warm garlic-corn roti, and one of several condiments, such as the cheesy cumin-chile cheddar fondue.

And let's not forget tapas. Spaniards, after all, are famous for sharing small plates of food. **Tapería Madrid** (*1471 Second Ave between 76th and 77th Sts, 212-794-2923*) helps New Yorkers relive their *viajes* to Spain's capital with a 20-dish menu of options such as *boquerones* (marinated anchovies) and grilled octopus.

French cuisine, on the other hand, traditionally means big meals laden with butter and cream—but our Gallic cousins can whip up tidbits as well. The sleek **L'Actuel** (*145 E 50th St between Lexington and Third Aves, 212-343-4200*) serves a wide selection of snack-size items from which you can easily assemble a meal. The *pot-au-feu tartine* and curried-chicken skewers are both good, but don't miss the city's best scrambled eggs: The buttery custard swims with chorizo. At the East Village bistro **Casimir** (*see page 146*), you can sidestep the usual steak frites in favor of what this place calls "paysan bites." Snack on warm sautéed chicken livers, or a few slices of grilled garlic sausage with a simple potato salad. You can also turn one of the popular side orders into your own paysan bite: Try the mashed potatoes, spinach sautéed with garlic and olive oil or—oh, go ahead—a basket of french fries.

Lots of slim pickin's You and your date can fill up on bite-size French cuisine at L'Actuel in midtown.

Necessities

return to Warner LeRoy's reopened and audaciously gaudy Russian Tea Room. Let the other tourists gawk at the Red Square diorama, the hulking bear-shaped aquarium, the ornate glasswork and the live orchestra on the second floor. You, meanwhile, should stick to the clubby main floor and settle into one of the supple leather booths. They're so comfortable they'll make you feel like a king…er, a czar.

Tavern on the Green

Central Park West at 67th St (212-873-3200). Subway: B, C to 72nd St; 1, 9 to 66th St–Lincoln Ctr. Mon–Thu noon–3pm, 5:30–10:30pm; Fri noon–3pm, 5–11pm; Sat 10am–3pm, 5–11pm; Sun 10am–3pm, 5:30–10:30pm. Average main course: $29. AmEx, DC, Disc, MC, V.

One of the most popular places for out-of-towners, this New York classic resembles an over-the-top casino: It's done to death with mirrors, Murano glass chandeliers, ornate furniture and fresh flowers. Despite the hubbub of birthday parties and camera flashes, the Tavern provides enough space between tables to actually enjoy the uninspired but decent food (though you'll have trouble catching the eye of your waiter). But you're not really paying for the food, of course; it's for the privilege of dining amid the fancy-shmancy decor on the edge of beautiful Central Park.

Windows on the World

1 World Trade Center, West St between Liberty and Vesey Sts, 107th floor (212-524-7011). Subway: E to World Trade Ctr; 1, 9, N, R to Cortlandt St. Mon–Thu noon–1pm, 5–9pm; Fri noon–1pm, 5–10:30pm; Sat noon–2pm, 5–10:30pm ; Sun noon–2pm. Average main course: $30. AmEx, DC, Disc, MC, V.

Thanks to former '21' chef Michael Lomonaco, Windows finally has food to match its spectacular view. Perched atop the World Trade Center, the restaurant caters mostly to those who don't mind vertigo from the bill or the hotel-dining-room decor. Still, there's no knocking the heavenly panorama.

Chic

Balthazar

80 Spring St between Broadway and Crosby St (212-965-1414). Subway: 6 to Spring St. Mon–Thu 7:30–11:30am, noon–5pm, 6pm–1:30am; Fri 7:30–11:30am, noon–5pm, 6pm–2:30am; Sat 7:30am–4pm, 6pm–2:30am; Sun 7:30am–4pm, 5:30pm–1:30am. Average main course: $20. AmEx, MC, V.

Forget seating hierarchies and canoodling celebrities: This replica of a Parisian brasserie has risen above the hype and settled into its true calling as a nonstop pleasure ride of early-morning pastries, evening oysters and cocktails, and late-night feasts. Ironically, as Balthazar mellows, it's becoming more exciting to those who arrive with hungry mouths and stomachs rather than just eyes and egos. If you can't snare a reservation (it's no easy task), come after midnight, when the dressed-up hordes have trundled off to bed. Then, the eatery eases into a quiet groove, and you're left to relax under the whirring ceiling fans and peruse Balthazar's abbreviated (and affordable) late-night menu.

Chic to chic See and be seen at Pastis.

Bond St

6 Bond St between Broadway and Lafayette St (212-777-2500). Subway: B, D, F, Q to Broadway–Lafayette St; 6 to Bleecker St. Mon–Sat 6–11:30pm; Sun 6pm–midnight. Lounge Mon–Fri 5pm–2am; Sat 6pm–2am; Sun 6pm–1am. Average sushi meal (6 pieces): $25. AmEx, MC, V.

Despite the rows of black Mercedes double-parked in front of it, Bond St does not scream *cool*. This Japanese-inspired tri-level space is so subdued that famous faces just slip into the shadows. Formerly of Nobu London, chef Linda Rodriguez prepares food that's similar to Nobu's (some gripe *too* similar). The vast selection of sushi is particularly good, and is also available in the candlelit basement lounge.

Canteen

142 Mercer St at Prince St (212-431-7676). Subway: N, R to Prince St, 6 to Spring St. Noon–2am. Average main course: $25. AmEx, DC, MC, V.

Like most things in Soho, Canteen catches your eye because of its looks. But once you're set up in a mod orange chair or cushy chocolate-colored banquette in the restaurant's roomy subterranean space, you'll realize that the food is also appealing. Choose from a menu of upscale (i.e., pricey) comfort food, such as macaroni and cheese and red-chili barbecued salmon. But the nicest touch at Canteen is its distinctly un-Soho service—it's actually friendly.

Clementine

1 Fifth Ave at 8th St (212-253-0003). Subway: N, R to 8th St–NYU. Sun–Thu 5pm–1:30am; Fri, Sat 5pm–2:15am. Bar Sun–Thu 5pm–2am; Fri, Sat 5pm–3am. Average main course: $22. AmEx, DC, MC, V.

If you can stand the mad crush at the bar, Clementine will reward you with some of the more interesting cooking in the city. Ask to sit in the slightly Deco main dining room (the smoky lounge up front is best for drinking only), and enjoy chef John Shenk's boldly flavored creations, such as coriander-scented fried clams with avocado salad. Yes, the parties of balding Sony execs with their 20-year-old armpieces can be annoying, but you'll be too busy licking barbecue sauce off your fingers to notice. Clementine also has an abbreviated late-night menu, served until 1:30am on weeknights and 2:30am on weekends.

Da Silvano

260 Sixth Ave between Houston and Bleecker Sts (212-982-2343). Subway: A, C, E, B, D, F, Q to W 4th St. 2–11:30pm. Average main course: $24. Average pasta: $16. AmEx, MC, V.

Why do so many midtown media honchos (Yo, Anna Wintour!) parade down to Da Silvano for lunch? There's the charm factor (exposed-brick walls, sleek sidewalk seating), and then there's the sophisticated, mostly Northern Italian food. Case in point: The gorgeous scallops are served in the shell with roe still attached. More authentically down-home Italian dishes include the stewed tripe, octopus salad, and, if you can afford it, the $25 pasta with summer truffles. Magazine execs and art directors aren't the only ones to have discovered this small, unpretentious place. You may rub elbows with celebrities and mere mortals, too.

Dok Suni's

119 First Ave between 7th St and St. Marks Pl (212-477-9506). Subway: L to First Ave; 6 to Astor Pl. Sun, Mon 4:30–11pm; Tue–Sat 4:30pm–midnight. Average main course: $12. Cash only.

Korean "home cooking" might not resemble anything you've ever cooked at home, but then, this smart downtowner feels more like a bar than a dining room, and the often brusque service feels somewhat less than domesticated. Still, as trendy Korean eateries sprout south of 14th Street (including sister location **DoHwa,** *55 Carmine St at Bedford St, 212-414-1224*), Dok Suni's continues to hold its own as a destination for hipsters and kimchi lovers. The menu includes such Korean staples as braised short ribs, grilled squid and, for comfort-food seekers, the classic rice dish bibimbop.

Florent

69 Gansevoort St between Greenwich and Washington Sts (212-989-5779). Subway: A, C, E to 14th St; L to Eighth Ave. Sun–Thu 9am–5am; Fri, Sat 24hrs. Average main course: $12. Cash only.

Long after Manhattan's best restaurants have hosed down their kitchens, reset their tables and turned off their lights, this retro French diner—wrapped in shiny chrome and located smack-dab in the middle of the Meatpacking District—shifts into high gear. Go at 4am on a Sunday morning and you'll have to fight for a seat. The club-kid staff squeezes between tables as the mixed crowd consumes big bowls of Prince Island mussels and plates of bulging omelettes. The food is not particularly memorable but Florent—not Times Square—remains the place to go for proof that New York really is the city that never sleeps.

Guastavino's

409 E 59th St between First and York Aves (212-980-2455, Club Guastavino 212-421-6644). Subway: N, R to Lexington Ave; 6 to 59th St. 11:30am–2:30pm, 5:30pm–11pm. Average main course: $25. Club Guastavino prix fixe: $60. AmEx, DC, Disc, MC, V.

In England, Sir Terence Conran's name inspires admiration and outright hostility. New Yorkers have been weighing in, too, ever since his diningplex known as Guastavino's opened in early 2000. The space, part of the Bridgemarket complex under the 59th Street Bridge, soars skyward and ends in a stunning, Guastavino-tiled ceiling. You can choose either the 300-seat ground-floor brasserie Guastavino's or the prix-fixe Club Guastavino upstairs. The service at the brasserie has improved by leaps and bounds, but the kitchen is uneven—the pan-global menu offerings are puzzlingly flavorless. However, that doesn't stop throngs of Windsor-knotted young things from filling every last seat. Chef Daniel Orr is clearly putting his efforts into the Club kitchen, which plays to his haute French strengths.

Isla

39 Downing St between Bedford St and Seventh Ave South (212-352-2822). Subway: 1, 9 to Houston St. Mon–Thu 5pm–1am; Fri, Sat 5pm–2am; Sun 5pm–midnight. Average main course: $20. AmEx, MC, V.

Unless you're making a detour to Florida, this is the closest you'll get to South Beach. White Naugahyde banquettes hug walls lined with pool-club tiling, and vintage 1950s orange plastic patio chairs sit near the bar. Owner Diane Ghioto, a former interior designer and *Elle* fashion editor, created the cabana vibe. Aaron Sanchez mans the kitchen, preparing nuevo Cubano dishes like plantain-encrusted jumbo shrimp and a four-person ceviche sampler presented in an ice-filled Lucite platter.

Markt

401 W 14th St at Ninth Ave (212-727-3314). Subway: A, C, E to 14th St; L to Eighth Ave. Mon–Fri 11:30am–4pm, 5:30pm–1am; Sat, Sun 10am–4pm, 5:30pm–1am. Average main course: $16. AmEx, DC, Disc, MC, V.

Markt hadn't been in business more than ten minutes before its 4,500 square feet were filled with downtowners of all stripes. Why? Well, it's not necessarily the food. While the restaurant serves all the

Necessities

usual Belgian suspects, nothing really knocks you out. Still, the huge wood-paneled eatery vibrates with energy, and the 70-foot marble-topped bar pumps out gallons of Belgian brews. On balmy nights, the French doors part to let in a breeze, and a few patrons dine alfresco (something of a questionable honor in the Meatpacking District).

Odeon

145 West Broadway between Thomas and Duane Sts (212-233-0507). Subway: A, C, 1, 2, 3, 9 to Chambers St. Mon–Thu 11:45am–2am; Fri 11:45am–3am; Sat 11:30am–3am; Sun 11:30am–2am. Average main course: $15. AmEx, DC, Disc, MC, V.

More than a decade after it appeared on the cover of *Bright Lights, Big City,* Odeon remains one of Tribeca's biggest draws. The large Deco dining room is always energized, and the bistro food, while not the best in town, is always reliable. Half the restaurant—including the random, always-on-premises celebrity—is eating the steak frites; other diners are munching on grilled tuna or simply nursing a cocktail. Jay McInerney might be a relic of the '80s; Odeon, thankfully, is not.

Pastis

9 Ninth Ave at Little West 12th St (212-929-4844). Subway: A, C, E to 14th St; L to Eighth Ave. Sun–Thu 9am–3am; Fri, Sat 9am–4am. Average main course: $16. AmEx, MC, V.

In the world of Balthazar owner Keith McNally, familiarity does not breed contempt; it breeds success. Walk into his latest bistro, Pastis (assuming you can get into the no-reservations joint), and you'll recognize numerous McNally touches, from his trademark distressed mirrors and aged plaster walls to an incessantly buzzing crowd. The workmanlike menu runs the gamut from rich to heavy: glazed pork belly on lentils, veal stew. It's all delightfully predictable—except for the rest rooms: thankfully, no attendants.

Raoul's

180 Prince St between Thompson and Sullivan Sts (212-966-3518). Subway: C, E to Spring St. 5:30pm–2am. Average main course: $22. AmEx, DC, MC, V.

If everything at Raoul's were about $5 cheaper—from the tiny cocktails to the superb $26 steak au poivre—you'd never leave the joint. After all, it's got all the elements that add up to a perfectly aged bistro: a long wooden bar, tiled floors, dim lighting. The restaurant draws a fair number of well-to-do gallery types, fortysomethings and moneyed youngsters, all of whom seem to be enjoying a perfect Manhattan evening of dinner and cocktails. Even as Club Monaco and Prada move in on its turf, Raoul's remains a slice of classic Soho.

71 Clinton Fresh Food

71 Clinton St between Stanton and Rivington Sts (212-614-6960). Subway: F to Delancey St; J, M, Z to Essex St. Mon–Thu 6–10:30pm; Fri–Sat 6–11:30pm. Average main course: $18. AmEx, MC, V.

The term *fresh food* conjures up certain images: a market in Italy, Sunday supper at grandma's. Not a pricey restaurant on a still-untouched block of the Lower East Side. But Fresh Food's Wylie Dufresne, formerly of Jean Georges, prepares inventive dishes that will make you yawn at all those tired downtown French bistros. Check out the gaggle of B-boys on the corner, and dig into black sea bass encrusted in crunchy rye-bread crumbs or seared scallops on black-olive risotto cake. It's all quality cooking—just not exactly grandma-style.

By Cuisine

American

Beacon

25 W 56th St between Fifth and Sixth Aves (212-332-0500). Subway: B, Q to 57th St; N, R to Fifth Ave. Mon–Thu noon–2pm, 5:30–10:30pm; Fri noon–2pm, 5:30–11pm; Sat 5:30pm–11pm. Average main course: $23. AmEx, DC, MC, V.

Beacon is one of those enormous, airy restaurants that offers blessed relief from the busy city. Its interior, comprising an open kitchen, a split-level dining room, a mezzanine and a private dining section, can be a sanctuary. Former Rainbow Room chef Waldy Malouf mans the eatery's wood-fired ovens, turning out supreme homemade bread and robust entrées, such as roasted suckling pig and glazed Argentine rib eye. For dessert, don't miss the peerless soufflés, especially the chocolate chip.

First

87 First Ave between 5th and 6th Sts (212-674-3823. Subway: F to Second Ave; 6 to Astor Pl. Mon–Thu 6pm–2am; Fri, Sat 6pm–3am; Sun 5pm–1am. Average main course: $15. AmEx, MC, V.

You can be fairly certain that two things will be true after you've dined at First: You will be drunk, and you'll be full. Order a round of teeny-weeny martinis (served on mounds of ice in glass beakers), then indulge in Sammy DeMarco's creative, rib-sticking takes on American standards. The best thing on the menu is the most pedestrian: DeMarco's spicy Buffalo "lollipop" wings. Thanks to prefryer surgery, the meat on the wing slides to one end of the bone when cooked, producing a moist, plump ball of chicken that pops off with one clean suck. Don't be surprised if you see a late-night gang of celeb chefs chowing down on them; First's mod-Gothic dining room is a restaurant-industry fave.

Gotham Bar and Grill

12 E 12th St between Fifth Ave and University Pl (212-620-4020). Subway: N, R, L, 4, 5, 6 to 14th St–Union Sq. Mon–Thu noon–2:15pm, 5:30–10:15pm; Fri noon–2:15pm, 5:30–11:15pm; Sat 5:30–11:15pm; Sun 5:30–10:15pm. Average main course: $30. AmEx, DC, MC, V.

Pairing style with substance, acclaimed chef Alfred Portale crafts modern American food that an architect would swoon over and anyone with an appetite will love. Start with his towering seafood salad, move on to crisp cod perched on a bed of pureed potatoes with snap peas and lobster essence and, by all means, end with his simple but sublime chocolate cake. While Gotham is certainly what you'd call a "fancy" restaurant, it's far from stuffy: Its large, slightly '80s-looking dining room remains casual, albeit in a moneyed sort of way. Which calls to mind Gotham's prices: If you find its steep bills prohibitive, try the three-course $20 prix-fixe lunch. It's one of the best bargains in town

Radio Perfecto

190 Ave B between 11th and 12th Sts (212-477-3366). Subway: L to First Ave. 6pm–midnight. Average main course: $9. Cash only.

Excellent roast chicken, fair prices and an inventive decor make this midsize bistro a welcome addition to Alphabet City's burgeoning restaurant scene. For dessert, try the peanut-butter surprise, a warm, gooey brownie bursting with coconut, chocolate chips and peanut butter.

Wild Blue

1 World Trade Center, 107th floor, West St between Liberty and Vesey Sts (212-524-7107). Subway: E to World Trade Ctr; N, R, 1, 9 to Cortlandt St. Mon–Thu 5:30–10pm; Fri, Sat 5:30–10:30pm. Average main course: $23. AmEx, DC, Disc, MC, V.

Like Windows on the World just down the hall, Wild Blue trades on chef Michael Lomonaco's spirited American cuisine and, of course, its high and mighty views of the city. But unlike Windows, Wild Blue is snug and actually tastefully decorated, with plenty of burnished wood and a vaulted ceiling. It's also blessedly cheaper, without subtracting much in food quality. Lomonaco's kitchen turns out dishes that pile-drive you with intense flavors. If you see the charred rib-eye steak or the knockout side of mustard–and–honey-roasted young beets on the ever-changing specials menu, grab 'em. (*See chapter* **Downtown.**)

American creative

Avenue

520 Columbus Ave at 85th St (212-579-3194). Subway: B, C to 86th St. Mon–Thu 7am–3pm, 5–11:30pm; Fri 7am–3pm, 5pm–12:30am; Sat 8am–3pm, 5pm–12:30am; Sun 8am–3pm, 5–11pm. Average main course: $14. AmEx, MC, V.

Catering to the neighborhood's stroller-pushing, chino-sporting residents, Avenue hawks food for every mood, hour and price range, from homemade sugared doughnuts to grilled foie gras. The place looks quasi French bistro, but chef Scott Campbell really can't be pigeonholed into any one cuisine. He's constantly developing offbeat but delicious creations, served in three portion sizes so you can sample a little of everything. Bring your morning paper, Broadway program or toddler and settle in.

Blue Ribbon Bakery

33 Downing St at Bedford St (212-337-0404). Subway: A, C, E, B, D, F, Q to W 4th St; 1, 9 to Houston St. Tue–Sun noon–2am. Average main course: $19. AmEx, DC, MC, V.

Blue Ribbon Bakery sells far more than just bread. Opened in April 1998 by Eric and Bruce Bromberg, this split-level restaurant serves everything from conventional entrées (rack of lamb, striped bass) to a medley of charcuterie-style tasting plates. If you have the chance, ask to sit downstairs. The candlelit ground-level café, with windows looking out onto the West Village, is pleasant, but the grottolike cellar is far more interesting. Whether you sit upstairs or down, remember that all those "little" plates of food can add up to a sizable bill. Variety is a Bromberg hallmark, their other restaurants are: **Blue Ribbon** (*97 Sullivan St between Spring and Prince Sts; 212-274-0404*) and **Blue Ribbon Sushi** (*see page 142 for review*).

Fifty Seven Fifty Seven

See page 131 for review.

Five Points

31 Great Jones St between Lafayette St and Bowery (212-253-5700). Subway: B, D, F, Q to Broadway–Lafayette St; 6 to Bleecker St. Mon–Sat 6pm–midnight. Average main course: $17. AmEx, DC, MC, V.

Zingy Mediterranean flavors accent the food at Five Points, incongruously named after Manhattan's

Pommes palm The frites and mayo are a real handful at Pommes Frites.

Necessities

most notorious 19th-century slum. As soon as this place opened, a young downtown crowd started lining up to dig into chef Marc Meyer's well-conceived dishes. The thick pork chop gets its kick from a lime-juice–and–honey marinade, and the lamb casserole is spiked with tangy preserved lemon. The decor here includes a fountain that feeds into a long, hollowed-out oak tree.

Gramercy Tavern

42 E 20th St between Broadway and Park Ave South (212-477-0777). Subway: N, R, 6 to 23rd St. Mon–Thu noon–2pm, 5:30–10pm; Fri noon–2pm, 5:30–11pm; Sat 5:30–11pm; Sun 5:30–10pm. Tavern Sun–Thu noon–11pm; Fri, Sat noon–midnight. Prix fixe: $62. AmEx, DC, Disc, MC, V.

Sitting down to an elegant meal in Manhattan doesn't have to mean dealing with stiff waiters and frosty hostesses. At Danny Meyer's Gramercy Tavern, the city's most welcoming upscale restaurant, you'll be set at ease by a bright, jovial dining room, a casual bar and relaxed, professional service. If you don't have reservations, you can snare a seat in the tavern arm of the restaurant, where a menu of affordable grilled meats and seafood is offered. Should you have been smart enough to phone a few weeks in advance, repair to the soothing main dining room for an evening of market-inspired haute cuisine that will send you (and even your snottiest foodie friends) to culinary heaven.

March

See page 133 for review.

Park View at the Boathouse

Central Park Lake, Park Drive North at E 72nd St (212-517-2233). Subway: 6 to 68th St–Hunter College. Mon–Thu noon–4pm, 5:30–10pm; Fri noon–4pm, 6–11pm; Sat 11am–3:45pm, 6–11pm; Sun 11am–3:45pm, 6–10pm. Average main course: $21. AmEx, Disc, MC, V.

The Boathouse finally has food befitting its idyllic Central Park setting. Chef John Villa prepares vibrant fusion cuisine, such as tuna tartare with ginger, lime chili and pear; and herb-crusted halibut in chive milk. Yes, the restaurant's still on the touristy side (how can it not be, given its location?), but it's hard to deny the appeal of dining and draining a Bloody Mary while ducks and gondolas float by on a lake in the middle of Manhattan.

Rainbow Grill

See page 135 for review.

River Café

1 Water St at Cadman Plaza West, Brooklyn (718-522-5200). Subway: A, C to High St. Mon–Sat noon–2:30pm, 6–11pm; Sun 11:30am–2:30pm, 6–11pm. Three-course prix fixe: $70. Tasting menu: $90. AmEx, DC, MC, V.

Situated beneath the Brooklyn Bridge on the banks of the East River, the River Café is more than just a restaurant—it's a destination. As much as for the food, you're shelling out big bucks for a drop-dead skyline view of Manhattan. Not to worry; chef Rick Laakkonen's cooking is divine. Bask in the view (and try to forget about the bill) as you savor an ultra-tender sea bass. Finish with the Brooklyn Bridge Marquise, an admittedly cheesy but undeniably delicious dark-chocolate minibridge set over a rich layered marquise. If you're an out-of-towner, this is the place to come for that big night out.

Veritas

43 E 20th St between Broadway and Park Ave South (212-353-3700; www.veritas-nyc.com). Subway: N, R, 6 to 23rd St. Mon–Sat 5:30–11pm, Sun 5–1-:30pm. Three-course prix fixe: $68. AmEx, MC, V.

The stark, stage-set decor at Veritas might take some warming up to, but Scott Bryan's cuisine does not. The former Luma chef creates rich, robust dishes, like braised veal cheeks atop incredibly smooth pureed celery root. Also alluring are Bryan's utterly professional staff and a 1,400-bottle wine list (on view at www.veritas-nyc.com). If there's a knock against the small restaurant, it's the prices. If that doesn't deter you, then call for reservations and enjoy a night of eating and drinking.

American regional

Charles' Southern Style Kitchen

2841 Frederick Douglass Blvd between 151st and 152nd Sts (212-926-4313). Subway: A, C, B, D to 155th St. Wed–Fri 1–11pm; Sat 1pm–midnight; Sun 1–8pm. Average main course: $5. AmEx, Disc, MC, V.

Buttressed by an all-you-can-eat-buffet dining room, this tiny, fluorescent-lit take-out sells the best fried chicken in New York, hands down. Charles Gabriel marinates his Perdue chickens for eight hours in a secret sauce and then dunks them in a massive, oil-filled cast-iron skillet. The result—intensely crunchy, well-seasoned poultry—proves that the South ain't got nothin' on Harlem.

Great Jones Café

54 Great Jones St between Lafayette St and Bowery (212-674-9304). Subway: B, D, F, Q to Broadway–Lafayette St; 6 to Bleecker St. Mon–Thu 5pm–midnight; Fri 5pm–1am; Sat noon–1am; Sun noon–midnight. Average main course: $8. Cash only.

Tiny (but easy to spot by its bright orange exterior and the bust of Elvis in the front window), Great Jones is one of the city's best Cajun restaurants. And because it's so small, its roadhouse interior always feels jumping: The jukebox is constantly cranking, there's always a crowd at the bar and some kind of catfish or po' boy is on special nightly. Wash down your blissfully salt- and fat-laden selections with a pink Hurricane, New Orleans's contribution to the cocktail pantheon. You might have a hard time scoring a table, especially if you're with a large group.

Hog Pit Barbecue NYC

22 Ninth Ave at 13th St (212-604-0092). Subway: A, C, E to 14th St; L to Eighth Ave. Sun–Thu

noon–11pm; Fri, Sat 5pm–1am. Bar noon–4am. Average main course: $12. AmEx, Disc, MC, V.
Break out your grungy country clothes when you head to the Hog Pit, where a Rebel flag (boo!) flies among stuffed boar and deer heads and flickering neon beer signs. Despite the fact that you're in Manhattan, it all feels pretty Dixie-fried. Dig into down-home fare like fried green tomatoes and scrumptious barbecue and fried chicken. Save room for a tantalizing wedge of blueberry pie or peach cobbler. The friendly servers tend to be skinny, attractive females; the crowd comprises a motley assortment of hipsters and regular folks looking for some BBQ. Bring a pocketful of change to spin a few cheatin' tunes on the country-only jukebox.

Mesa Grill

See page 133 for review.

Pink Tea Cup

42 Grove St between Bedford and Bleecker Sts (212-807-6755). Subway: 1, 9 to Christopher St–Sheridan Sq. 8am–midnight. Average main course: $11. Cash only.
A well-manicured West Village street isn't the most obvious place for a deliciously greasy soul-food joint, but a legion of devotees manages to find the Pink Tea Cup anyway. They line up here not for strainers of Earl Grey, but for such rib-sticking eats as breaded fresh catfish and fried pork chops with corn fritters. Try owner Serretta Ford's crunchy Southern fried chicken and you'll understand why the likes of Oprah, LL Cool J and Paul Reubens (a.k.a. Pee-Wee Herman) have left autographed photos. There's usually a wait for the weekend brunch; use it as a chance to decide whether you want pork chops or fried chicken with your pancakes.

Sylvia's

328 Malcolm X Blvd between 126th and 127th Sts (212-996-0660). Subway: 2, 3 to 125th St. Mon–Sat 8am–10:30pm; Sun 11am–8pm. Average main course: $10. AmEx, MC, V.
Look up "down-home cooking" in the dictionary and chances are you'll find a picture of Sylvia Woods. She's been the reigning Queen of Soul Food since opening her Harlem institution in 1962. After the hostess warmly greets you, order a lemonade and relax in the no-frills dining room. Choose your favorite from the comfort-food hall of fame: smothered pork chops, fried chicken, mac and cheese, sweet-potato pie—you won't be disappointed. The kitchen doesn't skimp on the fried chicken, so prepare to loosen your belt a notch or five.

Virgil's Real BBQ

152 W 44th St between Sixth Ave and Broadway (212-921-9494). Subway: B, D, F, Q to 42nd St; N, R, S, 1, 2, 3, 9, 7 to 42nd St–Times Sq. Sun, Mon 11:30am–11pm; Tue–Sat 11:30am–midnight. Average main course: $15. AmEx, MC, V.
One of Manhattan's great culinary deficiencies is a crushing lack of authentic barbecue spots. Because of zoning and clean-air regulations, genuine wood-burning smoke pits don't exist on the island. Even so, Virgil's does a surprising job at turning out decent 'cue, right in the middle of Times Square. The big meaty spareribs, served dry (i.e., dusted with a spice blend but no sauce) are tops on the menu. Sides such as cole slaw and baked beans arrive in abundance. So do the customers; expect the place to be mobbed.

Asian

Chinese

Canton

45 Division St between Bowery and Market St (212-226-4441). Subway: B, D, Q to Grand St, F to East Broadway. Sun, Wed, Thu noon–9pm; Fri, Sat noon–10:30pm. Average main course: $18. Cash only.
Put off by Chinatown's blinding fluorescent lights and heavy sauces? Reserve a table at this tastefully decorated eatery, where, for uptown prices, you'll receive excellent service and some of the city's finest Chinese food: impeccably crisp Peking duck in marshmallow-soft pancakes, sweet salt-baked scallops and stir-fried chicken with water chestnuts in fresh lettuce wraps.

The Cottage

360 Amsterdam Ave at 77th St (212-595-7450). Subway: 1, 9 to 79th St. Sun–Thu 11:30am–11:15pm; Fri, Sat 11:30am–midnight. Average main course: $8.75. AmEx, MC, V.
The Cottage (a.k.a. the West Side Cottage) is a Chinese restaurant in what looks like a diner with a makeover (note the faux-brick interior and cheesy realist-painting decor). But it's what's on the plate that counts, especially when you realize how little it's costing you. Dollar for dollar, the Cottage is one of the best spots for Chinese uptown.
Other locations: *2492 Broadway between 92nd and 93rd Sts (212-873-0211); 1034 Amsterdam at 11th St (212-662-1800); 2690 Broadway at 103rd St (212-316-2600).*

Joe's Shanghai

9 Pell St between Mott St and Bowery (212-233-8888). Subway: J, M, Z, N, R, 6 to Canal St. 11am–11:15pm. Average main course: $12. Cash only.
These days, Shanghai restaurants are opening in Manhattan faster than Banana Republics, and they're all indebted to this crowded, no-nonsense Chinatown favorite. Joe's plies you with characteristically heavy Shanghai specials like "lion's head" meatballs cooked in a rich brown sauce. But no meal is complete without Joe's steamed soup dumplings—balls of minced pork and crabmeat swimming in a rich, fragrant broth, all enveloped in a light, wontonlike wrapper. They're well worth the time you'll spend waiting for a table.
Other locations: *24 W 56th St between Fifth and Sixth Aves (212-333-3868); 82-74 Broadway between 45th and Whitney Aves, Elmhurst, Queens (718-639-6888); 136-21 37th Ave between Main and Union Sts, Flushing, Queens (718-539-3838).*

Shanghai Tang

77 W Houston St at Wooster St (212-614-9550). Subway: N, R to Prince St; 1, 9 to Houston St. 11:30am–1am. Average main course: $9. AmEx, MC, V.

Imported from Flushing, Queens, this block-long, bowling alley–narrow eatery serves authentic Shanghai cuisine, including punishingly rich braised pork shoulder and sautéed yellow eel. Plus, if you feel like turning Japanese, you can wander way, way to the back of the restaurant for a California or spider roll at the compact sushi bar.

Shun Lee Palace

155 E 55th St between Lexington and Third Aves (212-371-8844). Subway: E, F, N, R to Lexington Ave; 4, 5, 6 to 59th St. Noon–11:30pm. Average main course: $16. AmEx, DC, MC, V.

Michael Tong's plush, 28-year-old New York flagship continues to attract swarms of well-heeled patrons, who appreciate not only that they're enjoying one of the city's top Chinese meals, but also that it's being served on Oscar de la Renta–designed Limoges china. Sample perfectly rendered dishes like crisp, garlic-infused broad-bean sprouts or Ants Climb on Tree (a fiery chili-infused cellophane-noodle dish). Designer Adam Tihany's blue-and-earth-toned dining room is filled with Chinese antiques and a team of helpful, professional waiters.

Other locations: *Shun Lee, 43 W 65th between Central Park West and Columbus Ave (212-595-8895, Shun Lee Cafe 212-769-3888).*

Sweet-n-Tart Cafe

76 Mott St at Canal St (212-334-8088). Subway: J, M, Z, N, R, 6 to Canal St. 9am–midnight. Average main course: $5. Cash only.

Eat here now. Only three things on the menu top $6, and it's all so fresh, you can hear the broccoli screaming. Besides, you won't want to miss the novel flavors of dishes like beef with bitter melon. The restaurant's traditional *tong shui* soups come from a 1,000-year-old recipe that calls for high-quality ingredients and careful brewing; try the snow-frog–with–lotus-seed versions. To drink, choose from a large selection of fresh fruit and vegetable juices. There's plenty more seating at the nearby Sweet-n-Tart Restaurant, which is also a popular dim sum spot.

Other locations: *Sweet-n-Tart Restaurant, 20 Mott St between Park Row and Pell St (212-964-0380); Sweet-n-Tart Cafe, 136-11 38th Ave at Main St, Flushing, Queens (718-661-3380).*

Japanese

Bond St

See page 136 for review.

Blue Ribbon Sushi

119 Sullivan St between Spring and Prince Sts (212-343-0404). Subway: C, E to Spring St. Tue–Sun 4pm–2am. Average sushi meal (7 pieces, 1 roll): $16.50. Omakase (chef's choice) dinner: $75 minimum. AmEx, DC, MC, V.

Deservedly well-known and dauntingly crowded, the sushi arm of the budding Blue Ribbon empire (*see page 139*) ranks as one of the city's best raw-fish restaurants. The keys to success? Freshness, a constantly changing selection and creativity. All of the sushi and sashimi combinations are recommended, particularly those that highlight the daily and seasonal specials. The crowd and the decor are more Soho than Tokyo, but the attentive service and low-lit wood surroundings complement the spectacular food.

Honmura An

170 Mercer St between Prince and Houston Sts (212-334-5253). Subway: B, D, F, Q to Broadway–Lafayette St; N, R to Prince St. Tue 6–10pm; Wed, Thu noon–2:30pm, 6–10pm; Fri, Sat noon–2:30pm, 6–10:30pm; Sun 6–9:30pm. Average main course: $15. AmEx, DC, MC, V.

There's quiet Zen harmony to be found just off Houston Street—for a price. Climb the stairs to this soothing loftlike space and taste soba noodles the likes of which you've never tasted. Made on the premises, these strands of buckwheat are served in beautiful ceramic bowls with a variety of hot or cold broths and toppings, including sea urchin, giant prawn tempura, wild greens and *kombu* seaweed, and sliced duck and scallions. Wash down your meal with a bottomless cup of green tea.

Next Door Nobu

See page 133 for review

Obeca Li

62 Thomas St between Church St and West Broadway (212-393-9887; www.obecali.com). Subway: A, C, 1, 2, 3, 9 to Chambers St. Mon–Wed 6–11pm; Thu–Sat 6pm–midnight. Average main course: $20.50. AmEx, MC, V.

In this cavernous, multichambered Tribeca space, elaborately decorated in a variety of Asian themes, giggly young waiters serve all manner of delicious tastes. Under the guidance of Thai chef Noi Chort, the kitchen prepares gracefully fused Asian and French cuisine. Grilled squid, marinated short ribs and rare duck (a tender treat) are all flavored with miso; the sashimi is immaculately fresh. Obeca Li isn't cheap, but the inventive cooking merits the expense.

Oikawa

805 Third Ave at 50th St (212-980-1400). Subway: E, F to Lexington Ave; 6 to 51st St. Mon–Fri 11:30am–2:30pm, 5:30pm–12:30am; Sat 5:30–11pm. Average sushi meal (13 pieces): $18. AmEx, DC, Disc, MC, V.

Located in a glassy, mall-like midtown building, Oikawa may look sterile, but the food is thrilling. Returning to your local sushi hole will be a letdown after you've sampled the likes of shredded jellyfish, chopped shark's fin with plum sauce, and squid with spicy cod roe. Of the creative sushi, try the salmon-and-eel roll, gently fried, tempura-style.

Omen

113 Thompson St between Prince and Spring Sts (212-925-8923). Subway: C, E to Spring St. 6–11pm. Average main course: $16. AmEx.

Even the salads are impeccable at this calm, countrified Japanese retreat. The house salad, which is enlivened with seaweed and baby scallops, is the perfect accompaniment to an assortment of sashimi and udon specials. Order the herby *shiso* rice on the side, and try not to stare at the rock star sitting next to you.

Sandobe Sushi

330 E 11th St between First and Second Aves (212-780-0328). Subway: L to First Ave; 6 to Astor Pl. 5:30pm–12:30am. Average sushi meal (8 pieces, 1 roll): $11. Cash only.

When you leave this three-room restaurant, you will feel foolish for ever having eaten mediocre sushi. Chef Kirjin Kim's menu is the type that you'll gladly wait a half hour for (and chances are, you will), especially considering that his fish is some of the cheapest in the city. There are generous slabs of tuna and salmon, but the real stars are the rolls, in all the colors of the sushi rainbow. Unfortunately, every hipster in the East Village seems to know this, so it's almost always packed. If you can't deal with waiting, walk seven blocks south to Sandobe's more spacious sibling, **Jeollado** (*116 E 4th St between First and Second Aves; 212-260-7696*).

Yama–Houston

92 W Houston St between La Guardia Pl and Thompson St (212-674-0935). Subway: 1, 9 to Houston St. Mon–Thu 5:30–11:30pm; Fri, Sat 5:30–11:45pm; Sun 5:30–11pm. Average sushi meal (8 pieces, 1 roll): $15. AmEx, MC, V.

Even though this restaurant is underground, the view is great—beautiful people eating artfully arranged sushi in a dark, marble interior. Yama's quick, friendly service enhances the appeal of dishes such as the exceptionally light and crisp shrimp and vegetable tempura. It's a great restaurant for a date, though you may experience delayed gratification: With only six tables for two, groups of three or more are usually seated first. The long wait is more pleasantly spent at the original Yama near Irving Place or on quaint Carmine Street (the newest locale).

Other locations: *Yama, 122 E 17th St at Irving Pl (212-475-0969); 40 Carmine St between Bedford and Bleecker Sts (212-989-9330).*

Korean

Dok Suni's

See page 137 for review.

Malaysian

Nyonya

194 Grand St between Mott and Mulberry Sts (212-334-3669). Subway: B, D, Q to Grand St. 11am–11:30pm. Average main course: $8. Cash only.

Straddling the border of Little Italy and Chinatown, this bustling mess hall draws a mostly Asian crowd with its inexpensive Malaysian cuisine. Ask your sarong-wearing waitress for dishes like deep-fried red snapper sealed in a sweet-chili glaze. The din of the crowd and hustle of the open kitchen keep the room constantly abuzz. Don't be surprised if you find yourself making friends with neighboring diners.

Penang

38-04 Prince St at Main St, Flushing, Queens (718-321-2078). Subway: 7 to Flushing–Main St. Mon–Thu noon–midnight; Fri–Sat noon–1am; Sun 1pm–11pm. Average main course: $12. Cash only.

Unlike the Penangs in Manhattan, which veer dangerously close to tiki-bar territory with their thatched roofs and bamboo walls, the Flushing branch of this Malaysian chainlet is the genuine article: a no-frills eatery where the focus is on the superb cuisine. Chow down on whole crispy fish with ginger dip, and all manner of curries and chilies. And by all means, try the *roti canai*. The warm, flaky bread and peanutty curry sauce are as addictive as chips and salsa. They're so good, you'd return just for them. As for the Manhattan outlets, the food they serve is still quite tasty. You won't receive any props from your foodie friends for patronizing them, but you will enjoy yourself.

Other locations: *240 Columbus Ave at 71st St (212-769-3988); 1596 Second Ave between 82nd and 83rd Sts (212-585-3838).*

Pan-Asian

Kelley and Ping

127 Greene St between Prince and Houston Sts (212-228-1212). Subway: N, R to Prince St; B, D, F, Q to Broadway–Lafayette St; 6 to Bleecker St. Sun–Wed noon–11pm; Thu–Sat noon–midnight. Average main course: $6. AmEx, MC, V.

Here's the drill at this tried-and-trendy pan-Asian noodle house: Pick up your order at the counter, loom over slow eaters, and grab their seats as soon as they stand to gather their belongings. Despite the dog-eat-dog scene, the price and quality make a visit worthwhile. The place resembles a general store (you can buy the Thai dry goods that line one wall). The Bangkok curry is addictive, and the chicken satay and pad thai acceptable. The restaurant is noisy and popular with hip, young Soho tourists, but locals tolerate the scene for the quick, cheap eats—Beastie Boy Adam Yauch pops in to hunch over a bowl of noodles.

Rain

100 W 82nd St between Columbus and Amsterdam Aves (212-501-0776). Subway: B, C to 81st St; 1, 9 to 79th St. Mon–Thu noon–3pm; 6pm–midnight; Sat noon–4pm, 5pm–midnight; Sun noon–4pm, 5–10pm. Average main course: $16. AmEx, DC, Disc, MC, V.

When you're 80 blocks north of Chinatown, you can whine about the lack of good, cheap Asian restaurants, or you can head to Rain. With locations on the

Necessities

Upper East and Upper West Sides, Rain is ethnic eatery as interpreted by J. Crew. In other words, it's a neat, stylish place where uptowners will feel at ease. No matter which side of the park you're on, Rain remains a fine place to swill a Cosmo with a group of friends while sampling a bento-box assortment of pretty decent pan-Asian eats.
Other location: *Rain East, 1059 Third Ave between 62nd and 63rd Sts (212-223-3669).*

Republic

37 Union Square West between 16th and 17th Sts (212-627-7168). Subway: N, R, L, 4, 5, 6 to 14 St–Union Sq. Sun–Wed noon–11pm; Thu–Sat noon–midnight. Average main course: $7.50. AmEx, DC, MC, V.
This hip but affordable large restaurant facing Union Square specializes in noodles, and there are oodles to choose from, whether you want mellow (wonton broth noodles) or racy (barbecue pork on a bed of vermicelli). The long bar also works well for solo eaters.

Ruby Foo's

2182 Broadway at 77th St (212-724-6700). Subway: 1, 9 to 79th St. Sun–Thu 11am–12:30am; Fri, Sat 11am–1am. Average main course: $15. AmEx, MC, V.
Ruby Foo's high-octane pan-Asian decor evokes both classic chop-suey houses of old and the high-ceilinged decadence of other of-the-moment young-professional watering holes. Chef Junnajet Hurapan adds to the convivial spirit, mixing clever dim sum and meaty, fresh sushi on an East-meets-East fusion menu designed for sharing. Expect a wait even if you have made reservations.
Other location: *1626 Broadway at 49th St (212-489-5600).*

Thai

Amarin Cafe

See page 157 for review.

The Elephant

58 E 1st St between First and Second Aves (212-505-7739). Subway: F to Second Ave. Mon–Thu noon–3pm, 5:30pm–1am; Fri, Sat noon–3pm, 5:30pm–2:30am; Sun 5:30pm–1am. Average main course: $12. AmEx.
This French-Thai-Vietnamese bistro is tiny, but it thinks big. The cuisine features ambitious, often sculptural dishes, such as charcoal-grilled chicken marinated in lemongrass, and Thai spicy beef salad, a mini-tower of tender strips of steak with mint, cilantro and diced mango on a disk of jasmine rice. Its cheesy beaded curtains, woven beach mats on the wall and zebra-stripe furniture give the room a funky GI-bar air. Bask in it while sipping a lightly sweet and refreshing lychee-juice cocktail. Get there early or late to avoid a wait; the Elephant packs in a noisy crowd of hip locals and uptown yupsters.

Deli-cious The new Artie's makes pastrami from an old Lower East Side recipe.

Little Basil

39 Greenwich Ave at Charles St (212-645-8965). Subway: 1, 2, 3, 9 to 14th St. Noon–11:30pm. Average main course: $10. AmEx, DC, MC, V.
Little Basil may be the baby brother of the well-known Holy Basil in the East Village, but it's just as mature when it comes to preparing and presenting Thai food. The entrées and appetizers arrive with sauces drizzled around them in seductive designs, ready to be spooned onto the fragrant rice. Duck is a specialty here; the outstanding *pet kapraw* is a slightly sweet, deep-fried version. If you don't see what you want on the menu, ask the cooperative chef to take a crack at it.
Other location: *Holy Basil, 149 Second Ave between 9th and 10th Sts (212-460-5557).*

Vietnamese

Pho Bang

157 Mott St between Grand and Broome Sts (212-966-3797). Subway: J, M, Z, N, R, 6 to Canal St; B, D, Q to Grand St. 10am–10pm. Average main course: $6. Cash only.
Join the mostly Vietnamese clientele (always a good sign) and slurp away in the din of this always-crowded space. Pho Bang's menu offers the requisite Vietnamese starters—spring rolls, summer rolls, grilled beef on rice vermicelli—and all are skillfully cooked. But the real attraction is the *pho* (rice noodle) soup, which comes in 16 different variations (hint: *omosa* = tripe). If you're not in the mood for a massive bowl of this classic dish, have the *bánh mì cary ga* (curry chicken), served with a hunk of French bread. Then get wired for a walk through anarchic Chinatown by downing a sweet iced coffee.

Cyclo

203 First Ave between 12th and 13th Sts (212-673-3957). Subway: L to First Ave; 6 to Astor Pl.

Sun–Thu 5:30–10:45pm; Fri, Sat 5:30–11:45pm. Average main course: $11. AmEx, MC, V.
Yes, Cyclo will run you a bit more than the Vietnamese joints in Chinatown, but for a few extra bucks, you'll be rewarded with a stylishly simple interior, grooving music and absolutely no Formica. You'll also get Vietnamese food on par with the city's best, including whole crispy red snapper in a hot, sweet chili sauce and fragrant ginger chicken cooked in a clay pot. Service is efficient and unobtrusive, so you can really relax.

Eastern European

FireBird

365 W 46th St between Eighth and Ninth Aves (212-586-0244). Subway: A, C, E to 42nd St–Port Authority. Mon–Fri 11:30am–11pm; Sat, Sun 12:30pm–midnight. Average main course: $28. AmEx, DC, Disc, MC, V.
At this touristy, expensive Russian haunt on Restaurant Row, the waiters' uniforms include epaulets and gaiters, just like Vronsky, the sexy colonel in *Anna Karenina*. The ornately carved furniture and ostentatious tchotchkes are lavish to the point of parody, but the food is authentic and often delicious. Try not to fill up on the excellent complimentary potato bread. FireBird doesn't allow smoking or vodka bottles at tables, so it's more successful with visitors than with natural-born Russians.

Rasputin

2670 Coney Island Ave at Ave X, Brighton Beach, Brooklyn (718-332-8333). Subway: D to Neck Rd; F to Ave X. Mon–Thu 11am–9pm; Fri–Sun 7pm–3am. Banquet: $50. AmEx, Disc, MC, V.
If you want to party in Brighton Beach's Little Odessa, head directly to Rasputin, which bills itself as a "true supper club on the grand scale." Rasputin offers a glamorous, aqua-colored dining room equipped with balcony seating and a lighting grid that rivals any Broadway theater's. Your meal is an onslaught of iced vodka and French-Russian eats (French lobster salad and cheese-smothered sturgeon). The entertainment opens with a leggy chorus line high-kicking to "New York, New York," and closes with an entourage of scantily clad dancers prancing around the dance floor. And once they've finished, the dance floor is all yours—assuming you're not too drunk or full to dance.

Russian Samovar

256 W 52nd St between Broadway and Eighth Ave (212-757-0168). Subway: 1, 9 to 50th St; C, E to 50th St. Sun, Mon 5pm–midnight; Tue–Sat noon–midnight. Average main course: $20. AmEx, DC, Disc, MC, V.
Moody, broody billiard-room decor is the perfect backdrop for the passionate-sounding conversations of the Russian clientele here (Mikhail Baryshnikov is a co-owner). This is a Slavic home-away-from-home, where the food triggers potent memories. Consider the sweet and sloppy beef Stroganoff. It's not the lightest cuisine, and the prices aren't Brighton Beach bargain-basement. But the service is gracious, and the place does have its own distinctive style, with incongruous yet somehow perfect touches like a white baby-grand piano.

Russian Tea Room

See page 135 for review.

Veselka

144 Second Ave at 9th St (212-228-9682). Subway: 6 to Astor Pl. 24hrs. Average main course: $10. AmEx, Disc, MC, V.
This 24-hour old-timer attracts an assorted East Village crowd of students, insomniacs, families and the occasional Polish grandma. None of these folks ever leave hungry, especially after a combo plate, which includes soup, salad, stuffed cabbage, four pierogi and four slices of challah. The cold borscht is famous; for brunch, do yourself a favor and dive into the raspberry-cheese blintzes.

Ethiopian

Ghenet

284 Mulberry St between Prince and Houston Sts (212-343-1888). Subway: B, D, F, Q to Broadway–Lafayette St; N, R to Prince St; 6 to Bleecker St. Tue–Thu noon–4pm, 5–10:30pm; Fri, Sat noon–4pm, 5–11pm; Sun noon–3pm. Average main course: $9. AmEx, MC, V.
When it opened in 1998, Ghenet raised the bar for Ethiopian restaurants all over town, and it is still by far the best of the lot. The spongy *injera* is made with generous portions of *teff* (the expensive flour of a grain grown only in Ethiopia). The complex, hand-ground *berberé*—a combination of spices such as cardamom and dried chilies—is the basis for most of the stews. Any entrée, from the gently sautéed chicken (*doro aletcha*) to the rich lamb stew (*yebeg wot*), exemplifies the ideals of this cuisine. The family-style atmosphere has also made Ghenet popular with neighborhood hipsters, who have adopted the place for birthday parties and group dinners. And for those who do not eat meat, there are plenty of vegetarian choices.

French

Alison on Dominick Street

38 Dominick St between Varick and Hudson Sts (212-727-1188). Subway: 1, 9 to Canal St. Mon–Thu 5:15–10:30pm; Fri, Sat 5:15–10:45pm; Sun 5:15–9:30pm. Average main course: $30. AmEx, DC, MC, V.
There are popular French places below Houston Street—the ones that are impossibly crowded, noisy and overpriced. Alison on Dominick is the antidote. Reservations aren't difficult to get, either. Perhaps people are scared by the unfamiliar locale—but don't worry, the place is not hard to find. You'll be rewarded with a creative à la carte menu that's a welcome departure from the de rigueur steak frites found elsewhere. For instance, the Roquefort tart adds some oomph to a typically tender filet

Necessities

mignon. The quail salad's meat, glazed with cider and paprika, remains delicate inside its crunchy skin. For a change of taste at the end of the meal, go for the country cheese plate; the other desserts won't wow you.

Balthazar

See page 136 for review.

Casimir

103–105 Ave B between 6th and 7th Sts (212-358-9683). Subway: F to Second Ave; 6 to Astor Pl. Mon–Thu 5:30pm–midnight; Fri 5:30pm–1am; Sat 11:30am–4pm, 5:30pm–1am; Sun 11:30am–4pm, 5:30pm–midnight. Average main course: $13. AmEx.

Neither its tin ceilings, waning yellow light nor staff of young French guys sporting that just-rolled-out-of-bed look do much to differentiate Casimir from so many other New York bistros. What separates it from the pack is its crowd: On any given night, throngs of up-to-the-minute downtowners crowd around its tiny bar or flop down in its next-door Moroccan lounge, and many even sit down for dinner. Which is a good move: Casimir's bistro cuisine—cassoulet, steak frites, etc.—is quite good and, by New York standards, quite affordable.

Daniel

See page 129 for review.

Guastavino's

See page 137 for review.

Jean Claude

137 Sullivan St between Prince and Houston Sts (212-475-9232). Subway: C, E to Spring St. Sun–Thu 6:30–11pm; Fri, Sat 6:30–11:30pm. Average main course: $14. Cash only.

Just outside Jean Claude's red-trimmed storefront beautiful people jostle each other as they peer inside and try to gauge the wait for one of the dozen tables. Given the satisfying bistro food at these prices, you can't blame them. If you're single, this might be the place for you—after all, isn't having the chance to rub elbows with beautiful people what you're going out for? But here's a secret for the crowd-weary: Early in the evening—when the front window isn't obstructed by people—you and someone you love can reel in a fish entrée, such as snapper, monkfish or salmon. The average price is low because the menu is sans steak, so red-meat lovers must choose from leg of lamb or duck breast.

Manhattan transfers

A host of borough-jumping chefs have put Brooklyn on the culinary map

Not too long ago, you could have visited New York and eaten at its best and most high-profile restaurants without ever leaving Manhattan. But in recent years, a number of enterprising chefs and restaurateurs have waved goodbye to the city's most bustling borough and jumped ship to Brooklyn, land of cheap rents (well, *cheaper,* at least) and a pace of life that isn't so Indy 500.

The majority of them have relocated to spots on or near Smith Street, an emerging strip that cuts through the increasingly fashionable neighborhoods of Cobble Hill, Carroll Gardens and Boerum Hill. Make your way to this main drag and you can take your pick of a meal at **Sur** (*232 Smith St between Butler and Douglass Sts, Carroll Gardens, 718-875-1716*), an Argentine bistro framed by wood beams, exposed brick walls and flickering votive candles; a nibble at **Sweet Melissa Patisserie** (*276 Court St between Butler and Douglass Sts, Cobble Hill, 718-855-3410*), where you'll find impeccable pastries, the tastiest butterscotch pudding in NYC, and a soothing back garden; or a charming sit-down dinner at **Grocery** (*288 Smith St between Union and Sackett Sts, Carroll Gardens, 718-596-3335*), where partners Charles Keily and Sharon Patcher (both formerly of Manhattan must-eats Savoy and Gotham Bar and Grill) prepare top-notch creative American cuisine. For brunch, don't miss **Banania** (*241 Smith St at Douglass St, Carroll Gardens, 718-237-9100*), a bright and pleasant eatery that serves superb French-American food prepared by Danforth Houle, former kitchen hand at the now defunct, highly acclaimed Bouley. And if you simply must have some seared foie gras, reserve a table at **Saul** (*140 Smith St between Bergen and Dean Sts, Boerum Hill, 718-935-9844*), a sophisticated bistro run by Saul Bolton, formerly of Le Bernardin.

If you like your restaurants a bit edgier, hop on the L train to Williamsburg. Once a predominantly Jewish, Italian and Polish neighborhood, this industrial area has welcomed droves of artists who have converted warehouse spaces into studios. Equally industrious restaurateurs have breathed life into a trio of once-dilapidated, but now stunning, '20s-era dining cars. At **Diner**

Jean Georges

See page 131 for review.

Jules Bistro

65 St. Marks Pl between First and Second Aves (212-477-5560). Subway: 6 to Astor Pl. Mon–Fri 5:30pm–1am; Sat, Sun 11am–4pm, 5:30pm–1am. Average main course: $18. AmEx.

Live jazz, vintage movie posters and a bon vivant clientele—Jules is a slice of the French New Wave in the heart of the East Village. The kitchen serves archetypal bistro fare. Appetizers are *parfait,* from the unexpectedly rich and delicate salmon tartare to traditional offerings like escargot and pâté. Recommended main dishes include a number of simple but brilliantly executed items: steak frites with crispy shoestring fries and seared duck breast. The waitstaff's flirty charm adds to the Euro atmosphere and can compensate for lapses in service.

La Forêt

1713 First Ave between 88th and 89th Sts (212-987-9839). Subway: 4, 5, 6 to 86th St. Tue–Sat 5:30–11pm. Average main course: $14. Cash only.

Good, affordable bistros might not make waves south of 14th Street, but on this restaurant-starved strip of upper First Avenue, La Forêt is a godsend. Bouley-trained chef Vladimir Ribartchouk prepares creative French-inspired cuisine at eminently fair prices. Go for his potato-encrusted sea bass or his garlic-perfumed leg of lamb with a Vidalia-onion–and–apple curry sauce, and you'll say so long to Soho. Andrei Kondrashov, the restaurant's bearlike Russian owner and host, adds extra warmth to the sylvan-inspired nook.

Le Bernardin

See page 131 for review.

Les Deux Gamins

170 Waverly Pl at Grove St (212-807-7047). Subway: 1, 9 to Christopher St–Sheridan Sq. 8am–midnight. Average main course: $18. AmEx.

Even the American guys who kick back in this corner bistro seem French: Unshaven and with cigarettes dangling from their handsome faces. Both of the restaurant's worn-in rooms are usually filled at night, as those *mecs* and their head-turning girlfriends quaff liters of red wine and nibble on a variety of French staples. You can go low-budget (*croque monsieur*) or upscale (dry-aged steak au poivre). At weekend brunch, try to grab a sidewalk table, where you'll be able to keep one eye on the passing street life and the other on your cute French server.

(*85 Broadway at Berry St, 718-486-3077*), you'll find impressive French bistro cuisine along with a too-cool-for-school clientele hanging out at the bar, listening to DJ-spun records. Pilar Rigon, a onetime partner at Manhattan's perpetually mobbed Il Bagatto, opened **Miss Williamsburg Diner** (*206 Kent Ave between Metropolitan Ave and North 3rd St, 718-963-0802*), with her boyfriend, Massimiliano Bartoli, former executive chef at midtown's Osteria al Doge. The restaurant, on a barren block near the East River, is one of the most unexpected places in the city to find authentic northern Italian food, like handmade ravioli, fragrant risotto Milanese and thick pork chops sautéed in butter and rosemary. The newest of the converted diners is **Relish** (*255 Wythe St between North 3rd and Metropolitan Sts, 718-963-4546*), whose menu of "upscale comfort food" attracts its fair share of Williamsburg's famed hipsters. A fried-clam appetizer sounds like a predictably kitschy HoJo's reference but goes well beyond. Other basics, like the chicken and dumplings and nicely charred hanger steak, have quickly become customer favorites. But it's the space that makes Relish most alluring. Gleaming chrome details bathed in a warm red glow make it look more like a movie set than a lunch wagon. It's so stylish, it almost feels like you're in…Manhattan.

A peeling Banania is named for a French kids' drink.

Lucien

14 First Ave between 1st and 2nd Sts (212-260-6481). Subway: F to Second Ave. 10am–2am. Average main course: $14. AmEx, MC, V.

Lucien's menu doesn't stray too far from the bistro formula: steak frites, *moules marinières, tarte Tatin.* But as at most memorable bistros, the menu isn't really the point. Comfort, familiarity and flair are more important, and Lucien scores high on these counts. On a typical night, the banquettes are filled long after dinnertime with East Village locals, clearly in no rush to get home.

Max & Moritz

426A Seventh Ave between 14th and 15th Sts, Park Slope, Brooklyn (718-499-5557). Subway: F to Seventh Ave. Mon–Fri 5:30–11pm; Sat, Sun 11am–3:30pm, 5:30–11pm. Average main course: $13. AmEx, MC, V.

Brooklyn is awash in Manhattan-style bistros these days, but Max & Moritz was the first to chart the territory, and it remains one of the best. The pleasantly lit, compact dining room and spacious garden don't hurt a bit, but the real key to M & M's success is its European comfort fare. And there's a special Austrian menu on the first Tuesday of every month. You'll probably have to cool your heels on the sidewalk while waiting for a table, but remember: In Manhattan, food this good would run $25 an entrée—and you wouldn't be able to get in, anyway.

Pastis

See page 138 for review.

Patois

255 Smith St between Douglass and DeGraw Sts, Carroll Gardens, Brooklyn (718-855-1535). Subway: F, G to Carroll St. Tue–Thu 6–10:30pm; Fri, Sat 6–11:30pm; Sun 11am–3pm, 5–10pm. Average main course: $14. AmEx, MC, V.

Meet the restaurant responsible for Brooklyn's Smith Street renaissance (*see* **Manhattan transfers,** *page 146*). This petite bistro—with meet-your-neighbor tables and genuine French waiters—was a godsend to Cobble Hillers bored by the area's ho-hum dining options. But once the word got out and people started trekking here all the way from—gasp!—Manhattan, it became difficult to snag a table. Patois remains special for its consistently solid steak frites, grilled chicken, lamb chops and seared tuna. The escargot in puff pastry is the highlight of a seasonal appetizer list. And it's still a (cheap) thrill snaking through the kitchen to reach the year-round backyard garden and its thrift-store–chic lounge.

Payard Patisserie & Bistro

1032 Lexington Ave between 73rd and 74th Sts (212-717-5252). Subway: 6 to 77th St. Mon–Sat 7am–11pm. Average main course: $22. AmEx, Disc, MC, V.

If you call yourself a dessert junkie and you've never been to Payard, drop whatever you're doing and head over there—now. This is the kingdom of François Payard, former pastry chef at Daniel. It's a Willy-Wonka-goes-to-Paris wonderland of handmade chocolates, crisp fruit tarts, lush sorbets and mind-blowing designer creations. You can get the desserts to go—but why not savor them at one of the tiny café tables? And if you need a meal before your sweets, reserve a spot in the two-tiered dining room, which serves top-notch, upscale French fare.

Provence

38 MacDougal St at Prince St (212-475-7500). Subway: N, R to Prince St; 6 to Spring St. Sun–Thu noon–3pm, 6–10:30pm; Fri, Sat noon–3pm, 6pm–midnight. Average main course: $19. AmEx.

Located on a picturesque Soho street corner, this 13-year-old Provençal bistro wears its sponge-painted, country-house patina well. A mostly black-clad downtown crowd fills the warmly lit dining room (or vies for tables in the cozy garden). Chef Axel Grousset skillfully infuses Southeastern French classics with light, vibrant flavors. Traditionalists will appreciate the bouillabaisse and *coquilles St. Jacques*. Desserts worthy of the calories include Provence's version of *clafouti,* a traditional fruit custard studded with black cherries, and *calisson,* a Provençal almond tart.

Greek

Elias Corner

24-02 31st St at 24th Ave, Astoria, Queens (718-932-1510). Subway: N to Astoria Blvd. Mon–Sat 4pm–midnight; Sun 3pm–midnight. Average main course: $15. Cash only.

Elias's loyalists don't hesitate for a minute when they call this Greek establishment "the best fish restaurant in the city." You may agree, if you know how to order. First, study the fish on display for signs of freshness, then ask the name of the one that looks best and order it. The chef will brush it with olive oil, rub it with oregano and slap it on the grill. Squeeze a lemon over it and you have a perfect meal.

Estiatorio Milos

125 W 55th St between Sixth and Seventh Aves (212-245-7400). Subway: B, D, E to Seventh Ave. Mon–Sat 11:15am–11:45pm; Sun 5–10pm. Average fish price: $32 per pound. AmEx, DC, MC, V.

Milos strives to be an authentic Greek seafood restaurant and an efficient midtown expense-account spot. The kitchen's skillful preparations are beyond reproach; you will have a hard time finding fresher, more simply prepared seafood anywhere in the city. Like the Greek fish houses of Astoria, Queens, Milos lets you choose your entrée from the fresh catch reclining on ice at the rear of the vast, spartan room. Just pick whatever looks best. Your loup de mer, simply drizzled with olive oil, will have never tasted so good.

Molyvos

871 Seventh Ave between 55th and 56th Sts (212-582-7500). Subway: B, D, E to Seventh Ave; N, R to 57th St. Sun–Fri noon–3pm, 5:30–11:30pm; Sat noon–3pm, 5pm–midnight. Average main course: $21. AmEx, DC, Disc, MC, V.

Go fishing The trompe l'oeil sea view at Oceana will get you in the spirit.

Go ahead and judge Molyvos by its appearance; you'll probably be dead on. Manhattan's best Greek restaurant eschews the typical whitewashed walls and blue trim, opting instead for inviting terra-cotta tile floors and windows that swing open onto Seventh Avenue. The food is just as pleasing—superior Greek home cooking, refined for Manhattan taste buds. Begin your meal with complimentary feta–and–roasted-red-pepper spread; then move on to tiny tzatziki-smothered meatballs made with bulgur wheat pasta and zucchini, wood-grilled baby octopus, insanely rich and creamy moussaka and a pyramid of fried dough balls glazed with sticky sweet honey. The dishes aren't fancy—just plain delicious.

Periyali

35 W 20th St between Fifth and Sixth Aves (212-463-7890). Subway: F, N, R to 23rd St. Mon–Thu noon–3pm, 5:30–11pm; Fri noon–3pm, 5:30–11:30pm; Sat 5:30–11:30pm. Average main course: $20. AmEx, DC, MC, V.

A billowing ceiling canopy, white stucco walls and colorful banquettes—do you feel like you're on the Aegean yet? Periyali has been at the top of the Greek food chain for 14 years now, attracting a power-lunch crowd and casual Flatiron diners. Start by dipping hunks of warm country bread in herb-infused olive oil or pureed fava beans. As would be expected at a Greek restaurant, the grilling's great: Try the juicy grilled chicken-and-fennel brochettes with smoky eggplant-and-semolina salad, or *garides Santorini,* baked or grilled shrimp with tomato, scallions, feta and brandy. End the Grecian formula with moist orange semolina or black walnut cake—not-too-sweet alternatives to the honey-heavy baklava.

Trata

1331 Second Ave between 70th and 71st Sts (212-535-3800). Subway: 6 to 68th St–Hunter College. Sun–Thu noon–3pm, 5–11pm; Fri, Sat noon–3pm, 5pm–midnight. Average main course: $17. AmEx, DC, MC, V.

This mid-priced Greek restaurant, staffed by veterans of the far pricier Estiatorio Milos, will leave you wondering why anyone's ever felt the need to cook on anything other than a charcoal grill. Octopus, fresh sardines, peppers and a wide selection of fresh fish are displayed on a big bed of ice—until they hit the briquettes. Then they're drizzled with olive oil, lemon and herbs. Only the impersonal dining room detracts from Trata's blessed simplicity.

Indian

Ayurveda Cafe

706 Amsterdam Ave at 94th St (212-932-2400). Subway: B, C, 1, 9 to 86th St. 11:30am–11:30pm. Average main course: $6.95. AmEx, DC, MC, V.

Everything at this pint-size café is designed to create a feeling of balance, from the burbling fountain and cloud-covered ceiling to the preset vegetarian menu. Following the Indian holistic system of well-being known as Ayurveda, the kitchen builds each meal around six tastes: salty, sweet, sour, bitter, astringent and pungent. This translates into a platter loaded with tiny dishes; the selections change daily but include such items as spicy garbanzo beans, lentils, greens and a mildly sweet rice pudding. Surprisingly filling, the platter goes well with a thick, refreshing mango *lassi.* Be sure to open the ornate box at the doorway and extract a contemplative saying, which provides more provocative food for thought than the average fortune cookie.

Café Spice

72 University Pl at 11th St (212-253-6999). Subway: N, R, L, 4, 5, 6 to 14th St–Union Sq. Mon–Thu 11:30am–3pm, 5–10:30pm; Fri 11:30am–3pm, 5–11:30pm; Sat noon–11:30pm; Sun 1–10:30pm. Average main course: $15. AmEx, DC, MC, V.

In an earth-toned setting that's more Pottery Barn than 6th Street, the folks from uptown's Dawat offer high-quality renditions of prawn curry, tandoori chicken, *puri* and even wraps. Don't be fooled by the attempted trendiness of the interior: The food here is traditional and, unlike that of other newish Indian restaurants, fusion-free. All of the hearty, richly flavored and beautifully presented entrées include a square-meal accompaniment of nan, lentils, veggies and basmati rice.

Jackson Diner

37-47 74th St between Roosevelt and 37th Aves, Jackson Heights, Queens (718-672-1232). Subway: E, F, G, R to Jackson Hts–Roosevelt Ave; 7 to 74th St–Broadway. Sun–Thu 11:30am–10pm; Fri, Sat 11:30am–10:30pm. Average main course: $9. Cash only.

After 14 years in business, this esteemed house of *dosais* and dal ditched its funky, coffee-shop home for more spacious digs down the block. While the stylish lighting, earth-tone color scheme and chichi banquettes may be a treat for Queens residents, Manhattanites who trek to this Indian-food mecca might feel as if they've simply wound up back in Soho. Even so, Jackson Diner's authentic Indian food (much of it from veggie-friendly

Necessities

Stop carping Eat at Joe's Shanghai in Chinatown and you'll have no complaints.

South India) remains affordable and some of the best of its kind in any borough.

Pongal

110 Lexington Ave between 27th and 28th Sts (212-696-9458). Subway: 6 to 28th St. Mon–Fri noon–3pm, 5–10pm; Sat, Sun noon–10pm. Average main course: $8. MC, V.

You may see as many yarmulkes as saris at this unusual Indian restaurant, where the superb South Indian vegetarian cuisine is rich, flavorful and, would you believe, kosher? If you find the extensive menu a bit overwhelming, order a *thali*—Indian for "combination platter." Each offers eight to ten different dishes, including dessert, for less than $15. Because the food is so good at Pongal, however, the restaurant can often be extremely crowded, making for a less than relaxing dining experience.

Tabla

11 Madison Ave at 25th St (212-889-0667). Subway: N, R, 6 to 23rd St. Mon–Fri noon–2pm, 5:30–10:30pm; Sat 5:30–10:30pm; Sun 5:30–9:30pm. Bar Mon–Sat noon–11pm; Sun noon–10pm. Three-course prix fixe: $52. AmEx, DC, Disc, MC, V.

For the New York diner who has seen one too many tuna tartares, six too many "emulsions" of this or that, and a lifetime's worth of crème brûlées, relief exists in the form of Tabla. At this upscale Indian fusion restaurant opened by Danny Meyer (owner of Gramercy Tavern, Union Square Cafe and 11 Madison Park), flavors leap off the plate in guises you've never imagined. The familiar crab cake springs to life with Goan spices. For diners who want to experience Tabla without throwing down $52 for the prix-fixe dinner menu, consider the downstairs "bread bar," where you can munch on freshly baked olive-oil–and-rosemary nan with lemon-chive *raita* or a number of other condiments.

Thali

28 Greenwich Ave between 10th and Charles Sts (212-367-7411). Subway: A, C, E, B, D, F, Q to W 4th St. Noon–3pm, 6–10pm. Prix fixe: $10. Cash only.

There is no menu at this sparsely decorated, closet-size vegetarian restaurant. Just sit down and order tea, and within minutes, a server brings a large silver tray of *thali,* a traditional Indian meal consisting of curries, a lentil dish, chutney, pickles, bread, a pile of rice and dessert. You can be sure the food is fresh—the place has no storage area, so the ingredients are bought and prepared new each day. The food is good, but the deal is great.

Italian

al di là

248 Fifth Ave at Carroll St, Park Slope, Brooklyn (718-783-4565). Subway: M, N, R to Union St. Mon–Thu 6–10:30pm; Fri, Sat 6–11pm; Sun 6–10pm. Average main course: $12. MC, V.

All the pieces come together at this warm trattoria and—judging by the large crowds—everyone in Park Slope knows it. The rustic decor lures you in, while the expertly crafted Northern Italian food keeps you there for hours.

Andy's Colonial

2257 First Ave at 116th St (212-410-9175). Subway: 6 to 116th St. 11:30am–11pm. Average main course: $13. Cash only.

Andy's is a corner tavern with no printed menu, just a handful of tables and warm service. Co-owner Joe Medici (your bartender and waiter) will hand you a short list of specials. If those don't interest you, Joe will tell you that they can make "any kind of chicken or veal you'd like—marsala, parmigiana, you name it." Medici should know. He's got a friend in the kitchen: his 83-year-old father, Salvatore, the chef whom you'll spy through the open kitchen door hammering veal cutlets on a worn butcher block. All of Sal's entrées—from chicken *scarpariello* to linguine in silky clam sauce—make your hike to 116th Street worthwhile.

Babbo

See page 129 for review.

Bamonte's

32 Withers St between Union Ave and Lorimer St, Williamsburg, Brooklyn (718-384-8831). Subway: L to Lorimer St. Mon, Wed, Thu noon–10pm; Fri, Sat noon–11pm; Sun 1–10pm. Average main course: $14. MC, V.

You may never achieve the perfect Frankie Valli hair or pinkie-ring panache of many of the customers at Bamonte's, but that shouldn't keep you from this colorful 100-year-old eatery on a row-house–lined block of Williamsburg. Come on a weekend night and join the long tables of done-up ladies and clamoring fellas passing platters of light, crispy zucchini fritters, garlic-laden roasted peppers and spaghetti with meat sauce and meatballs. You'll love it—even if you're having a bad hair night.

Carmine's

2450 Broadway between 90th and 91st Sts (212-362-2200). Subway: 1, 2, 3, 9 to 96th St. Mon–Thu 11:30am–3pm, 5–11pm; Fri 11:30am–3pm, 5pm–midnight; Sat 11:30am–midnight; Sun 3–10pm. Average main course (family style): $18. AmEx, MC, V.

Plenty of pasta, oceans of red sauce and bucket-size cocktails are the hallmarks of Manhattan's two Carmine's, Southern Italian eateries that serve gargantuan, family-style portions of noodles in warm, celebratory settings. The spaghetti with meat sauce and sausage-and-peppers are average at best, but that has not deterred the crowds. Carmine's accepts reservations only for parties of six or more—and that's just on weekends and early evenings during the week. Otherwise, get ready to wait.

Other location: *200 W 44th St between Broadway and Eighth Ave (212-221-3800).*

Felidia

See page 131 for review.

Frank

88 Second Ave between 5th and 6th Sts (212-420-0202). Subway: F to Second Ave; 6 to Astor Pl. Mon–Thu 10:30am–3:45pm, 5pm–12:45am; Fri, Sat 10:30am–3:45pm, 5pm–1:45am; Sun 5pm–midnight. Average main course: $9. Cash only.

Inspired by his Neapolitan grandmother's cooking, chef-owner Frank Prisinzano serves superb, straightforward food at no-nonsense prices. Just as homespun is the tiny antique-filled storefront space. It's also packed with customers, so be prepared to wait for your *pappa di zucchine* (pureed zucchini soup), nutty risotto, and garlic-rosemary chicken. On cold or rainy nights, have a backup plan or you'll be stuck waiting on the sidewalk (the restaurant has no bar or foyer). In 2000, Prisinzano opened a next-door extension, **Vera,** but you still have to wait.

Il Bagatto

192 E 2nd St between Aves A and B (212-228-0977). Subway: F to Second Ave. Tue–Thu 6:30pm–midnight; Fri, Sat 6:30pm–1am; Sun 6–11pm. Average main course: $8. Cash only.

Cozy Il Bagatto was among the first restaurants to successfully lure reluctant uptowners into the bowels of Alphabet City. No surprise there—this always-jammed eatery serves hearty, flavorful food in a dark, cozy environment. The food overcomes the annoyance of having to wait for a table and deal with the harried, impatient staff. While you're cooling your heels (and you will have to), venture to the happening downstairs bar and take the edge off your appetite with a few cocktails and an order of bruschetta.

La Focacceria

128 First Ave between 7th St and St. Marks Pl (212-254-4946). Subway: L to First Ave; 6 to Astor Pl. Mon–Thu 1–10pm; Fri, Sat 10am–11pm. Average main course: $7. Cash only.

First, order a half carafe of the delicious house Chianti, fill your tumbler and drink to the abolition of long-stemmed glasses and overpriced wine lists. Next, scan the food choices on the wall. (This small, brightly lit, white-tiled pasta factory has been here since 1914 and still hasn't gotten around to printing a menu.) Everything's so cheap that you can probably afford to order appetizers, pasta and a main course, but portions are so big you won't have to.

Le Madri

168 W 18th St at Seventh Ave (212-727-8022). Subway: 1, 9 to 18th St. Noon–3pm, 5:30–11pm; closed for lunch Saturdays and Sundays in summer. Average main course: $29. Average pasta: $16. AmEx, DC, MC, V.

The rustic decor will tell you all you need to know about this restaurant: Arrangements of ripe fruits and vegetables dot the dining area, and the room's centerpiece is a hulking brick oven. Ahh, the joys of seasonal Tuscan cooking! The pasta is where the payoff is: The spinach gnocchi with basil and *cento pomodori* (100-tomatoes sauce) is flawlessly light and tastes of summer. In winter, roasted vegetables and black truffles play against butter-soft sheets of pappardelle.

Lupa

170 Thompson St between Houston and Bleecker Sts (212-982-5089). Subway: B, D, F, Q to Broadway–Lafayette St; 6 to Bleecker St. 11:30am–2:30pm, 5:30–11:30pm. Average main course: $12. AmEx, DC, MC, V.

Location is not everything. If it were, then Lupa might be lost in the sea of middling Italian eateries in the Village. What separates this trattoria from the pack are its owners (Mario Batali and Joe Bastianich of **Babbo,** *see page 129 for review;* and Jason Denton of **'Ino,** *see page 160 for review*) and its menu, a collection of Roman dishes that chef Mark Ladner fine-tuned while in Italy. Look for pastas such as bucatini with red onions and *guanciale* (cured pork). Also keep an eye out for oddball Babbo-esque creations, like homemade octopus head cheese.

Osteria al Doge

142 W 44th St between Sixth Ave and Broadway (212-944-3643). Subway: B, D, F, Q to 42nd St; N, R, S, 1, 2, 3, 9, 7 to 42nd St–Times Sq. Mon, Tue, Thu noon–11:30pm; Wed 11:30am–11:30pm; Fri noon–midnight; Sat 11:30am–midnight; Sun 4:30–10:30pm. Average main course: $16. AmEx, DC, Disc, MC, V.

The upstairs walls at Osteria al Doge are lined with pictures of Venice, and whether you sit at one of the long wooden tables up front or at a comfy leather banquette toward the back, you'll feel as if you're enjoying a solid meal in the canal-lined city (just ignore those *New Yorker* editors scattered about). The pastas, such as homemade farfalle with shrimp, fresh tomatoes and peas, are always reliable. Thin-crust pizzas are also available, as are heavier entrées, like herb-marinated sirloin steak. If you're rushed before the theater, you can gobble a free hard-boiled egg with your drink at the bar.

Pó

31 Cornelia St between Bleecker and 4th Sts (212-645-2189). Subway: A, C, E, B, D, F, Q to W 4th St. Tue 5:30–11pm; Wed, Thu 11:30am–2pm, 5:30–11pm; Fri, Sat 11:30am–2pm, 5:30–11:30pm; Sun 11:30am–2pm, 5–10pm. Average main course: $14. AmEx.

Chef Mario Batali (who has his own show on cable's TV Food Network) makes this tiny, romantic restaurant an unforgettable treat. The complimentary rosemary-laced white-bean bruschetta that's brought to the table as you're seated is a harbinger of the simple masterpieces to come. Batali favors intense (and often sweet) flavors, producing dishes like marinated quail with plums, frisée and pomegranate molasses, and a Fortune 500–rich white-bean ravioli with a balsamic-vinegar–brown-butter sauce. (To sample fancier, pricier, Batali creations, head to **Babbo;** *see page 129 for review.*)

Trattoria dell'Arte

900 Seventh Ave between 56th and 57th Sts (212-245-9800). Subway: N, R to 57th St. Mon–Fri 11:45am–11:30pm; Sat 11am–3pm, 5–11:30pm; Sun 11am–3pm, 5–10:30pm. Average main course: $28. Average pasta: $20. AmEx, MC, V.

You have to be in a certain mood to tackle the media–movie-biz cliques, potentially intense volume levels and steep bills at Trattoria dell'Arte. Even the decor gives attitude, with its dissonant peaches and teals in the downstairs dining room and Fellini-esque casts and sketches of body parts, including one of a huge breast. Food, anyone? Pizza with a wafer-thin crust is a specialty here. The antipasto bar offers a vast selection of fresh items. For dessert, try the hazelnut cannoli, its shell a crunchy complement to the ricotta stuffing.

Pizza

Lombardi's

32 Spring St between Mulberry and Mott Sts (212-941-7994). Subway: 6 to Spring St. Mon–Thu 11:30am–11pm; Fri, Sat 11:30am–midnight; Sun 11:30am–10pm. Large plain pizza: $12.50. Cash only.

Lombardi's is one of the few coal-oven pizzerias left in Manhattan. The pies can be too dry or a bit under-seasoned, but the place still ranks as one of Manhattan's best pizza parlors. Make sure you try the sublime three-cheese white pizza, and whichever pie you choose, ask for a topping of fresh garlic (it's free). In warm weather, try to get a table on the elevated deck out back.

Patsy's Pizzeria

2287 First Ave between 117th and 118th Sts (212-534-9783). Subway: 6 to 116th St. 11am–11pm. Large plain pizza: $10. Cash only.

You'll find some of the city's better thin-crust pizza at the various Patsy's scattered throughout Manhattan along with big family-style bowls of salad and pleasant settings. But if you really want to know why New York is the pizza capital of America, you'll have to visit the original Patsy's in East Harlem: Coal-oven pies don't get much better than at this 68-year-old stalwart. Amid time-warp decor, savor perfectly blackened and blistered crust (it's moist, chewy and a wee bit crispy) and a sweet sauce, the very essence of crushed plum tomatoes. See phone book for more locations.

Totonno Pizzeria Napolitano

1524 Neptune Ave between W 15th and W 16th Sts, Coney Island, Brooklyn (718-372-8606). Subway: B, D, F, N to Coney Island–Stillwell Ave. Wed–Sun noon–8:30pm. Large plain pizza: $14. Cash only.

This Coney Island institution, in business since 1924, is a bare-bones joint where everyone's a regular, except you. Don't worry about it—just sit back beneath the autographed head shots of baseball stars Derek Jeter, Tino Martinez et al., and let the brusque staff bring you a bubbling pizza straight from the coal-burning brick oven.

Other location: *1544 Second Ave between 80th and 81st Sts (212-327-2800).*

Two Boots Restaurant

37 Ave A between 2nd and 3rd Sts (212-505-2276). Subway: F to Second Ave. Mon–Fri 5pm–midnight; Sat, Sun noon–midnight. Large plain pizza: $13.95. AmEx, Disc, MC, V.

Two Boots, established in 1987, has become one of the most beloved pizza places in the city. Devotees flock to its funky locations for crispy cornmeal-crust pizza with spicy Cajun toppings (andouille sausage, crawfish tails) and goofy, film-geek names (Mr. Pink, Gelsemina, L'Avventura). Two Boots itself is named for the two boot-shaped places—Italy and Louisiana—whose disparate cuisines meld here with spunky results. The original, kid-friendly sit-down joint on Avenue A also has a full menu, with entrées such as pasta, shrimp Creole and fried-oyster po' boys—almost everything is battered, fried and then dipped into some hell-fire sauce. There are several Two Boots pizzerias around town that are excellent for getting just a slice (check phone book for other locations).

Kosher

Pongal

See page 150 for review.

Sammy's Roumanian

157 Chrystie St between Delancey and Rivington Sts (212-673-0330). Subway: B, D, Q to Grand St; J, M to Bowery. Sun–Thu 3:30–11pm; Fri, Sat 3:30pm–midnight. Average main course: $22. AmEx, MC, V.

You can find better steaks in Manhattan, but where else are you going to get Sammy's bar mitzvah–hall setting or its old-school waiters mixing chopped chicken liver tableside? Opt for the flavorful bone-in rib steak. Yes, you'll ingest massive amounts of cholesterol, but that bottle of vodka in a block of ice and the blaring Yiddish music should keep you from thinking about that impending heart attack.

Wolf & Lamb

10 E 48th St between Fifth and Madison Aves (212-317-0869). Subway: S, 4, 5, 6, 7 to 42nd St–Grand Central. Mon–Thu noon–11pm; Fri noon–3pm; Sun 2–11pm. Average main course: $19. AmEx, DC, Disc, MC, V.

Wolf & Lamb is a Diamond District restaurant that looks like it's a Soho bistro, owing to its exposed ventilation, red-brick walls and hardwood floors. Steaks are the main draw on the kosher menu. Less wonderful are several interesting, but not entirely successful twists on deli staples, like the ultralight knishes and the grilled pastrami on club bread. Nevertheless, those grilled steaks, heavily marinated in garlic and olive oil, are a carnivore's dream. The atmosphere is pleasantly chatty, and the customers are clearly enjoying themselves.

Latin American/Caribbean

Chicama

35 E 18th St between Broadway and Park Ave South (212-505-2233). Subway: L, N, R, 4, 5, 6 to 14th St–Union Sq. Mon–Thu noon–3pm, 6–12pm; Fri, Sat noon–3pm, 5:30pm–1am; Sun noon–3pm, 5:30–10pm. Average main course: $28. AmEx, V, MC

Filling ABC Carpet & Home's rustic, $2 million restaurant space is Peruvian-inspired Chicama, Douglas Rodriguez's first venture since bailing on the acclaimed Patria. Chicama's big draw is the ceviche bar. Arrive any time of day for the superb three-clam version, a pastalike mixture awash in green-tomato–and–parsley puree and crunchy pork *chicharrones*. Or sit down to a meal of suckling pig, pulled from NYC's only eucalyptus-burning rotisserie.

Chimichurri Grill

606 Ninth Ave between 43rd and 44th Sts (212-586-8655). Subway: A, C, E to 42nd St–Port Authority. Mon–Thu noon–11pm; Fri, Sat noon–11:30pm. Average main course: $18. AmEx, DC, MC, V.

The warm atmosphere is reason enough to squeeze into one of Chimichurri's 30 seats, but the simple, rich Argentine cuisine cinches the deal. You won't find a better empanada anywhere: Flaky and sinfully buttery, it's packed with a creamy meat filling. Main courses revolve around imported beef, the pride of the pampa. Shell steak, an 18-ounce hunk of chewy beef, springs to life with a spoonful of chimichurri, Argentina's pestolike herb mixture.

Coco Roco

392 Fifth Ave between 6th and 7th Sts, Park Slope, Brooklyn (718-965-3376). Subway: F to Seventh Ave. Sun–Thu noon–10:30pm; Fri, Sat noon–11:30pm. Average main course: $7. AmEx, Disc, MC, V.

Slowly rotating skewers of dripping, charred chicken will mesmerize you at this Peruvian outpost. But it's the other dishes on the menu that make Coco Roco one of the city's best South American joints: fluffy *papas rellenas*, stuffed with pork, roast corn and salsa; *arroz chaufa de mariscos*, a massive paella of seafood and rice; and *tacu-tacu de pescado*, sweet potato–crusted red snapper—to name but a few.

El Pollo

1746 First Ave between 90th and 91st Sts (212-996-7810). Subway: 4, 5, 6 to 86th St. 11am–11pm. Average main course: $6. AmEx, DC, MC, V.

Long before Boston Market rolled into town, El Pollo was turning out supreme rotisserie-roasted chicken. Steeped for more than 24 hours in a piquant Peruvian marinade, the birds are roasted until they're glistening with fat and so tender that a gentle tug nets you a mouthful of rich meat. And don't miss the fried plantains: The caramelized nuggets are as soft and sweet as pudding.

Esperanto

145 Ave C at 9th St (212-505-6559). Subway: L to First Ave; 6 to Astor Pl. Mon–Thu 6pm–1am; Fri–Sun 6pm–2:30pm; Sat, Sun 11am–4pm. Average main course: $13. V, MC.

Not all Latino cooking these days is of the nuevo variety. At Avenue C's bohemian-spirited Esperanto (owned by the proprietors of the down-the-block bar **Baraza,** *133 Ave C, 212-539-0811*), the food is pretty basic—and, for the most part, good. Thick-cut *chuletas* (pork-loin chops) arrive nicely charred with crisp *tostones*. Chunks of tender red snapper mingle with red peppers and cilantro in a ceviche awash in lime juice. Add it all up, and Esperanto should fare better than its namesake, the ill-fated international language.

Ipanema

13 W 46th St between Fifth and Sixth Aves (212-730-5848). Subway: B, D, F, Q to 47–50th Sts–Rockefeller Ctr. Noon–10pm. Average main course: $17. AmEx, DC, Disc, MC, V.

Pale yellow walls, hung with wood carvings of Brazilian houses, and an eternal bossa nova beat give Ipanema a patiolike feel, just right for ordering shrimp in some of the many available incarnations, such as the grilled and garlicky *camarão* Ipanema appetizer or the camarão Bahian, an entrée of the *frutos do mar* stewed with palm oil, tomatoes and coconut milk. Practice your Portuguese at the crowded bar, where you can order not only the usual lime-packed caipirinhas, but a fresh passion-fruit version, too.

Isla

See page 137 for review.

Jimmy's Bronx Cafe

281 W Fordham Rd between Cedar Ave and Major Deegan Expwy, Bronx (718-329-2000). Subway: 1, 9 to 207th St. Mon–Wed 10am–2am; Thu–Sun 10am–4am. Patio Thu–Sat 9pm–4am; Sun 5pm–4am. Average main course: $15. AmEx, DC, MC, V.

Enough with the Yankees and the zoo. The best reason to visit the Bronx is Jimmy's, a Puerto Rican entertainment mecca. After seeing a salsa band in the "Patio" nightclub (cover charges vary between $5 and $25), you can push through the doors to the café. One bite of the shrimp and lobster *asopao* and you'll understand why this gumbolike soup is Puerto Rico's national dish. The jade-green *berro con naranja* (orange-and-watercress juice) should give you the energy boost you need to start dancing to the city's top salsa and merengue bands.

Victor's Cafe 52

236 W 52nd St between Broadway and Eighth Ave (212-586-7714). Subway: C, E, 1, 9 to 50th St. Sun–Thu noon–midnight; Fri, Sat noon–1am. Average main course: $20. AmEx, DC, MC, V.

Nearly 30 years old, this estimable Theater District restaurant is the father of all of those fancy-pants pan-Latino joints cropping up all over Manhattan. Granted, it's not as hip as its upstart competitors, but you can still come here for a tasty pre- or post-theater meal. In the dark cocktail den, get in the mood with a *mojito,* Hemingway's favorite pre-Castro elixir, then let yourself go with thick black beans, crisp *tostones* and plenty more regional flavors, from porky and spicy to sweet and, well, porky.

Mexican

Lupe's East L.A. Kitchen

110 Sixth Ave at Watts St (212-966-1326). Subway: A, C, E, 1, 9 to Canal St. Sun–Tue 11:30am–11pm; Wed–Sat 11:30am–midnight. Average main course: $7.50. Cash only.

Sitting quietly in the no-man's-land where Soho gives way to the entrance of the Holland Tunnel, Lupe's is about as barrio-authentic as you can get without boarding a plane. No fancy hand-painted stoneware or passion-fruit margaritas from a Slurpee machine here, just cold *cervezas* and decent, hearty food on simple plates. You have a choice of bulging burritos and other Cal-Mex staples—just pick your favorite.

Rosa Mexicano

1063 First Ave at 58th St (212-753-7407). Subway: N, R to Lexington Ave; 4, 5, 6 to 59th St. Mon–Sat 5–11pm; Sun 5–10pm. Average main course: $20. AmEx, DC, MC, V.

When Josefina Howard cooks Mexican food, the result isn't a collection of leaden dishes smothered in melted cheese but rather a mix of fresh, vibrant flavors that jump off the plate. Savor plump bay-scallop ceviche, or dig into a grilled filet mignon topped with sweet roasted chilies. Service is efficient, and the decor strikes a mix between sophisticated and classic Mexican festive. No matter what you do, just remember to order the guacamole: Prepared tableside in a black stone mortar, it'll make you forget just how far north of the border you really are.

Zarela

953 Second Ave between 50th and 51st Sts (212-644-6740). Subway: E, F to Lexington Ave; 6 to 51st St. Mon–Thu noon–3pm, 5–11pm; Fri noon–3pm, 5–11:30pm; Sat 5–11:30pm; Sun 5–10pm. Average main course: $14.95. AmEx, DC, MC, V.

Ebullient celebrity chef Zarela Martinez presides over a fine Mexican restaurant that sometimes feels like the site of a rowdy, postcollegiate mixer. Martinez's famously authentic dishes, such as her *manchamanteles de pato* (roast duck in a red chili mole sauce), can open you up to new culinary horizons. But the crowds, the waits (even with reservations) and the rushed service can try your patience. The upstairs dining room is marginally calmer than the bar and seating downstairs, but you should come prepared for a party atmosphere.

Zocalo

174 E 82nd St between Lexington and Third Aves (212-717-7772). Subway: 4, 5, 6 to 86th St. Sun–Thu 6–10:30pm; Fri, Sat 6–11:30pm. Average main course: $20. AmEx, DC, MC, V.

The tequila bar might tempt, but saunter through the chain of orange-walled rooms buzzing with waiters, because you'll soon experience some refreshingly authentic Mexican dining. Standbys like guacamole are good; even better are the seafood and steaks cooked as they would be south of the border: The filet mignon comes well seasoned on a large hash-brown–and–corn patty, which soaks up the steak-sauce drippings. But be careful with the good and strong margaritas…on second thought, after a few you may not mind the bill, which can add up quickly.

Seafood

Aquagrill

210 Spring St at Sixth Ave (212-274-0505). Subway: C, E to Spring St. Tue–Thu noon–3pm, 6–10:45pm; Fri noon–3pm, 6–11:45pm; Sat noon–4pm,

6–11:45pm; Sun noon–4pm, 6–10:30pm. Average main course: $20. AmEx, MC, V.
A standard in Soho's world of the raw and the booked, Aquagrill is distinguished by its extremely fresh aquatic fare. Order your fish all gussied up (e.g., falafel-crusted salmon), or if you'd rather keep it simple, the kitchen will steam, grill or roast any selection on the menu. In warmer weather, ask to sit on the sidewalk deck. Otherwise, belly up to the raw bar: Oysters, ranging from the briny to the creamy, are FedExed in daily from around the world.

Blue Water Grill

31 Union Sq West at 16th St (212-675-9500). Subway: N, R, L, 4, 5, 6 to 14th St–Union Sq. Sun–Thu 11:30am–midnight; Fri, Sat 5:30pm–1am. Average main course: $18. AmEx, MC, V.
Blue Water, white noise. This immense, marbled restaurant (housed in a former bank) appeals to a young, attractive clientele that comes trawling for seafood—but boy, can these babies blab. If the noise level doesn't derange you, you'll enjoy the wide choice of fresh oysters (20 varieties, from as far away as Chile and Japan) and imaginative fish entrées (porcini-crusted rare tuna, mahimahi with lobster mashed potatoes). The bar really hops just after work, and you'll be seen to good advantage in the flattering low light, which makes the space seem grand but not grandiose.

Estiatorio Milos

See page 148 for review.

Le Bernardin

See page 131 for review.

Oceana

55 E 54th St between Madison and Park Aves (212-759-5941). Subway: E, F to Fifth Ave. Mon–Sat noon–2:30pm, 5:30–10:30pm. Prix fixe: $65. AmEx, DC, Disc, MC, V.
Dining at Oceana feels like eating aboard a ship—but don't think Long John Silver or tacky nautical decor. Imagine being ensconced in the cool, dark dining room of a great ocean liner and being served incredible just-caught seafood. Appetizers on chef Rick Moonen's $65 prix-fixe menu include lovingly marinated fresh anchovies (served with charred nan bread) and grilled baby octopus; the entrées include roasted monkfish served with foie gras and a massive bouillabaisse. The crowd is pure midtown expense-account—but since the bill can be downright titanic, what do you expect?

The Oyster Bar and Restaurant

See page 134 for review.

Pearl Oyster Bar

18 Cornelia St between Bleecker and 4th Sts (212-691-8211). Subway: A, C, E, B, D, F, Q to W 4th St. Mon–Fri noon–2:30pm, 6–11pm; Sat 6–11pm. Average main course: $18. MC, V.
Not much bigger than a bucket of steamers, Pearl serves some of the most straightforward and irresistible seafood in the city. Sidle up to the bar (the place has only one table) and savor a meaty lobster roll, littlenecks on ice and a cold German pilsner. It's simple pleasures like these that make Pearl shine.

Trata

See page 149 for review.

Spanish

El Quijote

226 W 23rd St between Seventh and Eighth Aves (212-929-1855). Subway: C, E, 1, 9 to 23rd St. Sun–Thu noon–midnight; Fri, Sat noon–1am. Average main course: $17. AmEx, DC, Disc, MC, V.
There is an undeniable glamour at this restaurant-bar—one that evokes near-forgotten flings and a pre-Franco world. The giant cactus out front will give you a sense of what you're in for: overload. The bar is decorated with over-the-top Castilian bric-a-brac. Let one of the bow-tied "Mr. Pro"–type bartenders execute a crisp martini for you, then settle in at one of the tables for some straight-faced old-school Spanish cuisine. Endearingly serious uniformed waiters serve cut-rate lobster specials and huge platters of paella.

Rio Mar

7 Ninth Ave at Little West 12th St (212-243-9015). Subway: A, C, E to 14th St; L to Eighth Ave. Sun–Thu noon–2am; Fri, Sat noon–3am. Average main course: $11. AmEx.
You can keep your freaking bowl of pretzels. When it comes to complimentary bar snacks, the Meatpacking District's Rio Mar—a raucous Spanish roadhouse and font of on-the-house olive oil—is without peer. You get an onslaught of greasy tapas: Swim with the *pulpo* (octopus), spear a few slugs of chorizo, shovel up some sweet tortilla. Rio Mar's rustic, inelegant fare is perfect with a pitcher or two (or six) of fruity sangria.

The Tapas Lounge

1078 First Ave at 59th St (212-421-8282). Subway: 4, 5, 6 to 59th St; N, R to Lexington Ave. Sun–Tue 5pm–midnight; Wed–Sat 5pm–3am. Average main course: $17. Average tapa: $8. AmEx.
The Tapas Lounge's dusky lighting, knee-high tables and deep, plush couches—kind of Spanish farmhouse meets Madrid bordello—make for comfortable canoodling (no small part of the tapas experience). The *comidas,* like the *tortilla española* (potato omelette) deserve your attention too, though. The two-tapas-per-person rule is waived if you sit at the bar. The open windows can be charming… depending on the wind direction: Exhaust from the Queensboro Bridge traffic directly overhead can spoil a date.

Steak houses

Gallagher's Steak House

228 W 52nd St between Broadway and Eighth Ave (212-245-5336). Subway: C, E, 1, 9 to 50th St.

Second best? If you can't get a reservation at Nobu, try Next Door Nobu—it *is* just as good.

Noon–midnight. Average main course: $30. AmEx, DC, Disc, MC, V.
Relive the days of Damon Runyon at Gallagher's, New York's premier steak house for more than 70 years. Discriminating beefhounds are encouraged to choose their own cuts from the walk-in refrigerator; go for the gusto and claim your King Loin—a massive 30-ounce slab, firm yet tender. Then choose from six different types of spuds and slather 'em with the tangy house steak sauce. You can puff a postprandial cigar at the bar.

Michael Jordan's— The Steak House NYC

Grand Central Terminal, West Balcony, 23 Vanderbilt Ave at 43rd St (212-655-2300). Subway: S, 4, 5, 6, 7 to 42nd St–Grand Central. Mon–Sat noon–10:30pm; Sat noon–10:30pm. Average main course: $27. AmEx, DC, MC, V.
It's tempting to view Michael Jordan's as a high-end All-Star Cafe, but the fact is (as much as Knicks fans might hate to admit it), the restaurant serves some of the best steak-house grub in the city. Chef David Walzog teams his high-quality, dry-aged beef with inventive appetizers and sides like crusty, tangy mac and cheese and crisp garlic-bread logs stacked atop a pool of Gorgonzola fondue. You can't go wrong with the rib eye or porterhouse for two. The problem with Jordan's is that because it's on the wall-less northwest balcony of Grand Central's main concourse, you miss that steak-house clubbiness. Then again, you *are* sitting in one of NYC's most storied landmarks, staring up at a starry-sky ceiling.

Old Homestead

56 Ninth Ave between 14th and 15th Sts (212-242-9040). Subway: A, C, E to 14th St; L to Eighth Ave. Mon–Thu noon–10:30pm; Fri, Sat noon–11:30pm. Average main course: $24.50. AmEx, DC, MC, V.
First-rate cuisine is the priority at this dog-eared 1868 landmark. Steaks, aged for four weeks (and available for shipment), hang on view in a front cooler. Order the prime rib—lean beef, slow-roasted on the bone to create a juicy two-and-a-half-inch–thick slab that puts the fatty cuts most restaurants serve to shame. The waitstaff runs the gamut from pompous to solicitous, but with more than a century of practice, Old Homestead knows what it's doing.

Peter Luger

See page 135 for review.

Sparks

210 E 46th St between Second and Third Aves (212-687-4855). Subway: S, 4, 5, 6, 7 to 42nd St–Grand Central. Mon–Thu noon–3pm, 5:30–11pm; Fri noon–3pm, 5–11:30pm; Sat 5–11pm. Average main course: $25. AmEx, DC, Disc, MC, V.
So Big Paul Castellano never did get to ingest his last saturated fats here; he was gunned down on the sidewalk outside in 1985. But even before the mob-hit headlines, Sparks had customers lining up, drawn by a 30-year history of superb steaks and big family dinners. The vast 1930s setting features carved wood, beveled glass and gas lamps, not to mention the second-largest wine cellar in America (which includes plenty of Jeroboams). Waiters are happy to improvise a lavish, off-the-menu chopped salad—and what better warm-up for a black-and-blue (charred outside, cold inside) sirloin than with a salad thick with bacon and blue cheese?

Vegetarian

See **Indian** for more non-meat restaurants.

Angelica Kitchen

300 E 12th St between First and Second Aves (212-228-2909). Subway: L to First Ave; N, R, 4, 5, 6 to 14th St–Union Sq. 11:30am–10:30pm. Average main course: $8. Cash only.

Serving both '60s holdouts and hard-core healthy New Yorkers since the mid-'70s, Angelica offers guilt-free dining at its finest. No dairy, eggs, refined sugars, meats or preservatives violate the delicious daily specials, and much of the produce hits the table a mere 48 hours after being picked. Service can be chilly, but the overall ambience is warmer and less sterile than that of most vegetarian restaurants. Even die-hard carnivores have been known to dive into flavorful, filling dishes like the Dragon Bowl—a tower of steamed vegetables over rice.

B&H Dairy

127 Second Ave between 7th St and St. Marks Pl (212-505-8065). Subway: 6 to Astor Pl. 7am–10pm. Average main course: $5. Cash only.

God bless B&H just for being there. Bless it for its little Formica lunch counter, for its airy bricks of challah and for its hot, chunky borscht. The tiny storefront doesn't look like much from the outside—or from the inside, for that matter—but one visit should make you an instant regular. Reliable diner specials and frantic but familial service make B&H ideal for a quick, low-maintenance lunch. Meat isn't served at B&H, but the whitefish salad is so good, you won't miss it.

Herban Kitchen

290 Hudson St between Dominick and Spring Sts (212-627-2257). Subway: C, E to Spring St; 1, 9 to Houston St. Mon–Thu 11am–4pm, 5–11pm; Fri 11am–4pm, 5pm–midnight; Sat 5pm–midnight; Sun 4–11pm. Average main course: $15. AmEx, DC, Disc, MC, V.

The name is a bit silly, but Soho's Herban Kitchen offers sumptuous, healthy food without the dippy health-food–restaurant vibe that undermines other veggie joints—Herban actually has a romantic feel, complete with candles and strewn dried flowers. All Herban's ingredients are organic, and daily specials emphasize seasonal produce from local farms. The creative menu also includes fish, poultry and beef entrées, in case you're in the company of a meat eater.

Kate's Joint

58 Ave B between 4th and 5th Sts (212-777-7059). Subway: F to Second Ave. 9am–1am. Average main course: $8. AmEx, DC, Disc, MC, V.

A funky neighborhood hangout, Kate's Joint proves vegetarian doesn't have to be synonymous with virtuous. Pig out here on vegan/vegetarian versions of old-fashioned diner grub, like Southern-fried unchicken cutlets (but be prepared for surly diner service, too). Not to wreck your diet or anything, but the macaroni and (soy) cheese is remarkably creamy; the homemade cobbler delicious. And you can wash everything down with a standard selection of beers.

Strictly Roots

2058 Adam Clayton Powell Jr. Blvd between 122nd and 123rd Sts (212-864-8699). Subway: 2, 3 to 125th St. Mon–Sat 11am–9pm. Average main course: $6. AmEx, DC, Disc, MC, V.

This Harlem diner serves "nothing that crawls, swims, walks or flies." Delicious food—such as the mock-beef stew—make it worth the visit. Don't miss the frothy shakes with names like Bad Man, served by friendly Rasta dudes.

Zen Palate

34 Union Sq East at 16th St (212-614-9291). Subway: N, R, L, 4, 5, 6 to 14th St–Union Sq. Mon–Thu 11am–11pm; Fri, Sat 11am–midnight; Sun noon–10:30pm. Average main course: $15. AmEx, DC, MC, V.

More sensuous than sanctimonious, Zen Palate treats your eyes and your stomach well. Relax in the serene upstairs dining room and savor innovative dishes such as the Red Mist (bean crêpe filled with soy protein and mushrooms, wrapped in seaweed and topped with a spicy red-pepper sauce). Equally good but cheaper and simpler food is served at the downstairs snack bar and at sidewalk tables. Beware the pretheater rush at the midtown location.

Other locations: *663 Ninth Ave at 46th St (212-582-1669); 2170 Broadway between 76th and 77th Sts (212-501-7768).*

Cheap Eats

Sometimes, you don't get what you pay for—you get a hell of a lot more. And it's even true in New York City, where, if you know where to go, you can taste-test everything from authentic shwarma and Peruvian *pollo* to thick hand-formed burgers—each for less than $10. You and your wallet will love what you find. (Each of the following have main courses or the equivalent of $10 or less—many more cheap eats are in the **By Cuisine** listings starting on page 138.)

Amarin Cafe

617 Manhattan Ave between Driggs and Nassau Sts, Williamsburg, Brooklyn (718-349-2788). Subway: G to Metropolitan Ave; L to Lorimer St. Sun–Thu 11am–10:30pm; Fri, Sat 11am–11pm. Average main course: $6.50. Cash only.

Amarin's bland decor—beige and Formica everything—is probably an asset; if the atmosphere were half as enticing as the food, you'd never get a table. Munch on piquant green-papaya salad and light, fresh vegetarian pad thai—all of which seem to have been airlifted in straight from the Gulf of Thailand.

Necessities

Corner Bistro

331 W 4th St at Jane St (212-242-9502). Subway: A, C, E to 14th St; L to Eighth Ave. 11:30am–4am. Average burger: $4. Cash only.

No wonder the crowds keep coming back to this smoky tavern seven nights a week—the jaw-stretching Bistro Burger is one of the tastiest and messiest things you'll ever wrap your hands around. Eight ounces of flame-broiled ground chuck are topped with gooey American cheese, a tangle of crisp bacon and a thick round of raw onion and served on a tiny paper plate. The best time to savor your burger in peace is mid-afternoon, when streams of sunlight cut through the dust.

Cosí Sandwich Bar

Paramount Plaza, 1633 Broadway at 51st St (212-397-2674). Subway: N, R to 49th St; 1, 9 to 50th St. Mon–Thu 7am–10pm; Fri 7am–9pm; Sat noon–5pm; Sun noon–6pm. Average sandwich: $7. AmEx, DC, MC, V.

In the perfect sandwich, it's not just the filling that matters, but also the bread. At Cosí, a sporty, Parisian-inspired chain that's multiplying faster than a calculator, dough receives royal treatment. Brick ovens produce warm and tasty flatbread that's sprinkled with salt crystals and then split open, releasing a cloud of aromatic steam. What gets stuffed inside is up to you: Join the throngs in line and tell the deft counterpeople to insert smoked ham, marinated mushrooms, roasted peppers, pesto chicken—you name it. Check the phone book for other locations.

Ecco-La

1660 Third Ave at 93rd St (212-860-5609). Subway: 6 to 96th St. Noon–11:30pm. Average main course: $9. AmEx, MC, V.

The first room at Ecco-La is cheerful, noisy and boldly colorful; the second is quiet and decorated with gilt-framed pictures and upholstered chairs. Choose your room according to your mood and enjoy the simple menu, which offers endless variations of pastas and sauces, most for under $10.

Flor de Mayo

2651 Broadway between 100th and 101st Sts (212-663-5520). Subway: 1, 9 to 103rd St. Noon–midnight. Average main course: $8. AmEx, DC, MC, V.

Restaurants serving Chinese and Spanish food are a plentiful half-breed in New York. What sets Flor de Mayo apart from its Chino-Latino peers is a moist and flavorful Peruvian roasted chicken: You won't find a better bird in town. Get a side of rice and garbanzo beans and you won't find a better meal—for the price.

Havana Chelsea

188 Eighth Ave between 19th and 20th Sts (212-243-9421). Subway: C, E to 23rd St. Mon–Sat 8am–10:30pm; Sun noon–9:30pm. Average main course: $7. Cash only.

This narrow, hole-in-the-wall Cuban diner has a big heart. Contented, chatty customers, many of them *Cubanos,* line the Formica counter and huddle around the flimsy, speckled tables. The delicious sandwiches come in big, bigger and biggest and are perfect for take-out. But for the full experience, order a hot meal such as the *ropa vieja,* shredded beef in a tangy tomato sauce (it's not on the menu, but ask

Curry favor Score points for choosing to eat Indian food at Jackson Diner in Queens.

for it) or the gargantuan order of roast chicken. Entrées come with beans and pillowy yellow rice scooped out of funky stainless steel heating drawers. The service here tends toward the laid-back, so settle in, amuse yourself with the place mats featuring dated, right-wing facts about Cuba, and sip on a tropical *batido* (shake), a smooth, viscous concoction made with condensed milk.

Mama's Food Shop

200 E 3rd St between Aves A and B (212-777-4425). Subway: F to Second Ave. Mon–Sat 11am–10:30pm. Average main course: $7. Cash only.
Mama's was the first nostalgia-food joint to spring up in the East Village. In 1999, Mama's gave birth to Stepmama (a grill across the street) and Mama's Milk (a smoothie/coffee bar next door). If you're yearning for milky whipped spuds and chunky meat loaf, Mama's serves them in generous portions.

Mamoun's Falafel

119 MacDougal St between Bleecker and 3rd Sts (212-674-8685). Subway: A, C, E, B, D, F, Q to W 4th St. 10am–5am. Average falafel: $2.50. Cash only.
Good Middle Eastern eateries abound in New York, but if you're near MacDougal Street, the clear choice is Mamoun's. The location is as narrow and dark as a root cellar, and there's always a line, but the spicy, crispy falafel heaped with tomatoes, lettuce and tahini would be worth the wait at twice the price. Mamoun's, which is actually Syrian, is also one of the few places that has real shwarma (spit-roasted layers of marinated lamb) instead of the oversize-hot-dog-on-a-spike known as a gyro.

Margon

136 W 46th St between Sixth and Seventh Aves (212-354-5013). Subway: B, D, F, Q to 47–50th Sts–Rockefeller Ctr. Mon–Fri 7am–4:45pm; Sat 7am–2pm. Average main course: $6. Cash only.
This crowded Cuban lunch counter offers much-needed deliverance from the usual midtown lunch hustle. Line up for Cuban sandwiches, octopus salad, tripe and pig's feet, or soft beef pot roast—all served with great amounts of beans (black or red) and rice. Sharing tables with strangers is encouraged, as long as you don't hog the hot sauce.

Nha Trang

87 Baxter St between White and Walker Sts (212-233-5998, 212-962-9149). Subway: J, M, Z, N, R, 6 to Canal St. 10am–10pm. Average main course: $6. Cash only.
The cafeterialike setting may not be much to look at, but Nha Trang makes some of the most compelling Vietnamese food in New York. It's not exactly an experience to linger over—the efficient waitstaff serves your table faster than you can say "Pho"—but that means dishes like the addictive fried spring rolls arrive steaming hot. The *canh chua tom* (Saigon-style hot-and-sour soup) is a can't-miss.

Pepe Rosso to Go

149 Sullivan St between Prince and Houston Sts (212-677-4555). Subway: C, E to Spring St. 11am–11pm. Average main course: $8. Cash only.
This quartet of stripped-down eateries serves the kind of simple and utterly satisfying Italian food that should be easy to find but never is. At the tiny Sullivan Street location, you'll have to fight for what few seats there are, and be prepared for brusque, harried service from the young Italian counter guys. To quote the budding chainlet's motto: No Diet Coke, no decaf coffee, no skim milk—just good food.
Other locations: *Pepe Giallo to Go, 253 Tenth Ave between 24th and 25th Sts (212-242-6055); Pepe Rosso, 110 St. Marks Pl between First Ave and Ave A (212-677-6563); Pepe Verde, 559 Hudson St between Perry and 11th Sts (212-255-2221).*

Pommes Frites

123 Second Ave between 7th St and St. Marks Pl (212-674-1234). Subway: 6 to Astor Pl. Sun–Thu 11:30am–midnight; Fri, Sat 11:30am–1am. Regular fries: $2.50. Cash only.
It's only fitting that this grungy closet—and not some hotshot restaurateur—sparked New York City's obsession with authentic Belgian frites. The squat fries are hand-cut, plunged into a deep-fryer (twice) and served with ketchup or about 30 mayo-based toppings. The frites remain the perfect tonic to a night out in the East Village.

Radio Perfecto

See page 139 for review.

Sugar Shack

2611 Frederick Douglass Blvd at 139th St (212-491-4422). Subway: B, C to 135th St. Tue–Thu 5–11pm; Fri, Sat 11am–1am; Sun 11am–5pm. Average main course: $10. AmEx, MC, V.
Have the tour-bus crowds at Sylvia's put you off? Do you ache for a more chilled-out soul-food experience? Saunter up to Sugar Shack, where the food is pure American goodness, and the plush red couches, beautiful artwork, glamorous waitresses and low lighting befit the elegant Strivers' Row neighborhood. Will it be chicken and waffles or the herb-and-spice–smothered chicken? Leave room for the sweet-potato–pecan pie; you won't find it like this south of 125th Street.

Cafés

Amy's Bread

672 Ninth Ave between 46th and 47th Sts (212-977-2670). Subway: C, E to 50th St. Mon–Fri 7:30am–7pm; Sat 8am–6pm; Sun 9am–4pm. Average sandwich: $4.50. Cash only.
Serious bread heads know Amy's for its astounding loaves, rounds and rolls. Amy also transforms the lowly sandwich. For example, the humble grilled-cheese sandwich morphs into cheddar on country sourdough with tomato, cilantro and spicy

chipotle pepper sauce. For dessert, grab one of the heavenly brownies.

Other location: *Inside Chelsea Market, 75 Ninth Ave between 15th and 16th Sts.*

Cafe Gitane

242 Mott St at Prince St (212-334-9552). Subway: N, R to Prince St; 6 to Spring St. 9am–midnight. Average main course: $7.50. AmEx, MC, V.

Across from old St. Patrick's Cathedral on a tree-lined strip of Mott Street, Cafe Gitane is a key feature of gentrified Nolita's hipster landscape. Downtown Francophones fill the air with smoke, breeze through *Paris Match* and sip powerful coffee at all hours. (For a caffeine jolt, guzzle a turbo-charged Americano.) Most people come here to socialize, but the café does offer a small menu of Mediterranean dishes, such as grilled chicken atop couscous. The waitstaff is slow, but it doesn't really matter, since Gitane so perfectly captures that Parisian café lounge-and-look feel.

Ceci-Cela

55 Spring St between Lafayette and Mulberry Sts (212-274-9179). Subway: 6 to Spring St. Mon–Fri 7am–7pm; Sat 8am–7pm; Sun 9am–7pm. Pain au chocolat: $1.95. Cash only.

Tucked into a narrow space that's barely visible amid Spring Street's ever-increasing bustle, Ceci-Cela offers luscious daily-made pastries in a funky, relaxed setting. Line up for the flaky *pain au chocolat* (simply the best in town), exquisite fresh-berry tarts, and rich mini éclairs.

City Bakery

22 E 17th St between Fifth Ave and Broadway (212-366-1414). Subway: N, R, L, 4, 5, 6 to 14th St–Union Sq. Mon–Sat 7:30am–6pm. Average sandwich: $5.75. AmEx, Disc, MC, V.

What to pillage first? The succulent salad bar full of Union Square Greenmarket goodies or the seductive sweets counter? City Bakery has the take-out (or eat-in) foods of your dreams: cosmopolitan sandwiches and soups, salads, legendary lemonade and hot chocolate, and a lemon tart that one-ups the French.

Drip

489 Amsterdam Ave at 83rd St (212-875-1032). Subway: B, C to 81st St; 1, 9 to 79th St. Mon–Fri 9pm–1am; Sat, Sun 9pm–3am. Average drink: $6. MC, V.

Containers of Cheez Whiz and other American food classics salute you from the walls of this *Jetsons*-esque coffee bar/bar/dating service. Dating service? Yup, for $10 you can fill out a form that is stored in one of the many folders scattered around the room. Although light fare is available (chocolate cake, lemon bars, sandwiches), the drinks—alcoholic and non—are what float this lounge. Long Island iced tea is served in a mason jar and the Cap'n Crunch milk shake may keep you on the wagon.

Hungarian Pastry Shop

1030 Amsterdam Ave at 111th St (212-866-4230). Subway: B, C, 1, 9 to 110th St–Cathedral Pkwy. Mon–Fri 8am–11:30pm; Sat 8:30am–11:30pm; Sun 8:30am–10pm. Average pastry: $2. Cash only.

A Morningside Heights original, this plain-looking coffee shop offers coffee, tea and pastries (made in-house) to Columbia University students and teachers, and other locals. Ignore the pretentious coeds at the next table pretending to study Kant and pull out that Jackie Collins novel you've been dying to read.

'Ino

21 Bedford St between Sixth Ave and Downing St (212-989-5769). Subway: 1, 9 to Houston St. Mon–Fri 8am–2am; Sat, Sun 11am–2am. Average sandwich: $6.50. Cash only.

Next time you're at Film Forum, skip the concessions; around the corner on Bedford Street, 'Ino offers inspired Italian snacks for the price of a medium popcorn. Modeled after a bruschetteria the owners visited in Italy, 'Ino's wooden, amber-lit interior is made for basic pleasures like grazing and wine-sipping. The selection of bruschettas ($2) changes daily, but expect toppings like fontina, olive pesto and sweet onion. 'Ino also offers pressed sandwiches and about 20 wines (all available by the half carafe, and most by the glass).

L-Cafe

187–189 Bedford Ave between North 6th and North 7th Sts, Williamsburg, Brooklyn (718-388-6792). Subway: L to Bedford Ave. Mon–Fri 9am–midnight; Sat, Sun 10am–midnight; take-out Mon–Fri 7am–8pm; Sat, Sun 9am–8pm. Average main course: $7. AmEx, MC, V.

It used to be that finding a table at Williamsburg's L-Cafe was as fruitless an endeavor as pushing through the crowd at CBGB. But since expanding in 1999, it's easier to pop in for breakfast, lunch or dinner. Everything on the menu is affordable and tasty, from Scotch eggs to the four-cheese baked macaroni.

Le Gamin Café

1 Main St at the East River, Dumbo, Brooklyn (718-722-2979). Subway: F to York St. Sun–Tue 8am–6pm; Wed–Sat 8am–10:30pm. Average main course: $7. Cash only.

Located just a few steps from the East River, the newest Le Gamin offers the chainlet's familiar menu of crêpes, sandwiches and salads in an enormous split-level space—big enough to house all the bohos in Dumbo—plus, live music during weekend brunch. There's a Gamin in almost every artsy neighborhood in Manhattan; the tiny Soho spot was the first. The Chelsea branch, which is a more comfortable size, attracts many stylish types from the nearby London Towers apartment complex. Francophiles *de l'est* can take refuge at the one in the East Village. However, the West Village gets the full-service kitchen of **Les Deux Gamins** (*see page 147*).

Other locations: *50 MacDougal St between Prince and Houston Sts (212-254-4678); 183 Ninth Ave at 21st St (212-243-8864); 536 E 5th St between Aves A and B (212-254-8409).*

Once Upon a Tart

135 Sullivan St between Prince and Houston Sts (212-387-8869). Subway: C, E to Spring St. Mon–Fri 8am–8pm; Sat 9am–8pm; Sun 9am–6pm. Average sandwich: $6. AmEx, DC, Disc, MC, V.

What's in a name? At this tiny Soho café, it's more than just tasty vegetable tarts (eight variations in all). Soups, salads and sandwiches—along with freshly baked desserts: macaroons, cookies, brownies and, of course, fruit tarts—make this an ideal place to rest during a Soho shopping binge.

Palacinka

28 Grand St between Thompson St and Sixth Ave (212-625-0362). Subway: C, E to Spring St. 10am–midnight. Average crêpe: $6.50. Cash only.

More European than Eurotrash, this boho-chic café on the edge of Soho seduces stray shoppers with its 1930s general-store vibe and its wonderful crêpes. You'll find the best of various crêpe traditions—French, Italian and the oft-overlooked Yugoslavian—in the tasty repertoire. And the name? Palacinka (pal-uh-CHIN-ka) is a dessert crêpe served in the Balkans.

Tea & Sympathy

108–110 Greenwich Ave between 12th and 13th Sts (212-989-9735). Subway: F, 1, 2, 3, 9 to 14th St; L to Sixth Ave. 11:30am–10:30pm. Average main course: $10.50. Cash only.

Once upon a time, English tea parlors welcomed only proper pinky pointers. At this teensy West Village fixture, you'll spot sippers of all stripes. In what feels like an oversize dollhouse, grown-up tea partyers pour jasmine from whimsical pots whilst the charmingly chipper waitstaff spoils them with scones and clotted cream. But you can also get dainty finger sandwiches and manly English dishes like shepherd's pie and bangers and mash.

No burritos Rosa Mexicano's *cocina* is *alto.*

Delis

Artie's Delicatessen

2290 Broadway between 83rd and 84th Sts (212-579-5959). Subway: 1, 9 to 86th St. Mon–Thu 11am–midnight; Fri 11am–1am; Sat, Sun 9:30am–1am. Average sandwich: $6.95. AmEx, MC, V.

A new old-fashioned eatery? That's Artie's—it opened at the end of 1999, but has the trappings of a traditional deli: hanging salamis, overstuffed sandwiches and a hot dog grill. The pastrami, made from a recipe bought at auction from an old Lower East Side eatery called Schmulke Bernstein, is the main attraction, along with silky chicken soup with a matzo ball as big as a softball.

Carnegie Deli

854 Seventh Ave at 55th St (212-757-2245). Subway: N, R to 57th St. 6:30am–4am. Minimum: $12.50 per person. Cash only.

Consider the Carnegie Deli Reuben: a football-helmet–size dome of molten Swiss cheese, sauerkraut, pastrami and (somewhere within this mass) a couple slices of rye. Such is the norm at New York's most famous deli, where crusty waiters and walls of celebrity eight-by-tens create the ambience. Better pastrami, hot dogs and knishes can be had downtown at Katz's or Second Avenue Deli, but for price (the Reuben costs $17.95) and sheer size (all of Carnegie's sandwiches are comically large), this Theater District legend stands alone.

Ess-a-Bagel

359 First Ave at 21st St (212-260-2252). Subway: 6 to 23rd St. Mon–Fri 6am–10pm; Sat, Sun 7am–5pm. Plain bagel: 60¢. AmEx, DC, Disc, MC, V.

Let's talk about the ideal bagel: It should be big as a salad plate, have a crust that's a little chewy but still breakable and have no—or almost no—space in the hole. The fat-fingered guys making dumb jokes behind the counter at Ess-a-Bagel's original downtown location serve such a bagel. It is perfection at 60 cents a pop (if you get it stuffed with smoked-whitefish salad, tomatoes and red onions, it's $4.15). Large chandeliers, faux-wood paneling and a gurgling cauldron of boiling bagels add to the downtown ambience, but the pudgy, doughy rings are just as good at the midtown location.

Other location: *831 Third Ave between 50th and 51st Sts (212-980-1010).*

Katz's Delicatessen

205 E Houston St at Ludlow St (212-254-2246). Subway: F to Second Ave. Sun–Tue 8am–10pm; Wed, Thu 8am–11pm; Fri, Sat 8am–3am. Pastrami sandwich: $7.95. AmEx, MC, V (catering and shipping only).

This venerable, cafeteria-style New York deli, immortalized in *When Harry Met Sally…*, stands at the invisible portal of the Lower East Side. Other than the fact that there aren't too many Jewish guys working here anymore, the lunch hall, with its hanging salamis and scores of autographed photos, looks like it hasn't changed in 50 years. Grab a meal ticket at the door and stride up to the mile-long counter, where gifted surgeons slice open blackened hunks of pastrami. Katz's also has the city's best hot dog (crispy on the outside, juicy and tangy within). Wash it all down with an egg cream—an old-fashioned drink with a misleading name—or a bottle of Katz's own brews (pilsner, lager and pale ale).

Second Avenue Deli

156 Second Ave at 10th St (212-677-0606). Subway: L to Third Ave; 6 to Astor Pl. Sun–Thu 7am–midnight; Fri, Sat 7am–3am. Average main course: $12. AmEx, DC, Disc, MC, V.

Even after a makeover by hotshot designer Adam Tihany, this warhorse still looks pretty much like a deli. One major change: The second room, off to the right, is now a photo-filled shrine to legendary Yiddish actress Molly Picon (you might remember her as Roger Moore's meddling mom in *The Cannonball Run*). You're not going to find a better brisket sandwich in town, or better kishkes, matzo ball soup, chopped liver and so on and so forth. The crowds, especially on weekends, testify to the quality of the food. Posters on the door remind patrons that the 1996 murder of owner Abe Lebewohl remains unsolved. Drink a Dr. Brown's Cel-Ray soda, the time-honored celery-flavored tonic, in his honor.

Diners

Cheyenne Diner

411 Ninth Ave at 33rd St (212-465-8750). Subway: A, C, E to 34th St–Penn Station. 24hrs. Average main course: $7. AmEx, DC, Disc, MC, V.

Cheyenne is the kind of place that cigarette-ad location scouts would give a lung for—and locals feel lucky it remains on Manhattan soil: a silver-sided, pink-neon–signed breadbox of a diner. Brunch specials come with juice, fruit salad, coffee and megacaloric helpings of eggs and meat. Enjoy the indulgence, the gunmetal-gray housing and the delightfully crappy view of Ninth Avenue.

Comfort Diner

214 E 45th St between Second and Third Aves (212-867-4555). Subway: S, 4, 5, 6, 7 to 42nd St–Grand Central. Mon–Fri 7am–11pm; Sat 9am–11pm. Average main course: $9. AmEx, DC, Disc, MC, V.

At Manhattan's Comfort Diners, you'll find cushy vinyl booths, chrome siding and a smattering of good old American knickknacks. Still, don't expect some shoddy '50s-style theme restaurant. Comfort's kitchens crank out crackling-good fried chicken, excellent moist meat loaf and thick milk shakes. The Upper East Side location also has a bar—which means you can enjoy a Bloody Mary at brunch with those buttermilk pancakes and bacon.

Other location: *142 E 86th St at Lexington Ave (212-369-8628).*

Boyish charm Le Gamin tempts you to hang around for hours, Paris-style.

Empire Diner

210 Tenth Ave at 22nd St (212-243-2736). Subway: C, E to 23rd St. 24hrs. Average main course: $12. AmEx, DC, Disc, MC, V.

This West Chelsea all-nighter is the essence of preserved Americana, with no sign of peeling chrome. Come at night, when the place glows, to sample above-average diner fare. At 3am, everything tastes fine and a little illicit. It's a shame the rest of the city isn't like this—as shiny and as edgily smooth as early Tom Waits.

M&G Soul Food Diner

383 W 125th St at Morningside Ave (212-864-7326). Subway: A, C, B, D to 125th St. 8:30am–11:30pm. Average main course: $8. Cash only.

M&G's fried chicken, which is served with a stack of fluffy pancakes, is almost more crust than meat—and that's a good thing. The deeply seasoned, hot-and-crispy coating is excellent, and it makes a perfect foil to the sweet syrup drizzled over the flapjacks. The feel of M&G is equally appealing: faux-wood paneling, a Formica-topped lunch counter, a few tiny tables—and a hair net–wearing staff whose Richard Roundtree cool is matched only by that of the jukebox, stocked with the likes of Curtis Mayfield and Barry White.

Tom's Restaurant

782 Washington Ave between John St and Sterling Pls, Prospect Heights, Brooklyn (718-636-9738). Subway: 2, 3 to Eastern Pkwy–Brooklyn Museum. Mon–Sat 6:30am–4pm. Average main course: $7.50. Cash only.

In April 1968, Martin Luther King Jr. was assassinated, and Washington Avenue, on the border of Prospect Park and Crown Heights erupted into riots. "It was about 5 o'clock when it all broke loose," remembers Gus Vlahavas, the owner of Tom's, which has been around since 1937. "All these neighborhood people were holding hands in a line so nobody could touch the restaurant." What compelled locals to protect Tom's? It could have been the food—breakfasts of crab cakes, eggs and grits; overstuffed club sandwiches; classic meat loaf and the rare house special, lime rickeys. It also could have been the rock-bottom prices. But it was probably devotion to the Vlahavas family that forged the human chain. FYI, Suzanne Vega says this is the hangout that inspired her to write "Tom's Diner."

Restaurants by neighborhood

Financial District
Wild Blue, page 139
Windows on the World, page 136

Tribeca
Bouley Bakery, page 129
Danube, page 129
Grace, page 134
Next Door Nobu, page 133
Nobu, page 133
Obeca Li, page 142
Odeon, page 138

Lower East Side
Katz's Delicatessen, page 161
Sammy's Roumanian, page 153
71 Clinton Fresh Food, page 138

Chinatown–Little Italy
Canton, page 141
Joe's Shanghai, page 141
Lombardi's, page 152
Nha Trang, page 159
Nyonya, page 143
Pho Bang, page 144
Sweet-n-Tart Café, page 142

Soho
Alison on Dominick Street, page 145
Aquagrill, page 155
Balthazar, page 136
Blue Ribbon, page 139
Blue Ribbon Sushi, page 142
Café Gitane, page 160
Canteen, page 136
Ceci-Cela, page 160
Herban Kitchen, page 157
Ghenet, page 145
Honmura An, page 142
Jean Claude, page 146
Kelley and Ping, page 143
Le Gamin Café, page 160
Lupe's East L.A. Kitchen, page 154
Mercer Kitchen, page 131
Omen, page 143
Once Upon a Tart, page 161
Palacinka, page 161
Pepe Rosso to Go, page 159
Provence, page 148
Raoul's, page 138
Shanghai Tang, page 142

Noho
Bond St, page 136
Five Points, page 140
Great Jones Café, page 140

East Village
Angelica Kitchen, page 157
B&H Dairy, page 157
Casimir, page 146
Cyclo, page 145
Dok Suni's, page 137
The Elephant, page 144
Esperanto, page 153
First, page 138
Frank, page 151
Holy Basil, page 144
Il Bagatto, page 151
Jeollado, page 143
Jules Bistro, page 147
Kate's Joint, page 157
La Focacceria, page 151
Le Gamin Café, page 160
Lucien, page 148
Mama's Food Shop, page 159
Pepe Rosso, page 159
Pomme Frites, page 159
Radio Perfecto, page 139
Sandobe Sushi, page 143
Second Avenue Deli, page 162
Tasting Room, page 134
Two Boots Restaurant, page 152
Veselka, page 145

Greenwich Village
Babbo, page 129
Café Spice, page 149
Clementine, page 137
Da Silvano, page 137
Gotham Bar and Grill, page 138
Lupa, page 151
Mamoun's Falafel, page 159
Yama–Houston, page 143

West Village
Blue Ribbon Bakery, page 139
Corner Bistro, page 158
DoHwa, page 137
Florent, page 137
Hog Pit Barbecue NYC, page 141
'Ino, page 160
Isla, page 137
Junno's, page 134
Les Deux Gamins, page 147
Little Basil, page 144
Pastis, page 138
Pearl Oyster Bar, page 155
Pepe Verde, page 159
Pink Tea Cup, page 141
Pó, page 152
Rio Mar, page 155
Tea & Sympathy, page 161
Thali, page 150
Yama, page 143

Chelsea
Amy's Bread, page 159
El Quijote, page 155
Empire Diner, page 162
Havana Chelsea, page 158
Le Madri, page 151
Le Gamin Café, page 160
Markt, page 137
Old Homestead, page 156
Pepe Giallo to Go, page 159
Periyali, page 149

Gramercy–Flatiron
Blue Water Grill, page 155
City Bakery, page 160
Ess-a-Bagel, page 161
Chicama, page 153
Gramercy Tavern, page 140
Mesa Grill, page 133
Pongal, page 150
Republic, page 144
Tabla, page 150
Veritas, page 140
Yama, page 143
Zen Palate, page 157

Midtown East
An American Place, page 129
Comfort Diner, page 162
Ess-a-Bagel, page 161
Felidia, page 131
Fifty Seven Fifty Seven, page 131
Four Seasons, page 134
Guastavino's, page 137
L'Actuel, page 135
March, page 133
Métrazur, page 134
Michael Jordan's—The Steak House NYC, page 156
Oceana, page 155
Oikawa, page 142
The Oyster Bar and Restaurant, page 134
Rain East, page 144
Rosa Mexicano, page 154
Shun Lee Palace, page 142
Sparks, page 156
The Tapas Lounge, 155
Vong, page 131
Wolf & Lamb, page 153
Zarela, page 154

Midtown West
Amy's Bread, page 159
Aquavit, page 129
Beacon, page 138
Carmine's, page 151
Carnegie Deli, page 161
Cheyenne Diner, page 162
Chimichurri Grill, page 153
Cosí Sandwich Bar, page 158
Estiatorio Milos, page 148
Firebird, page 145
Gallagher's Steak House, page 156
Ipanema, page 154
Le Bernardin, page 131
Margon, page 159
Molyvos, page 149
Osteria al Doge, page 152
Rainbow Grill, page 135
Ruby Foo's, page 144
Russian Samovar, page 145
Russian Tea Room, page 135
Thalia, page 134
Trattoria dell'Arte, page 152
'21', page 133
Victor's Café 52, page 154
Virgil's Real BBQ, page 141
Zen Palate, page 157

Upper West Side
Artie's Delicatessen, page 161
Avenue, page 139
Ayurveda Cafe, page 149
Carmine's, page 151
The Cottage, page 141
Drip, page 160
Flor de Mayo, page 158
Hungarian Pastry Shop, page 160
Jean Georges, page 131
Joe's Shanghai, page 141
Penang, page 143
Rain, page 144
Ruby Foo's, page 144
Shun Lee, page 142
Tavern on the Green, page 136
Zen Palate, page 157

Upper East Side
Café Boulud, page 129
Comfort Diner, page 162
Daniel, page 129
Ecco-La, page 158
Elaine's, page 133
El Pollo, page 153
Jo-Jo, page 131
La Forêt, page 147
Park View at the Boathouse, page 140
Payard Patisserie & Bistro, page 148
Penang, page 143
Rain East, page 144
Tapería Madrid, page 135
Totonno Pizzeria Napolitano, page 152
Trata, page 149
Zocalo, page 154

Above 116th St
Andy's Colonial, page 151
Charles' Southern Style Kitchen, page 140
M&G Soul Food Diner, page 162
Patsy's Pizzeria, page 152
Strictly Roots, page 157
Sugar Shack, page 159
Sylvia's, page 141

Brooklyn
See also **Manhattan transfers,** *page 146*
al di là, page 150
Amarin Cafe, page 157
Bamonte's, page 151
Coco Roco, page 153
L-Cafe, page 160
Le Gamin Café, page 160
Max & Moritz, page 148
Patois, page 148
Peter Luger, page 135
Rasputin, page 145
River Café, page 140
Tom's Restaurant, page 162
Totonno Pizzeria Napolitano, page 152

Queens
Elias Corner, page 148
Jackson Diner, page 149
Joe's Shanghai, page 141
Penang, page 143
Sweet-n-Tart Cafe, page 142

The Bronx
Jimmy's Bronx Café, page 154

Necessities

Shopping & Services

These merchants can fulfill all of your basic needs (and a few more)

People may say they come to New York for the museums and the cultural highs, but deep down, they're really here for the shopping. After all, New York is the shopping capital of the world (especially now that the sales tax on clothing applies only to items costing more than $110!). Some visitors come for the city's gargantuan department stores; others for the high fashion and still others for cheap Levi's and good deals on electronics. Regardless of your agenda, as you're making your way through the myriad options, it helps to think like a New Yorker. If an object catches your eye, keep in mind that you don't have to buy it. Simply put it on hold and come back when the time is right. Or do what many locals do—buy the item to possibly return it later. Just be sure to check store policy, because some will only give credit toward a new purchase. So, on your mark, get set, spend!

SHOP TILL YOU DROP

New Yorkers are the smartest kind of shoppers: They wait for end-of-season discounts, shop at discount emporiums such as Daffy's, TJ Maxx and Century 21, and sneak off to sample sales during lunch hour. What do they know that you don't? Department stores usually hold sales at the end of seasons; August and February are the best months. The post-Christmas reductions tend to occur earlier in December than they used to, but most shopkeepers think all holidays (Fourth of July, Easter, Labor Day, etc.) are good excuses for a sale.

▶ Designers' sample sales are some of the best sources of low-priced chic clothes. For information about who's selling where, see ***Time Out New York***'s Check Out section.

▶ You can also get the ***S&B Report*** ($10 per issue; 877-579-0222, www.lazarshopping.com). Or call the **SSS Sample Sales** hotline (212-947-8748).

Necessities

What's my line? The season's hottest designs are on the Co-op floor of Barneys New York.

NTRY-ROCK STAR JOANNA
ACKS PREGNANT WOMAN
DIESEL
FOR SUCCESSFUL LIVING
Is this only the beginning of
The Luxury of Dirt Terror?
by KEITH REINHARD
Country-rock star Joanne, who reached number one on the world's country-rock charts with "Dirty Country Girl " last summer, has had a remarkable career. Her new CD "The Luxury of Dirt" has been climbing the charts rapidly. But everything seems to be falling to pieces. IT'S REAL has the full story. Wednesday night as Joanna was trying to enter the club The Twitty Twit, she was denied entry. "She was wearing dirty clothes", the bouncer Mikey Bündefeldt explains. According to anonymous witnesses, Joanna then argued that dirt has become a luxury in this shiny, flashy world.
Joanna then raised her right hand as if she was about to hit the bouncer who then professionally avoided the assault which caused Joanna to fall. In her fall she violently grabbed another woman who was queuing for the club which caused them both to fall. The innocent woman who, it appeared, could have been pregnant, had to seek medical advice the following morning, a spokesman from the lawfirm Suit & Case told It's Real.
o one is going
to talk dirty to me"
says victim
bouncer Mikey.
Inside report: by BOB SCARPELLI
"Joanna laughed and said her dirty jeans were a luxury, but I've been working the door for 5 years and noone is going to talk dirty to me", Mikey Bündefeldt, the bouncer at the club The Twitty Twit says and you know he's honest about it.
Get the full
story in your own
free copy of It's Real!
At your local Diesel dealer
or at www.diesel.com
IT'S REAL
TOMORROW'S TRUTH TODAY
Number 105 in a series of Diesel "How to..." guides to successful living. For more information: call Diesel Headquarters 212 755 9200 www.diesel.com This advertisement is pure fiction. The characters, names, incidents, dialogue and plot are used fictitiously. Any resemblance to actual persons or companies is purely coincidental.
DIESEL STORES: 60TH STREET @ LEXINGTON AVE 212 308-0055

Farhi and wide Nicole Farhi brings British style to New York at her 60th Street shop.

Downtown shops stay open an hour or two later than those uptown (they open later in the morning, too). Thursday is the universal—though unofficial—shop-after-work night; most stores are open till 7pm, if not later.

Keep in mind that certain stores listed below have multiple locations. If a shop has more than two branches, we'll tell you to check the business pages in the phone book for other addresses.

▶ **Fashion,** starting below, includes everything from "Downtown boutiques" to places that are "Strictly for men."

▶ **Fashion Services,** page 188, lists shoe repair places, dry cleaners, etc.

▶ **Accessories,** page 190, includes shops devoted to selling hats, jewelry and the like.

▶ **Health & Beauty,** page 195, lists our recommended places to get good haircuts, massages and other services.

▶ Looking for unique gifts, such as a camera, or something for your home? See **Objects of Desire,** page 200.

Fashion

Department stores

Barneys New York

660 Madison Ave at 61st St (212-826-8900). Subway: N, R to Fifth Ave; 4, 5, 6 to 59th St. Mon–Fri 10am–8pm; Sat 10am–7pm; Sun 11am–6pm. AmEx, MC, V.

All the top designers are represented at this haven of New York style. In late 1999, Barneys extended its Co-op department, which houses a great selection of lesser-known—though still high-end—labels and cute dressing rooms adorned with Tic Tac containers. Barneys also sells hip home furnishings and fancy children's clothes. In May 2000, it opened a Co-op outpost at the location where it holds its highly recommended Warehouse Sale every August and February. **Other location:** *Barneys Co-op, 236 W 18th St between Seventh and Eighth Aves (212-593-7800).*

Bergdorf Goodman

754 Fifth Ave at 58th St (212-753-7300). Subway: E, F, N, R to Fifth Ave. Mon–Wed, Fri 10am–7pm; Thu 10am–8pm; Sat 10am–6pm. AmEx, JCB, MC, V.

While Barneys aims to attract a young, trendy crowd, Bergdorf's is dedicated to an elegant, understated one—with lots of money to spare. As department stores go, it's one of the best for clothes and accessory shopping; it's intimate on a large scale. The famed men's store is across the street. In late 1999, the store opened its "Floor of Beauty," which is giving the Sephora chain some major competition.

Bloomingdale's

1000 Third Ave at 59th St (212-355-5900). Subway: N, R to Lexington Ave; 4, 5, 6 to 59th St. Mon, Tue 10am–8:30pm; Wed–Fri 10am–10pm; Sat 10am–7pm; Sun 11am–7pm. AmEx, MC, V.

This gigantic, glitzy department store has everything you could ever want to buy. The ground floor features designer handbags, scarves, hosiery, makeup and jewelry, and upstairs you'll find furniture, linens, two floors of shoes, designer names and a variety of cheaper goods. Brace yourself for crowds—Bloomingdale's is the third most popular tourist attraction in NYC, after the Empire State Building and the Statue of Liberty.

Felissimo

10 W 56th St at Fifth Ave (212-956-4438). Subway: B, Q to 57th St. Mon–Wed, Fri, Sat 10am–6pm; Thu 10am–8pm. AmEx, JCB, MC, V.

This five-story townhouse is a Japanese-owned, eco-savvy specialty store that stocks a collection of covetable items. Choose from jewelry, furnishings, doggie toys, clothing and collectibles. Assistance is available in nine languages.

Henri Bendel

712 Fifth Ave at 56th St (212-247-1100). Subway: N, R to Fifth Ave; 4, 5, 6 to 59th St. Mon–Wed, Fri, Sat 10am–7pm; Thu 10am–8pm; Sun noon–6pm. AmEx, DC, Disc, JCB, MC, V.

Bendel's is a sweet-smelling sliver of heaven. Its lavish quarters resemble a plush townhouse—there are elevators, but it's nicer to saunter up the elegant, winding staircase. The first floor features a slew of makeup lines, including some harder-to-find ones, such as Awake and BeneFit. Prices are comparable with those in other upscale stores, but somehow things look more desirable here. It must be those darling shopping bags in the store's signature brown-and-white-stripe.

Jeffrey New York

449 W 14th St between Ninth and Tenth Aves (212-206-1272). Subway: A, C, E to 14th St; L to Eighth Ave. Mon–Wed, Fri 10am–8pm; Thu 10am–9pm; Sat 10am–7pm; Sun 1–6pm. AmEx, MC, V.

Jeffrey Kalinsky, a former Barneys shoe buyer, has spiced up Meatpacking District shopping (*see* **Meat street manifesto,** *below*) with his namesake shop, a branch of the Atlanta original. More of an oversize boutique than a department store, Jeffrey's 14,000-square-foot store is stocked with plenty of Ann Demeulemeester, Alexander McQueen and Helmut Lang; its centerpiece is the shoe salon, which includes Prada, Manolo Blahnik and Robert Clergerie.

Meat street manifesto

The frontier for stylish shopping is now the Meatpacking District

New Yorkers have patented the technique of turning remote industrial areas into coveted locales. Since Soho and Tribeca have gone to the masses, city slickers have set their sights on the Meatpacking District, named for the beef, veal and pork wholesalers that line the streets. Today, cognoscenti patrol the neighborhood, frequenting new art galleries and exclusive restaurants. Local shops mostly sell handcrafted furniture and housewares, in keeping with the artsy vibe. The unblocked view of the Hudson River is reason enough to make the trip, but be prepared for a few surprises. Fetid odors from the remaining meatpackers still permeate the air, despite expensive perfumes worn by art-buying visitors. Streets run crooked. And if you think that's a transvestite prostitute on the corner...it is.

This once-forsaken region of Manhattan might be daunting, but it's easily covered in one day. The entire Meatpacking District is the size of a small park, a few blocks south of 14th Street, from Ninth Avenue to the Hudson River. Begin your tour at the corner of 14th Street and Ninth Avenue, where you'll find Belgian-food hot spot **Markt** (*see chapter* **Restaurants, Chic**).

Walking west on 14th Street toward Tenth Avenue (stay on the north side of the street), you will pass a strip of galleries that includes **Katzen/Stein** (*421 W 14th St between Ninth and Tenth Aves, 212-989-6616*), **Cynthia Broan** (*423 W 14th St between Ninth and Tenth Aves, 212-633-6525*) and **Long Fine Art** (*427 W 14th St between Ninth and Tenth Aves, 212-337-1940*). Don't be intimidated if you're not wearing the latest Gucci—browsing is free. You can assuage your bruised ego either by sampling a homestyle apple pie at **Little Pie Company** (*407 W 14th St between Ninth and Tenth Aves, 212-414-2324*) or by putting down the plastic for a Helmut Lang suit or a pair of strappy Manolos

Lord & Taylor

424 Fifth Ave between 38th and 39th Sts (212-391-3344). Subway: B, D, F, Q to 42nd St; 7 to Fifth Ave. Mon, Tue 10am–7pm; Wed 9am–8:30pm; Thu, Fri 10am–8:30pm; Sat 9am–7pm; Sun 11am–7pm. AmEx, Disc, MC, V.

Lord & Taylor is a conservative, rather old-fashioned department store, the kind where you go to buy sensible underwear—and not much else. It was here that the Fifth Avenue tradition of dramatic Christmas window displays began.

Macy's

151 W 34th St between Broadway and Seventh Ave (212-695-4400). Subway: B, D, F, Q, N, R to 34th St–Herald Sq; 1, 2, 3, 9 to 34th St–Penn Station. Mon–Sat 10am–8:30pm; Sun 11am–7pm. AmEx, MC, V.

This place doesn't have the cheapest or the hippest merchandise in New York, but it's still worth the trip. Macy's calls itself the biggest department store in the world—it occupies an entire city block. You'll find everything from designer labels to cheap, colorful knockoffs; there's also a pet shop, a fish market, a Metropolitan Museum gift shop and a juice bar. Beware the aggressive perfume sprayers and resign yourself to getting hopelessly lost. The store has its own concierge service (*212-560-3827*) to help you maximize your shopping potential.

Saks Fifth Avenue

611 Fifth Ave between 49th and 50th Sts (212-753-4000). Subway: B, D, F, Q to 47–50th Sts–Rockefeller Ctr; E, F to Fifth Ave. Mon–Wed, Fri, Sat 10am–7pm; Thu 10am–8pm; Sun noon–6pm. AmEx, DC, Disc, JCB, MC, V.

Saks is the classic upscale American department store. It features all the big names in women's fashion (and some of the better lesser-known ones), an excellent menswear department, two standout shoe departments, fine household linens, a large kids' section and some of the best customer service in town. The ground floor is packed with accessories and has a stylish beauty area, where personal consultations and makeovers are available.

Takashimaya

693 Fifth Ave between 54th and 55th Sts (212-350-0100). Subway: E, F to Fifth Ave. Mon–Sat 10am–7pm. AmEx, DC, Disc, JCB, MC, V.

The New York branch of this Japanese department store opened in 1993 and has been giving traditional Fifth Avenue retailers a run for their money ever since. The five-story palace mixes Eastern and Western aesthetics and extravagance. The first two floors offer 4,500 square feet of art gallery space and a men's and women's signature collection, as well as Japanese makeup and exotic plants; the top floor is dedicated to designer accessories.

Hoof it Get great shoes at Jeffrey New York.

at **Jeffrey New York** (*see page 168*), a minimalist megaboutique owned by a former Barneys New York shoe buyer. Sneak around the corner to 15th Street's **Lucy Barnes** (*422 W 15th St between Ninth and Tenth Aves, 212-647-0149*). It's technically outside the Meatpacking District, but British designer Barnes's extravagant to-the-floor skirts and brightly colored tank tops meet the neighborhood style quotient. Her husband runs a hip, neighboring gallery, **Gavin Brown's enterprise** (*see chapter* **Art Galleries**), where his **Passerby** bar (*212-206-7321*) gets a groove going through the night—its color-blocked floor lights up in synch with the booming bass.

Head a few blocks south to Gansevoort Street—a hotbed of design activity. **Gansevoort Gallery** (*72 Gansevoort St between Greenwich and Washington Sts, 212-633-0555*) stocks pricey 1950s antique furniture that once cluttered doctors' waiting rooms. Two doors down is the first Manhattan outpost of Brooklyn's **Breukelen** (*see* **Gift shops**, *page 207*), a shop carrying contemporary Spanish light fixtures and exclusive Italian furniture. Across the street, **Florent,** the stylish late-night diner that was a neighborhood pioneer (*see chapter* **Restaurants, Chic**), borders the display window of **H55** (the shop is actually one block up at *17 Little West 12th St between Ninth Ave and Washington St, buzzer #12; 212-462-4559*). Follow Gansevoort to Washington Street, where **Auto** (*805 Washington St between Gansevoort and Horatio Sts, 212-229-2292*), a simple, white-

Uptown's brands

BCBG Max Azria

770 Madison Ave at 66th St (212-717-4225). Subway: 6 to 68th St–Hunter College. Mon–Wed, Fri, Sat 10am–7pm; Thu 10am–8pm; Sun noon–6pm. AmEx, DC, Disc, MC, V.

A favorite of young Hollywood stars, the BCBG Max Azria collection has graced the pages of *In Style* countless times. Look for the sexy separates, dresses and shoes. This location is under renovation until September 2000; a temporary store is open at 744 Madison Ave between 64th and 65th Sts.

Bottega Veneta

635 Madison Ave between 59th and 60th Sts (212-371-5511). Subway: N, R to Fifth Ave; 4, 5, 6 to 59th St. Mon–Fri 10am–6pm; Sat 11am–6pm. AmEx, DC, Disc, JCB, MC, V.

For gear that screams luxury but remains logo-free, fashion hounds shop here. The ready-to-wear line was recently given a makeover, and now, BV has become one to watch (and want).

Burberry

9 E 57th St between Fifth and Madison Aves (212-371-5010). Subway: N, R to Fifth Ave. Mon–Fri 9:30am–7pm; Sat 9:30am–6pm; Sun noon–6pm. AmEx, DC, Disc, JCB, MC, V.

Classic Burberry's gone hip. Wave goodbye to the trench coat every commuter wears on rainy days and say hello to cute doggie coats in the company's signature plaid, as well as a fabulous new women's collection.

Calvin Klein

654 Madison Ave at 60th St (212-292-9000). Subway: N, R to Lexington Ave; 4, 5, 6 to 59th St. Mon–Wed, Fri, Sat 10am–6pm; Thu 10am–8pm; Sun noon–6pm. AmEx, Disc, MC, V.

This minimalist flagship store is totally Calvin: footwear, housewares and, of course, the couture lines.

Celine

51 E 57th St between Madison and Park Aves (212-486-9700). Subway: N, R to Fifth Ave. Mon–Sat 10am–6pm. AmEx, DC, Disc, JCB, MC, V.

American designer Michael Kors recently took over this traditional French house and dramatically revitalized the entire line, making it more casual but as luxurious as ever.

Chanel

15 E 57th St between Fifth and Madison Aves (212-355-5050). Subway: N, R to Fifth Ave. Mon–Wed, Fri 10am–6:30pm; Thu 10am–7pm; Sat 10am–6pm. AmEx, DC, JCB, MC, V.

The spirit of Mademoiselle Chanel lives on at this opulent flagship store. There's even the Chanel Suite, a Baroque salon modeled after the divine Coco's private apartment on the Rue Cambon in Paris.

Chloé

850 Madison Ave at 70th St (212-717-8220). Subway: 6 to 68th St–Hunter College. Mon–Sat 10am–6pm. AmEx, MC, V.

Meat street manifesto (continued)

walled store, carries silk-lined wool throws and leather pillows by up-and-coming designers, plus coffee-table–toppers, such as back issues of *Flair* magazine. More treats for the eye can be found—and bought—at **Alleged Gallery** (*809 Washington St between Gansevoort and Horatio Sts, 646-486-1110*), where rare British, French and Japanese magazines are sold amid avant-garde art (look out for shows of fashion designer Susan Cianciolo's textile works). If you want something more functional, consider a canopied Chinese marriage bed two blocks south at 12th Street's Asian furniture showroom **Béyül** (*353 W 12th St between Greenwich and Washington Sts, 212-989-2533*). Ladies lucky enough to be in town for Diane Von Furstenberg's biannual sample sales can snap up cheap wrap dresses at her trilevel headquarters (*389 W 12th St between Washington St and West Side Hwy, 212-753-1111*). Before leaving the block, stop for a margarita at the legendary Mexican chow hall **Tortilla Flats** (*676 Washington St at 12th St, 212-243-1053*).

Follow Greenwich Street back uptown until it becomes Ninth Avenue; the less expensive shops will bring you back to reality. At jeweler **Boucher** (*9 Ninth Ave between Little West 12th and 13th Sts, 212-206-3775*), you can browse for pastel gemstone baubles along with people in the middle of a two-hour wait for a table at **Pastis,** the restaurant next door (*see chapter* **Restaurants, Chic**). Stroll down the block to **Bahay** (*24 Ninth Ave between 13th and 14th Sts, 212-989-9412*) for handmade ceramic sushi trays and chopstick holders. Don't leave without downing a few beers at the **Village Idiot** (*355 W 14th St between Eighth and Ninth Aves, 212-989-7334*), where line-dancing inebriated cowboys are the norm. Then mosey over to the famed steakhouse **Old Homestead** (*See chapter* **Restaurants, Steak houses**) for a $100 Porterhouse gift box. That puts you back at the junction of Ninth Avenue and 14th Street—tipsy, maxed-out and beefed-up.

When Stella McCartney commandeered this French fashion house several years ago, the label quickly became a sexy must-have. The flagship duplex sells everything from sunglasses and McCartney's new signature scent, Innocence, to groovy slip dresses.

Christian Dior

21 E 57th St between Fifth and Madison Aves (212-931-2950). Subway: N, R to Fifth Ave. Mon–Wed, Fri, Sat 10am–6pm; Thu 10am–7pm; Sun 11am–5pm. AmEx, JCB, MC, V.

John Galliano has breathed new life into Dior's formerly predictable designs. This elegant boutique carries couture and the ready-to-wear line.

Diesel

770 Lexington Ave at 60th St (212-308-0055). Subway: N, R to Lexington Ave; 4, 5, 6 to 59th St. Mon–Sat 10am–8pm; Sun noon–6pm. AmEx, DC, Disc, JCB, MC, V.

This 14,000-square-foot emporium will satisfy any denim craving you might have. In addition to jeans and stylish accessories and vinyl clothing, there are shoes, under- and outerwear, and refreshments of the coffee variety.

Other location: *Diesel Style Lab, 416 West Broadway between Prince and Spring Sts (212-343-3863).*

DKNY

655 Madison Ave at 60th St (212-223-3569). Subway: N, R to Lexington Ave; 4, 5, 6 to 59th St. Mon–Wed, Fri, Sat 10am–7pm; Thu 10am–9pm; Sun noon–6pm. AmEx, DC, JCB, MC, V.

Donna Karan's department store–like DKNY flagship seems to have it all: an organic café serving shots of wheatgrass, Donna-approved reads, luxe Marie Papier stationery, vintage furniture and Ducati motorcycles. Oh, and did we mention you can buy DKNY clothing?

Dolce & Gabanna

825 Madison Ave between 68th and 69th Sts (212-249-4100). Subway: 6 to 68th St–Hunter College. Mon–Wed, Fri, Sat 10am–6pm; Thu 10am–7pm. AmEx, JCB, MC, V.

Italian design-house Dolce & Gabanna is the label of choice for such famous pretty young things as Christina Ricci and Heather Graham. For a price, why not make it yours?

Emporio Armani

601 Madison Ave between 57th and 58th Sts (212-317-0800). Subway: N, R to Lexington Ave; 4, 5, 6 to 59th St. Mon–Fri 10am–8pm; Sat 10am–7pm; Sun noon–6pm. AmEx, DC, JCB, MC, V.

The postmodern decor serves as a stark backdrop for top Armani designs. The store also houses the chic Armani Café.

Other location: *110 Fifth Ave at 16th St (212-727-3240).*

Fendi

720 Fifth Ave at 56th St (212-767-0100). Subway: N, R to Fifth Ave. Mon–Sat 10am–6pm. AmEx, DC, JCB, MC, V.

Sure, 1999 should have been dubbed the "Year of the Baguette," after the house of Fendi's best-selling pocketbook. But the Italian line also wows its fans with fab furs and a statement-making ready-to-wear line.

Gianni Versace

647 Fifth Ave between 51st and 52nd Sts (212-317-0224). Subway: E, F to Fifth Ave. Mon–Sat 10am–6:30pm. AmEx, DC, MC, V.

Housed in the former Vanderbilt mansion, this is one of the largest (28,000 square feet) boutiques in New York City. Go and stare longingly at the mosaics, even if you can't afford the clothes.

Other location: *815 Madison Ave between 68th and 69th Sts (212-744-6868).*

Giorgio Armani

760 Madison Ave at 65th St (212-988-9191). Subway: 6 to 68th St–Hunter College. Mon–Wed, Fri, Sat 10am–6pm; Thu 10am–7pm. AmEx, MC, V.

This enormous boutique features all three Armani collections: the signature Borgonuovo—tailored suits, evening wear and a bridal line—as well as Classico and Le Collezioni.

Givenchy

954 Madison Ave at 75th St (212-772-1040). Subway: 6 to 77th St. Mon–Sat 10am–6pm. AmEx, DC, MC, V.

With talented English designer Alexander McQueen holding the scissors, the styles are no longer quite as understated as when Hubert de Givenchy created Audrey Hepburn's to-die-for ensembles.

Gucci

685 Fifth Ave at 54th St (212-826-2600). Subway: E, F to Fifth Ave. Mon–Wed, Fri 10am–6:30pm; Thu, Sat 10am–7pm; Sun noon–6pm. AmEx, DC, JCB, MC, V.

When Tom Ford revitalized Gucci a few years back, he made the old-lady label hip again. No fashionista is without at least a pair of shoes from this wildly popular line. Ford also designed the look of the company's new New York flagship store.

Issey Miyake

992 Madison Ave between 77th and 78th Sts (212-439-7822). Subway: 6 to 77th St. Mon–Fri 10am–6pm; Sat 11am–6pm; Sun noon–5pm. AmEx, MC, V.

This minimalist store houses Issey Miyake's breathtaking women's and men's collections and accessories.

Joseph

804 Madison Ave between 67th and 68th Sts (212-570-0077). Subway: 6 to 68th St–Hunter College. Mon–Wed, Fri, Sat 10am–6:30pm; Thu 10am–7pm. AmEx, DC, MC, V.

London-based retailer Joseph enjoys success on both sides of the Atlantic. His extremely popular perfect-fitting pants (which start around $225) are in every fashion editor's closet. This store carries the entire ready-to-wear line. Joseph also has two shops that sell just pants; check the phone book for locations.

Moschino

803 Madison Ave between 67th and 68th Sts (212-639-9600). Subway: 6 to 68th St–Hunter College. Mon–Sat 10am–6pm. AmEx, MC, V.
Moschino means expensive and irreverent clothes for men and women. And you can always pick up a pencil kit for $5. Really.

Nicole Farhi

10 E 60th St between Madison and Fifth Aves (212-223-8811). Subway: N, R to Fifth Ave. Mon–Fri 10am–7pm; Sat 10am–6pm; Sun noon–5pm. AmEx, Disc, MC, V.
London-based designer Nicole Farhi creates clothing worth holding on to—her fabrics are durable, and her designs are seasonless. Like her fashions, her home collection, also available here, mixes modern with ethnic-inspired items. If shopping for the Nicole Farhi lifestyle tuckers you out, head to the shop's basement for a bite to eat at her namesake restaurant.

Polo Ralph Lauren

867 Madison Ave at 72nd St (212-606-2100). Subway: 6 to 68th St–Hunter College. Mon–Wed, Fri, Sat 10am–6pm; Thu 10am–8pm. AmEx, DC, Disc, JCB, MC, V.
Ralph Lauren spent $14 million turning the old Rhinelander mansion into an Ivy League superstore, filled with oriental rugs, English paintings, riding whips, leather chairs, old mahogany and fresh flowers. The homeboys, skaters and other young blades who've adopted Ralphie's togs head straight to Polo Sport across the street.
Other location: *Polo Sport, 888 Madison Ave at 72nd St (212-434-8000).*

Prada

841 Madison Ave at 70th St (212-327-4200). Subway: 6 to 68th St–Hunter College. Mon–Wed, Fri, Sat 10am–6pm; Thu 10am–7pm. AmEx, MC, V.
Prada remains the label of choice for New York's fashion set (yes, you still have to put your name on a waiting list to buy the latest shoe styles). If you're only interested in the accessories, skip the crowds at the two larger stores and stop by the small 57th Street location. If you're downtown, see if the new branch next to the Soho Guggenheim has opened.
Other locations: *724 Fifth Ave between 56th and 57th Sts (212-664-0010); 45 E 57th St between Park and Madison Aves (212-308-2332).*

Shanghai Tang

714 Madison Ave between 63rd and 64th Sts (212-888-0111). Subway: N, R to Fifth Ave; 4, 5, 6 to 59th St. Mon–Sat 10am–7pm; Sun noon–6pm. AmEx, MC, V.
The luxe Hong Kong superstore has relocated to a town house. Owner David Tang worships color, so expect lots of it. Along with silk Chinese dresses and jackets, there are unique gifts and housewares, including lamps constructed from Chinese lanterns.

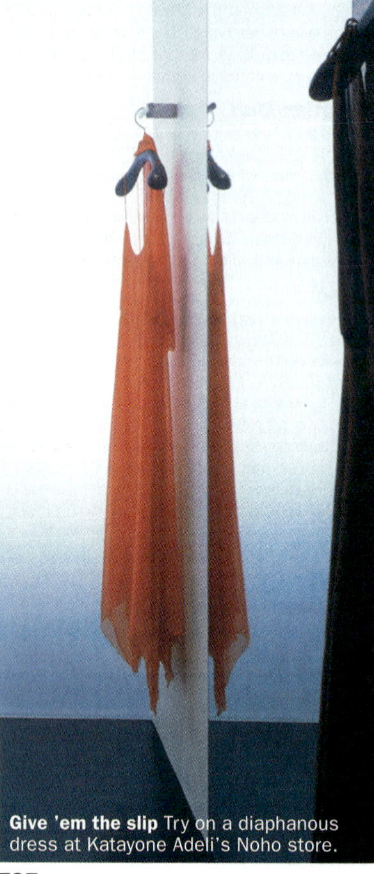

Give 'em the slip Try on a diaphanous dress at Katayone Adeli's Noho store.

TSE

827 Madison Ave at 69th St (212-472-7790). Subway: 6 to 68th St–Hunter College. Mon–Wed, Fri, Sat 10am–6pm; Thu 10am–7pm. AmEx, MC, V.
Stop by for the most fab cashmere knits and other hip styles by house designer Hussein Chalayan.

Valentino

747 Madison Ave at 65th St (212-772-6969). Subway: 6 to 68th St–Hunter College. Mon–Sat 10am–6pm. AmEx, MC, V.
Celebrities and socialites just adore Valentino. Can you be as elegant as Sharon Stone? Only if you have enough money, honey.

Vera Wang

991 Madison Ave at 77th St (212-628-3400). Subway: 6 to 77th St. By appointment only. AmEx, MC, V.

Wang's famous wedding dresses and gowns are lusted after by many, but sold to the few who can afford them at her exclusive boutique. Her admirers include celebs like Alicia Silverstone and Mariah Carey.

Yves Saint Laurent

855–859 Madison Ave between 70th and 71st Sts (212-988-3821). Subway: 6 to 68th St–Hunter College. Mon–Sat 10am–6pm. AmEx, DC, JCB, MC, V.

Gucci's Tom Ford was recently named creative director of Yves Saint Laurent; expect him to breathe new life into an old label. For now, the fashions are a bit ladies-who-lunch chic but still glamorous enough to be sought after.

Downtown trendsetters

A Détacher

262 Mott St between Houston and Prince Sts (212-625-3380). Subway: B, D, F, Q to Broadway–Lafayette St; 6 to Bleecker St. Tue–Sun noon–7pm. MC, V.

A Détacher is designer Mona Kowalska's placid boutique, featuring her own line of "minimalist but constructed" women's clothing and designer knickknacks.

agnès b.

116 Prince St between Wooster and Greene Sts (212-925-4649). Subway: N, R to Prince St. 11am–7pm. AmEx, MC, V.

Agnès b. is known for simple designs for women (stores carry accessories and makeup, too). The timeless styles will probably spend more time outside your closet than in it. *For* **agnès b. homme,** *see page 184.*

Other locations: *1063 Madison Ave between 80th and 81st Sts (212-570-9333); 13 E 16th St between Fifth Ave and Union Sq West (212-741-2585).*

Anna Sui

113 Greene St between Prince and Spring Sts (212-941-8406). Subway: C, E to Spring St; N, R to Prince St. Mon–Sat 11:30am–7pm; Sun noon–6pm. AmEx, DC, JCB, MC, V.

Judging from her frequent sweeps of East Village thrift stores and flea markets throughout the city, Anna Sui's ideas come directly from the past. Her clothes and makeup line, displayed in a lilac-and-black boutique, are popular with funky rich kids and rock stars.

The best Spots to max out your credit card

Financial District

The **Winter Garden** at the World Financial Center is one of the few indoor shopping centers in Manhattan. There's also a whole world of underground shops below the **World Trade Center** towers.

Soho

Shopping becomes more serious as you head north to Soho. A herd of chain stores has joined big-name designers like Prada and Helmut Lang (so much so that vanguard labels such as Comme des Garçons have relocated to West Chelsea). If you wish to avoid crowds, head to **Nolita,** the neighborhood just east of Soho; its indie-designer boutiques are the first stops for fashionistas.

Chinatown

Canal Street is the place to go for fake Rolexes and Prada bags, as well as for the best DJ mix tapes, electronics, sports shoes and T-shirts. Along **Mott and Mulberry Streets,** you can pick up made-in-China slippers, parasols and lanterns.

Lower East Side

Quickly becoming the home for cutting-edge designers, the Lower East Side is still considered a bargain hunter's paradise. Not to be missed: **Orchard Street** between Houston and Delancey Streets, where you'll find leather goods, luggage, designer clothes, belts, shoes and yards of fabric.

The Villages

The **East Village** has trendy boutiques, along with an abundance of secondhand shops. Check out East 7th and 9th Streets for clothes, furnishings and young designers. Head west to **Greenwich Village** for quaint shops filled with jazz records and rare books—and don't forget to visit Balducci's or the **Meatpacking District,** just north of the West Village (*see* **Meat street manifesto,** *page 168*).

Flatiron

Another cluster of boutiques and chains can be found on Fifth Avenue and Broadway between 14th and 23rd Streets.

Fifth Avenue

The **midtown** stretch of Fifth Avenue is where you'll find the city's famed department stores—Henri Bendel, Saks Fifth Avenue, Bergdorf Goodman—along with famous jewelers Tiffany, Cartier and Bulgari.

Necessities

APC

131 Mercer St between Prince and Spring Sts (212-966-9685). Subway: N, R to Prince St. Mon–Sat 11am–7pm; Sun noon–6pm. AmEx, JCB, MC, V.

APC is France's answer to the Gap. Here, you'll find basic essentials in muted colors with minimal styling in a store designed by Julian Schnabel. The French heritage is evident in the prices, which tend to be on the high side.

Atsuro Tayama

120 Wooster St between Prince and Spring Sts (212-334-6002). Subway: C, E to Spring St; N, R to Prince St. Mon–Sat 11am–7pm; Sun noon–6pm. AmEx, MC, V.

Former Yohji Yamamoto assistant designer Atsuro Tayama has been creating his own looks since 1982. Choose from modern, asymmetrical dresses, sheer shirts and billowy skirts.

Betsey Johnson

138 Wooster St between Prince and Spring Sts (212-995-5048). Subway: C, E to Spring St; N, R to Prince St. Mon–Sat 11am–7pm; Sun noon–7pm. AmEx, MC, V.

When the Betsey Johnson flagship opened on Wooster Street, her tiny Thompson Street store closed. But the larger location has room not only for her mid-priced line but for her signature collection, Ultra, as well. In a departure from her usual design scheme—the hot-pink walls of her other shops—sunshine yellow livens up this boutique. Check the phone book for other locations.

Catherine

468 Broome St at Greene St (212-925-6765). Subway: C, E to Spring St; N, R to Prince St. Mon–Wed 11am–7pm; Thu–Sat 11am–8pm; Sun noon–8pm. AmEx, MC, V.

If chain stores take over the universe, take refuge at Catherine. This colorful shop showcases everything from tile-topped cocktail tables and vintage glass vases to beaded silk pillows and chocolate—not to mention the breathtaking fashions of owner-designer Catherine Malandrino.

Christopher Totman

262 Mott St between Houston and Prince Sts (212-925-7495). Subway: B, D, F, Q to Broadway–Lafayette St; 6 to Bleecker St. Mon–Sat 11am–7pm; Sun noon–6pm. AmEx, MC, V.

A trip to Christopher Totman's shop will transport you halfway around the world—fabrics from India and knits from Peru make his men's and women's collections ($20–$500) an anomaly in an era of sleek, high-tech fabrics.

Comme des Garçons

520 W 22nd St between Tenth and Eleventh Aves (212-604-9200). Subway: C, E to 23rd St. Tue–Sat 11am–7pm; Sun noon–6pm. AmEx, MC, V.

This austere store is devoted to Rei Kawakubo's architecturally constructed, quintessentially Japanese designs for men and women. It's no surprise that the boutique is in the new art mecca of Chelsea: Kawakubo's clothing is hung like art, and the space is very gallerylike.

Costume National

108 Wooster St between Prince and Spring Sts (212-431-1530). Subway: C, E to Spring St; N, R to Prince St. Mon–Sat 11am–7pm; Sun noon–6pm. AmEx, MC, V.

This minimalist, but not plain, collection features Italian fashions designed by Ennio Capasa, who collaborated with architect Cosimo Antoci on the look of this 3,000-square-foot space.

Cynthia Rowley

112 Wooster St between Prince and Spring Sts (212-334-1144). Subway: C, E to Spring St; N, R to Prince St. Mon–Sat 11am–7pm; Sun noon–6pm. AmEx, MC, V.

Rowley's ultrafeminine dresses, pants, shirts and accessories can all be found in this bright, youthful boutique. Her menswear line is also on display here.

Daryl K

21 Bond St at Lafayette St (212-777-0713). Subway: B, D, F, Q to Broadway–Lafayette St; 6 to Bleecker St. Mon–Sat 11am–7pm; Sun noon–6pm. AmEx, MC, V.

Daryl Kerrigan's vinyl pants, colored cords, hip-hugger bootlegs and graffiti-inspired T-shirts attract rock & rollers and rocking regulars. Her much-anticipated menswear collection, Fir, hit stores in late 1999, and resurfaces on the racks only occasionally. The East 6th Street locale is where last season's goods end up, often at half price.

Other location: *208 E 6th St between Bowery and Second Ave (212-475-1255).*

D&G

434 West Broadway between Prince and Spring Sts (212-965-8000). Subway: C, E to Spring St; N, R to Prince St. Mon–Sat 11am–7pm; Sun noon–6pm. AmEx, MC, V.

While most of Milan's heavies still prefer the Upper East Side, some (like D&G) are choosing Soho as the home of their more youthful, less pricey lines. Custom-mixed disco, opera and house music play as gals and guys shop for jeans, suits, collection dresses and shoes.

Helmut Lang

80 Greene St between Spring and Broome Sts (212-925-7214). Subway: C, E to Spring St; N, R to Prince St. Mon–Sat 11am–7pm; Sun noon–6pm. AmEx, MC, V.

This 3,000-square-foot store houses Austrian designer Helmut Lang's cool suits and dresses, and recently launched accessories collection. The casual Helmut Lang Jeans line, which features denim pants, killer jean jackets and sweaters, is also available.

Jill Stuart

100 Greene St between Prince and Spring Sts (212-343-2300). Subway: C, E to Spring St; N, R to Prince St. Mon–Sat 11am–7pm; Sun noon–6pm. AmEx, MC, V.

Jill Stuart's first freestanding American boutique features her young, modern womenswear (including shoes and handbags), as well as supersweet children's clothes.

Jussara

125 Greene St between Houston and Prince Sts (212-353-5050). Subway: N, R to Prince St. Mon–Sat 11am–7:30pm; Sun noon–7pm. AmEx, MC, V.

Although of Korean descent, Jussara Lee was raised in Brazil, which explains a lot about her style: romantic modernism. The shop has garment racks with terra-cotta shingle roofs, a tall balcony, a stone fountain and benches. Her tweed and velvet jackets, coats and dresses are flirty without being too revealing.

Katayone Adeli

35 Bond St between Bowery and Lafayette St (212-260-3500). Subway: B, D, F, Q to Broadway–Lafayette St; 6 to Bleecker St. Mon–Sat 11am–7pm; Sun noon–6pm. AmEx, MC, V.

Say good-bye to the days of searching through Barneys' racks for a pair of Katayone Adeli's perfect side-slit pants. Now, you only have to plunk down your credit card to buy her basics-with-a-twist.

Louis Vuitton

114–116 Greene St between Prince and Spring Sts (212-274-9090). Subway: C, E to Spring St; N, R to Prince St. Mon–Fri 11am–7pm; Sun noon–5pm. AmEx, DC, Disc, JCB, MC, V.

When French luxury-goods company Louis Vuitton hired American Marc Jacobs as artistic director, everyone knew the staid monogrammed luggage and accessories were sure to get a spin. The revamped styles come in cherry red and pearly white; at the Soho outpost, a full range of men's and women's ready-to-wear collections is also on display. **Other location:** *49 E 57th St between Park and Madison Aves (212-371-6111).*

Marc Jacobs

163 Mercer St between Houston and Prince Sts (212-343-1490). Subway: N, R to Prince St. Mon–Sat 11am–7pm; Sun noon–6pm. AmEx, MC, V.

Marc Jacobs's first Manhattan boutique, housed in a former art gallery, is long and narrow, with white walls and distant ceilings. The impeccable designs displayed here include Jacobs's collections of both men's and women's ready-to-wear, accessories and shoes.

Zabête's the best You'll want it all, from accessories to suits, at the Kirna Zabête boutique.

Mayle
252 Elizabeth St between Houston and Prince Sts (212-625-0406). Subway: B, D, F, Q to Broadway–Lafayette St; 6 to Bleecker St. Tue–Sat noon–7pm; Sun noon–6pm. AmEx, MC, V.
Mayle, a Nolita-based, model-owned store, epitomizes the neighborhood: The clothes are desirable, elegant, whimsical and a touch trendy.

Miu Miu
100 Prince St between Mercer and Greene Sts (212-334-5156). Subway: N, R to Prince St. Mon–Sat 11am–7pm; Sun noon–6pm. AmEx, MC, V.
This is the first home for Miuccia Prada's secondary line, Miu Miu. Secondary, yes; cheap, no. Still, $225 for the season's most coveted shoes isn't that bad.

P.A.K
229 Mott St between Prince and Spring Sts (212-226-5167). Subway: 6 to Spring St. Tue–Sat noon–7:30pm; Sun 1–6pm. AmEx, MC, V.
Combine Jil Sander's feminine tailoring, Calvin Klein's minimalist store aesthetic and Banana Republic's prices, and you get P.A.K. Designer Corey Pak's clothes are funky yet practical elements with which to build a wardrobe.

Philosophy di Alberta Ferretti
452 West Broadway between Houston and Prince Sts (212-460-5500). Subway: C, E to Spring St; N, R to Prince St. Mon–Sat 11am–7pm; Sun noon–6pm. AmEx, MC, V.
This four-level store features mother-of-pearl–colored walls and cascading water—elements that echo the layering, translucence and craft in Ferretti's collection of delicate womenswear.

Pleats Please
128 Wooster St at Prince St (212-226-3600). Subway: N, R to Prince St. Mon–Sat 11am–7pm; Sun 11am–6pm. AmEx, MC, V.
New Yorkers can't seem to get enough of Japanese designer Issey Miyake's mid-priced line of accordion-pleated clothing. The billowing pants, skirts and dresses are featherweight, machine-washable and wrinkle-proof.

Plein Sud
70 Greene St between Spring and Broome Sts (212-431-8800). Subway: C, E to Spring St; N, R to Prince St. Mon–Sat 11am–7pm; Sun noon–6pm. MC, V.
This newly opened shop is as beautiful as the 12-year-old French line it houses. Think: sexy. Madonna, Jennifer Lopez and Mary J. Blige are all fans.

Prada Sport
116 Wooster St between Prince and Spring Sts (212-925-2221). Subway: C, E to Spring St; N, R to Prince St. Mon–Sat 11am–7pm; Sun noon–6pm. AmEx, DC, JCB, MC, V.
Prada's sportswear collection is a line of waterproof and windproof garments that look as good on the sidewalk as they do on the slopes. This is the former Comme des Garçons space, and it retains the same sleek vibe.

Product
71 Mercer St between Broome and Spring Sts (212-274-1494). Subway: C, E to Spring St; N, R to Prince St. Mon–Sat 11am–7pm; Sun noon–6pm. AmEx, MC, V.
Product is a hip clothier for women that features wonderful stretchy fabrics, clean lines and frivolous accessories. Expect very good-looking clothes that aren't as expensive as those at APC, which is just up the block. Sales are frenzied and frequent.
Other location: *219 Mott St between Prince and Spring Sts (212-219-2224).*

Red Tape
333 E 9th St between First and Second Aves (212-529-8483). Subway: L to First Ave; 6 to Astor Pl. Noon–8pm. AmEx, MC, V.
Rebecca Danenberg's basics for downtown denizens have always won hanger space in NYC's hippest boutiques. Go straight to the source—her first store, Red Tape—for a collection that is a touch rock & roll, a bit feminine and altogether street-friendly.

Tocca
161 Mercer St between Prince and Houston Sts (212-343-3912). Subway: N, R to Prince St. Mon–Sat 11am–7pm; Sun noon–6pm. AmEx, MC, V.
What girl doesn't melt at the sight of Tocca's window? Colorful dresses and separates are displayed in this gorgeous cerulean boutique. Also on sale are children's and home lines previously available only in the Tokyo store.

Tracy Feith
209 Mulberry St between Spring and Kenmare Sts (212-334-3097). Subway: 6 to Spring St. Mon–Sat 11am–7pm; Sun noon–6pm. AmEx, MC, V.
Tracy Feith, known for his darling dresses, recently relocated to a larger, 1,500-square-foot shop nearby. The additional space hasn't gone to waste: Feith fans will find not only the primary women's line, but also menswear, kid's clothes and whimsical accessories.

Vivienne Tam
99 Greene St between Prince and Spring Sts (212-966-2398). Subway: C, E to Spring St; N, R to Prince St. Mon–Fri 11am–7pm; Sat 11:30am–7:30pm; Sun noon–7pm. AmEx, MC, V.
Cantonese-born Vivienne Tam's first U.S. boutique is decidedly exotic, featuring oxblood walls and a massive Chinese character cut out of a partition (it means "double happiness"). Her long, transparent, mandarin-colored dresses, flowing skirts and sheer knit sweaters bring out the girlie-girl in every woman.

Vivienne Westwood
71 Greene St between Spring and Broome Sts (212-334-5200). Subway: C, E to Spring St; N, R to

Prince St. Mon–Sat 11am–7pm; Sun noon–6pm. AmEx, DC, JCB, MC, V.
Vivienne Westwood set up shop for the first time in New York in 1999. Known for her experimental draping, Savile Row–style tailoring and impeccable construction, Westwood has been setting fashion trends since 1971. This location doubles as her showroom.

Wang

219 Mott St between Prince and Spring Sts (212-941-6134). Subway: 6 to Spring St. Tue–Sun noon–7pm. AmEx, MC, V.
Wang, a boutique owned by Sally and Jennifer Wang, carries the sisters' simple, chic clothes.

Yohji Yamamoto

103 Grand St at Mercer St (212-966-9066). Subway: J, M, Z, N, R, 6 to Canal St. Mon–Sat 11am–7pm; Sun noon–6pm. AmEx, DC, MC, V.
Yohji Yamamoto's flagship store is a huge, lofty space filled with his trademark well-cut designs.

Zero

225 Mott St between Prince and Spring Sts (212-925-3849). Subway: 6 to Spring St. Tue–Sat 12:30–7:30pm; Sun 12:30–6pm. AmEx, MC, V.
Ground zero for downtown hipsters, Zero sells offbeat clothing, much of it based on simple geometric shapes.

Boutique bonanza

Antique Boutique

712–714 Broadway at Waverly Pl (212-995-5577). Subway: N, R to 8th St–NYU. Mon–Thu 11am–9pm; Fri, Sat 11am–10pm; Sun noon–8pm. AmEx, DC, Disc, JCB, MC, V.
For years, Antique Boutique was style headquarters for Long Island ravers who were in for the weekend. But now Antique Boutique has regained its cool, with the reopening of its basement room (which used to house stinky buy-by-the-pound thriftwear). Clothing by designers new to the boutique's repertoire are on display alongside fashion bibles like *Visionaire*.

Bond 07

7 Bond St between Broadway and Lafayette Sts (212-677-8487). Subway: B, D, F, Q to Broadway–Lafayette St; 6 to Bleecker St. Mon–Sat 11am–7pm; Sun noon–7pm. AmEx, MC, V.
Selima Salaun, of Le Corset and Selima Optique fame (*see* **Lingerie,** *page 182* and **Eyewear emporiums,** *page 190*), has branched out from undies and

Sex (shopping) in the city

Add some spice to your New York visit

Despite Mayor Rudolph Giuliani's crackdown on NYC's many girlie parlors a couple years back, retail sex-paraphernalia stores still abound. If you're like most, you've walked by these various stores but have never had the courage to venture in. So join us, fellow sex-shop virgins, as we take you on a beginner's tour of some of our city's hot spots. This journey will lead you from a cluttered boutique hawking leather-based debauchery to a nest of vibrators hidden floors above midtown mediocrity. What will you learn? Well, that there are plenty of places to indulge your fantasies, whether "normal" or downright frightening. You will also realize that dildos have a much more prominent position in our fair society than you were probably aware of. Let's embark, shall we?

Situated among the bodegas of the Lower East Side, the fashionable **Toys in Babeland** (*94 Rivington St at Ludlow St, 212-375-1701*) is a boutique that caters to lesbians but accommodates all lifestyles. "We get a crowd that ranges from very vanilla to girls who are coming in to buy strap-on dildos to fuck their boyfriends," says salesperson Alicia Relles. Perusers can fondle sample dildos and vibrators set out on tables: models range from the cheap but handy Pocket Rocket ($21) to the expensive but popular Rabbit Pearl ($72). You'll find handwritten cards next to certain items, with messages such as "Blackie is my old, faithful, favorite first dildo," (is this a remarkably progressive Cracker Barrel Country Store?). Other standouts include the horsetail butt plug ($40–$90), which you insert into your booty with a horsetail extending out of it. There are shelves of erotic fiction (including the provocative trilogy Anne Rice wrote as A.N. Roquelaure) and instruction manuals for tantric massage and secret sexual positions.

Next stop on our journey is one of the city's most famous sex shops, the West Village's 27-year-old **Pink Pussycat Boutique** (*167 W 4th St between Sixth and Seventh Aves, 212-243-0077*). The shop is bright and flashy in a Vegasy kind of way. Pink Pussycat hawks the usual variety of vibrators, dildos and handcuffs, but unlike Toys in Babeland, products are stored in glass cases, and a

eyewear, this time offering a carefully edited selection of clothing, accessories and vintage 20th-century French furniture.

Calypso on Broome

424 Broome St between Crosby and Lafayette Sts (212-274-0449). Subway: 6 to Spring St. Mon–Sat 11am–7pm; Sun noon–6pm. AmEx, MC, V.

While customers can still shop at the original Calypso, this location (which is about four times the size) features more upscale merchandise (less resort wear) and totally different vendors. Stop by either shop for gorgeous slip dresses, suits, sweaters and scarves, many from unknown French designers. Check the phone book for other locations. For children's versions, see **Calypso Enfants,** *page 185.*

DDC Lab

180 Orchard St between Houston and Stanton Sts (212-375-1647). Subway: F to Second Ave. Mon–Wed noon–7pm; Thu–Sat noon–9pm; Sun noon–6pm. AmEx, Disc, MC, V.

This airy shop specializes in items you can't get anywhere else in New York, such as a pair of Nike sneakers commemorating Hong Kong's transfer to Chinese rule.

Dressing Room

49 Prince St between Lafayette and Mulberry Sts (212-431-6658). Subway: N, R to Prince St; 6 to Spring St. Mon–Sat 1–7pm; Sun 1–6pm. AmEx, MC, V.

The Dressing Room, one of Nolita's first clothing boutiques, set the rest of the 'hood in motion. It carries girlie goodies, from frilly panties and feather necklaces to nylon skirts and denim duds.

Hedra Prue

281 Mott St between Houston and Prince Sts (212-529-7324). Subway: B, D, F, Q to Broadway–Lafayette St; 6 to Bleecker St. Mon–Sat 11am–7pm; Sun noon–7pm. AmEx, MC, V.

A shopping trip to Nolita isn't complete unless you check out the wares at Hedra Prue. This shop stocks downtown's latest and greatest young designer styles and accessories.

Intermix

125 Fifth Ave between 19th and 20th Sts (212-533-9720). Subway: N, R to 23rd St. Mon–Sat 11am–8pm; Sun noon–6pm. AmEx, Disc, JCB, MC, V.

Intermix is a Flatiron fave. The buyers have amazing taste; designers carried here include Plein Sud, Kostum, Catherine and Bloom.

seated security guard glares at you while you browse. The beginner might not feel so welcome. The crowd is a mix of Bleecker Street locals, groups of friends out for a goof and curious couples. The eclectic staff ranges from standoffish to genuinely caring; it depends on who you talk to.

The West Village is rife with get-yo-freak-on landmarks, one of the most respected being the **Leather Man** (*111 Christopher St between Bleecker and Hudson Sts, 212-243-5339*). Although this shop is a fetishistic, gay-male mecca, the staff by no means shuns straight adventurers. "This is a place where one can have an intelligent conversation about adult toys," says salesperson Rob Hansen. The preeminent custom-leather clothier on the ground floor can stitch up anything in leather. Descend the circular stairwell, and you'll enter another world. On a counter containing scores of dildos rests a huge fake penis—if it were fluorescent orange, it could be used as a traffic cone. Lashes, paddles and masks fill out the collection.

No sex-shop tour would be complete without a visit to a sleazy porn-video palace,

Games people play Accessorize at Toys in Babeland.

so head to **Harmony** (*139 Christopher St at Greenwich St, 212-366-9059*), a joint where the aura of creepiness and perversion is exactly what you'd expect from a sex store located near the West Side Highway. Desperate-looking men shuffle around

Other location: *1003 Madison Ave between 77th and 78th Sts (212-249-7858).*

Jade

240 Mulberry St between Houston and Prince Sts (212-925-6544). Subway: B, D, F, Q to Broadway–Lafayette St; N, R to Prince St; 6 to Bleecker St. Mon–Sat 11am–7pm; Sun noon–6pm. AmEx, DC, MC, V.

Christiane Celle snatched up property in überhip Nolita long before it was hot; first she opened Calypso, then Jade. Here, she sells Chinese-style clothing.

Kirna Zabête

96 Greene St between Prince and Spring Sts (212-941-9656). Subway: C, E to Spring St; N, R to Prince St. Mon–Sat 11am–7pm; Sun noon–6pm. AmEx, MC, V.

Just when you think you've finalized your list of top ten favorite shops, along comes one that throws the tally off. Founded by 28-year-old fashion veterans (in NYC, that's not an oxymoron) Sarah Hailes and Beth Shepherd, Kirna Zabête includes more than 50 designers from around the globe, including Hussein Chalayan, Olivier Theyskens and Bruce.

Language

238 Mulberry St between Prince and Spring Sts (212-431-5566). Subway: N, R to Prince St; 6 to Spring St. Tue–Sat noon–8pm; Sun, Mon noon–6pm. AmEx, DC, Disc, MC, V.

Language, the clothing boutique–cum–furniture store–cum–art gallery, is a can't-miss for shoppers who buy into the lifestyle-shopping aesthetic. Would you like a teak salt-and-pepper shaker to go with that Chloé dress?

Louie

68 Thompson St between Spring and Broome Sts (212-274-1599). Subway: C, E to Spring St. Tue–Sat noon–7pm; Sun noon–6pm. AmEx, MC, V.

At Laura Pedone's boutique, every design is an original. Louie is often the launching pad for young, unknown clothiers.

Min-K

334 E 11th St between First and Second Aves (212-253-8337). Subway: L to First Ave; 6 to Astor Pl. Mon, Wed–Sun noon–8:30pm. AmEx, MC, V.

Unless you shop in Japan, you probably won't recognize any of the labels sold at this new East Village boutique. Min-K owner Minji Kim makes frequent trips to Tokyo to pick up the latest and greatest

Sex (shopping) in the city (continued)

eyeing devices like a Fake Vagina with Real Hair ($20–$300) and Double Anal Beads ($3–$60). There is the usual stock of dildos, blow-up dolls and lubricants. This is not the type of place where you ask questions; you bring your penis pump or dildo to the counter, get it thrown in a brown bag, and escape into the night, clutching your new best friend.

Compared with Harmony, the **Pleasure Chest** (*156 Seventh Ave South between Charles and Perry Sts, 212-242-2158*) seems like a suburban gift shop. Indeed, according to salesperson Jo, patrons here are more "mainstream American." Her definition of mainstream might be a bit skewed, however. "A businessman came in on his lunch break to buy a blow-up doll for his daughter's boyfriend to protect her virginity," says Jo. "He asked me to gift wrap it for him." Like the Pussycat, the Chest is heavy on gag items, such as a fake Beanie Babies rabbit with an enormous phallus ($22); Naughty Checkers ($24), with game pieces shaped like penises and breasts; and elephant underwear (complete with the trunk to hold your trunk, $18).

The ladies will reach full climax at 25-year-old **Eve's Garden** (*119 W 57th St between Sixth and Seventh Aves, suite 1201, 212-757-8651*), a friendly shop that caters mostly to women, but also to gay and straight couples. Eve's Garden has the most relaxed and hassle-free atmosphere of all these shops. It even distributes a mail-order catalog (*800-848-3837*), which carries most of what's in the store (dildos are referred to as "dils for does"). "We want to maintain a discreet and comfortable environment," says salesperson Kim. Eve's Garden is on the 12th floor of an office building. "When people come into the building for a [dental] appointment," says Kim, "they will often swing by to get a dildo after getting their teeth cleaned." There's a variety of lubricants, such as the nontoxic, flavored For Play ($15), which heats up with friction, and a crowd-pleasing selection of silicone Japanese vibrators (they're hypoallergenic and have rotating shafts and vibrating clitoral stimulators; $75–$150). Just because there are no blow-up dolls doesn't mean that Eve's isn't fun. The wireless, remote-control vibrating panties ($90) are sure to give any woman a buzz.

streetwear, from leg warmers to Scandinavian-print sweater dresses.

Olive & Bette's

252 Columbus Ave between 71st and 72nd Sts (212-579-2178). Subway: B, C, 1, 2, 3, 9 to 72nd St. Mon–Sat 10am–7pm; Sun 11am–6pm. AmEx, MC, V.

Olive & Bette's is the store that has succeeded in getting even the most uptown-phobic girls to trot up to 71st Street or even to its 80th Street location. That's because they have all you could want: underwear, outerwear, jewelry and even itty-bitty decals for your nails.

Other location: *1070 Madison Ave between 80th and 81st Sts (212-717-9655).*

Patricia Field

10 E 8th St at Fifth Ave (212-254-1699). Subway: N, R to 8th St–NYU. Mon–Sat noon–8pm; Sun 1–7pm. AmEx, Disc, MC, V.

Patricia Field is brilliant at working club and street fashion. (Plus, she and her partner, Rebecca Field, are responsible for the clothes seen on *Sex and the City*). Her store, run by an ambisexual staff, has an eclectic mix of original jewelry, makeup and club gear. There's always something new, the clothing is gorgeous and durable, and the wigs are the most outrageous in town.

Scoop

532 Broadway between Prince and Spring Sts (212-925-2886). Subway: N, R to Prince St. Mon–Sat 11am–8pm; Sun 11am–7pm. AmEx, MC, V.

Scoop is the ultimate fashion editor's closet. Clothing from Tocca, Daryl K, Susan Lazar, Diane Von Furstenberg and plenty of others are arranged by hue, not label.

Other location: *1275 Third Ave between 73rd and 74th Sts (212-535-5577).*

Steven Alan

60 Wooster St between Spring and Broome Sts (212-334-6354). Subway: C, E to Spring St; N, R to Prince St. 11am–7pm. AmEx, MC, V.

Steven Alan's stock is coveted by hip girls from all over town. This is an excellent place to scout fashion's next big things.

TG-170

170 Ludlow St between Houston and Stanton Sts (212-995-8660). Subway: F to Second Ave. Noon–8pm. AmEx, MC, V.

Terry Gillis has an eye for emerging designers: She was the first to carry Rebecca Danenberg, Pixie Yates and Built by Wendy. Gillis also has her own line—called TG-170, of course—consisting of simple separates in unusual fabrics.

Trash & Vaudeville

4 St. Marks Pl between Second and Third Aves (212-982-3590). Subway: 6 to Astor Pl. Mon–Fri noon–8pm; Sat 11:30am–9pm; Sun 1–7:30pm. AmEx, MC, V.

This punk staple has two floors of stretchy tube dresses, leathers, snakeskin boots, collar tips, jewelry and other accessories.

Zao

175–179 Orchard St between Houston and Stanton Sts (212-505-0500). Subway: F to Second Ave. Sun–Thu 11am–7pm; Fri, Sat 11am–9pm. AmEx, MC, V.

Zao's buyers scour the planet for groundbreaking talent and offer fashion's next big things a forum for their designs, regardless of medium. At Zao, you'll not only find clothing from London's Central St. Martin's grads but also art, music and fashion publications. Wowie zao-y!

Leather goods

Carla Dawn Behrle

89 Franklin St between Church St and Broadway (212-334-5522). Subway: 1, 9 to Franklin St. Tue–Sat noon–7pm. AmEx, MC, V.

Carla Dawn Behrle's Tribeca shop features leather pants, skirts and dresses that can be best described as duds for that modern Bond girl (or boy). Among the celebs who have donned Behrle's designs are the Spice Girls, Bono and the Edge.

Coach

342 E 57th St at Madison Ave (212-754-0041). Subway: N, R to Lexington Ave; 4, 5, 6 to 59th St. Mon–Sat 10am–7pm; Sun 11am–6pm. AmEx, MC, V.

The colorful, butter-soft leather briefcases, wallets and handbags found here are exceptional. This and the 63rd Street (off Madison Avenue) location are the only Coach stores in Manhattan to stock the company's outerwear collection. Check the phone book for other locations.

Il Bisonte

72 Thompson St between Spring and Broome Sts (212-966-8773). Subway: C, E to Spring St. Sun, Mon noon–6pm; Tue–Sat noon–6:30pm. AmEx, MC, V.

Stylish, durable bags, belts and saddlebags from the famous Florentine company are sold here.

Jutta Neumann

317 E 9th St between First and Second Aves (212-982-7048). Subway: L to First Ave; 6 to Astor Pl. Tue–Sat noon–8pm. AmEx, MC, V.

Jutta Neumann designs leather sandals and bags as well as belts and jewelry. Haven't you always wanted a leather choker?

New York City Custom Leather

168 Ludlow St between Houston and Stanton Sts (212-375-9593). Subway: F to Second Ave. By appointment only. Cash only.

Fashion bugs buzz to Agatha Blois's shop to custom-order camouflage-print jackets with rabbit hoods and lace-up corsets with feminine rose inlays.

Lingerie

Enelra

48½ E 7th St between First and Second Aves (212-473-2454). Subway: 6 to Astor Pl. Sun–Thu noon–8pm; Fri, Sat noon–9pm. AmEx, MC, V.
During the 1980s, Madonna was a regular. You'll find plenty of corsets, bras and slinky slips, as well as fluffy marabou mules.

La Perla

777 Madison Ave between 66th and 67th Sts (212-570-0050). Subway: 6 to 68th St–Hunter College. Mon–Sat 10am–6pm. AmEx, MC, V.
Every woman deserves the luxury of La Perla, a high-end line of Italian lingerie, but few can afford it. Surrounded by marble walls and columns, customers at this Upper East Side boutique can expect lots of specialized attention from the staff. Bras start at about $200 and lace corsets can run to more than $500.

La Petite Coquette

51 University Pl between 9th and 10th Sts (212-473-2478). Subway: L, N, R, 4, 5, 6 to 14th St–Union Sq. Mon–Wed, Fri, Sat 11am–7pm; Thu 11am–8pm; Sun noon–6pm. AmEx, MC, V.
There are too many goodies for the eye (and body) to take in at La Petite Coquette. At this tiny lingerie boudoir, customers can flip through panels of pinned-up bras and panties before making a selection. Once you know what you like, owner Rebecca Apsan will order it for you.

Le Corset by Selima

80 Thompson St between Spring and Broome Sts (212-334-4936). Subway: C, E to Spring St. Mon–Wed, Fri 11am–7pm; Thu 11am–8pm; Sat noon–7pm; Sun noon–6pm. AmEx, DC, MC, V.
In addition to Selima Salaun's slinky designs, this spacious boutique stocks antique camisoles, Renaissance-inspired girdles and of-the-moment lingerie designers such as Collette Dinnigan.

Lingerie & Company

1217 Third Ave between 70th and 71st Sts (212-737-7700). Subway: 6 to 68th St–Hunter College. Mon–Sat 9:30am–7pm; Sun noon–5pm. AmEx, Disc, MC, V.
Sibling team Mark Peress and Tamara Watkins take a look at your body (and ask a few questions) before giving lingerie recommendations.

Religious Sex

7 St. Marks Pl between Second and Third Aves (212-477-9037). Subway: 6 to Astor Pl. Mon–Wed noon–8pm; Thu–Sat noon–9pm; Sun 1–8pm. AmEx, Disc, MC, V.
Religious Sex is a playpen for the fetishist in all of us. The store carries mesh tops with *fuck* printed all over them, panties that are smaller than eye patches and rubber corsets that will all but ensure a dangerous liaison.

Swimwear

Liza Bruce

80 Thompson St between Spring and Broome Sts (212-966-3853). Subway: C, E to Spring St. Mon–Sat 11am–6pm. AmEx, MC, V.
Twenty years ago, British-raised swimwear designer Liza Bruce gave women a reason to throw out their floral-patterned Gottex numbers. At her new Soho store, girls can pop in for a suit in July—when they really need one. The boutique also carries Bruce's ready-to-wear line.

Malia Mills

199 Mulberry St between Spring and Kenmare Sts (212-625-2311). Subway: 6 to Spring St. Noon–7pm. AmEx, MC, V.
Ever since one of her designs made it onto the cover of *Sports Illustrated*'s swimsuit issue a couple of years ago, Malia Mills's swimwear has become a staple for those who spend their New Year's on St. Barth.

Streetwear

Active Wearhouse

514 Broadway between Spring and Broome Sts (212-965-2284). Subway: N, R to Prince St; 6 to Spring St. Mon–Sat 9am–9pm; Sun 10am–8pm. AmEx, Disc, JCB, MC, V.
Active Wearhouse has become the place to pick up the latest in footwear from Adidas, New Balance, Nike, Saucony and others. The store also sells clothing; the North Face section is especially strong. Active's sister shop Transit stocks the same in its subway-themed store (*see* **Shoes,** *page 193*).

alife

178 Orchard St between Houston and Stanton Sts (646-654-0628). Subway: F to Second Ave. Noon–8pm. AmEx, MC, V.
This shop, run by the graphic design team Artificial Life, sells footwear from Tsubo, Snipe and Dry Shod, one-of-a-kind accessories by Suckadelic and Nuflow, CDs by club-friendly artists and rare Japanese action figures.

Canal Jean

504 Broadway between Spring and Broome Sts (212-226-1130). Subway: N, R to Prince St; 6 to Spring St. Mon–Thu, Sun 10am–8pm; Fri, Sat 10:30am–9pm; Sun 11am–9pm. AmEx, DC, MC, V.
Browse the vast acreage of jeans, T-shirts and other basics, plus new (e.g., French Connection) and vintage clothing and accessories, socks, bags and fun jewelry. Canal's prices are definitely worth the trip.

Final Home

242 Lafayette St between Prince and Spring Sts (212-966-0202). Subway: 6 to Spring St. Mon–Sat noon–8pm; Sun 1–7pm. AmEx, MC, V.
Kosuke Tsumura's Final Home shop opened just in time to outfit paranoid New Yorkers for the new mil-

lennium. The shop carries unisex essentials with more pockets, zippers, twists and turns than one of the *Choose Your Own Adventure* books (one coat has 44 pockets).

Memes

3 Great Jones St between Broadway and Lafayette St (212-420-9955). Subway: B, D, F, Q to Broadway–Lafayette St; 6 to Bleecker St. Noon–8pm. AmEx, MC, V.

Tetsuo Hashimoto believes it takes more than a Kangol hat and a pair of Adidas to establish street cred. His shop, Memes, offers refined men's streetwear, more fitted than typical baggy offerings but by no means uptight.

Nylonsquid

222 Lafayette St between Spring and Broome Sts (212-334-6554). Subway: 6 to Spring St. Sun–Thu noon–7pm; Fri, Sat noon–8pm. AmEx, MC, V.

Nylonsquid gives new meaning to Cool Britannia. London-based sneaker and clothing distributors Mick Hoyle and John Chatters originally wanted to open a showroom but opted instead for a retail space that doubles as one.

Phat Farm

129 Prince St between West Broadway and Wooster St (212-533-7428). Subway: C, E to Spring St; N, R to Prince St. Mon–Sat 11am–7pm; Sun 11am–6pm. AmEx, MC, V.

This store showcases Def Jam Records impresario Russell Simmons's classy and conservative take on hip-hop couture: phunky-phresh oversize and baggy clothing. For gals, there's the Baby Phat line.

Recon

237 Eldridge St between Houston and Stanton Sts (212-614-8502). Subway: F to Second Ave. Tue–Sun noon–7pm. AmEx, JCB, MC, V.

This joint venture of famed graffiti artists Stash, Futura 2000 and Bleu opened in 1998, offering graf junkies a chance to wear the work of their favorite artists. In addition to clothes, Recon carries accessories like backpacks and toiletries.

SSUR

219A Mulberry St between Prince and Spring Sts (212-431-3152). Subway: N, R to Prince St; 6 to Spring St. Mon–Fri noon–7pm; Sat noon–7:30pm; Sun 1–6pm. AmEx, MC, V.

Designer Russ Karablin's gallery-turned-shop combines military-surplus antichic with streetwear style. SSUR is Russ spelled backward.

Stüssy

104 Prince St between Mercer and Greene Sts (212-274-8855). Subway: N, R to Prince St. Mon–Thu

Unique boutique Zao sells fashion-forward clothes as well as CDs, art and style journals.

noon–7pm; Fri, Sat 11am–7pm; Sun noon–6pm. AmEx, MC, V.
Check out the fine hats, T-shirts and other skate and surf gear that Sean Stüssy is famous for.

Supreme

274 Lafayette St between Houston and Prince Sts (212-966-7799). Subway: B, D, F, Q to Broadway–Lafayette St; N, R to Prince St. Mon–Sat 11:30am–7pm; Sun noon–6pm. AmEx, MC, V.
Sunshine lights up the racks and shelves of the latest skatewear, mostly from East Coast brands like Independent, Zoo York, Chocolate and the shop's eponymous line. Of course, there are decks and the necessary skate accessories, too.

Triple Five Soul

290 Lafayette St between Houston and Prince Sts (212-431-2404). Subway: B, D, F, Q to Broadway–Lafayette St; N, R to Prince St. 11am–7pm. AmEx, MC, V.
"Jungle boogie" is the phrase that first comes to mind at this urban-meets-rainforest–themed shop. The bamboo bike in the window is from Vietnam, but the clothing and accessories inside are from New York designers. Triple Five Soul also offers curvier versions of its menswear for the ladies.

Union

172 Spring St between West Broadway and Thompson St (212-226-8493). Subway: C, E to Spring St. Mon–Sat 11am–7pm; Sun noon–7pm. AmEx, MC, V.
Can't make it to London? The folks at Union have brought the city to you. The store is the exclusive dealer of the Duffer of St. George, the famed streetwear sold at the British shop of the same name. Union also sells Maharishi, 68 and Brothers, and the Union label.

X-Large

267 Lafayette St between Prince and Spring Sts (212-334-4480). Subway: N, R to Prince St; 6 to Spring St. Noon–7pm. AmEx, Disc, MC, V.
New Yorkers were thrilled when X-Large graduated from its closet-size shop on Avenue A and moved into these sleek digs, which now house the X-Large label for boys and Mini for girls.

Strictly for men

Although chic department stores (*see* **Department stores**, *page 167*) such as Barneys New York and Bergdorf Goodman have enormous men's sections (Bergdorf's is even housed in a separate building across the street from the main shop), it's not always easy or comfortable for guys to search for new duds. At many fashion boutiques, the men's collections are either limited or tucked away in the back. The following shops offer stylish clothing for men only. At these stores, it's the women who will find themselves waiting on the couch outside the dressing room. See also **Streetwear,** *page 182.*

agnès b. homme

79 Greene St between Spring and Broome Sts (212-431-4339). Subway: C, E to Spring St; N, R to Prince St. Mon–Sat 11am–7pm; Sun noon–6pm. AmEx, DC, MC, V.
The films of Jean-Luc Godard and his contemporaries are clearly a primary inspiration for agnès b.'s designs. Men's basics include the classic snap cardigan sweater and striped long-sleeved T-shirts that will make you feel like Picasso in his studio.

Brooks Brothers

346 Madison Ave at 44th St (212-682-8800). Subway: S, 4, 5, 6, 7 to 42nd St–Grand Central. Mon–Wed, Fri, Sat 9am–7pm; Thu 9am–8pm; Sun noon–6pm. AmEx, Disc, MC, V.
This famous men's store is still where prepsters head for high-quality button-down shirts and chinos, but it's also the place to buy a classic men's tuxedo. The staff will almost guarantee it'll last you for decades.
Other locations: *1 Church St between Cortlandt and Liberty Sts (212-267-2400); 666 Fifth Ave between 52nd and 53rd Sts (212-261-9440).*

D/L Cerney

13 E 7th St between Second and Third Aves (212-673-7033). Subway: 6 to Astor Pl. Noon–8pm. AmEx, MC, V.
This vintage shop specializes in menswear from the 1940s to the 1960s, plus new, timeless original designs for the swanky groom.
Other location: *222 West Broadway between Franklin and White Sts (212-941-0530).*

INA Men

See **INA,** page 188.

Jack Spade

See **Jack Spade,** page 190.

Nova USA

100 Stanton St at Ludlow St (212-228-6844). Subway: F to Second Ave. Noon–7pm. AmEx, Disc, MC, V.
Tony Melillo's casual menswear is for sale here, including his superpopular judo pants and other basics in fleece, wool crepe and cotton twill.

Paul Smith

108 Fifth Ave between 15th and 16th Sts (212-627-9770). Subway: L, N, R, 4, 5, 6 to 14th St–Union Sq. Mon–Wed, Fri, Sat 11am–7pm; Thu 11am–8pm; Sun noon–6pm. AmEx, Disc, MC, V.
Stop by Paul Smith for the relaxed-English-gentleman look. These designs are exemplary for their combination of elegance, quality and wit. Accessories are also available.

Sean

132 Thompson St between Houston and Prince Sts (212-598-5980). Subway: C, E to Spring St. Mon–Thu, Sat 11am–8pm; Fri 11am–9pm; Sun noon–7pm. AmEx, MC, V.
Sean Cassidy (it's not who you're thinking) discovered French designer Pierre Emile Lafaurie during

visits to Paris; he fell in love with Lafaurie's men's suits, cotton shirts and corduroy jackets. Now Cassidy devotes his shop to Lafaurie's designs.
Other location: *224 Columbus Ave between 70th and 71st Sts (212-769-1489).*

Seize sur Vingt

243 Elizabeth St between Houston and Prince Sts (212-343-0476). Subway: B, D, F, Q to Broadway–Lafayette St; N, R to Prince St; 6 to Bleecker St. Tue–Sun noon–7pm. AmEx, MC, V.
This charming boutique offers a selection of menswear that falls somewhere between suits and jeans. Men's shirts come in vibrant colors and are made with impeccable details: mother-of-pearl buttons and square, short collars designed to look good with the top button undone.

Ted Baker London

107 Grand St at Mercer St (212-343-8989). Subway: J, M, Z, N, R, 6 to Spring St. Mon–Wed 11:30am–7pm; Thu 11:30am–7:30pm; Fri, Sat noon–7:30pm; Sun noon–6:30pm. AmEx, DC, MC, V.
The Brits behind this label present a modern, restrained line of men's clothing whose focus is short- and long-sleeved shirts in bright colors. Customers should not overlook the rest of the collection, which has been popular in England for more than a decade.

Thomas Pink

520 Madison Ave at 53rd St (212-838-1928). Subway: E, F to Fifth Ave. Mon–Fri 10am–7pm; Thu 10am–8pm; Sat 10am–6pm; Sun 11am–5pm. AmEx, DC, JCB, MC, V.
This shirt shop opened on London's Jermyn Street two decades ago. The younger American shop looks tony and British; it's also modern and user-friendly. Pink's shirts are offered in bold, dynamic colors that may be paired with more conservative suits.

Children's clothes

For **Children's toys,** see page 201.

Bonpoint

1269 Madison Ave at 91st St (212-722-7720). Subway: 6 to 96th St. Mon–Sat 10am–6pm. AmEx, MC, V.
Perfect for toddlers with expense accounts, this Upper East Side institution carries frilly white party dresses and starched sailor suits.
Other location: *811 Madison Ave at 68th St (212-879-0900).*

Calypso Enfants

284 Mulberry St between Houston and Prince Sts (212-965-8910). Subway: B, D, F, Q to Broadway–Lafayette St; N, R to Prince St. Mon–Sat 11am–7pm; Sun noon–6pm. AmEx, MC, V.
Fans of Calypso—and its ultrafeminine women's clothing, bags and accessories (*see* **Calypso on Broome,** *page 179*)—positively adore this francophone children's boutique. There's the same French style here: Tiny wool coats that look as if they leapt from the pages of *Madeline.*

Hoyt & Bond

248 Smith St between Douglass and DeGraw Sts, Carroll Gardens, Brooklyn (718-488-8283). Subway: F, G to Carroll St. Tue, Wed 10am–6pm; Thu–Sat 10am–7pm; Sun 11am–6pm. MC, V.
Hipsters with kids need places to shop, too. Designer Elizabeth Beer's store features both her line of children's clothing (A-line skirts, color-saturated ponchos, kiddie cowboy hats) and women's pieces (chic angora and wool kerchiefs and mittens).

Lilliput

240 Lafayette St (212-965-9567) and 265 Lafayette St between Prince and Spring Sts (212-965-9201). Subway: N, R to Prince St; 6 to Spring St. Sun, Mon noon–6pm; Tue–Sat 11am–7pm. AmEx, Disc, MC, V.
Now on both sides of the street, this stylish source for kids and babies sells secondhand as well as new clothing.

Little O

1 Bleecker St between Bowery and Mott St (212-673-0858). Subway: B, D, F, Q to Broadway–Lafayette St; 6 to Bleecker St. Tue–Sat 12:30–7:30pm; Sun 1–7pm. MC, V.

Young in old As an alternative to cookie-cutter children's styles, Little O sells only vintage.

Necessities

Model/mom Debbie Deitering dug to the bottom of vintage bins to provide hipster parents with a chic alternative to cookie-cutter, crayon-colored fashions for tots. Items at the store come from several decades.

Space Kiddets

46 E 21st St between Park Ave South and Broadway (212-420-9878). Subway: N, R, 6 to 23rd St. Mon, Tue, Fri 10:30am–6pm; Wed, Thu 10:30am–7pm; Sat 10:30am–5:30pm. AmEx, MC, V.

This shop strives for a unique combination: clothing that is cool, practical, comfortable and fun for kids. In addition to one-of-a-kind toys and selected secondhand frocks, Space Kiddets now features a preteen collection for girls on the second floor.

Z'Baby Company

100 W 72nd St at Columbus Ave (212-579-2229). Subway: B, C, 1, 2, 3, 9 to 72nd St. Mon–Sat 10:30am–8pm; Sun 11am–6:30pm. AmEx, MC, V.

Uptown yuppies clothe their newborns and kids up to size seven in Z'Baby's styles. Sonia Rykiel is among the designers who trim their cuts down to size.

Other location: *996 Lexington Ave at 72nd St (212-472-2229).*

Necessities

Maternity wear

Liz Lange Maternity

958 Madison Ave between 75th and 76th Sts (212-717-9030). Subway: 6 to 77th St. Mon–Sat 10am–7pm; Sun noon–5pm. AmEx, MC, V.

Liz Lange is the mother of stylish maternity wear. Catering to such high-profile clients as Cindy Crawford (who loved anything tight and black), Lange aspires to take nonpregnant styles and modify them. Her inspiration in fashion? Jackie O., whose fresh, feminine style she imitates.

Pumpkin Maternity

225 Lafayette St at Spring St (917-237-0567). Subway: 6 to Spring St. By appointment only. AmEx, Disc, MC, V.

Former rocker Pumpkin Wentzel manages a by-appointment showroom where her merchandise hangs behind a peach-colored curtain. Casual, tailored and machine-washable, Wentzel's line features essentials for the expectant mother who craves the feel of real denim against her skin: Pumpkin Maternity sells recycled and reengineered vintage Levi's. If you like what you see, place an order, and Wentzel will ship your gear within a month.

Designer discount

Century 21 Department Store

22 Cortlandt St at Broadway (212-227-9092). Subway: N, R, 1, 9 to Cortlandt St. Mon–Wed 7:45am–7:30pm; Thu 7:45am–8:30pm; Fri 7:45am–8pm; Sat 10am–7:30pm; Sun 11am–6pm. AmEx, Disc, MC, V.

Some discerning shoppers report finding clothes by Helmut Lang and Donna Karan here, but you have to visit every ten days or so to get such bargains. Rack upon rack is heavy with discounted designer and name-brand fashions. Also sold cheap: housewares and appliances, underwear, accessories, cosmetics, fragrances and women's shoes. With the exception of the designer section, there are no fitting rooms. Dress accordingly.

Other location: *472 86th St between Fourth and Fifth Aves, Bay Ridge, Brooklyn (718-748-3266).*

Daffy's

111 Fifth Ave at 18th St (212-529-4477). Subway: L, N, R, 4, 5, 6 to 14th St–Union Sq. Mon–Sat 10am–9pm; Sun noon–7pm. Disc, MC, V.

There are three floors packed with current mainstream fashions, from evening gowns and leather jackets to Calvin Klein and French lingerie, as well as men's suits and shirts. Prices are much lower than at retail stores, and there are often substantial markdowns. The kids' clothes are fabulous. Check the phone book for other locations.

Find Outlet

361 W 17th St between Eighth and Ninth Aves (212-243-3177). Mon–Sat 10am–7pm. AmEx, MC, V.

Ike Rodriguez and Ingrid deGranier have changed the way New Yorkers shop for designer samples and season-old stock. The duo's store feels like a hip boutique yet offers items at 50 to 80 percent off retail. Designers include Lotta, Cashmere Studio and Paul & Joe.

Belly high Liz Lange Maternity offers stylish clothes for mothers-to-be.

TJ Maxx

620 Sixth Ave between 18th and 19th Sts (212-229-0875). Subway: F to 14th St; L to Sixth Ave. Mon–Sat 9:30am–9pm; Sun 11am–7pm. AmEx, DC, MC, V.

This discount designer clothes store, with its brightly lit Woolworth's-like appearance, is less of an obvious treasure trove than Century 21 (*see above*), but if you're prepared to sift through the junk, you will undoubtedly find some fabulous purchases. Maxx also stocks household goods, luggage and shoes.

Outlet malls

These outlet malls require a visit to the outlying suburbs, but most offer shuttle buses from Manhattan. See chapter **Directory** for more travel information.

Clinton Crossing

Clinton, CT (860-664-0700; www.chelseagca.com). Travel: By car, take I-95 north to exit 63 (Clinton), make two lefts, and Clinton Crossing is on the left. Jan–Mar Sun–Wed 10am–6pm; Thu–Sat 10am–9pm. Apr–Jun Mon–Sat 10am–9pm; Sun 10am–6pm. Jul, Aug Mon–Sat 10am–9pm; Sun 10am–8pm. Sept–Dec Mon–Sat 10am–9pm; Sun 10am–6pm.

An upscale shopping center on the Connecticut shoreline, Clinton Crossing is operated by Chelsea Premium Outlet Centers, which also runs Liberty Village and Woodbury Commons. Though modeled after a country village, complete with (albeit synthetic) shingled cottages and cobblestone streets, Clinton Crossing keeps its urban edge with designer shops such as Donna Karan and Versace and a Barneys New York Outlet. Besides the 36 clothing outlets (including Brooks Brothers, Calvin Klein, Danskin, Fila and Malo), you can pick up half-priced Coach leather goods or housewares at Crate & Barrel. All Chelsea Premium Outlet Centers advertise discounts of 25 to 65 percent.

Liberty Village

Flemington, NJ (908-788-5729; www.chelseagca.com). Travel: By bus, take Trans-Bridge Bus Lines (800-962-9135; round-trip $23.30, children under 12 $11.60, seniors $10.80) from Port Authority Bus Terminal. Call for directions by car. Mon–Wed 10am–6pm; Thu–Sat 10am–9pm; Sun 10am–6pm.

Liberty, an hour from the city, is a modest collection of 60 stores (Donna Karan, Ellen Tracy, Cole-Haan), but customers wrestle with smaller crowds than they would at bigger locations like Woodbury Commons. Erected in 1981, Liberty is the nation's oldest outlet village. New Jersey does not charge sales tax on clothing and shoes, so you can shop guilt- and tax-free. Unfortunately, a 6 percent sales tax is charged on accessories, home furnishings and gift items.

Tanger Outlet Center

Riverhead, NY (800-407-4894; www.tangeroutlet.com). Travel: By bus, take Sunrise Coach Lines (800-527-7709; round-trip $29, children under 5 free) to Tanger's entrance gate. By train, take the LIRR (round-trip $20.50–$30.50) from Penn Station to Riverhead. Call for directions by car. Mon–Sat 10am–9pm; Sun 10am–7pm.

This Long Island shopping oasis, 60 miles from Manhattan, is the perfect detour from the road to the Hamptons (*see chapter* **Trips Out of Town**). Tanger is 153 outlets in two separate malls—Tanger I and Tanger II—that are connected by a trolley. Tanger's array of department stores, clothing brands such as Levi's and BCBG and specialty names like Samsonite and Natori provide enough merchandise to suit any discriminating shopper, and discounts here can reach 70 percent off.

Woodbury Commons

Central Valley, NY (914-928-4000; www.chelseagca.com). Travel: By bus, take Short Line Buses (800-631-8405, 212-736-4700; www.shortlinebus.com; round-trip $22.45, children $12.45, ask about special packages) from Port Authority Bus Terminal, 42nd St at Eighth Ave. Call for directions by car. Jan–Mar Sun–Wed 10am–6pm; Thu–Sat 10am–9pm. Apr–Dec Mon–Sat 10am–9pm; Sun 10am–8pm.

This is a designer haven, harboring the Giorgio Armani General Store, Gucci and Versace outlets, and Space, which carries such hot-ticket names as Prada and Miu Miu. Discounted items from the Gap, Banana Republic, Adidas, Nike and Patagonia will appeal to traditional mall dwellers, while department-store regulars can revel in Woodbury's Barneys New York Outlet and the 32,679-square-foot Off 5th–Saks Fifth Avenue Outlet.

Vintage and secondhand clothes

The cardinal rule of secondhand-clothes shopping is: The less you browse, the more you have to pay. Although we've included a few in our listings, the shops along lower Broadway tend to ask inflated prices for anything except the most mundane '70s disco shirts. The alternatives, too numerous and ever-changing to list here, are the many small shops in the East Village and on the Lower East Side. These nooks (along with the now-famous Domsey's in Brooklyn) are where real bargains can be found. Salvation Army and Goodwill stores are also worth checking out—as is any place with the word *thrift* in its name. **Flea markets** also have a lot of vintage/antique clothing; *see page 202.*

Alice Underground

481 Broadway at Broome St (212-431-9067; www.aliceundergroundnyc.com). Subway: N, R to Prince St; 6 to Spring St. 11am–7:30pm. AmEx, MC, V.

This vintage mainstay houses a good selection of gear from the 1940s through the 1960s in all sorts of fabrics and in varied condition. Prices are high, but the bins at the front and back are always worth rummaging through. There's also a nice selection of bedding.

Allan & Suzi

416 Amsterdam Ave at 80th St (212-724-7445). Subway: 1, 9 to 79th St. Mon–Fri noon–8pm; Sat noon–7pm; Sun noon–6pm. AmEx, Disc, JCB, MC, V.
Models drop off their worn-once Comme des Garçons, Muglers and Gaultiers here. The platform-shoe collection is unmatched. A great store, but not cheap.

Anna

150 E 3rd St between Aves A and B (212-358-0195). Subway: F to Second Ave. Mon–Fri 1–8pm; Sat, Sun 1–7pm. AmEx, MC, V.
Anna is Kathy Kemp's middle name. Her shop, a haven for fashion stylists, usually stocks whatever is Kemp's current rage. Recently, she has also been carrying reworked vintage clothing as well as some pieces by local designers.

Domsey's Warehouse

431 Kent Ave at S 9th St, Williamsburg, Brooklyn (718-384-6000; www.domsey.com). Subway: J, M, Z to Marcy Ave. Mon–Fri 9am–5:30pm; Sat 9am–6:30pm; Sun 11am–5:30pm. Disc, MC, V.
Domsey's Warehouse, which recently expanded into New Jersey, has let the quality of its preworn duds fall in recent years. Still, it's usually easy to turn up something worthwhile. Choose from a huge selection of used jeans, jackets, military and industrial wear, ball gowns, shoes and hats. Especially notable are the Hawaiian shirts, the sports-gear windbreakers and the unreal prices on cowboy boots.
Other location: *90 Smith St, Perth Amboy (732-376-1551).*

Filthmart

531 E 13th St between Aves A and B (212-387-0650). Subway: L to First Ave; N, R, 4, 5, 6 to 14th St–Union Sq. Mon, Tue 12:30–7pm; Wed–Sun 12:30–8pm. Disc, MC, V.
This newish East Village store specializes in white-trash and rock & roll memorabilia from the 1960s through the early 1980s. Expect lots of leather, denim and T-shirts. Also check out the excellent pinball machine selection.

INA

101 Thompson St between Prince and Spring Sts (212-941-4757). Subway: C, E to Spring St. Noon–7pm. AmEx, MC, V.
In the market for an Alexander McQueen dress worn by Naomi Campbell? You'll find it at INA—though you won't know it was her's. For the past eight years, INA on Thompson has reigned supreme over the downtown consignment scene. The cheery Soho location features drastically reduced couture pieces, while the Nolita site tends to carry clothing that's more trendy. And be sure to visit the men's store on Mott Street.
Other locations: *21 Prince St between Mott and Elizabeth Sts (212-334-9048); INA Men, 262 Mott St between Houston and Prince Sts (212-334-2210).*

Instant replay INA Men and the other INA shops sell designer clothes on consignment.

Keni Valenti Retro-Couture

247 W 30th St between Seventh and Eighth Aves (212-967-7147; www.kenivalenti.com). Subway: A, C, E, 1, 2, 3, 9 to 34th St–Penn Station. By appointment only. AmEx, DC, Disc, MC, V.
By virtue of sheer volume and quality, Valenti is New York's premier dealer of retired evening gowns. This by-appointment-only showroom caters to models and actresses, but the space is also a mecca for anyone passionate about Halston, Courrèges and Giorgio Sant'angelo. Prices start in the thousands.

Rags-a-Go-Go

218 W 14th St between Seventh and Eighth Aves (646-486-4011). Subway: A, C, E to 14th St; L to Eighth Ave. Mon–Sat 11am–7pm; Sun 11am–6pm. AmEx, Disc, JCB, MC, V.
Do you like arranging your clothing by color? Then you'll love this place, where all the secondhand streetwear—sweatshirts, cords, tank tops, uniforms—are grouped according to hue. What's more, there's only one price for each type of clothing (e.g., all shirts are $12; all Ts are $6).
Other locations: *75 E 7th St between First and Second Aves (212-254-4771); 119 St. Marks Pl between First Ave and Ave A (212-254-4772).*

Resurrection

123 E 7th St between First Ave and Ave A (212-228-0063). Subway: L to First Ave; 6 to Astor Pl. Mon–Sat 1–9pm; Sun 1–8pm. AmEx, MC, V.
This vintage boutique is a Pucci wonderland; Kate Moss and Anna Sui are regulars. Owner Katy Rodriguez rents the space from the Theodore Wolinnin Funeral Home next door. Two dressing rooms take the place of the altar, and as you walk along the racks of leopard coats, 1940s dresses and beaded cardigans, you'll find yourself stepping on the metal outline of a coffin lifter. But don't worry: Rodriguez's shop looks more like a jewel box than a haunted house.
Other location: *217 Mott St between Prince and Spring Sts (212-625-1374).*

Screaming Mimi's

382 Lafayette St between 4th and Great Jones Sts (212-677-6464). Subway: N, R to 8th St–NYU; 6 to

Astor Pl. Mon–Sat noon–8pm; Sun noon–6pm. AmEx, DC, Disc, MC, V.
This was where Cyndi Lauper shopped in the 1980s. The prices are reasonable for what you're getting, and the selection is more carefully chosen than at the Broadway stores around the block. The window displays are always worth a look.

Fashion Services

Clothing rental

One Night Out/Mom's Night Out

147 E 72nd St between Lexington and Third Aves (212-988-1122). Subway: 6 to 68th St–Hunter College. Mon–Wed, Fri 10:30am–6pm; Thu 10:30am–8pm; Sat 11am–5pm. AmEx, DC, Disc, MC, V.
One Night Out rents brand-new evening wear to uptown socialites and downtown girls trying to pass for the same ($150 to $425). Across the hall, Mom's Night Out provides the service to expectant mothers, for $195 to $225.

Zeller Tuxedos

201 E 56th St at Third Ave, second floor (212-355-0707). Subway: N, R to Lexington Ave; 4, 5, 6 to 59th St. Mon–Fri 9am–6:30pm; Sat 10am–5pm. AmEx, MC, V.
Armani, Ungaro and Valentino tuxes are available for those who didn't think to pack theirs. Check the phone book for other locations.

Laundry

Dry cleaners

Madame Paulette Dry Cleaners

1255 Second Ave between 65th and 66th Sts (212-838-6827). Subway: 6 to 68th St–Hunter College. Mon–Fri 7:30am–7pm; Sat 8am–5pm. AmEx, MC, V.
Madame Paulette gives your designer frocks an incredibly gentle touch. This 40-year-old luxury dry cleaners knows how to treat a society lady's things.

Meurice Garment Care

31 University Pl between 8th and 9th Sts (212-475-2778). Subway: N, R to 8th St–NYU. Mon–Fri 7:30am–7pm; Sat 7:30am–5pm. AmEx, MC, V.
Don't be fooled by the old-fashioned washboards adorning the walls. Laundry is serious business here. Meurice's roster of high-profile clients includes Armani and Prada, and the company handles all kinds of delicate stain removal and other repair jobs.
Other location: *245 E 57th St between Second and Third Aves (212-759-9057).*

Midnight Express Cleaners

212-921-0111, 800-798-7248. Mon–Fri 9am–7pm; Sat 9am–1pm. AmEx, MC, V.
Telephone Midnight Express, and your laundry will be picked up anywhere below 96th Street at a mutually convenient time and returned to you the next day. It costs $6.95 for a man's suit to be cleaned, including pickup and delivery. MEC also does laundry in bulk. There are various minimum charges, depending on your location.

Laundromats

Most neighborhoods have coin-operated laundromats, but in New York it costs about the same amount to drop off your wash and let someone else do the work. Check the yellow pages for specific establishments.

Ecowash

72 W 68th St between Columbus Ave and Central Park West (212-787-3890). Subway: B, C to 72nd St; 1, 9 to 66th St–Lincoln Ctr. 7:30am–10pm. Cash only.
For the environmentally inclined, Ecowash uses only natural and nontoxic detergent. You can wash your own duds, starting at $1.75, or drop off up to seven pounds for $6.50 (each additional pound is 75 cents).

Repairs

Clothing repair

Raymond's Tailor Shop

306 Mott St between Houston and Bleecker Sts (212-226-0747). Subway: B, D, F, Q to Broadway–Lafayette St; 6 to Bleecker St. Mon–Fri 7:30am–7:30pm; Sat 9am–6:30pm. Cash only.
Raymond's can alter or repair "anything that can be worn on the body." There's also an emergency service, and pick-up and delivery are free in much of Manhattan.

R&S Cleaners

Call 212-674-6651 for information. Cash only.
This cash-only pick-up and delivery service specializes in cleaning, repairing and tailoring leather jackets. Prices start at $35, and cleaning generally takes about a week.

Jewelry and watch repair

Zig Zag Jewelers

1336A Third Ave between 76th and 77th Sts (212-794-3559). Subway: 6 to 77th St. Mon–Fri 11am–7:30pm; Sat 10am–6:30pm; Sun noon–6pm. AmEx, DC, Disc, JCB, MC, V.
These experts won't touch costume jewelry, but they'll restring and reclasp your broken Harry Winstons and Bulgaris. Watch repairs are always trustworthy; estimates are free, and new batteries cost between $10 and $30.
Other location: *963 Madison Ave between 75th and 76th Sts (212-472-6373).*

Shoe repair

Andrade Shoe Repair

103 University Pl between 12th and 13th Sts (212-529-3541). Subway: L, N, R, 4, 5, 6 to 14th St–Union Sq. Mon–Fri 7:30am–7pm; Sat 9am–6:30pm. Cash only.
Andrade is a basic—but trustworthy—shoe-repair chain. Check phone book for other locations.

Shoe Service Plus

15 W 55th St between Fifth and Sixth Aves (212-262-4823). Subway: E, F to Fifth Ave. Mon–Fri 7:30am–7pm; Sat 10am–5pm. AmEx, DC, Disc, JCB, MC, V.
This shop is bustling with customers. And no wonder: The staff here will give just as much attention to your battle-weary combat boots as to your pricey delicate Manolos.

Necessities

Accessories

Eyewear emporiums

Alain Mikli Optique

880 Madison Ave between 71st and 72nd Sts (212-472-6085). Subway: 6 to 68th St–Hunter College. Mon–Sat 10am–6pm. AmEx, JCB, MC, V.
French frames for the bold and beautiful are available from this 12-year-old Madison Avenue outlet.

Myoptics

123 Prince St between Greene and Wooster Sts (212-598-9306). Subway: N, R to Prince St. Mon–Sat 11am–7pm; Sun noon–6pm. AmEx, Disc, MC, V.
Plastics are hot at Soho's Myoptics; look for styles by Matsuda, Oliver Peoples and Paul Smith. Check the phone book for other locations.

Selima Optique

59 Wooster St between Spring and Broome Sts (212-343-9490). Subway: C, E to Spring St. Mon–Wed, Fri, Sat 11am–7pm; Thu 11am–8pm; Sun noon–7pm. AmEx, DC, JCB, MC, V.
Selima Salaun's wear-if-you-dare frames are popular with such famous four-eyes as Sean Lennon and Lenny Kravitz (both of whom have frames named for them). Salaun also stocks Alain Mikli, Matsuda, Face à Face and others.
Other location: *84 East 7th St between First and Second Aves (212-260-2495).*

Sol Moscot Opticians

118 Orchard St at Delancey St (212-477-3796). Subway: F to Delancey St; J, M, Z to Essex St. 9am–5:30pm. AmEx, DC, Disc, MC, V.
At this 75-year-old family-run optical emporium, expect to find the same big-name designer frames stocked at the pricier uptown boutiques for at least 20 percent off. Sol Moscot also carries vintage varieties that start at $29.
Other locations: *69 W 14th St at Sixth Ave (212-647-1550); 107-20 Continental Ave between Queens Blvd and Austin St, Forest Hills, Queens (718-544-2200).*

Zeitlin Optik

40 E 52nd St between Madison and Park Aves (212-319-5166). Subway: E, F to Fifth Ave. Mon–Fri 10am–6pm; Sat 10am–5pm. AmEx, DC, MC, V.
Marc Zeitlin's 14-year-old boutique stocks not-so-recognizable brands from around the world: Buvel and Mugen from Japan, Binocle from France, and Marwitz from Germany. Don't see what you want? Zeitlin will whip you up a custom pair.

Handbags

See also **Leather goods,** page 181.

Amy Chan

247 Mulberry St between Prince and Spring Sts (212-966-3417). Subway: B, D, F, Q to Broadway–Lafayette St; 6 to Spring St. Noon–7pm. AmEx, JCB, MC, V.
Although she had designed everything from shoes to waist and vest bags (years before Miu Miu and Helmut Lang showed them), designer Amy Chan's career really took off a few years back when she launched a collection of handbags made from Chinese silks, sari fabric and feathers. Her bags are now the centerpiece of her Nolita boutique.

Blue Bag

266 Elizabeth St between Houston and Prince Sts (212-966-8566). Subway: B, D, F, Q to Broadway–Lafayette St; 6 to Bleecker St. 11am–7pm. AmEx, Disc, JCB, MC, V.
Blue Bag is the walk-in handbag closet of your dreams. Its delicious bags (not all blue) are popular with Linda Evangelista and Kate Moss.

Jack Spade

56 Greene St between Spring and Broome Sts (212-625-1820). Subway: C, E to Spring St; N, R to Prince St. Mon–Sat 11am–7pm; Sun noon–6pm. AmEx, MC, V.
Jack Spade is not Kate's brother or long-lost cousin, but a fictional muse created by her husband, Andy. This shop is for the guy who's always eyed his gal's weekend bag, laptop tote or canvas accessory.

Jamin Puech

252 Mott St between Houston and Prince Sts (212-334-9730). Subway: B, D, F, Q to Broadway–Lafayette St; 6 to Bleecker St. Mon–Sat 11am–7pm; Sun noon–6pm. AmEx, JCB, MC, V.
Looking for a precious accessory or two? Make tracks to this tiny boutique, which sells exquisite creations by French partners Benoit Jamin and Isabel Puech. The selection includes flirty sequined bags, large leather totes and colorful boas.

Kate Spade

454 Broome St at Mercer St (212-274-1991). Subway: 6 to Spring St. Mon–Sat 11am–7pm; Sun noon–6pm. AmEx, MC, V.
Popular handbag designer Kate Spade sells her clas-

sic boxy tote as well as other chic numbers in this stylish store. Prices range from $80 to $400. Spade also stocks shoes, pajamas and rain slickers.

Kazuyo Nakano

223 Mott St between Prince and Spring Sts (212-941-7093). Subway: 6 to Spring St. 12:30–6pm. AmEx, JCB, MC, V.

Kazuyo Nakano started working on the assembly line at her father's kimono-bag factory in Kyoto straight out of high school. Now, nearly 20 years later, Nakano has her own handbag shop. Many of her fun and functional designs are embroidered with flowers.

Hats

Amy Downs Hats

227 E 14th St between between Second and Third Aves (212-598-4189). Subway: L to Third Ave; N, R, 4, 5, 6 to 14th St–Union Sq. Wed–Sun 1–6pm. Cash only.

Downs's soft wool and felt hats are neither fragile nor prissy. In fact, feel free to crumple them up and shove them into your bag (after purchasing them, of course)—they just won't die. Check out her trademark Twister, a cone-shaped hat with tassels.

Eugenia Kim

203 E 4th St between Aves A and B (212-673-9787). Subway: F to Second Ave. Wed–Sun 2–8pm. AmEx, MC, V.

Spotted on the street two years ago wearing one of her own creations, Eugenia Kim was besieged by shopowners who wanted to sell her hats. Now, you can go directly to the source for her funky cowboy hats, feather cloches and more.

The Hat Shop

120 Thompson St between Prince and Spring Sts (212-219-1445). Subway: C, E to Spring St; N, R to Prince St. Mon–Sat noon–7pm; Sun 1–6pm. AmEx, JCB, MC, V.

Linda Pagan isn't a hat designer herself, merely a hat junkie, and her delightful boutique is a cross between a millinery shop and a department store. Not only are customers able to choose from 40 different designers, they receive scads of personal attention, too.

Kelly Christy

235 Elizabeth St between Houston and Prince Sts (212-965-0686). Subway: B, D, F, Q to Broadway–Lafayette St; 6 to Bleecker St. Tue–Sat noon–7pm; Sun noon–6pm. AmEx, MC, V.

The selection, for both men and women, is lovely, and the atmosphere is relaxed. Try on anything you like; Christy is more than happy to help and give you the honest truth.

Knox Hats

620 Eighth Ave between 40th and 41st St (212-768-3781). Subway: A, C, E to 42nd St–Port Authority. Mon–Sat 10am–7pm; Sun 10am–4:30pm. AmEx, DC, MC, V.

Since the esteemed Madison Avenue hatter Worth & Worth closed its retail store in 1999, gentlemen have been forced to seek out new locations for quality headgear. One spot that certainly has a wide variety is the family-owned Knox Hats, which claims to have 1,000 hats in its window display.

Jewelry

Bulgari

730 Fifth Ave at 57th St (212-315-9000). Subway: N, R to Fifth Ave. Mon–Sat 10am–5:30pm. AmEx, DC, JCB, MC, V.

Bulgari offers some of the world's most beautiful adornments—everything from watches and chunky gold necklaces to leather goods and stationery.

Other location: *783 Madison Ave between 66th and 67th Sts (212-717-2300).*

Cartier

653 Fifth Ave at 52nd St (212-446-3459). Subway: E, F to Fifth Ave. Mon–Fri 10am–6pm; Sat 10am–5:30pm. AmEx, DC, JCB, MC, V.

Cartier bought its Italianate building, one of the few remnants of this neighborhood's previous life as a classy residential area, for two strands of oriental pearls. All the usual Cartier items—jewelry, silver, porcelain—are sold within.

Other locations: *Trump Tower, 725 Fifth Ave between 56th and 57th Sts (212-308-0843); 828 Madison Ave at 69th St (212-472-6400).*

Fragments

107 Greene St between Prince and Spring Sts (212-334-9588). Subway: C, E to Spring St; N, R to Prince St. Mon–Fri 11am–7pm; Sat noon–7pm; Sun noon–6pm. AmEx, MC, V.

Fragments rocks. And we're not just talking diamonds. Over the years, buyers Janet Goldman and Jimmy Moore have assembled an exclusive stable of

Me, me, me Go ahead, be selfish and buy yourself a piece of jewelry at Me & Ro.

35 artists. The jewelers first offer their designs (which are never *too* trendy) at the Soho store, before Goldman and Moore sell them to department stores like Barneys.

Ilias Lalaounis

733 Madison Ave at 64th St (212-439-9400). Subway: N, R to Lexington Ave; 4, 5, 6 to 59th St. Mon–Sat 10am–5:30pm. AmEx, MC, V.

This Greek jewelry designer's work is inspired by his native country's ancient symbols as well as American Indian and Arabic designs.

Kara Varian Baker

215 Mulberry St between Prince and Spring Sts (212-431-5727). Subway: 6 to Spring St. Wed–Sat noon–7pm; Sun noon–5pm. AmEx, Disc, JCB, MC, V.

Kara Varian Baker's store feels more like a New Age living room than a trendy boutique. Famous for her chunky sterling-silver lockets, Baker also designs classic pearl necklaces and avant-garde pieces with colorful stones.

L'Atelier

89 E 2nd St between First Ave and Ave A (212-677-4983). Subway: F to Second Ave. Mon–Fri 11am–7pm; Sat noon–6:30pm. AmEx, MC, V.

All of the precious-metals adornments at this small East Village jewel box are made on-site.

Manny Winick & Son

19 W 47th St at Fifth Ave (212-302-9555). Subway: B, D, F, Q to 47–50th Sts–Rockefeller Ctr. Mon–Fri 10am–5:30pm; Sat 10am–4:30pm. AmEx, Disc, MC, V.

Traditional jewelry made from precious stones is sold alongside more sculptural contemporary pieces.

Me & Ro

239 Elizabeth St between Houston and Prince Sts (917-237-9215). Subway: B, D, F, Q to Broadway–Lafayette St; 6 to Bleecker St. Tue–Sat 11am–6pm; Sun noon–6pm. AmEx, MC, V.

After nine years of selling their merchandise at other people's shops, Robin Renzi and Michele Quan, the dynamic duo behind Me & Ro jewelry, opened their first boutique in fall 1999. Their designs are inspired by ancient Chinese, Tibetan and Indian traditions (such as tying bells around the wrist as a form of protection). Their celeb following includes Madonna and Julia Roberts.

Piaget

730 Fifth Ave at 57th St (212-246-5555). Subway: N, R to Fifth Ave. Mon–Sat 10am–6pm. AmEx, DC, JCB, MC, V.

This giant boutique full of glittering jewels would surely make any girl swoon—as well as the person paying for that perfect diamond.

Push

240 Mulberry St between Prince and Spring Sts (212-965-9699). Subway: 6 to Spring St. Tue–Sat noon–7pm; Sun 1–6pm. AmEx, DC, JCB, MC, V.

Karen Karch's charming rings, most of which are simple, narrow diamond settings, make spending two months' salary on an engagement band obsolete. If you're not getting hitched, the store still has plenty to offer.

Reinstein/Ross

122 Prince St between Greene and Wooster Sts (212-226-4513). Subway: N, R to Prince St. Mon–Sat 11:30am–7pm; Sun noon–6pm. AmEx, MC, V.

Most of the sleek, handmade engagement and wedding bands at Reinstein/Ross are made with the store's custom alloys, such as 22-karat "apricot" gold. The designs look like they came from the Met's Roman collection.

Other location: *29 E 73rd St between Fifth and Madison Aves (212-772-1901).*

Robert Lee Morris

400 West Broadway between Spring and Broome Sts (212-431-9405). Subway: C, E to Spring St; N, R to Prince St. Mon–Fri 11am–6pm; Sat 11am–7pm; Sun noon–6pm. AmEx, Disc, MC, V.

Robert Lee Morris is one of the foremost contemporary designers; his bright Soho gallery is filled with strong, striking pieces.

Ted Muehling

47 Greene St between Broome and Grand Sts (212-431-3825). Subway: C, E to Spring St; N, R to Prince St. Tue–Sat noon–6pm. AmEx, MC, V.

Ted Muehling creates beautiful organic shapes in the studio behind the store, where he also sells the work of other artists.

Tiffany & Co.

727 Fifth Ave at 57th St (212-755-8000). Subway: N, R to Fifth Ave. Mon–Wed, Fri, Sat 10am–6pm; Thu 10am–7pm. AmEx, DC, JCB, MC, V.

Tiffany's heyday was around the turn of the century, when Louis Comfort Tiffany was designing his famous lamps and sensational Art Nouveau jewelry. Today, the big stars are Paloma Picasso and Elsa Peretti. Three stories are stacked with precious jewels, silver accessories, chic watches, stationery and porcelain.

Luggage

Need more luggage because you bought too much stuff? Before you head for the nearest Samsonite dealer, check out the many shops on Orchard and Canal Streets that sell cheapo luggage. None stand out, but they are good, quick fixes. Other, more expensive options are listed below.

Bag House

797 Broadway at 11th St (212-260-0940). Subway: L, N, R, 4, 5, 6 to 14th St–Union Sq. Mon–Sat 11am–7pm; Sun 1–6pm. AmEx, DC, MC, V.

All manner of bags, from the tiniest tote to something you could stow a small family in, are available here.

Flight 001

See page 212 for listing.

Innovation Luggage

300 E 42nd St at Second Ave (212-599-2998). Subway: S, 4, 5, 6, 7 to 42nd St–Grand Central. Mon–Fri 9am–8pm; Sat 10am–7pm; Sun 11am–6pm. AmEx, Disc, MC, V.

This chain carries the newest (but not necessarily chicest) models of top-brand luggage, including Tumi, Samsonite, Andiamo and Dakota. Check the phone book for other locations.

Shoes

West 8th Street has shoe stores lining both sides of the block between Broadway and Sixth Avenue. Don't want to shop-hop? For the latest in swanky shoes, swing by Barneys New York or Jeffrey New York. For sheer variety, Saks Fifth Avenue wins, toes down (*see* **Department stores,** *page 167*). Below, you'll find sneakers, boots and designer knockoffs. For **Shoe repair,** *see page 190.*

Billy Martin's

810 Madison Ave at 68th St (212-861-3100). Subway: 6 to 68th St–Hunter College. Mon–Fri 10am–7pm; Sat 10am–6pm; Sun noon–5pm. AmEx, DC, MC, V.

Founded in 1978 by the late many-time Yankee manager Billy Martin, this Western store features heaps of cowboy boots in all colors and sizes.

Christian Louboutin

941 Madison Ave between 74th and 75th Sts (212-396-1884). Subway: 6 to 77th St. Mon–Sat 10am–6:30pm. AmEx, MC, V.

Louboutin, famous for his sexy, superpricey red-soled shoes, brought his French foot sensibilities to the Upper East Side in 1999. Serious shoe hounds should come prepared with several hundred dollars.

Chuckies

399 West Broadway between Spring and Broome Sts (212-343-1717). Subway: C, E to Spring St. Mon–Sat 11am–8pm; Sun noon–8pm. AmEx, MC, V.

An alternative to department store shoe floors, Chuckies carries an exhaustive supply of high-profile labels. Stock ranges from old-school Fendis to up-and-coming Ernesto Espositos.
Other location: *1073 Third Ave between 63rd and 64th Sts (212-593-9898).*

David Aaron

529 Broadway between Prince and Spring Sts (212-431-6022). Subway: N, R to Prince St; 6 to Spring St. Mon–Thu 11am–8pm; Fri, Sat 11am–8:30pm; Sun 11am–7:30pm. AmEx, Disc, MC, V.

Want the latest footwear fashions for a bargain? Stop by this shop, which blatantly copies the hottest styles mere weeks after they appear in stores.

Jimmy Choo

645 Fifth Ave, entrance on 51st St (212-593-0800). Subway: E, F to Fifth Ave. Mon–Sat 10am–6pm. AmEx, MC, V.

Jimmy Choo, famed for conceiving Princess Diana's custom-shoe collection, is conquering America with his three-year-old emporium. The plush space features Choo's chic boots, sexy pumps and kittenish flats—none of which sells for less than $350.

J.M. Weston

812 Madison Ave at 68th St (212-535-2100). Subway: 6 to 68th St–Hunter College. Mon–Wed, Fri, Sat 10am–6pm; Thu 10am–8pm; Sun 1–5. AmEx, MC, V.

Weston shoes, exquisitely handmade in 34 styles, appeal to a range of men from Woody Allen to Yves Saint Laurent. "Westons don't fit you; you fit them," notes Robert Deslauriers, the man who established the Manhattan store of this Paris institution. The shop also stocks women's shoes.

Manolo Blahnik

31 W 54th St between Fifth and Sixth Aves (212-582-3007). Subway: E, F to Fifth Ave. Mon–Fri 10:30am–6pm; Sat 10:30am–5pm. AmEx, MC, V.

Made by the high priest of glamour, these timeless shoes—in innovative designs and maximum taste—will put style in your step.

McCreedy & Schreiber

37 W 46th St between Fifth and Sixth Aves (212-719-1552). Subway: B, D, F, Q to 47–50th Sts–Rockefeller Ctr; 7 to Fifth Ave. Mon–Sat 9am–7pm; Sun 11am–5pm. AmEx, DC, Disc, MC, V.

This well-known quality men's shoe store is good for traditional American styles: Bass Weejuns, Sperry Topsiders, Frye boots and the famous Lucchese boots, in everything from goatskin to crocodile.
Other location: *213 E 59th St between Second and Third Aves (212-759-9241).*

Otto Tootsi Plohound

413 West Broadway between Prince and Spring Sts (212-925-8931). Subway: C, E to Spring St; N, R to Prince St. Mon–Fri 11:30am–7:30pm; Sat 11am–8pm; Sun noon–7pm. AmEx, DC, JCB, MC, V.

One of the best places for the latest in shoe styles, Tootsi carries a wide range of trendy imports for both women and men. Prices for some pairs are tolerable, but beware of the impulse to splurge.
Other locations: *137 Fifth Ave between 20th and 21st Sts (212-460-8650); 38 E 57th St between Park and Madison Aves (212-231-3199).*

Sigerson Morrison

242 Mott St between Houston and Prince Sts (212-219-3893). Subway: B, D, F, Q to Broadway–Lafayette St; 6 to Bleecker St. Mon–Sat 11am–7pm; Sun noon–6pm. AmEx, MC, V.

Stop by this cultish women's shoe store for delicate styles in the prettiest colors: ruby red, crocodile olive, shiny pearl and baby blue.

Stephane Kélian

158 Mercer St between Prince and Houston Sts (212-925-3077). Subway: N, R to Prince St. Mon–Sat 11am–7pm; Sun noon–6pm. AmEx, DC, JCB, MC, V.

Check out this funky French shoe master's latest looks for men and women at his quiet Soho boutique. **Other location:** *717 Madison Ave between 63rd and 64th Sts (212-980-1919).*

Timberland

709 Madison Ave at 63rd St (212-754-0434). Subway: N, R to Fifth Ave; 4, 5, 6 to 59th St. Mon–Sat 9:30am–7pm; Sun noon–6pm. AmEx, Disc, MC, V.

The complete American line of Timberland shoes and boots for men and women is sold here. The company's rugged outdoor apparel is also available.

Transit

655 Broadway between Bond and Bleecker Sts (212-358-8726). Subway: 6 to Bleecker St. Mon–Sat 9am–8:30pm; Sun 10am–7:30pm. AmEx, DC, Disc, MC, V.

Customers enter this NYC subway–inspired sneaker shop via a turnstile. In addition to Nike, Adidas and New Balance, the store carries designer kicks from Donna Karan and Polo Ralph Lauren.

Health & Beauty

Bath, body and beauty booty

Alcone

235 W 19th St between Seventh and Eighth Aves (212-633-0551). Subway: 1, 9 to 18th St. Mon–Sat 11am–6pm. AmEx, MC, V.

Frequented by make-up artists, Chelsea's Alcone offers brands and products you won't find elsewhere in the city, such as Visiora foundation and the German brand Kryolan. It's full of items that might belong on a horror-movie set (fake-blood and bruise kits, for instance), but mere mortals shop for its premade palettes (trays of a dozen or more eye, lip and cheek colors). Not to miss: Alcone's own sponges.

Aveda

233 Spring St between Sixth Ave and Varick St (212-807-1492). Subway: C, E to Spring St; 1, 9 to Houston St. Mon–Fri 10am–7pm; Sat 10am–6pm; Sun 11am–6pm. AmEx, DC, MC, V.

This is a spacious, tranquil boutique filled with an exclusive line of hair- and skin-care products, makeup, massage oils and cleansers, all made from flower and plant extracts. Check the phone book for other locations.

The Body Shop

773 Lexington Ave at 61st St (212-755-7851). Subway: N, R to Lexington Ave; 4, 5, 6 to 59th St. Mon–Sat 10am–8pm; Sun 11am–6pm. AmEx, Disc, MC, V.

The Body Shop, as most everyone knows, is the premier place for natural beauty products in no-nonsense, biodegradable plastic bottles. Check the phone book for other locations.

Face Stockholm

110 Prince St at Greene St (212-966-9110). Subway: N, R to Prince St. Mon–Sat 11am–8pm; Sun noon–7pm. AmEx, MC, V.

Along with a full line of shadows, lipsticks, tools and blushes (at very reasonable prices), Face offers two services: makeup applications and lessons. Phone for an appointment or just stop by and check it out yourself.

Other locations: *687 Madison Ave at 62nd St (212-207-8833); 226 Columbus Ave between 70th and 71st Sts (212-769-1420).*

5S

98 Prince St between Mercer and Greene Sts (212-925-7880). Subway: N, R to Prince St. Mon–Thu 11am–7pm; Fri, Sat 11am–8pm; Sun noon–7pm. AmEx, JCB, MC, V.

The newish makeup and skin-care line 5S, by Japanese cosmetics giant Shiseido, takes a novel approach to beauty. Products are divided into five "senses of well-being" categories, ranging from energizing to nurturing.

Fresh

1061 Madison Ave between 80th and 81st Sts (212-396-0344). Subway: 6 to 77th St. Mon–Sat 10am–7pm; Sun noon–6pm. AmEx, MC, V.

Fresh, one of the soap industry's leaders, is a Boston company that bases its soaps, lotions and other products on natural ingredients such as honey, milk and sugar. Head to this bilevel store to stock up on cyclamen- and freesia-scented soap, and to sample the company's makeup and fragrance lines.

Other location: *57 Spring St between Lafayette and Mulberry Sts (212-925-0099).*

Kiehl's

109 Third Ave between 13th and 14th Sts (212-677-3171). Subway: L, N, R, 4, 5, 6 to 14th St–Union Sq. Mon–Wed, Fri 10am–6:30pm; Thu 10am–7:30pm; Sat 10am–6pm. AmEx, DC, MC, V.

Kiehl's is a New York institution; it has called this Third Avenue shop home since 1851. Stop by to try the company's luxurious face moisturizer, lip balm or Creme with Silk Groom, and you'll be hooked for life. The staff is knowledgeable and friendly, and extremely generous with free samples.

L'Occitane

1046 Madison Ave at 80th St (212-396-9097). Subway: 6 to 77th St. Mon–Sat 10am–7pm; Sun noon–6pm. AmEx, DC, MC, V.

Fans of L'Occitane, a 25-year-old line of bath and beauty products made in Provence, flock to this shop to pick up brick-size soaps, massage balm and shea-butter hand cream. Check the phone book for other locations.

M•A•C

14 Christopher St between Sixth and Seventh Aves (212-243-4150). Subway: 1, 9 to Christopher St–Sheridan Sq. Mon–Wed, Fri, Sat 11am–7pm; Thu 11am–8pm; Sun noon–6pm. AmEx, MC, V.

Makeup Art Cosmetics, a Canadian company, is

Necessities

Scent of a woman English-import Creed stocks hundreds of fragrances.

committed to the development of cruelty-free products and is famous for its lipsticks and eyeshadows in otherwise unobtainable colors. The enormous Soho branch is a bit like an art gallery and features nine makeover counters.
Other location: *113 Spring St between Greene and Mercer Sts (212-334-4641).*

Make Up Forever

409 West Broadway between Prince and Spring Sts (212-941-9337). Subway: C, E to Spring St; N, R to Prince St. Mon–Sat 11am–7pm; Sun noon–6pm. AmEx, MC, V.
Make Up Forever, a French line introduced in the United States a few years ago, is popular with women and drag queens alike. Colors range from bold purples and fuchsias to muted browns and soft pinks; the mascara is a must-have.

Ricky's

718 Broadway at Washington Pl (212-979-5232). Subway: N, R to 8th St–NYU. Mon–Thu 8am–11pm; Fri–Sun 8am–midnight. AmEx, DC, Disc, JCB, MC, V.
Stock up on tools and extras such as Tweezerman tweezers, cheap containers for traveling, empty make-up palettes, odd-shaped cotton swabs (e.g., ones with a flat head) and makeup cases that look like souped-up tackle boxes. Ricky's in-house makeup line, Mattése, offers fake lashes, glitter, nail polish and other items in colors and packaging similar to that of M•A•C. Check the phone book for other locations.

Sephora

555 Broadway between Prince and Spring Sts (212-625-1309). Subway: N, R to Prince St. Mon–Wed, Sat 10am–8pm; Thu, Fri 10am–9pm; Sun noon–7pm. AmEx, Disc, JCB, MC, V.
Sephora, the French beauty chain that is slowly working its way across America, has given downtown gals a reason to stay put: it has everything. The 8,000-square-foot makeup library looks like the first floor of a department store, but no one is standing behind the display cases (staffers hang back until you choose to seek them out). The flagship store is at Rockefeller Center; check the phone book for other locations.

Shiseido Studio

155 Spring St between Wooster St and West Broadway (212-625-8820). Subway: C, E to Spring St. Sun, Mon noon–6pm; Tue 11am–6pm; Wed–Sat 11am–7pm.
A beauty store without one product for sale? It may sound crazy, but the folks behind the supersuccessful Shiseido makeup and skin-care lines have opened a 3,800-square-foot consumer learning center aimed at educating shoppers about skin care. Visitors are encouraged to test more than 330 items—cosmetics, fragrances and more.

Shu Uemura

121 Greene St between Prince and Spring Sts (212-979-5500). Subway: C, E to Spring St; N, R to Prince St. Mon–Sat 11am–7pm; Sun noon–6pm. AmEx, MC, V.
The entire line of Shu Uemura Japanese cosmetics is for sale at this stark, well-lit Soho boutique. Most hit Shu Uemura for its selection of brushes, lipsticks, blushes and eye shadows, but for a real eye-opening experience, check out the best-selling eyelash-curler.

Perfumeries

Creed

9 Bond St between Broadway and Lafayette St (212-228-1940). Subway: B, D, F, Q to Broadway–Lafayette St; 6 to Bleecker St. Mon–Sat 11:30am–7:30pm; Sun noon–6pm. AmEx, MC, V.

In this city, you'd be hard-pressed to find many affordable items that are two-and-a-half centuries old. But now that the 240-year-old English perfume house Creed has set up shop, you'll find many pedigreed items—and they smell good, too. Customers are encouraged to walk the 9,000-square-foot gallery and test the hundreds of fragrances. This is Creed's first new store in 100 years.

Demeter

83 Second Ave between 4th and 5th Sts (212-505-1535). Subway: F to Second Ave. Mon–Sat noon–7pm. MC, V.

If you follow the smell of dirt, tomatoes, and gin and tonics along lower Second Avenue, it doesn't mean you're near a restaurant dumpster. Your nose could have led you to Demeter Fragrances' anything-but-chichi boutique. In addition to its famous single-note scents like Prune, Crème Brûlée and Holy Water, the shop carries Demeter's full range of bath and body products.

Pharmacists

For 24-hour pharmacies, see chapter **Directory, Health and medical facilities.**

C.O. Bigelow Apothecaries

414 Sixth Ave between 8th and 9th Sts (212-533-2700). Subway: A, C, E, B, D, F, Q to W 4th St. Mon–Fri 7:30am–9pm; Sat 8:30am–7pm; Sun 8:30am–5:30pm. AmEx, DC, Disc, MC, V.

One of the grand old New York pharmacies, Bigelow is the place to find soaps, creams, perfumes, hygiene products, over-the-counter remedies, hair accessories, makeup—you name it.

Zitomer

969 Madison Ave between 75th and 76th Sts (212-737-4480). Subway: 6 to 77th St. Mon–Fri 9am–8pm; Sat 9am–7pm; Sun 10am–6pm. AmEx, DC, Disc, JCB, MC, V.

Zitomer has every bath, beauty and health product under the sun. The second floor has children's clothing and toys. The store also sells underwear, socks and panty hose.

Salons and spas

Some swanky salons free up their $200 chairs one night a week for those willing to become cut

Blissed out You'll have to plan ahead if you want to visit Bliss 57 for a spa treatment.

or color guinea pigs for trainees. Not to worry—there's much supervision, and the results are usually wonderful. Best of all, it costs a fraction of the usual price. All of the following have model nights, with prices starting at $30 (usually payable in cash only). Phone for details about their next model night, but know that you may well have to join a three-month waiting list. **Louis Licari** (*212-327-0639*). **Peter Coppola Salon** (*212-988-9404*). **Frédéric Fekkai Beauté de Provence** (*212-753-9500*).

In addition to those salons, which all offer superb cuts and color, the salons below are a few NYC standouts.

Devachan

558 Broadway between Prince and Spring Sts, second floor (212-274-8686). Subway: N, R to Prince St. Tue–Fri 11am–7pm; Sat 10am–5pm. AmEx, MC, V.

This cozy, intimate salon is where celebrities and socialites go to hide their roots. Cuts start at $80; color starts at $60. The salon doubles as a spa—book an appointment for a kick-butt pore-picking or just settle for the killer scalp massage offered when your color is rinsed out.

Miano Viel Salon and Spa

16 E 52nd St between Fifth and Madison Aves, second floor (212-980-3222). Subway: E, F to Fifth Ave. Tue 9am–6pm; Wed 9am–5:30pm; Thu, Fri 9am–7pm; Sat 9am–5pm. MC, V.

You could pay more than $300 in one sitting, but Damian Miano and Louis Viel know how to treat a girl's tresses.

Parlor

102 Ave B between 6th and 7th Sts (212-673-5520). Subway: F to Second Ave; L to First Ave. Tue–Fri noon–9pm; Sat 11am–7pm. AmEx, MC, V.

Cuts are about $75 at this hipster–meets–glamour-puss East Village beauty parlor.

Privé

310 West Broadway between Grand and Canal Sts (212-274-8888). Subway: A, C, E to Canal St. Tue–Fri 10am–8pm; Sat 10am–7pm; Sun 11am–6pm. AmEx, MC, V.

No need to head uptown for luxe locks. Laurent D., famous for tending to the tresses of celebs like Gwyneth Paltrow, scored prime retail space in the SoHo Grand Hotel for his first New York salon. Haircuts with Laurent cost $185, with others $90 to $125. Highlights start at $125.

Suite 303

Chelsea Hotel, 222 W 23rd St between Seventh and Eighth Aves (212-633-1011). Subway: C, E, 1, 9 to 23rd St. Tue–Sat noon–6:45pm. Cash only.

Owned by three ex-Racine stylists, Suite 303 is located in the wonderfully spooky Chelsea Hotel. Haircuts start at $60. Highlights start at $110.

Ultra

233 E 4th St between Aves A and B (212-677-4380). Subway: F to Second Ave. Call ahead for hours. AmEx, DC, MC, V.

It's no wonder the music industry flocks to Ultra. This tiny salon's anonymous, mint-green storefront has the feel of a low-profile club. Cuts start at $75, color at $60, highlights $85 and up.

Cheap cuts & blow-drys

Astor Place Hair Stylists

2 Astor Pl at Broadway (212-475-9854). Subway: N, R to 8th St–NYU; 6 to Astor Pl. Mon–Sat 8am–8pm; Sun 9am–6pm. Cash only.

This is the classic New York hair experience. An army of barbers does everything from neat trims to shaved designs, all to pounding music—usually hip-hop. You can't make an appointment; just take a number and wait outside with the crowd. Sunday mornings are quiet. Cuts start at $11, blow-drys at $15.

Jean Louis David

1180 Sixth Ave at 46th St (212-944-7389). Subway: B, D, F, Q to 47–50th Sts–Rockefeller Ctr. Mon–Wed, Fri 10am–7pm; Thu 10am–8pm. MC, V.

Everything happens fast at this chain. Models flicker in and out of view on a television screen. Stylists scurry about in white lab coats. Best of all, a shampoo, trendy cut and blowout can be yours, without an appointment, for under $30. A shampoo and blowout costs $23.39. Check the phone book for other locations.

Nails

Rescue

21 Cleveland Pl between Spring and Kenmare Sts (212-431-3805). Subway: 6 to Spring St. Tue, Wed 11am–7pm; Thu, Fri noon–8pm; Sat, Sun 10am–6pm. AmEx, MC, V.

Are your hands in a state of emergency? Run to Rescue. This charming garden-level space has been open for only two years—and neighbors are still discovering its intensive treatments. The Ultra TLC manicure ($28) is worth every penny.

Spas

Feeling frazzled? After long days of battling vicious city crowds and being always on the go, you may want to pamper your weary body with a visit to a spa. Most treatments start at $60, but no matter how ridiculously relaxed you feel afterward, don't forget to leave a tip (15 to 20 percent).

Avon Centre Spa

Trump Tower, 725 Fifth Ave between 56th and 57th Sts, sixth floor (212-755-2866). Subway: N, R to

Fifth Ave. Mon, Tue, Fri, Sat 9am–6pm; Wed, Thu 10am–8pm. AmEx, MC, V.
Forget Skin-So-Soft Avon: This is just the type of place you'd expect to find in glitzy Trump Tower. It offers not only face and body treatments but also highlights with top colorist Brad Johns, and the famous eyebrow pluckings of Eliza Petrescu.

Bliss 57

19 E 57th St between Fifth and Madison Aves, third floor (212-219-8970). Subway: B, Q to 57th St; E, F to Fifth Ave. Mon–Fri 9:30am–8:30pm; Sat 9:30am–6:30pm. AmEx, MC, V.
This new uptown sister of Soho's hippest spa is the ultimate in tony retreats. The sleekly designed Bliss 57 takes indulgence to a new level, offering multiple services at once—to cut down on the time that your necessary coddling requires. Want a manicure in tandem with your facial? Done. How about an underarm wax as well? No problem. Just prepare to plop down—and max out—the plastic.
Other location: *Bliss, 568 Broadway between Houston and Prince Sts, second floor (212-219-8970).*

Carapan

5 W 16th St between Fifth and Sixth Aves, garden level (212-633-6220). Subway: L, N, R, 4, 5, 6 to 14th St–Union Sq. 10am–9:45pm. AmEx, MC, V.
Carapan, which means "a beautiful place of tranquillity where one comes to restore one's spirit" in the language of the Pueblo Indians, offers reiki, craniosacral therapy and manual lymphatic drainage.

Helena Rubinstein

135 Spring St between Greene and Wooster Sts (212-343-9963). Subway: C, E, 6 to Spring St. Tue 11am–7pm; Wed 11am–9pm; Thu, Fri 11am–8pm; Sat 10am–6pm; Sun noon–6pm. AmEx, MC, V.
Head downstairs past HR's street-level Beauty Gallery, which sells makeup and skin-care products, to enter a quiet, plush oasis. Change into a soft robe behind privacy curtains in the locker room and await your treatments in a sleek lounge supplied with magazines, cookies and ice water. To prepare for reentry into the real world, take a steam shower or a sample from the skin-care and perfume trays in the bathroom.

The Mezzanine Spa at Soho Integrative Health Center

62 Crosby St between Spring and Broome Sts (212-431-1600). Subway: 6 to Spring St. Mon–Fri 8am–8pm; Sat, Sun noon–8pm. AmEx, MC, V.
The brainchild of dermatologist Dr. Laurie Polis, the spa is located inside her luxurious doctor's office, giving beauty clients the expertise of a medical pro. The Mezzanine includes four facial rooms and two wet rooms for rinse-requiring services, such as the volcanic mud treatment. The spa's signature therapy is the Diamond Peel: a device that exfoliates the face using suction and microcrystals.

Prema Nolita

252 Elizabeth St between Houston and Prince Sts (212-226-3972). Subway: B, D, F, Q to Broadway–Lafayette St; 6 to Bleecker St. Tue–Sat 11am–8pm; Sun 11am–6pm. AmEx, MC, V.
Owned by beauty-biz veteran Celeste Induddi and her two partners, Prema Nolita may be the tiniest spa in the city. In the front of the shop, shelves display cult skin-care lines Jurlique and Anne Semonin. At the back, there's a single treatment room, offering a lavish list of services.

Objects of Desire

Cameras and electronics

When shopping for cameras and other electronics, it helps if you know exactly what you want before venturing inside the shop: If you look lost, you will certainly be given a hard sell. When buying a major item, check newspaper ads for price guidelines (start with the inserts in the Sunday *New York Times*). It pays to go to a reputable shop, but if you're brave, you can get small pieces such as Walkmans for cheap in the questionable establishments along Canal Street, but don't expect a warranty. Another reason to go to a more reputable place is to get reliable (and essential) advice about the devices' compatibility with systems in the country where you want to use it.

B&H Photo

420 Ninth Ave between 33rd and 34th Sts (212-444-5040). Subway: A, C, E to 34th St–Penn Station. Mon–Thu 9am–7pm; Fri 9am–2pm; Sun 10am–5pm. AmEx, Disc, MC, V.
If you can deal with the odd hours (B&H is also closed on all Jewish holidays), long lines and a bit of a schlepp, this emporium is the ultimate one-stop shop for all your photographic, video and audio needs. This is the favorite shop of up-and-coming professional photographers.

Bang & Olufsen

927 Broadway between 21st and 22nd Sts (212-388-9792). Subway: N, R to 23rd St. Mon–Fri 9:30am–7pm; Sat 9:30am–6pm; Sun noon–5pm. AmEx, MC, V.
Sleek and Swedish-efficient, Bang & Olufsen's upscale home electronics are must-haves for any design-mad techie. Favorites include the yellow dolomite, four-inch-deep BeoSound 2000 stereo and the BeoCom 6000 cordless phone, with a 1,200-yard range (slightly larger than a pack of cigarettes, the phone has an interior antenna and stores up to 200 numbers).
Other location: *952 Madison Ave at 75th St (212-879-6161).*

Harvey

2 W 45th St between Fifth and Sixth Aves (212-575-5000). Subway: B, D, F, Q to 42nd St. Mon–Wed, Fri 9:30am–6pm; Thu 9:30am–8pm; Sat 10am–6pm; Sun noon–5pm. AmEx, MC, V.

Harvey offers chain-store variety without the lousy warranties and mass-market stereo components. There are lots of high-end products, but plenty of realistically priced items, too.

Other location: *888 Broadway at 19th St, inside ABC Carpet & Home (212-228-5354).*

J&R Electronics

23 Park Row between Beekman and Ann Sts (212-238-9000, 800-221-8180). Subway: J, M, Z to Fulton St; 2, 3 to Park Pl; 4, 5, 6 to Brooklyn Bridge–City Hall. Mon–Wed, Fri, Sat 9am–7pm; Thu 9am–7:30pm; Sun 10:30am–6:30pm. AmEx, Disc, MC, V.

This block-long row of shops carries everything (from PCs and TVs to CDs) for your home-entertainment needs.

The Wiz

726 Broadway between Washington and Waverly Pls (212-677-4111). Subway: N, R to 8th St–NYU; 6 to Astor Pl. Mon–Fri 10am–9:30pm; Sat 9am–9:30pm; Sun 11am–6pm. AmEx, DC, Disc, MC, V.

Thanks to the Wiz's claim that it will match or beat any advertised price on electronic equipment, even the illegal importers on Canal Street have a hard time keeping up. Check the phone book for other locations.

Photo processing

Photo-developing services can be found on just about any city block. Most drugstores (Rite Aid and CVS, for example) and megastores such as Kmart offer this service, although the best results should be expected from those that develop on the premises.

Duggal

9 W 20th St between Fifth and Sixth Aves (212-242-7000). Subway: F, N, R to 23rd St. Mon–Fri open 24 hours; Sat, Sun 9am–6pm. AmEx, MC, V.

Duggal has amassed a large and dedicated following, ranging from artists such as David LaChapelle to big-name companies like American Express and Armani. Started by Indian immigrant Baldev Duggal some 40 years ago, this around-the-clock shop focuses on being able to develop any type of film—and do it flawlessly (the prices reflect that).

Gadget repairs

Computer Solutions Provider

45 W 21st St between Fifth and Sixth Aves, second floor (212-463-9744; www.cspny.com). Subway: F, N, R to 23rd St. Mon–Fri 9am–6pm. AmEx, MC, V.

Specialists in Macs, IBMs and all related peripherals, CSP's staffers can recover your lost data and soothe you through all manner of computer disasters. They perform on-site repairs.

Panorama Camera Center

124 W 30th St between Sixth and Seventh Aves (212-563-1651). Subway: 1, 9 to 28th St. Mon–Fri 9am–6pm; Sat 11am–3pm. AmEx, MC, V.

All kinds of camera and camcorder problems can be solved here, with an eye to speed if necessary.

Photo-Tech Repair Service

110 E 13th St between Third and Fourth Aves (212-673-8400; www.phototech.com). Subway: L, N, R, 4, 5, 6 to 14th St–Union Sq. Mon, Tue, Thu, Fri 8am–4:45pm; Wed 8am–6pm; Sat 10am–3pm. AmEx, Disc, MC, V.

Photo-Tech has been servicing the dropped, cracked and drowned since 1959. With 19 on-site technicians at your disposal, Photo-Tech guarantees that all camera wrongs can be righted, no matter the brand of equipment. Expect to pay $5 to replace a battery cover or $100 to get that Canon Elph back into shape. Rush services are available, but repairs generally take one to two weeks.

Children's toys

Enchanted Forest

85 Mercer St between Spring and Broome Sts (212-925-6677). Subway: N, R to Prince St. Mon–Sat 11am–7pm; Sun noon–6pm. AmEx, DC, Disc, JCB, MC, V.

Browse through this gallery of beasts, books and handmade toys in a magical forest setting.

FAO Schwarz

767 Fifth Ave between 58th and 59th Sts (212-644-9400). Subway: N, R to Fifth Ave; 4, 5, 6 to 59th St. Mon–Sat 10am–6pm; Sun 11am–6pm. AmEx, DC, Disc, MC, V.

This famous toy emporium, which has been supplying New York kids with playthings since 1862, stocks more stuffed animals than would invade your worst nightmare. There are also kites, dolls, games, miniature cars, toy soldiers, bath toys and so on.

Kidding Around

60 W 15th St between Fifth and Sixth Aves (212-645-6337). Subway: F to 14th St; L to Sixth Ave. Mon–Fri 10am–7pm; Sat 11am–7pm; Sun 11am–6pm. AmEx, Disc, MC, V.

This quaint shop offers loyal customers playful toys and a small collection of kid's clothing.

Other location: *68 Bleecker St between Broadway and Lafayette St (212-598-0228).*

Penny Whistle Toys

448 Columbus Ave between 81st and 82nd Sts (212-873-9090). Subway: B, C to 81st St; 1, 9 to 79th St. Mon–Fri 10am–7pm; Sat 10am–6pm; Sun 11am–5pm. AmEx, MC, V.

The bubble-blowing teddy bear stationed outside is a neighborhood favorite. Expect more jigsaw puzzles and Play-Doh than video games.

Other location: *1283 Madison Ave between 91st and 92nd Sts (212-369-3868).*

Flea markets

For bargain-hungry New Yorkers, rummaging through flea markets qualifies as a religious experience. There's no better way to walk off that Bloody Mary brunch than by wandering through aisles of vinyl records, 8-track tapes, clothes, books and furniture.

Although Mayor Giuliani has clamped down on the number of illegal street vendors working in the city, you might still get lucky: East Village vendors are persistent, if unreliable. Try looking along Second Avenue and Avenue A at night or lower Broadway on weekend afternoons for used clothes, records and magazines. And when the weather's nice, there are sidewalk or stoop sales. Although not as common in Manhattan, stoop sales are held on Saturdays in parts of Brooklyn (Park Slope, especially) and Queens. If you have a car, you'll quickly spot the signs attached to trees and posts; if not, local free papers usually found in grocery stores provide the hours, dates and addresses. Sidewalk shopping is popular with the natives, and they're serious, so head out early.

Necessities

Annex Antiques Fair & Flea Market

Sixth Ave between 25th and 26th Sts (212-243-5343). Subway: F to 23rd St. Sat, Sun 9am–5pm.
Designer Anna Sui hunts regularly at the Annex, as do plenty of models and the occasional dolled-down celebrity. Divided into scattered sections, one of which charges $1, the market has shrunk a bit due to building on part of the site. All areas feature heaps of secondhand clothing (some of it actually antique-quality), old bicycles, platform shoes, birdcages, vinatge eyeglass frames, funky tools and those always-necessary accessories: hats, purses, gloves and compacts. Don't miss the Garage—the nearby indoor market is a trove of unusual items: a pristine 1960s clock was unearthed here not too long ago at a deep, deep discount. The garage is heaven, especially on a cold day.
Other location: *The Garage, 112 W 25th St between Sixth and Seventh Aves (212-243-5343).*

Antique Flea & Farmer's Market

P.S. 183, 67th St between First and York Aves (212-721-0900). Subway: 6 to 68th St–Hunter College. Sat 6am–6pm.
This is a small market, but one that's good for antique lace, silverware and tapestries. Fresh eggs, fish and vegetables are often also available.

I.S. 44 Flea Market

Columbus Ave between 76th and 77th Sts (212-721-0900). Subway: B, C to 72nd St; 1, 9 to 79th St. Sun 10am–6pm.
Sadly, this flea isn't what it used to be. New merchandise, like dried flowers, T-shirts and tube socks, has slowly pushed out the secondhand wonders. But with more than 300 stalls, you're still likely to find something.

Soho Antique Fair & Collectibles Market

Grand St at Broadway (212-682-2000). Subway: J, M, Z, N, R, 6 to Canal St. Sat, Sun 9am–5pm.
This flea market opened in 1992, and although it's smaller than the sprawling Sixth Avenue market, you just might walk away with more. Vintagewear, collectible radios, linens and all manner of kitsch cover a parking lot. There isn't a huge selection (when the weather's bad, the choice is hit-or-miss), but prices are fair. Sunday is always best.

Florists

Although every corner deli sells flowers—especially carnations—they usually last just a few days. For arrangements that stick around a while and don't contain baby's breath, check out some of Manhattan's better florists.

Blue Ivy

206 Fifth Ave between 25th and 26th Sts, fifth floor (212-448-0006). Subway: N, R to 28th St. Mon–Sat 9am–7pm. AmEx, DC, Disc, MC, V.
Simon Naut, a former chief floral designer for the Ritz-Carlton Hotel, joined forces with graphic artist Michael Jackson to open this upscale floral shop. Arrangements start at $50.

City Floral

1661 York Ave between 87th and 88th Sts (212-410-0303). Subway: 4, 5, 6 to 86th St. Mon–Fri 8am–6:15pm; Sat 8am–5pm; Sun 9am–noon. AmEx, DC, Disc, JCB, MC, V.
City Floral, a full-service florist specializing in exotic flowers and gourmet fruit baskets, is a member of Interflora, a worldwide delivery network.

Elizabeth Ryan Floral Designs

411 E 9th St between Ave A and First Ave (212-995-1111). Subway: L to First Ave; 6 to Astor Pl. Mon–Fri 10am–7pm; Sat 10am–6pm. AmEx, MC, V.
Elizabeth Ryan has arranged her shop like one of her gorgeous bouquets, and the results are simply magical. Fork out $40 (or up to whatever you can afford) for an original bouquet and request your favorite blooms.

Perriwater Ltd.

960 First Ave at 53rd St (212-759-9313). Subway: E, F to Lexington Ave; 6 to 51st St. Mon–Fri 9am–6pm; Sat 10am–6pm. AmEx, MC, V.
Proprietor Patricia Grimley doesn't believe that white flowers should be reserved for weddings; she loves the pure effect of an all-white arrangement for any occasion.

Renny

505 Park Ave at 59th St (212-288-7000). Subway: N, R to Lexington Ave; 4, 5, 6 to 59th St. Mon–Sat 9am–6pm. AmEx, MC, V.

"Exquisite flowers for the discriminating" is the slogan. Customers include David Letterman, Calvin Klein and myriad party-givers.

Spruce

75 Greenwich Ave between Seventh Ave South and Eighth Ave (212-414-0588). Subway: 1, 9 to Christopher St–Sheridan Sq. Mon–Fri 9am–8pm; Sat 11am–7pm. AmEx, MC, V.

For an untraditional arrangement, ask for some roses encircled by a ring of wheatgrass. It can be whipped up on the premises.

VSF

204 W 10th St between Bleecker and W 4th Sts (212-206-7236). Subway: A, C, E, B, D, F, Q to W 4th St. Mon–Fri 10am–5pm; Sat 11am–4pm. AmEx, Disc, MC, V.

VSF stands for very special flowers, and very special they are. Dried-flower arrangements, exotic bonsai, miniature topiary and extravagant bouquets are the store specialities.

Food and drink

Although New York is urban to the core, there is no shortage of farm-fresh, high-quality produce, meats and grains. Listed below are a few better-known city markets. Check out *Time Out New York*'s annual *Eating & Drinking Guide* for a more complete list of markets and everything edible.

A. Zito & Sons Bakery

259 Bleecker St at Seventh Ave South (212-929-6139). Subway: 1, 9 to Christopher St–Sheridan Sq. Mon–Sat 6am–7pm; Sun 6am–3pm. Cash only.

If you're lucky, you'll stop in at Zito when the fresh bread is being brought up from the two 110-year-old brick ovens downstairs. Even if the bread isn't hot, buy two loaves: one for the walk back to your hotel room and the other so you have something to show for your trip to the store. If you're in good health, try the heart attack in a loaf—prosciutto bread loaded with chunks of cured ham, black pepper and rendered lard. There's a deli area, serving hot or cold heros and salads, but Zito's bread is, well, it's bread and butter.

Balducci's

424 Sixth Ave at 9th St (212-673-2600). Subway: A, C, E, B, D, F, Q to W 4th St. 7am–8:30pm. AmEx, MC, V.

Solidly rooted in Southern Italian traditions, Balducci's is a New York institution. A fraction of the size of your typical suburban megamarket, this gourmet shop is as cramped and bustling as a midtown subway platform during rush hour. Prickly pears, blood oranges and porcini mushrooms overflow crowded bins, $40 bottles of extra-virgin olive oil are racked to the ceiling, and slabs of foie gras and boxes of white truffles at $100 an ounce pack the refrigerated glass cases. Heaven couldn't be better stocked. Across the street is a Balducci's café that also sells yummy prepared foods.

Dean & DeLuca

560 Broadway at Prince St (212-431-1691). Subway: N, R to Prince St. Mon–Sat 10am–8pm; Sun 10am–7pm. AmEx, MC, V.

Dean & DeLuca's flagship store (the only one that isn't just a fancy coffee bar) continues to provide the most sophisticated collection of specialty food products in New York City. The grandiose appearance of the place and its epic range of products are reflected in the prices, which are sky-high. But downtown residents and international visitors don't seem to mind. After all, where else can you be assured that you are choosing from the highest-quality products on the market?

Foodworks

10 W 19th St between Fifth and Sixth Aves (212-352-9333). Subway: F, N, R to 23rd St. Mon–Fri 8am–8:30pm; Sat, Sun 11am–6:30pm. AmEx, MC, V.

This is a Flatiron standby for gourmet sandwiches, soups and sushi to go. There's also a nice selection of flowers and Japanese candy.

Gourmet Garage

2567 Broadway between 96th and 97th Sts (212-663-0656). Subway: 1, 2, 3, 9 to 96th St. 7am–9pm. AmEx, Disc, MC, V.

Gourmet Garage is the Manhattan version of Trader Joe's, the California-based chain of bargain-basement gourmet markets that has a handful of stores in Westchester and on Long Island. It's not comprehensive: You won't find a dozen different cuts of steak or ten types of mushrooms. What you will find is a select range of produce, meats and fish, and a line of house-brand prepared foods offered at fair prices. Stop in regularly to find unusual imported condiments and other dry goods on special. Check the phone book for other locations.

Grace's Marketplace

1237 Third Ave at 71st St (212-737-0600). Subway: 6 to 68th St–Hunter College. Mon–Sat 7am–8:30pm; Sun 8am–7pm. AmEx, DC, MC, V.

Grace's Marketplace has been a gourmet stronghold of the Upper East Side since 1985. Grace's core customer is a solidly affluent, high-maintenance society matron, but the store appeals to all fans of high-quality produce, meats and fish. Grace's also stocks the unusual, such as Boutargue pressed carp roe and long flatbreads called "tongue of mother-in-law." The bread selection is fab, but Grace herself doesn't do the baking—she chooses the best from 37 selected purveyors.

Greenmarkets

212-477-3220. Mon–Fri 9am–6pm.

There are more than 20 open-air markets sponsored by city authorities in various locations and on different days. The most famous is the one at Union Square (*17th St between Broadway and Park Ave South; Mon, Wed, Fri, Sat 8am–6pm*), where small producers of organic cheeses, honey, vegetables, herbs and flowers sell their wares from the backs of their flatbed trucks. Arrive early, before the good stuff sells out.

Guss' Pickles

35 Essex St between Grand and Hester Sts (212-254-4477). Subway: F to East Broadway. Mon–Thu, Sun 9am–6pm; Fri 9am–3:30pm. MC, V.

Once upon a time, there was a notorious rivalry between two pickle merchants, Guss and Hollander, but eventually it was settled. Guss put his name over the door of the old Hollander store and became the undisputed Pickle King, selling them sour or half-sour and in several sizes. Also excellent are the sauerkraut and pickled peppers and watermelon rinds.

Kam Man Food Products

200 Canal St at Mott St (212-571-0330). Subway: J, M, Z, N, R, 6 to Canal St. 9am–9pm. MC, V.

This shop has a good selection of fresh and preserved Chinese, Thai and other Asian foods, as well as utensils and kitchenware.

Kitchen Market

218 Eighth Ave between 21st and 22nd Sts (212-243-4433). Subway: C, E, to 23rd St. Mon–Sat 9am–10:30pm; Sun 11am–10:30pm. Cash only.

Don't let the scary Day of the Dead skeletons in the window keep you from entering this narrow Chelsea storefront: It's chock-full of essential Mexican goodies. Kitchen Market sells a selection of *moles,* salsas and tortillas, as well as lots of Mexican knickknacks. Must-have items for south-of-the-border cooking include *nopales* (cactus leaves), tomatillos, jicama and a range of fresh and dried chilies; yuppified treats like chipotle *queso* dip, red-chili honey and banana soda are also sold. And be sure to try one of Kitchen's *Norte* specialties: an authentic San Francisco–style burrito.

Li-Lac

120 Christopher St between Bleecker and Hudson Sts (212-242-7374). Subway: 1, 9 to Christopher St–Sheridan Sq. Mon–Fri 10am–8pm; Sat noon–8pm; Sun noon–5pm. AmEx, Disc, MC, V.

Handmade chocolates par excellence are the specialty here. Take home an edible Statue of Liberty for $20.

McNulty's Tea and Coffee

109 Christopher St between Bleecker and Hudson Sts (212-242-5351). Subway: 1, 9 to Christopher St–Sheridan Sq. Mon–Sat 10am–9pm; Sun 1–7pm. AmEx, Disc, MC, V.

The original McNulty began selling tea here in 1895; in 1980, the shop was taken over by the Wong family. Of course, coffee is included in the bevy of stimulants, but the real draw is the tea. From the rarest, the White Flower Pekoe (it's harvested once a year in China and costs $25 per pound) to a simple Darjeeling or a box from Fortnum & Mason, this is a tea haven.

Myers of Keswick

634 Hudson St between Horatio and Jane Sts (212-691-4194). Subway: A, C, E to 14th St; L to Eighth Ave. Mon–Fri 10am–7pm; Sat 10am–6pm; Sun noon–5pm. AmEx, V.

This charming English market is a frequent stop for Brits and local Anglophiles. While some come looking for a hint of home or a jolly good meet-and-greet, others flock to the store for old-fashioned English

Yes, Sir! New Yorkers can't get enough of the new Terence Conran Shop.

fare—shepherd's pie, Cornish pasties and steak-and-kidney pies. Other specialties include homemade pork bangers and Cumberland sausages. Shelves are lined with jars of clotted cream, PG Tips tea, scone mix, HP sauce (England's answer to A.1.) and "memory cards" emblazoned with the image of Her Majesty Queen Elizabeth II.

Raffeto's Corporation

144 Houston St at MacDougal St (212-777-1261). Subway: A, C, E, B, D, F, Q to W 4th St. Tue–Fri 9am–6:30pm; Sat 9am–6pm. Cash only.

In business since 1906, Raffeto's is the source of much of the designer pasta that is sold in gourmet shops all over town. The staff sells special ravioli, tortellini, fettuccine, gnocchi and manicotti in any quantity to anyone who calls in, with no minimum order.

Russ & Daughters

179 Houston St between Allen and Orchard Sts (212-475-4880). Subway: F to Second Ave. Mon–Sat 9am–7pm; Sun 8am–5:30pm. MC, V.

You'll feel like a circus seal when the jovial men behind the counter of this legendary Lower East Side shop start tossing you bits of lox and gravlax, but who's complaining? Russ & Daughters sells eight kinds of smoked salmon and many other Jewish foodstuffs. The house specialty is the herring, soaked in your choice of schmaltz, red wine, lemon-ginger sauce or mustard-dill marinade. Russ & Daughters' clientele has changed a bit since the store opened in 1914—you'll now see as many shaved heads as naturally bald ones—but the food hasn't.

Zabar's

2245 Broadway at 80th St (212-787-2000). Subway: 1, 9 to 79th St. Mon–Fri 8am–7:30pm; Sat 8am–8pm; Sun 9am–6pm. AmEx, MC, V.

Zabar's is more than just a market—it's a New York landmark worthy of a name-check in syrupy Nora Ephron movies and campaign stops by would-be elected officials. You certainly won't escape lightly wallet-wise, but you can't argue with the topflight food. Besides the famous smoked fish and rafts of Jewish delicacies, Zabar's has fabulous coffee, bread and cheese selections. Plus, it's the only market of its kind that offers an entire floor of housewares.

Liquor stores

Most supermarkets and corner delis sell beer and aren't too fussy about ID, though you do need to show proof that you are over 21 if asked (and don't carry open alcohol containers in the streets—that's a sure bust these days). To buy wine or spirits, you need to go to a liquor store. Most liquor stores don't sell beer, nor are they open on Sundays.

Astor Wines & Spirits

12 Astor Pl at Lafayette St (212-674-7500). Subway: N, R to 8th St–NYU; 6 to Astor Pl. Mon–Sat 9am–9pm. AmEx, JCB, MC, V.

This is a modern wine supermarket that would serve as the perfect blueprint for a chain, were it not for a law preventing liquor stores from branching out. There's a wide range of wines and spirits.

Best Cellars

1291 Lexington Ave between 86th and 87th Sts (212-426-4200). Subway: 4, 5, 6 to 86th St. Mon–Thu 10am–9pm; Fri, Sat 10am–10pm. AmEx, MC, V.

This wine shop stocks only 100 selections, but each one is delicious and has been tasted by the owners (who tested more than 1,500 bottles). The best part is that they're all under $10.

Sherry-Lehmann

679 Madison Ave at 61st St (212-838-7500). Subway: N, R to Lexington Ave; 4, 5, 6 to 59th St. Mon–Sat 9am–7pm. AmEx, MC, V.

Perhaps the most famous of New York's numerous liquor stores, Sherry-Lehmann has a vast selection of Scotches, brandies and ports, as well as a superb range of French, American and Italian wines.

Warehouse Wines & Spirits

735 Broadway between 8th St and Waverly Pl (212-982-7770). Subway: N, R to 8th St–NYU; 6 to Astor Pl. Mon–Thu 9am–8:45pm; Fri, Sat 9am–9:45pm. AmEx, MC, V.

For the best prices in town for wine and liquor, look no further. Grab a cart, because you'll need it.

For the home

ABC Carpet & Home

888 Broadway at 19th St (212-473-3000; www.abchome.com). Subway: N, R to 23rd St. Mon–Fri 10am–8pm; Sat 10am–7pm; Sun 11am–6:30pm. AmEx, MC, V.

The selection is unbelievable, and often, so are the steep prices. But this New York shopping landmark really does have it all: accessories, linens, rugs, antique (Western and Asian) and reproduction furniture, and more (there are more carpets in the store across the street). If you are determined to get cheaper prices, trek to ABC's warehouse outlet in the Bronx

Other location: *1055 Bronx River Ave between Westchester Ave and Bruckner Blvd, Bronx (718-842-8770).*

Area I.D. Moderne

262 Elizabeth St between Houston and Prince Sts (212-219-9903). Subway: B, D, F, Q to Broadway–Lafayette St; 6 to Bleecker St. Tue–Sun noon–7pm. AmEx, MC, V.

Area I.D. sells home accessories and ready-made furniture (think 1950s modern) but also offers interior-decoration and design services. What sets this store apart is that all of its furniture has been reupholstered in luxurious fabrics (Ultrasuede and mohair, for example).

Bennison Fabrics

76 Greene St between Spring and Broome Sts (212-941-1212). Subway: C, E to Spring St. Mon–Fri 9am–5pm. MC, V.

Bennison is an unusual downtown shop that sells a classic but innovative range of fabrics silk-screened in England. Prices are steep, and the fabrics—usually 70 percent linen, 30 percent cotton—end up in some of the best-dressed homes in town.

Chelsea Garden Center Home Store

435 Hudson St at Leroy St (212-727-7100). Subway: 1, 9 to Houston St. 10am–6:30pm. AmEx, MC, V.
The Chelsea Garden Center's 8,000-square-foot sun-filled garden, home and lifestyle store has plenty of indoor plants, furniture, books, tools and pottery that'll brighten up your host's pad, once winter sets in.
Other locations: *321 Bowery at 2nd St (212-777-4500); 207 Ninth Ave between 22nd and 23rd Sts (212-741-6052).*

Felissimo

See **Department stores,** page 167.

Fishs Eddy

889 Broadway at 19th St (212-420-9020). Subway: N, R to 23rd St. Mon–Sat 10am–9pm; Sun 11am–8pm.
Fishs Eddy sells virtually indestructible, well-priced china that you may also find in your favorite hotel or diner.
Other location: *2176 Broadway at 77th St (212-873-8819).*

Gracious Home

1217 and 1220 Third Ave between 70th and 71st Sts (212-988-8990). Subway: 6 to 68th St–Hunter College. Mon–Fri 8am–7pm; Sat 9am–7pm; Sun 10am–6pm. AmEx, DC, MC, V.
If you need a new curtain rod, place mat or drawer pull—or any other household accessory—this is the place to find it. (Gracious Home will even deliver to your hotel at no charge.)
Other location: *1992 Broadway at 67th St (212-231-7800).*

Kartell

45 Greene St between Broome and Grand Sts (212-966-6665). Subway: A, C, E, J, M, Z, N, R, 6 to Canal St. Tue–Sat 11am–7pm; Sun noon–6pm. AmEx, MC, V.
If you think "good plastic" is an oxymoron, visit Kartell. Its furniture, crafted from the most durable of substances, will set you straight.

Knoll

105 Wooster St at Prince St (212-343-4000). Subway; N, R to Prince St. Mon–Fri 10am–6pm. AmEx.
Knoll sells classic and contemporary furniture that you'll find in almost every Soho loft.

Making Light

89 Grand St at Greene St (212-965-8817). Subway: A, C, E, J, M, Z, N, R, 6 to Canal St. Tue–Sat 11am–7pm; Sun noon–6pm. Amex, MC, V.
Does the synthesis of language and light make you think of Times Square? Munich native Ingo Maurer wants you to think Soho—not lame-o. His clever lamps and fixtures incorporate neon words and LED phrases.

MoMA Design Store

44 W 53rd St between Fifth and Sixth Aves (212-767-1050). Subway: E, F to Fifth Ave. 10am–6:30pm. AmEx, JCB, MC, V.
At the Museum of Modern Art's recently remodeled design store, you'll find calendars, glasses, jewelry, coatracks—you name it—in the most whimsical shapes and colors.

More and Moss

146 Greene St between Houston and Prince Sts (212-226-2190). Subway: N, R to Prince St. Tue–Fri 11am–7pm; Sat, Sun noon–6pm. AmEx, MC, V.
Do you insist on impeccable design for even the most prosaic objects? Murray Moss's museumlike emporium, which recently expanded next door, features the best of what the contemporary design world has to offer, including streamlined clocks, curvy sofas and witty salt-and-pepper shakers.

Portico Home

72 Spring St between Broadway and Lafayette St (212-941-7800). Subway: 6 to Spring St. Mon–Sat 10am–7pm; Sun noon–6pm. AmEx, Disc, MC, V.
Portico features clean, country-chic furniture and bed and bath accessories. Check the phone book for other locations.

Restoration Hardware

935 Broadway at 22nd St (212-260-9479). Subway: N, R to 23rd St. Mon–Sat 10am–8pm, Sun 11am–7pm.
If you're in the market for a shiny hammer, a funky yet durable corkscrew or a comfy leather club chair, Restoration Hardware has what you need; it's a must-stop for the happy homemaker.
Other location: *103 Prince St at Greene St (212-431-3518).*

Rhubarb Home

26 Bond St between Lafayette St and Bowery (212-533-1817). Subway: B, D, F, Q to Broadway–Lafayette St; 6 to Bleecker St. Mon–Sat noon–7pm; Sun 2–6pm. AmEx, DC, MC, V.
Stacy Sindlinger scouts flea markets and yard sales for impeccably battered furniture. Chipped worktables, French Deco mirrors, even a baker's table have all been in her shop at one time or another.

The Terence Conran Shop

415 E 59th St at First Ave (212-755-9079). Subway: N, R to Lexington Ave; 4, 5, 6 to 59th St. Mon–Fri 10am–8pm; Sat 10am–7pm; Sun noon–7pm. AmEx, MC, V.
Sir Terence Conran returned to New York in fall 1999 with this witty design store under the Queensboro Bridge (Conran used to have a shop here in the '80s). As in Europe, he offers an overwhelming selection of trendy products—new and antique—for every room of the house: cabinets, sofas, rugs, dishes, lighting…the list goes on.

Totem Design

71 Franklin St between Broadway and Church St (212-925-5506). Subway: 1, 9 to Franklin St. Mon–Sat 11am–7pm; Sun noon–5pm. AmEx, MC, V.

Totem offers sleek, one-of-a-kind furniture, lighting and accessories that will blend seamlessly with your flea-market treasures.

Urban Archeology

143 Franklin St between Varick and Hudson Sts (212-431-4646). Subway: A, C, E to Canal St; 1, 9 to Franklin St. Mon–Fri 8am–6pm; Sat 10am–4pm. AmEx, MC, V.

Old buildings saved! Or rather, picked to pieces and sold for parts. This store carries refurbished architectural artifacts, from Corinthian columns and lobby-size chandeliers to bathtubs and doorknobs, as well as reproductions of popular favorites.

Other locations: *285 Lafayette St between Houston and Prince Sts (212-431-6969); 239 E 58th St between Second and Third Aves (212-371-4646).*

Waterworks Collection

475 Broome St between Greene and Wooster Sts (212-274-8800). Subway: C, E to Spring St. Mon–Sat 10am–6pm; Sun noon–6pm. AmEx, MC, V.

Given their awkward shapes and sizes, bathrooms can be the hardest rooms to organize. With that in mind, the folks at Waterworks stock an array of items, from secretaries to silver-plated shaving brushes, that make bathrooms pleasant.

Wyeth

151 Franklin St between Varick and Hudson Sts (212-925-5278). Subway: A, C, E to Canal St; 1, 9 to Franklin St. Mon–Sat 11am–6pm. AmEx, DC, MC, V.

This Tribeca shop is known for its collection of metal lamps, chairs and tables stripped of old paint, sanded and burnished to a soft finish. The hardware is nickel-plated.

Gift shops

Alphabets

47 Greenwich Ave between Charles and Perry Sts (212-229-2966). Subway: 1, 9 to Christopher St–Sheridan Sq. Sun–Thu noon–8pm; Fri, Sat noon–10pm. AmEx, MC, V.

Hilarious postcards, wrapping paper and tiny treasures pack the shelves at Alphabets, together with a range of goofy T-shirts and offbeat souvenirs of New York.

Other locations: *115 Ave A between 7th and 8th Sts (212-475-7250); 2284 Broadway between 82nd and 83rd Sts (212-579-5702).*

Breukelen

369 Atlantic Ave between Hoyt and Bond Sts, Boerum Hill, Brooklyn (718-246-0024). Subway: A, C, G to Hoyt–Schermerhorn. Tue–Sun noon–7pm. AmEx, DC, MC, V.

This contemporary design store crops up unexpectedly in the middle of Atlantic Avenue's popular three-block stretch of antiques stores. While the collection isn't limited to any single style, everything—pet dishes, table lamps, tumblers—fits a simple, clean, pared-down aesthetic.

Other location: *68 Gansevoort St between Greenwich and Washington Sts (212-645-2216).*

Daily 235

235 Elizabeth St between Prince and Houston Sts (212-334-9728). Subway: B, D, F, Q to Broadway–

Orient yourself The best knickknacks this side of the Pacific are available at Pearl River Mart.

Lifesaver For gifts of Americana and more, stop at Love Saves the Day in the East Village.

Lafayette St; 6 to Bleecker St. Mon–Sat noon–8pm; Sun noon–6pm. AmEx, DC, Disc, MC, V.
This store is stocked with stuff you probably don't need but buy anyway. There's soap, matchbook-size games, condoms, books on photography, voodoo dolls—and that's just a sampling.

Felissimo

See **Department stores,** page 167.

Frenchware

98 Thompson St between Prince and Spring Sts (212-625-3131). Subway: C, E to Spring St. Tue–Sun noon–7pm. AmEx, DC, JCB, MC, V.
If names like Tintin, Astérix and Le Petit Prince give you a happy jolt, here's a news flash: Frenchware, a *charmant* den for Francophiles, carries *chocolat* bowls bearing those icons, Ricard pitchers and a lot more.

Gaston

125 Grand St between Broadway and Crosby Sts (212-219-3846; www.gastonnyc.com). Subway: J, M, Z, N, R, 6 to Canal St. Mon–Sat 11am–7pm; Sun noon–6pm. AmEx, MC, V.
Gaston Marticorena is a young-gun home-furnishings-and-accessories designer who's famous for items with double functions: Candles double as vases, chairs boast built-in magazine racks and animal-shaped children's toys have bottle-opening backsides. Marticorena mans this whimsical shop in a landmark building just east of Soho.

Hammacher Schlemmer

147 E 57th St between Third and Lexington Aves (212-421-9000). Subway: E, F to Lexington Ave; 4, 5, 6 to 59th St. Mon–Sat 10am–6pm. AmEx, DC, Disc, JCB, MC, V.
Here are two floors of bizarre and ingenious toys and gadgets for home, car, sports and leisure, each one supposedly the best of its kind. It's the perfect place to buy a gift that will permanently attach a smile to anyone's face. In December, the store opens its doors on Sunday for drooling holiday shoppers.

Karikter

19 Prince St between Elizabeth and Mott Sts (212-274-1966). Subway: N, R to Prince St; 6 to Spring St. 11am–7:30pm. AmEx, MC, V.
Babar and Astérix paraphernalia are the main draw at this Euro-style Nolita housewares shop. But grown-up goodies are also available—the four-foot, $2,200 Tintin rocketship is joined by chic and affordable items such as Philippe Starck–designed flyswatters and colorful Mendolino toilet brushes.

Love Saves the Day

119 Second Ave at 7th St (212-228-3802). Subway: 6 to Astor Pl. 1–7:30pm. AmEx, MC, V.
This shop has more kitsch toys and tacky novelties than you can shake an Elvis doll at. There are Elvis lamps with pink shades, ant farms, lurid machine-made tapestries of Madonna, glow-in-the-dark crucifixes and Mexican Day of the Dead statues.

Metropolitan Opera Shop

136 W 65th St at Broadway (212-580-4090). Subway: 1, 9 to 66th St–Lincoln Ctr. Mon–Sat 10am–10pm; Sun noon–6pm. AmEx, Disc, MC, V.
Located in the Metropolitan Opera at Lincoln Center, this shop sells CDs, cassettes and laser discs of—you guessed it—operas. There's also a wealth of opera memorabilia.

Mxyplyzyk

123–125 Greenwich Ave at 13th St (212-989-4300). Subway: A, C, E to 14th St; L to Eighth Ave. Mon–Sat 11am–7pm; Sun noon–5pm. AmEx, MC, V.
The name doesn't mean anything, although it's similar to the name of a character from *Superman*

comics. Mxyplyzyk offers a hodgepodge of chic lighting, furniture, toys, stationery, housewares and gardening items.

Pearl River Mart

277 Canal St at Broadway (212-431-4770). Subway: J, M, Z, N, R, 6 to Canal St. 10am–7:30pm. AmEx, Disc, MC, V.

In this downtown emporium, you can find all things Chinese, from clothing, gongs, pots, woks and teapots, to groceries, medicinal herbs, bedroom slippers and traditional stationery.

Other location: *200 Grand St between Mott and Mulberry Sts (212-966-1010).*

Pop Shop

292 Lafayette St between Houston and Prince Sts (212-219-2784). Subway: B, D, F, Q to Broadway–Lafayette St; 6 to Bleecker St. Tue–Sat noon–7pm; Sun noon–6pm. AmEx, MC, V.

Famed pop iconographer Keith Haring's art lives on in this shop, which sells T-shirts, bags, pillows and jigsaw puzzles—all emblazoned with Haring's famous cartoony crayon-colored characters.

Shì

233 Elizabeth St between Prince and Houston Sts (212-334-4330). Subway: B, D, F, Q to Broadway–Lafayette St; 6 to Bleecker St. Mon–Sat noon–7pm; Sun noon–6pm. AmEx, MC, V.

At Shi—which means "is" in Chinese—everything has been selected for its unique design, from the bullet-shaped hanging glass vases to crisp Caravane silk bedding.

Tink

42 Rivington St between Eldridge and Forsyth Sts (212-529-6356). Subway: F to Delancey St; J, M, Z to Essex St. Wed–Sat 2–8pm; Sun 2–7pm. Cash only.

Illustrator Claudia Pearson's Lower East Side studio-turned–international gift shop showcases artifacts from Bali, South Africa and Samoa.

White Trash

304 E 5th St between First and Second Aves (212-598-5956). Subway: F to Second Ave; 6 to Astor Pl. Tue–Sat 2–9pm; Sun 1–8pm. MC, V.

After holding a monthly yard sale at First Avenue and 4th Street for a while, "white trash" connoisseurs Kim Wurster and Stuart Zamsky opened this popular store, to the delight of those in dire need of Jesus night-lights, Noguchi lamps and 1950s kitchen tables. Recently, mid-century luxury barware and coffee tables have joined the vintage crop.

Music

Superstores

HMV

57 W 34th St at Sixth Ave (212-629-0900). Subway: B, D, F, Q, N, R to 34th St–Herald Sq; 1, 2, 3, 9 to 34th St–Penn Station. Mon–Sat 9am–10pm; Sun 11am–9pm. AmEx, Disc, MC, V.

One of the biggest record stores in North America, HMV has a jaw-dropping selection of vinyl, cassettes, CDs and videos. Check the phone book for other locations.

J&R Music World

See **Cameras and electronics,** page 200.

Tower Records

692 Broadway at 4th St (212-505-1500, 800-648-4844; www.towerrecords.com). Subway: N, R to 8th St–NYU. 9am–midnight. AmEx, Disc, MC, V.

Tower Records is a source for all the current sounds on CD and tape. Visit the clearance store down the block on Lafayette Street for marked-down stuff in all formats, including vinyl (especially classical). Check the phone book for other locations.

Virgin Megastore

52 E 14th St at Broadway (212-598-4666; www.virginmega.com). Subway: L, N, R, 4, 5, 6 to 14th St–Union Sq. Mon–Sat 9am–1am; Sun 10am–11pm. AmEx, Disc, JCB, MC, V.

As enormous record stores go, this one is pretty good. Check out the Virgin soda machine and keep an eye out for dates of in-store performances. There's a great selection of U.K.-import CDs. Books and videos are available.

Other location: *1540 Broadway between 45th and 46th Sts (212-921-1020).*

Multigenres

Bleecker Bob's

118 W 3rd St between MacDougal St and Sixth Ave (212-475-9677; www.bleeckerbobs.com). Subway: A, C, E, B, D, F, Q to W 4th St. Sun–Thu noon–1am; Fri, Sat noon–3am. AmEx, MC, V.

Bleecker Bob's is an institution, but unfortunately it has coasted on its reputation for at least a decade. Still, it's where to go when you really can't find what you want anywhere else.

Etherea

66 Ave A between 4th and 5th Sts (212-358-1126). Subway: F to Second Ave. Mon–Thu noon–10:30pm; Fri, Sat noon–11:30pm; Sun noon–10pm. AmEx, DC, MC, V.

Etherea has taken over the space that used to be Adult Crash. The stock is mostly indie, experimental, electronic and rock records.

Mondo Kim's

6 St. Marks Pl between Second and Third Aves (212-598-9985; www.kimsvideo.com). Subway: 6 to Astor Pl. 9am–midnight. AmEx, MC, V.

This minichain of movie-and-music stores offers a great selection for collector geeks: indie, electronic, prog, kraut, soundtracks and used CDs. Check the phone book for other locations.

Other Music

15 E 4th St between Broadway and Lafayette St (212-477-8150; www.othermusic.com). Subway: N, R to 8th

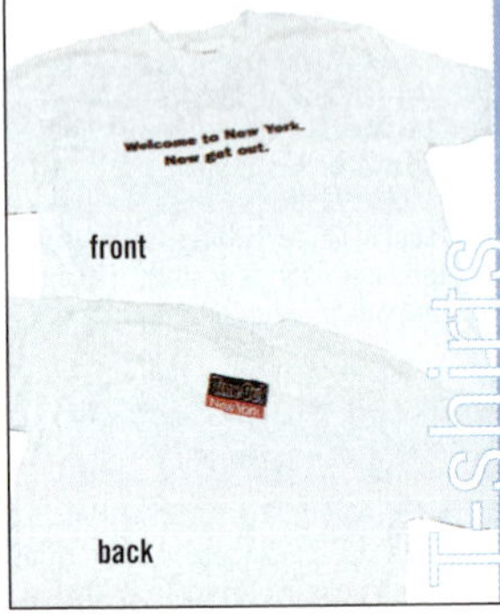

St–NYU; 6 to Astor Pl. Mon–Thu, Sat noon–9pm; Fri noon–10pm; Sun noon–7pm. AmEx, MC, V.
Excluding the big chains, perhaps the most famous record store in NYC is Other Music. No other venue has risen to the challenge of turn of the century genremania quite like this joint. Owned by three former Kim's slaves (*see* **Mondo Kim's,** *page 209*), it stocks a full selection of indie, ambient, psychedelia, noise and French pop.

St. Marks Sounds

16 St. Marks Pl (212-677-2727) and 20 St. Marks Pl (212-677-3444) between Second and Third Aves. Subway: 6 to Astor Pl. Mon–Fri noon–10pm; Sat noon–11pm; Sun noon–9pm. Cash only.
Sounds, consisting of two neighboring stores, is the best bargain on the block. The eastern branch stocks catalog releases, while new releases take up the west.

Subterranean Records

5 Cornelia St between 4th and Bleecker Sts (212-463-8900; www.strnyc.com). Subway: A, C, E, B, D, F, Q to W 4th St. Noon–8pm. AmEx, MC, V.
At this just-off-Bleecker shop you'll find both new, used and live recordings.

Classical

Gryphon Record Shop

233 W 72nd St between Broadway and West End Ave (212-874-1588; www.gryphonrecordshop.com). Subway: 1, 2, 3, 9 to 72nd St. Mon–Wed, Fri, Sat 11am–7pm; Thu 11am–10pm; Sun 12:30–6:30pm. MC, V.
This solidly classical store has traditionally been vinyl only, but the 21st century has brought in a wave of CDs. Gryphon also carries a sprinkling of jazz and show music.

Dance

Dance Tracks

91 E 3rd St at First Ave (212-260-8729). Subway: F to Second Ave. Mon–Thu noon–9pm; Fri noon–10pm; Sat noon–8pm; Sun 1–6:30pm. AmEx, Disc, MC, V.
Stocked with Euro imports hot off the plane (nearly as cheap to buy here) and with racks of domestic house, dangerously enticing bins of Loft/Paradise Garage classics and private decks to listen on, Dance Tracks is a must.

Satellite Records

342 Bowery between Great Jones and Bond Sts (212-780-9305; www.satelliterecords.com). Subway: B, D, F, Q to Broadway–Lafayette St; 6 to Bleecker St. Mon–Sat 1–9pm; Sun 2–8pm. AmEx, Disc, MC, V.
The racks here are a mess, but sort through them and you'll eventually find every 12-inch you've ever wanted.

Hip-Hop and R&B

Beat Street Records

494 Fulton St between Bond St and Elm Pl, Downtown Brooklyn (718-624-6400; www.beatstreet.com). Subway: A, C, G to Hoyt–Schermerhorn; 2, 3, 4, 5 to Nevins St. Mon–Wed 10am–7pm; Thu–Sat 10am–7:30pm; Sun 10am–6pm. AmEx, Disc, MC, V.
See **From Jamaica with love,** page 308.

Fat Beats

406 Sixth Ave between 8th and 9th Sts, second floor (212-673-3883; www.fatbeats.com). Subway: A, C, E, B, D, F, Q to W 4th St. Mon–Thu noon–9pm; Fri, Sat noon–10pm; Sun noon–8pm. MC, V.
See **From Jamaica with love,** page 308.

Jazz

Jazz Record Center

236 W 26th St between Seventh and Eighth Aves, room 804 (212-675-4480; www.jazzrecordcenter.com). Subway: C, E to 23rd St; 1, 9 to 28th St. Mon–Sat 10am–6pm. Disc, MC, V.
Quite simply, Jazz Record Center is the best jazz store in the city, selling current and out-of-print records. Worldwide shipping is available.

Showtunes

Footlight Records

113 E 12th St between Third and Fourth Aves (212-533-1572; www.footlight.com). Subway: L, N, R, 4, 5, 6 to 14th St–Union Sq. Mon–Fri 11am–7pm; Sat 10am–6pm; Sun 11am–5pm. AmEx, DC, MC, V.
This spectacular store specializes in vocalists, Broadway cast recordings, film soundtracks, bossa nova and French pop.

World Music

World Music Institute

49 W 27th Street between Broadway and Sixth Ave, suite 930 (212-545-7536; www.heartheworld.org). Subway: N, R to 28th St. Mon–Fri 10am–6pm. AmEx, MC, V.
The square footage is sparse, but WMI employs experts who can order sounds from any remote corner of the earth, usually within six weeks.

Specialty stores

Arthur Brown & Brothers

2 W 46th St between Fifth and Sixth Aves (212-575-5555; www.artbrown.com). Subway: B, D, F, Q to 47–50th Sts–Rockefeller Ctr; 7 to Fifth Ave. Mon–Fri 9am–6:30pm; Sat 10am–6pm. AmEx, DC, Disc, MC, V.
Pens of the world are all on the same page at Arthur Brown, which has one of the largest selections anywhere, including Mont Blanc, Cartier, Dupont, Porsche and Schaeffer.

Big City Kites

1210 Lexington Ave at 82nd St (212-472-2623; www.bigcitykites.com). Subway: 4, 5, 6 to 86th St. Mon–Fri 11am–6:30pm; Thu 11am–7:30pm; Sat 10am–6pm. AmEx, Disc, JCB, MC, V.

Act like a kid again and go fly a kite. There are more than 150 to choose from.

Evolution

120 Spring St between Greene and Mercer Sts (212-343-1114; www.evolutionsoho.com). Subway: C, E to Spring St. 11am–7pm. AmEx, DC, MC, V.

If natural history is an obsession, look no further. Insects in Plexiglas, giraffe skulls, seashells and wild-boar tusks are among the items for sale in this relatively politically correct store—the animals died of natural causes or were culled.

Necessities

Fetch

43 Greenwich Ave between Charles and Perry Sts (212-352-8591; www.fetchny.com). Subway: A, C, E, B, D, F, Q to W 4th St; 1, 9 to Christopher St–Sheridan Sq. Mon–Fri noon–8pm; Sat 11am–7pm; Sun noon–6pm. AmEx, MC, V.

This luxury shop for dogs and cats carries everything from silken coats to aromatherapy perfume for Fido and Fritz. Most of Fetch's specialty foods—such as bone-shaped peanut-butter treats and Kitty Calamari—can be eaten by people, too. If you enjoy sharing culinary moments with your pet, bon appétit!

Flight 001

96 Greenwich Ave between 12th and Jane Sts (212-691-1001; www.flight001.com). Subway: A, C, E to 14th St; L to Eighth Ave. Mon–Sat noon–8pm; Sun noon–6pm. AmEx, DC, JCB, MC, V.

This one-stop travel shop in the West Village has all the sleekness of the Concorde. The requisite traveler's guidebooks and luggage join such glam products as vacuum-packed shower gel pouches and pocket-sized aromatherapy kits. Did you forget something? Flight 001's "travel essentials" wall features packets of Woolite, mini dominoes and everything in between.

Game Show

1240 Lexington Ave between 83rd and 84th Sts (212-472-8011). Subway: 4, 5, 6 to 86th St. Mon–Wed, Fri, Sat 11am–6pm; Thu 11am–7pm; Sun noon–5pm. AmEx, MC, V.

Scads of board games are sold here, including some guaranteed to leave you intrigued or offended (a few are quite naughty).

Other location: *474 Sixth Ave between 11th and 12th Sts (212-633-6328).*

Jerry Ohlinger's Movie Material Store

242 W 14th St between Seventh and Eighth Aves (212-989-0869). Subway: A, C, E, 1, 2, 3, 9 to 14th St; L to Eighth Ave. 1–7:45pm. AmEx, Disc, MC, V.

Ohlinger has an extensive stock of "paper material" from movies past and present, including photos, programs, posters and fascinating celebrity trivia.

Flying high Get your travel goods at Flight 001.

Kate's Paperie

561 Broadway between Prince and Spring Sts (212-941-9816). Subway: N, R to Prince St. Mon–Sat 10am–7pm; Sun 11am–7pm. AmEx, JCB, MC, V.

Kate's is the ultimate paper mill—there are more than 5,000 papers to choose from. It's also the best outpost for stationery, journals, photo albums, stamps and more.

Other locations: *8 W 13th St between Fifth and Sixth Aves (212-633-0570); 1282 Third Ave between 73rd and 74th Aves (212-396-3670).*

Kate Spade Paper

59 Thompson St between Spring and Broome Sts (212-965-8654). Subway: C, E to Spring St. Mon–Sat 11am–7pm; Sun noon–6pm. AmEx, MC, V.

Bag lady Kate Spade's personal calendars and bound agendas come in leather, as well as novelty animal prints and her signature nylon. Also look for note cards illustrated by British dame Laura Stoddart.

Nat Sherman

500 Fifth Ave at 42nd St (212-764-5000). Subway: S, 4, 5, 6, 7 to 42nd St–Grand Central; 7 to Fifth Ave. Mon–Fri 9am–7pm; Sat 10am–6:30pm; Sun 11am–5pm. AmEx, DC, MC, V.

Just across the street from the glorious New York Public Library, Nat Sherman specializes in slow-burning cigarettes, cigars and smoking accouterments, from cigar humidors to smoking chairs. Upstairs is the famous smoking room, where you can test your tobacco.

Paramount Vending

297 Tenth Ave at 27th St (212-935-9577). Subway: C, E to 23rd St. Mon–Fri 10am–6pm. AmEx, MC, V.

Wondering where to get a new jukebox or a secondhand arcade game? This is the place.

Pearl Paint

308 Canal St between Church St and Broadway (212-431-7932; www.pearlpaint.com). Subway: J, M, Z, N, R, 6 to Canal St. Mon–Wed, Fri 9am–7pm; Thu 9am–8pm; Sat 9am–6:30pm; Sun 9:30am–6pm. AmEx, Disc, MC, V.

This artist's mainstay is as big as a supermarket and

features everything you could possibly need to create your masterpiece—even if it's just in your hotel room. **Other location:** *207 E 23rd St between First and Second Aves (212-592-2179).*

Poster America Gallery

138 W 18th St between Sixth and Seventh Aves (212-206-0499). Subway: 1, 9 to 18th St. Tue–Sat noon–6pm; Sun 1–5pm. AmEx, MC, V.
PAG stocks original advertising posters from both sides of the Atlantic, dating as far back as 1880.

Quark Spy Center

537 Third Ave between 35th and 36th Sts (212-889-1808; www.quarkfiles.com). Subway: 6 to 33rd St. Mon–Fri 10am–6:30pm; Sat noon–5pm. AmEx, DC, MC, V.
Quark is a little creepy but worth a visit if you're interested in donning some body armor or bugging your ex-spouse's house. It's for those with elaborate James Bond fantasies.

Rand McNally Map & Travel Center

150 E 52nd St between Lexington and Third Aves (212-758-7488; www.randmcnally.com). Subway: E, F to Lexington Ave; 6 to 51st St. Mon–Fri 9am–7pm; Sat 10am–6pm; Sun noon–5pm. AmEx, Disc, MC, V.
Rand McNally stocks maps, atlases and globes, even those from rival publishers.
Other location: *555 Seventh Ave between 39th and 40th Sts (212-944-4477).*

Sam Ash Music

155, 159, 160 and 163 W 48th St between Sixth and Seventh Aves (212-719-2299; www.samashmusic.com). Subway: B, D, F, Q to 47–50th Sts–Rockefeller Ctr. Mon–Fri 10am–8pm; Sat 10am–7pm; Sun noon–5pm. AmEx, Disc, MC, V.
This 75-year-old musical-instrument emporium dominates its midtown block with four neighboring shops. In addition to new, vintage and custom guitars, Sam Ash deals in stereo equipment, turntables and all manner of sheet music.
Other locations: *2600 Flatbush Ave at Hendrickson Pl, Marine Park, Brooklyn (718-951-3888); 113-25 Queens Blvd at 76th Rd, Forest Hills, Queens (718-793-7983).*

Sony Style

550 Madison Ave between 55th and 56th Sts (212-833-8800). Subway: E, F to Fifth Ave. Mon–Sat 10am–7pm; Sun noon–6pm.
For the latest from Sony, including futuristic boom boxes, paper-thin TV screens, innovative earphones and Sony's own VAIO personal computer line (created to interact with other company products), stop by this interactive midtown flagship. Downstairs, watch one of the big screen TVs with surround sound while lounging on a Polo Ralph Lauren leather couch.

Stack's Coin Company

123 W 57th St between Sixth and Seventh Aves (212-582-2580; www.stacks.com). Subway: B, Q, N, R to 57th St. Mon–Fri 10am–5pm. Cash only.
The oldest and largest coin dealer in the United States, Stack's deals in rare and ancient coins from around the world.

Tender Buttons

143 East 62nd St between Third and Lexington Aves (212-758-7004). Subway: N, R to Lexington Ave; 4, 5, 6 to 59th St. Mon–Fri 10:30am–6pm; Sat 10:30am–5pm. Cash only.
This is probably the best collection of buttons you'll find on the Eastern seaboard. Search through dozens of varieties of sailor buttons for your pea coat or ask to see the special antique collection upstairs.

Terra Verde

120 Wooster St between Prince and Spring Sts (212-925-4533). Subway: N, R to Prince St. Mon–Sat 11am–7pm; Sun noon–6pm. AmEx, MC, V.
Manhattan's first eco-market combines art and activism. Architect William McDonough renovated this Soho space, using nontoxic building materials and formaldehyde-free paint. Get your chemical-free linens, natural soaps and solar radios here.

Tiny Doll House

1146 Lexington Ave between 79th and 80th Sts (212-744-3719). Subway: 6 to 77th St. Mon–Fri 11am–5:30pm; Sat 11am–4pm. AmEx, MC, V.
Everything in this shop is tiny: miniature furniture and furnishings for dollhouses, including chests, beds, kitchen fittings and cutlery. Even adults will love it.

West Marine

12 W 37th St between Fifth and Sixth Aves (212-594-6065; www.westmarine.com). Subway: B, D, F, Q, N, R to 34th St–Herald Sq. Mon–Fri 10am–6pm; Sat 10am–4pm. AmEx, Disc, MC, V.
Get your basic marine supplies, fishing gear and deck shoes here, or shell out $250 to $2,000 for a fisherman's Global Positioning System.

Sports

Blades, Board and Skate

659 Broadway between Bleecker and Bond Sts (212-477-7350; www.blades.com). Subway: B, D, F, Q to Broadway–Lafayette St; 6 to Bleecker St. Mon–Sat 11am–8pm; Sun noon–6pm. AmEx, Disc, JCB, MC, V.
This is where to come for those pesky in-line skates, as well as for a wide range of skateboard and snowboard equipment and clothing. Check the phone book for other locations.

Gerry Cosby & Company

2 Pennsylvania Plaza, inside Madison Square Garden (212-563-6464, 800-548-4003; www.cosbysports.com). Subway: A, C, E, 1, 2, 3, 9 to 34th St–Penn Station. Mon–Fri 9:30am–7:30pm; Sat 9:30am–6pm; Sun noon–5pm. AmEx, Disc, MC, V.
Cosby features a huge selection of official teamwear and other sporting necessities. The store remains open during evening Knicks, Rangers and NY Liberty games.

Doggy style Make all of your pet's fantasies come true with a gift from the pet store Fetch.

Niketown

6 E 57th St between Fifth and Madison Aves (212-891-6453, 800-671-6453). Subway: N, R to Fifth Ave. Mon–Fri 10am–8pm; Sat 10am–7pm; Sun 11am–6pm. AmEx, Disc, JCB, MC, V.

Every 23 minutes, a huge screen drops down and plays a Nike ad, and interactive CD-ROMs help you make an informed shoe choice. Don't scoff: There are 1,200 kinds of footwear to choose from.

Paragon Sporting Goods

867 Broadway at 18th St (212-255-8036). Subway: L, N, R, 4, 5, 6 to 14th St–Union Sq. Mon–Sat 10am–8pm; Sun 11am–6:30pm. AmEx, DC, Disc, MC, V.

A full line of sports equipment and sportswear is available at this three-floor store. There's a good range of swimwear, surfwear, tennis rackets, climbing gear and shoes.

Studio stores

Disney Store

711 Fifth Ave at 55th St (212-702-0702; www.disneystore.com). Subway: E, F, N, R to Fifth Ave. Mon–Sat 10am–8pm; Sun 11am–7pm. AmEx, Disc, JCB, MC, V.

This is where all your favorite Disney characters come to life (in great quantity)—Mickey, Minnie, Goofy, etc. At the Fifth Avenue store, the largest of them all, you can peruse all of Disney's toys and souvenirs. Check the phone book for other locations.

Warner Bros. Studio Store

1 E 57th St at Fifth Ave (212-754-0300; www.wbstore.com). Subway: E, F, N, R to Fifth Ave. Mon–Sat 10am–7pm; Sun noon–7pm. AmEx, Disc, JCB, MC, V.

The outlet for anything and everything that has a Warner Bros. character slapped on it features baseball hats, T-shirts and a few surprises.

Other locations: *330 World Trade Center between Vesey and Cortlandt Sts, concourse level (212-775-1442); 1 Times Square at the corner of 42nd St and Seventh Ave (212-840-4040).*

Tattoos and piercing

Tattooing was made legal in New York only in April 1998; piercing is completely unregulated, so be discriminating.

Fun City

124 MacDougal St between Bleecker and 3rd Sts (212-674-0754). Subway: A, C, E, B, D, F, Q to W 4th St. Mon–Thu, Sun noon–midnight; Fri, Sat noon–2am. AmEx, Disc, MC, V.

This is no doctor's office, but the folks at Fun City can be trusted. Tattoos and custom piercings are available.

Other location: *94 St. Marks Pl between First Ave and Ave A (212-353-8282).*

NY Adorned

47 Second Ave at 3rd St (212-473-0007). Subway: F to Second Ave. Sun–Thu noon–8pm; Fri, Sat noon–10pm. AmEx, MC, V.

The waiting area of this beautiful store looks like the lobby of a clean hipster hotel. Along with piercing, Adorned offers tattooing and mendhi designs.

Venus Modern Body Art

199 E 4th St between Aves A and B (212-473-1954). Subway: F to Second Ave. 1–9pm. AmEx, Disc, MC, V.

Venus has been tattooing and piercing New Yorkers since 1993, long before body art became de rigueur. It offers an enormous selection of jewelry to choose from—diamonds in your navel and platinum in your tongue, anyone? Piercings range from $15 to $35, plus jewelry.

Entertainment

Feature boxes

Roaring good time One of the best musicals on Broadway is *The Lion King*.

New York by Season

Whether you prefer the leaves of autumn or the flowers of spring, New York blooms with perennial activity

As each season turns, one of New York's multiple personalities emerges. Winter's holiday parties and slushy traffic jams melt into the flowers and in-line skates of spring. Summer is hot, sweaty and slower, with garden restaurants, outdoor concerts and neighborhood fairs (not to mention air-conditioning) providing welcome relief from the sizzling streets. The pace picks up again in the fall, when New Yorkers enjoy the last of the sun's long rays and the beginning of the opera, dance and music seasons.

The festivals, parades and events listed below are held regularly. Don't forget to confirm that an event is happening before you set out.

▶ Check the websites **www.timeout.com** and **www.timeoutny.com** for more information on seasonal events.
▶ The website of NYC & Company–the Convention & Visitors Bureau (**www.nycvisit.com**) has additional info.
▶ For team sports seasons, see chapter **Sports & Fitness**.

Spring

International Artexpo

Jacob K. Javits Convention Center, Eleventh Ave between 34th and 39th Sts; enter at 37th St (800-331-5706; www.artexpos.com). Subway: A, C, E to 34th St–Penn Station. Mid-March.

The world's largest art exhibition and sale, the Artexpo features original artwork, fine-art prints, limited-edition lithographs and more by some 2,400 artists, from Picasso to Robert Indiana.

Whitney Biennial

Whitney Museum of American Art, 945 Madison Ave at 75th St (212-570-3600). Subway: 6 to 77th St. Late Mar–early Jun.

Every two years, the Whitney showcases what it deems to be the most important recent American art, generating much controversy in the process. The 2000 installation featured everything from an ant farm to a giant sculpture made of tires. The next show is in 2002.

St. Patrick's Day Parade

Fifth Ave between 44th and 86th Sts (212-484-1222). Mar 17.

New York becomes a sea of green for the annual

MacDaddy Irish-Americans proudly wear green on St. Patrick's Day, March 17.

Entertainment

Hat attack Easter tradition demands that you don fancy duds and a special bonnet.

U.S. holidays

Plan around these red-letter days

Although most banks and government offices close on these major U.S. holidays (except Election Day), stores and restaurants are usually open. If you will be in New York around a holiday, be sure to call ahead to find out if there are special hours on these days.

New Year's Day January 1

Martin Luther King Jr. Day third Monday in January

Presidents' Day third Monday in February

Memorial Day last Monday in May

Independence Day July 4

Labor Day first Monday in September

Columbus Day second Monday in October

Election Day first Tuesday after first Monday in November

Veterans' Day November 11

Thanksgiving fourth Thursday in November

Christmas Day December 25

Entertainment

Irish-American day of days, starting at 11am with the parade up Fifth Avenue and extending late into the night in bars all over the city.

Ringling Bros. and Barnum & Bailey Circus

Madison Square Garden, Seventh Ave at 32nd St (212-465-6741). Subway: A, C, E, 1, 2, 3, 9 to 34th St–Penn Station. Late Mar–early May.

The Barnum & Bailey half of this famous three-ring circus annexed the line "the Greatest Show on Earth" back in its early days in New York City. Don't miss the free midnight parade of animals through the Queens-Midtown Tunnel and along 34th Street that traditionally opens and closes the show's run.

Easter Parade

Fifth Ave between 49th and 57th Sts (212-484-1222). Easter Sunday.

The annual Easter Parade kicks off at 11am. Try to get a spot around St. Patrick's Cathedral, which is the best viewing platform—but get there early.

New York Antiquarian Book Fair

Park Ave between 66th and 67th Sts (212-777-5218). Subway: 6 to 68th St–Hunter College. April.

More than 170 international booksellers exhibit rare books, maps, manuscripts and more.

New York International Auto Show

Jacob K. Javits Convention Center, Eleventh Ave between 34th and 39th Sts; enter at 35th St (800-282-3336; www.nyauto.com). Subway: A, C, E to 34th St–Penn Station. April.

Cars from the past, present and future are on display during this annual rite of spring.

New York City Ballet Spring Season

New York State Theater, 20 Lincoln Center Plaza, 65th St at Columbus Ave (212-870-5570). Subway: 1, 9 to 66th St–Lincoln Ctr. Late Apr–Jun.

The NYCB's spring season usually features a new ballet, in addition to repertory classics by George Balanchine and Jerome Robbins, among others (*see chapter* **Theater & Dance**).

Marijuana March

Starts at Washington Square Park, Washington Sq Park South at Thompson St (212-677-7180). Subway: A, C, E, B, D, F, Q to W 4th St. First Saturday in May.

This annual parade for pot legalization is sponsored by Cures not Wars, an alternative-drug-policy advocacy group.

Bike New York: The Great Five Boro Bike Tour

Starts at Battery Park, finishes on Staten Island (212-932-0778). Early May.

Every year, thousands of cyclists take over the city for a 42-mile (68km) bike ride through the five boroughs. Traffic is rerouted, and you'll feel like you're in the Tour de France—sort of. (You must register in advance.)

You Gotta Have Park

Parks throughout the city (212-360-3456). May.
This is an annual celebration of New York's public spaces, with free events in the major parks of all five boroughs. It heralds the start of a busy schedule of concerts and other events in green places all around the city.

Bang on a Can Festival

Various venues (212-777-8442; www.bangonacan.org). Starts in early May with events throughout the year.
Think of Bang on a Can as the annual showcase for the rambunctious side of classical music. The highlight of every festival is the daylong BoaC Marathon, where you might catch art-music heads like Ben Neill or Fred Frith following a revamped interpretation of a Xenakis, Cage or Stockhausen piece performed by Sonic Youth's Thurston Moore or Lee Ranaldo.

Vision Festival

Venue changes annually (www.visionfestival.org). Mid-May.
The Lower East Side–based Vision Festival is the only full-fledged avant-garde jazz event in town. Organized by Iron Man bassist William Parker and his wife, dancer Patricia Nicholson, the multimedia event brings together some of the biggest draws in free jazz (Matthew Shipp, Peter Brøtzmann, Joseph Jarman) with dancers, poets and visual artists.

Ninth Avenue International Food Festival

Ninth Ave between 37th and 57th Sts (212-581-7029). Subway: A, C, E to 42nd St–Port Authority. Mid-May.
A glorious mile of gluttony. Hundreds of stalls serve every type of food. Fabulously fattening.

Military Salute Week

Intrepid *Sea-Air-Space Museum, Pier 86, 46th St at West Side Hwy (212-245-2533, recorded info 212-245-0072). Subway: A, C, E to 42nd St–Port Authority. Last week in May.*
All branches of the military visit New York for this celebration of the armed forces. The U.S. Navy and ships from other countries sail past the Statue of Liberty. Also, expect maneuvers, parachute drops, air displays and various ceremonies. During the week, you can visit some of the ships at Pier 86.

Lower East Side Festival of the Arts

Theater for the New City, 155 First Ave at 10th St (212-254-1109). Subway: L to First Ave; 6 to Astor Pl. Last weekend in May.
This annual arts festival and outdoor carnival celebrates the neighborhood that helped spawn the Beats, Method acting and Pop Art. It features performances by more than 20 theatrical troupes and appearances by local celebrities.

Summer

Toyota Comedy Festival

Various locations (888-33-TOYOTA). Early to mid-June.

Sea me! The Mermaid Parade in Coney Island celebrates the arrival of summer.

Entertainment

Win oar lose The Liberty Challenge brings some Hawaiian style to New York City.

Hundreds of America's funniest men and women perform at 30 venues around the city. The information line operates from May to mid-June only.

Puerto Rican Day Parade

Fifth Ave between 44th and 86th Sts (212-484-1222). Second Sunday in June.
Featuring colorful floats and marching bands, this parade has become one of the city's liveliest street celebrations.

Museum Mile Festival

Fifth Ave between 82nd and 104th Sts (212-606-2296). Second Tuesday in June.
Several major museums host this open-house festival. Crowds are attracted by the free admission and the highbrow street entertainment.

Central Park SummerStage

Rumsey Playfield, Central Park; enter at 72nd St at Fifth Ave (212-360-2777; www.summerstage.org). Subway: 6 to 77th St. Jun–Aug.
Enjoy free weekend afternoon concerts featuring top international performers and a wide variety of music; there are a few benefit shows for which admission is charged. Some years, dance and spoken-word events are offered on weekday nights as well.

Metropolitan Opera Parks Concerts

Various locations (212-362-6000). June.
The Metropolitan Opera presents two different operas at open-air evening concerts in Central Park and other parks throughout the five boroughs and New Jersey. The performances are free. To get a good seat, you need to arrive hours early and be prepared to squabble.

Bell Atlantic New York Jazz Festival

Knitting Factory and various venues (212-219-3006; www.jazfest.com). Early June.
This used to be called the What Is Jazz? Festival. Now you never know what corporate heading Knitting Factory owner-impresario Michael Dorf will be putting in front of his annual fest—it's been Texaco and Heineken in the past. Whoever sponsors it, the event is guaranteed to be the most sprawling of the year. Dorf mixes the biggest names in jazz (Joe Henderson, the Art Ensemble of Chicago, Dave Holland, McCoy Tyner) with alterna-draws such as P-Funk All-Stars, Jon Spencer Blues Explosion and Galactic—that's the difference between this series and that of his rival/mentor George Wein's JVC Jazz Festival.

JVC Jazz Festival

Various locations (212-501-1390; www.festivalproductions.net). Mid-June.
The direct descendant of the original Newport Jazz Festival, the JVC bash has become a New York institution. Not only does the festival fill big-time halls like Carnegie and Avery Fisher with big draws (João Gilberto, Herbie Hancock, Cassandra Wilson), it also spreads jazz throughout the city by offering gigs in Harlem and half-price deals at downtown clubs like the Village Vanguard and Sweet Basil. JVC also sponsors free concerts by more adventurous musicians (like Marc Ribot and James Carter) in Bryant Park.

Gay and Lesbian Pride March

From Columbus Circle, along Fifth Ave to Christopher St (212-807-7433). Late June.
Every year, New York's gay and lesbian community parades through the streets of midtown to Greenwich Village to commemorate the Stonewall uprising of 1969. The celebrations have expanded into a week's worth of goings-on, and in addition to a packed club schedule, there's an open-air dance party on the West Side piers. The event draws thousands of visitors to the city.

Liberty Challenge

Pier 25, North Moore St at West St (212-580-0442; www.libertychallenge.org). Late June.
Top teams from Manhattan and around the world come to the city for this outrigger canoe race from lower Manhattan to the Statue of Liberty and back. It's Waikiki on the Hudson: Besides buff paddlers from Hawaii (where the sport originated), you can check out booths selling Hawaiian food and gifts, and paddling gear.

Midsummer Night Swing

Lincoln Center Plaza, Broadway between 64th and 65th Sts (212-875-5766). Subway: 1, 9 to 66th St–Lincoln Ctr. Late Jun–Jul.
Dance under the stars Tuesday through Saturday evenings beside the fountain at picturesque Lincoln Center. Each night is devoted to a different style of dance, from swing to square. If you have two left feet, don't worry—performances are preceded by free dance lessons.

New York Shakespeare Festival

Delacorte Theater, Central Park at 81st St (212-539-8750, 212-539-8500; www.publictheater.org). Subway: B, C to 81st St; 6 to 77th St. Late Jun–Sept.
The free Shakespeare Festival is one of the high-

lights of a Manhattan summer, with big-name stars pulling on their tights for a whack at the Bard. There are two plays each year, with at least one written by Shakespeare (*see chapter* **Theater & Dance**).

Bryant Park Free Summer Season

Bryant Park, Sixth Ave at 42nd St (212-768-4242; www.bryantpark.org). Subway: B, D, F, Q to 42nd St; 7 to Fifth Ave. Jun–Aug.

This reclaimed park, a lunchtime oasis for midtown's office population, is the site of a packed season of free classical music, jazz, dance and film. Best of all are the Monday-night open-air movies.

Mermaid Parade

From the Cyclone roller coaster at West 10th St to West 16th St, Coney Island, Brooklyn (718-372-5159; www.coneyisland.com). Subway: B, D, F, N to Coney Island–Stillwell Ave. Saturday after summer solstice.

If your taste runs to the wild and free, don't miss Coney Island's annual showcase of bizarreness, consisting of elaborate floats, paraders dressed as sea creatures, kiddie-costume contests and other über-kitschy celebrations to kick off the summer.

Macy's Fireworks Display

Locations to be announced (212-494-4495). Jul 4 at 9:15pm.

The highlight of Independence Day is this spectacular fireworks display. Look up in wonder as $1 million worth of pyrotechnics light up the night.

Nathan's Famous Fourth of July Hot Dog–Eating Contest

Nathan's Famous, 1310 Surf Ave at Stillwell Ave, Coney Island, Brooklyn (718-946-2202). Subway: B, D, F, N to Coney Island–Stillwell Ave. Jul 4.

The winner of this Coney Island showdown is the man or woman who can stuff the most wieners down his or her gullet in 12 minutes.

Digital Club Festival

Various venues (www.digitalclubfestival.com). July.

This weeklong affair (previously called the MacFest and the IntelFest) is organized by Knitting Factory mogul Michael Dorf and Irving Plaza founder Andrew Rasiej. It features hundreds of bands at more than 20 Manhattan venues. While the festival doesn't feature big headliners, it's a chance for visitors to check out the local talent all at once.

Lincoln Center Festival

Lincoln Center, 65th St at Columbus Ave (212-875-5928). Subway: 1, 9 to 66th St–Lincoln Ctr. July.

Dance, music, theater, opera, kids' events and more are all part of this ambitious festival held in and around the Lincoln Center arts complex.

Seaside Summer Concert Series

Asser Levy Seaside Park, Sea Breeze Ave at Ocean Pkwy, Brighton Beach, Brooklyn (718-469-1912). Subway: D, F to W 8th St–NY Aquarium. July.

Vintage pop-music acts perform in Brighton Beach beside the ocean during this music series.

Washington Square Music Festival

Washington Square Park, La Guardia Pl at 4th St (212-431-1088). Subway: A, C, E, B, D, F, Q to W 4th St. Tuesdays at 8pm in July.

This open-air concert season, featuring mainly chamber-orchestra and big-band music, has been running in Greenwich Village for years.

New York Philharmonic Concerts

Various locations (212-875-5709). July.

The New York Philharmonic presents a varied program, from Mozart to Weber, in many of New York's larger parks. The bugs are just part of the deal.

New York Renaissance Faire

Sterling Forest, Tuxedo, NY (914-351-5171). Travel: George Washington Bridge to Rte 4 West, then Rte 17 North to Exit 15A to Rte 17A; buses also available from Manhattan. Early Aug–late Sept.

The Ren Faire is for those who prefer wild knights to wild nights. More than 500 costumed daredevils, artisans, jousters on horseback and mud-pit enthusiasts liven up this annual festival.

Thursday Night Concert Series

Main Stage, South Street Seaport, South St at Fulton St (212-732-7678). Subway: A, C to Broadway–Nassau; J, M, Z, 2, 3, 4, 5 to Fulton St–. Jun–Aug.

Free outdoor concerts by emerging artists—presenting all types of music—are held on Thursdays throughout the summer at the South Street Seaport. (For more information on the Seaport, *see chapter* **Downtown**.)

Summergarden

Museum of Modern Art, 11 W 53rd St between Fifth and Sixth Aves (212-708-9400). Subway: E, F to Fifth Ave. Fri, Sat 8:30pm; Jul–Aug.

Listen to free classical concerts, organized with the Juilliard School, in the museum's sculpture garden.

Celebrate Brooklyn! Performing Arts Festival

Prospect Park Bandshell, 9th St at Prospect Park West, Park Slope, Brooklyn (718-855-7882; www.brooklynx.org). Subway: F to Seventh Ave. Fri, Sat; late Jul–late Aug.

Nine weeks of free outdoor events—music, dance, film and spoken word—are presented in Brooklyn's answer to Central Park.

Mostly Mozart

Avery Fisher Hall, Lincoln Center, 65th St at Columbus Ave (212-875-5399). Subway: 1, 9 to 66th St–Lincoln Ctr. Late Jul–Aug.

For more than a quarter century, the Mostly Mozart festival has mounted an intensive four-week schedule of performances of work by the genius and his fellow baroque wig-wearers. There are also lectures and other side attractions.

Lincoln Center Out-of-Doors

Outdoor venues in and around Lincoln Center, 65th St at Columbus Ave (212-875-5108). Subway: 1, 9 to 66th St–Lincoln Ctr. August.

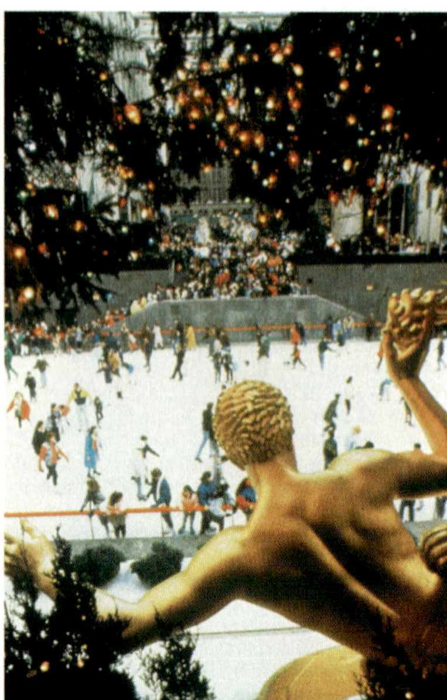

Lighten up The Rockefeller Center Christmas tree brightens midtown in winter.

The parks and plazas of Lincoln Center play host to a variety of dance and music performances, special events and children's entertainment during this three-week-long festival.

Central Park Zoo Chill Out Weekend

Central Park Wildlife Center, enter at Fifth Ave at 64th St (212-861-6030). Subway: N, R to Fifth Ave. Early August.

Stay cool and check up on the polar bears and penguins during Central Park Zoo's two-day party.

Harlem Week

Throughout Harlem (212-862-8477). Subway: 2, 3, 4, 5, 6 to 125th St. Early to mid-August.

The largest black and Latino festival in the world features music, film, dance, fashion, exhibitions and sports. The highlight is the street festival on Fifth Avenue between 125th and 135th streets, which includes an international carnival of arts, entertainment and great food. Don't miss the jazz, gospel and R&B performances. (For more on Harlem, *see chapter* **Uptown** *and* **Movin' on up,** *page 70.*)

Fringe Festival

Various locations downtown (212-420-8877). Mid- to late August.

The young Fringe Festival has emerged as a major venue for up-and-coming talent in the performing-arts world.

Hong Kong Dragon Boat Festival

The Lake at Flushing Meadows–Corona Park, Queens (718-539-8974). Subway: 7 to Main St–Flushing. Mid-August.

This Hong Kong tradition now makes waves here. Teams from the New York area paddle colorful 39-foot teak crafts with dragon heads at the bow and tails at the stern to the banging of drums.

Macy's Tap-o-Mania

Macy's Herald Square, Broadway at 34th St (212-494-5247). Subway: B, D, F, Q, N, R to 34th St–Herald Sq. Late August.

Thousands of hoofers converge outside Macy's flagship Herald Square store for this annual attempt to break the Guinness World Record for the largest assemblage of tap dancers to dance a single routine.

U.S. Open

USTA National Tennis Center, Flushing, Queens (info and tickets 718-760-6200). Subway: 7 to Willets Point–Shea Stadium. Late Aug–early Sept.

The final Grand Slam event of the year, the U.S. Open is also one of the most entertaining tournaments on the international tennis circuit. Tickets are hard to come by, however.

Panasonic Village Jazz Festival

Throughout Greenwich Village (www.villagejazzfestival.com). Late August.

This seven- to ten-day festival features performers at most of the Village's many jazz clubs and includes lectures and films. It culminates in a free concert in Washington Square Park.

West Indian Day Carnival

Eastern Pkwy from Utica Ave to Grand Army Plaza, Prospect Park, Brooklyn (718-625-1515). Subway: 3, 4 to Utica Ave. Labor Day weekend.

This loud and energetic celebration of Caribbean culture offers a children's parade on Saturday and ends with an even bigger march of flamboyantly costumed revelers on Labor Day.

Wigstock

Pier 54, West St between 12th and 13th Sts (212-439-5139). Subway: A, C, E, to 14th St; L to Eighth Ave. Labor Day weekend.

Viva drag, glamour and artificial hair! Anyone who can muster some foundation and lipstick dresses up as a woman, and real girls had better be extra fierce to cope with the competition. Having outgrown its origins in the East Village's Tompkins Square Park, Wigstock now rages at Pier 54, near the West Village.

Richmond County Fair

Historic Richmond Town, 441 Clarke Ave between Richmond and Arthur Kill Rds, Staten Island (718-351-1611). Travel: Staten Island Ferry, then S74 bus to St. Patrick's Pl. Labor Day weekend.

This is an authentic county fair, just like the ones in rural America, with arts and crafts and extra-large produce and strange agricultural competitions.

Fall

Downtown Arts Festival

Various lower Manhattan locations (212-243-5050; www.simonsays.org). September.
The former Soho Arts Festival has expanded from a September block party to a mammoth event of art exhibitions, gallery tours and critical forums, as well as performance-art happenings, experimental video shows and good old-fashioned readings.

CMJ Music Marathon, MusicFest and FilmFest

Various venues. (646-485-6600, 877-6-FESTIVAL; www.cmj.com). September.
Hundreds of bands play at this four-day industry schmoozefest. *CMJ* (*College Music Journal*) publishes a trade and a consumer mag that track college-radio airplay, retail sales, etc. The festival books hip young things in genres such as rock, indie rock, hip-hop, electronica and alternative country. This is one of the most important industry confabs for music-biz pros.

Broadway on Broadway

43rd St at Broadway (212-768-1560). Subway: N, R, S, 1, 2, 3, 9, 7 to 42nd St–Times Sq. Sunday after Labor Day.
For one day at least, Broadway is remarkably affordable, as the season's new productions offer a sneak (free!) peek at their latest theatrical works right in the middle of Times Square.

Guinness Fleadh

Downing Stadium, Randall's Island (212-860-1828; www.guinnessfleadh.com). Travel: 4, 5, 6 to 125th St, then M35 bus to stadium. September.
At this outdoor Irish and Irish-American music fest, the Guinness flows freely and the bands rock. Past Fleadhs (pronounced "flah") have featured Ireland natives such as Sinéad O'Connor, Van Morrison and Shane MacGowan, as well as non-Irishmen (not even close) Lucinda Williams and Hootie & the Blowfish. Now that the Fleadh's held in September (and not rainy June), it's not such a mudfest (*see chapter* **Music, Summer venues**).

New York City Century Bike Tour

Begins at Harlem Meer, Central Park, 110th St at Lenox Ave (212-629-8080; www.transalt.org). Subway: 2, 3 to 110th St. Early September.
This 100-mile ride through the city benefits, and is organized by, Transportation Alternatives, a local group dedicated to promoting cycling and making the city safe for riders. Shorter routes are also an option.

Brooklyn BeerFest

Outside the Brooklyn Brewery, 79 North 11th St between Berry St and Wythe Ave, Williamsburg, Brooklyn (718-486-7422; www.brooklynbrewery.com). Subway: L to Bedford Ave. Mid-September.
Taste more than 100 beers from around the world at this annual ale festival hosted by the Craft Brewers Guild. Industry insiders will be around to explain the finer points of hops and barley.

Mayor's Cup

New York Harbor (212-748-8590). Subway: 1, 9 to South Ferry; 4, 5 to Bowling Green. Mid-September.
Classic schooners and yachts unfurl their sails in this annual race.

German-American Steuben Parade

Fifth Ave from 63rd to 86th Sts (516-239-0741). Subway: N, R to Fifth Ave. Mid-September.
This parade celebrates German-American contributions to the U.S.

New York Is Book Country

Various locations (www.bookreporter.com/nyisbookcountry). Mid- to late September.
This literary festival ends with a massive street fair on Fifth Avenue.

Feast of San Gennaro

Mulberry St from Houston to Canal Sts (212-484-1222). Subway: J, M, Z, N, R, 6 to Canal St. Third week in September.
Celebrations for the patron saint of Naples last ten days, from 11am to 11pm daily, with fairground booths, stalls and plenty of Italian food and wine.

Atlantic Antic

Boerum Hill–Brooklyn Heights, Brooklyn (718-875-8993). Subway: N, R to Court St; 2, 3, 4, 5 to Borough Hall. Last Sunday in September.

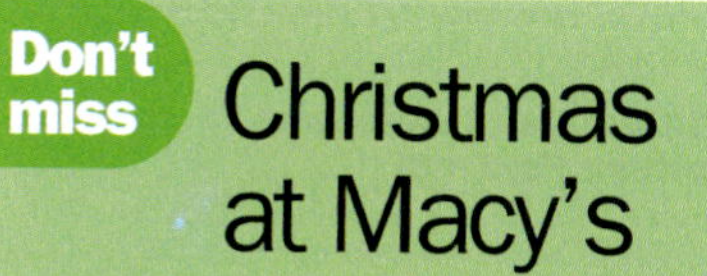
Don't miss
Christmas at Macy's

What it takes to deck the halls of Macy's main floor

Lights: 86,325

Christmas trees: 86

Feet of garland: 1,178

Feet of ribbon: 27,000

Ornaments: 9,100

Wreaths: 2

Menorahs: 2

Hours of labor: 2,500 (for design, preparation, installation, maintenance and removal)

Source: American Christmas Decorations

This multicultural street fair on Brooklyn's Atlantic Avenue features live entertainment and waterfront art exhibitions.

New York Film Festival

Alice Tully Hall, Lincoln Center, 65th St at Columbus Ave (212-875-5610; www.filmlinc.com). Subway: 1, 9 to 66th St–Lincoln Ctr. Late Sept–early Oct.

One of the film world's most prestigious events, the festival is a showcase for major directors from around the world. More than two dozen American and foreign films are given New York, U.S. or world premieres, and the festival usually features rarely seen classics. Tickets for films by known directors are often hard to come by.

Columbus Day Parade

Fifth Ave between 44th and 86th Sts (212-484-1222). Columbus Day.

To celebrate the first recorded sighting of America by Europeans, the whole country gets an Italian-flavored holiday (though not always a day off from work)—and the inevitable parade up Fifth Avenue.

Dumbo: Art Under the Bridge

Various locations in Dumbo, Brooklyn, at the East River between the Manhattan and Brooklyn Bridges (718-624-3772). Subway: A, C to High St; F to York St. Mid-October.

The Dumbo area of Brooklyn (Down Under the Manhattan Bridge Overpass) becomes one big art happening for a weekend. Open studios, DJs, fashion shows, music, theater, film and dance events are just some of the attractions.

Williamsburg Arts and Culture Festival

Various locations in Williamsburg, Brooklyn (718-486-7372). Subway: L to Bedford Ave. Mid-October.

North Brooklyn's artsy neighborhood hosts fashion shows, open studio tours and happenings at area galleries, restaurants and shops during this weekend-long festival.

Big Apple Circus

Damrosch Park, Lincoln Center, 65th St at Columbus Ave (212-721-6500). Subway: 1, 9 to 66th St–Lincoln Ctr. Late Oct–early Jan.

The audience sits within 50 feet of the lone ring at this long-running classic circus.

Halloween Parade

Starts on Sixth Ave from Broome to Spring Sts, up to 23rd St. Oct 31 at 7pm.

Anyone can participate in this parade (and about 25,000 people do every year)—just wear a costume and line up at the beginning of the route around 6pm with the rest of the fascinating characters. For more information, call the *Village Voice* (212-475-3300).

New York City Marathon

Starts at the Staten Island side of the Verrazano-Narrows Bridge (212-860-4455; www.nycmarathon.org). First Sunday in November at 10:45am.

A crowd of 30,000 marathoners runs through all five boroughs over a 26.2-mile (42km) course. The race finishes at Tavern on the Green, in Central Park at West 67th Street.

Autumn Blues Festival

Symphony Space, 2537 Broadway at 95th St (212-864-5400; www.heartheworld.org). Subway: 1, 2, 3, 9 to 96th St. Early November.

New York is by no means a blues town comparable to Memphis or Chicago. But each year, the World Music Institute and Symphony Space invite blues artists—whether wizened living links to a vanishing rural tradition or new jacks with worldly influences—to show how they connect the dots.

Macy's Thanksgiving Day Parade

From Central Park West at 77th St to Macy's, Broadway at 34th St (212-695-4400). Thanksgiving Day at 9am.

Bring the kids to this one: The parade features enormous inflated cartoon-character balloons, elaborate floats and Santa Claus, who makes his way to Macy's department store, where he'll spend the next month in Santaland. If you can, stop by for Inflation Eve the night before to watch the big balloons take shape on West 77th and 81st Streets between Central Park West and Columbus Aves.

Winter

The Nutcracker

New York State Theater, Lincoln Center, 65th St at Columbus Ave (212-870-5570). Subway: 1, 9 to 66th St–Lincoln Ctr. Thanksgiving–first week of January.

The New York City Ballet's performance of this famous work, assisted by students from the School of American Ballet, is a much-loved Christmas tradition (*see chapter* **Dance**).

Christmas Tree Lighting Ceremony

Rockefeller Center, Fifth Ave between 49th and 50th Sts (212-484-1222). Subway: B, D, F, Q to 47–50th Sts–Rockefeller Ctr. First week of December.

Five miles of lights festoon a giant evergreen in front of the GE Building. The tree, ice skaters and the shimmering statue of Prometheus make this the city's most enchanting Christmas spot.

Messiah Sing-In

Avery Fisher Hall, Lincoln Center, 65th St at Columbus Ave (212-333-5333). Subway: 1, 9 to 66th St–Lincoln Ctr. Mid-December.

Around Christmas—usually a week before—the National Choral Council rounds up 21 conductors to lead huge audiences (sometimes 3,000-strong) in a rehearsal and performance of Handel's *Messiah*. No experience is necessary, and you can buy the score on-site. Call for date and time.

Christmas Spectacular

Radio City Music Hall, 1260 Sixth Ave at 50th St (212-247-4777). Subway: B, D, F, Q to 47–50th Sts–Rockefeller Ctr. Nov–early Jan.

This famous long-running show features the fabulous high-kicking Rockettes in tableaux and musical numbers that exhaust the thematic possibilities of Christmas.

New Year's Eve Ball Drop

Times Square (212-768-1560; www.timessquarebid.org). Subway: N, R, S, 1, 2, 3, 9, 7 to 42nd St–Times Sq. Dec 31.

A traditional New York year ends and begins in Times Square, culminating with the dropping of the ball—encrusted with 504 Waterford Crystal triangles, weighing 1,070 pounds and illuminated by 600 multicolored halogen bulbs; it was created specially for the 1999–2000 bash. If teeming hordes of drunken revelers turn you on, by all means go. The surrounding streets are packed by 9pm.

New Year's Eve Fireworks

Central Park (212-860-4455). Dec 31.

The best viewing points for this explosive display are Central Park at 72nd Street, Tavern on the Green (Central Park West at 67th St) and Fifth Avenue at 90th Street. The fun and festivities, including hot cider and food, start at 10:30pm.

New Year's Eve Midnight Run

Starts at Tavern on the Green, Central Park West at 67th St (212-860-4455). Subway: B, C to 72nd St; 1, 9 to 66th St–Lincoln Ctr. Dec 31.

A five-kilometer jaunt through the park, the New York Road Runners Club's Midnight Run also features a masquerade parade, a pre- and post-race live DJ, fireworks, prizes and a champagne toast at the run's halfway mark.

New Year's Day Marathon Poetry Reading

The Poetry Project at St. Mark's Church in-the-Bowery, 131 E 10th St at Second Ave (212-674-0910; www.poetryproject.com). Subway: 6 to Astor Pl. Jan 1.

Big-name bohemians and downtown habitués such as Patti Smith, Richard Hell and Richard Foreman traditionally grace the stage for this all-day spectacle of poetry, music, dance and performance art.

Chinese New Year

Around Mott St, Chinatown (212-484-1222). Subway: J, M, Z, N, R, 6 to Canal St. First day of the full moon between Jan 21 and Feb 19.

The city's Chinese population celebrates the lunar new year in style, with dragon parades, performers and delicious food throughout Chinatown. Since private fireworks were banned in 1995, the celebrations don't have quite the bang they once did.

Winter Antiques Show

Seventh Regiment Armory, Park Ave at 67th St (718-665-5250; www.winterantiquesshow.com). Subway: 6 to 68th St–Hunter College. Mid-January.

This is the most prestigious of New York's antiques fairs, with an eclectic selection of items ranging from ancient works to Art Nouveau. The show's vast American collections come from all over the country. Sales benefit the East Side House Settlement.

Outsider Art Fair

The Puck Building, 295 Lafayette St at Houston St (212-777-5218). Subway: B, D, F, Q to Broadway–Lafayette St; 6 to Bleecker St. Late January.

A highlight of the annual art calendar, this three-day extravaganza draws crowds of buyers and browsers from all over the world. The fair's 35 dealers exhibit outsider, self-taught and visionary art in all media, at prices that range from $500 to $350,000.

New York Independent Film and Video Festival

Madison Square Garden, Seventh Ave at 32nd St (212-777-7100; www.nyfilmvideo.com). Subway: A, C, E, 1, 2, 3, 9 to 34th St–Penn Station. Early February. Also held in early June and mid-Sepember.

This cultural extravaganza of film, art and fashion kicks off with a mammoth happening at the Garden. Then, for nine days various venues around the city hold screenings, concerts and fashion shows.

New York International Children's Film Festival

Call for location (212-349-0330; www.gkids.com). Mid-February.

Launched in 1998, this popular festival shows films aimed at children age 3 to 18.

The Armory Show

Call for location (212-777-3338). Late February.

Though it debuted in 1999, this international art festival is already one of the biggest weekends on the avant-garde calendar. The original (and controversial) 1913 Armory Show introduced cutting-edge art to New York, and this fair carries on the name and the tradition of showcasing visual groundbreakers from galleries around the world.

The Art Show

Seventh Regiment Armory, Park Ave at 67th St (212-766-9200, ext 248). Subway: 6 to 68th St–Hunter College. Late February.

Begun in 1989 and organized by the Art Dealers Association of America, this is one of New York's largest art fairs. Exhibitors offer paintings, prints and sculptures dating from the 17th century to the present. Proceeds go to the Henry Street Settlement, a Lower East Side social-services agency.

Empire State Building Run-Up

Empire State Building, 350 Fifth Ave at 34th St (212-860-4455). Subway: B, D, F, Q, N, R to 34th St–Herald Sq; 6 to 33rd St. Late February.

Runners speed up the 1,576 steps from the lobby to the 86th floor. Australian Paul Crake set the 9:53 record in 2000.

Art Galleries

The city's economic boom has spurred an art boom—reverberating everywhere from elite uptown galleries to raw nonprofit spaces

Blessed with an abundance of galleries that exhibit everything from old and modern masters to contemporary experiments in new media, New York is an art lover's dream. You'll find galleries not just amid the refined residences of upper Madison Avenue and the glossy boutiques of 57th Street but also in areas you might not expect: in postindustrial West Chelsea, on the scruffy Lower East Side, in the meatpacking hinterland of Greenwich Village, even under the ramps that lead up to the Brooklyn Bridge. Real-estate values have forced relocations and forged a few new partnerships. While uptown galleries remain stable and sedate, occasionally taking on new artists, gallerists in the cast-iron district of Soho—until recently the world capital of the contemporary art market—have had to compete with mushrooming numbers of retail shops, restaurants and hotels. Consequently, dozens of Soho galleries have defected to more spacious (and quieter) quarters in West Chelsea, the former warehouse district now almost entirely dedicated to the exhibition and sale of contemporary art. There are still notable holdouts in Soho, though, and on weekends the neighborhood fills with a colorful mix of shoppers, tourists and art enthusiasts—often the same people.

Tribeca has its own odd assortment of small galleries and fine, art-friendly restaurants, and with more artists priced out of Manhattan studios, the Brooklyn neighborhoods of Williamsburg and Dumbo (Down Under the Manhattan Bridge Overpass) are offering freewheeling, often festive delights in quirky new artist-run spaces. Williamsburg now even boasts bona fide galleries of its own. In fact, the art world's structure resembles that of the film industry: uptown corporate studios bearing the names Gagosian, PaceWildenstein and Marlborough; major independent productions in Chelsea and Soho; and smaller art-house upstarts and satellite productions on the fringes.

There has also been a curatorial shift. A number of galleries have reduced their emphasis on American (particularly New York) artists and taken on a more global perspective. Photography continues to enjoy a renaissance, along with so-called outsider art. And traditional, object-oriented exhibitions share the bill with multidisciplinary, often site-specific artworks that incorporate several media at once (especially video), adding a theatrical flavor to viewing and collecting. Finally, the past year has seen a resurgence of painting, a trend that looks as if it will continue.

Opening times listed are from September to May or June. Summer visitors should keep in mind that most galleries are only open Monday to Friday from late June to early September; some close at the end of August. Call before visiting.

▶ For weekly reviews and listings, gallerygoers should pick up a copy of ***Time Out New York.***
▶ Monthly notices can be found in such magazines as ***Artforum*** ($7), ***Flash Art*** ($7), ***Art in America*** ($5) and ***Art Now Gallery Guide*** (free for the asking at most galleries or $4.95 at museum bookstores).
▶ If you are interested in the art market, look to the monthlies ***Art and Antiques*** ($4.95), ***Art & Auction*** ($3.95) and ***ArtNews*** ($6).

Upper East Side

Most galleries on the Upper East Side are well established and sell masterworks priced for millionaires. Still, anyone can look for free, and many works are treasures that could swiftly vanish into someone's private collection. Check the auction-house ads for viewing schedules of important collections before they go on the block.

Gagosian

980 Madison Ave at 76th St (212-744-2313). Subway: 6 to 77th St. Tue–Sat 10am–6pm. Summer hours Tue–Fri 10am–6pm.

The prince of 1980s success, Larry Gagosian is still one of New York's major players in contemporary art, showing new work by such artists as Francesco Clemente and David Salle, and the young painting queen of the moment, Cecily Brown. He has also been hugely successful in the resale market and has a gigantic new gallery in Chelsea (*see page 232*).

Leo Castelli

59 E 79th St between Madison and Park Aves (212-249-4470). Subway: 6 to 77th St. Tue–Sat 10am–6pm.

Still life in Chelsea Matthew Marks's 22nd Street gallery makes art lovers stop and stare.

Castelli returned his operation to its original uptown space shortly before he died in 1999. World-famous Castelli is known for representing such seminal Pop figures as Jasper Johns, Roy Lichtenstein and James Rosenquist, as well as conceptual artists Lawrence Weiner and Joseph Kosuth. It seems more like a museum than a contemporary gallery.

M. Knoedler & Co. Inc.

19 E 70th St between Fifth and Madison Aves (212-794-0550). Subway: 6 to 68th St–Hunter College. Sept–May Tue–Fri 9:30am–5:30pm; Sat 10am–5:30pm. Summer hours Mon–Fri 9:30am–5:30pm.

Knoedler represents name abstractionists and Pop artists including Frank Stella, Nancy Graves, David Smith, Helen Frankenthaler and Donald Sultan, as well as a selection of emerging artists.

Michael Werner

4 E 77th St between Fifth and Madison Aves (212-988-1623). Subway: 6 to 77th St. Sept–May Mon–Sat 10am–6pm. Jun–Aug Mon–Fri 10am–6pm.

In early 2000, Werner relocated his gallery to a slightly grander townhouse than the prior one, but this genteel addition to his successful operation in Germany continues to offer finely curated exhibitions of work by such protean European art stars as Marcel Broodthaers, Sigmar Polke and Per Kirkeby.

Salander-O'Reilly Galleries

20 E 79th St at Madison Ave (212-879-6606). Subway: 6 to 77th St. Sept–late Jun Mon–Sat 9:30am–5:30pm. Summer hours Mon–Fri 9:30am–5:30pm.

An extensive artist base, including important European and American realists, makes these galleries a must.

Yoshii

17 E 76th St between Fifth and Madison Aves (212-744-5550). Subway: 6 to 77th St. Call for times.

A recent relocation from 57th Street has not affected the nature of this small gallery. Yoshii presents lively shows by contemporary artists in painting, photography, sculpture and installation, as well as terrific historical surveys featuring work by such important modernists as Picasso and Giacometti.

Zwirner & Wirth

32 E 69th St between Fifth and Madison Aves (212-517-4178). Subway: 6 to 68th St–Hunter College. Sept–May Tue–Sat 10am–6pm. Call for summer hours.

Gallerist David Zwirner has prospered in Soho, and now, with a partner from Switzerland, he's opened a space uptown that's devoted to blue-chip artists and the lucrative secondary market. The gallery launched with an exhibit of Gerhard Richter's work; it also shows other contemporary masters, such as Martin Kippenberger and Mario Merz.

57th Street

The home of Carnegie Hall, exclusive boutiques and numerous art galleries, 57th Street is a beehive of cultural and commercial activity—ostentatious and expensive but fun.

DC Moore Gallery

724 Fifth Ave between 56th and 57th Sts (212-247-2111). Subway: E, F, N, R to Fifth Ave. Tue–Sat 10am–5:30pm.

This airy gallery, overlooking Fifth Avenue, shows prominent 20th-century and contemporary artists, such as Milton Avery, Paul Cadmus, Robert Kushner, Jacob Lawrence and George Platt Lynes.

Lawrence Rubin Greenberg Van Doren

730 Fifth Ave at 57th St (212-445-0444). Subway: E, F, N, R to Fifth Ave. Tue–Sat 10am–6pm.

The name might make it sound like a law firm, but this relatively new gallery represents such diverse artists as Roy Lichtenstein and Dorothea Rockburne, as well as younger artists.

Marian Goodman

24 W 57th St between Fifth and Sixth Aves (212-977-7160). Subway: B, Q, N, R to 57th St. Mon–Sat 10am–6pm.

Work by acclaimed European contemporary painters, sculptors and conceptualists predominates here, usually in striking installations. The impressive roster of gallery artists includes Christian Boltanski and Rebecca Horn, as well as Jeff Wall, Juan Muñoz and Gabriel Orozco. This is a 57th Street must-see.

Marlborough

40 W 57th St between Fifth and Sixth Aves, second floor (212-541-4900). Subway: B, Q, N, R to 57th St. Sept–May Mon–Sat 10am–5:30pm. Summer hours Mon–Fri 10am–5:30pm.

Modernist bigwigs are the staple at this monolithic international gallery. On view are works by Larry Rivers, Red Grooms, Marisol, R.B. Kitaj, Magdalena Abakanowicz and more—much more. **Marlborough Graphics,** at the same address, is just as splendiferous. (For the Chelsea location, *see page 234.*)

Mary Boone

745 Fifth Ave between 57th and 58th Sts, fourth floor (212-752-2929). Subway: E, F, N, R to Fifth Ave. Tue–Fri 10am–6pm; Sat 10am–5pm.

This former Soho celeb continues to attract major attention. In 1999, the New York Police Department found cause to arrest her for showing a Tom Sachs work consisting of a bowl of live bullets sitting on the gallery's counter. Still, Boone was hardly ruffled. Her list of contemporary artists includes Eric Fischl, Ross Bleckner, Barbara Kruger and hipster Damian Loeb. Boone is also showcasing the ideas of independent curators, who organize stellar group shows that include new photography, sculpture and painting.

PaceWildenstein

32 E 57th St between Madison and Park Aves (212-421-3292; www.pacewildenstein.com). Subway: N, R to Fifth Ave; 4, 5, 6 to 59th St. Sept–May Tue–Fri 9:30am–6pm; Sat 10am–6pm.

The heavyweight of dealerships, this gallery giant offers work by some of the 20th century's most significant artists: Picasso, Mark Rothko, Alexander Calder, Ad Reinhardt, Lucas Samaras, Agnes Martin and Chuck Close, along with Julian Schnabel, Kiki Smith and Elizabeth Murray. **Pace Prints and Primitives,** at the same address, publishes prints—from Old Masters to big-name contemporaries—and has a fine collection of African art. (For the Soho branch, *see page 238.*)

Chelsea

The growth of the West Chelsea art district has been nothing short of phenomenal. Until 1993, the nonprofit Dia Art Center was the area's only major claim to art. Now, new galleries seem to open every month. All this activity has inevitably attracted trendy restaurants and shops such as Comme des Garçons, a repercussion that, in light of Soho's history, may someday threaten to overthrow art's domination of the neighborhood. For now, though, West Chelsea is the ideal spot to observe the latest breakthroughs in video, installation, painting and sculpture. Some galleries have such distinctive architecture that it's worth the trip just to see them—and to catch the light from the nearby Hudson River. Keep in mind that the subways take you only as far as Eighth Avenue—so you'll have to walk at least one long avenue farther to get to the galleries. Otherwise, catch a cab.

AC Project Room

453 W 17th St between Ninth and Tenth Aves, second floor (212-645-4970). Subway: A, C, E to 14th St; L to Eighth Ave. Tue–Sat 10am–6pm.

This innovative artist-run space, a recent addition to Chelsea, attracts a cross-generational mix of New York–based artists working in diverse forms.

Alexander and Bonin

132 Tenth Ave between 18th and 19th Sts (212-367-7474; www.alexanderandbonin.com). Subway: A, C, E to 14th St; L to Eighth Ave. Tue–Sat 10am–6pm.

This long, cool drink of an exhibition space features contemporary painting, sculpture, photography and works on paper by an interesting group of international artists, including Doris Salcedo, Willie Doherty, Paul Thek, Mona Hatoum, Rita McBride, Silvia Plimack Mangold and Jennifer Bolande.

Andrea Rosen Gallery

525 W 24th St between Tenth and Eleventh Aves (212-627-6000). Subway: C, E to 23rd St. Sept–Jun Tue–Sat 10am–6pm. Summer hours Mon–Fri 10am–6pm.

Count on this place to show you the young heroes of the decade; this is where Rita Ackermann's endearing but unsettling waifs, John Currin's equally unsettling young babes, Andrea Zittel's compact model homes and Wolfgang Tillmans's disturbing fashion photos all found their way into the limelight.

560 Broadway
First Stop Soho

Janet Borden, Inc. 431-0166	Specializing in Contemporary Photography.
Bridgewater/Lustberg & Blumenfeld 941-6355	Contemporary Art: Paintings, Photography, Sculpture and Works on Paper.
Cavin Morris 226-3768	Specializing in Art by International Self-Taught Artists Including Old Masters and the Next Wave.
DFN Gallery 334-3400	Contemporary Art including Paintings, Sculpture and Works on Paper.
Donahue Sosinski 226-1111	Contemporary Painting and Sculpture.
Monique Goldstrom 941-9175	Modern & Contemporary Masters including 19th and 20th Century Photography.
Kathryn Markel 226-3608	Contemporary Paintings and Works on Paper.
Sears Peyton 966-7469	Unique Works on Paper by Contemporary American Artists.

Barbara Gladstone

515 W 24th St between Tenth and Eleventh Aves (212-206-9300). Subway: C, E to 23rd St. Tue–Sat 10am–6pm.

Barbara Gladstone is strictly blue-chip and presents often spectacular shows of high-quality painting, sculpture, photography and video by established artists, including Richard Prince, Matthew Barney, Rosemarie Trockel, Anish Kapoor, Ilya Kabokov and Vito Acconci.

Bill Maynes

529 W 20th St between Tenth and Eleventh Aves, eighth floor (212-741-3318). Subway: C, E to 23rd St. Tue–Sat 11am–6pm.

Bill Maynes is a bright, energetic fellow whose lovely gallery offers a great downtown view toward New York Harbor. He shows youngish painters and sculptors, who take traditional media to quirky, emotionally affecting new heights.

Bonakdar Jancou Gallery

521 W 21st St between Tenth and Eleventh Aves (212-414-4144; www.bonakdarjancou.com). Subway: C, E to 23rd St. Tue–Sat 10am–6pm.

In her dreamy, skylighted Chelsea gallery, British-born Bonakdar presents odd, often disturbing—and just as often quite distinguished—installations by such vanguard artists as Ernesto Neto, Charles Long, Uta Barth and Matt Collishaw.

Brent Sikkema

530 W 22nd St between Tenth and Eleventh Aves (212-929-2262). Subway: C, E to 23rd St. Tue–Sat 10am–6pm.

Former owner of the late Soho gallery Wooster Gardens, Brent Sikkema followed the mass exodus to Chelsea. Here, he mounts evocative and politically charged shows of work by American, British and European artists, including Kara Walker and Yinka Shonibare.

Casey Kaplan

416 W 14th St between Ninth and Tenth Aves (212-645-7335). Subway: A, C, E to 14th St; L to Eighth Ave. Sept–Jul Tue–Sat 10am–6pm.

This gallery is one of the latest to move out of Soho, where, in only four years, the young Kaplan made his gallery one of the brightest spots on the downtown art map, introducing work by artists based primarily in New York and Los Angeles. Among the most notable: Amy Adler and photographer Anna Gaskell.

Charles Cowles

537 W 24th St between Tenth and Eleventh Aves (212-925-3500). Subway: C, E to 23rd St. Sept–Jun Tue–Sat 10am–6pm. Summer hours Mon–Fri 10am–5pm.

Newly relocated from Soho, this gallery shows modern and contemporary paintings, sculptures and installations, including work by Beverly Pepper,

Mary, Mary, quite contrary Stargaze at the Mary Boone Gallery, whose owner was arrested in 1999 for showing a Tom Sachs artwork involving live ammunition.

Darren Watterston, Vernon Fisher, Charles Arnoldi, Howard Ben Tré, Beatrice Caracciolo, Doug Martin and Tom Hollond.

Cheim & Read

521 W 23rd St between Tenth and Eleventh Aves (212-242-7727). Subway: C, E to 23rd St. Tue–Sat 10am–6pm.

Louise Bourgeois and Jenny Holzer are examples of the high-profile artists that John Cheim and Howard Read (expatriates from 57th Street's Robert Miller Gallery) have put on view in their cool and sensibly human-scale gallery. Look for a high concentration of photographers, such as Jack Pierson, Adam Fuss and August Sander, along with contemporary sculptors and painters such as Lynda Benglis and Louise Fishman.

Cristinerose Gallery

529 W 20th St between Tenth and Eleventh Aves, second floor (212-206-0297). C, E to 23rd St. Tue–Sat 11am–6pm.

This quirky gallery consistently mounts engaging shows, spotlighting high-IQ artists whose work focuses on the materials used.

Fredericks Freiser

504 W 22nd St between Tenth and Eleventh Aves (212-633-6555). Subway: C, E to 23rd St. Tue–Sat 11am–6pm.

Formerly the Jessica Fredericks Gallery, this space was renamed to reflect the fact that both Fredericks and her partner/spouse Andrew Freiser work out of this small gallery on the ground floor of an art-dedicated townhouse. They have effectively developed a new generation of collectors of work by midcareer and emerging artists from New York and Los Angeles; their roster includes Michael Bevilacqua, Marnie Weber, Robert Overby and John Wesley.

Gagosian Chelsea

555 W 24th St between Tenth and Eleventh Aves (212-741-1111). Subway: C, E to 23rd St. Sept–Jun Tue–Sat 10am–6pm. Summer hours Mon–Fri 10am–6pm.

This is Larry Gagosian's humongous (20,000-square-foot) contribution to 24th Street's row of high-end galleries (for the uptown location, *see page 227*). He launched in 1999 with a powerful show of Richard Serra's monumental sculpture, and followed up with Anselm Kiefer and Damien Hirst exhibitions. Whatever he shows, you can be sure it will be big, beautiful and expensive.

Gavin Brown's enterprise

436 W 15th St between Ninth and Tenth Aves (212-627-5258). Subway: A, C, E to 14th St; L to Eighth Ave. Tue–Sat 10am–6pm.

Londoner Gavin Brown champions young hopefuls in an admirably antiestablishment gallery that has managed to establish such artists as Rirkrit Tiravanija and Elizabeth Peyton, while showcasing veteran talents such as Stephen Pippin and Peter Doig. Stop by to look at the art and have a drink at Passerby, the gallery's chic bar.

Marks of excellence Big-name contemporary

Gorney, Bravin and Lee

534 W 26th St between Tenth and Eleventh Aves (212-352-8372). Subway: C, E to 23rd St. Tue–Sat 10am–6pm.

This large new gallery gathers the energies of owners Jay Gorney, Karin Bravin and John P. Lee. Its stable of artists include such established names as Fabian Marcaccio, Moira Dryer, Kenneth Emil Lukas, Catherine Opie, Martha Rosler and Jessica Stockholder.

Greene/Naftali

526 W 26th St between Tenth and Eleventh Aves, eighth floor (212-463-7770). Subway: C, E to 23rd St. Tue–Sat 10am–6pm.

Carol Greene's airy aerie has wonderful light, a spectacular view and a history of rock-'em–sock-'em group shows of a somewhat conceptualist nature, as well as fine solo work by American painters and installation specialists.

cey Moffatt are for sale at Matthew Marks's 24th Street gallery.

Henry Urbach Architecture

526 W 26th St between Tenth and Eleventh Aves (212-627-0974). Subway: C, E to 23rd St. Wed–Sat noon–6pm.

Henry Urbach mounts quirky, conceptual shows that almost always have a photographic or architectural bent.

Holly Solomon Gallery

Chelsea Hotel, 22 W 23rd St between Seventh and Eighth Aves, room 425 (212-924-1191). Subway: C, E, 1, 9 to 23rd St. Call for appointment.

The once-reigning doyenne of the Soho scene has closed her gallery and set up an office in a room at the Chelsea Hotel. Solomon may hold shows in nearby rooms or in other venues, but for now, viewing her remarkable stock is by appointment only.

John Weber

529 W 20th St between Tenth and Eleventh Aves, second floor (212-691-5711). Subway: C, E to 23rd St. Tue–Sat 10am–6pm.

Weber shows strong conceptual and minimalist work, with an emphasis on sculpture. Artists include Hans Haacke, Daniel Buren and Alice Aycock.

Klemens Gasser & Tanja Grunert, Inc.

524 W 19th St between Tenth and Eleventh Aves (212-807-9494). Subway: C, E to 23rd St. Tue–Sat 10am–6pm.

Grunert and her husband, Grasser, ran a gallery in Cologne. Now living in New York, the couple has opened shop in Chelsea and continues to present consistently good shows that focus on European artists.

Linda Kirkland

504 W 22nd St between Tenth and Eleventh Aves (212-627-3930). Subway: C, E to 23rd St. Thu–Sat 11am–6pm.

The brains behind the conversion of this 1860 townhouse, Linda Kirkland runs a nifty operation on the third floor, which she gives over to the work of the fastest emerging artists on the street; she also holds group shows in all media.

Luhring Augustine

531 W 24th St between Tenth and Eleventh Aves (212-206-9100). Subway: C, E to 23rd St. Sept–May

Tue–Sat 10am–6pm. Summer hours Mon–Fri 10am–6pm.
Luhring Augustine's gracious, skylighted Chelsea gallery (designed by the area's architect of choice, Richard Gluckman) features work from an impressive stable of artists that includes the Germans Albert Oehlen, Gerhard Richter and Günther Förg, Britons Rachel Whiteread and Fiona Rae, and Americans Janine Antoni, Christopher Wool, Larry Clark and Paul McCarthy.

Marlborough Chelsea

211 W 19th St between Seventh and Eighth Aves (212-463-8634). Subway: C, E to 23rd St; 1, 9 to 18th St. Tue–Sat 10am–5:30pm.
The 57th Street gallery's satellite branch displays new sculpture and painting (for uptown location, *see page 229*).

Matthew Marks

523 W 24th St between Tenth and Eleventh Aves (212-243-0200). Subway: C, E to 23rd St. Tue–Sat 10am–6pm. Summer hours Mon–Fri 10am–6pm.
The ambitious Matthew Marks, the driving force behind Chelsea's rebirth as an art center, has two galleries. The 24th Street gallery is a 9,000-square-foot, two-story space featuring new work by contemporary painters, photographers and sculptors, including Lucian Freud, Nan Goldin, Sam Taylor-Wood, Gary Hume, Andreas Gursky, Katharina Fritsch and Tracey Moffatt. The other is a beautifully lit, glass-fronted converted garage devoted to large-scale work by such blue-chip modernist heroes as Willem de Kooning, Ellsworth Kelly, Brice Marden and Terry Winters.
Other location: *522 W 22nd St between Tenth and Eleventh Aves (212-243-1650).*

Getting the hang of it

Nonprofit galleries are where many young artists get their start

The scene is familiar: A brightly lit open gallery crammed with an odd assortment of chic hipsters and old-guard couples in suits and Rolexes. Flanked by a gallerist, a young artist stands in one corner smiling and greeting visitors, trying hard to live up to the hype. In most other cities, this probably would seem strange; here, it's the natural blend of money and talent that has made New York the world's contemporary art center for close to half a century.

But this tableau is hardly representative of the whole New York art world—certainly not that of emerging artists. In fact, New York has long depended on a small pool of far less glamorous nonprofit galleries where unknowns can experiment and show their wares. For them, this is the real art world, the crucible where ideas are forged and mulled over long before they hit the big time. And if a show flops, it's not the career blow it would be at a higher-profile gallery. Actually, the art on view at the nonprofits is not so different from what you would find elsewhere; the boundaries between the wacky and the accepted are blurring. (The 2000 Whitney Biennial featured ant farms and an installation of a simulated rainstorm). What you will find are smaller pieces with lower production values—which is what makes them affordable. So whether you're just browsing or looking to buy, the nonprofits are worth a visit. Following are some of the best (for a complete listing and other nonprofits, *see page 239*).

One of the oldest of the batch is **Artists Space** (*38 Greene St between Broome and Grand Sts, 212-226-3970*) in the heart of Soho. It's now famous for having nurtured the careers of such artists as Cindy Sherman and Laurie Anderson, but in the 28 years it has been showing the work of emerging talent, many, many artists—famous and not-so-famous—have passed through. With new director Barbara Hunt at the helm, there's a good chance that this venerable institution will be mounting more profile-raising exhibitions.

Around the corner on Broadway is the **Thread Waxing Space** (*476 Broadway between Prince and Spring Sts, 212-966-9520*), which offers a diverse program of readings, performance, video and symposia, in addition to serving as a gallery. Photo-collages by Beck and his grandfather Al Hansen were on view here. Other recent shows have included an exhibition devoted to gym culture and a roundup of works coming out of Yaddo, the famous art colony that has nurtured the best of American writers and artists. You might also want to check out the exhibition catalogs on sale at the front desk—they are a great way to get to know what's hot in emerging art and can give you a good overview of recent activities.

The Drawing Center (*35 Wooster St between Broome and Grand Sts, 212-219-*

Max Protetch Gallery

511 W 22nd St between Tenth and Eleventh Aves (212-633-6999). Subway: C, E to 23rd St. Tue–Sat 10am–6pm.

Relocated from Soho, Max Protetch Gallery has been hosting excellent group shows of contemporary work imported from China and elsewhere. Protetch also shows important new painting, sculpture and ceramics. This is also one of the few galleries that leaves room for architectural drawings and installations.

Metro Pictures

519 W 24th St between Tenth and Eleventh Aves (212-206-7100). Subway: C, E to 23rd St. Sept–May Tue–Sat 10am–6pm. Jun, Jul Tue–Fri 10am–6pm. Closed August.

This great playground for artists features the keenly critical, cutting-edge work of Cindy Sherman, Fred Wilson and Laurie Simmons, along with Carroll Dunham's wildly polymorphous painting, Mike Kelley's sublime conflation of pathos and perversity, Jim Shaw's California kitsch and Tony Oursler's eerie, eye-popping video projections.

Murray Guy

453 W 17th St between Ninth and Tenth Aves (212-463-7372). Subway: A, C, E to 14th St; L to Eighth Ave. Tue–Sat 10am–6pm.

The dynamic duo of Margaret Murray and Janice Guy mounts elegant shows with such artists as Francis Cape, Mette Tronvoll and Beat Streuli.

Pat Hearn Gallery

530 W 22nd St between Tenth and Eleventh Aves (212-727-7366). Subway: C, E to 23rd St. Tue–Sat 11am–6pm.

Vanguard gallerist Pat Hearn helped establish the

High art Installation works come out on top at Dia Center for the Arts in Chelsea.

2166) is the country's only nonprofit institution devoted to the undervalued art of drawing. As such, it exhibits work by the already-famous. It has one of the strongest programs of any gallery in New York, an eclectic mix of old and new. Recent exhibitions have included shows of seminal film director Sergei Eisenstein's early drawings and outsider art by James Castle. Slated for November 2000 is the French surrealist artist and poet Henri Michaux and in April 2001, James Ensor.

Two long-time champions of young artists have exhibition space in Soho. **Art in General** (*79 Walker St at Broadway, 212-219-0473*) and **Exit Art** (*548 Broadway between Prince and Spring Sts, 212-966-7745*) have shows that tend to be sprawling cornucopias mostly by unknowns, often fresh out of art schools and new to the city scene. There is bound to be something you've never seen before at these galleries, though the quantities can be exhausting. Art in General emphasizes cultural diversity, and at Exit Art you can expect the best in multimedia cross-pollinations—as well as a tapas bar.

All gallery tours go through Chelsea, and on your way from Soho, you should stop by the West Village's **White Columns** (*320 W 13th St between Eighth Ave and Hudson St, 212-924-4212*), which gets its name from the structures in its original space. The gallery favors thematic group shows, and its openings are popular with the large young art community. Director Paul Ha and curator Lauren Ross often spot trends before anyone else does.

Last but not least, there's **Dia Center for the Arts** (*548 W 22nd St between Tenth and Eleventh Aves, 212-989-5566*), which organizes exhibitions and poetry readings. In the 1960s and '70s, the Dia Foundation funded many now-famous artworks, including Walter De Maria's *Earth Room* (*141 Wooster St between Houston and Prince Sts, second floor*)—one of New York's secret gems—which the center still maintains at great cost. It's open to the public September through June. And in 2001, the center plans to open a new branch, in a converted 1929 factory on the Hudson River in Beacon, New York. It will house Dia's permanent collection of work by the likes of Andy Warhol, Dan Flavin, Donald Judd and Cy Twombly.

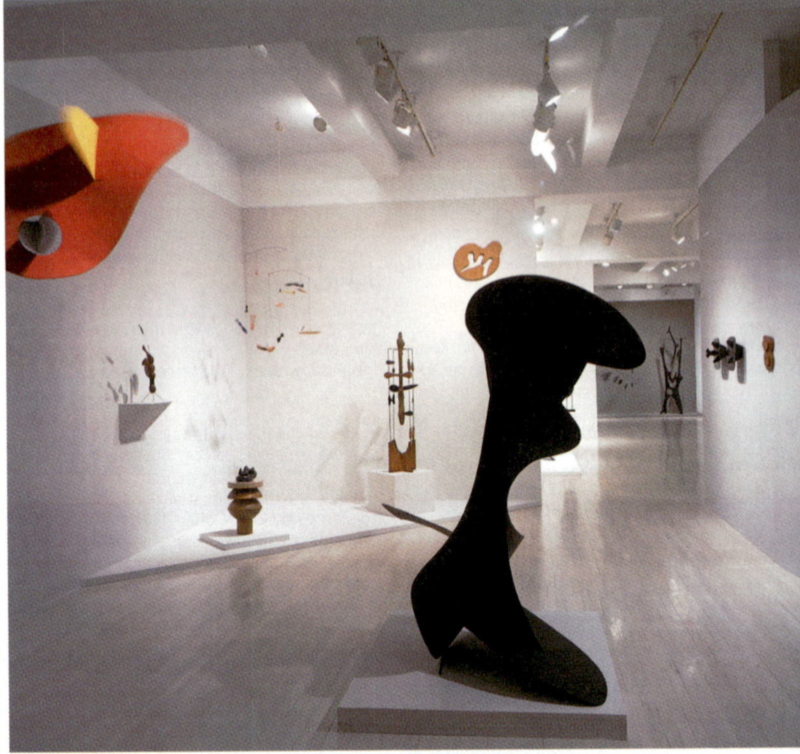

Modern love PaceWildenstein in midtown and Soho sells the modern masters.

East Village and Soho art scenes before moving up to Chelsea to continue presenting her roster of rigorous abstractionists and conceptualists. She represents Mary Heilmann, Jutta Koettker, Joan Jonas, Renee Green and Lincoln Tobier.

Paula Cooper Gallery

534 W 21st St between Tenth and Eleventh Aves (212-255-1105). Subway: C, E to 23rd St. Tue–Sat 10am–6pm. Call for summer hours.

Cooper opened the first art gallery in Soho and, as an early settler in West Chelsea, built one of the grander temples of art. Now, perhaps to compete with other big names in the area, she's opened a second space across the street. She is known for the predominantly minimalist, largely conceptual work of artists whose careers have flourished under her administration. They include Donald Judd, Carl Andre, Jonathan Borofsky, Dan Walsh and Rudolf Stingel, as well as photographers Andres Serrano and Zoe Leonard.

Other location: *521 W 21st St between Tenth and Eleventh Aves (212-255-5247).*

Paul Kasmin

293 Tenth Ave at 27th St (212-563-4474). Subway: C, E to 23rd St. Sept–Jun Tue–Sat 10am–6pm. Summer hours Mon–Fri 10am–6pm.

Another dealer who fled Soho's shopping hordes, Kasmin puts on group shows involving up-and-coming artists and more established names such as Caio Fonseca, Mark Innerst and Donald Baechler. Also, look for solo exhibitions by Alessandro Twombly, Suzanne McClelland, Nancy Rubins, Elliott Puckette and Aaron Rose, whose reputations—and prices—increase with every new appearance.

Paul Morris Gallery

465 W 23rd St between Ninth and Tenth Aves (212-727-2752). Subway: C, E to 23rd St. Tue–Sat 11am–6pm.

Paul Morris's gallery in Chelsea's London Terrace complex is a shoebox compared to his former digs on West 20th Street, but his impressive roster of emerging talents makes the traditional art that's exhibited in the neighboring larger galleries look terribly old-hat.

Postmasters Gallery

459 W 19th St between Ninth and Tenth Aves (212-727-3323). Subway: C, E to 23rd St. Tue–Sat 11am–6pm.

Another Soho-gone-West Chelsea addition, Postmasters is an intriguing international gallery run by Magdalena Sawon. She presents techno-savvy art, most of which has conceptual leanings. Artists include Spencer Finch, Sylvie Fleury, Alix Pearstein and Claude Wampler.

Robert Miller

524 W 26th St between Tenth and Eleventh Aves (212-980-5454). Subway: C, E to 23rd St. Sept–May Tue–Sat 10am–6pm. Call for summer hours.

This former 57th Street stalwart contracted the Chelsea bug. At Miller's new space, you'll see work you might otherwise expect to see in a museum: Lee Krasner, Al Held, Alice Neel, Joan Mitchell and Philip Pearlstein, as well as popular photographers such as Diane Arbus, Robert Mapplethorpe and Bruce Weber.

Rupert Goldsworthy Gallery

453 W 17th St between Ninth and Tenth Aves, second floor (212-414-4560). Subway: A, C, E to 14th St; L to Eighth Ave. Tue–Sat 11am–6pm.

This British gallerist has been in the business for years and has the eye to show for it. You won't be disappointed by his cool, often theme-based shows.

Sonnabend Gallery

536 W 22nd St between Tenth and Eleventh Aves (212-627-1018). Subway: C, E to 23rd St. Sept–Jun Tue–Sat 10am–6pm. Summer hours Tue–Fri 11am–5pm.

This elegant old standby has also taken flight from Soho to Chelsea. Look for strong new work from artists such as Haim Steinbach, Ashley Bickerton, Gilbert & George, John Baldessari and Matthew Weinstein.

303 Gallery

525 W 22nd St between Tenth and Eleventh Aves (212-255-1121). Subway: C, E to 23rd St. Tue–Sat 10am–6pm.

This savvy gallery features critically acclaimed international artists working in several media. They include photographers Thomas Ruff, Maureen Gallace, Thomas Demand and Collier Schorr; sculptor Daniel Oates; painters Sue Williams and Karen Kilimnik; and video artist Doug Aitken, winner of the 1999 Venice Biennale Grand Prize.

Venetia Kapernekas Fine Arts, Inc.

526 W 26th St between Tenth and Eleventh Aves, suite 814 (212-462-4150). Subway: C, E to 23rd St. Tue–Sat 11am–6pm.

This gallery adds some flare to an already art-packed building, hanging cross-generational shows mixing the work of young artists like Yvette Brackman with that of the more established, such as video artist Michel Auder.

Soho

Despite a large number of defections to Chelsea, you can still find something of interest and import on every street in Soho, along with such solid institutions as the downtown branch of the Guggenheim, the Museum for African Art and the New Museum for Contemporary Art. What follows is a selection of the better galleries in the community.

American Fine Arts, Colin deLand

22 Wooster St between Grand and Canal Sts (212-941-0401). Subway: A, C, E, J, M, Z, N, R, 6 to Canal St. Tue–Sat noon–6pm.

Dealer Colin deLand mounts what are arguably the most unusual exhibitions in Soho. His shows retain a refreshingly ad-hoc feel that belies the consistently strong quality of the work. Artists include filmmaker John Waters and the subversive collective Art Club 2000.

Anton Kern

558 Broadway between Prince and Spring Sts, second floor (212-965-1706). Subway: N, R to Prince St; 6 to Spring St. Sept–Jul Tue–Sat 10am–6pm. Closed August.

The son of artist Georg Baselitz, Gladstone Gallery protégé Kern presents installations by young American and European artists whose futuristic, site-specific installations have provided the New York art world with some of its most visionary shows.

Bronwyn Keenan

3 Crosby St at Howard St (212-431-5083). Subway: J, M, Z, N, R, 6 to Canal St. Tue–Sat 11am–6pm.

Among the younger dealers in New York, Keenan may have the sharpest eye for new talent. While work can be inconsistent, shows tend to be bigger than the sum of their parts, making this gallery a worthwhile stop more often than not.

CRG Art

93 Grand St between Mercer and Greene Sts (212-966-4360). Subway: A, C, E, J, M, Z, N, R, 6 to Canal St. Sept–Jul Tue–Sat 11am–6pm. By appointment only in August.

Carla Chammas, Richard Desroche and Glenn McMillan's premises represent such eminent risk-takers as Jim Hodges, Sandra Scolnik and Robert Beck.

▶ If you want to view larger collections of art, check out chapter **Museums**.

▶ See chapter **Downtown** for more information on the ever-changing Soho neighborhood.

Curt Marcus Gallery

578 Broadway between Houston and Prince Sts (212-226-3200). Subway: B, D, F, Q to Broadway–Lafayette St; N, R to Prince St; 6 to Bleecker St. Sept–Jun Tue–Sat 10am–6pm. Call for summer hours.
This is a place for the peculiar but appealing, from Richard Pettibone's Shakerish objects and the mysterious pinhole photography of Barbara Ess to the intricate inkblots of filmmaker/conceptualist Bruce Connor.

David Zwirner

43 Greene St between Broome and Grand Sts (212-966-9074). Subway: A, C, E, J, M, Z, N, R, 6 to Canal St. Sept–May Tue–Sat 10am–6pm. Summer hours Mon–Fri 10am–6pm.
This maverick German expatriate's shop has been the hot spot on Greene Street since it opened in 1993. The shows are a barometer of what's important in art—not just in New York but internationally. The stable of cutting-edge talent includes Raymond Pettibon, Jason Rhoades, Toba Khedoori and Stan Douglas.

Deitch Projects

76 Grand St between Wooster and Greene Sts (212-343-7300). Subway: A, C, E, J, M, Z, N, R, 6 to Canal St. Tue–Sat noon–6pm.
Jeffrey Deitch is known for spotting new talent and setting trends; his openings attract stellar crowds. He continues to focus on emerging artists who create elaborate, often outrageously provocative multimedia installations. Of late, Deitch's roster of the young and hip has included street artist Barry McGee and the fabulous Vanessa Beecroft.

Friedrich Petzel

26 Wooster St between Grand and Canal Sts (212-334-9466). Subway: A, C, E, J, M, Z, N, R, 6 to Canal St. Sept–Jun Tue–Sat 10am–6pm. Call for summer hours.
Locals have nicknamed this "the morphing gallery" for its emphasis on the conceptually based art of mutating forms seen in work by Jorge Pardo. But with painter Richard Phillips and photographers Sharon Lockhart and Dana Hoey now on board, Petzel is on the leading edge of his generation of dealers.

Lehmann Maupin

39 Greene St between Broome and Grand Sts (212-965-0753). Subway: A, C, E, J, M, Z, N, R to Canal St; 6 to Spring St. Tue–Sat 10am–6pm.
Rem Koolhaas designed this flexible project space, which features epic group shows of hip Americans and Europeans. It may be the most eclectic of the high-end galleries in Soho.

Nolan/Eckman

560 Broadway at Prince St, sixth floor (212-925-6190). Subway: N, R to Prince St; 6 to Spring St. Sept–Jun Tue–Fri 10am–6pm; Sat 11am–6pm. By appointment only in summer.
This small but high-level gallery shows primarily work on paper by established contemporary artists from the U.S. and Europe.

PaceWildenstein

142 Greene St between Prince and Houston Sts (212-431-9224). Subway: B, D, F, Q to Broadway–Lafayette St; N, R to Prince St; 6 to Bleecker St. Sept–Jun Tue–Sat 10am–6pm. Summer hours Mon–Thu 10am–5pm; Fri 10am–4pm.
This luxurious downtown branch of the famous 57th Street gallery is where you'll find grand-scale installations by such big-time contemporaries as Robert Irwin, Sol LeWitt, Joel Shapiro, Julian Schnabel, George Condo, John Chamberlain and Robert Whitman. (For the uptown location, *see page 229.*)

Ronald Feldman Fine Arts

31 Mercer St between Grand and Canal Sts (212-226-3232). Subway: J, M, Z, N, R, 6 to Canal St. Sept–Jun Tue–Sat 10am–6pm. Call for summer hours.
Feldman's history in Soho is marked by landmark shows by such artists as Komar & Melamid, Ida Applebroog, Leon Golub and Hannah Wilke, but he also puts on more avant-garde installations by Eleanor Antin, Roxy Paine, Nancy Chunn and Carl Fudge.

Sean Kelly

43 Mercer St between Broome and Grand Sts (212-343-2405). Subway: J, M, Z, N, R, 6 to Canal St. Sept–Jun Tue–Sat 11am–6pm. Summer hours Mon–Fri 10am–5pm.
This Brit expat's project-oriented gallery offers exhibitions by established conceptualists, including Ann Hamilton, Lorna Simpson and Marina Abramovic, and also showcases emerging talents such as Cathy de Monchaux and James Casebere.

Sperone Westwater

142 Greene St between Houston and Prince Sts, second floor (212-431-3685). Subway: B, D, F, Q to Broadway–Lafayette St; N, R to Prince St; 6 to Bleecker St. Sept–mid-Jun Tue–Sat 10am–6pm. Summer hours Mon–Fri 10am–6pm.
This stronghold of painting is one of the best places to see work by the Italian neo-Expressionists Luigi Ontani and Mimmo Paladino. Among the gallery's other illustrious contemporaries are Frank Moore, Jonathan Lasker, Susan Rothenberg and Richard Tuttle.

Brooklyn

Artists living and/or working in the postindustrial blue-collar neighborhoods of Brooklyn have opened up several galleries. Some summer weekends, area artists sponsored by the Dumbo Arts Center hold group exhibitions in their studios or at big, carnival-style art fairs. Williamsburg, long known as a flourishing, insular artist's community, has had an influx of high-style gentrification. One subway stop from Manhattan, the neighborhood still offers a number of worthwhile galleries mixed in with new restaurants and boutiques. Brooklyn may be the best place to see on-the-verge artists without any unnecessary pomp and circumstance.

Flipside

84 Withers St between Leonard and Lorimer Sts, third floor, Williamsburg (718-389-7108). Subway: L to Lorimer St. Sun 1–6pm. Call for summer hours.
This intimate artist-run gallery features work in all media by accomplished homegrown talent.

GAle GAtes et al.

37 Main St between Front and Water Sts, Dumbo (718-522-4596). Subway: F to York St. Wed–Sun noon–6pm.
The first and most energetic gallery to open in Dumbo, this huge nonprofit complex on the Brooklyn waterfront hosts group exhibitions and performances of all sorts by a wide variety of local artists.

Momenta

72 Berry St between North 9th and North 10th Sts, Williamsburg (718-218-8058). Subway: L to Bedford Ave. Mon, Fri–Sun noon–6pm.
The most professional and imaginative organization in Williamsburg, Momenta presents strong solo and group exhibitions by an exhilarating mix of emerging artists. Catch their dynamic work here before it's snapped up by Manhattan dealers.

Pierogi 2000

177 North 9th St between Bedford and Driggs Aves, Williamsburg (718-599-2144). Subway: L to Bedford Ave. Sept–Jul Mon, Fri–Sun noon–6pm and by appointment. Closed August.
Strong monthly openings at this artist-run gallery tend to attract the whole neighborhood.

Roebling Hall

390 Wythe Ave at South 4th St, Williamsburg (718-599-5352). Subway: L to Bedford Ave. Sat–Mon noon–6pm.
Directors Joel Beck and Christian Viveros-Fauné cook up cutting-edge, alternative shows at this Williamsburg hot spot—a must-see on the Brooklyn gallery circuit.

The Rotunda Gallery

33 Clinton St between Pierrepont St and Cadman Plaza West, Brooklyn Heights (718-875-4047; www.brooklynx.org/rotunda). Subway: 2, 3, 4, 5 to Borough Hall. Tue–Fri noon–5pm; Sat 11am–4pm.
This beautiful Brooklyn Heights gallery is the borough's oldest as well as its foremost nonprofit exhibition space. Monthly shows feature innovative sculpture, painting, site-specific installation, photography and video by Brooklyn-based artists, always in top-quality presentations.

Williamsburg Art & Historical Center

135 Broadway at Bedford Ave (718-486-7372). Subway: J, M, Z to Marcy Ave; L to Bedford Ave. Sat, Sun noon–6pm. Monday by appointment.
At the foot of the Williamsburg Bridge sits this art center, built to acknowledge the presence of more than 3,000 artists and performers living in the neighborhood. Housed in a four-story 1867 building, it includes an art gallery and a performance theater.

Nonprofit spaces

See also **Getting the hang of it,** page 234.

Apex Art

291 Church St between Walker and White Sts (212-431-5270). Subway: 1, 9 to Franklin St. Sept–Jul Tue–Sat 11am–6pm. Closed August.
At this unconventional gallery, the impulse comes from independent critics who experiment with cleverly themed shows in all media. Exhibitions are chosen annually by anonymous submission to a jury of previous curators. The results are truly interesting and unpredictable—a slate of work that rarely follows the prevailing fashions.

Art in General

79 Walker St between Broadway and Lafayette St (212-219-0473; www.artingeneral.org). Subway: J, M, Z, N, R, 6 to Canal St. Sept–May Tue–Sat noon–6pm. Closed July, August.
See **Getting the hang of it,** page 234.

Artists Space

38 Greene St between Grand and Broome Sts, third floor (212-226-3970; www.artistsspace.org). Subway: A, C, E, J, M, Z, N, R, 6 to Canal St. Sept–Jul Tue–Sat 11am–6pm. Closed August.
See **Getting the hang of it,** page 234.

Dia Center for the Arts

548 W 22nd St between Tenth and Eleventh Aves (212-989-5566; www.diacenter.org). Subway: C, E to 23rd St. Mid-Sept–mid-Jun Wed–Sun noon–6pm. $6.
See **Getting the hang of it,** page 234.

The Drawing Center

35 Wooster St between Broome and Grand Sts (212-219-2166). Subway: C, E, 6 to Spring St. Tue–Fri 10am–6pm; Sat 11am–6pm. Closed August.
See **Getting the hang of it,** page 234.

Exit Art: The First World

548 Broadway between Prince and Spring Sts, second floor (212-966-7745). Subway: B, D, F, Q to Broadway–Lafayette St; N, R to Prince St; 6 to Bleecker St. Tue–Fri 10am–6pm; Sat 11am–6pm. Call for summer hours.
See **Getting the hang of it,** page 234.

Grey Art Gallery and Study Center at New York University

100 Washington Sq East between Waverly and Washington Pls (212-998-6780; www.nyu.edu/greyart). Subway: A, C, E, B, D, F, Q to W 4th St; N, R to 8th St–NYU. Tue, Thu, Fri 11am–6pm; Wed 11am–8pm; Sat 11am–5pm. Closed mid-July, August. Suggested donation $2.50.
NYU's museum-laboratory has a collection of nearly

6,000 works that cover all the visual arts. Exhibition subjects run from fine art and cultural trends to quirky personalities in the history of art.

International Center of Photography

1133 Sixth Ave at 43rd St (212-768-4682; www.icp.org). Subway: B, D, F, Q to 42nd St; 7 to Fifth Ave. Tue–Thu 10am–5pm; Fri 10am–8pm; Sat, Sun 10am–6pm. $6, students and seniors $4, voluntary contribution Fri 5–8pm.

The International Center of Photography is growing along with photography's popularity. Its galleries, once split between its midtown and uptown locations, are now consolidated in its expanded and redesigned midtown building, which reopens in November 2000. Having outgrown its uptown landmark building (*1130 Fifth Ave at 94th St*), the center will move its school and library of thousands of biographical and photographic files, as well as back issues of photography magazines, to a new facility at the end of 2001. ICP, which began in the 1960s as the International Fund for Concerned Photography, contains work by photojournalists Robert Capa, Werner Bischof, David Seymour and Dan Weiner, who were all killed on assignment. Their work was preserved and exhibited by Cornell Capa, brother of Robert, who went on to found the ICP in 1974. It's no surprise that exhibitions are strong on news and documentary photography. There are two floors of exhibition space for retrospectives devoted to single artists, such as the ever-popular Weegee. Exhibitions change throughout the year

Sculpture Center

167 E 69th St between Lexington and Third Aves (212-879-3500). Subway: 6 to 68th St–Hunter College. Tue–Fri 11am–6pm; Sat 10am–5pm.

This is one of the best places to see work by emerging and midcareer sculptors. Newly installed leadership should continue to place it in the forefront of all things 3D.

Thread Waxing Space

476 Broadway between Grand and Broome Sts, second floor (212-966-9520). Subway: J, M, Z, N, R to Canal St; 6 to Spring St. Tue–Sat 10am–6pm.

See **Getting the hang of it,** page 234.

White Columns

320 W 13th St between Eighth Ave and Hudson St (212-924-4212). Subway: A, C, E to 14th St; L to Eighth Ave. Sept–Jul Wed–Sun noon–6pm. Closed August.

See **Getting the hang of it,** page 234.

Photography

In the past decade, there has been a renewal of interest in art photography in New York, along with notable strides forward in the medium. For an overview, look for the bimonthly directory *Photography in New York International* ($4). (For public collections, *see chapter* **Museums**).

Ariel Meyerowitz

580 Broadway between Prince and Houston Sts (212-625-3434). Subway: B, D, F, Q to Broadway–Lafayette St; N, R to Prince St; 6 to Spring St. Wed–Sat 11am–6pm; Tuesday by appointment.

Ariel Meyerowitz was the director of the James Danziger Gallery for many years before it closed. Now, striking out on her own, she is looking to establish herself at the forefront of photography gallerists.

Edwynn Houk Gallery

745 Fifth Ave between 57th and 58th Sts, fourth floor (212-750-7070). Subway: N, R to Fifth Ave. Sept–Jul Tue–Sat 11am–6pm. Closed last three weeks of August.

This highly respected specialist in 20th-century vintage and contemporary photography has two professional-looking rooms in which to show such artists as Sally Mann, Dorothea Lange, Man Ray, Alfred Stieglitz, Brassaï, Cartier-Bresson, Danny Lyon and Elliott Erwitt, all of whom command top dollar.

Howard Greenberg & 292 Gallery

120 Wooster St between Prince and Spring Sts, second floor (212-334-0010). Subway: C, E, 6 to Spring St; N, R to Prince St. Tue–Sat 11am–6pm.

These connecting galleries exhibit one enticing show after another of name 20th-century photographers, including Berenice Abbot, William Klein, Robert Frank, Ralph Eugene Meatyard and Imogen Cunningham.

Janet Borden

560 Broadway at Prince St, sixth floor (212-431-0166). Subway: N, R to Prince St. Sept–Jun Tue–Sat 11am–5pm. July Tue–Fri 11am–5pm. Closed August.

No tour of contemporary photography can be complete without a visit to this Soho stalwart, where the latest work by Oliver Wassow, Jan Groover, Tina Barney and Sandy Skoglund, among others, is regularly on view.

Julie Saul Gallery

560 Broadway at Prince St (212-431-0747). Subway: N, R to Prince St. Tue–Sat 11am–6pm.

Come here for well-conceived contemporary photography shows featuring clean and smart installation.

Pace/MacGill

32 E 57th St between Madison and Park Aves, ninth floor (212-759-7999). Subway: N, R to Lexington Ave; 4, 5, 6 to 59th St. Sept–late Jun Tue–Fri 9:30am–5:30pm; Sat 10am–6pm. Summer hours Mon–Thu 9:30am–5:30pm; Fri 9am–4pm.

This is a gallery that never misses. Look for well-known names such as Richard Avedon, William Wegman, Joel-Peter Witkin and Walker Evans, in addition to important contemporaries Harry Callahan, Philip-Lorca DiCorcia and Kiki Smith.

Yancey Richardson Gallery

560 Broadway at Prince St (212-343-1255). Subway: N, R to Prince St. Tue–Sat 11am–6pm.

This intimate gallery shows contemporary, often experimental, American, European and Japanese photographers, each with a solid following.

Books & Poetry

Whether you're a rhymer, a reader or a listener, New York's literary scene offers wordy fun, chapter and verse

"I have taken a liking to this abominable place," confessed Mark Twain about the city in which he married, made his fortune and died. His conversion was probably helped by the fact that New Yorkers took such a liking to him.

New York has always been a literary town, a place where the published few are sought-after guests at dinner parties, and where both best-selling authors and up-and-comers gather at writers' haunts like Elaine's to exchange gossip and be seen. Why, Norman Mailer once even ran for mayor. As the publishing capital of the United States, New York creates literary stars the way Los Angeles creates movie stars. Million-dollar advances and Hollywood options bring fame and gossip-column coverage to authors (and, in some cases, to their editors). The literary crème de la crème mingles in the fashion world; even the soigné mid-'90s literary breakfasts hosted by Harry Evans, then Random House president and publisher, were held not within the book-lined walls of some dusty scholarly establishment but at the ultrachic department store Barneys.

Still, you don't have to be part of the literati to get literary satisfaction in New York. Whether you want to hear Bret Easton Ellis or Jane Hamilton reading from their latest novels, poets trying out their new work or speakers dazzling (or boring) audiences with intellectual pyrotechnics, there's always a place to do so, often for free (literary events are among the best entertainment deals in the city).

Spoken word, formerly known as performance poetry, is a popular New York pastime. Not since the Beats reinvented the American oral tradition have poets attracted so much media attention or been as fashionable. Spoken word's mainstays are the often-raucous slams (in which selected audience members award points to competing poets) and open-mike nights (when unknowns get five minutes to do their thing before the crowd). Slammer Reg E. Gaines is a graduate of this scene. He made his name with his rap-inspired poetry for the smash-hit musical *Bring in 'da Noise, Bring in 'da Funk*. You'll find the most innovative performance poetry in the ongoing reading series and festivals; in these, poets cross-pollinate their verses with performance art, theater, dance and music, particularly rap and jazz.

Dead poets (and novelists) get an airing, too, in the form of marathon readings, a truly New York tradition. Annual readings often star a stream of big-name personalities. Past readers at Symphony Space's Joycean Bloomsday event have included Frank McCourt and Claire Bloom. You can also celebrate Good Friday with a reading of Dante's *Inferno* at the Cathedral of St. John the Divine, complete with devil's food cake. Also, watch for one-time-only marathons, which are usually held in celebration of a literary anniversary.

New York's bookstores—especially the superstores—have become meccas for anyone seeking a good read, a cappuccino and a comfortable lounge chair, or a café table around which to spend a literate evening with like-minded friends. Some of these stores have become known among bookishly inclined lonely hearts as hot pickup spots (a few Barnes & Noble stores stay open until midnight). Many feature literary events, including author readings, talks and signings, and discussions of arcane matters, such as setting and location in fiction. Also, the New York Public Library hosts poetry and author readings, listed in the brochure *Events for Adults,* available free at all branches. Some reading series take long summer breaks, so call to confirm events before setting out.

- For the most comprehensive listings of book and poetry events, get the monthly ***Poetry Calendar,*** free at many bookstores, or find it online at the Academy of American Poets site (www.poets.org).
- For weekly listings, check the Books and Around Town sections of ***Time Out New York.***
- See chapter **Gay & Lesbian** for more bookstores.

Author readings

In today's cutthroat publishing climate, where books either make the best-seller lists or die early deaths, authors are clamoring for the chance to promote their latest titles at bookstores, some of which schedule almost daily events. These are always free, usually in the early evening, and they're well attended; arrive early if you want a seat. At the superstores, events range from lowbrow to highbrow: You're as likely to catch a supermodel promoting her new exercise book as you are one of your favorite novelists. The following offer frequent author readings, talks and signings.

Barnes & Noble

33 E 17th St between Park Ave South and Broadway (212-253-0810). Subway: L, N, R, 4, 5, 6 to 14th St–Union Sq. 10am–10pm.
Calendars of events for each branch (nine in Manhattan alone) are available in-store. Check phone book for more locations.

Bluestockings

172 Allen St between Stanton and Rivington Sts (212-777-6028; www.bluestockings.com). Subway: F to Second Ave. Tue–Sat noon–8pm; Sun 2–8pm.
See chapter **Gay & Lesbian.**

Borders Books and Music

5 World Trade Center at Church and Vesey Sts (212-839-8049). Subway: E to World Trade Ctr; N, R, 1, 9 to Cortland St. Mon–Fri 7am–8:30pm; Sat 10am–8:30pm; Sun 11am–8:30pm.
Calendars of events for each branch are available in-store.
Other locations: *461 Park Ave at 57th St (212-980-6785); 576 Second Ave at 32nd St (212-685-3938).*

Corner Bookstore

1313 Madison Ave at 93rd St (212-831-3554). Subway: 6 to 96th St. Mon–Thu 10am–8pm; Fri 10am–7pm; Sat, Sun 11am–6pm.
Pick up a calendar of upcoming readings.

A Different Light

151 W 19th St between Sixth and Seventh Aves (212-989-4850). Subway: 1, 9 to 18th St. 11am–10pm.
See chapter **Gay & Lesbian.**

Posman Books

1 University Pl between Waverly Pl and 8th St (212-533-2665). Subway: N, R to 8th St–NYU. Mon–Fri 10am–8pm; Sat, Sun noon–6pm.
A haunt of New York University students, Posman presents lesser-known novelists and poets.

Rizzoli Bookstore

454 West Broadway between Prince and Houston Sts (212-674-1616). Subway: C, E to Spring St; N, R to Prince St. Mon–Sat 10:30am–8pm; Sun noon–7pm.
Soho's arty bookstore and its midtown and downtown sisters are prime spots for catching high-profile novelists, photographers and artists on book tours.
Other locations: *31 W 57th St between Fifth and Sixth Aves (212-759-2424); World Financial Center, 200 Vesey St at North End Ave (212-385-1400).*

Three Lives & Co.

154 W 10 St at Waverly Pl (212-741-2069). Subway: A, C, E, B, D, F, Q to W 4th St. Mon, Tue 1–8pm; Wed–Sat 10:30am–8:30pm; Sun 1–7pm.
Hear established novelists read in this cozy West Village bookstore.

Reading series

The following host fiction and poetry readings; some also offer lectures.

The Algonquin

59 W 44th St between Fifth and Sixth Aves (212-840-6800, 800-555-8000). Subway: B, D, F, Q to 42nd St; 7 to Fifth Ave. Mon 7pm. $25, $50 with dinner.
This literary landmark hosts Spoken Word on Monday nights, and many big names pass through. Past evenings have included Israel Horovitz's birthday party and a reading by Ethan Hawke of Nicole Burdette's plays.

Housing Works Used Books Café

126 Crosby St between Houston and Prince Sts (212-334-3324). Subway: B, D, F, Q to Broadway–Lafayette St; 6 to Bleecker St. Call for schedule of events. Free.
If you like a little social consciousness with your literary readings, check out the impressive lineup of writers at this organization dedicated to raising money for the HIV-positive homeless. Housing Works also has a series of lectures by the organization Fairness and Accuracy in Reporting. Buy a donated book or a cup of coffee to support Housing Works' efforts.

KGB

85 E 4th St between Second and Third Aves (212-505-3360). Subway: F to Second Ave; 6 to Astor Pl. Mon 7:30pm. Free.
This funky East Village bar hosts a weekly reading series that features luminaries of the downtown poetry scene.

Makor

35 W 67th St between Columbus Ave and Central Park West (212-601-1000; www.makor.org). Subway: 1, 9 to 66th St–Lincoln Ctr. Call for schedule of events.
Mingling is easy at this Jewish-oriented cultural center, though the events have nothing to do with dating per se. Its calendar includes dozens of events from poetry slams and book-discussion groups to gallery talks and theme brunches. Some events are free; some aren't.

National Arts Club

15 Gramercy Park South between Third Ave and Park Ave South (212-475-3424). Subway: 6 to 23rd St. Call for schedule of events. Free.
When this private club opens its doors to the public, it may be for contemporary writers on the publicity circuit or devotees of the W.B. Yeats Society.

Novel approach Binnie Kirshenbaum reads her newest fiction to the literary set.

A jacket or business attire is required to enter the elegant landmark building.

New School for Social Research

66 W 12th St between Fifth and Sixth Aves (212-229-5488). Subway: F to 14th St; L to Sixth Ave. Admission varies.

The New School's occasional spoken-word series is sometimes organized by one of New York's slickest and most venerable spoken-word-and-music artists, Sekou Sundiata, a New School faculty member. The school also holds lecture series. The Academy of American Poets also hosts readings (at the Tishman Auditorium) by some of the country's best-known writers.

92nd Street Y Unterberg Poetry Center

1395 Lexington Ave at 92nd St (212-996-1100). Subway: 6 to 96th St. Admission varies.

The Academy of American Poets and the Y cosponsor regular readings with such luminaries as Edward Albee, Athol Fugard, David Mamet and Alice Walker. Panel discussions and lectures by high-profile academics are also held.

Selected Shorts: A Celebration of the Short Story

Symphony Space, 2537 Broadway at 95th St (212-864-5400). Subway: 1, 2, 3, 9 to 96th St. Late Jan–late May, every other Wednesday at 6:30pm. $18, seniors $15. Call for schedule of events.

Accomplished actors tackle short stories for one of the longest-running programs at Symphony Space, a large Art Deco theater. The selected works range from classic to cutting edge, and past readers have included William Hurt, Blair Brown and Cynthia Nixon. Purchase tickets early, since events usually sell out.

Writer's Voice/West Side YMCA

5 W 63rd St between Central Park West and Broadway (212-875-4124). Subway: A, C, B, D, 1, 9 to 59th St–Columbus Circle. $5, under 18 free.

Events include readings by poets, playwrights and novelists, as well as popular open-mike nights. The Y also offers highly regarded writers' workshops and publishes its own literary magazine.

Spoken word

Dia Center for the Arts

548 W 22nd St between Tenth and Eleventh Aves (212-989-5566). Subway: C, E to 23rd St. One Friday a month at 7pm. $6, students and seniors $2.50.

Dia's Readings in Contemporary Poetry series features established American poets; past readers have included Adrienne Rich, Robert Creeley and John Ashbery.

Dixon Place

309 E 26th St at Second Ave (212-532-1546). Subway: 6 to 28th St. Call for dates and times. Admission varies.

Ellie Covan hosts a performance salon in a small theater, which is a bit hidden from the street. Open-mike nights are held on the first Wednesday of every month, and poets often mix with storytellers, fiction writers, dancers and performance artists.

A Gathering of Tribes

285 E 3rd St between Aves B and C (212-674-3778; www.tribe.org). Subway: F to Second Ave. Sun 5–7pm. Free.

Poetry readings and poetry parties are held on Sunday evenings. A Gathering of Tribes also publishes its own poetry magazine and is home to an art gallery.

A Little Bit Louder

Thirteen, 35 E 13th St at University Pl (212-979-6677). Subway: L, N, R, 4, 5, 6 to 14th St–Union Sq. Mon 7pm. $5.

Each week, the mod lounge Thirteen hosts a stimulating poetry forum dedicated to slam. Come for the open-mike nights or the occasional theme readings, which in the past have featured women only and prominent slam-circuit favorites.

Nuyorican Poets Cafe

236 E 3rd St between Aves B and C (212-505-8183). Subway: F to Second Ave. Call for dates and times. Admission varies.

The now-famous Nuyorican goes beyond open mikes and slams with multimedia events, staged readings, hip-hop poetry nights and more. Elbow your way past the slumming media execs on the hunt for new talent. Slams are held every Friday night and the first Wednesday of every month.

Poetry Project

St. Mark's Church in-the-Bowery, 131 E 10th St at Second Ave (212-674-0910; www.poetryproject.com). Subway: L to Third Ave; 6 to Astor Pl. Call for dates and times. Admission varies.

The legendary Poetry Project, whose hallowed walls first heard the likes of Allen Ginsberg and Anne Waldman, remains a thriving center for hearing the new and worthy. Living legends like Jim Carroll and Patti Smith still read here.

Segue at Double Happiness

Double Happiness, 173 Mott St between Broome and Grand Sts (212-941-1282). Subway: B, D, Q to Grand St; 6 to Spring St. Oct–May Sat 4–6pm. $4.

The Segue Foundation's long-standing poetry series now finds a home in a bar—the funky, cavernous Double Happiness in Chinatown (for review, *see chapter* **Bars**).

Talks and lectures

Brecht Forum

122 W 27th St between Sixth and Seventh Aves, tenth floor (212-242-4201; www.brechtforum.org). Subway: 1, 9 to 28th St.

This old-style leftist institution offers lectures, forums, discussions and bilingual poetry readings.

Books and crannies Read (to yourself) in the New York Public Library's reading room, which was restored in 1999.

The Brooklyn Public Library

Grand Army Plaza, Eastern Pkwy at Flatbush Ave, Park Slope, Brooklyn (718-230-2100; www.brooklynpubliclibrary.org). Subway: 2, 3 to Grand Army Plaza.

Brooklyn's main library branch offers lectures and readings of impressive scope.

New School for Social Research

See **Reading series** *for listings.*

The New School hosts esoteric lectures by visiting savants.

92nd Street Y

See **Reading series** *for listings.*

The Y offers regular lectures by and dialogues between top-notch speakers on subjects ranging from literature and the arts to feminism, politics and international scandals. The literary likes of Susan Sontag and Wole Soyinka have spoken here.

New York Public Library, Celeste Bartos Forum

Fifth Ave between 40th and 42nd Sts (212-930-0855). Subway: B, D, F, Q to 42nd St; 7 to Fifth Ave. Admission varies.

Several annual lecture series feature renowned writers and thinkers, including quite a few Guggenheim fellows, speaking on issues of contemporary culture, science and the humanities.

Tours

Mark Twain Annual Birthday Tour

Meet at the southwest corner of Broadway and Spring St (212-873-1944). Subway: N, R to Prince St. Late November. $15.

The tour, led by Twain aficionado Peter Salwen ends with a birthday toast at one of the great American novelist's New York City homes.

Greenwich Village Literary Pub Crawl

Meet at the White Horse Tavern, 567 Hudson St at 11th St (212-613-5796). Subway: 1, 9 to Christopher St–Sheridan Sq. Sat 2pm. $12, students and seniors $9. No reservations required.

The two-and-a-half-hour crawl to the watering holes of legendary village writers is guided by actors from the New Ensemble Theatre Co., Inc. These thespians give a history of the establishment and its literary patrons before performing pieces from each author's work.

Greenwich Village Past and Present

Meet at Washington Sq Arch, Washington Sq Park, Fifth Ave at Waverly Pl. Call Street Smarts N.Y. at 212-969-8262 for more information. Subway: A, C, E, B, D, F, Q to W 4th St. Call for dates and times.

This walk takes you past homes and hangouts of Village writers past and present.

Cabaret & Comedy

Let them entertain you: Torch singers set you on fire and stand-ups leave you senseless with laughter

Cabaret venues

New York is the cabaret capital of the U.S., and quite possibly of the world. Few, if any, other cities can offer a dozen different shows on any given night. In the strict New York sense, the term *cabaret* covers both the venue and the art form. It's an intimate club where songs are sung, generally by one person, but sometimes by a small ensemble. The songs are usually drawn from what's known as the Great American Songbook—the vast repertoire of the American musical theater—and are supplemented with the occasional new number by a contemporary composer. More than anything, cabaret is an act of intimacy: The best singers are able to draw the audience in until each member feels he or she is being serenaded.

The Golden Age of cabaret in New York was the 1950s and early 1960s. The advent of rock music and changing tastes eventually made cabaret an art form for the connoisseur, but these days, plenty of fans and performers are keeping it alive. Today's venues basically fall into two groups: classic, elegant, expensive boîtes like the Oak Room and Cafe Carlyle, where you'll spend $30 to $60 just to get in and hear the likes of Bobby Short, Rosemary Clooney and Andrea Marcovicci; and less formal neighborhood clubs like Don't Tell Mama and Danny's Skylight Room, where up-and-coming singers—many of them enormously talented—perform for enthusiastic fans who pay much lower cover charges.

Classic nightspots

Cafe Carlyle

Carlyle Hotel, 35 E 76th St at Madison Ave (212-744-1600, 800-227-5737). Subway: 6 to 77th St. Tue–Sat 8:45, 10:45pm. Closed Jul–mid Sept. Cover $60, no drink minimum. AmEx, DC, MC, V.

This is the epitome of chic New York, especially when Bobby Short, Eartha Kitt or Betty Buckley do their thing. (Woody Allen sits in as clarinetist with Eddie Davis and His New Orleans Jazz Band at the early Monday night show—but call ahead, he might be off making a movie.) Don't dress down; the Carlyle is a place to plunk down your cash and live the high life. To drink in some atmosphere more cheaply, try Bemelmans Bar across the hall, which always has a fine pianist, such as Barbara Carroll or Peter Mintun, Tuesday to Saturday from 9:45pm to 12:45am with a $10 cover. (*See chapter* **Accommodations**.)

Feinstein's at the Regency

540 Park Ave at 61st St (212-339-4095). Subway: B, Q, N, R to Lexington Ave; 4, 5, 6 to 59th St. Tue–Thu

Entertainment

White light Tony Award–winner Lilias White sings torch songs at Arci's Place.

Altered states Surf Reality hosts mind-bending comedy on the Lower East Side.

8:30pm; Fri, Sat 8:30, 11pm. Cover $60, $50 food-and-drink minimum.
Michael Feinstein's swanky new room in the Regency hotel draws lots of top performers: Rosemary Clooney, sexy singer-guitarist John Pizzarelli, and the crown prince of cabaret himself. Note: A night here quickly adds up—the cover charge alone is steep, and then comes a pricey dinner.

The FireBird Cafe

363 W 46th St between Eighth and Ninth Aves (212-586-0244). Subway: A, C, E to 42nd St–Port Authority. Show times vary. Cover $30, $15 drink minimum. AmEx, DC, Disc, MC, V.
This classy joint, which opened in early 1998, is next door to the regally appointed Russian restaurant of the same name (*see chapter* **Restaurants** *for review*). If the caviar and the mosaic reproduction of Klimt's *The Kiss* don't ignite your passions, rely on the first-rate performers who include Tom Anderson, Steve Ross and Barbara Brussell. On Sundays, the ASCAP Songwriter's Series, a showcase for new works, brings in a lineup of promising novices as well as big Broadway names (like Steven Schwartz of *Godspell*).

The Oak Room

Algonquin Hotel, 59 W 44th St between Fifth and Sixth Aves (212-840-6800). Subway: B, D, F, Q to 42nd St. Tue–Thu 9pm; Fri, Sat 9, 11:30pm, dinner compulsory at first Fri, Sat show. Cover $50, $15 drink minimum. AmEx, DC, Disc, MC, V.
This resonant banquette-lined room, overseen by the solicitous Arthur Pomposello, is the place to savor the cream of cabaret performers, among them Andrea Marcovicci, Maureen McGovern and the witty Mary Cleere Haran. (*See chapter* **Accommodations**.)

The Supper Club

240 W 47th St between Broadway and Eighth Ave (212-921-1940). Subway: C, E, 1, 9 to 50th St; N, R to 49th St. Fri, Sat 8pm–4am. Show times vary. Cover $20 on Fri, $25 on Sat, $15 after 11pm, no drink minimum. AmEx, DC, MC, V.
Dine and dance to a 16-piece big band in this beautifully restored ballroom. The decor and better-than-average food attract a glamorous crowd of pre-theater *dahlings*. The strikingly azure Blue Room is the setting for swing-dance lessons.

Emerging talents

Arci's Place

450 Park Ave South between 30th and 31st Sts (212-532-4370). Subway: 6 to 33rd St. Sun, Mon 8pm; Tue–Thu 9pm; Fri, Sat 8:30, 11pm. Cover $25, $15 food-and-drink minimum.
The Italian food is top-notch at this intimate Park Avenue restaurant, and so is the talent: Karen Mason, Wesla Whitfield and Marilyn Volpe have all played New York's newest cabaret.

Danny's Skylight Room

346 W 46th St between Eighth and Ninth Aves (212-265-8133; www.dannysgrandseapalace.com). Subway: A, C, E to 42nd St–Port Authority. Show times vary. Cover $8–$15, $10 food-and-drink minimum. AmEx, DC, MC, V.
A pastel nook of the Grand Sea Palace restaurant, "where Bangkok meets Broadway" on touristy Restaurant Row, Danny's features pop-jazz, pop and cabaret, with the accent on the smooth. In addition to up-and-comers, this is a good place to catch a few mature cabaret and jazz standbys like Blossom Dearie and Dakota Staton.

Don't Tell Mama

343 W 46th St between Eighth and Ninth Aves (212-757-0788). Subway: A, C, E to 42nd St–Port Authority. Mon–Sun 4pm–4am, 4 to 8 shows a night. No cover for piano bar; $3–$20 in cabaret room, two-drink minimum (no food served). AmEx, MC, V.
Showbiz pros like to visit this Theater District venue. The acts range from strictly amateurish to potential stars of tomorrow. The nightly lineup can include pop, jazz or Broadway singers, female impersonators, magicians, revues or comedians.

Judy's Chelsea

169 Eighth Ave between 18th and 19th Sts (212-929-5410). Subway: C, E to 23rd St; 1, 9 to 18th St. Mon–Thu, Sun 8:30pm; Fri, Sat 8:30, 11pm. Cover varies, $10 food-and-drink minimum. AmEx, MC, V.

The venerable Theater District haunt Judy's lost its lease in 1998, but resurfaced downtown in a fabulous space. The outré folksinger Go Mahan often performs here, and the geek-chic Lounge-O-Leers keep piano-bar patrons laughing with grooved-out versions of Top 40 hits. Co-owner/singer Judy Kreston (just one of the many Judys after whom the place is named) and pianist David Lahm often perform on Saturday nights.

Triad

158 W 72nd St between Broadway and Columbus Ave (212-799-4599). Subway: B, C, 1, 2, 3, 9 to 72nd St. 5:30pm, show times vary. Cover varies, two-drink minimum. AmEx, Disc, MC, V ($10 minimum).

This Upper West Side cabaret has been the launching pad for many successful revues over the years, several of which (*Forever Plaid, Forbidden Broadway*) have moved to larger spaces Off Broadway. Dinner is available, and there's an occasional singer or benefit show in the downstairs lounge.

Upstairs at Rose's Turn

55 Grove St between Seventh Ave South and Bleecker St (212-366-5438). Subway: 1, 9 to Christopher St–Sheridan Sq. 4pm–4am, show times vary. Cover $5–$15, two-drink minimum. Cash only.

Upstairs at Rose's Turn is a dark room with zero atmosphere. The emphasis tends to be on comedy, or pocket-size one-act musicals—like *Our Lives & Times,* a hilarious spoof on current events.

Alternative venues

The Duplex

61 Christopher St at Seventh Ave South (212-255-5438). Subway: 1, 9 to Christopher St–Sheridan Sq. Show times vary. Piano bar 9pm–4am daily. Cover $6–$12, two-drink minimum. Cash only.

New York's oldest cabaret has been going strong for 50-plus years, and it sets the pace for campy, good-natured fun. The Duplex attracts a mix of regulars and tourists, who laugh and sing along with classy drag performers, comedians and rising stars.

Joe's Pub

425 Lafayette St between Astor Pl and 4th St (212-539-8770). Subway: N, R to 8th St–NYU; 6 to Astor Pl. 6pm–4am. Show times vary. Cover varies. AmEx, MC, V.

This plush club and restaurant in the Public Theater manages to be hip and elegant at the same time. While you can hear chanteuses such as Patti LuPone, Faith Prince and Lea DeLaria at the 8:30pm show, other past performers include pop stars Duran Duran and indie songstress Aimee Mann. Late-night shows start at 11pm; Tuesday is salsa night, Wednesday is reggae, and on Thursdays downtown notables—model Rachel Williams and artist Tom Sachs, for instance—take over the turntables in the Celebrity DJ series. You can rub elbows with the likes of Puff Daddy and Madonna, who dropped in to check out Me'Shell Ndegéocello.

Torch

137 Ludlow St between Rivington and Stanton Sts (212-228-5151). Subway: F to Delancey St; J, M, Z to Essex St. Mon–Fri 8pm–midnight; Sat, Sun 7pm–3am. Show times vary. No cover. AmEx, DC, MC, V.

Monday nights, this Lower East Side bar/restaurant is where you'll find Nicole Renaud, an enchanting Parisian songbird. Renaud's crystalline voice, clever playlist (music from *The Umbrellas of Cherbourg,* anyone?) and bizarrely beautiful costumes make for a decidedly off-beat evening. Best of all, there's no cover. Avoid the pricey food, but splurge on a delicious fleur-de-lis cocktail and savor the Gallic atmosphere.

Wilson's

201 W 79th St between Broadway and Amsterdam Ave (212-769-0100). Subway: 1, 9 to 79th St. Show times vary. Cover $5–$10, no minimum. AmEx, DC, Disc, MC, V.

Don't let the cruisy atmosphere at this Upper West Side bar and bistro fool you. It's true cabaret when Judy Barnett is onstage. Her velvety powerhouse of a voice and inventive jazz arrangements will have you cheering.

Comedy venues

No joke: The business of comedy is booming in New York City. Small, out-of-the-way clubs and bars have been nurturing a new generation of performers who flirt with the avant-garde. Many of the talented fringe performers who started out in the alternative clubs of the Lower East Side are gradually making their way into bigger clubs and mainstream outlets. Marc Maron, who does edgy stand-up, frequently appears on such talk shows as *Late Show with David Letterman,* and the Upright Citizens Brigade has a weekly half-hour show on Comedy Central, as well as its own theater, where the troupe performs and produces shows for up-and-coming talent.

You can still catch off-beat performers at some smaller venues, along with established stars like Colin Quinn, Janeane Garofalo and David Cross. The following clubs offer a wide range of comedy styles—from traditional stand-up to some very twisted entertainment.

Show times vary, so it's always best to call ahead.

Boston Comedy Club

82 W 3rd St between Thompson and Sullivan Sts (212-477-1000; www.thebostoncomedyclub.com). Subway: A, C, E, B, D, F, Q to W 4th St. Mon $8, two-drink minimum; Tue–Thu $8, one-drink minimum;

Fri, Sat $12, two-drink minimum; Sun $7, two-drink minimum. AmEx, MC, V.
This rowdy basement-level room is a late-night option. The bill can include as many as ten different acts. Monday's first show is a new-talent showcase.

Carolines on Broadway

1626 Broadway between 49th and 50th Sts (212-757-4100). Subway: C, E, 1, 9 to 50th St; N, R to 49th St. $12–$27, two-drink minimum. AmEx, DC, MC, V.
A cornerstone of Times Square's tourist attractions, Caroline's colorful lounge is the place to see TV and movie faces—Damon Wayans, Jay Mohr and Janeane Garofalo have all performed here—or comics with broad appeal like Wendy Liebman. Billy Crystal and Jay Leno honed their craft at the original Carolines in Chelsea.

Chicago City Limits Theatre

1105 First Ave between 60th and 61st Sts (212-888-5233; www.chicagocitylimits.com). Subway: N, R to Lexington Ave; 4, 5, 6 to 59th St. Mon $10, Wed–Sun $20. AmEx, MC, V.
Founded in the Windy City, this popular group moved to New York in 1979 and has been delighting audiences ever since with a combination of current-events–driven sketch routines and audience-inspired improvisation. There's no drink minimum, because the theater doesn't serve alcohol.

Comedy Cellar

117 MacDougal St between 3rd and Bleecker Sts (212-254-3480; www.comedycellar.com). Subway: A, C, E, B, D, F, Q to W 4th St. Sun–Thu $7; Fri, Sat $12, two-drink minimum. AmEx, MC, V.
Amid the coffeehouses of MacDougal Street, this well-worn underground lair recalls the counterculture vibe of another era, before the neighborhood became besieged by bridge-and-tunnel partiers. Still, the Comedy Cellar regularly provides an excellent roster of popular local talent.

Comic Strip Live

1568 Second Ave between 81st and 82nd Sts (212-861-9386; www.comicstriplive.com). Subway: 4, 5, 6 to 86th St. Sun–Thu $10; Fri, Sat $14, $10 drink minimum. AmEx, DC, Disc, MC, V.
This saloonlike stand-up club is known for separating truly funny talents from the mere wanna-bes. Monday is audition night—comic hopefuls can sign up in the first week of May and November (call to confirm dates) in hopes of becoming a regular.

Dangerfield's

1118 First Ave between 61st and 62nd Sts (212-593-1650). Subway: N, R to Lexington Ave; 4, 5, 6 to 59th St. Sun–Thu $12.50; Fri, Sat $15; Sat last show $20, no food-and-drink minimum. AmEx, DC, MC, V.
Opened by comedian Rodney Dangerfield in 1969, this glitzy lounge is now one of New York's oldest and most formidable clubs. Food is served and there's $4 parking—an NYC deal.

Gotham Comedy Club

34 W 22nd St between Fifth and Sixth Aves (212-367-9000). Subway: F, N, R, 1, 9 to 23rd St. $8–$15, two-drink minimum. AmEx, MC, V.
This elegant, intimate and comfortable club books a lineup of top comedians from all over the country, including Irish–New Yorker Colin Quinn (*Saturday Night Live*), legend Robert Klein and weirdo Lewis Black (*The Daily Show*). Jerry Seinfeld stays sharp with occasional unannounced Saturday appearances.

New York Comedy Club

241 E 24th St between Second and Third Aves (212-696-5233). Subway: 6 to 23rd St. Sun–Thu $5; Fri, Sat $10, two-drink minimum. AmEx, MC, V.
The New York Comedy Club takes a democratic approach: a packed lineup and a bargain cover price. Fridays at 11pm and Saturdays at midnight, you can catch the city's top African-American comedians, and the last Friday of every month is Hispanic night.

PS NBC

HERE, 145 Sixth Ave between Spring and Dominick Sts (212-647-0202). Subway: C, E, to Spring St. Free.
This is your chance to see the TV stars of tomorrow, today. The NBC network takes up residence in this cool downtown theater Monday through Thursday to audition new talents that it's considering for network projects. Shows are free (just like TV), and the talent is almost first-rate (unlike TV). Call for schedules.

Stand-Up NY

236 W 78th St at Broadway (212-595-0850). Subway: 1, 9 to 79th St. Sun–Thu $7; Fri, Sat $12, two-drink minimum. AmEx, MC, V.
A somewhat sterile but small and intimate place, Stand-Up NY always features a good mix of club-circuit regulars and new faces.

Surf Reality

172 Allen St between Stanton and Rivington Sts, 2nd floor (212-673-4182; www.surfreality.org). Subway: F to Second Ave. Call for ticket prices.
The center of the Lower East Side alternative universe, Surf Reality features a lot of comedy—but probably nothing like you've ever seen before. Bring an open mind and you'll be entertained by acts such as TV Head, which has been described as "creepy and endearing."

Upright Citizens Brigade Theater

161 W 22nd St between Sixth and Seventh Aves (212-366-9176; www.uprightcitizens.org). Subway: F, 1, 9 to 23rd St. Tue–Sun. Most shows are $5; call for exact ticket prices.
The home of Comedy Central's crazy and brilliant sketch group, the UCB Theater features inexpensive, high-quality sketch comedy and improv six nights a week. The original foursome still performs every Sunday for free; their disciples (the UCB calls them "cult members") entertain the rest of the week.

Clubs

After suffering some damaging blows during the past few years, New York's anything-goes nightlife is bouncing back

The quelling of New York bohemia at the hands of Mayor Rudolph Giuliani is pretty well known by now—his urban clean-up has wiped out much of what made New York's nightlife scene so unique. But a lot of the blame must also go to the city's fantastically robust economy: Sky-high rents have made this historically Manhattan-centric city more culturally decentralized. More and more hipsters have been forced to move to the outer boroughs, and it's become harder and harder to open a club in Manhattan. As a result, it's slowly become socially acceptable to go clubbing in Brooklyn, Queens and the Bronx; concurrently, the number of smaller lounge-style venues in Manhattan has swelled.

PLAY IT SAFE

In pre-Giuliani times, weapons were the only items verboten in clubs, but the current climate has forced some clubs to police their patrons' drug use as well, so if getting high is your cup of E, be careful—drugs are illegal. And, of course, leave the guns and knives at home.

It should be said that while New York isn't nearly as dangerous as it used to be, this is still a city where anything can happen. If you're leaving a club at an ungodly hour, you might want to take a taxi or call a car service as you leave. Here are three of the latter with easily memorized numbers: **Lower East Side Car Service** (*212-477-7777*), **New Day** (*212-228-6666*) and **Tel Aviv** (*212-777-7777*). More car services are listed in chapter **Directory.**

Many of the more risqué events shun publicity (and hence may not be listed here), so if you're interested in events of a semi-illegal nature, it's best to ask around.

Alcohol is sold until 4am, and some after-hours clubs are open late enough to reopen their bars at 8am (noon on Sunday), the earliest allowed by law. There are also a number of illegal drinking dens (not surprisingly, we can't list these); ask around at last call if you want another round. Wherever you go, most people won't arrive before midnight (some clubs don't even open their doors until well past 4am). Still, one of the city's most popular events, **Body & Soul,** is a reaction to that; it runs at Vinyl on Sundays from 3pm until 11pm, allowing club dinosaurs and weekday clock-punchers to be in bed early (*see page 257*).

The thong show Shake your bare booty to Latin/tribal house at La Nueva Escuelita.

Entertainment

THE SOUND OF NEW YORK

New Yorkers are a cynical, hard-to-impress bunch. But despite the perennial been-there-done-that attitude, New York's club scene is proud of its history and traditions. Most natives in their late twenties or early thirties grew up on disco and old-school rap, and DJs program a fair number of "classics" in their sets. While some clubs seem overly nostalgic for legendary, long-gone nightspots like Paradise Garage (a famed gay disco and the source of the British term for gospel-influenced vocal house music), classics give props to the past and connect the musical dots between then and now.

New York DJs offer an eclectic mix of hip-hop, reggae, soul, house, disco, drum 'n' bass and Latin during the course of a night (though less so in the big clubs). The crowds, too, tend to be varied (though certain clubs are populated almost exclusively by white gay musclemen). A gay sensibility is common in clubs, and a "straight" night often means "mixed."

Although glamour-oriented clubs do have door policies, most upscale joints these days are more concerned with how much you have in your wallet than what brand of trousers you've got on. You still may want to dress up, though, since door policies can change like the weather. Hetero-heavy venues often refuse entry to groups of men in order to maintain a desirable gender balance. Bottle service—in which you must purchase an entire bottle of liquor (usually at a couple of hundred dollars a pop) to sit down at a table—is one trend that has spread as the bonuses of dot-com and Wall Street types have metastasized.

Mother, may I? Sure! Have a girl's night out at Clit Club, Friday nights at Mother.

While Friday and Saturday are, of course, the biggest nights to go out, many hipsters and locals stick to midweek clubbing to avoid the throngs of suburbanites (a.k.a. the bridge-and-tunnel crowd) who overwhelm Manhattan every weekend. Besides, a number of the more interesting events happen during the week.

STAY IN THE KNOW

The club scene is mercurial: Parties move weekly, and clubs can differ wildly from night to night. For example, a primarily gay establishment may "go straight" once a week because a promoter can fill the place on a slow night. Calling ahead is a good idea, as is consulting the most recent issue of *Time Out New York* or the monthly style magazine *Paper.* The gay listings magazine *HX* (Homo Xtra) is also good for club reviews, albeit with a gym-queen–oriented slant.

Parties, especially roving events, may change venues at a moment's notice, and keeping up can be a challenge. Calling the various hot lines can help keep your finger on the pulse of New York nightlife. Rave clothing and record store **Liquid Sky** has a popular phone line (*212-343-0532*) with details on rave-oriented nights. **Mello**'s line is another good one to call for a variety of parties (*212-330-9018*). Other rave lines include **New York at Night** (*212-465-3299*), **Digital Domain** (*212-592-3676*) and **Solar Luv** (*212-629-2078*). **Atom** (*212-501-ATOM*) covers a variety of events, from hip-hop and rave to gay parties (such as Café Con Leche). **E-Man** (*212-330-8101*) tracks a selection of underground house clubs, mostly—but by no means exclusively—of the mixed-to-gay variety. **Giant Step** (*212-714-8001*) focuses on acid jazz, drum 'n' bass, trip-hop and the like. **Mixed Bag Productions** (*212-604-4224*) has a role in many events: In addition to running Konkrete Jungle, MBP helps promote various jungle, acid jazz and trip-hop parties, including larger-scale ravelike events.

Admission prices for the clubs listed below vary according to the night, but usually range from $5 to $25. When no closing time is listed, assume the club stays open until the party fizzles out. FYI, the term *club* is used to describe discos and live-music venues (*see also chapter* **Music**).

▶ An up-close look at queer nightlife can be found in chapter **Gay & Lesbian.**

▶ Reviews of the hottest roving parties are in **Disco to go,** page 254.

▶ To find out the latest in the club scene, pick up a copy of ***Time Out New York.***

Entertainment

Center of it all Dance to the house mixes of star DJs like Danny Tenaglia at Centro-Fly.

Entertainment

Clubs

Baktun

418 W 14th St between Ninth Ave and Washington St (212-206-1590). Subway: A, C, E to 14th St; L to Eighth Ave. Hours vary with event.

Although it's a cramped little sweatbox, Baktun has recently blossomed into a reliable source for quality music in a fun, not-too-serious atmosphere. Fridays are generally given over to deep-ish house, with four similarly formatted monthly parties rotating weeks. Saturdays, you'll find drum 'n' bass, while midweek events tend to lean toward abstract beats and trip-hop. There are also frequent art shows here, plus a well-appointed video booth from which projectionists add trippy visuals to the party.

Centro-Fly

45 W 21st St between Fifth and Sixth Aves (212-627-7770). Subway: F, N, R to 23rd St. Hours vary with event.

The spectacularly designed Centro-Fly opened in late 1999 to rave reviews. Its eye-popping Op Art decor and just-right size—unlike Twilo and Tunnel, it's large but not gargantuan—mean it can strike the right balance between big-club excitement and quality music. Thursday's **Subliminal Sessions**—helmed by Erick "More" Morillo and his Subliminal label—is the best night, with music by More himself and some of the world's best house DJs as guests (Danny Tenaglia, Derrick Carter, etc.). The crowd is as beautiful as the club (which means that hordes of yuppies and suburban schlubs can't be far behind), making Centro-Fly one of New York's most deservedly talked-about discos.

Cheetah

12 W 21st St between Fifth and Sixth Aves (212-206-7770). Subway: F, N, R to 23rd St. Hours vary with event.

Drink prices are outrageous and the crowd can tend toward model-worshippers and Eurotrash, but the cheetah-print booths and indoor waterfall are fun. **Purr,** a hip-hop/R&B/classics party on Monday, is popular for its attractive, racially mixed crowd of trendy downtown heteros on the make. Plenty of models and celebs, too. Call for details on nightly parties, or check out the Clubs section in *Time Out New York.*

Copacabana

617 W 57th St between Eleventh and Twelfth Aves (212-582-2672). Subway: A, C, B, D, 1, 9 to 59th St–Columbus Circle. Jun–Aug Tue 6pm–3am; Thu–Sat 6pm–4am. Sept–May Tue 6pm–3am; Fri 6pm–5am; Sat 10pm–5am.

The truly legendary Copa is an upscale disco catering to a 25-and-up, mainly black and Hispanic clientele. Although this isn't the exact same space Barry Manilow sang about (the club moved across town to its present space a few years back), the look and feel have been preserved with remarkable faithfulness. Live bands play salsa and merengue every night, and DJs fill the gaps with hip-hop, R&B, disco and Latin sounds. The dress code requires that customers look "casual but nice": no jeans, sneakers or work boots, and gents must wear shirts with collars. (*See chapter* **Music: Popular music.**)

Divas

222 E 14th St between Second and Third Aves (212-473-6590). Subway: L to Third Ave; N, R, 4, 5, 6 to 14th St–Union Sq. Hours vary with event.

Divas is bizarre in just about every way: the name (it sounds more appropriate for a gay sports bar in the sticks), the layout (the DJ booth and dance floor are at opposite ends of the club, separated by a 30-foot bar) and the scene. Currently, Tuesday nights draw a freaky, sexually polymorphous crowd of cross-dressers, club kids and their admirers, while Saturdays feature solid deep house and a much more music-oriented clientele.

Don Hill's

511 Greenwich St at Spring St (212-334-1390). Subway: C, E to Spring St; 1, 9 to Houston St. Tue–Sun 10pm–4am.

Don Hill's is half dance club, half live-music venue, and its best night, **Squeezebox** (now monthly), combines both: It's a gay rock party, with live bands and a drag queen DJ spinning glammy, punky, scummy rock for a mixed (but queer in appearance and sensibility) crowd. Other nights are devoted to pedestrian '80s pop or live bands.

Exit

605 W 55th St between Eleventh and Twelfth Aves (212-582-8282). Subway: A, C, B, D, 1, 9 to 59th St–Columbus Circle. Hours vary with event.

A massive, hangarlike space with a lovely roof deck, Exit has housed several other clubs, all of which became quickly popular with knuckleheads. Chalk it up to the amount of people needed to fill this place. Still, special events and the occasional stint by a reliable promoter warrant its inclusion here. Worth keeping in mind.

Krystal's

89-25 Merrick Blvd between 89th and Jamaica Aves, Jamaica, Queens (718-523-3662). Subway: E, J, Z to Jamaica Ctr. Mon, Tue, Fri, Sat 10pm–4am.

If you don't mind traveling to the outer boroughs, you can get a slightly grittier taste of the city's musical life. Krystal's, in the Caribbean section of Queens, is where you'll hear a hot mix of hip-hop and reggae, played for a boisterous local audience.

La Kueva

28-26 Steinway St at 28th Ave, Astoria, Queens (718-267-9069). Subway: G, R to Steinway St; N to 30th Ave. 10pm–4am

Every Thursday, Chichi Rock throws out a Latin and American "rock & roll/new-wave lifeline" from the DJ booth at this Latin rock joint. Expect a selection of the above, "from Kennedy's death 'til today."

La Nueva Escuelita

301 W 39th St at Eighth Ave (212-631-0588). Subway: A, C, E to 42nd St–Port Authority. Thu–Sun 10pm–5am.

Escuelita used to be a seedy Latin drag club. Now, it's a rather less seedy Latin drag club, but no less entertaining. Though La Nueva Escuelita is oriented toward gay and lesbian Latinos, all are welcome. The music is generally high-energy, and heavy on the merengue and banging Latin/tribal house. The drag shows are not to be missed. The Sunday tea dance is hosted by the incomparable Harmonica Sunbeam, a hilarious drag queen comedian with an off-the-wall fashion sensibility and universal comic appeal.

The Lounge

Lenox Lounge, 288 Lenox Ave between 124th and 125th Sts (212-722-9566). Subway: 2, 3 to 125th St. Tue, Thu 11pm–4am.

Go to the heart of Harlem for this twice-a-week gay hip-hop night—a phenomenon that's not nearly as unique as you might think. House, reggae, R&B and disco classics are thrown into the musical mix, and there's a more party-minded atmosphere than at other spots in the area or, for that matter, at Chelsea gay clubs. It's a solidly black crowd, but new faces are welcome regardless of their complexion. DJs include NFX, Cat and veteran spinner Andre Collins.

Mother

432 W 14th St at Washington St (212-366-5680). Subway: A, C, E to 14th St; L to Eighth Ave. Hours vary with event.

Run by longtime club royals Chi Chi Valenti and Johnny Dynell (a popular DJ), Mother is home to a variety of highly imaginative events. Jackie 60, the club's nine-year-old Tuesday-night tradition, took its last bow just before New Year's Eve 1999, but its replacement, **Queen Mother,** is just as entertaining, if not yet steeped in legend like its predecessor. **Clit Club** is a Friday-night lesbian institution, and Saturday's **Click+Drag** is a brilliant crossbreeding of technological and sexual fetishism. A vague dress code exists on Tuesdays and Saturdays—according to that week's theme—but it's selectively enforced.

Nell's

246 W 14th St between Seventh and Eighth Aves (212-675-1567). Subway: A, C, E, 1, 2, 3, 9 to 14th St; L to Eighth Ave. 10pm–4am.

More than a decade old, Nell's is much the same as it's always been. Its formula is laid-back jazz and funky soul (often with live bands) upstairs, where there's a limited dining menu, and DJ-supplied hip-hop, R&B, reggae, house and classics below. The crowd is multiracial (leaning to black), dressed up, straight and ready to spend.

NV

289 Spring St at Hudson St (212-929-NVNV). Subway: C, E to Spring St; 1, 9 to Houston St. Wed–Fri 4:30pm–4am; Sat 8pm–4am.

NV, located just west of Soho, caters mainly to yuppies, sports stars and model-worshippers, but worthwhile parties do take place on occasion. The Sunday-night **Passion** event draws an upscale, good-looking mixed-to-black crowd that grooves to hip-hop, R&B and classics.

Octagon

555 W 33rd St at Eleventh Ave (212-947-0400). Subway: A, C, E to 34th St–Penn Station. Hours vary with event.

Another rent-a-club, Octagon is a cool space that's been around forever and hosts any and every kind of party, depending on who's got the money to book the space. The best and most reliable night is Friday; **U + Me,** a long-running deep-house night catering mainly to gay black men, is lots of fun. There's also a side room featuring hip-hop.

Ohm

16 W 22nd St between Fifth and Sixth Aves (212-229-2000). Subway: F, N, R to 23rd St. Thu–Sat 8pm–4am.

Although promoters come and go, Ohm is essentially a mainstream, aggressively hetero scene. Expect to hear Euro-house on the main floor, and hip-hop and pop down in the basement.

One51

151 E 50th St between Third and Lexington Aves (212-753-1144). Subway: E, F to Lexington Ave; 6 to 51st St. Mon–Sat 5pm–4am.

A midtown supper club–cum–disco, One51 is chiefly the domain of businessmen, Europeans and old-money types. The joint is pleasant enough in its own way: The upstairs lounge is comfy, and the DJs—who spin mostly well-known dance hits—are good at what they do. Downstairs, the dining room is turned over to dancing once the last table is cleared. If the neoswing thing is your bag, New York's top swing promoter runs Thursday nights. Dressing up is advised, though casual-but-neat attire is okay too.

Planet 28

215 W 28th St between Seventh and Eighth Aves (212-726-8820). Subway: A, C, E to 34th St–Penn Station; 1, 9 to 28th St. Hours vary with event.

Planet 28 features everything from gay, black voguing balls (the fierce **Clubhouse** event on Wednesday is as close to *Paris Is Burning* as you're likely to get) to rave and hip-hop nights. The events change often, so check ahead.

Roxy

515 W 18th St between Tenth and Eleventh Aves (212-645-5156). Subway: A, C, E to 14th St; L to Eighth Ave. Hours vary with event.

Originally a roller disco (and still one on Wednesday nights), the Roxy gained worldwide fame in the early '80s as the epicenter of the downtown hip-hop culture clash. Later, it became a cheesy Latin freestyle

Disco to go

Take the party anywhere with these mobile blowouts

There's nothing like a fully kitted out nightclub with all the bells and whistles, but there's also something to be said for the spontaneity and novelty of parties that aren't held in traditional nightclubs. New Yorkers are partying in unusual locations these days, from antiques shops to bowling alleys, to say nothing of the myriad restaurants that host club-style events. There are also a number of ongoing parties that don't stick to one location but rove around to all kinds of spots. Here are some of the city's best.

Beige

B Bar, 40 E 4th St at Bowery (212-475-2220). Subway: 6 to Astor Pl. Tue 11pm.

DJs serve up a groovy, just-this-side-of-camp soundtrack that can include anything from gay show-tune standards to 1980s electro-disco classics. Expect fashionistas, clubbies and off-duty drag queens. Hilarious and very visual.

Halcyon

227 Smith St between Butler and Douglass Sts, Carroll Gardens, Brooklyn (718-260-9299). Subway: F, G to Bergen St. Tue–Thu 12pm–12am, Fri–Sun 12pm–2am.

An interesting mishmash of retail and entertainment experiences comprise this friendly Brooklyn establishment: It's a record emporium that boasts a fine selection of current and classic dance music on both vinyl and CD; an antiques shop (the walls are covered with various space-age housewares and tchotchkes for sale); and a café/coffee bar. Various local DJs (including some rather well-known names) spin records every night, and patrons are welcome to just hang out and groove to the music on the many couches and chairs. Saturday afternoons, Halcyon hosts an open-turntable session for DJ wanna-bes, who are later upstaged by a pro who shows the room how it's done.

Konkrete Jungle

Various locations (212-604-4224; www.konkretejungle.com). Mon 10:30pm; $10, $8 with invite.

Konkrete Jungle is the longest-running drum 'n' bass night in the city, but you have to be quick to keep up with this peripatetic party. The music is more hardstep than deep or jazzy jungle, and the crowd tends toward the youngish. Call for details.

Night Strike

Bowlmor Lanes, 110 University Pl between 12th and 13th Sts (212-255-8158). Subway: L, N, R, 4, 5, 6 to 14th St–Union Sq. Mon 10pm.

Scenesters exchange their platforms for bowling shoes, while DJs spin house and techno. There's something humanizing about a crowd of full-on night-crawlers letting their

club, then a hugely popular gay club. Scotto, cofounder of NASA, one of the city's first rave-style parties, has recently started **Drop.com** (cleverly promoting his website) on Fridays, bringing in a variety of high-profile guest DJs from the house, techno and drum 'n' bass worlds. The queens have returned on Saturdays, packing the place as they used to do.

Sapphire

249 Eldridge St between Houston and Stanton Sts (212-777-5153). Subway: F to Second Ave. 7pm–4am.

Sapphire was one of the first trendy Lower East Side DJ bars, and it was unbearable (i.e. crowded). It's gotten a lot better, now that the club has fallen out of fashion. The music is fairly typical most of the week—hip-hop, reggae, acid jazz, R&B and disco classics—though Monday's **Sleaze Factor** party, with pumping deep house and soulful techno, has slowly become a must. Sleaze Factor also brings in top-notch guest DJs, offering clubgoers the chance to dance to world-famous spinners like Carl Craig and the Shamen's Mr. C.

Shine

285 West Broadway at Canal St (212-941-0900). Subway: A, C, E to Canal St. Hours vary with event.

A slew of clubs have operated in Shine's location, and none have been particularly great. The space itself just isn't that workable. It does have a dance floor, a stage and a DJ booth, though, and its more interesting parties make good use of all three. The **Giant Step** organization has recently revived its famous weekly showcase of acid jazz/trip-hop/eclectic beats; it's now on Mondays, with DJ Ron Trent and various guest DJs and musicians. Tuesday's **Prohibited Beats** explores the world of live drum 'n' bass, with super drummer JoJo Mayer leading a troupe of live musicians.

Sin Sin

248 E 5th St at Second Ave (212-253-2222). Subway: F to Second Ave. Hours vary with event.

hair down and hanging out the classic American white-trash way: drinkin', bowlin' and shootin' the shit.

Organic Grooves

Various locations (212-439-1147). Fri 10:30pm. Prices vary.

The Go Global folks throw their parties at any old space, from Lower East Side antiques shops to Brooklyn's decrepit waterfront. DJ Sasha spins soupy, trippy dub funk and acid jazz, while live musicians noodle to the records. It's hippieish but funky nonetheless. The crowd makeup is more sexually straight and racially mixed (and it's not a bad-looking bunch, either).

Pure Country

Tennessee Mountain, 121 W 45th St between Sixth Ave and Broadway (212-869-4545). Subway: B, D, F, Q to 47–50th Sts–Rockefeller Ctr. Mon 6:30–11pm. $10.

Urban cowboys can kick up their boot heels at this bastion of Southern cookin', thanks to Rona Kaye (formerly of Denim & Diamonds) and DJ Alan Kohn. Yee-haw!

Tsunami

Various locations (212-439-8124; www.tsunami-trance.com). Days and prices vary.

If Goa trance is your bag, Tsunami is the name you want to know. The all-night events are irregularly scheduled but usually feature top trance DJs and live performers.

Turntables on the Brooklyn Side

Various locations (212-560-5593; www.rhythmlove.com). Days and prices vary.

An offshoot of Organic Grooves, Turntables on the Brooklyn Side (so called until they move the party out of the borough) is similarly fixated on mid-tempo, mellow breakbeats, with a distinctly hippieish sensibility.

Vampyros Lesbos

The Cooler, 416 W 14th St between Ninth and Tenth Aves (212-229-0785). Subway: A, C, E to 14th St; L to Eighth Ave. Thu 9pm, $7.

The Vampyros Lesbos party is a Thursday-night homage to the early-'70s soft-core porn/horror flicks of Spanish director Jess Franco. DJ Franc O spins a selection of loungecore, exotica, strip-hop and other kitschy, groovy stuff from Franco films and their ilk. The crowd, meanwhile, does its best to be decadent, while slides of soft-core nudes and album sleeves illuminate the walls. The party has been moving around lately, so call to verify its location.

Wasabi Wednesday

Avenue A Sushi, 103 Ave A between 6th and 7th Sts (212-982-8109). Subway: F to Second Ave. Wed 7:30pm. Free.

This venue, a holdover from the '80s, combines all of the era's boho hallmarks: it's a sushi restaurant that doubles as an art gallery and video bar, and it's covered in black tile, mirrors and neon. There's no dancing, but DJ Bruce Tantum works the room into a chopstick-brandishing frenzy with house, lounge, drum 'n' bass, disco and the indescribable. All the while, a bizarre mix of videos (Japanese pornimation, Russ Meyer films, *Showgirls*) play.

Mad platter Twilo DJ Sasha mans the decks.

Also known as the Leopard Lounge, Sin Sin has a restaurant on the ground floor and a cozy little bar/disco upstairs, complete with a postage stamp–size parquet dance floor. DJs spin every night, with Sunday's **Aspara** event being the best party. It's nominally a fetish-oriented lesbian shindig, but men are generally welcome, if they're well-behaved. The crowd is, in fact, a very mixed, very downtown bunch, and the hard house tracks fit the vaguely sleazy mood perfectly.

S.O.B.'s.

204 Varick St at Houston St (212-243-4940). Subway: 1, 9 to Houston St. Hours vary with event.

The venerable S.O.B.'s (it stands for Sounds of Brazil) opened in the mid-'80s as the so-called world-beat boom began. Although its bread and butter is still presenting concerts by Latin, Caribbean and African artists, the club has also been involved with more discotheque-oriented events. Thursday's **Basement Bhangra** night is a popular weekly showcase of the hybrid of Western club sounds (hip-hop, house, drum 'n' bass) and traditional subcontinental pop and folk music. Saturday nights are given over to live Brazilian bands (see chapter **Music: Popular music**).

Sound Factory

618 W 46th St between Eleventh and Twelfth Aves (212-643-0728). Subway: C, E to 50th St. Hours vary with event.

This new incarnation of the legendary Sound Factory has been open since 1997, and the sound system has gotten even better. However, the club does not have DJ Junior Vasquez, and for many that means it will never be the Sound Factory. Unlike the original Factory's streetwise black and Latin gay audience, the new Factory crowd is mostly straight and suburban. DJ Jonathan Peters spins an attack-oriented brand of hard house, with snare rolls and breakdowns occurring every other minute. The club is also keeping alive the long New York after-hours tradition of free munchies, offering a generous spread of fruit, cookies, potato chips, coffee and more, although it now has a full bar.

Speeed

20 W 39th St between Fifth and Sixth Aves (212-719-9867). Subway: B, D, F, Q to 42nd St; 7 to Fifth Ave. Hours vary with event.

Speeed opened early in 1998 with much fanfare, and then, well.... While it never achieved "in" status, it has a full lineup of mostly mainstream parties with hip-hop on the ground floor and house in the basement. Events change often here, and worthwhile nights do pop up on occasion.

Studio 84

3534 Broadway at 145th St (212-234-8484). Subway: 1, 9 to 145th St. Wed–Sun 9pm–4am.

Who needs techno when you've got merengue? That's the frenzied, 150-beats-per-minute dance music you hear blasting out of the speakers at this genuine Dominican dance hall. Though its light-speed tempo and insane arrangements can be daunting to first-timers, there's no denying merengue's sex appeal. Salsa, Latin house, hip-hop and reggae are also played here, and every Thursday there's a gay-themed party.

Thirteen

35 E 13th St at University Pl (212-979-6677). Subway: L, N, R, 4, 5, 6 to 14th St–Union Sq. Mon–Sun 10pm–4am.

This tiny joint features a variety of nights that offer everything from the usual hip-hop/R&B/classics formula to rock and house music. Parties come and go, but Sunday night's **Shout!** has survived them all by playing Northern soul, freakbeat, 1960s psychedelic rock, garage punk and various other genres commonly (albeit often wrongly) associated with mods.

True

28 E 23rd St between Madison Ave and Park Ave South (212-254-6117). Subway: N, R, 6 to 23rd St. Tue–Fri 6pm; Sat 10pm.

Although it is one of Manhattan's smaller dance clubs, True fills a definite need. The best night is Tuesday, when the early-evening Latino Café party turns into **Super Funk,** attracting a fun music-industry crowd (it's a good bet that you'll rub elbows at the bar with the likes of Todd Terry or Masters at Work). You'll mostly hear deep but pumping house spun by guest DJs ranging from local up-and-comers to the internationally known likes of Benji Candelario.

Tunnel

220 Twelfth Ave at 27th St (212-695-4682). Subway: C, E to 23rd St. Fri 10pm–6am; Sat 11pm–noon; Sun 10pm–4am.

A stunningly massive place with equally impressive decor—there's a unisex bathroom complete with a bar and banquettes, a coffeehouse and the mind-blowing, psychedelic Cosmic Cavern, designed by pop artist Kenny Scharf (it's got floor-to-ceiling fake fur, Lava lamps, Internet terminals, black-light paintings and a fountain). A 1996 police raid dealt a blow to Tunnel's spirit (not to mention its trendy cachet), from which the club never fully recovered, but it's such an incredible space that it deserves at least one visit. Head for one of the many smaller rooms, which feature more interesting music, decor and people.

Twilo

530 W 27th St between Tenth and Eleventh Aves (212-268-1600). Subway: C, E to 23rd St. Hours vary with event.

With little else besides an immense sound system and dance floor, Twilo was designed to be a temple of music. Unfortunately, it wants to be both underground and trendy, a bit of an oxymoronic goal. Friday, the straight (i.e., mixed) night, draws lots of suburban ex-ravers. The music can be excellent, but the hype-driven booking policy yields uneven results; the upstairs lounge, on the other hand, has hosted everything from drum 'n' bass to loungecore. On Saturdays, Twilo attempts to restore the magic of the old Sound Factory with Junior Vasquez. But while the original Factory sound was hard, brutal and funky, Junior's music now is largely fluffy HiNRG.

205 Club

205 Chrystie St at Stanton St (212-473-5816). Subway: F to Second Ave. Hours vary with event.

The 205 Club, like Sapphire, is basically a nondescript bar that was so regularly hassled by the authorities for dancing-patron violations that it took the extraordinary step of obtaining a cabaret license. It's still a bit of a Bowery dive, but now you'll hear everything from African music and reggae to hip-hop, drum 'n' bass and funk.

Vinyl

6 Hubert St at Hudson St (212-343-1379). Subway: A, C, E, 1, 9 to Canal St. Hours vary with event.

For sheer star power, you probably can't beat Vinyl's weekly lineup of legendary DJs. Timmy Regisford spins Paradise Garage retreads and R&B-flavored house for a devoted crowd every Saturday, while Fridays belong to the brilliant Danny Tenaglia, who spins everything from Garage disco classics to hard but funky techno. Wednesdays, "Little" Louie Vega spins at **Dance Ritual**, and Sunday afternoon's **Body & Soul** throbs from 3pm to 11pm. Inhibited dancers beware: Vinyl's liquor license was revoked in 1997, so no buying courage (or rhythm) in a bottle here.

The Warehouse

141 E 140th St between Grand Concourse and Walton Ave, Bronx (718-992-5974). Subway: 4 to 138th St. Sat 10pm–6am.

Most visitors to New York don't include a visit to a gay, black hip-hop and house club in the South Bronx on their itineraries. But the adventurous and streetwise visitors will find the Warehouse a uniquely New York experience. Plummeting crime rates notwithstanding, the South Bronx is still probably one of the city's—hell, the nation's—worst areas. Once inside the club, though, you'll find a peaceful, friendly, attitude-free crowd.

Wetlands

161 Hudson St at Laight St (212-966-4225). Subway: A, C, E, 1, 9 to Canal St. Hours vary with event.

Mainly a live rock venue (*see chapter* **Music: Popular music**), Wetlands was founded on admirably progressive ideals. It holds frequent fund-raisers and follows environmentally correct policies (no plastic cups, a nonsmoking lounge, etc.). So, yes, it's still kinda hippie-dippy, but the place does host rap, reggae, jungle and trance nights, so it's worth checking out.

Lounges

bOb

235 Eldridge St between Houston and Stanton Sts (212-777-0588). Subway: F to Second Ave. 7pm–4am.

bOb features everything from the standard hip-hop/reggae/classics to exotica and film-noir soundtracks. The space doubles as an art gallery.

Serena

222 W 23rd St between Seventh and Eighth Aves (212-255-4646). Subway: C, E, 1, 9 to 23rd St. Tue–Sat 6pm–4am; Sun, Mon 6pm–2am.

A very trendy and elegantly done-up joint in the basement of the legendary Chelsea Hotel, Serena attracted legions of devoted scenesters its first few months in business. The hoi polloi were close on their heels. Tuesday's **Velveteen** party is still full of fashionistas and celebrities; Jonny Sender, a widely respected veteran DJ (and former bass player in Konk), spins a cool, eclectic mix of music for what is essentially a superficial, musically illiterate crowd.

Void

16 Mercer St at Howard St (212-941-6492). Subway: J, M, Z, N, R, 6 to Canal St. Wed, Thu 8pm–2am; Fri, Sat 8pm–3am.

Void, as you might expect from the name, is dark, stark and minimalist. A giant video screen engulfs one wall, and there are monitors embedded in the cocktail tables. Musically, you get DJs spinning armchair techno or live bands playing jazz.

XVI

16 First Ave between 1st and 2nd Sts (212-260-1549). Subway: F to Second Ave. Hours vary with event.

XVI's incredibly funky basement used to be a social club called Sweet 16, which the former proprieter's kids helped decorate. The place is from a different time: all mirrored tiles, stone floors, exotic paintings and gaudy brick arches. DJs play on the ground floor and downstairs, though the music tends to be considerably more pedestrian than the decor.

Film & TV

New York is ready for its close-up, on the silver screen or the boob tube

Do you feel like you're on a movie set when you walk the mean streets of New York? If the answer is yes, it's no surprise—many corners of the city have added gritty drama to the big and small screen, from Martin Scorsese's Gotham classic *Taxi Driver* to the latest installment of *Sex and the City*.

The prospect of running into an actual film shoot here is high. The rise in film projects in the area has been so meteoric during the past six years that New York could well be renamed Cine City: 209 movies were made here in 1999, compared with just 69 in 1993. The film-friendly mayor improved relations between production companies and local labor unions, which has led to the film-business boom. Whether it's big-name Hollywood projects like the romantic comedy *Autumn in New York* (starring Richard Gere and Winona Ryder) or small indie pictures, there's always some project filming on location in one of the five boroughs.

Besides providing an urban backdrop, New York is allowing filmmakers to bypass Hollywood altogether—western Queens has re-emerged as a vital film-production center. It's the location of **Silvercup Studios** (where *Sex and the City* and *The Sopranos* are produced) and **Kaufman Astoria Studios,** where Rudolph Valentino and the Marx Brothers made the smash hits of their day, and where hits like TV's *Sesame Street* and the film *Ransom* are shot.

There are also network and cable TV studios scattered around midtown Manhattan. MTV's Times Square studio and NBC's *Today* studio at Rockefeller Center are always mobbed with spectators. Other studios include CBS's *The Early Show,* taped in the GM Building (*767 Fifth Ave between 58th and 59th Sts*), and ABC's *Good Morning America* studio on Times Square (*1500 Broadway between 43rd and 44th Sts*).

If you have behind-the-camera aspirations, the city also happens to be a great place to develop your own fabulous filmmaking career. Besides New York University's world-renowned graduate film program, several shorter-term production courses and workshops, such as those offered by **New York Film Academy** (*212-674-4300*) and the **Reel School** (*212-965-9444*), are worth investigating. As you explore the city's sights you might stumble across a film set, so remember that when the director yells "Action!" it's time to shut up and watch.

For viewing the finished product, there are hundreds of screens throughout the metropolis, from the Anthology Film Archives (*see page 262*), one of the nation's premier showcases for experimental film, to the new 25-screen AMC Empire movie complex (*234 W 42nd St between Seventh and Eighth Aves, 212-398-3939*). Many movies open in New York (and Los Angeles) before they're shown elsewhere to build word of mouth—or, if it's at the end of the year, for Oscar consideration. So catch a flick when you're in town and be a part of the buzz machine.

That's the ticket

New Yorkers are famously knowledgeable about film; on opening nights for blockbusters (or a Woody Allen picture), lines often wind around the corner and SOLD OUT signs are posted on ticket-sellers' windows. On summer weekends, it seems that *every* movie sells out long before its scheduled show times. To avoid disappointment, call the automated 777-FILM ticket system well in advance. This adds $1.50 per ticket to your bill, but if it's a movie you're dying to see, you may feel it's worth it. Once at the cinema, head to the automated ticket booth to swipe your credit card (*AmEx, MC, V*) and get your tickets.

Note: There are "ticket buyers' lines" and "ticket holders' lines." The first showings on Saturday or Sunday (around noon) are less crowded, even for brand-new releases. Finally, since a handful of theaters in Manhattan are reserved-seating only, be sure to call ahead before you go.

▶ For information on how to be an audience member for NYC-based shows, see **Crowd pleasers**, page 260.

▶ See chapter **New York by Season** for details of film festivals throughout the year.

▶ For up-to-date movie reviews and cinema listings, check out ***Time Out New York***.

Popular cinemas

There are scores of first-run movie theaters located throughout the city. New releases come and go relatively quickly; if a film does badly, it might only show for a couple of weeks. Tickets usually cost $9.50, with discounts for children and senior citizens (often restricted to weekday afternoons). See **That's the ticket,** page 258, for tips on getting into sought-after screenings.

Cineplex Odeon Encore Worldwide

340 W 50th St between Eighth and Ninth Aves (212-50-LOEWS, ext 610). Subway: C, E, 1, 9 to 50th St. All tickets $4. AmEx, MC, V.

This is the "second-chance" cinema—these six screens show movies that are a few months old and have closed everywhere else. At four bucks a flick, it's the best movie deal in town.

Clearview's Ziegfeld

141 W 54th St between Sixth and Seventh Aves (212-777-FILM, ext 602). Subway: B, Q to 57th St; E, F to Fifth Ave. $9.50, children and seniors $6. AmEx, MC, V.

Rich in history, and still the grandest picture palace in town (it is, after all, named after the Follies), the Ziegfeld is often the venue for glitzy New York premieres. It is also a reserved-seating theater, so remember to order your tickets in advance or get there early.

Loews Kips Bay

570 Second Ave at 32nd St (212-50-LOEWS, ext 558). Subway: 6 to 33rd St. $9.50, children and seniors $6. AmEx, MC, V.

Thanks to the steep inclines of stadium seating, you can always see the screen, no matter how tall the guy in front of you is. Mainstream and slightly off-center Hollywood films are the standards at this recently built megaplex named for Jacobus Kip, an affluent 17th-century farmer.

Sony Lincoln Square & IMAX Theatre

1992 Broadway at 68th St (212-50-LOEWS, ext 638). Subway: 1, 9 to 66th St–Lincoln Ctr. $9.50, children and seniors $6. IMAX tickets $9.50, seniors $7.50, children $6. AmEx, MC, V.

Sony has constructed an entertainment center that's more a theme park than a dull old multiplex. Fiberglass decorations conjure up classic movie sets, a gift shop sells movie memorabilia, and the troop of popcorn vendors could bloat entire armies. Oh, and there are 12 fairly large screens. The center's eight-story IMAX screen accommodates 3-D films of the usual show-off-the-technology variety. These ultravivid underwater adventures and city-of-the-future fantasies are usually 35 to 45 minutes long. Services for the hearing impaired are available. For another IMAX theater, see page 262.

United Artists Union Square 14

Broadway at 13th St (212-253-2225). Subway: L, N, R, 4, 5, 6 to 14th St–Union Sq. $9.50, children and seniors $6.50. AmEx, MC, V.

What this venue lacks in character it makes up for with such amenities as comfortable stadium seating and digital sound in all 14 theaters.

Revival and art houses

For a city of its size, New York has shockingly few venues that screen art films and old movies. The following are the most popular.

Angelika Film Center

18 W Houston St at Mercer St (212-777-FILM, ext 531). Subway: B, D, F, Q to Broadway–Lafayette St; 6 to Bleecker St. $9, children and seniors $5.50. Cash only at box office.

Entertainment

Wham, BAM, thank you, ma'am Brooklynites love BAM Rose Cinemas' lineup of classic films.

Popular with local NYU students, the Angelika is a six-screen cinema, featuring primarily new American independent and foreign films. There's an espresso-and-pastry bar to hang out in before or after the show. It's a zoo on weekends, so come extra early or buy your tickets by phone.

BAM Rose Cinemas

30 Lafayette Ave between Flatbush Ave and Fulton St, Fort Greene, Brooklyn (718-623-2770). Subway: B, M, N, R to Pacific St; D, Q, 2, 3, 4, 5 to Atlantic Ave; G to Fulton St. $8.50, children and seniors $5.50. Cash only.

First-run art flicks finally arrived in Brooklyn when the beautiful, four-screen BAM Rose Cinemas opened in late 1998. The venue is affiliated with the Brooklyn Academy of Music.

Cinema Classics

332 E 11th St between First and Second Aves (212-675-6692; www.cinemaclassics.com). Subway: L to First Ave; N, R, 4, 5, 6 to 14th St–Union Sq. $5, includes double features. Cash only.

It may be shabby and cramped, but this tiny East Village venue's imaginative old-film programs (lots of noir series) draw a serious batch of film buffs. The $5 double bills can't be beat.

Cinema Village

22 E 12th St between Fifth Ave and University Pl (212-924-3363, box office 212-924-3364). Subway: L, N, R, 4, 5, 6 to 14th St–Union Square. $8.50, children and seniors $5.50. Cash only at box office.

Cinema Village specializes in American indies and foreign films that don't find their way into the Angelika and Lincoln Plaza cinemas. The theater also hosts mini festivals and runs horror films at midnight on weekends.

Film Forum

209 W Houston St between Sixth Ave and Varick St (212-727-8110, box office 212-727-8112). Subway: 1, 9 to Houston St. $9, children and seniors $5. Cash only at box office.

On Soho's edge, the three-screen Film Forum offers some of the best new films, documentaries and art

Crowd pleasers

Drown out the canned laughter with your genuine giggles at these TV shows

Tickets are available to all sorts of TV shows taped in New York studios. If you make requests by mail, be sure to include your name, address, and day and evening telephone numbers.

The Daily Show

356 W 58th St between Eighth and Ninth Aves (212-586-2477; www.comedycentral.com/dailyshow). Subway: A, C, B, D, 1, 9 to 59th St–Columbus Circle. Mon–Thu 5:30pm.

If you're a fan of this Comedy Central series, reserve tickets three months ahead of time by phone; or call on the Friday before you'd like to attend to see if there are any canceled tickets. You must be at least 18, with photo ID.

Late Night with Conan O'Brien

Mailing address: NBC Tickets, 30 Rockefeller Plaza, New York, NY 10112 (212-664-4000; www.nbc.com/conan). Subway: B, D, F, Q to 47–50th Sts–Rockefeller Ctr. Tue–Fri 5:30pm.

Send a postcard for tickets. A limited number of same-day tix are distributed at 9am. You must be at least 16.

Late Show with David Letterman

Mailing address: Ed Sullivan Theater, 1697 Broadway, New York, NY 10019 (212-975-1003; www.cbs.com/lateshow). Subway: B, D, E to Seventh Ave; N, R to 49th St; 1, 9 to 50th St. Mon–Thu 5:30pm, Fri 8pm.

Send a postcard six to eight months in advance, or apply for tickets online; standby tickets are available by calling 212-247-6497 at 11am on the day of taping. You must be at least 16, with photo ID.

MTV

1515 Broadway at 44th St (212-258-8000; www.mtv.com). Subway: N, R, S, 1, 2, 3, 9, 7 to 42nd St–Times Sq.

Call MTV or watch the music channel for info about being in the audience or participating in a show.

The Ricki Lake Show

Mailing address: 226 W 26th St, fourth floor, New York, NY 10001 (212-352-8600). Subway: 1, 9 to 28th St. Wed, Thu 3pm and 5pm; Fri 1pm and 3pm.

Call or send requests by postcard for tickets one month in advance. Standby tickets are available 90 minutes before taping; wait outside the studio (*221 W 26th St between Seventh and Eighth Aves*). You must be at least 18, with photo ID.

The Rosie O'Donnell Show

Mailing address: NBC Tickets, 30 Rockefeller Plaza, New York, NY 10112 (212-664-4000; rosieo.warnerbros.com).

movies around. Series or revivals, usually brilliantly curated, are also shown.

Lincoln Plaza Cinemas

30 Lincoln Plaza, entrance on Broadway between 62nd and 63rd Sts (212-757-2280, box office 212-757-0359). Subway: A, C, B, D, 1, 9 to 59th St–Columbus Circle. $9, children and seniors $5.50. Cash only at box office.

Commercially successful European films can be seen here alongside biggish American independent productions. All six theaters are wheelchair accessible and equipped with assisted-listening devices for the hearing impaired.

Paris Theatre

4 W 58th St between Fifth and Sixth Aves (212-688-3800). Subway: N, R to Fifth Ave. $9, children and seniors $5.50. Cash only at box office.

Situated beside Bergdorf Goodman and across from the Plaza Hotel, the Paris has a stylish program of European art-house movies, in addition to such eminently revivable films as Fellini's *8½*. In winter, beware: There's no indoor waiting area.

Quad Cinema

34 W 13th St between Fifth and Sixth Aves (212-255-8800, box office 212-255-2243). Subway: F to 14th St; L to Sixth Ave. $8.50, children and seniors $5.50. Cash only at box office.

Four small screens show a broad selection of foreign films, American independents and documentaries—a preponderance dealing with sexual and political issues. Oftentimes, these are movies you can't see anywhere else. Children under five are not admitted.

Screening Room

54 Varick St at Laight St (212-334-2100). Subway: 1, 9 to Canal St. $9, children and seniors $6. Cash only.

Attached to a swanky bistro, this small, cozy theater is perfect for the ultimate dinner-and-movie date (it has love seats for two). It shows a mix of first-run films and revivals, and *Breakfast at Tiffany's* plays every Sunday.

Is that your final answer? Watch them sweat live on *Who Wants to Be a Millionaire.*

Subway: B, D, F, Q to 47–50th Sts–Rockefeller Ctr. Mon–Thu 10am.

A ticket lottery is held March through June; only postcards received during those months are accepted. You will be notified one to two weeks in advance of taping if you have seats. A few same-day standby seats are available at 8am (but fans start lining up at 5am) from the 49th Street entrance, between Rockefeller Plaza and Sixth Avenue. No children under five admitted.

Saturday Night Live

Mailing address: NBC Tickets, 30 Rockefeller Plaza, New York, NY 10112 (212-664-4000; www.nbc.com/snl). Subway: B, D, F, Q to 47–50th Sts–Rockefeller Ctr. Dress rehearsals at 7:30pm, live at 10:15pm.

A ticket lottery is held in August, and only postcards received that month are accepted. You will be notified one to two weeks in advance of taping if you have seats. A few same-day standby tickets, for the dress rehearsal and the live show, are distributed at 9:15am (but people start lining up at around 5am). You must be at least 16.

Who Wants to Be a Millionaire

Mailing address: Who Wants to Be a Millionaire, Columbia University Station, P.O. Box 250225, New York, NY 10025 (212-735-5369; www.abc.com). Mon–Thu 5pm.

Send postcards only to request tickets. You must be at least 18, and present a valid ID at the taping. Tickets are mailed out about two weeks before the scheduled taping.

Entertainment

A slice of celluloid Pizza, popcorn and great pictures at Two Boots Pioneer Theater.

Two Boots Pioneer Theater

155 E 3rd St at Ave A (212-254-3300). Subway: F to Second Ave. $9; children, seniors and students $5. Tickets half-price with dinner at Two Boots Restaurant next door. Cash only.

The pizza chain Two Boots opened the East Village's only first-run alternative film center in 2000, and the programming has been as tasty as the pies.

Museums and societies

American Museum of the Moving Image

See chapter **Museums** *for listings.*

The first museum in the U.S. devoted to moving pictures is in Queens. More than 700 films and videos are shown each year, covering everything from Hollywood classics and series devoted to a single actor or director to oddball industrial-safety films. The schedule is inspired and entertaining.

Anthology Film Archives

32 Second Ave at 2nd St (212-505-5110). Subway: F to Second Ave. $8; students, seniors and members $5. Cash only.

Anthology is one of New York's treasures, housing the world's largest collection of written material documenting the history of independent and experimental film and video. The Archives are sponsored by some of the biggest names in film, and host a full program of screenings, festivals, talks, lectures and concerts.

► Special film series and experimental films often appear in museums and galleries other than those listed here. See also chapter **Museums.**

Brooklyn Museum of Art

See chapter **Museums** *for listings.*

The Brooklyn Museum of Art's intelligent, eclectic roster concentrates primarily on the works of foreign filmmakers.

Film Society of Lincoln Center

Lincoln Center, 65th St between Broadway and Amsterdam Ave (212-875-5600; www.filmlinc.com). Subway: 1, 9 to 66th St–Lincoln Ctr. $9, members $5. Cash only.

The Society was founded in 1969 to promote film and to support filmmakers. It operates the Walter Reade Theater (built in 1991), a state-of-the-art showcase for contemporary film and video—with the most comfortable theater seats in New York. Programs are usually organized around a theme, often with a decidedly international perspective. Each autumn, the society hosts the New York Film Festival (*see chapter* **New York by Season**).

Solomon R. Guggenheim Museum

See chapter **Museums** *for listings.*

The Guggenheim is building a reputation for programming series that are insightful and provocative, a notable example being 1998's well-received tribute to the motorcycle in cinema. It's worth a look.

IMAX Theater

American Museum of Natural History. See chapter **Museums** *for listings. Combined museum and film admission $15, seniors $10.50, children $8.50. AmEx, DC, V.*

The IMAX screen is four stories high, and the daily programs concentrate on the natural world. On weekends, it is usually crowded with children and their parents. For another IMAX theater, see page 259.

Metropolitan Museum of Art

See chapter **Museums** *for listings.*

The Met offers a full program of documentary films on art (many of which relate to exhibitions) in the Uris Center Auditorium (near the 81st Street entrance). On weekends, there are occasional themed series.

Millennium

66 E 4th St between Second Ave and Bowery (212-673-0090). Subway: F to Second Ave; 6 to Astor Pl. $7, members $5. Cash only.

This media-arts center screens avant-garde works, sometimes introduced by the films' directors, as part of the Personal Cinema Series, which runs from September through June (Fridays and Saturdays at 8 pm). The center also loans out filmmaking equipment, holds classes and workshops, and has a gallery showing works by and about media artists.

Museum of Modern Art

See chapter **Museums** *for listings.*

MoMA was one of the first museums to recognize film as an art form. Its first director, Alfred H. Barr, believed that film was "the only great art peculiar to the 20th century." Film scholars and researchers delve into the museum's massive film archives (appointments must be requested in writing). MoMA has about 25 screenings a week, often in series on the work of a particular director, or other themes. Entry is free with museum admission ($10), and the theater is usually much less crowded than the galleries. An infrared listening system is available for free to the hard-of-hearing.

Museum of Television & Radio

See chapter **Museums** *for listings.*

Television and radio works, rather than film, are archived here. The museum's collection includes more than 30,000 TV programs, which can be viewed at private consoles. A number of programs are shown daily in the museum's two screening rooms and its 63-seat video theater. Screenings are Tue–Sun at 1pm, Thu at 6pm and Fri at 7pm.

Whitney Museum of American Art

See chapter **Museums** *for listings.*

In keeping with its practice of showing the best in contemporary American art, the Whitney runs a varied schedule of film and video works. Its exhibitions often have a strong moving-image component, including the famous Biennial showcase of contemporary artworks. Entry is free with museum admission ($12.50).

Foreign-language films

Most or all of the previous institutions will screen films in languages other than English, but the following show only foreign films.

Asia Society

See chapter **Museums** *for listings.*

The Society shows films from India, China and other Asian countries, as well as Asian-American films. While the museum undergoes renovation, films are being shown at venues throughout the city. Call 212-517-ASIA.

French Institute–Alliance Française

55 E 59th St between Park and Madison Aves (212-355-6160). Subway: N, R to Lexington Ave; 4, 5, 6 to 59th St. Tue–Fri 11am–7pm; Sat, Sun 11am–3pm. $7. AmEx, MC, V.

The Institute shows movies from back home. They're usually subtitled (and never dubbed).

Goethe-Institute/German Cultural Center

See chapter **Museums** *for listings.*

A paragovernmental German cultural and educational organization, the Goethe-Institute shows German films in various locations around the city, as well as in its own opulent auditorium.

Japan Society

333 E 47th St between First and Second Aves (212-752-0824). Subway: E, F to Lexington Ave; 6 to 51st St. $8; seniors, students and members $5. AmEx, MC, V.

The Japan Society Film Center organizes a full schedule of Japanese films, including two or three big series each year.

Film festivals

Every September and October since 1963, the **Lincoln Center Film Society** has hosted the prestigious New York Film festival (*www.filmlinc.com*). The Film Society, with the Museum of Modern Art, also sponsors the highly regarded **New Directors, New Films** festival each spring, to show works by on-the-cusp filmmakers from around the world.

Several smaller, but just as anticipated, festivals occur throughout the year in the city. In October the fledgling **ResFest Digital Film Festival** (*www.resfest.com*) puts the spotlight on films using new technology and storytelling techniques (mainly shorts, and many of them animated). January brings the annual **New York Jewish Film Festival** (*212-875-5600*). Held at the Walter Reade Theater (*see* **Film Society of Lincoln Center,** *page 262*), the festival screens works from Jewish filmmakers living abroad. The **Gen Art Film Festival** (*212-290-0312; www.genart.org*), a weeklong late-spring showcase of quality independent films, is followed by the more established **New York Lesbian and Gay Film Festival** in early June (*212-254-7228*). **Bryant Park** (*Sixth Ave between 40th and 42nd Sts*) has free summertime Monday-night screenings (8:30pm) of classics on a giant screen.

The best Screens

We rate these cinemas tops for...

Blockbusters
Clearview's Ziegfeld or Loews Kips Bay

Foreign films
Paris or BAM Rose Cinemas

Romantic movies
Clearview's Ziegfeld

Cheap movies
Cineplex Odeon Encore Worldwide

Dinner dates
Screening Room

Midnight movies
Angelika Film Center

Classics
Museum of Modern Art

Documentaries
Film Forum

Gay & Lesbian

From Chelsea to the East Village and beyond, queer New York tempts with many places to eat, drink and be Mary

The much-chanted phrase "We're here, we're queer, get used to us" is outdated. It's safe to say that New York is definitely used to its boisterous rainbow contingent. In the city, from the floor of the New York Stock Exchange to the big design and fashion houses on Seventh Avenue, it is impossible to ignore the fact that openly gay men and women are a powerful part of what makes New York one of the world's financial and cultural centers. As the site of the 1969 Stonewall riots and the birthplace of the American gay-rights movement, New York City is a queer mecca and contains the headquarters of more than 500 lesbian, gay, bisexual and transgender social and political organizations.

During the annual celebration of **Gay Pride,** which takes place the last weekend in June (although the festivities begin the week prior), the Empire State Building is lit up in glorious lavender. This event draws hundreds of thousands of visitors to the city. The Pride March, which takes place on a Sunday, attracts up to a half-million spectators. A number of Manhattan businesses now fly the lesbian- and gay-friendly rainbow flag in tribute. Pride is a great time to visit New York: You'll feel as if everyone here is queer.

Arrive during the summer months to sample lesbian and gay resort culture on **Fire Island,** which is only a short trip from the center of town (*see chapter* **Trips Out of Town**); the stellar lineup of celluloid delights at the increasingly important **New York Lesbian & Gay Film Festival** in June (*212-254-7228*); and the cross-dressing extravaganza **Wigstock** (around Labor Day), presided over by the irrepressible Lady Bunny.

An essential stop for any lesbian or gay visitor to New York is the **Lesbian & Gay Community Services Center** (*see page 266*), a downtown nexus of information and activity that serves as a meeting place for more than 300 groups and organizations. There you can pick up copies of New York's free weekly gay and lesbian publications. And don't miss *Time Out New York*'s lively Gay & Lesbian listings for the latest happenings around town. In 2000, *TONY* received a Media Award from the Gay & Lesbian Alliance Against Defamation honoring the magazine's overall gay and lesbian coverage.

Although the sizable gay and lesbian population of New York is quite diverse, the lesbian and gay club and bar scenes often don't reflect this, since they are frequently gender-segregated and, like their straight counterparts, tend to attract the single 35-and-under crowd. However, the social alternatives are plentiful—among them burgeoning queer coffee-bar, bookstore and restaurant scenes, as well as dozens of gay and lesbian films and plays that are presented in mainstream venues (*see chapters* **Cabaret & Comedy, Film & TV** *and* **Theater & Dance**).

There's no doubt about it: New York is a nonstop city with a multitude of choices for queer entertainment. Enjoy!

▶ For more information about annual gay events such as Wigstock and the Pride March, see chapter **New York by Season.**

▶ If you're interested in New York's drag circuit, see **The royal treatment** page 270.

▶ For a complete listing of New York's nightlife, check out chapter **Clubs.** For strictly gay listings, see **Boys' Life,** page 266, or **Dyke Life,** page 272.

Books and media

Publications

New York's gay weekly magazines are *HX* (*Homo Xtra*) and *Next*—both of which include extensive information on bars, dance clubs, sex clubs, restaurants, cultural events and group meetings…and loads of personals. *HX* also devotes a few pages to lesbian listings. The newspaper *LGNY* (*Lesbian & Gay New York*) offers feisty political coverage with an activist slant. The *New York Blade News,* a sister publication of *The Washington Blade,* also focuses on queer politics and news. All four are free at gay and lesbian venues and shops. *MetroSource* ($4.95) is a bimonthly glossy with a guppy slant, covering interior decorating, designer fashions and exotic travel.

National publications include the stylish *Out* ($4.95) and the newsy *The Advocate* ($3.95), both

Entertainment

monthlies. *Girlfriends* ($4.95) and *Curve* ($3.95) are colorful, fun monthly magazines for lesbians. Also look for the rather tacky (and irregularly published) *Bad Attitude* ($7) and the far better sex quarterly *On Our Backs* ($5.95).

Fodor's Gay Guide to New York City ($12) is an excellent source of opinionated information about queer NYC and the surrounding areas. Daniel Hurewitz's *Stepping Out*, which details nine walking tours of gay and lesbian NYC, is another invaluable source. Both books—as well as the above-mentioned magazines—are available at **A Different Light** and at the **Oscar Wilde Memorial Bookshop** (*see below*).

Television

There's an abundance of gay-related broadcasting, though nearly all of it is amateurishly produced and appears on public-access cable channels. Programming varies by cable company, so you may not be able to watch all these shows on a hotel TV. At night, Channel 35 (in most of Manhattan) switches over to sexually explicit programs, which include the infamous Robin Byrd hosting her *Men for Men* soft-core strip shows. Manhattan Neighborhood Network (channels 34, 56, 57 and 67 on all Manhattan cable systems) has plenty of gay shows, ranging from zany drag queens milking their 15 minutes of fame to serious discussion programs. *HX* and *Next* provide the most current TV listings.

Bookshops

Most New York bookshops have gay sections (*see chapter* **Books & Poetry**), but the following cater especially to gays and lesbians.

A Different Light Bookstore & Café

151 W 19th St between Sixth and Seventh Aves (212-989-4850). Subway: 1, 9 to 18th St. 11am–10pm. AmEx, Disc, MC, V.

This is the biggest and best gay-and-lesbian bookshop in New York. It's great for browsing and has plenty of free readings, film screenings and art openings. Besides books, there are videos, calendars, greeting cards and a vast array of magazines.

Bluestockings

172 Allen St at Stanton St (212-777-6028). Subway: F to Second Ave. Mon noon–6pm; Tue–Sat noon–8pm; Sun 2–8pm. AmEx, Disc, MC, V.

This funky Lower East Side bookstore devoted to women's literature (it's named after an 18th-century feminist group) has established itself as a popular cultural center, with readings and events throughout the week. You'll find everything from dyke-hero comic books to groundbreaking feminist manifestos.

Oscar Wilde Memorial Bookshop

15 Christopher St between Sixth and Seventh Aves (212-255-8097). Subway: 1, 9 to Christopher St–Sheridan Sq. Mon–Sat 11am–8pm; Sun noon–7pm. AmEx, Disc, MC, V.

New York's oldest gay-and-lesbian bookshop is chock-full of books and magazines, and offers many discounts.

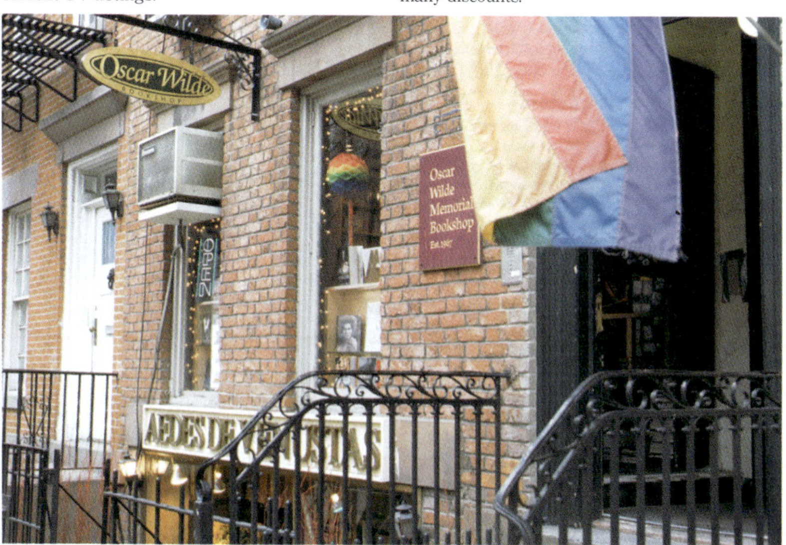

You can speak its name The Oscar Wilde Memorial Bookshop is the city's oldest gay bookshop.

Entertainment

Centers and phone lines

Audre Lorde Project Center

85 S Oxford St at Lafayette Ave, Fort Greene, Brooklyn (718-596-0342). Subway: C to Lafayette Ave. Mon 10am–6pm; Tue–Thu 10am–9pm; Fri 10am–6pm; Sat 1:30–9pm.

Officially known as the Audre Lorde Project Center for Lesbian, Gay, Bisexual, Two-Spirit & Transgender People of Color Communities, this community center provides a plethora of resources for queer people of color. Call for information about events and group meetings.

Barnard Center for Research on Women

101 Barnard Hall, 3009 Broadway at 117th St (212-854-2067). Subway: 1, 9 to 116th St–Columbia University. Mon–Fri 9am–5pm.

An academic center with a distinctly off-putting name, this is where to explore scholarly feminism—a calendar of classes, lectures and film screenings is available. The library has an extensive archive of feminist journals and government reports.

Gay & Lesbian Switchboard of New York Project

212-989-0999; www.glnh.org. Mon–Fri 6–10pm.

This is a phone-information service only. Callers who need legal help can be referred to lawyers, and there's information on bars, restaurants and hotels. The switchboard is especially good at giving peer counseling to people who have just come out or who may be considering suicide. There are also details on all sorts of other gay and lesbian organizations. Outside New York (but within the U.S.), callers can contact the switchboard's sister toll-free line, the Gay & Lesbian National Hotline at 888-THE-GLNH.

Gay Men's Health Crisis

119 W 24th St between Sixth and Seventh Aves (212-367-1000, AIDS advice hot line 212-807-6655; www.gmhc.org). Subway: 1, 9 to 23rd St. Advice hot line Mon–Fri 9am–9pm, Sat noon–3pm. Recorded information in English and Spanish at other times. Office Mon–Fri 10am–9pm.

This was the first organization in the world to take up the challenge of helping people with AIDS. It has a threefold mission: to push the government to increase services, to help those who are sick by providing services and counseling to them and their families, and to educate the public to prevent the further spread of HIV. There are 250 staff members and 1,400 volunteers. Support groups usually meet in the evenings.

Lesbian & Gay Community Services Center

208 W 13th St between Sixth and Seventh Aves (212-620-7310; www.gaycenter.org). Subway: F, 1, 2, 3, 9, to 14th St; L to Sixth Ave. 9am–11pm.

Founded in 1983, the Center, which was renovated in 2000, provides political, cultural, spiritual and emotional sustenance to the gay and lesbian community. While it principally offers programs and support for locals, there's plenty to interest the visitor, including a free information packet for tourists and those new to the city. You'll be amazed at the diversity of groups (around 300) that meet here. The Center also houses the National Museum and Archive of Lesbian and Gay History, and the Vito Russo lending library.

Lesbian Herstory Archive

P.O. Box 1258, New York, NY 10116 (718-768-3953; fax 718-768-4663). By appointment only.

Newly housed in the Park Slope area of Brooklyn (which is known as "Dyke Slope" for its large and growing lesbian population), the Herstory Archive, started by Joan Nestle and Deb Edel in 1974, includes more than 10,000 books (theory, fiction, poetry, plays), 1,400 periodicals and many items of personal memorabilia. You, too, can donate a treasured possession and become part of Herstory.

Michael Callen–Audre Lorde Community Health Center

356 W 18th St between Eighth and Ninth Aves (212-271-7200; www.callen-lorde.org). Subway: A, C, E to 14th St; L to Eighth Ave. Mon 12:30–8pm; Tue, Thu, Fri 9am–4:30pm; Wed 8:30am–8pm.

Formerly known as Community Health Project, this is the country's largest (and New York's only) health center primarily serving the gay, lesbian, bisexual and transgender community. The center offers an exhaustive list of services, including comprehensive primary care, HIV treatment, free adolescent services, STD screening and treatment, mental health services, and peer counseling and education.

NYC Gay & Lesbian Anti-Violence Project

240 W 35th St between Seventh and Eighth Aves, suite 200 (212-714-1184, 24-hour hot line 212-714-1141; www.avp.org). Subway: A, C, E, 1, 2, 3, 9 to 34th St–Penn Station. Mon–Thu 10am–8pm; Fri 10am–6pm.

The project provides support for the victims of antigay and antilesbian attacks. Working with the police department's bias unit, project volunteers offer advice on seeking police help. Short- and long-term counseling is available.

Boys' Life

While the Christopher Street area of the West Village has quaint historical gay sites such as the **Stonewall** (*see page 269*), friendly show-tune piano cabarets and unpretentious stores full of rainbow knickknacks and slogan T-shirts, over the past several years, the gay epicenter has shifted to Chelsea, which flaunts an attitude that can be daunting.

Entertainment

Gym dandies The buff and the beautiful work out at Chelsea's American Fitness Center.

The neighborhood's main drag is Eighth Avenue between 16th and 23rd Streets, a strip lined with businesses catering to upwardly mobile gay men: gyms, sexy clothing and trendy home-furnishing stores, tanning and grooming salons, galleries, cafés, bars and mid-range restaurants for brunch, business lunches and late dinners. The cult of the body reigns in Chelsea, and it's a kick to watch the perfectly toned men strut their stuff down Eighth Avenue. True, some of the gym bunnies adopt a creepy pecking order and ignore the existence of all those without muscles. However, the stereotype of Chelsea being a vast sea of supermen is exaggerated, and all types of queers converge on the neighborhood to check out the scene.

Most of Manhattan's dance clubs are either in Chelsea, or a hop, skip and jump away from it, and feature a big gay house/techno night during the weekend. During these bacchanals, sybarites can spin and twirl with upwards of 500 half-naked men until the wee hours of the morning.

In reaction to Chelsea, a counterculture community of punk-rock-glitter-fashion boys and theatrical drag queens thrives in the East Village, in a network of small, divey bars. The scene has an arty, bohemian vibe, and there are many equally lovely men to be found there, from 1970s macho butches to Bowie-type androgynes. The crowd tends to be even younger than in Chelsea (although some men may appear to be younger than they are) and is more mixed, both racially and sexually.

Some habitués of Chelsea and the East Village do mix. Men of all ages, shapes and sizes frequent the city's leather/fetish bars and clubs, such as the **Spike** in Chelsea and the **Lure** in an area of the West Village known as the Meatpacking District (*see* **Bars,** *page 268*). If you're a devotee of the leather scene, you might want to plan your trip around either the New York Mr. Leather Contest, which takes place in the autumn, or the Black Party at **Saint at Large**—a special all-night leather-and-S/M–themed circuit party that attracts thousands of people every March (*see page 270*).

For open-air cruising, try the **Ramble** in Central Park, located between the 79th Street transverse and the Lake (but beware of police entrapment). And although the city has made every effort to clean up Times Square and turn it into an extension of Disney World, you can for the moment still find nude male burlesque at the **Gaiety** (*201 W 46th St between Broadway and Eighth Ave, 212-221-8868*). This west-midtown area—once known as Hell's Kitchen but now known by the less threatening moniker Clinton—shows signs of being the next hot homo habitat. Take a stroll up Ninth Avenue between 42nd and 57th Streets to explore.

Don't worry if you're just just an average T-shirt-and-jeans–type gay man. Not only will you feel comfortable in almost any gay space, you'll be surprised at how much cruising happens on the streets while you're walking around town, and how easy it is to turn a glance into a conversation.

Accommodations

Chelsea Mews Guest House

344 W 15th St between Eighth and Ninth Aves (212-255-9174). Subway: A, C, E to 14th St; L to Eighth Ave. Singles and doubles $125–$200 (slightly higher during Gay Pride). Cash only.

Built in 1840, this guest house has accommodations exclusively for gay men. The rooms are comfortable and well furnished and have semiprivate bathrooms. Smoking is not allowed.

Chelsea Pines Inn

317 W 14th St between Eighth and Ninth Aves (212-929-1023; fax 212-620-5646). Subway: A, C, E to 14th St; L to Eighth Ave. Doubles and triples $89–$139 plus tax (slightly higher during Gay Pride and holidays). AmEx, DC, Disc, MC, V.

This centrally located inn near the West Village and Chelsea welcomes gay male guests and lesbians. Vintage movie posters set the mood, and the 23 rooms are clean and comfortable; some have private bathrooms, and all have radios, televisions and air-conditioning (essential in the summer).

Colonial House Inn

318 W 22nd St between Eighth and Ninth Aves (212-243-9669, 800-689-3779). Subway: C, E to 23rd St. $80–$114 with shared bath; $125 with private bath. Prices higher on the weekends. MC, V.

This beautifully renovated 1880s townhouse sits on a quiet street in the heart of Chelsea. It's run by, and primarily for, gay men. Colonial House is a great place to stay, even if some of the cheaper rooms are small. Major bonuses: free continental breakfast in the "Art Gallery Lounge" and a rooftop deck (nude sunbathing allowed!).

Incentra Village House

32 Eighth Ave between 12th and Jane Sts (212-206-0007). Subway: A, C, E to 14th St; L to Eighth Ave. $99–$179 ($20 more during Gay Pride and some holidays). AmEx, MC, V.

Two cute 1841 townhouses, perfectly situated in the West Village, make up this guest house run by gay men (lesbians and gay men are welcome). The rooms (singles, doubles and suites) are spacious, with private bathrooms and kitchenettes; some have working fireplaces. There's also a 1939 Steinway baby grand piano for show tune–spouting queens. While interestingly decorated, the rooms aren't always maintained at the height of cleanliness.

Bars

Most bars in New York offer theme nights, drink specials and happy hours, and the gay ones are no exception. Don't be shy, remember to tip the bartender, and carry plenty of business cards. *See chapters* **Bars** *and* **Cabaret & Comedy.**

East Village

Beige

B Bar, 40 E 4th St at Bowery (212-475-2220). Subway: B, D, F, Q to Broadway–Lafayette St; 6 to Bleecker St. Tue 10pm–4am. AmEx, MC, V.

Superpopular and supertrendy, Beige is packed to the gills with a frantic mix of the fabulous, sexy, pretentious and tacky. Everyone has an agenda, whether it's to dress to impress, network for a job or get laid, and the ensuing dynamics are quite spirited. It's mostly a gay male affair, but plenty of stylish gals (some of them are even dykes) join in the fun. Wear your Tuesday best, or you'll feel out of place at this groovy fete.

Boiler Room

86 E 4th St between First and Second Aves (212-254-7536). Subway: F to Second Ave. 4pm–4am. Cash only.

For most self-respecting East Village boys, a stop here on the weekends isn't just an option—it's a moral imperative. Probably the most intensely cruisey of East Village bars, this unassuming joint is busy on weeknights and absolutely mobbed on Friday and Saturday nights. The jukebox features a varied selection of new hits and classics, and there are video-game machines for the easily bored.

The Cock

188 Ave A at 12th St (212-946-1871). Subway: L to First Ave. 9:30pm–4am. Cash only.

This lively, deliberately seedy haunt carries on the East Village raunch tradition with cheap drinks, spicy shows and a bevy of stylishly sexy boys (What? You thought the name referred to a rooster?), and even a few girls. The music ranges from campy '80s to full-bore rock & roll.

Cher and Cher alike New York's drag performers will make you believe.

Wonder Bar

505 E 6th St between Aves A and B (212-777-9105). Subway: F to Second Ave. 6pm–4am. Cash only.

At its best, this groovy lounge hosts an appealingly diverse mix of people—most shockingly, men *and* women—making it an ideal hangout. The only downside is that most nights the smoke is as thick as the crowd. DJs spin soul, trip-hop and classics.

West Village

Bar d'O

29 Bedford St at Downing St (212-627-1580). Subway: A, C, E, B, D, F, Q to W 4th St; 1, 9 to Houston St. 7pm–3am. Cash only.

Thursdays, Saturdays and Sundays at this dark, cozy, candlelit haunt feature intimate cabaret performances by the city's most talented drag queens. (The cast varies, but you can almost always count on catching Joey Arias, Jackie Beat, Raven O and Sherry Vine—all of whom really sing, not lip-synch). On Mondays, the joint becomes a lesbian lounge, Pleasure, one of the most vibrant spots for New York dyke life. The music in the small, smoky room is a slow-grind, hip-hop groove, and the place is full of rap stars who truly believe in "ladies first."

The Lure

409 W 13th St between Ninth and Tenth Aves (212-741-3919). Subway: A, C, E to 14th St; L to Eighth Ave. 8pm–4am. Cash only.

This newfangled fetish bar attracts a broad, energetic, sometimes posey bunch. Wednesdays it hosts Pork, a raunchy party for the younger set; you'll find men in uniforms, fetish performances and more mystery than most NYC bars offer. Most other nights, a strict (and very amusing) dress code is enforced: don leather or rubber, and don't even think about those sneakers or cologne.

Stonewall

53 Christopher St between Sixth and Seventh Aves (212-463-0950). Subway: 1, 9 to Christopher St–Sheridan Sq. 3pm–4am. Cash only.

This is a landmark bar, next door to the actual location of the 1969 gay rebellion against police harassment. If you don't already know it, ask the bartender to talk you through the story. Play some pool, chat up the other customers (they're nice), then check out the upstairs bar that frequently features go-go boys. Over the last couple of years, the bar has shed its ho-hum image to become a lively place to linger.

Chelsea

Barracuda

275 W 22nd St between Seventh and Eighth Aves (212-645-8613). Subway: C, E to 23rd St. 4pm–4am. Cash only.

This Chelsea bar—which actually feels more like the East Village—continues to draw hordes of boys. More comfy and friendly than its neighborhood competition, the space is split in two, with a traditional bar area up-front and a frequently redecorated lounge in back, plus a pool table, pinball machine and nightly DJs. Various drag-queen celebrities perform shows throughout the week. Boys on a budget, take note: There's never a cover.

g

223 W 19th St between Seventh and Eighth Aves (212-929-1085). Subway: 1, 9 to 18th St. 4pm–4am. Cash only.

This pleasant lounge is one of Chelsea's most popular destinations, especially for the well-scrubbed, fresh-faced set. Don't miss the trendy juice/power-drink bar. (Can an in-house pedicurist be far behind?) One word of warning: Late in the evening, the space is often filled to capacity, while outside, there's an intimidating line of unfortunates waiting to get in. Go early to stake your place at the bar.

The Spike

120 Eleventh Ave at 20th St (212-243-9688). Subway: C, E to 23rd St. 9pm–4am. Cash only.

The Spike was once the quintessential late-1970s Levi's/leather gay bar. Today, however, it's pretty soft around the edges, since the new clones are all hanging out at the Lure (*see above*). Still, the Spike has taken on a newer and more varied generation of cruisers and preclubbers. Weekend evenings retain an easygoing and fairly traditional leather flavor.

Midtown

The Townhouse

See page 272 for review.

Uptown

The Works

428 Columbus Ave between 80th and 81st Sts (212-799-7365). Subway: B, C to 81st St; 1, 9 to 79th St. 2pm–4am. Cash only.

The major hangout for young gay men on the Upper West Side draws a decidedly yuppity under-40 crowd. On Sunday evenings, there's a popular beer blast: Between 6pm and 1am, you pay $5 to drink all the brew you can manage. Part of the proceeds benefit the homebound AIDS patient meal-delivery service God's Love We Deliver.

Clubs

A number of New York clubs have gay nights; many of those we list are one-nighters rather than permanent venues. There's also a large number of fund-raising parties and other events worth looking out for. For more clubs, the majority of which are gay-friendly, plus more information about some of those listed below, *see chapter* **Clubs.**

Dance clubs

La Nueva Escuelita

301 W 39th St at Eighth Ave (212-631-0588). Subway: A, C, E to 42nd St–Port Authority. Thu–Sat 10pm–5am; Sun 7pm–5am. MC, V.

Extravagant drag floorshows are performed Thursday through Saturday at this Latin showpalace, with Sunday reserved for solo performers. The always-enthusiastic audience responds to their fave queens and go-go dancers with a nonstop barrage of tips, and there's also sweaty dancing to salsa, merengue and house. On Friday nights the crowd is predominantly lesbian.

Mother

432 W 14th St at Washington St (212-366-5680). Subway: A, C, E to 14th St; L to Eighth Ave. Tue–Sun 10:30pm–4:30am. Hours and prices vary with event.

This is one of the remaining vestiges of truly twisted New York nightlife. Queer (but not necessarily gay) revelers gather here every week for clever fetish, dress-up and performance-oriented theme nights, such as Tuesday's Queen Mother (which replaced the legendary Jackie 60 party); Saturday's Click & Drag, a cyber-fetish costume parade (you must conform to the dress code, or at least wear all black—

call for info); and Friday night's women's party, Clit Club (*see* **Dyke life,** *page 272*).

Saint at Large

To get on the mailing list, call 212-674-8541 or visit www.saintatlarge.com.

The now-mythical Saint, with its huge aluminum-domed interior, was one of the first venues where New York's gay men enjoyed dance-floor freedom. The club closed, but the clientele keeps its memory alive with a series of four huge circuit parties each year. These parties—the S/M-tinged Black Party, the White Party (those names refer not to skin color but to the mood of the events), Halloween and New Year's Eve—attract legions of muscle-bound and image-conscious gay men from around the U.S.

Twilo

530 W 27th St between Tenth and Eleventh Aves (212-268-1600). Subway: C, E to 23rd St. Sat 11pm, $30.

Crowds of gay men flock to this futuristic fete every Saturday night (and well into Sunday morning) to worship at the shrine of super-DJ Junior Vasquez. Cavernous and always bursting at the seams, with a sound system that keeps you shivering for days, this is a sure bet for boogying boys.

Roxy

515 W 18th St between Tenth and Eleventh Aves (212-645-5156). Subway: A, C, E to 14th St; L to Eighth Ave. Sat 11pm, $20.

Hordes of muscle boys and club crawlers pack Saturday nights at this venerable pleasure pit. The winning formula—the requisite go-go boys and DJs spinning happy house music—guarantees a satisfying megaclub experience.

Sex clubs

Despite the city's crackdown on adult businesses, a few bathhouses and sex clubs for men still exist. Apart from the barlike **J's Hangout** (*675 Hudson St at 14th St, 212-242-9292*)—which is less blatantly sexual and more of an after-hours desperation cruise—there is the **West Side Club** bathhouse (*27 W 20th Street between Fifth and Sixth Aves, 212-691-2700*) in Chelsea and its sister establishment, the **East Side Club** (*227 E 56th St at Second Ave, 212-753-2222*). For more current details, consult *HX* magazine's Getting Off section.

Entertainment

The royal treatment

Drag kings and queens rule New York nightlife with majestic flair

The art of female (and to a much lesser extent, male) illusion has been an integral part of New York's gay scene since the glory days of the Bowery burlesque halls. However, in 1927, when Mae West attempted to bring her gender-bending play *The Drag* to Broadway, the uproar was so great that she was forced to cancel production. That same year, the New York State legislature banned any play "depicting or dealing with the subject of sex degeneracy or sex perversion."

Fast-forward some 70-odd years, and it's obviously a brave new world—why, even Mayor Rudy Giuliani dolled up as a Monroe-esque character for a benefit dinner (granted, he was pretty scary looking). And as sure as every queen worships Barbra Streisand, audiences clamor to attend New York drag-themed theatrical productions such as *Hedwig and the Angry Inch* and *Dame Edna*, not to mention top-notch cabarets like Fez and Bar d'O (*see page 269*), where female impersonators reign supreme. Beyond that, two wildly popular restaurants—Lucky Cheng's and Lips—are "manned" by transgender waitstaffs (*see pages 271 and 272*) and any trendy club worth its salt has at least one colorful queen on the payroll.

Drag moved beyond nightclub status into the realm of mainstream novelty in 1993—the year RuPaul went from lip-synching Cher at New York City's Pyramid Club to working listeners nationwide with her catchy video and dance hit, "Supermodel." Suddenly, every talk show, TV sitcom and jet-set party jumped on the drag bandwagon, and New York's gender illusionists were happy to oblige. So far, none has achieved the glory of her majesty RuPaul, but a bevy of riotously entertaining queens rule the town as her ladies-in-waiting.

Topping the list of triumphants is the big, blond and bawdy Lady Bunny, the mastermind behind the annual outdoor drag festival Wigstock (*see chapter* **New York by Season**). In her court are the lovely Kevin Aviance—the new Grace Jones—who dazzles at clubs such as the Roxy (*see above*) with hypnotic dance songs like her hit "Din Da Da," and tireless queen of nightlife Girlina, who seems to host every

Restaurants and cafés

Few New York restaurants would bat an eye at a same-sex couple enjoying an intimate dinner. The neighborhoods mentioned above have hundreds of great eating places that are de facto gay restaurants, and many that are gay-owned and operated. Below are a few of the most obviously gay places in town. See chapter **Restaurants** for more dining options.

Big Cup

228 Eighth Ave between 21st and 22nd Sts (212-206-0059). Subway: C, E to 23rd St. Sun–Thu 7am–1am; Fri, Sat 8am–2am. Cash only.
A bustling coffee joint with a modest selection of sweets and sandwiches, Big Cup is a place where one can hang out for hours during the day and witness the unique Chelsea lifestyle, but at night the throng can be overwhelming. During summer months, the choked sidewalk outside is a popular hangout, especially for youngsters who aren't yet allowed into bars.

Eighteenth & Eighth

159 Eighth Ave at 18th St (212-242-5000). Subway: A, C, E to 14th St; L to Eighth Ave; 1, 9 to 18th St. Sun–Thu 9am–midnight; Fri, Sat 9am–12:30am. Average main course: $12. AmEx, MC, V.
Health-conscious, high-carbo food makes this small restaurant one of the great success stories of Chelsea. It's always full of cute, cruisey boys and girls, and the wait for a table is sometimes shockingly long.

Food Bar

149 Eighth Ave between 17th and 18th Sts (212-243-2020). Subway: A, C, E to 14th St; L to Eighth Ave; 1, 9 to 18th St. 11am–4pm, 5pm–midnight. Average main course: $13. AmEx, MC, V.
Don't let the tan, buffed and beautiful boys who parade in and out of this stylish eatery dissuade you from checking it out. While its patrons may seem to have come direct from the Roxy, and more than a smattering of women would certainly be a welcome sight, Food Bar serves excellent grub; its weekend brunch menu is particularly tasty. Just be sure to check your teeth before putting the make on any of your many muscular neighbors.

Lips

2 Bank St at Greenwich Ave (212-675-7710). Subway: 1, 2, 3, 9 to 14th St. Mon–Thu

Hair today Lady Bunny (right) and Polly Grip are stars of New York nightlife.

hot party in town. Jimmy James renders absolutely flawless vocal impersonations of Barbra, Eartha and Judy; Justin Bond and sidekick Kenny Mellman provide a mix of camp and pathos in their lounge act called *Kiki and Herb;* and cable-access star Brini Maxwell puts audiences in hysterics with her drag version of Martha Stewart.

Besides the big-name entertainers,there are scores of other drag participants. The annual Night of 1000 Gowns, which is run by the Imperial Court, is a surreal spectacle as hundreds of glamorous "gals" partake in the crowning of a new empress.

Likewise, the drag-king scene has its stars, such as Shaft lookalike Dréd—who strips to reveal her sexy body. Then there's the portly and political Murray Hill; and last but not least, the pompadoured Mo B. Dick, who was featured as a go-go club manager in John Waters's film *Pecker.*

The king scene peaked in the mid-'90s at Club Casanova, and has waned since the venue's demise. But various lesbian parties often feature kings, and each spring the lesbian House of Moshood throws a ball with several male-impersonation categories.

D-day (as in *Drag* day) in New York comes on Halloween. Everyone in town, from dedicated souls who spend their entire year perfecting a thematic costume to frat brothers who slap on a wig for the first time, struts the crowded streets—everyone, that is, except for the year-round drag queens, who view the spooky holiday as "amateur night."

Coffee talk Tall, dark espressos aren't the only reason to stop in Chelsea's Big Cup.

5:30pm–midnight; Fri, Sat 5:30pm–2am; Sun 11:30am–4pm, 5:30pm–midnight. Average main course: $16. AmEx, DC, MC, V.
The attraction at this drag-theme eatery is not the food, and it's certainly not the service; it's the novelty of having a dish named for a drag queen delivered to your table by a drag queen who at any moment will let loose in an old-fashioned lip-synch. It's about as mainstream as drag gets, but the loud show tunes and camp classics playing on video monitors will satisfy queens who relish the overblown.

Lucky Cheng's

24 First Ave between 1st and 2nd Sts (212-473-0516). Subway: F to Second Ave. Sun–Thu 6pm–midnight (drag shows at 8, 9:30 and 11pm); Fri, Sat 6pm–1am (shows at 7:30 and 11pm). Average main course: $15. AmEx, DC, Disc, MC, V.
This sprawling Chinese restaurant is such a phenomenon that tour buses are often seen parked outside. The gimmicks: a transgender waitstaff and drag shows in the basement lounge. Straight people will probably dig it more than seasoned queers. Ditto for La Nouvelle Justine (*212-673-8908*), the adjoining S/M-themed eatery.

The Townhouse

206 E 58th St at Third Ave (212-826-6241). Subway: N, R to Lexington Ave; 4, 5, 6 to 59th St. Mon–Thu noon–3:30pm, 5–11pm; Fri, Sat noon–3:30pm, 5pm–midnight; Sun noon–4pm, 5–11pm. Average main course: $20. AmEx, DC, MC, V.
If you're a reasonably attractive man under 40, you're likely to be greeted—or at least ogled—by one of the soused middle-aged regulars chatting up the bartenders at this "gentlemen's" restaurant. The bar is like a gay version of '21'—it's so discreet, there's even a secret exit for paranoid closet cases. But the gay men who come here for happy hour are a jovial bunch who would feel equally at home belting out show tunes at the Monster in the West Village. In the dining room beyond the bar, you'll spot couples in various stages of courtship; the flirty service makes this a good place for solo diners as well. The American menu is ambitious but not always successful. A tender roasted chicken with polenta fries and spinach is one of the best options. The famous dress code (no hats, workout clothes, sleeveless shirts, cut-offs or torn clothing of any type) is strictly enforced.

Gyms

See chapter **Sports & Fitness** for more fitness facilities, including YMCAs.

American Fitness Center

128 Eighth Ave at 16th St (212-627-0065). Subway: A, C, E to 14th St; L to Eighth Ave; 1, 9 to 18th St. Mon–Fri 6am–midnight; Sat, Sun 8am–9pm. $15 per day, weekly pass $55. AmEx, Disc, MC, V.
This fully equipped supergym is barbell-bunny heaven. It's vast and spotless, with 15,000 square feet (1,400 square meters) of free-weight space, acres of cardiovascular machines and countless aerobics classes.

David Barton

552 Sixth Ave between 15th and 16th Sts (212-727-0004). Subway: F to 14th St. Mon–Fri 6am–midnight; Sat 9am–9pm; Sun 10am–11pm. $15 per day, weekly pass $75. AmEx, MC, V.
Barton, husband of party promoter Susanne Bartsch, mixes fitness with fashion and nightlife at his gyms. Sleek locker rooms, artfully lit weight rooms and pumping music may make you feel as if you should have a cocktail instead of another set of reps. Besides free weights, Barton offers the three essential C's: classes, cardio equipment and cruising.

Dyke Life

The most exciting aspect of lesbian life in New York is that the women you'll see out and about in bars, clubs, restaurants, bookshops, community meetings and lesbian cabarets will truly defy all stereotypes. While lesbian culture is not as visible or as geographically concentrated as that of gay men, it is also far less segregated (with some exceptions), either by age or race, and is far more friendly and welcoming.

If you're into community activism, you'll find plenty to spark your interest (although the glory days of outrageous civil disobedience have passed): Just check in at the **Lesbian & Gay Community Services Center** (*see page 266*). The Center also offers a wide range of support groups and 12-step meetings for people in recovery. But if you're a dyke who's not into the activist or recovery scene and just wants to have some unbridled fun, New York City has plenty to offer.

The full-time East Village lesbian bar **Meow Mix** (*see below*) is a welcome gathering spot for alternadykes. And the unflappable promoter Caroline Clone continues to offer women large-scale dance parties including **Her/SheBar** and **Lovergirl**. The idea that lesbians want more for their money has also given old, standard bars in the West Village a reason to try a little harder. Meanwhile, lesbian discos are getting progressively larger and are no longer held only in funky, out-of-the-way dives. Unfortunately, the rising popularity of these clubs doesn't guarantee they'll be around for long, so check the lesbian bar guide in *HX* or *Time Out New York* for the most current information. Some women's bars and clubs strive for an all-women environment—better to check ahead if you're planning on bringing your male friends.

Outside Manhattan, Park Slope in Brooklyn remains a sort of lesbian residential hub, and includes the **Lesbian Herstory Archive** and the **Audre Lorde Project** (*see page 266*). The neighborhood is lovely, and there is an abundance of relaxed coffeehouses and cafés.

If you're staying in Brooklyn and plan to travel into Manhattan to take advantage of dyke nightlife, take a taxi back. Though stories of how dangerous New York is at night are greatly exaggerated, it's still not a good idea to ride the subway alone late at night. (*See chapter* **Directory, Safety** *or* **NYC Gay & Lesbian Anti-Violence Project,** *page 266*.)

Accommodations

See **Colonial House Inn,** page 267, and **Incentra Village House,** page 268.

Markle Residence for Women

123 W 13th St between Sixth and Seventh Aves (212-242-2400). Subway: F, 1, 2, 3, 9 to 14th St; L to Sixth Ave. $133–$225 per week, including two meals (one-month minimum). MC, V.

Offering women-only Salvation Army accommodations in a pleasant Greenwich Village location, the Markle has clean, comfortable rooms, all of which have telephones and private bathrooms.

Bars and lounges

See **Beige** and **Wonder Bar,** page 268.

Crazy Nanny's

21 Seventh Ave South at Leroy St (212-366-6312). Subway: 1, 9 to Christopher St–Sheridan Sq. 4pm–4am. AmEx, MC.

An old faithful, Nanny's is a loud neon-lit bar and disco with TV screens and a pool table downstairs; there's a DJ and a big-screen TV upstairs. Nanny's has also started staging theme nights; depending on who is DJing, the crowd might be predominantly black women or a mixed, trendy bunch of fags and dykes. It's a good place to hang out and have a frosty cold one, especially after a softball game on a weekend afternoon. Daily happy hour with two-for-one drinks is from 4 to 7pm.

Henrietta Hudson

438 Hudson St at Morton St (212-924-3347). Subway: 1, 9 to Christopher St–Sheridan Sq. Mon–Fri 4pm–4am; Sat, Sun 3pm–4am. AmEx, Disc, MC, V.

This is a watering hole for middle-class suburban girls with lots of hair. Women love it for cruising; it's laid out so you can eye everyone at once, then make your choice and make a move.

Julie's

204 E 58th St between Second and Third Aves (212-688-1294). Subway: N, R to Lexington Ave; 4, 5, 6 to 59th St. 5pm–4am. Cash only.

Julie's is an incredibly discreet, elegant bar for mature, professional, often-closeted women in search of the same. It stays open as late as 4am if business is good. Hors d'oeuvres are served from 5 to 8pm.

Meow Mix

269 Houston St at Suffolk St (212-254-0688). Subway: F to Second Ave. Mon 5pm–4am; Tue–Fri, Sun 8pm–4am; Sat 4pm–4am. Cash only.

The hippest lesbian establishment in Manhattan, Brooke Webster's alternative dyke bar has been named-dropped by everyone from Ellen DeGeneres to Fran Drescher. But it's also a haven for individuals of all stripes. The place appeals to youngish,

Howdy time Cowgirl Hall of Fame is a lesbian fave for eats and greets.

Cat power Hip, young dykes crowd into Meow Mix for drinks, live music and performances.

edgy women and their male friends. There's a laid-back vibe even when the space plays host to raucous parties, go-go dancers, live bands (like Sexpod and the Lunachicks), readings and performances. Be on the lookout for slumming celebs. (*See chapter* **Music: Popular music.**)

Clubs

Great club nights are the holy grail of New York City—something that's fabulous one week sucks or is closed down the next, and so the search continues. These are the current lesbian hot spots, but don't panic if they're not around in a few months' time—there are bound to be new nights and venues blossoming in their place. Check the lesbian listings in *HX* or *Time Out New York* for current info.

Clit Club

Mother (see page 269 for listings). Fri 10pm–5am.
The longest-running lesbian night (founded in 1990) is still going strong, with new weekly midnight performances ranging from sexy stripteases to obscure performance art. Quality DJs and bodacious go-go girls are still standard here. Renovations have transformed this once-dark dive into a larger, more user-friendly space. The only males who come by are the Mother regulars: gays and cross-dressers who hang out here other nights of the week. Similarly, dykes are welcome at Mother any night.

Lovergirl

Bar 85, 504 W 16th St between Tenth and Eleventh Aves (212-631-1000). Subway: A, C, E to 14th St; L to Eighth Ave. Sat 10pm–4:30am.
This popular women's party attracts a multiracial crowd that enthusiastically shakes its groove thang to the funky beat. Inspiring the revelers is an array of sexy go-go gals sporting the latest in fashionable g-strings.

Restaurants and cafés

Cowgirl Hall of Fame

519 Hudson St at 10th St (212-633-1133). Subway: 1, 9 to Christopher St–Sheridan Sq. Mon–Fri 5–11pm; Sat, Sun 11am–4pm, 5–11pm. Bar Sun–Thu 5pm–midnight; Fri, Sat 5pm–2am. Average main course: $11. AmEx, MC, V.
In name and spirit, Cowgirl Hall of Fame is a great girl place, though everyone will enjoy it. With its Tex-Mex and comfort food, country music jukebox and cowgirl memorabilia–covered walls, the place is pure country kitsch. Women with kids come again and again because their high-chair and entertainment needs are ably met by the sympathetic single-parent owner, Sherri. The preclub scene revs up on frozen margaritas at the steer horn–decorated bar; in the warmer months, the sidewalk tables are great for people-watching.

Rubyfruit

531 Hudson St between Washington and Charles Sts (212-929-3343). Subway: 1, 9 to Christopher St–Sheridan Sq. Mon–Fri 3pm–2am; Sat 11:30am–4am; Sun 11:30am–2am. Average main course: $20. Average drink: $5. AmEx, DC, JCB, MC, V.
A warm and energetic band of women patronizes Rubyfruit, the only dedicated lesbian bar and restaurant in town. Though the food is solidly good, it's not the main selling point. The congenial customers and a varied program of cabaret and music make this a good place for fun-loving old-school dykes.

Kids' Stuff

Sure, New York City is the ultimate adult playground, but it's also a gigantic amusement park for children

New York is a noisy, nonstop, loudmouthed, horn-honking, in-your-face city where anything goes and everything seems possible—which could be why so many kids think it was made for them. It's the perfect environment for short attention spans and experience-hungry spirits, and possibly the only city in the world where a child can wake up in the morning and make breakfast for animals in a zoo kitchen, practice an obscure Indian dance in the afternoon and go to a pajama-party storytime before bed. Kids don't get bored in New York. They get overscheduled.

Given the ultracompetitive nature of the city, it's not surprising that educational value is often the focus of play. From September through May, museums and other institutions offer lots of hands-on learning. In summer, the emphasis shifts to unmitigated fun, though there's still plenty to inspire: free outdoor theater in parks and parking lots, Lincoln Center's wonderful Out-of-Doors festival, Central Park's SummerStage and much more.

There are also the unscheduled pleasures of the street—especially when you venture farther afield than Disneyfied midtown. If you let them, kids will have a ball scaling industrial loading bays, ogling street performers, swinging around subway poles or just wandering around and taking it all in. Especially during the warm months, street life feeds all of a child's senses and provides endless stories to take home.

The local public libraries and bookstores hold excellent programs for children. Pick up a copy of *Events for Children* from any branch of the New York Public Library for extensive listings of free storytellings, puppet shows, films and workshops in libraries. The Donnell Library, home of the Central Children's Room, is the best place for events; it also houses the original Winnie the Pooh and other toys that belonged to Christopher Robin (*see chapter* **Museums**). All Barnes & Noble and Borders megastores have regular free story-reading hours and other activities; pick up a calendar in any branch (*see chapter* **Books &**

Entertainment

The great pumpkin Learn how gardens grow at the Brooklyn Botanic Garden.

Poetry). You might also invest in a copy of Alfred Gingold and Helen Rogan's slim but invaluable paperback, *The Ultra Cool Parents Guide to All of New York,* and their equally slim but invaluable *New York's 50 Best Museums for Cool Parents and Their Kids* (City & Co.), which also includes museums' web addresses. For a guide to restaurants that welcome children, check out Sam Freund and Elizabeth Carpenter's *Kids Eat New York* (Little Bookroom). Sam was nine and very into entertainment value when he compiled this book with his mom.

Although there's no shortage of events and activities designed specifically for kids, don't pass by some of the cutting-edge stuff for adults; many zany Off-Broadway shows are sure hits with children, as are most new-media art shows.

▶ For more ideas on where to take the kids, check out chapters **Uptown, Central Park, New York by Season, Sports & Fitness** and **Trips Out of Town.**

Amusement parks

Astroland

1000 Surf Ave at W 8th St, Coney Island, Brooklyn (718-372-0275). Subway: B, D, F, N to Coney Island–Stillwell Ave. Winter, phone for details; summer noon–midnight (weather permitting). $1.75 single kiddie rides. Cash only.

Coney Island's amusement park is rather run-down and tacky (to some), but a delight to children nonetheless. In summer, ride the frightening Cyclone roller coaster (younger kids will prefer the Tilt-a-Whirl), watch a snake charmer, get sticky cotton-candy fingers, bite into a Nathan's Famous hot dog and, if you can navigate the boom boxes, enjoy the sun and sand.

Arts festivals

Central Park SummerStage

See chapter **New York by Season, Summer.**

International Festival of Puppet Theater

212-439-7529, ext 2000. Sept 2002.

This biennial festival of puppet theater from several continents is produced by the Jim Henson Foundation. Although its central component is cutting-edge productions for adults, children will also enjoy the rich blend of offerings. Watch for other puppet activity piggybacking on the festival.

New York International Fringe Festival

Various venues in the East Village and Lower East Side. 212-420-8888, call 888-FRINGE-NYC for schedule. Three weeks in August. $11, children $7.

Fringe Jr, the kids' component of this downtown festival, grows bigger every year, paralleling the growing number of children living in the area. There's now a slew of shows just for children, and several on the adult program that are recommended for older children. Though some of the productions are a bit ragged around the edges, they're imaginative and, on the whole, intelligent. Fort Fringe Jr is a kind of clubhouse at the festival's main venue, where youngsters can play, create and participate in workshops. Most exciting of all to many kids is Fringe Al Fresco, the festival's free outdoor and store-window performance and installation component (watch out for human chess games and roving robots). Every year, Fringe Al Fresco kicks off with a block-long street-theater performance.

Niño Nada Festival

Various Lower East Side locations (212-269-4849). Late Aug–early Oct.

The downtown Pure Pop Theater Festival, scheduled to overlap with the New York International Fringe Festival, was launched in 1999 by the hip Lower East Side performance space Todo con Nada. Its Niño Nada children's festival offers family entertainment with a rock & roll sensibility—Niñapalooza.

Lincoln Center Out-of-Doors

Lincoln Center Plaza, Broadway at 65th St (212-875-5108). Subway: 1, 9 to 66th St–Lincoln Ctr. August. Free.

New Yorkers who attend this open-air festival know that they're as likely to find a dance company doing hip-hop moves as they are to catch a sitar concert. Kids' performances and participatory days are scheduled throughout the festival. The annual highlights are the Iced Tea Dance (a chance for children to try ballroom dancing with help from the pros); Homemade Instrument Day, when you can see wonderfully weird electronic creations and make and play your own instrument; and Play Day, when subway musicians emerge into the light of day and giant puppets perform. Get that sunblock ready.

New York International Children's Film Festival

For schedule and film information or to buy tickets, call 212-349-0330 or go to www.gkids.com. February.

This festival has experienced tremendous growth since it started in 1998, and it now screens an exciting mix of shorts and features (many of them premieres) from indie filmmakers around the world. A retrospective rounds out the event. Kids determine the festival winners by filling in ballots after each short-film program; these programs also include Q&A sessions with the filmmakers. In 2000,

Look at me! Older children show off their acting skills as part of the TADA! Youth Ensemble.

NYICFF was a two-weekend affair, with additional winter school-break screenings later; there's a good chance the festival will be longer in 2001. Programs are age-specific, from ages two to teen.

Circuses

Check the local papers for details of when the artsy, animal-free, French-Canadian **Cirque du Soleil** is in town (usually April). The music, costumes and staging are pure fantasy, though younger children might be frightened by the stylish clowns. Tickets are snapped up fast. If you're hankering for something more New York, look out for free outdoor summer performances by Brooklyn's raucous, alternative **Circus Amok.**

Big Apple Circus

Damrosch Park, Lincoln Center (212-268-2500, tickets from Centercharge 212-721-6500, Ticketmaster 212-307-4100). Subway: 1, 9 to 66th St–Lincoln Ctr. Prices vary. AmEx, MC, V.

New York's own traveling circus was founded 13 years ago as a traditional, one-act-at-a-time alternative to the Ringling Bros.' three-rings-at-once extravaganza. Big Apple prides itself on being a true family affair, with acts that feature the founder's two children and his equestrian wife. Clown Bello Noch supplies the panache that's recently been missing from the international guest-artist acts. The circus has a regular winter season (Oct–Jan) in Damrosch Park and, budget permitting, travels to other city parks in early spring.

Ringling Bros. and Barnum & Bailey Circus

Madison Square Garden, Seventh Ave at 32nd St (212-465-6741; www.ringling.com). Subway: A, C, E, 1, 2, 3, 9 to 34th St–Penn Station. April. $10.50–$42.75. AmEx, DC, Disc, MC, V.

The original (and most famous) American circus has three rings, lots of glitz and plenty to keep kids glued to their seats. Barnum's famous sideshow was revived in 1998. It's extremely popular, so reserve seats well in advance.

UniverSoul Big Top Circus

Venue and performance schedule changes year to year (800-316-7439 or Ticketmaster 212-307-7171). $13–$25. AmEx, DC, Disc, MC, V.

This African-American circus has all the requisite clowns, animal acts and hoopla, with a plus: instead of the usual circus music, you get hip-hop, R&B and salsa. Owned and operated by the man who promoted the Commodores, UniverSoul is the result of a two-year worldwide search for black circus performers.

Museums and exhibitions

Even museums that are not entirely devoted to children provide a wealth of activity. For example, kids will love exploring the revamped dinosaur halls and stunning new **Rose Center for Earth and Space** (which includes the planetarium) at the **American Museum of Natural History.** Kids should also visit the **Liberty Science Center** (don't miss the Touch Tunnel), the **New York Transit Museum** and the ***Intrepid* Sea-Air-Space Museum,** which has a collection of military paraphernalia housed on an aircraft carrier. All of the major art museums offer weekly family tours and/or workshops (with the exception of the **Guggenheim,** which has occasional exhibit-related events for children); tours at the **Brooklyn Museum of Art** and **Metropolitan Museum** include sketching in the galleries; the Metropolitan and **MoMA** also have short-film programs that are thematically related to that week's gallery exploration. Be sure to ask for free printed family guides at each art museum you visit.

Brooklyn Children's Museum

145 Brooklyn Ave at St. Mark's Ave, Brooklyn (718-735-4400). Subway: 3 to Kingston Ave. Weekends only, a free shuttle bus runs hourly from the Brooklyn Museum of Art and the Grand Army Plaza subway station. Winter Wed–Fri 2–5pm; Sat, Sun 10am–5pm. Summer Mon, Wed, Fri–Sun 10am–5pm. Winter and spring school vacations 10am–5pm. Suggested donation $4. Cash only.

Founded in 1899 and redesigned in 1996, BCM was the world's first museum designed specifically for children. Its focus today is on opening kids' eyes to world cultures—especially those of the city's immigrant population—through a mix of hands-on exhibits and items from its permanent collection. You reach the exhibits via a walkway through which a neon-lit stream of water also passes; shy kids can acclimate themselves gradually to the museum by operating water wheels and damming the stream with stones. In the music studio, children play instruments from around the globe, as well as synthesizers, and dance on the keys of a walk-on piano. A new gallery houses exhibitions from museums around the country. There are special workshops daily and weekly performances (the museum's summertime rooftop-performance series is on Fridays at 6pm).

Children's Museum of the Arts

182 Lafayette St between Broome and Grand Sts (212-274-0986). Subway: 6 to Spring St. Wed–Sun noon–5pm. $5, Wed 5–7pm pay what you wish. AmEx, MC, V.

The under-seven crowd loves the Children's Museum of the Arts. It has a floor-to-ceiling chalkboard, art computers and vast stores of art supplies—perfect for young travelers pining for their crayons and, if you happen to be gallery-hopping in Soho, a great place to stop by with little ones. Visual- and performing-arts workshops led by local artists are scheduled regularly, many in conjunction with the museum's exhibitions of children's art from other nations. Children must be accompanied by adults.

▸ For general listing information, see **Pushing all the right buttons,** page 280, and the **Museums** chapter.

Children's Museum of Manhattan

212 W 83rd St between Broadway and Amsterdam Ave (212-721-1234). Subway: 1, 9 to 86th St. Tue–Sun 10am–5pm. $5. AmEx, Disc, MC, V.

The Children's Museum of Manhattan promotes literacy of every kind through its dynamic and playful hands-on exhibits. Through May 2001, "Body Odyssey" lets kids discover (theoretically, at least) what's going on inside them by allowing children to crawl through models of blood vessels and to fling "platelets" at each other. The late, great Charles Schulz's Peanuts gang is immortalized in the hands-on "Good Grief!" exhibition. Bigger kids can head to the state-of-the-art media lab, where they team up to make their own TV shows: Kids operate the cameras, edit tape and play at being talk-show hosts or studio-audience members. Workshops are scheduled for weekends and during school vacations.

Lefferts Homestead Children's Museum

Prospect Park, Flatbush Ave near Empire Blvd, Brooklyn (718-965-6505). Subway: D to Prospect Park. Spring–fall, call for hours. Free.

For a change of pace and an entirely different sense of New York, check out Lefferts Homestead, a restored 17th-century farmhouse that has housed Dutch settlers, African-Americans and Lenape Indians over the years. Not far from Prospect Park zoo and the park's restored carousel, Lefferts gives kids a hands-on neighborhood history through its exhibit, "Who Lived Here?" Visitors play with cooking tools in a Dutch kitchen, hunt for barnyard implements in a hay-strewn model barn, play with toys that young residents might have owned and try out the beds—including a Lenape bed made of saplings, straw and animal skin. On summer weekends, there's storytelling under a tree, as well as hoop games and gardening.

Lower East Side Tenement Museum

Children's tours Sat, Sun noon, 1, 2, 3pm. $8, children $6. See chapter **Museums** *for listings.*

Housed in an old tenement building that was home to successive families of new immigrants, this museum offers a weekly interactive children's tour of the Sephardic Confino family's former home. The tour is led by 13-year-old Victoria Confino (actually, a staff member), who teaches visitors about New York in the early 1900s by dancing the fox-trot, playing games with them, and forever answering the question, "Where does everyone sleep?" Recommended for ages 7 to 14.

New York Hall of Science

See chapter **Museums, Arts and culture** for listings.

Panorama of New York City

Queens Museum of Art, Flushing Meadows–Corona Park, Queens (718-592-9700). Subway: 7 to Willets Pt–Shea Stadium. Wed–Fri 10am–5pm; Sat, Sun noon–5pm. $4, students and seniors $2, children free.

Swingers club Kids have a high time getting frisky at Central Park playgrounds.

On the site of two World's Fairs, near the archaic-looking, once-modern Unisphere, is an unremarkable museum that houses an amazing architectural-scale model of the city. The museum's main attraction has thousands of tiny buildings, bridges and highways, and little lights that glow when the model skyline darkens. The museum holds occasional panorama-related workshops during the summer months. (*See chapter* **Museums.**)

Socrates Sculpture Park

Broadway at Vernon Blvd, Long Island City, Queens (718-956-1819). Subway: N to Broadway. 10am–sunset. Free.

Unlike most art exhibitions, this outdoor, city-owned spread of large-scale contemporary sculpture is utterly devoid of snarling guards and "don't touch" signs. Children can climb on, run through and sit astride works that seem to have been plopped haphazardly on the grounds of this four-acre park. *See chapter* **The Outer Boroughs.**

Sony Wonder Technology Lab

See **Pushing all the right buttons,** page 280.

Music

Carnegie Hall Family Concerts

Carnegie Hall, 154 W 57th St at Seventh Ave (212-903-9600). Subway: B, D, E to Seventh Ave; B, Q to 57th St; N, R, to 57th St. $5. Monthly, fall to spring.

Even kids who profess to hate classical music are usually impressed by a visit to Carnegie Hall (one youngster wrote a postconcert thank-you letter to "Dear Mr. Hall"), and its thematic Family Concert series, featuring world-class performers, works hard to appeal to youngsters. Preconcert activities include a workshop and storytelling. Ages 6 and up.

Growing Up with Opera

John Jay Theater, 899 Tenth Ave at 59th St (212-769-7008). Subway: A, C, B, D, 1, 9 to 59th St–Columbus Circle. $15–$25. AmEx, MC, V.

Short operas, some written specially for young audiences, are sung in English by the Metropolitan Opera Guild, whose members meet kids after the performance; only three or four concerts are held from fall through spring. The guild has recently added a participatory series for preschoolers (tickets $10), staged in smaller theaters around the city.

Jazz for Young People

Alice Tully Hall, Lincoln Center, 65th St at Columbus Ave (212-875-5599, tickets 212-721-6500). Subway: 1, 9 to 66th St–Lincoln Ctr. $10–$15. AmEx, MC, V.

These participatory concerts, led by trumpeter and jazz ambassador Wynton Marsalis and modeled on the Young People's Concerts (*see below*), help children figure out answers to such questions as "What is jazz?"

Little Orchestra Society

Florence Gould Hall, 55 E 59th St between Madison and Park Aves (212-971-9500). Subway: N, R to Lexington Ave; 4, 5, 6 to 59th St. $32. AmEx, MC, V.

"Lolli-Pops" presents participatory orchestral concerts for children ages three to five, combining classical music with dance, puppetry, theater and mime. A spectacular *Amahl and the Night Visitors* (with live sheep) is presented every Christmas. "Happy Concerts" for ages five and up are staged at Avery Fisher Hall.

New York Philharmonic Young People's Concerts

Avery Fisher Hall, Lincoln Center, 65th St at Columbus Ave (212-875-5656). Subway: 1, 9 to 66th St–Lincoln Ctr. $6–$16. AmEx, MC, V.

Musicians address the audience directly during these legendary educational concerts, made popular by the late Leonard Bernstein. Each concert is preceded by an hour-long "Children's Promenade," during which kids meet orchestra members and try out their instruments.

Outdoor activities

Brooklyn Botanic Garden

See chapter **The Outer Boroughs** *for listings.*

The garden's highlight is the 13,000-square-foot (1,200-square-meter) Discovery Garden, where children can play at being botanists, make toys out of natural materials, weave a wall and get their hands dirty.

New York Botanical Garden

See chapter **Outer Boroughs, Bronx** *for listings.*

The immense Children's Adventure Garden, opened in spring 1998, is a whimsical (think frog-shaped fountains) "museum of the natural world" with interactive "galleries," both indoors and out. Children also run under Munchy, a giant topiary; poke around in a touch tank; and plant, weed, water and harvest in the Family Garden. If it's too cold to wander outside, ask for a kid's guide and audio tour to the Enid A. Haupt Conservatory (admission $3.50), the spectacular glass house where you can see papyrus, cocoa and bananas grow all year long.

Nelson Rockefeller Park

Hudson River at Chambers St (212-267-9700). Subway: A, C, 1, 2, 3, 9 to Chambers St. 10am–sunset. Free.

River breezes keep this park several degrees cooler than the rest of the city—a big plus in the summer. There's plenty for kids to do here besides watch the boats. (Saturday's a good day for ocean liners.) They can play on Tom Otterness's quirky sculptures in the picnic area (near the Chambers Street entrance), enjoy one of New York's best playgrounds and participate in art, sports or street-game activities (call for times and locations). Other activities, such as kite-flying and fishing, are planned throughout the summer. Two blocks north on Pier 25, also known as the Children's Pier, are a miniature-golf course, a sand-and-sprinkler area for overheated tots and a snack shack; it's easy to imagine being on a beach vacation here. The River Project (*212-941-5901*) on Pier 26 admits children on weekends; they can examine small creatures under microscopes and feed the aquarium fish.

Riverbank State Park

Riverside Drive at 145th St (212-694-3600). Subway: 1, 9 to 145th St. Outdoor pool and carousel, spring through fall only. Call for hours and prices.

Pushing all the right buttons

These interactive museums encourage kids to look—and touch

Like *family-friendly* and *edutainment,* the word *interactive* has been so overused in the promotion of things kid-related that it's become almost meaningless. There's even a noun version, *interactives,* and New York has plenty of them, all promising to educate and entertain a wired generation of youngsters who prefer to learn by doing. Still, while most interactives are entertaining, many struggle to be more than just point-and-click exercises.

New York's best-designed, most eye-opening interactive spots are environments that invite children to experiment, create and experience themselves and the world in brand-new ways. A couple are off the beaten path, but they're well worth the trek. **The Brooklyn** and **Manhattan Children's Museums** (see *Museums*) also offer some fairly stimulating interactive play.

Sony Wonder Technology Lab

Sony Plaza, 550 Madison Ave between 55th and 56th Sts (212-833-8100). Subway: E, F to Fifth Ave; 6 to 51st St. Tue, Wed, Fri, Sat 10am–6pm; Thu 10am–8pm; Sun noon–6pm. Free.

This three-story digital wonderland really *is* a lab: Sony Wonder lets visitors (or "media trainees") experiment with state-of-the art communication technology as they design their own video games, assist in endoscopic surgery, crisis-manage an earthquake, edit a TV show, operate robots and play sound engineer in the digital-recording studio, where they can remix Celine Dion's hit song "Power of Love." In the High Definition Interactive Theater, the audience directs the action in a video adventure.

The lab manages to put visitors—not technology—at the center of the experience: You enter through a log-in station where you record your name, voice and image on a magnetic card; when you swipe the card at each of the six workstations, your image appears on a monitor and a voice welcomes you. Kids in the eight-and-up age range will think this place is mad cool, and will probably get the most out of it. But it's also a great playground for younger children who like touching things and seeing their faces on giant monitors.

To avoid long waits, get here soon after noon on weekdays (school and camp groups have priority in the mornings; Thursdays are your best bet) and early on weekends (except in summer, when Saturdays and Sundays are relatively traffic-free).

New York Hall of Science

See chapter **Museums, Arts and culture** *for listings.*

Located in the mysterious Space Pavilion of the 1964 World's Fair and flanked by

Entertainment

Who'd have thought that a new park built on top of a sewage-treatment plant could be so good? Riverbank's 26 waterfront acres offer two great playgrounds, nice picnic spots, a carousel designed by children and a wading pool, plus an Olympic-size outdoor pool (with a four-foot-deep shallow end), winter ice skating and year-round in-line skating.

Central Park

Manhattanites don't have gardens; they have parks. The most popular (and populous) is Central Park, where there are plenty of special places and programs designed just for children. **Arts in the Park** (*212-988-9093*) organizes an extensive summer program of children's arts events in several parks throughout the city. Don't miss the beautiful antique carousel ($1 a ride) and the lively **Heckscher playground** (just one of 20), which has handball courts, horseshoe pitches, several softball diamonds, a puppet theater, a wading pool and a crèche (*see* **Uptown, Central Park**).

Charles A. Dana Discovery Center

See chapter **Uptown** *for listings.*

Take the kids fishing at the restored and stocked Harlem Meer; the season runs from April through October. Poles and bait are supplied (with a parent's ID) to children ages five-and-up until 90 minutes before closing; staff is available to help bait hooks. Other activities include bird-watching and workshops such as kite-making or sun-printing (1–3pm most weekends).

Conservatory Water

Central Park at 74th St near Fifth Ave. Subway: 6 to 77th St. Jul–Aug Sun–Fri 11am–7pm; Sat 2–7pm (weather permitting).

outdated models of rocket ships, the Hall of Science offers curious minds some terrific adventures. The most popular of its interactive exhibits is the immense outdoor Science Playground, which is modeled after an even bigger one in Bombay. Here, youngsters engage in whole-body science exploration, discovering principles of balance, gravity, energy and so on as they play on a giant seesaw and turn a huge Archimedes screw to push water uphill. The playground is open late spring through fall for ages six and up, but there's plenty for younger children to explore indoors, including a giant bubble machine. In the new Marvelous Molecules exhibit, kids find out what they're made of by testing the DNA in their hair or mapping their bodies' warmest spots with an infrared camera. In the process, they learn that they're really no different from cockroaches or broccoli. Little ones who aren't old enough to understand can make space stations in the molecule-building area.

A spectacular scale-model diorama of New York City is located in the nearby Queens Museum of Art (*see page 278 and photo, page 86*). It's a great attraction for the child who can still be awed by something that can't be touched.

American Museum of the Moving Image

See chapter **Museums, Arts and culture** *for listings.*

The American Museum of the Moving Image doesn't do much to publicize "Behind the Screen," its main attraction. So kids can usually put themselves in the starring role here without too much competition. In the first section of the exhibition, they'll see a history of the technological wizardry behind Hollywood's products. By looking at early stop-motion photography and working zoetropes (early animation toys that create the illusion of movement), kids will learn that moving images don't actually move; they'll also get a chance to test for themselves the phenomenon known as "persistence of vision" by making a flip-book of computerized-photo self-portraits and by creating animated shorts at a digital-animation stand. Kids can also dub sound at a sound-editing workstation, put their voice in Groucho's mouth with an automated dialogue replacement system or see themselves imaged in various bizarre landscapes through chroma-key technology (otherwise known as blue screen).

An even bigger hit with young AMMI visitors is "Computer Space," a hands-on exhibition of video-arcade games ranging from the relatively ancient PacMan and Pong to the very latest. And don't forget to check out Tut's Fever Movie Palace, designed by New York artist Red Grooms to emulate the neo-Egyptian movie houses popular in the 1930s. With any luck, you may catch one of the vintage films screened here daily.

Stuart Little Pond, named after E.B. White's storybook mouse of the same name, is the city's model-yacht racing mecca. When the boatmaster is around, rent one of the remote-controlled vessels ($10/hour), but be warned—it's not as speedy as Nintendo. Nearby, a large bronze statue of Alice in Wonderland provides excellent climbing opportunities

Henry Luce Nature Observatory

See chapter **Uptown** *for listings.*

This is the newest children's hot spot in Central Park, with telescopes, microscopes and simple hands-on exhibits that teach about the plants and animals living (or hiding) in the surrounding area. Workshops are held on weekend afternoons, spring through fall (1–3pm). Kids (with a parent's ID) can borrow a discovery kit—a backpack containing binoculars, a bird-watching guide and various cool tools.

North Meadow Recreation Center

Central Park at 79th St (212-348-4867). Subway: A, C, B to 81st St. Mon–Fri 9am–7pm; Sat, Sun 10am–6pm. Free.

Borrow (with ID) a fun-in-the-park kit containing a Frisbee, hula hoop, Wiffle ball and bat, jump rope, kickball and other diversions.

Stories at the Hans Christian Andersen Statue

Central Park at Conservatory Water (212-929-6871, 212-340-0906). Subway: 6 to 77th St. Jun–Sept Sat 11am; July Wed 11am. Free.

Children have gathered for generations at the foot of the Hans Christian Andersen statue for Saturday stories read by master tale-tellers from all over America—a real New York tradition, not to be missed. On Wednesdays, children's librarians read their favorite stories.

NY Skateout

Classes meet at Central Park entrance at Fifth Ave at 72nd St (212-486-1919; www.nyskate.com). Subway: 6 to 68th St–Hunter College. Skate lessons Mar–Nov Sat, Sun 9am. Dec–Feb Sat, Sun 10am. $25 for a two-hour class. Reservations are essential.

Classes are offered for beginners and more advanced skaters (ages five and up). Once they get the hang of it, children skate in supervised groups around the park's loop road. NY Skateout is dedicated to skating safety: Don't even think of showing up without all the gear. Call for information on equipment rental.

Wildman's Edible Park Tours

Various city parks, including Central and Prospect Parks. Call for meeting place, time and instructions (718-291-6925). Mar–Nov. $10, children $5. Cash only.

Irrepressible urban forager and naturalist "Wildman" Steve Brill was once arrested for munching Central Park's dandelions; now his eat-as-you-go foraging tours are sanctioned by the parks commissioner. His tours aren't meant specifically for kids, but youngsters delight in his joke-laden banter; besides, he pays them special attention, and lets them shake fruit off branches and dig for roots with big shovels.

Play spaces

For older kids itching to burn some energy, try Chelsea Piers, which has a gymnasium, roller rink and half-pipe for in-line skating and skateboarding (*see chapter* **Sports & Fitness**).

Playspace

2473 Broadway at 92nd St (212-769-2300). Subway: 1, 2, 3, 9 to 96th St. Mon–Sat 9:30am–6pm; Sun 10am–6pm. $6.50. Cash only.

In this play space with huge plate-glass windows, children ages six and under build in the immense sandbox, ride on toy trucks, dress up and climb on the jungle gym. This is not a drop-off center, but the play is supervised, and parents can relax—read, even—in a small café to the side. There are also drop-in games, art classes and storytimes. Admission is good for the entire day: You can leave and come back.

Rain or Shine

209 E 29th St between Second and Third Aves (212-532-4420). Subway: 6 to 28th St. Call for hours; open play and open gym are generally daily during school vacations. Play $6.95 per two-hour session; gym and play $15 per two-hour session. Reservations required.

This large, airy place is devoted to imaginative play for kids ages six months to six years; they'll find a dress-up area, a giant playhouse, ride-on toys and an art room, as well as peers looking for playmates. Open hours in the gym, which has a rock-climbing wall, are for children ages 9 months to 12 years.

Theater

Several small theaters and repertory companies offer weekend-matinee family performances. Most of these are musical productions of questionable value. Check magazine or newspaper listings for details (*see chapter* **Directory**). The following are the best of New York's family theaters and series.

Family Matters

Dance Theater Workshop, 219 W 19th St between Seventh and Eighth Aves (212-924-0077). Subway: C, E to 23rd St; 1, 9 to 18th St. $12, children $8. AmEx, MC, V.

Curated by a pair of choreographer-parents for ages 6 and up, Family Matters is designed to kick-start children's imaginations and get them doing their own thing. The series blends diverse forms of dance, music, theater and art in a thematic, variety-show format, and features work by experimental artists who don't usually perform for kids but whose sensibilities and style are quirky, fun or wild enough to entertain young audiences.

Hop to it Have natural fun in the New York Botanical Garden's Adventure Garden.

Joyce Theater

175 Eighth Ave at 19th St (212-242-0800). Subway: A, C, E to 23rd St. Late Mar–late Apr, first two weeks in August, two weeks in December. $35 for evening performances; $25, children $15 for weekend matinee. AmEx, DC, Disc, MC, V.

This is the home of the Feld Ballet, which was founded some 25 years ago by Eliot Feld (you might remember him as Baby John in *West Side Story*). Feld has auditioned extensively in the New York City elementary-school system and has also provided free training to thousands of kids with raw talent. The best of these students now make up his Ballet Tech company, and they lend a decidedly New York attitude to Feld's edgy, athletic ballet style. The Kids Dance matinees, performed by teen students, are designed with young audiences in mind; don't miss, especially, the Feld's NoTCRACKER season in December, a nutty alternative to the traditional tutued thing.

Los Kabayitos Children's Theater

CSV Cultural Center, 107 Suffolk St between Delancey and Rivington Sts (212-260-4080, ext 14). Subway: F to Delancey St; J, M, Z to Essex St. $10, children $6. Cash only. Call for reservations and showtimes.

New York's only Latino children's theater was founded in 1999 by the Society of the Educational Arts in a lively Lower East Side cultural center. English- and Spanish-language performances of traditional and new Latin American musical-theater plays alternate every weekend (the theater is dark during school vacations).

New Amsterdam Theater

214 W 42nd St between Seventh and Eighth Aves (212-307-4100). Subway: A, C, E to 42nd St–Port Authority; N, R, S, 1, 2, 3, 9, 7 to 42nd St–Times Square. Wed–Fri 8pm; Wed, Sat 2pm; Sun 1, 6:30pm. $25–$90. AmEx, DC, Disc, MC, V.

Disney laid claim to 42nd Street by renovating this splendid theater, an Art Deco masterpiece. Its inaugural and perpetually sold-out show, *The Lion King*, is directed by wizardly puppeteer Julie Taymor.

New Victory Theater

209 W 42nd St between Broadway and Eighth Ave (212-382-4020; tickets Telecharge 212-239-6200). Subway: A, C, E to 42nd St–Port Authority; N, R, S, 1, 2, 3, 9, 7 to 42nd St–Times Square. $10–$30. AmEx, MC, V.

New York's only year-round, full-scale young people's theater (and the first of the new 42nd Street theaters to be reclaimed from porndom when it opened, fully renovated, in 1995), the New Victory is a gem that shows the very best in international theater and dance at junior prices (which is why you'll see plenty of adults sans kids in the audience). The theater's winter-holiday season never fails to be thrilling—and it sells out fast.

Puppetworks

338 Sixth Ave at 4th St, Park Slope, Brooklyn (718-965-3391). Subway: M, N, R to Union St. Sat, Sun 12:30, 2:30pm. $7, ages 2–18 $5. Cash only.

This company, established in 1938, offers two plays a season, alternating weekly. The productions are based on classic tales, such as *Beauty and the Beast* or *Alice in Wonderland,* and are usually performed with marrionettes, with a classical-music accompaniment. Puppetworks performs occasional seasons in Greenwich Village, too; call for information.

Swedish Cottage Marionette Theater

Central Park West at 81st St (212-988-9093). Subway: B, C to 81st St. Sept–May Tue–Fri 10:30am, noon; Sat 1pm. Jun–Aug Mon–Fri 10:30am, noon. $5, ages 2–12 $4. Cash only.

Run by New York's Department of Parks and Recreation, this intimate theater in an old Swedish schoolhouse was recently renovated. Reservations are essential.

TADA! Youth Ensemble

120 W 28th St between Sixth and Seventh Aves (212-627-1732). Subway: 1, 9 to 28th St. Dec, Jan, Mar, Jul, Aug; call for times. $12, under 17 $6. Cash only.

This group presents musicals performed by and for children. The ensemble casts, ages eight and up, are drawn from open auditions. The shows are well-presented, high-spirited and extremely popular. Reservations are advised; call for details about weeklong musical-theater workshops.

Carolines Kids' Klub

See chapter **Cabaret & Comedy** *for listings.*

The Kids' Klub offers a more or less monthly (except in summer) schedule of stand-up comedy by kids ages 8 to 14 at Carolines, one of New York's premier stand-up spots. As you may expect, these children tend to be smartass types—very funny, fairly slick, slightly hyper—and school-food and parent jokes predominate. Call for reservations.

Zoos

Bronx Zoo/Wildlife Conservation Society

See chapter **The Outer Boroughs** *for listings.*

Some 4,000 animals representing 543 species live in reconstructed natural habitats at the Bronx Zoo—one of the world's largest and most magnificent. Inside is the Bronx Children's Zoo, scaled down for the very young, with lots of domesticated animals to pet, plus exhibits that show you the world from an animal's point of view. Camel and elephant rides are available from April to October. Don't miss the sea-lion feeding (daily at 3pm).

Central Park Wildlife Center

Fifth Ave at 64th St (212-861-6030). Subway: N, R to Fifth Ave. Mon–Fri 10am–5pm; Sat, Sun 10:30am–5:30pm. $3.50, ages 3–12 50¢, under 3 free, seniors $1.25. Cash only.

This small zoo (featuring 130 species) is one of the highlights of the park. You can watch seals frolic above and below the waterline, crocodiles snap at swinging monkeys, and huge polar bears swim endless laps like true neurotic New Yorkers. The chilly penguin house is a favorite summer retreat for hot kids. The Tisch Children's Zoo has 27 pettable species of animals.

New York Aquarium for Wildlife Conservation

Surf Ave at W 8th St, Coney Island, Brooklyn (718-265-3405). Subway: D, F to W 8th St–NY Aquarium. Summer 10am–6pm; winter 10am–5pm. $8.75, children and seniors $4.50. Cash only.

Although the aquarium is rather shabby, kids always enjoy seeing the famous Beluga whale family. There's also a re-creation of the Pacific coastline and an intriguing glimpse of the kinds of things that manage to live in the East River, plus the usual dolphin show and some truly awesome sharks. Watch the dolphins being fed daily at 11:30am and 3pm. Added bonus: Coney Island's Astroland is just a short stroll on the boardwalk away (*see page 276*).

Baby-sitting

Babysitters' Guild

212-682-0227. 9am–9pm. Cash only.

Long- or short-term baby-sitters cost $15 and up an hour, and you can hire a sitter who speaks any one of 16 languages. If you tell the agency folk you need a sitter more than once during your stay, they'll do their best to book the same person for you each time.

Avalon Nurse Registry & Child Service

212-245-0250. Mon–Fri 8:30am–5:30pm; Sat, Sun 9am–8pm. Cash only.

Avalon arranges full- or part-time nannies and baby-sitters. A sitter (four-hour minimum) costs $15 per hour for one or two children in nonresidential places (e.g., a hotel room) and $20 per hour for three or more children, plus travel expenses. The agency recommends that you call at least 24 hours in advance.

Pinch Sitters

212-260-6005. Mon–Fri 7am–5pm. Cash only.

Pinch Sitters specializes in temporary and occasional child care, mainly by creative types moonlighting between engagements, and mainly for creative types with unpredictable schedules. Although some days are fully booked as much as a week in advance, you can usually call in the morning for an evening sitter or the previous afternoon for a daytime sitter; the agency can sometimes get you a sitter within the hour. Charges are $14 an hour, and there's a four-hour minimum.

Museums

Whether you're into Manet or the moon, New York has a museum to fan your interests

New York's museums are arguably the best in the world. More than 60 institutions hold collections of everything from Gutenberg bibles (three of them) and ancient Etruscan jewelry to Plains Indians buckskins and salsa records; others feature hands-on science exhibits. The buildings themselves are equally impressive and eclectic. The spiral uptown Guggenheim is a real jaw-dropper, and the granite cube of the Whitney Museum, with its cyclops-eye window and concrete moat, is a striking contrast to the surrounding architecture.

It is usually self-defeating to try to cram several museum visits into a single day, or even to try to see every exhibit at a major museum such as the Metropolitan Museum of Art or the American Museum of Natural History. Pace yourself: Some museums have excellent cafés or restaurants, so you can break for coffee or a complete meal. Sarabeth's at the Whitney, Sette MoMA at the Museum of Modern Art, the Museum Café in the Morgan Library and the Jewish Museum's Café Weissman are all good reasons to take a breather from the collections. And while it might be traditional to save museums for a rainy day, most also offer a gloriously air-conditioned respite from the summer heat.

Though entry usually costs no more than the price of a movie ticket, museum admission prices may still come as a shock to visitors. This is because most New York museums are funded privately and not by government money; in fact the **New York Historical**

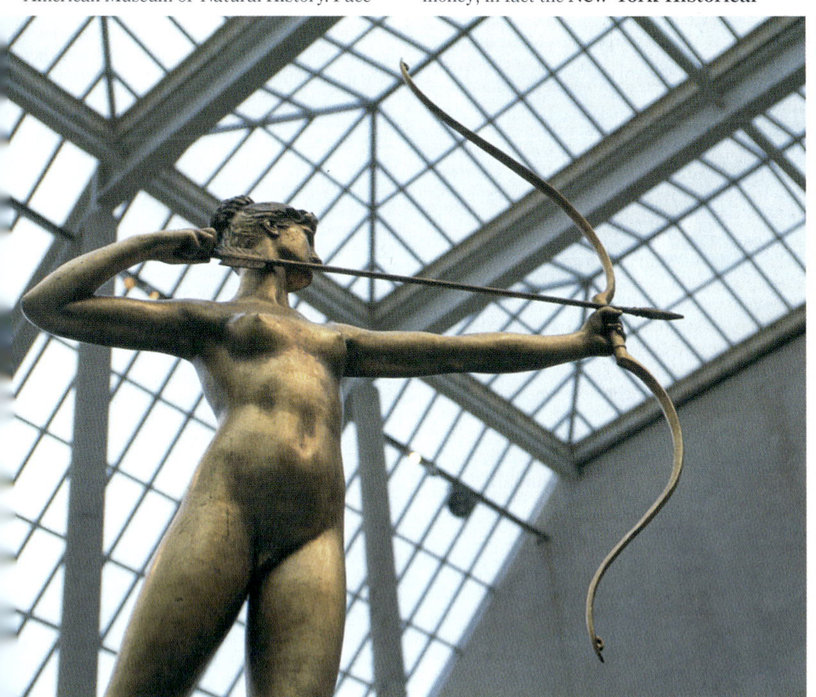

Hunting for art Follow Diana's aim through 5,000 years of art at the Metropolitan.

Metal head The Met has some 15,000 objects in its Arms and Armor collection.

Society, the city's oldest museum, had to close for two years when funding fell short (it is now open again). Even so, most of the city's major art institutions, including the **Whitney,** the **Museum of Modern Art** and the **International Center for Photography** (*see chapter* **Art Galleries**), offer the public at least one evening a week when admission is free or by voluntary donation. And while the city's crown jewel, the **Metropolitan Museum,** has a suggested donation, it is pay-what-you-wish at all times. That means you can get in for as little as 25 cents!

Many of New York's best-known museums—such as the **Frick Collection,** the **Morgan Library,** the **Schomburg Center for Research in Black Culture,** the Whitney and the **Guggenheim**—started out as private collections. **The Cloisters,** at the northern tip of Manhattan in **Fort Tryon Park,** was John D. Rockefeller's gift to the city. Its reconstructed Gothic monastery houses the Met's beautiful collection of medieval art. When the sun's shining and the sky's a deep blue, bring a picnic lunch, admire the red-tile roof and inhale the delicate scents of the garden. It's a treat.

Try not to miss the audio tour at the provocative **Ellis Island Museum,** the eye-opening exhibitions at the **Museum of Jewish Heritage** and the tour at the **Lower East Side Tenement Museum** (*see chapter* **Downtown**). All give visitors insight into NYC's immigrant history. Across the Hudson River, New Jersey's **Liberty Science Center,** with its interactive exhibits and rooftop terrace overlooking Manhattan and the Statue of Liberty, is an unexpected pleasure. If you go on the weekend, when the ferry service is operating, you can admire the Statue of Liberty during the ride.

Don't hesitate to visit the museums if you have kids in tow; most have special events for children if they aren't already kid-friendly (*see chapter* **Kids' Stuff**).

The prize for most neglected museum has to go to the **Brooklyn Museum of Art.** But thanks to the controversy over 1999's "Sensation!" show, which featured the work of young British artists, the museum is enjoying a higher profile. Its size and grandeur come as a pleasant surprise as you emerge from the subway station just outside the **Brooklyn Botanic Garden,** but there's an even greater surprise inside: the excellent exhibits (even without dung-flecked paintings of the Virgin Mary). It's the second-largest museum in New York, but it rarely draws the huge crowds that head for exhibits in Manhattan. And that's a shame, because its Egyptian collection rivals that of the Met, and its recent temporary shows have been first-class.

One of the best features of the city's museums is that they do not rest on their fantastic reputations; they constantly change, expand and enhance themselves. One of the most dramatic examples of this is the **American Museum of Natural History**'s construction of the **Rose Center for Earth and Space** (*see* **Space is the place,** *page 288*). This new facility centers around the high-tech **Hayden Planetarium**—a space theater housed in an 87-foot sphere, visible through a clear glass enclosure. Other additions include the Hall of the Universe and the Hall of Planet Earth.

The art museums are just as forward-thinking: MoMA recently teamed with Queens's hot showcase for young talents, **P.S. 1 Center for Contemporary Art,** and the **Dia Center for the Arts** has announced plans to open a satellite facility upstate (*see chapter* **Art Galleries**).

Most of New York's museums are closed on New Year's Day, Presidents' Day, Memorial Day, Independence Day, Labor Day, Columbus Day, Thanksgiving and Christmas Day. Some change their opening hours in summer, so it's wise to check before setting out.

If you're planning a multimuseum tour over several days that includes the American Museum of Natural History, the Museum of Modern Art, the Guggenheim Museum and the ***Intrepid*** **Sea-Air-Space Museum,** it's well worth investing in a CityPass—for $32 ($21.75 for seniors and $24 for youth ages 12 to 17) you can go to all four, as well as the **Empire State Building Observatory** and the **Top of the World Trade Center.** You'll save $36. It's available at the entrance of any of the participating attractions or online at www.citypass.net/ny.htm.

▶ See chapter **Art Galleries** for more places to see art.
▶ See chapters **Downtown, Midtown, Uptown** and **Outer Boroughs** for ideas on other sights to see while in the neighborhood.
▶ For reviews and listings of current shows, see ***Time Out New York*** or go to **www.timeout.com.**

Major institutions

American Museum of Natural History

Central Park West at 79th St (212-769-5000, recorded information 212-769-5100; www.amnh.org). Subway: B, C to 81st St; 1, 9 to 79th St. Mon–Thu, Sun 10am–5:45pm; Fri, Sat 10am–8:45pm. Suggested donation $10, students and seniors $7.50, children $6. AmEx, MC, V.

The fun begins right in the main rotunda, as a towering barosaur, rearing high on its hind legs, protects its young from an attacking allosaurus. It's an impressive welcome to the largest museum of its kind in the world, and a reminder to visit the dinosaur halls on the fourth floor. During the museum's 1995–96 renovation (by the firm responsible for much of the Ellis Island Museum), several specimens were remodeled in light of recent discoveries. The Tyrannosaurus rex, for instance, was once believed to have walked upright, Godzilla-style; now it stalks, head down, with its tail parallel to the ground, and is altogether more menacing. The rest of the museum is equally dramatic. The Hall of Biodiversity examines world ecosystems and environmental preservation. But the real star of the renovation is the Rose Center for Earth and Space, which opened in February 2000 (*see* **Space is the place,** *page 288*). There's also a particularly good Native American section and a stunning collection of gems, including the obscenely large Star of India blue sapphire. An IMAX theater shows bigger-than-life nature programs (*see page 262*), and there are always innovative temporary exhibitions, in addition to an easily accessible research library with vast photo and print archives and friendly, helpful staff.

Brooklyn Museum of Art

200 Eastern Pkwy at Washington Ave, Park Slope, Brooklyn (718-638-5000; www.brooklynart.org). Subway: 2, 3 to Eastern Pkwy–Brooklyn Museum. Wed–Fri 10am–5pm; Sat 11am–9pm; Sun 11am–6pm. Suggested donation $4, students $2, seniors $1.50. AmEx, MC, V (in gift shop only).

The Brooklyn Museum, founded 177 years ago, appended the word *Art* to its name in 1997 to draw wider attention to the world-class collections inside this gorgeous 19th-century Beaux Arts building (and having withstood attacks for exhibiting the controversial "Sensation!: Young British Artists from the Saatchi Collection" has certainly helped). The African art and pre-Columbian textile galleries are especially impressive, and the Native American collection is outstanding. There are many works from the ancient Middle East and extensive holdings of American painting and sculpture by such masters as Winslow Homer, Thomas Eakins and John Singer Sargent. Don't miss the Egyptian galleries: The Rubin Gallery's gold-and-silver–gilded ibis coffin, for instance, is sublime. Two floors up, the Rodin sculpture court is surrounded by paintings by French contemporaries such as Monet and Degas. There's also an informal café (which closes at 4pm) and a children's museum.

The Cloisters

Fort Tryon Park, Fort Washington Ave at Margaret Corbin Plaza, Washington Heights (212-923-3700; www.metmuseum.org). Subway: A to 190th St. Mar–Oct Tue–Sun 9:30am–5:15pm; Nov–Feb Tue–Sun 9:30am–4:45pm. Suggested donation $10 (includes admission to the Metropolitan Museum of Art on the same day), under 12 free if accompanied by an adult. Cash only.

The Cloisters houses the Met's medieval art and architecture collections in an unexpectedly tranquil, rural setting. The museum, overlooking the Hudson River, is a convincing Roman structure, even though

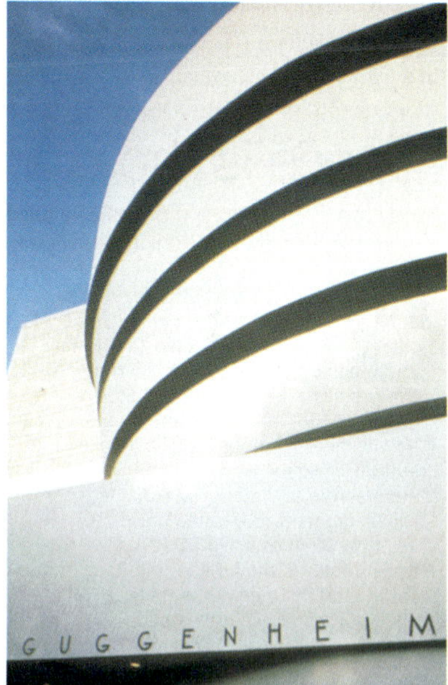

The Wright stuff The Guggenheim's building is a work of art in its own right.

it was constructed a mere 60 years ago. Don't miss the famous unicorn tapestries or the *Annunciation Triptych* by Robert Campin.

Cooper-Hewitt National Design Museum

2 E 91st St at Fifth Ave (212-849-8400). Subway: 4, 5, 6 to 86th St. Tue 10am–9pm; Wed–Sat 10am–5pm; Sun noon–5pm. $5, under 12 free, no admission charge Tue 5–9pm. Cash only.

The Smithsonian's National Design Museum is worth a visit for both its content and its architecture—the turn-of-the-century building once belonged to Andrew Carnegie. Architects responded to his request for "the most modest, plainest and roomy house in New York" by designing a 64-room mansion in the style of a Georgian country house. Recent exhibitions have included a retrospective of the masterful American designs of Charles and Ray Eames. This is the only museum in the U.S. devoted exclusively to historical and contemporary design; its changing exhibitions are always interesting. Sign language interpretation is available on request (*212-849-8387*).

Frick Collection

1 E 70th St at Fifth Ave (212-288-0700). Subway: 6 to 68th St–Hunter College. Tue–Sat 10am–6pm; Sun 1–6pm. $7, students and seniors $5, under 10 not admitted, ages 10–16 must be accompanied by an adult. Cash only.

This private, predominantly Renaissance collection, housed in an opulent residence once owned by industrialist Henry Clay Frick, is more like a stately home than a museum. American architect Thomas Hastings designed the 1914 building in 18th-century European style. The paintings, sculptures and furniture on display are consistently world-class—among them works by Gainsborough, Rembrandt, Renoir, Vermeer, Whistler and the French cabinetmaker Jean-Henri Riesener. The indoor garden court and reflecting pool are especially lovely.

Guggenheim

See **Solomon R. Guggenheim Museum,** page 290.

Metropolitan Museum of Art

1000 Fifth Ave at 82nd St (212-535-7710; www.metmuseum.org). Subway: 4, 5, 6 to 86th St. Tue–Thu, Sun 9:30am–5:15pm; Fri, Sat 9:30am–8:45pm. Suggested donation $10, students and seniors $5, under 12 free. Cash only. No strollers on Sundays.

It could take days, even weeks, to cover the Met's 1.5 million square feet (139,354.5 square meters) of exhibition space, so try to be selective. Egyptology fans should head straight for the Temple of Dendur. There's an excellent Islamic art collection and more than 3,000 European paintings, including major works by Rembrandt, Raphael, Tiepolo and Vermeer (five of them, including *Young Woman with a Water Jug*) The Greek and Roman halls have gotten a facelift, and the museum has also been adding to its galleries of 20th-century painting. Each year, a selection of contemporary sculptures is installed in the open-air roof garden (open between May and October); have a sandwich there while taking in the panorama of Central Park. On weekend evenings, enjoy a classical quintet performing on the mezza-

Space is the place

Hayden Planetarium's out-of-this world addition is the new star in New York's museum galaxy

It's never been so marvelous to feel so small. When the American Museum of Natural History's shiny **Rose Center for Earth and Space** opened in February 2000, Gothamites feared the worst: *Star Wars* meets Action Park. But even the most jaded New Yorkers and tourists will be lulled into a state of childlike wonder by the soaring architecture and humbling exhibits explaining our place in the universe.

The $210 million, 333,500-square-foot Rose Center is the largest, most expensive project the institution has undertaken in its 130-year history. The project is based on some pretty big expectations: "Pilgrims will come here—not for religion, but for science and education," says its architect, James Polshek, who lovingly calls his great glass addition to the museum a "cosmic cathedral." Inside the glass cube, Polshek's iconic 87-foot aluminum sphere—which houses the rejuvenated Hayden Planetarium—seems to float in thin air.

The giant silvery globe is divided into two theaters. On top is the Hayden Planetarium, loaded with specially made Mark IX projector that can cast 3-D images of nearly 10,000 stars from any point in the universe. The show *Passport to the Universe*, narrated by Tom Hanks, takes viewers on a 3-D journey past Saturn's rings, into the Orion Nebula, where new stars are born, moves out to the farthest reaches of known space and then returns to Earth on a shortcut through a black hole (if you get motion sickness, then you might want to close your eyes during

nine overlooking the Great Hall. And don't forget the Costume Institute or the new Howard Gilman Photography Gallery. Foreign-language tours are available (*212-570-3711*).

The Morgan Library

29 E 36th St between Madison and Park Aves (212-685-0008). Subway: 6 to 33rd St. Tue–Thu 10:30am–5pm; Fri 10:30am–8pm; Sat 10:30am–6pm; Sun noon–6pm. $7, seniors and students $5, under 12 free. Cash only.

This beautiful Italianate museum—also an extraordinary literary-research facility—was once the private library of financier J. Pierpont Morgan. Mostly gathered during Morgan's trips to Europe, the collection includes three Gutenberg Bibles, original Mahler manuscripts and the gorgeous silver, copper and cloisonné 12th-century Stavelot triptych. A subtly colorful marble rotunda with a carved 16th-century Italian ceiling separates the three-tiered library from the rich red study. Guided tours are available Tuesday through Friday at noon. There's also a modern conservatory attached to the museum, with a tranquil courtyard café.

Museum of Modern Art

11 W 53rd St between Fifth and Sixth Aves (212-708-9400; www.moma.org). Subway: E, F to Fifth Ave. Mon, Tue, Thu, Sat 10:30am–5:45pm; Fri 10:30am–8:15pm. $10, students and seniors $6.50, under 16 free, voluntary donation Fri 4:30–8:15pm. Cash only.

The Museum of Modern Art, or MoMA for short, holds the finest and most comprehensive collection of 20th-century art in the world. The permanent collection is exceptionally strong on works by Matisse, Picasso (his *Les Desmoiselles d'Avignon* hangs here), Miró and later modernists. In 2000, the curators rearranged the museum's works for MoMA 2000, a series of exhibitions stretching into 2001 to celebrate the millennium. The photo collection has major holdings by just about every important figure in the medium. The film and video department is outstanding, with a collection of more than 14,000 films; it hosts 20-plus screenings a week in two plush theaters. Get your tickets early (*see chapter* **Film & TV**). The elegant Italian restaurant Sette MoMA (*212-708-9710*) overlooks the lovely Abby Aldrich Rockefeller Sculpture Garden; an informal café is on the ground floor. Free gallery talks begin at 1pm and 3pm daily (except Wednesday) and on Thursday and Friday evenings at 6pm and 7pm. A sculpture touch-tour for visually impaired visitors is by appointment (*212-708-9864*). Take note: On Mondays, when many other museums are closed, MoMA is open.

Other location: *P.S. 1 Contemporary Art Center, 22-25 Jackson Ave at 46th Ave, Long Island City, Queens (718-784-2084). Subway: E, F to 23 St–Ely Ave; 7 to 45 Rd–Court House Sq.*

Known for its cutting-edge exhibitions and international studio program, this alternative contemporary art space was recently acquired by MoMA. Its first exhibition was an overview of emerging artists from the New York area.

National Museum of the American Indian

George Gustav Heye Center, U.S. Custom House, 1 Bowling Green between State and Whitehall Sts

Universe-ity The Rose Center explains it all.

this). In the Big Bang Theater on the lower level, a short light show narrated by Jodie Foster explains the birth of the universe. From here, visitors exit the sphere and step onto the Cosmic Pathway, a ramp that spirals down to a cluster of exhibits below. Along the way, a 360-foot display marks the approximate age of the universe in billion-year increments, beginning with the Big Bang and ticking up to the present. To illustrate the brief span of mankind, the final panel displays a strand of human hair, the thickness of which symbolizes the length of our existence.

Another "wow" component to see is the Scales of the Universe walkway, which floats along the perimeter of the cube's second floor. It gives visitors a sense of the relative size of the universe's components by using the grand sphere as a reference point. For example, if the sphere represents the sun, then a soccer ball–size model represents the Earth. The idea came from a letter that Princeton University astrophysicist Henry Norris Russell sent to the museum in 1915. No doubt he was trying to get tickets in advance, which is what you should do if you want to get into this place.

Entertainment

(212-668-6624; www.conexus.si.edu). Subway: N, R to Whitehall St; 1, 9 to South Ferry; 4, 5 to Bowling Green. Mon–Wed, Fri–Sun 10am–5pm; Thu 10am–8pm. Free.
The galleries, resource center and two workshop rooms of this museum, a branch of the Smithsonian Institution's sprawling organization of museums and research institutes, occupies two floors of the grand rotunda in the exquisite 1907 U.S. Custom House. Located just around the corner from Battery Park and the Ellis Island ferry, it offers displays based on a permanent collection of documents and artifacts that offer valuable insights into the realities of Native American history. Exhibitions are thoughtfully explained, usually by Native Americans. Of special interest is "All Roads Are Good," which reflects the personal choices of storytellers, weavers, anthropologists and tribal leaders. Only 500 of the collection's one million objects are on display at any time, which is one reason that, despite the building's lofty proportions, the museum seems surprisingly small. A main branch, on the Mall in Washington, D.C., will open in 2002.

Natural History Museum

See **American Museum of Natural History,** page 287.

New Museum of Contemporary Art

583 Broadway between Houston and Prince Sts (212-219-1222; www.newmuseum.org). Subway: B, D, F, Q to Broadway–Lafayette St; N, R to Prince St; 6 to Bleecker St. Wed, Sun noon–6pm; Thu–Sat noon–8pm. $5, under 18 free, Thu 6–8pm free. AmEx, DC, Disc, MC, V.
Since its founding in 1977, this Soho institution has been the focus of controversy. It quickly became a lightning rod for its fusion of art, technology and political correctness in major group shows that gravitated heavily toward the experimental, the conceptual and the latest in multimedia presentations. Even its window displays draw crowds. A $3 million renovation and expansion of its Victorian cast-iron building has given it a friendlier entrance, an airy second-floor exhibition space and an intimate downstairs bookshop and reading room that's visible from the street. The museum continues to mount important midcareer retrospectives for underrecognized artists, although it has adopted a broader, more international outlook. Its retrospective of Brazilian artist Cildo Meireles in early 2000 was particularly successful.

Solomon R. Guggenheim Museum

1071 Fifth Ave at 88th St (212-423-3500). Subway: 4, 5, 6 to 86th St. Sun–Wed 9am–6pm; Fri, Sat 9am–8pm. $12, students and seniors $7, under 12 free, voluntary donation Fri 6–8pm. AmEx, MC, V.
Designed by Frank Lloyd Wright, the Guggenheim itself is a stunning piece of art. In addition to works by Kandinsky, Picasso, van Gogh, Degas and Manet, the museum owns Peggy Guggenheim's trove of Cubist, Surrealist and Abstract Expressionist works and the Panza di Biumo collection of American Minimalist and Conceptual art from the 1960s and '70s. The photography collection began with the donation of more than 200 works by the Robert Mapplethorpe Foundation. In 1992, a new ten-story tower increased the museum's space to include a sculpture gallery (with great views of Central Park) and a café. Since then, the Guggenheim has made news with its ambitious global expansion (*see chapter* **Soar Subjects**), its penchant for sweeping historical presentations (such as its elegant overview of 5,000 years of Chinese art) and its in-depth retrospectives of such major American artists as Robert Rauschenberg. Admission prices are some of the highest in the city; but if you are willing to fork over $16 for a dual ticket, you're also granted entry to the Guggenheim's Soho branch. Even if you don't want to pay to see the collection inside, visit the uptown museum to admire the stunning white building coiled among the turn-of-the-century mansions on Fifth Avenue.

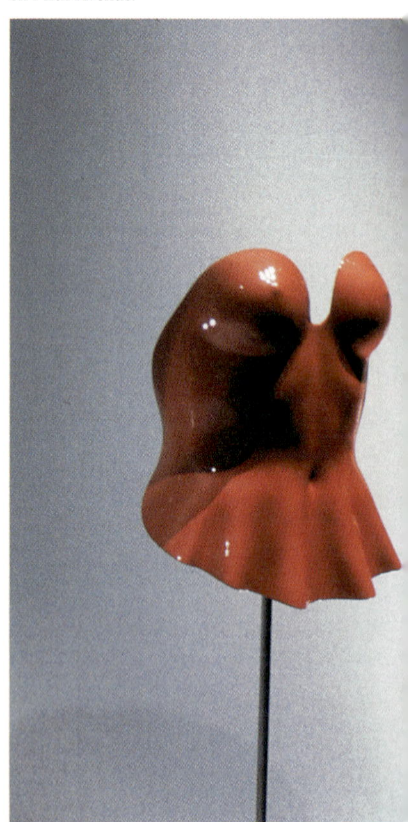

Other location: *Guggenheim Museum Soho, 575 Broadway at Prince St (212-423-3500).*
The Soho Guggenheim opened in 1992 to showcase selections from the permanent collection, as well as to mount temporary exhibitions. For a while, it has been showing Andy Warhol's version of Da Vinci's *The Last Supper*, which is nothing short of startling.

Whitney Museum of American Art

945 Madison Ave at 75th St (212-570-3600, recorded information 212-570-3676; www.whitney.org). Subway: 6 to 77th St. Wed, Fri–Sun 11am–6pm; Thu 1–8pm. $12.50, students and seniors $10.50, children under 12 free, Thu 6–8pm free. AmEx, MC, V.
Like the Guggenheim, the Whitney sets itself apart first with its unique architecture: a gray granite cube designed by Marcel Breuer. Inside, the Whitney is a world unto itself, one whose often controversial exhibitions not only measure the historical importance of American art but mirror the culture of the moment. In 2000, major donor Marylou Whitney withdrew her financial support—to a protest against a work in the Biennial Exhibition. When Gertrude Vanderbilt Whitney, a sculptor and art patron, opened the museum in 1931, she dedicated it to living American artists; its first exhibition showed the work of eight artists. Today, the Whitney holds approximately 12,000 pieces by nearly 2,000 artists, including Edward Hopper (the museum owns his entire estate), Andrew Wyeth, Arshile Gorky, Georgia O'Keeffe, Jackson Pollock, Alexander Calder, Alice Neel, Louise Nevelson, Jasper Johns, Andy Warhol, Agnes Martin and Jean-Michel Basquiat. The museum is also perhaps the country's foremost showcase for American independent film and video artists. Over the past decade, it has vastly expanded its collection of contemporary photography as well. Still, the Whitney's reputation rests mainly on its temporary shows, particularly the show everyone loves to hate: the Biennial. Held every even-numbered year, it remains the most prestigious assessment of contemporary American art in the U.S. The next one is slated for 2002. There are free guided tours daily;

Ab fab Try to squeeze in a visit to the Museum at FIT.

the expanded gift shop next door is now accessible through a lobby passage. Sarabeth's (*212-570-3670*), the museum café, is open daily till 4:30pm and offers a lively up-from-below view of Madison Avenue, along with food that is pricey but excellent.

Whitney Museum of American Art at Philip Morris

120 Park Ave at 42nd St (212-878-2550). Subway: S, 4, 5, 6, 7 to 42nd St–Grand Central. Mon–Fri 11am–6pm; Thu 11am–7:30pm; sculpture court Mon–Sat 7:30am–9:30pm; Sun 11am–7pm. Free.

The Whitney's midtown branch, located in a lobby gallery, is devoted to changing solo projects by contemporary artists. The curators have done a great job mounting exciting shows by working artists.

Art and design

American Academy and Institute of Arts and Letters

Audubon Terrace, Broadway between 155th and 156th Sts (212-368-5900). Subway: 1, 9 to 157th St. Thu–Sun 1–4pm. Free.

This organization honors 250 American writers, composers, painters, sculptors and architects. Edith Wharton, Mark Twain and Henry James were once members; today's list includes Terrence McNally, John Guare, Kurt Vonnegut and Alison Lurie. It's not actually a museum, but there are annual exhibitions open to the public and a magnificent library of original manuscripts and first editions, open to researchers by appointment only.

American Craft Museum

40 W 53rd St between Fifth and Sixth Aves (212-956-3535). Subway: E, F to Fifth Ave. Tue, Wed, Fri–Sun 10am–6pm; Thu 10am–8pm. $5. Cash only.

This is the country's leading art museum for 20th-century crafts in clay, glass, metal, fiber and wood. There are temporary shows on the four bright and spacious floors, and one or two exhibitions from the permanent collection each year, concentrating on a specific medium. The shop, though small, sells some unusually stylish jewelry and ceramics.

Dahesh Museum

601 Fifth Ave at 48th St (212-759-0606; www.daheshmuseum.org). Subway: B, D, F, Q to 47–50th Sts–Rockefeller Ctr. Tue–Sat 11am–6pm. Free.

This jewel-box museum houses the private collection of Salim Moussa Achi, a Lebanese philosopher with a consuming passion for European Academic art. The collection focuses on Orientalism, landscapes, scenes of rural life, and historical or mythical images painted by 19th- and early-20th-century artists whose work you won't see in public collections anywhere else.

Forbes Magazine Galleries

62 Fifth Ave at 12th St (212-206-5548). Subway: L, N, R, 4, 5, 6 to 14th St–Union Sq. Tue, Wed, Fri, Sat 10am–4pm. Free. Under 16 must be accompanied by an adult.

The late magazine publisher Malcolm Forbes assembled this wonderful private collection of treasures. Besides toy boats and soldiers, the galleries showcase historic presidential letters and—best of all—a dozen Fabergé eggs and other superbly intricate pieces by the famous Russian jeweler and goldsmith Peter Carl Fabergé. Gallery hours are subject to change, so call to check before visiting.

Isamu Noguchi Garden Museum

32-37 Vernon Blvd at 33rd Rd, Long Island City, Queens (718-204-7088; www.noguchi.org). Travel: N to Broadway. Or shuttle bus from the Asia Society, 725 Park Ave at 70th St, every hour on the half-hour 11:30am–3:30pm. Apr–Oct Wed–Fri 10am–5pm; Sat, Sun 11am–6pm. Suggested donation $4. Cash only.

Sculptor Isamu Noguchi designed stage sets for Martha Graham and George Balanchine, as well as sculpture parks and immense works of great simplicity and beauty. Noguchi's studios are now a showcase for his pieces—in 12 small galleries and a sculpture garden. There's a guided tour at 2pm (*718-721-1932*), and films are shown throughout the day.

Municipal Art Society

457 Madison Ave between 50th and 51st Sts (212-935-3960, tour information 212-439-1049; www.mas.org). Subway: E, F to Fifth Ave; 6 to 51st St. Mon–Wed, Fri, Sat 11am–5pm. Free.

This center for urban design was founded in 1980. It functions as a gallery, bookshop and lecture forum with exhibitions on architecture, public art and community-based projects. The MAS is also headquarters of the Architectural League and the Parks Council. Its greatest attraction may be its location: inside the historic Villard Houses, opposite St. Patrick's Cathedral.

The Museum at FIT

Seventh Ave at 27th St (212-217-5800; www.fitnyc.suny.edu). Subway: 1, 9 to 28th St. Tue–Fri noon–8pm; Sat 10am–5pm. Free.

The Fashion Institute of Technology has the world's largest collection of costumes and textiles. Recent exhibitions have been devoted to designers such as Bob Mackie and Norman Norell, but others have included a look at the importance of the little black dress and the history of corsets.

Museum of American Folk Art

2 Lincoln Sq, Columbus Ave between 65th and 66th Sts (212-977-7298, www.folkartmuseum.org). Subway: 1, 9 to 66th St–Lincoln Ctr. Tue–Sun 11:30am–7:30pm. Free.

The exhibits are exquisite. The range of decorative, practical and ceremonial folk art encompasses pottery, trade signs, delicately stitched log-cabin quilts and even windup toys. The craftsmanship is often breathtaking. There are occasional lectures, demonstrations and performances, and a museum shop next door. The museum will be moving into a new

Bowl me over Shopping is as interesting as exploring the exhibits at the Museum for African Art.

site in 2001, though it will still hold some exhibits in the Lincoln Center branch.

National Academy of Design

1083 Fifth Ave at 89th St (212-369-4880). Subway: 4, 5, 6 to 86th St. Wed, Thu, Sat, Sun noon–5pm; Fri 10am–6pm. $8, under 5 free, no admission charge Fri 5–8pm. Cash only.

Housed in an elegant Fifth Avenue townhouse, the Academy comprises the School of Fine Arts and a museum containing one of the world's foremost collections of 19th- and 20th-century American art (painting, sculpture, architecture and engraving). The permanent collection includes works by Mary Cassatt, John Singer Sargent and Frank Lloyd Wright. Temporary exhibitions are impressive.

Nicholas Roerich Museum

319 W 107th St at Riverside Dr (212-864-7752, www.roerich.org). Subway: 1, 9 to 110th St–Cathedral Pkwy. Tue–Sun 2–5pm. Donation requested.

Nicholas Roerich was a Russian-born philosopher, artist, architect, explorer, pacifist and scenery painter who collaborated with Nijinsky, Stravinsky and Diaghilev. The Roerich Peace Pact of 1935, an international agreement on the protection of cultural treasures, earned him a Nobel Peace Prize nomination. Roerich's wife bought this charming townhouse specifically as a museum to house her late husband's possessions. Paintings are mostly from his Tibetan travels and display his interest in mysticism. It's a fascinating place, although Roerich's intriguing life story tends to overshadow the museum.

Queens Museum of Art

New York City Building, Flushing Meadows–Corona Park, Queens (718-592-9700; queensmuse.org). Subway: 7 to 111th St. Wed–Fri 10am–5pm; Sat, Sun noon–5pm. Suggested donation $4, students and seniors $2, children under 5 free. Cash only.

Located on the site of the 1964–65 World's Fair, the Queens Museum recently completed a thorough $15 million renovation. In addition to the art collections and fine, site-specific temporary exhibitions, the museum offers a permanent miniature model of New York City. It's fun to try to find where you're staying—rent binoculars for $1 apiece. Dusk falls every 15 minutes, revealing tiny illuminated buildings and a fluorescent Central Park. The model is constantly updated; there had been some 60,000 changes at the last count.

Studio Museum in Harlem

144 W 125th St between Seventh Ave and Malcolm X Blvd (212-864-4500). Subway: 2, 3 to 125th St. Wed–Fri 10am–5pm; Sat, Sun 1–6pm. $5, no admission charge first Saturday of each month. Cash only.

The Studio Museum started out in 1967 as a rented loft space. During the next 20 years, it expanded onto two floors of a 60,000-square-foot (5,500-square-meter) building—a gift from a New York bank—and became the first black fine-arts museum in the country. Today, it shows changing exhibitions by African-American, African and Caribbean artists and continues its prestigious artists-in-residence program.

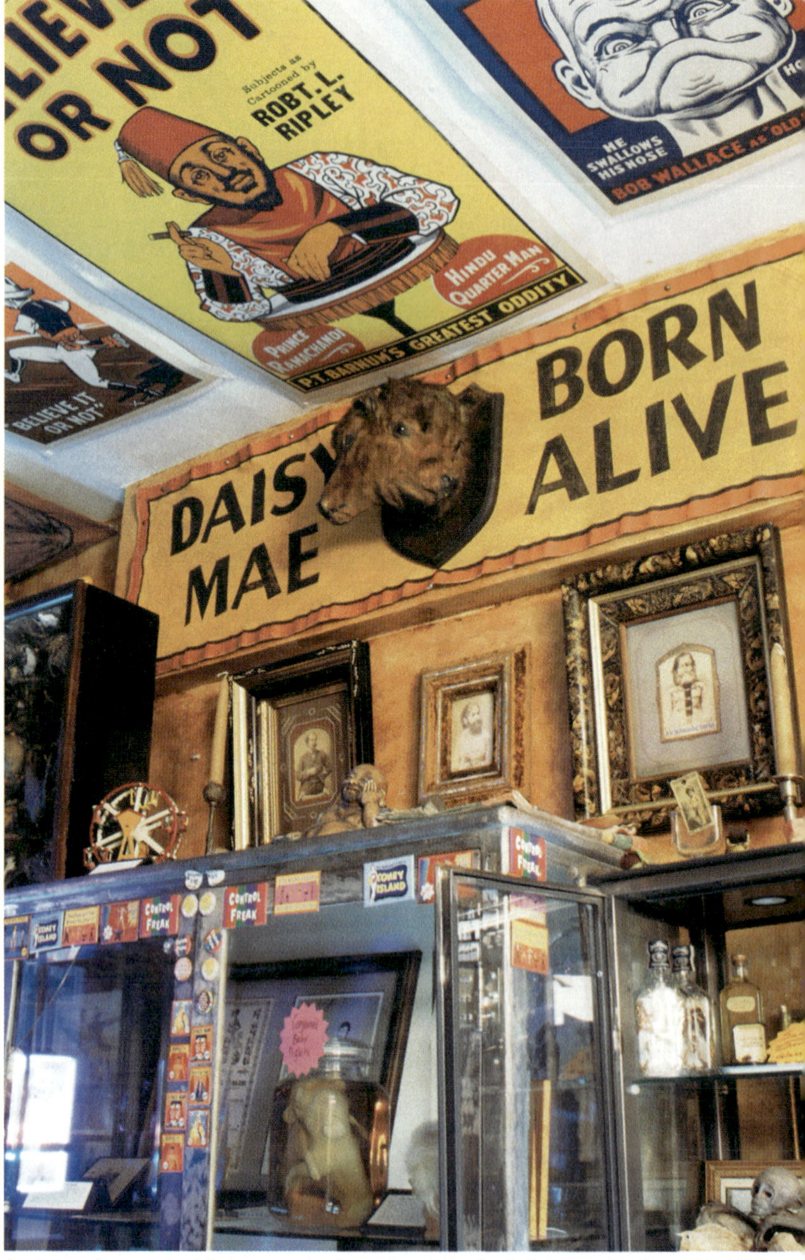

Geek love One man's sideshow passion is on view at the Freakatorium on the Lower East Side.

Arts and culture

Ethnic

Asia Society

502 Park Ave at 59th St (212-517-2742, www.asiasociety.org). Subway: N, R to Lexington Ave; 4, 5, 6 to 59th St. Mon–Sat 10am–6pm. $4, students and seniors $2, under 12 free.

While the main building undergoes renovation, the Asia Society is temporarily located at 502 Park Avenue. The stalwart eight-story headquarters at 725 Park Avenue, which will reopen in fall 2001, reflects the society's importance in promoting Asian-American relations. It sponsors study missions and conferences, and promotes public programs on both continents. Galleries show major art exhibitions from public and private collections, including the permanent Mr. and Mrs. John D. Rockefeller III collection of Asian art. Asian musicians and performers often play here; call for a schedule.

China Institute in America

125 E 65th St between Park and Lexington Aves (212-744-8181; www.chinainstitute.org). Subway: 6 to 68th St–Hunter College. Mon–Sat 10am–5pm; Sun 1–5pm. Suggested donation $3, students $2, children under 12 free. AmEx, MC, V.

Consisting of just two small gallery rooms, the China Institute is somewhat overshadowed by the Asia Society. But its exhibitions, ranging from works by Chinese women artists to selections from the Beijing Palace Museum, are impressive. The society also offers lectures and courses on such subjects as cooking, calligraphy and Confucianism.

French Institute–Alliance Française

55 E 59th St between Madison and Park Aves (212-355-6160; www.fiaf.org). Subway: B, Q, N, R to Lexington Ave; 4, 5, 6 to 59th St. Tue–Fri 11am–7pm; Sat, Sun 11am–3pm. Free.

This is the New York home for all things French: The institute (a.k.a. the Alliance Française) holds the city's most extensive all-French library and offers numerous language classes and cultural seminars. There are also French film screenings (*see chapter* **Film & TV**) and live dance, music and theater performances.

Garibaldi-Meucci Museum

420 Tompkins Ave between Chestnut Ave and Shaughnessy Ln, Staten Island (718-442-1608). Travel: Staten Island Ferry, then S52 bus. Tue–Fri, Sat, Sun noon–5pm. Suggested donation $3.

The 1840s Gothic Revival home of Italian inventor Antonio Meucci, this museum is also the former refuge of Italian patriot Antonio Garibaldi.

Goethe-Institut/German Cultural Center

1014 Fifth Ave at 82nd St (212-439-8700; www.goethe.de). Subway: 4, 5, 6 to 86th St. Library: Tue, Thu noon–7pm; Wed, Fri noon–5pm. Gallery: Tue, Thu 10am–7pm; Wed, Fri 10am–5pm. Free.

Goethe-Institut New York is just one branch of a German multinational cultural organization founded in 1951. Located across the street from the Metropolitan Museum in a landmark Fifth Avenue mansion, it mounts shows featuring German-born contemporary artists, as well as concerts, lectures and film screenings (*see chapter* **Film & TV**). A library offers books in German or English, German periodicals, videos and audiocassettes.

Hispanic Society of America

Audubon Terrace, Broadway between 155th and 156th Sts (212-926-2234; www.hispanicsociety.org). Subway: 1 to 157th St. Tue–Sat 10am–4:30pm; Sun 1–4pm. Library: Tue–Sat 10am–4:30pm. Free.

Two limestone lions flank the entrance to this majestic building in Hamilton Heights, a gentrified area of Harlem. Outside, an equestrian statue of El Cid, Spain's medieval hero, stands on the Beaux Arts terrace between the society's two buildings. Inside, there's an ornate Spanish Renaissance court and an upper gallery lined with paintings by El Greco, Goya and Velázquez. The collection is dominated by religious artifacts, including a number of 16th-century tombs from the monastery of San Francisco in Cuéllar, Spain.

International Salsa Museum

2127 Third Ave at 116th St (212-472-2652; after 5pm 212-289-1368). Subway: 6 to 116th St. Noon–7pm. Donation suggested.

This small museum, tucked away in Spanish Harlem, is dedicated to all aspects of Latin music. The collection includes musical instruments, photography, personal mementos, recordings and literature.

Jacques Marchais Museum of Tibetan Art

338 Lighthouse Ave off Richmond Rd, Staten Island (718-987-3500; www.tibetanmuseum.com). Travel: Staten Island Ferry, then S74 bus to Lighthouse Ave, then walk up the hill 15 minutes. Apr–Nov Wed–Sun 1–5pm; Dec–March Wed–Fri 1–5pm. $3. Cash only.

This mock Tibetan temple stands on a hilltop high above sea level. It contains a fascinating Buddhist altar and the largest collection of Tibetan art in the West, including religious objects, bronzes and paintings. There's a comprehensive English-language library containing books on Buddhism, as well as on Tibetan and Asian art. The landscaped gardens include a zoo of stone animals (with birdhouses and a wishing well) and offer good views.

Japan Society

333 E 47th St between First and Second Aves (212-752-3015; www.japansociety.org). Subway: E, F to Lexington Ave; 6 to 51st St. Tue–Sun 11am–6pm (during exhibitions only). Suggested donation $5. Cash only.

The Japan Society promotes cultural exchange programs and special events, plus exhibitions two or three times a year. The gallery shows both traditional and contemporary Japanese art. The society's film center is a major showcase for Japanese cinema in the U.S. (*see chapter* **Film & TV**). There's also a library and language center in the lower lobby wing.

Museum of Jewish Heritage: A Living Memorial to the Holocaust

18 First Pl at Battery Pl, Battery Park City (212-968-1800; www.mjhnyc.org). Subway: 1, 9 to Rector St. Sun–Wed 9am–5pm; Thu 9am–8pm; Fri and holiday eves 9am–3pm; closed Sat and Jewish holidays. $7, students and seniors $5, under 5 free, Sunday free. Advance ticket purchase recommended; call the museum or Ticketmaster (212-307-4007). AmEx, MC, V.

You don't have to be Jewish to appreciate the contents of this institution, built in a symbolic six-sided shape (recalling the Star of David), under a tiered roof. Opened in 1997, it offers people of all backgrounds one of the most moving cultural experiences in the city. The well-thought-out exhibits feature 2,000 photographs, hundreds of surviving cultural artifacts and plenty of archival films that vividly detail the crime against humanity that was the Holocaust. The exhibition continues beyond those dark times into days of renewal, ending in an upper gallery that is flooded with daylight and gives especially meaningful views of Lady Liberty in the harbor. It's an unforgettable experience. Closed-captioned video is available.

Jewish Museum

1109 Fifth Ave at 92nd St (212-423-3230). Subway: 4, 5, 6 to 86th St. Mon, Wed, Thu, Sun 11am–5:45pm; Tue 11am–8pm. $8, under 12 free, no admission charge Tue 5–8pm. Cash only.

A fascinating collection of art, artifacts and media installations, the Jewish Museum is housed in the 1908 Warburg Mansion, which was renovated in 1993 to include the underground Café Weissman. Recent exhibitions have included a look at turn-of-the-century Berlin as a Jewish cultural center and works by John Singer Sargent from the collection of a prominent Jewish London gallerist. The museum commissions a contemporary artist or group of artists to install a new show each year, and the results are always stellar. The permanent exhibition tracks the Jewish cultural experience through exhibits ranging from a 16th-century mosaic wall from a Persian synagogue and a filigreed silver circumcision set to an interactive Talmud—there's even a Statue of Liberty Hanukkah lamp. Most of this eclectic collection was rescued from European synagogues before World War II.

Those were the days Step into the past as you walk through the New York Historical Society.

El Museo del Barrio

1230 Fifth Ave between 104th and 105th Sts (212-831-7272). Subway: 6 to 103rd St. Wed–Sun 11am–5pm. $4, students and seniors $2. AmEx, MC, V.

At the top of Museum Mile, not far from Spanish Harlem (the neighborhood from which it takes its name), El Museo del Barrio is dedicated to the work of Latino artists in the United States as well as that of Latin Americans. Pepón Osorio was the subject of a recent exhibition. Typical exhibitions are contemporary and consciousness-raising; El Museo also sponsors community events like the festive annual celebration of the Mexican Day of the Dead (Nov 1).

Museum for African Art

593 Broadway between Houston and Prince Sts (212-966-1313; www.africanart.org). Subway: B, D, F, Q to Broadway–Lafayette St; N, R to Prince St; 6 to Bleecker St. Tue–Fri 10:30am–5:30pm; Sat, Sun noon–6pm. $5, under 2 free, Sun free. MC, V (over $10).

This tranquil museum was designed by Maya Lin, who also created the stunningly simple Vietnam Veterans' Memorial in Washington, D.C. Exhibits change about twice a year; the quality of the works shown is high, and they often come from amazing private collections. There's an unusually good bookshop with a children's section.

Yeshiva University Museum

2520 Amsterdam Ave at 185th Street (212-960-5390). Subway: 1 to 181st St. Tue–Thu 10:30am–5pm; Sun noon–6pm. $3. Cash only.

The museum usually hosts one major exhibition a year and several smaller ones, mainly on Jewish themes.

Historical

American Numismatic Society

Audubon Terrace, Broadway at 155th Sts (212-234-3130; www.amnumsoc.org). Subway: 1 to 157th St. Tue–Fri 9am–4:30pm. Free.

The collection covers 26 centuries of filthy lucre.

Brooklyn Historical Society

128 Pierrepont St at Clinton St, Brooklyn Heights, Brooklyn (718-254-9830; www.brooklynhistory.org).

ubway: N, R to Court St; 2, 3, 4, 5 to Borough Hall. Ion, Thu–Sat noon–5pm. $2.50, Mon free. Cash only.
What do Woody Allen, Mae West, Isaac Asimov, Iel Brooks and Walt Whitman have in common? nswer: They were all—along with Al Capone, arry Manilow and Gypsy Rose Lee—born in rooklyn. Thus they merit tributes in this tiny useum dedicated to Brooklyn's past glories. The ociety's historic brownstone is undergoing reno-ation and will reopen in fall 2001. In the meantime, vents and exhibits are being held at other venues; all for locations.

'raunces Tavern Museum

4 Pearl St at Broad St, second and third floors 212-425-1778). Subway: 1, 9 to South Ferry. Ion–Fri 10am–4:45pm; Sat noon–4pm. $2.50, nder 6 free. Cash only.
'his tavern used to be George Washington's water-ng hole and was a prominent meeting place for nti-British groups before the Revolution. The 18th-entury building, which has been partly recon-tructed, is unexpectedly quaint, considering its etting on the fringes of the Financial District. Most f its artifacts are displayed in period rooms. The hanging exhibitions are often interesting.

he Freakatorium

7 Clinton St between Stanton and Rivington Sts 212-375-0475; www.freakatorium.com). Subway: to Delancey St; J, M, Z to Essex St. Mon–Fri 1am–6pm. Free.
Not a formal museum by any stretch of the imagi-ation, the Freakatorium is a funky little storefront n the Lower East Side. It's jammed with sideshow nemorabilia, such as the vest and cane of Tom 'humb and a matchstick-and-foil cathedral made y John "Elephant Man" Merrick. Up on a wall, the wo heads of the calf Daisy Mae survey the room. 'he collection is the personal obsession of Johnny 'ox, himself a sideshow performer—he's a human lockhead and sword swallower.

.ower East Side 'enement Museum

0 Orchard St at Broome St (212-431-0233; www.tenement.org). Subway: F to Delancey St; J, M, to Essex St. Visitor center open Tue–Fri 1–4pm; at, Sun 11am–4:30pm. $8, students and seniors 6. AmEx, MC, V.
'or a fascinating look at the history of immigra-ion, visit this 19th-century tenement. The building, n the heart of what was once Little Germany, con-ains three reconstructed apartments belonging to German Jewish dressmaker, a Sicilian Catholic amily and an orthodox Jewish brood. Take the tour f you want to see the tenement itself. They're con-lucted Tuesday through Friday every half hour rom 1 to 4pm. Book ahead—the tours always sell ut. A tour designed for families runs Saturday and unday every hour noon to 3pm. The museum also as a gallery, shop and video room, and organizes ocal-heritage walking tours.

Merchant's House Museum

29 E 4th St between Lafayette St and Bowery (212-777-1089; www.merchantshouse.com). Subway: 6 to Astor Pl. Thu–Mon 1–5pm. $5, under 12 free. Cash only.
Seabury Tredwell was the merchant in question. He made his fortune selling hardware and bought this elegant Greek Revival house three years after it was built in 1832. The house has been virtually untouched since the 1860s; the decor is spare (except for the lavish canopied four-poster beds) and the ornamentation tasteful.

Mount Vernon Hotel Museum and Garden

421 E 61st St at First Ave (212-838-6878). Subway: N, R to Lexington Ave; 4, 5, 6 to 59th St. Tue–Sun 11am–4pm. $4, students and seniors $3, under 5 free. Cash only.
This 18th-century coach house was once part of a farm owned by Abigail Adams Smith, the daughter of John Adams, the second president of the U.S. (She and her husband never actually lived here; financial circumstances forced them to sell the estate before they moved in.) It later became a country hotel where New Yorkers went for a bucolic retreat. The house is filled with period articles and furniture (Abigail died in 1813), and there's an adjoining formal garden. The museum is run by the Colonial Dames of America.

Museum of the City of New York

1220 Fifth Ave at 103rd St (212-534-1672; www.mcny.org). Subway: 6 to 103rd St. Wed–Sat 10am–5pm; Sun noon–5pm. Suggested donation $5; students, children and seniors $4; families $10. Cash only.
Several ongoing exhibitions showcase the vast, fascinating history of New York City. Recent installations have examined George Washington's time in NYC, the centennial of Noël Coward's birth and the last 100 years of city history.

New York Historical Society

2 W 77th St at Central Park West (212-873-3400; www.nyhistory.org). Subway: B, C to 81st St. Tue–Sun 11am–5pm. Suggested donation $5. Cash only.
New York's oldest museum, which had been closed for several years after running out of money, is back in business. Founded in 1804, it was one of America's first cultural/educational institutions. Exhibitions include everything from Paul Robeson's diaries to a display about Pocahontas. The permanent collection includes such items as Tiffany lamps (which were made in Queens), lithographs and a lock of George Washington's hair.

Skyscraper Museum

Currently closed, the museum will move into its new permanent site in Battery Park City in 2001. (212-968-1961; www.skyscraper.org). Call for information or visit the website.
When it opens its permanent home in Battery Park City, this unique museum will provide a lavish history of the world's tallest buildings—past, present

and future—through photos, architectural drawings, builders' records and other artifacts.

South Street Seaport Museum

Visitor center, 12 Fulton St at South St on the East River (212-748-8600; www.southstseaport.org). Subway: A, C to Broadway–Nassau; J, M, Z, 2, 3, 4, 5 to Fulton St. Apr 1–Sept 30 Mon, Wed, Fri–Sun 10am–6pm; Thu 10am–8pm. Oct 1–Mar 31 Mon, Wed–Sun 10am–5 pm. $6, seniors $5, students $4, children under 12 $3.

The museum sprawls across 11 blocks along the East River—an amalgam of galleries, historic ships, 19th-century buildings and a visitors' center. The staff (mostly volunteers) is friendly, and it's fun to wander around the rebuilt streets, popping in to see an exhibition on tattooing before climbing aboard the four-masted 1911 *Peking*. The Seaport itself is pretty touristy, but still a charming place to spend an afternoon. Near the Fulton Fish Market building, there are plenty of cafés to choose from.

The Statue of Liberty and Ellis Island Immigration Museum

Ellis Island (212-363-3200). Reached via the Circle Line–Statue of Liberty Ferry (212-269-5755), departing every half hour from Battery Park promenade at the southern tip of Manhattan. Subway: N, R to Whitehall St; 1, 9 to South Ferry; 4, 5 to Bowling Green. First ferry leaves Manhattan at 9am; last ferry leaves at 3:30pm. 9am–5pm. $7, seniors $6, ages 3–17 $3, under 3 free.

An interesting museum devoted to the statue's history is contained in its pedestal. On the way back to Manhattan, the tour boat takes you to the Immigration Museum on Ellis Island, through which more than 12 million people entered the country. The exhibitions are an evocative and moving tribute to anyone who headed for America with dreams of a better life. The audio tour (available in five languages; $3.50) is excellent. (*See chapter* **Downtown.**)

Waterfront Museum

290 Conover St at Pier 45, Red Hook Garden Pier, Red Hook, Brooklyn (718-624-4719; www.waterfrontmuseum.org). Travel: A, C, F to Jay St–Borough Hall; M, N, R to Court St; 2, 3, 4, 5 to Borough Hall; then B61 bus from either Jay at Willoughby St or Atlantic at Court St to Beard St; walk one block west to Conover St.; barge is two blocks south. Garden Pier open daily 24 hours; barge open during special events only. Call for schedule. Free.

Documenting New York's history as a port, this museum is located on a 1914 Lehigh Valley Railroad Barge. Listed on the National Register of Historic Places, it's the only surviving wooden barge of its kind afloat today. See superb views of Manhattan and the busy New York harbor.

Media

American Museum of the Moving Image

35th Ave at 36th St, Astoria, Queens (718-784-0077; www.ammi.org). Subway: G, R to Steinway St; N to 36th Ave. Tue–Fri noon–5pm; Sat, Sun 11am–6pm. $8.50, students and seniors $5. Cash only.

About a 15-minute subway ride from midtown Manhattan, AMMI is one of the city's most dynamic and entertaining institutions. Built within the restored complex that once housed the original Astoria Studios (where commercial filmmaking got its start and continues today), it offers an extensive daily film and video program that should satisfy even the most demanding cinephile. If you're curious about the mechanics and history of movie and television production, the core exhibition, "Behind the Screen," will give you interactive insight into every aspect of it—storyboarding, directing, editing, sound-mixing and marketing. Make your own short at a digital animation stand. The museum has a café, but there are other places to eat nearby; Astoria is the largest Greek community outside Europe, and the neighborhood boasts some terrific Hellenic restaurants.

Museum of Television and Radio

25 W 52nd St between Fifth and Sixth Aves (212-621-6600; www.mtr.org). Subway: B, D, Q to 47–50th Sts–Rockefeller Ctr; E, F to Fifth Ave. Tue, Wed, Fri–Sun noon–6pm; Thu noon–8pm. $6, students and seniors $4, children under 14 $3. Cash only.

This is a living, working archive of more than 60,000 radio and TV programs. Head to the fourth-floor library and use the computerized system to access a favorite *Star Trek* or *I Love Lucy* episode. The assigned console downstairs will play up to four of your choices within two hours. The radio listening room works the same way. There are also special public seminars and screenings. It's a must for TV and radio heads.

Newseum/NY

580 Madison Ave between 56th and 57th Sts (212-317-7503, recorded information 212-317-7596; www.freedomforum.org). Subway: E, F, N, R to Fifth Ave. Mon–Sat 10am–5:30pm. Free.

These are the branch galleries of a Washington, D.C., center for media studies, and the entrance through a pleasant, glass-enclosed atrium of a midtown office tower hardly prepares visitors for the intensity of what lies ahead. Newseum/NY presents topical photography exhibitions that illuminate, with no small emotional impact, the work of prize-winning news photographers and correspondents the world over. Sponsored by the Freedom Forum, it also presents accompanying film and lecture series that encourage public discussion of First Amendment issues. Exhibitions change several times a year. Documentaries screen at 1pm every Monday and Friday and run about an hour.

Subway stories Discover underground New York history at the Transit Museum.

Military

Intrepid Sea-Air-Space Museum

USS Intrepid, *Pier 86, 46th St at the Hudson River (212-245-0072; www.intrepidmuseum.org). Subway: A, C, E to 42nd St–Port Authority. Oct 31–Mar 31 Tue–Sun 10am–5pm; Apr 1–Oct 30 10am–5pm; last admission at 4pm. $10. AmEx, MC, V.*

This museum is located on the World War II aircraft carrier *Intrepid,* whose decks are crammed with space capsules and various aircraft. There are plenty of audiovisual shows, and hands-on exhibits appealing to children.

New York Public Library

The multitentacled New York Public Library, founded in 1895, comprises four major research libraries and 82 local and specialty branches, making it the largest and most comprehensive library system in the world. The library grew from the combined collections of John Jacob Astor, Samuel Jones Tilden and James Lenox. Today, it holds 50 million items, including nearly 18 million books. About a million items are added to the collection each year. Unless you're interested in a specific subject, your best bet is to visit the system's flagship building, officially called the Humanities and Social Sciences Library. The newest branch, the Science, Industry and Business Library, opened in 1996. Information on all branches of the library can be found at www.nypl.org.

Humanities and Social Sciences Library

455 Fifth Ave at 42nd St (recorded information 212-869-8089). Subway: B, D, F, Q to 42nd St; 7 to Fifth Ave. Mon, Thu–Sat 10am–6pm; Tue, Wed 11am–6pm. Free.

This landmark Beaux Arts building is what most people mean when they say "the New York Public Library." The famous stone lions out front are wreathed with holly at Christmas; during the summer people sit on the steps or sip cool drinks at the outdoor tables beneath the arches. The free guided tours of the building at 11am and 2pm include the beautiful and recently renovated Rose Main Reading Room. The Bill Blass Public Catalogue Room was recently restored and renovated and now contains computers for surfing the Internet. Special exhibitions are frequent and worthwhile, and lectures in the Celeste Bartos Forum are always well attended.

Donnell Library Center

20 W 53rd St between Fifth and Sixth Aves (212-621-0618). Subway: E, F to Fifth Ave. Mon, Wed, Fri 10am–6pm; Tue, Thu 10am–8pm; Sat 10am–5pm; Sun 1–5pm. Free.

This branch of the NYPL has an extensive collection of records, films and videotapes, with appropriate screening facilities. The Donnell specializes in foreign-language books—in more than 80 languages—and there's a children's section of more than 100,000 books, films, records and cassettes, as well as the original Winnie the Pooh dolls.

Library for the Performing Arts

Lincoln Center, 111 Amsterdam Ave between 65th and 66th Sts (212-870-1630). Subway: 1, 9 to 66th St–Lincoln Ctr. Free.

This facility, with outstanding research and circulating collections covering music, drama, theater and dance, is closed until late 2000 for renovations. For the circulating collection, visit the Mid-Manhattan Library (*455 Fifth Ave at 40th St*); for the research materials, go to the Library Annex (*521 W 43rd St between Tenth and Eleventh Aves*).

Science, Industry and Business Library

188 Madison Ave between 34th and 35th Sts (212-592-7000). Subway: 6 to 33rd St. Mon, Fri 10am–6pm; Tue, Thu 11am–8pm; Wed 11am–7pm; Sat noon–6pm. Free.

The world's largest public information center devoted to science, technology, economics and business occupies the first floor and lower level of the old B. Altman department store. Opened in 1996 after a $100 million renovation, the new Gwathmey Siegel–designed branch of the NYPL has a circulating collection of 50,000 books and an open-shelf reference collection of 60,000 volumes. Aiming to help people who own small businesses, the library also specializes in digital technologies and the Internet. The library provides a free 30-minute tour on Tuesdays at 2pm.

Schomburg Center for Research in Black Culture

515 Malcolm X Blvd at 135th St (212-491-2200). Subway: 2, 3 to 135th St. Mon–Sat 10am–6pm; Sun 1–5pm. Free.

This extraordinary trove of vintage literature and historical memorabilia relating to black culture and the African diaspora was founded by its first curator, Puerto Rico–born bibliophile Arthur Schomburg, who established the collection in 1926. The Schomburg Center also hosts live jazz concerts, films, lectures and tours.

Science and technology

Liberty Science Center

251 Phillip St, Jersey City, NJ (201-200-1000; www.lsc.org). Travel: Call for directions. Tue–Sun 9:30am–5:30pm. $9.50, students $8.50, children 2–18 and seniors $7.50.

This excellent museum has innovative exhibitions and America's largest, most spectacular IMAX cinema. From the observation tower you get great views of Manhattan and an unusual sideways look at the Statue of Liberty. The center emphasizes hands-on science, so get ready to elbow your way among the excited kids. On weekends, take the ferry.

New York Hall of Science

47-01 111th St at 46th Ave, Flushing Meadows, Queens (718-699-0005; www.nyhallsci.org). Subway: 7 to 111th St. Jul 1–Aug 31 Mon 9:30am–2pm; Tue–Sun 9:30am–5pm. Sept 1–Jun 30 Mon–Wed 9:30am–2pm; Thu–Sun 9:30am–5pm. $7.50, seniors and children $5, Sept 1–Jun 30 Thu, Fri 2–5pm free. AmEx, MC, V.

Since opening during the 1964–65 World's Fair, the New York Hall of Science has built the largest collection of interactive science exhibits in the city; it's now considered one of the top science museums in the country. The emphasis here is on education, and stimulating exhibits successfully demystify science for the school children who usually fill the place. The museum includes a 48-foot-high entrance rotunda, a dining pavilion and a 300-seat auditorium.

Urban services

Fire Museum

278 Spring St at Varick St (212-691-1303; www.nyfd.com/museum.html). Subway: 1, 9 to Houston St. Tue–Sun 10am–4pm. Suggested donation $4. AmEx, MC, V.

This small but cheerful museum is located in an old three-story firehouse whose pole still gleams. See a few vintage fire engines and several displays of fire-fighting ephemera dating back 100 years.

New York Transit Museum

Schermerhorn St at Boerum Pl, Brooklyn Heights, Brooklyn (718-243-3060; www.mta.nyc.ny.us/museum/index.html). Subway: A, C, G to Hoyt–Schermerhorn Sts; F to Jay St; M, N, R to Court St; 2, 3, 4, 5 to Borough Hall. Tue, Thu, Fri 10am–4pm; Sat, Sun noon–5pm. $3. Cash only.

Don't look for a building—the Transit Museum is underground in an old 1930s subway station. Its entrance, down a flight of stairs, is beneath the Board of Education building, across from the black-and-white–striped New York City Transit Authority building. Nose around among vintage subways with wicker seats and canvas straps, antique turnstiles and plenty of ads and public service announcements—including one explaining that spitting "is a violation of the sanitary code." So there! The museum closed in May 2000 for renovation. Work is scheduled to last about six months; call for more information.

New York Police Museum

25 Broadway between Morris St and Battery Pl (212-301-4440). Subway: J, M, Z to Broad St; 1, 9 to Rector St; 4, 5 to Bowling Green. 10am–6pm. Free.

The NYPD's museum dedicated to itself features exhibits on the history of the department and the tools (and transportation) of the trade. It's also the only place in the city where the public can buy officially licensed NYPD paraphernalia, like a lovely police-logo golf shirt.

Music

Sweet symphonies, power pop, sassy salsa, badass blues, jazz in its many permutations—New York has it all, live and on stage *now*

New York makes so much music that sometimes the natives take it for granted. There really is no style of music that can't be found here. As the unofficial capital of the world, the city profits from an endless influx of people and ideas from every corner of the globe, and music fans here are all the luckier for it.

Many music venues don't stick to one kind of music—at Carnegie Hall, for instance, you could hear Yo-Yo Ma one night and Shirley Bassey the next. So we've categorized venues according to the primary genre, and cross-referenced where necessary. Because the classical and opera music scene is so big and well defined, its own section starts on page 317.

Popular Music

Popular songs and beats of all sorts spill out of every bar, club and arena in town; traffic noise notwithstanding, music really is the sound of the city.

With the advent of DJ culture, many clubs are getting adventurous with their musical presentation. Some, like **Joe's Pub,** have local celebrities and artists DJ entire evenings. Others, like the Lower East Side's **Tonic,** have opened separate rooms to accommodate DJs. And at the **Knitting Factory,** with several acts booked every night, there's bound to be something unique and to your liking.

It is refreshing that so many clubs have diverse booking policies, though if you're interested in only one sound, there are plenty of legendary clubs that cater to you. Jazz fan? Try **Birdland** or the **Blue Note.** If you're a rocker, **CBGB** and the **Continental** are musts. Looking for Latin rhythms? Visit **S.O.B.'s** or **Copacabana.** Whatever your tastes, the options are plentiful, which is why we've broken down the most vital music outlets for you here. (*See* **Find your groove** *page 315*).

Rules to follow: Whether you want to drink or not, always bring a photo ID (driver's license or passport will do)—many clubs will ask you to prove that you are 21 or over, no matter how old you look.

Tickets for shows are generally available at the door. For larger events, it's wise to buy

Ion storm Meet the Magnetic Fields, just one of the bands that perform at Bowery Ballroom.

Entertainment

through Ticketmaster over the phone or at outlets throughout the city (*see chapter* **Directory, Tickets**). Tickets for some events are also available through www.ticketweb.com. You can buy tickets online from websites of specific venues (web addresses are included in venue listings where available). See page 317 for more ticket details, and remember: It's always a good idea to call first for info and times, which can change without notice.

> ▶ For annual music events such as the JVC Jazz Festival, see chapter **New York by Season.**
> ▶ For more live-music venues, see chapters **Clubs, Cabaret & Comedy** and **Gay & Lesbian.**
> ▶ For information on specific shows, check the current issue of ***Time Out New York.***

Arenas

Continental Airlines Arena

East Rutherford, NJ (201-935-3900). Travel: NJ Transit bus from Port Authority Bus Terminal, Eighth Ave at 42nd St, $3.25 each way (212-564-8484). From $22.50. Cash only.

New Jersey's answer to Madison Square Garden is the Meadowlands Complex. Not quite as enormous as Giants Stadium, the CAA recently played host to Bruce Springsteen and the E Street Band's much-ballyhooed 15-night homecoming. Along with high-tech productions by the likes of Janet Jackson and Backstreet Boys, the arena is also the sight of radio-sponsored hip-hop extravaganzas.

Madison Square Garden

Seventh Ave at 32nd St (212-465-6741; www.thegarden.com). Subway: A, C, E, 1, 2, 3, 9 to 34th St–Penn Station. $22.50–$75. AmEx, DC, Disc, MC, V.

Awright, Noo Yawk! Are you ready to rock & roll? The acoustics here may be more suited to the crunch of hockey and the slap of basketball, but MSG is the most famous rock venue in the world. Ricky Martin, Marc Anthony, Cher and Bette Midler are but a few who've sold out this place recently. Be warned: The cost of good seats has been known to exceed $100.

Nassau Veterans Memorial Coliseum

1255 Hempstead Turnpike, Uniondale, Long Island (516-794-9303). Travel: Long Island Rail Road (718-217-5477) from Penn Station, Seventh Ave at 32nd St, to Hempstead, then N70, N71 or N72 bus. From $22.50. AmEx, Disc, MC, V.

Nassau Coliseum doesn't have a lot of character, but that quality isn't usually required for "enormodomes," is it? Many of the same shows that play MSG and the Continental Airlines Arena come here, too, and the Coliseum is probably the quintessential place to hear Billy Joel, the pride of Long Island.

Rock, Pop & Soul

Apollo Theatre

253 W 125th St between Adam Clayton Powell Jr. and Frederick Douglass Blvds (Seventh and Eighth Aves) (212-749-5838). Subway: A, C, B, D, 1, 9 to 125th St. $9–$30. AmEx, MC, V.

In its heyday, there was no place as atmospheric as this classic Harlem spot to see R&B acts. Its Wednesday's Amateur Night launched stars such as Ella Fitzgerald and Michael Jackson. Now, the show (taped for TV's *Showtime at the Apollo*) is full of comedians and soul singers hitting as many notes as they can before reaching the right one. Still, it's a fun way to see the Apollo audience in all its cheering and jeering glory. There's an obvious police presence, especially for hip-hop gigs featuring the likes of DMX and Method Man. Don't worry about venturing to Harlem at night. If Korn can do it, so can you.

Arlene Grocery

95 Stanton St between Ludlow and Orchard Sts (212-358-1633). Subway: F to Second Ave; J, M, Z to Essex St. Free. Cash only at bar.

Named for the actual Lower East Side market that it replaced, Arlene Grocery runs as many as seven or eight groups a night through its top-notch sound system. As you might expect, lots of them will never make it, but you could also catch worthy local popsters such as Mach Five or Sean Altman, as well as the popular metal and punk karaoke nights.

Baby Jupiter

170 Orchard St at Stanton St (212-982-2229). Subway: F to Second Ave; J, M, Z to Essex St. Free–$5. MC, V.

Up front, the Lower East Side's Baby Jupiter is a bustling restaurant, but when you walk through the curtains to the live music space, the vibe is laid-back. Plenty of tables, chairs and sofas make you feel right at home for shows by a diverse mix of artists; everyone from singer-songwriters like Leona Naess to funk and hip-hop groups like Anti-Pop Consortium have stopped in. The sound isn't great, but the atmosphere (and prices) at this joint can't be beat.

Baggot Inn

82 W 3rd St between Thompson and Sullivan Sts (212-477-0622). Subway: A, C, E, B, D, F, Q to W 4th St. $5. AmEx, MC, V.

The Baggot Inn has refurbished its interior and its booking policies of late: Good Irish rock can be heard, as well as the bad bar-band fare that's all too typical of the Bleecker Street scene.

BAMcafé/Brooklyn Academy of Music

See page 317 for listings.

Entertainment

The boys from Brazil The samba and salsa bands at S.O.B.'s will get you onto the dance floor.

The Brooklyn Academy of Music used to save the jazz, funk and pop-based world music for the fall Next Wave Festival. Now the BAMcafé, a comfy upstairs lounge, hosts live music on a weekly basis. The mix of genres includes folk, cabaret and spoken word. Performers have included poet Carl Hancock Rux and avant blues griot Mark Anthony Thompson's Chocolate Genius (*see chapters* **New York by Season** *and* **Theater & Dance**).

Beacon Theatre

2124 Broadway at 74th St (212-496-7070). Subway: 1, 2, 3, 9 to 72nd St. $30–$80. Cash only at box office.

The Beacon is almost like the legendary Fillmore East transplanted to the Upper West Side. What else can you say about the site of the Allman Brothers' annual monthlong residency? In recent times, the lovely gilded interiors have seen such varied geniuses as Nick Cave, Brian Wilson and Caetano Veloso.

Bitter End

147 Bleecker St at Thompson St (212-673-7030; www.bitterend.com). Subway: A, C, E, B, D, F, Q to W 4th St. $5. AmEx, Disc, MC, V.

The ne plus ultra of Bleecker Street joints. Although the B-52's are known to play the occasional warm-up gig here (as do faded pop stars à la John Waite), the Bitter End will forever feature singer-songwriters who are just jazzed to be on the same stage where Dylan strummed and sang all those years ago.

BMW Bar

199 Seventh Ave between 21st and 22nd Sts (212-229-1807). Subway: 1, 9 to 23rd St. Free.

Beer and wine aren't the only thing this Chelsea bar serves. BMW Bar also features live acoustic rock, blues, country and folk music, performed regularly by locals Ken Hypes, Rick Johnson and Joe Romby.

Bottom Line

15 W 4th St at Mercer St (212-228-6300). Subway: N, R to 8th St–NYU. $15–$25. Cash only.

Words of warning: Catch the management on a bad night or attend a particularly crowded event, and you'll find yourself a prisoner at the Riker's Island of rock. Nonetheless, Allan Pepper's cabaret-style club has persisted for 25 years, longer than any similar venue. Why? It's the city's premier acoustic venue. Roots music, singer-songwriter stylings, the occasional jazz or fusion gig and Buster Poindexter all find a home here.

Bowery Ballroom

6 Delancey St between Bowery and Chrystie St (212-533-2111). Subway: 6 to Spring St; J, M to Bowery. $10–25. V, MC bar only.

Since opening in 1998, Mercury Lounge's roomy outpost has become the city's most coveted venue for rock, hip-hop and neo-soul acts (Jonathan Richman, the Roots, Broadcast) as well as for DJ sets by the likes of the Chemical Brothers and Fatboy Slim. Besides splendid acoustics and sightlines, there are spacious bars downstairs and overlooking the stage. It's ideal for those "I loathe this band but still want to drink here" moments. The box office is at **Mercury Lounge** (*see page 309*).

Brownies

169 Ave A between 10th and 11th Sts (212-420-8392; www.browniesnyc.com). Subway: 6 to Astor Pl; L to First Ave. $7–$10. AmEx, Disc, MC, V.

This East Village underground rock hot spot has transformed itself over the past couple of years. While the booking still includes longtime indie faves (Versus, Antietam, Papas Fritas) and popular Long Island bands, Brownies now also hosts DJ parties (hip-hop and electronica) several nights a week, starting at 11pm. And dig that shiny copper bar!

Carnegie Hall

See page 317 for listings.

Although a gig at Carnegie Hall is still synonymous with hitting the big time, nowadays many of the venue's showcases are simply reminders that the hall's acoustics were designed for classical music—period. But that doesn't stop veteran folkies like the Band from playing here annually, and it didn't stop Carnegie's honchos from launching a yearlong jazz program, directed by star trumpeter Jon Faddis. Other nights, you might catch world-famous musicians such as the Buena Vista Social Club.

CBGB

315 Bowery at Bleecker St (212-982-4052; www.cbgb.com). Subway: B, D, Q to Broadway–Lafayette St; F to Second Ave; 6 to Bleecker St. $3–$12. Cash only.

Despite the declining quality of its bookings and soundpersons, this venue will forever be an attraction—it is, after all, the birthplace of punk. The brave staff still endures auditions on Sundays and Mondays, but the usual offerings are local indie and punk bands, vintage big names such as Tom Tom Club and hip traveling acts like Royal Trux.

CB's 313 Gallery

313 Bowery at Bleecker St (212-677-0455). Subway: B, D, F, Q to Broadway–Lafayette St; 6 to Bleecker St. $6–$10. AmEx, MC, V.

The Gallery is CBGB's more cultivated cousin. It's just as long and narrow, but it's festooned with local artists' work instead of graffiti and layers of posters. Acoustic fare, local singer-songwriters and the like dominate.

C-Note

157 Ave C at 10th St (212-677-8142). Subway: F to Second Ave; L to First Ave; 6 to Astor Pl. Free.

This joint has a mix of singer-songwriter fare, guitar-based pop and jazz. It also occasionally hosts CD release parties for local bands and special events such as the Women in Music Fest.

Continental

25 Third Ave at St. Marks Pl (212-529-6924). Subway: N, R to 8th St–NYU; 6 to Astor Pl. Free–$6. Cash only.

The Continental's walls are crammed with photos of its past performances—people like the Ramones and Wendy O. Williams—and big names like Iggy Pop still drop in from time to time. You're more likely, though, to catch a local posthardcore act. Even so, punk-scene legends such as the Rattlers (from NYC) and Fear and the Real Kids (from elsewhere) would rather kick out the jams on the great sound system here than just about anywhere else.

The Cooler

416 W 14th St between Ninth Ave and Washington St (212-229-0785; www.thecooler.com). Subway: A, C, E to 14th St; L to Eighth Ave. Free–$15. AmEx, MC, V.

It's easy to miss this basement space's street-level door (look for the LIVE MUSIC sign), but once you get in you'll be struck by the former meat locker's dark atmosphere. There are drawbacks—too hot, too cold, too crowded to see who's on the low stage—but the often intriguing bills mix avant rock with electronic music and hip-hop. Look out for appearances by Prince Paul and a variety of Sonic Youth–related projects, as well as the popular kitsch-funk Vampyros Lesbos parties. Mondays are free.

Don Hill's

511 Greenwich St at Spring St (212-334-1390). Subway: C, E to Spring St; 1, 9 to Houston St. $5–12. AmEx, DC, MC, V.

See chapter **Clubs** for review.

Downtime

251 W 30th St between Seventh and Eighth Aves (212-695-2747). Subway: 1, 9 to 28th St. $5–$12. AmEx, MC, V.

During the week, run-of-the-mill rock bands play in this vertically spacious bar with an upstairs lounge and pool table. But locals such as Lo-Fi Lee book swing and fun "horror rock" events, too, mixing classic films with cool bands. The club has also been throwing Goth-oriented parties for new records by the Cure and the like.

Elbow Room

144 Bleecker St between Thompson St and La Guardia Pl (212-979-8434). Subway: A, C, E, B, D, F, Q to W 4th. $5–$10. AmEx, MC, V.

Yet another dive on Bleecker Street, the Elbow Room

achieved A-list status in 1998, when its Wednesday night karaoke parties drew the likes of Courtney Love and Claire Danes to the mike—and inspired a short-lived VH1 special in the process. Local music of all stripes rules every other night of the week.

Fez

Inside Time Café, 380 Lafayette St at Great Jones St (212-533-2680). Subway: B, D, F, Q to Broadway–Lafayette St; 6 to Bleecker St. $5–$18, plus two-drink minimum. AmEx, MC, V.

Fez is one of the city's finest venues for lounge/cabaret acts. Located downstairs from the back of the restuarnt Time Café, it hosts a variety of local events, such as the popular Loser's Lounge tribute series. On Thursdays, the Mingus Big Band introduces a new generation of listeners to the robust, sanctified jazz of the late Charles Mingus. Its dinner-theater–style seating leaves little standing room, so make reservations and arrive early. (*See chapter* **Bars.**)

Hammerstein Ballroom at the Manhattan Center

Manhattan Center, 311 W 34th St between Eighth and Ninth Aves (212-564-4882). Subway: A, C, E to 34th St–Penn Station. $10–$20. Cash only.

Built inside the Moonie-owned Manhattan Center, the Hammerstein Ballroom is a multitiered space that is slightly larger than midsize venues like Irving Plaza, yet nowhere near as massive as Madison Square Garden. This is the venue of choice for dance acts (Prodigy, Underworld, Fatboy Slim), hip-hop and R&B (Eminem, the Roots, Kelis) and, of course, rawk & roll (Marilyn Manson, Kid Rock, Ben Folds Five). Security is a hassle, and the sound pretty much sucks, but hey, the sightlines can't be beat.

Irving Plaza

17 Irving Pl at 15th St (212-777-6800). Subway: L, N, R, 4, 5, 6 to 14th St–Union Sq. $10–$30. Cash only.

For a while, Irving Plaza was unique: a midsize venue that was often the first stop on the path to superstardom for aspiring national touring acts. Now there's competition, but Irving is still nothing to sniff at. Elegant decor, an upstairs lounge and a giant screen playing videos and TV-footage collages from the Emergency Broadcast Network complement a sterling booking reputation. The Beta Band, Macy Gray, Luscious Jackson, Squeeze and loads of up-and-coming acts have played here. Jay-Z threw his release party for *Vol. 3...Life and Times of S. Carter* here, too.

Stylin' The Knitting Factory features rock, funk and jazz—just what Vernon Reid plays.

Izzy Bar

116 First Ave at between 10th and 11th Sts (212-228-0444). Subway: L to First Ave; 6 to Astor Pl. $5–$10. AmEx, MC, V.

Initially a haven for left field jazz acts, Izzy Bar has become one of NYC's better temples of groove. In addition to some smoking nights geared toward lovers of house and drum 'n' bass, funk bands and jazz-tinged jam sessions keep the party going.

Joe's Pub

425 Lafayette St between 4th St and Astor Pl (212-539-8770). Subway: 6 to Astor Pl; N, R to 8th St–NYU. $12–$35. AmEx, DC, Disc, MC, V.

Named in honor of Public Theater founder Joseph Papp, Joe's Pub features eclectic entertainment (Rickie Lee Jones, Youssou N'Dour, Me'Shell NdegéOcello, Charlie Hunter) in a posh, neocabaret setting. Even when the bar is crowded, this small room maintains its quiet cool, as downtown hipsters unwind on comfy couches. Beware: Seating is limited and the door policy is selectively strict. (See chapter **Cabaret & Comedy**.)

Knitting Factory/The Old Office/ The KnitActive SoundStage

74 Leonard St between Broadway and Church St (212-219-3055; www.knittingfactory.com). Subway: A, C, E to Canal St; 1, 9 to Franklin St. $5–$20. AmEx, MC, V ($15 minimum charge).

On some nights, you can traverse entire galaxies of music just by going from one room to another. The main performance space could host a basic rock or indie act (Lou Reed, Elf Power) or genre jumper (Arto Lindsay, Vinicius Cantuária), while the smaller KnitActive Soundstage and Old Office might feature poetry, alternative cinema or jazz artists (Tim Berne, any number of John Zorn protégés or sidemen). The café and bar are open throughout the day, and the main room holds 250 people.

L'Amour

1545 63rd St between Fifteenth and Sixteenth Aves, Bay Ridge, Brooklyn (718-837-9506). Subway: N to New Utrecht Ave; B to 62nd St.

This hard-rock landmark reopened in late 1999 to host the kind of metal shows that made it famous back in the '80s. In its heyday, L'Amour was ground zero for metal, and was the only place to hear such bands as Queensrÿche and Metallica, along with local regulars Anthrax, Twisted Sister and M.O.D. Ask a veteran what went on in those days. One person who can attest to the club being a "crazy, wild place" is Sebastian Bach, who has played here.

The Living Room

84 Stanton St at Allen St (212-533-7235). Subway: F to Second Ave; J, M, Z to Essex St. Free. Cash only.
The Living Room is a cozy lounge-type space, and as you'd expect from the name, its singer-songwriters play right there, up close and personal. The ambience is low-key and friendly, and when out-of-towners (such as Trailer Bride) drop in, a hat is often passed around for gas money. Keep an eye out for quality locals like Jenifer Jackson and Timothy "Speed" Levitch (from the documentary *The Cruise*), who play regularly.

Luna Lounge

171 Ludlow St between Houston and Stanton Sts (212-260-2323). Subway: F to Second Ave. Free. Cash only.
This popular Lower East Side hangout has a bustling bar up front and a stage in the back. The music is always free, so there's a fair share of dreck, but the cozy confines make it go down easy and there are still good pop performances by the likes of Frank Bango and Richard X. Heyman.

Makor

35 W 67th St at Columbus Ave (212-601-1000). Subway: 1, 9 to 66th St. $5–$12. AmEx, MC, V.
Makor isn't your average Jewish cultural center. Of course, it has its share of klezmer and folkloric events, but the plush music room in the basement also hosts plenty of funk, jazz and world music. Past performers range from groovehounds Medeski Martin & Wood to the Cuban diva Albita.

Manitoba's

99 Ave B between 6th and 7th Sts (212-982-2511). Subway: F to Second Ave; L to First Ave. Free. AmEx, DC, Disc, MC, V.
Ever since the Avenue B Social Club got a name change from its new owner, the Dictators' legendary Handsome Dick Manitoba, Beat Rodeo, Adam Roth and other great local acts have set up weekly residencies, packing fans into this small, friendly room. Power-popper Jonnie Chan & the New Dynasty Six, country stylist Tom Clark and the rootsy Simon & the Bar Sinisters play regularly.

Maxwell's

1039 Washington St, Hoboken, NJ (201-798 0406). Travel: PATH train to Hoboken; NJ Transit bus #126 from Port Authority Bus Terminal. $5–$12. AmEx, DC, MC, V.
Maxwell's has been the most consistently forward-looking rock club in the metropolitan area for the past 15 years. Since it's in another state, many visiting acts play a date here as well as at the Bowery

From Jamaica with love

The originator of the city's block-rockin' beats actually came from a Caribbean island

Hip-hop and New York are inextricably linked, but if you go way back, the beat's seed was planted in 1967, when a 13-year-old Jamaican arrived in the Bronx. Clive "Herc" Campbell, already skilled on turntables, would grow up to become DJ Kool Herc, the undisputed godfather of hip-hop.

As an adolescent coming of age in Jamaica's Trenchtown ghetto, Herc learned how to DJ and operate sound systems while peeking through the fences at blues dances and watching dub and talk-over masters such as U Roy, Prince Buster and King George. After he and his family moved to the Bronx, Herc's mother introduced him to the Motown sound and American R&B heavyweights such as James Brown.

In 1973, Herc made his humble debut at his sister's birthday party, held in the West Bronx housing project that his family called home. Word of his performance spread. Applying techniques he picked up in Jamaica to his own powerful sound system, Herc became a bona fide DJ star. Fans flocked to his parties, held at now-defunct clubs like the Executive Playhouse, Hevalo and the Twilight Zone.

What distinguished Herc from other New York DJs was his unique playlist, which he guarded vigilantly, going so far as to soak the labels off his records—a technique used by Jamaican DJs to skunk the competition. Instead of spinning trendy disco hits, Herc created entirely new music by piecing together snippets of obscure old funk, soul and R&B records. Partygoers responded so strongly to the drum- and percussion-drenched breaks of songs like "Apache" that he began to cut back and forth between copies of the same record to extend the effect. The technique came to be known as the breakbeat—the foundation of hip-hop.

By 1975, younger DJs like Grandmaster Flash—who went on to record such seminal hits as "The Message" and "White Lines"—were modifying Herc's new sound. As a student at Samuel Gompers Vocational High

Ballroom, Knitting Factory, etc. It can get a little close when it's crowded, but hey, it's a landmark. The dining room serves edible bar food. Music ranges from garage and punk to indie and roots.

Meow Mix

269 Houston St at Suffolk St (212-254-0688). Subway: F to Second Ave. $5. Cash only.

The music at this brew-fueled neighborhood dyke bar ranges from trashed-up glam to singer-songwriter fare and an anything-goes DJ aesthetic. The last Sunday of every month features popular tribute shows, which showcase downtown bands who give it up for anybody from Kiss to the Jackson 5. (*See chapter* **Gay & Lesbian.**)

Mercury Lounge

217 Houston St at Ave A (212-260-4700; www.mercuryloungenyc.com). Subway: F to Second Ave. $6–$12. MC, V.

Squeeze past the narrow bar up front to get to the brick-walled live-music room in back. The sound is great, you can see from just about any spot, and the staff actually treat you nicely (you can get a glass of water for free!). The music ranges from the rumbling blues of 20 Miles to the classic, dark NYC sound of Kid Congo Powers or the Gunga Din, with all manner of singer-songwriters and a mix of others thrown in.

Nell's

246 W 14th St between Seventh and Eighth Aves (212-675-1567; www.nells.com). Subway: A, C, E, 1, 2, 3, 9 to 14th St; L to Eighth Ave. $10–$15. AmEx, MC, V (for drinks only).

Nell's plush interior, modeled after a Victorian gentlemen's club, was the place to be seen in the late 1980s—if you could get in. In the 1990s (and still packed nightly), the crowd type shifted from international jet set to hip-hop royalty. The late Notorious B.I.G. shot a video here and Tupac Shakur reportedly got a blow job on the dance floor. Nowadays, Nell's mostly offers local funk, reggae, world and Latin acts, as well as a weekly open mike R&B night. Don't count out this New York City institution just yet. (*See chapter* **Clubs.**)

Nightingale Bar

213 Second Ave at 13th St (212-473-9398). Subway: L to First Ave. $5. Cash only.

The mother of all NYC dives, this bar has a stage that's about six inches off the ground. When seeing a band here, there's no way to avoid feeling as though you're up there with them. This is the place that, for better or worse, gave the world Blues Traveler and the Spin Doctors. Don't miss the Fleshtones whenever they play here.

School in the Bronx, Flash played a key role in the evolution of hip-hop when he designed and assembled a cue monitor for his mixer. "My peek-a-boo system, which I later found out was called a cue monitor, allowed me to prehear a passage of music in my headphones before I pushed it out to the people," Flash explains. "I was able to play a section of music on one record, prehear it on the other, and when it was getting ready to go off, segue the other record in on time. I could take a section of a song that was maybe ten seconds and make it five minutes long if I cared to."

Nowadays, however, the MC has replaced the DJ as the most prominent member of the standard hip-hop group. "I think a lot of it has to do with modern technology," says Flash. "Some MCs today prefer to use a DAT [Digital Audio Tape player], because it sounds cleaner and doesn't skip if you're jumping around onstage. But I feel that people still come to see the DJ, even if he makes a couple of mistakes—it's part of the realism. The DJ sets the atmosphere and has to entertain a crowd that's cool and waiting for something to happen. We set the atmosphere so that the MCs can just take it to the next level when they come onstage."

Think you can take it to the next level yourself? Pick up the same music New York's hottest DJs buy at the following record stores, which specialize in hip-hop.

Beat Street

494 Fulton St between Bond St and Elm Pl, Brooklyn (718-624-6400). Subway: A, C, G to Hoyt–Schermerhorn Sts; 2, 3 to Hoyt St. Mon–Sat 9:30am–7pm; Sun 9:30am–6pm. AmEx, Disc, MC, V.

Beat Street, a block-long basement with two DJ booths, has the latest vinyl to go with that phat new sound system. CDs run the gamut from gospel to dancehall. But it's the reggae boom shots, 12-inch singles and new hip-hop albums that make this the first stop for local DJs seeking killer breakbeats and samples.

Etherea

66 Ave A between 4th and 5th Sts (212-358-1126). Subway: F to Second Ave. Mon–Thu noon–10:30pm; Fri, Sat noon–11:30pm; Sun noon–11pm.

Etherea is dominated by indie, experimental, electronic and rock records, with smaller sections of hip-hop and jazz. The selection of used vinyl is particularly good.

New Jersey Performing Arts Center

1 Center St at the waterfront, Newark, NJ (888-466-5722). Travel: PATH train to Newark, then take Loop shuttle bus two stops to center. $12–$100. AmEx, DC, MC, V.

NJPAC, the sixth largest performing arts center in the U.S., features everything from the Buena Vista Social Club and jazz singer-pianist Diana Krall to Irish pop star Mary Black and the Grammy-winning a capella quintet Sweet Honey in the Rock (*see page 318*).

9C

700 E 9th St at Ave C (212-358-0048). Subway: F to Second Ave; L to First Ave; 6 to Astor Pl. Free–$5. Cash only.

Deep in the heart of Alphabet City, this unassuming watering hole hosts a weekly Opry-style hootenany hosted by Greg Garing, who looks like Peter Murphy and sings like Ira Louvin. Garing has had less impact here than he did in Nashville, where he singlehandedly kick-started a grassroots hoots scene, but something great happens every once in a while.

92nd Street Y

See page 318 and chapter **Books & Poetry** *for listings.*

The Y's popular music schedule extends to gospel, various indigenous folkloric styles and jazz of the mainstream variety. Jazz in July, the program's centerpiece, entices swingers young and old into the comfy surroundings, as does the Lyrics & Lyricists Series, which celebrates the tunesmiths who wrote the American popular songbook.

Radio City Music Hall

1260 Sixth Ave at 50th St (212-247-4777). Subway: B, D, F, Q to 47–50th St–Rockefeller Ctr. From $25. AmEx, MC, V.

After a multimillion-dollar restoration, this awe-inspiring Art Deco hall is more dazzling than ever. Walking through Radio City Music Hall is almost as exciting as watching the superstars who perform here. Although the posh assigned seating isn't ideal for rock acts Beck and Radiohead, it's tailor-made for vocally oriented performers k.d. lang and D'Angelo. The hall also hosts the annual Christmas Spectacular (*see chapter* **New York by Season**).

Roxy

515 W 18th St between Tenth and Eleventh Aves (212-645-5156; tickets sold through Ticketmaster, 212-307-7171; www.roxynyc.com). Subway: A, C, E to 14th St; L to Eighth Ave. $12–$20.

Mainly a dance club, and once the cradle of hip-hop, Roxy doesn't have live performances regularly, but De La Soul, Moby and Femi Kuti have all taken bows at this roller rink. (*See chapter* **Clubs**.)

Entertainment

From Jamaica with love (continued)

Fat Beats

406 Sixth Ave between 8th and 9th Sts, second floor (212-673-3883). Subway: A, C, E, B, D, F, Q to W 4th St. Mon–Fri noon–9pm; Sat, Sun noon–10pm. MC, V.

Fat Beats is to local hip-hop what church is to gospel music: the foundation. Twin Technics 1200 turntables command the center of this tiny West Village shrine to vinyl. Everyone—Q-Tip, DJ Evil Dee, DJ Premier, Beck, Mike D, Marilyn Manson—shops here regularly for treasured hip-hop, jazz and reggae releases, as well as underground magazines like *Stress* and cult flicks like *Wild Style*. And Fat Beats is the one spot where you're almost certain to find regular customer and former Ultramagnetic MC Kool Keith wearing a cape, silver boots and...a sock.

Joe's CDs

11 St. Marks Pl between Second and Third Aves (212-673-4606). Subway: 6 to Astor Pl. Mon–Thu 11am–11pm; Fri, Sat 11am–midnight; Sun 11am–9pm.

On a block riddled with rock-oriented CD stores, Joe's compensates with sizable sections of reasonably priced techno, hip-hop and acid-jazz titles. Another room features a wall of not-bad used and advance CDs and other curiosities (all $2.99 or less).

Other location: *96 Christopher St at Bleecker St (212-414-4099). Subway: 1, 9 to Christopher St–Sheridan Sq. Mon–Fri 11am–10pm; Sat, Sun 11am–11pm.*

MoonSka

84 E 10th St between Third and Fourth Aves (212-673-5538). Subway: 6 to Astor Pl. Noon–8pm. AmEx, Disc, DC, MC, V.

This East Village dive stocks the most diverse selection of ska in New York—if not the country. The inventory reflects everything from ska's Jamaican origins to the godforsaken shift that occurred when groups like the Mighty Mighty Bosstones and Sublime appropriated the sound and reduced it to '90s pop.

Superpower

4905 Church Ave between Utica Ave and E 49th St, Crown Heights, Brooklyn

Shine

285 West Broadway at Canal St (212-941-0900; www.shinelive.com). Subway: A, C, E, 1, 9 to Canal St. $6–$15. AmEx, MC, V (for drinks only).
One of Tribeca's hottest nightspots, Shine has a red velvety interior that's frequented by the likes of Puff Daddy, Jennifer Lopez and Leonardo DiCaprio. It hosts gigs by local bands of questionable merit and more than a few of yesteryear's one-hit wonders. Plus, there are infrequent stands by up-and-comer bands (New Radicals and Dot Allison) and the odd old-timer (Iggy Pop).

Sidewalk

94 Ave A at 6th St (212-473-7373). Subway: F to Second Ave; 6 to Astor Pl. Free. AmEx, MC, V.
They call it "the Fort at Sidewalk," possibly because you have to wend your way through several rooms of diners and drinkers to get to the music space, way in back. Once you're there, anything goes, with the music supplied by host Lach and the "antifolk" scene he spearheads. Open mikes and jam sessions occur frequently, in case you have the mind to drop by with your acoustic guitar, and a passel of antifolkies hit the floor (there's no stage) every night.

S.O.B.'s

204 Varick St at Houston St (212-243-4940; www.sobs.com). Subway: 1, 9 to Houston St. $10–$25. AmEx, DC, Disc, JCB, MC, V.

(718-282-7746). Travel: 2, 5 to Church Ave, then B35 bus to Utica Ave. Mon–Fri 9am–9pm; Sat 9am–11pm. AmEx, Disc, DC, MC, V.
The city's most comprehensive reggae store and distributor carries a full selection of the latest CDs and tapes, but vinyl is the big draw. Pick out brand-spanking-new dancehall from Sizzla, Beenie Man and Buju Banton or rootsy classics by the likes of Joe Higgs and the Congos. You can even have the in-house DJ spin the latest 45s.

Upstairs

2968 Ave X at Nostrand Ave, Sheepshead Bay, Brooklyn (718-567-3333). Subway: D to Sheepshead Bay. Mon–Fri 9am–7pm; Sun 10am–5pm. AmEx, Disc, MC, V.
A DJ's paradise, this huge store stocks an estimated 20,000 records, including classics like A Tribe Called Quest's *People's Instinctive Travels and the Paths of Rhythm* and Boogie Down Productions' *Criminal Minded.* Upstairs attracts a host of curious collectors from around the world, so the vinyl tends to disappear from the shelves shortly after it arrives.

S.O.B.'s stands for "Sounds of Brazil," but that's not the only kind of music you'll dance to at the city's premier spot for musicians from south of the border. Besides samba, there's reggae (Sugar Minott, the Congos), other Caribbean stuff (Sweet Micky, Malavoi), Afropop (Kanda Bongo Man, Ricardo Lemvo and Makina Loca) and even hip-hop (Jeru the Damaja). Mondays—La Tropica Nights—are devoted to salsa's biggest names. The safari-themed restaurant's dance floor sees its share of hip-hoppers and well-heeled denizens who stop by after work to sample contemporary jazz and R&B.

The Supper Club

240 W 47th St between Eighth Ave and Broadway (212-921-1940). Subway: N, R, S, 1, 2, 3, 9, 7 to 42nd St–Times Sq. $12–$15. AmEx, MC, V.
The gorgeous, ornate Supper Club has acoustics that are clean enough to please such particular artists as Amel Larrieux, Rufus Wainwright and Beck. (*See chapter* **Cabaret & Comedy**.)

Symphony Space

2537 Broadway at 95th St (212-864-1414). Subway: 1, 2, 3, 9 to 96th St. $10–$25. AmEx, MC, V.
Symphony Space is the venue for all kinds of music, but the 1,000-seat hall is probably best known for the multiculti concerts presented by the World Music Institute. The crowds clap as hard for Gypsy revelers Taraf de Haidouks as they do for the earth-shaking gospel brass band McCollough's Sons of Thunder. Many of the city's homesick nationals end up dancing onstage with the visiting stars by concert's end. (*See page 320.*)

The Theater at Madison Square Garden

Seventh Ave at 32nd St (212-465-6741). Subway: A, C, E, 1, 2, 3, 9 to 34th St–Penn Station. Prices vary. AmEx, DC, Disc, MC, V.
This is the smaller, classier extension of Madison Square Garden, and since it's not an arena, it also sounds better. The theater hosts celebrations such as a Caribbean All-Stars Festival and pop divas (Lauryn Hill, Whitney Houston, Joni Mitchell), who probably could sell out the Garden anyway but want that quasi–dinner theater vibe.

Town Hall

123 W 43rd St between Sixth and Seventh Aves (212-840-2824). Subway: B, D, F, Q to 42nd St; N, R, S, 1, 2, 3, 9, 7 to 42nd St–Times Sq. $15–$25. AmEx, MC, V.
A venerable theater with ear-pleasing acoustics, Town Hall was conceived as the people's auditorium, and its democratic bookings keep that spirit alive. In addition to shows by folk stars such as Kate and Anna McGarrigle, you can also catch showcases by disco institutions like Martha Wash, French atmospherists Air and Fred Hersch, and plenty of Celtic and world-beat events.

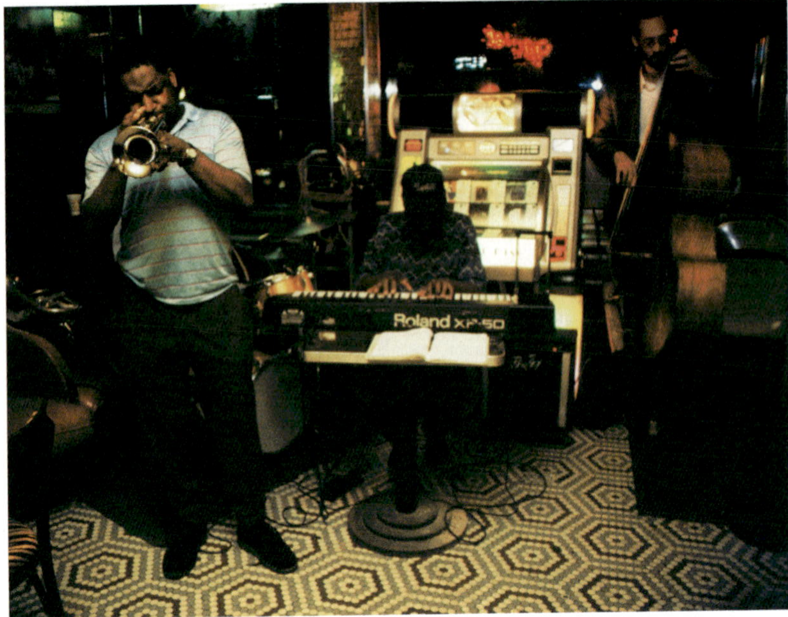

X marks the spot Old-school jazz still rules at Lenox Lounge, where Malcolm X once hung out.

Tonic

107 Norfolk St between Delancey and Rivington Sts (212-358-7503; www.tonic107.com). Subway: F to Delancey St; J, M, Z to Essex St. $8–$12. Cash only.
Tonic, a former kosher winery, is one of the premier spots for experimental jazz and rock. Hordes of working jazz musicians, including Susie Ibarra and Matthew Shipp, play in many permutations with each other and with guests. John Zorn and Michael Gira are just two musicians who've curated the Sunday songwriter series. The Subtonic lounge downstairs features DJs and a killer vibe (the booths are old wine casks). Check your expectations at the door—at Tonic, anything really can happen.

Westbeth Theater Center Music Hall

151 Bank St between West and Washington Sts (212-741-0391; www.westbeththeater.com). Subway: A, C, E to 14th St; L to Eighth Ave. $8–$35. Cash only.
The Westbeth is a 500-capacity space with decent sound that has seen shows from Pavement, Elliott Smith and Beth Orton—and hosted the garage-rock festival called Cavestomp. It has a nice bar area outside the main room, where you can hang if you're not digging the opening act.

Wetlands Preserve

161 Hudson St at Laight St (212-966-4225; www.wetlands-preserve.org). Subway: A, C, E, 1, 9 to Canal St. Free–$15. AmEx, MC, V (drinks only).
Deadheads seeking to keep the vibe alive flock here for Dead cover bands and musicians peripherally connected to the band. The club also regularly books ska, funk, reggae, jungle, hip-hop and hardcore marathons—making it a haven for urban sounds of all types. The Roots have been hosting a popular weekly free-form jam geared toward female hip-hoppers. And activists can feast on the wealth of information on the community bulletin board.

Windows on the World

1 World Trade Center, West St between Liberty and Vesey Sts (212-524-7000; www.windowsonthe world.com). Subway: A, C to Chambers St; E to World Trade Ctr; N, R, 1, 9 to Cortlandt St. $5. AmEx, MC, V (drinks only).
Windows is a romantic bar in which to sip very expensive drinks, sample dull food and dance to local DJs, funk and Latin-pop bands atop the World Trade Center—on the 107th floor, actually. The Dust Brothers, Kid Creole and the Coconuts and other big names play here on occasion. The dress code is "cocktail casual," which means no jeans or sneakers. (*See chapters* **Restaurants** *and* **Clubs**.)

Jazz & Experimental

Birdland

315 W 44th St between Eighth and Ninth Aves (212-581-3080; www.birdlandjazz.com). Subway: A,

C, E to 42nd St–Port Authority. $15–$25. AmEx, MC, V.
The flagship venue for midtown's recent jazz resurgence, Birdland hosts many of jazz's biggest names amid the neon bustle of Times Square. The dining area's three tiers allow for maximum visibility, so patrons can experience everyone from Pat Metheny and Terence Blanchard to Chico O'Farrill while also enjoying pretty fine cuisine. To compete with the Monday-night big bands in residence elsewhere, the club has enlisted the Toshiko Akiyoshi Jazz Orchestra, featuring Lew Tabackin.

Blue Note

131 W 3rd St between MacDougal St and Sixth Ave (212-475-8592; www.bluenote.net). Subway: A, C, E, B, D, F, Q to W 4th St. $10–$65, plus $5 minimum. AmEx, DC, Disc, MC, V.
"The jazz capital of the world" is how this famous club describes itself, and the big names who play here are often greeted as if they're visiting heads of state. Recent acts have included Chaka Khan, Roberta Flack and Michel Legrand. All this comes at a price: Dinner will cost you more than $25 a head.

Cornelia Street Café

29 Cornelia St between Bleecker and 4th Sts (212-989-9318). Subway: A, C, E, B, D, F, Q to W 4th St. $5–$10. AmEx, DC, MC, V.
Cornelia Street Café may be avant-garde, but it's accessible too. There's something about walking down the stairs of this Greenwich Village eatery that brings out the calm in some of the scene's most adventurous players (Tony Malaby, Tom Varner). The result is dinner music with a contemporary edge.

Deanna's

107 Rivington St between Ludlow and Essex Sts (212-420-2258). Subway: F to Delancey St; J, M, Z to Essex St. $6. AmEx.
From the lounge in front to the oak tables and grand piano at its center, Deanna's resembles a speakeasy. Its stylish grandeur creates the perfect atmosphere in which to hear some of the local jazz scene's finest musicians, but arguably the biggest draw is proprietor Deanna Kirk, a fine singer who can croon with the best of them and periodically gets onstage to prove it.

Stanley H. Kaplan Penthouse at Lincoln Center

165 W 65th St at Eighth Ave, tenth floor (212-875-5400). Subway: 1, 9 to 66th St–Lincoln Ctr. Tickets available from Alice Tully Hall box office. AmEx, DC, Disc, MC, V.
If you thought Lincoln Center only housed grand concert halls, you should come hear one of the jazz events at the Kaplan Penthouse. A 100-seat room with a terrace that offers a scenic view of the Hudson River, the Penthouse is the specialty room for the Lincoln Center jazz program's series of duets and solo recitals. It's like having Tommy Flanagan, Geri Allen, Sir Roland Hanna or Chucho Valdés while away the evening in your living room.

Iridium

48 W 63rd St at Columbus Ave (212-582-2121; www.iridiumjazz.com). Subway: 1, 9 to 66th St–Lincoln Ctr. $25–$30, plus $10 minimum. AmEx, DC, Disc, JCB, MC, V.
This club's location—across the street from Lincoln Center—guarantees that its lineups are generally top-notch. Amid a decor that's a little Art Nouveau and a little Dr. Seuss, Iridium lures upscale crowds with a bill that's split between household names and those known only by the jazz-savvy. Monday nights belong to the legendary guitarist, inventor and icon Les Paul, who often ends up sharing the stage with one of the guitar heroes who swear by his prize invention, the Gibson solid-body electric guitar.

The Jazz Standard

116 E 27th St between Park Ave South and Lexington Ave (212-576-2232; www.jazzstandard.com). Subway: 6 to 28th St. $10–$20, plus $10 minimum at tables. AmEx, DC, MC, V.
The bilevel Jazz Standard is a club for all jazz tastes. Upstairs, there's a restaurant/lounge piping in the kind of cool sounds that enhance dinner and conversation. Downstairs, talented instrumentalists (Gary Bartz, Benny Golson, David "Fathead" Newman) hold sway in the 130-plus–capacity music room. The fine acoustics and unobstructed sightlines will delight jazz vets and rookies alike.

Knitting Factory/The Old Office/ The KnitActive SoundStage

See page 307 for listings.

Lenox Lounge

288 Lenox Ave between 124th and 125th Sts (212-427-0253). Subway: 2, 3 to 125th St. $10. Cash only.
Onetime Lenox Lounge regular Billie Holiday might not recognize this Art Deco paradise in the wake of its recent renovation, but she wouldn't be put off by its retrofied "new" look. Although the jazz here isn't always traditional, the hardbop outfits that jam here (Cecil Payne, James Spaulding, John Hicks) make no bones about carrying on an old tradition. (*See* **Movin' on up,** *page 70.*)

Merkin Concert Hall

See page 318 for listings.
Just across the street from Lincoln Center, Merkin's smaller, equally elegant digs provide an intimate setting for jazz and experimental music (Matthew Shipp) not likely to be heard at Avery Fisher Hall.

Roulette

228 West Broadway at White St (212-219-8242; www.roulette.org). Subway: C, E to Canal St; 1, 9 to Franklin St. $10. Cash only.
Ever thought you might want live music in your living room? Well, improvising trombonist/Roulette proprietor Jim Staley has saved you the trouble. The atmosphere in his ten-year-old salon is relaxed—until the music starts up. The players, Staley's friends, represent an encyclopedia of world-famous music experimentalists. You're as likely to hear

Entertainment

computer-music pioneers such as David Behrman as you are avant-jazzers like Dave Douglas.

Smalls

183 W 10th St at Seventh Ave South (212-929-7565). Subway: 1, 9 to Christopher St–Sheridan Sq. $10. Cash only.

The spot where jazz new jacks rub elbows with their college-student counterparts and Beat-era nostalgists, Smalls books high-profile up-and-comers (Jason Lindner, Myron Walden, James Hurt) and established stars (Lee Konitz). There's no liquor license, but you can bring your own booze or sample some of the juices at the bar.

St. Nick's Pub

773 St. Nicholas Ave at 149th St (212-283-9728). Subway: A, C, B, D to 145th St. $5. Cash only.

St. Nick's may be the closest thing to an old-fashioned juke joint you're likely to find in the city: It's got live music six nights a week, charmingly makeshift decor and mature patrons who take their hedonistic impulses seriously. It's possible to hear practically every type of music here (except hip-hop), but Monday night's amazing jam session with Patience Higgins's Sugar Hill Jazz Quartet is the draw. (*See* **Movin' on up,** *page 70.*)

Sweet Basil

88 Seventh Ave South between Bleecker and Grove Sts (212-242-1785; www.sweetbasil.com). Subway: 1, 9 to Christopher St–Sheridan Sq. $17.50–$20, plus $10 minimum. AmEx, MC, V.

Sweet Basil is one reason that many people consider Seventh Avenue South to be a prime stretch of jazz real estate; past players have included Abdullah Ibrahim and the late Art Blakey. The club now showcases young players (Abraham Burton, Renee Rosnes, Marc Cary) as well as veterans. It serves dinner, and there's a weekend jazz brunch.

Swing 46

349 W 46th St between Eighth and Ninth Aves (212-262-9554). Subway: A, C, E to 42nd St–Port Authority. Thu–Sat $12; Sun–Wed $7. MC, V.

You don't have to don a zoot suit or a poodle skirt to make the scene at this midtown bastion of retro, but it certainly enhances the vibe. Seven nights' worth of bands that jump, jive and wail await you here, so be sure to wear your most comfortable shoes. Dancing is a must.

Tonic

See page 312 for listings.

Up Over Jazz Café

351 Flatbush Ave at Seventh Ave, Park Slope, Brooklyn (718-398-5413). Subway: D, Q to Seventh Ave; 2, 3 to Grand Army Plaza. Cash only.

Up Over Jazz Café bucks one of the more established jazz club traditions: It's upstairs rather than in the basement. The differences stop there. Up Over is one of Brooklyn's key jazz rooms, mainly because its good sightlines and warm sound system have lured name players (John Hicks, Mike LeDonne, Freddie Hubbard) who usually confine their NYC appearances to Manhattan.

Village Vanguard

178 Seventh Ave South at Perry St (212-255-4037). Subway: A, C, E, 1, 2, 3, 9 to 14th St; L to Eighth Ave. $15–$20, plus $10 minimum. Cash only.

This basement club is still going strong after 65 years. Its stage—a small but mighty step-up that has seen the likes of John Coltrane, Bill Evans and Miles Davis—hosts the crème de la crème of mainstream jazz talent. The Monday-night regular is the 17-piece Vanguard Jazz Orchestra, which has now held the same slot (originally as the Thad Jones/Mel Lewis Jazz Orchestra) for more than 30 years.

Reggae, World & Latin

Copacabana

617 W 57th St between Eleventh and Twelfth Aves (212-582-2672; www.copacabana.com). Subway: A, C, B, D, 1, 9 to 59th St–Columbus Circle. $5–$40. AmEx, MC, V (for table reservations only).

It's no surprise that the Copa's reputation precedes it. For decades, it has been the venue that introduced the superstars of Latin music to the tourist masses. The Copa can get expensive, but after an ecstatic night of dancing to, say, Tony Vega or Victor Manuelle, you're not likely to leave disappointed. (*See chapter* **Clubs**.)

Gonzalez y Gonzalez

625 Broadway between Bleecker and Houston Sts (212-473-8787; www.gonzalezygonzalez.com). Subway: B, D, F, Q to Broadway–Lafayette St; 6 to Bleecker St. Free. AmEx, MC, V.

Gonzalez may seem like just a kitschy Tex-Mex restaurant, but in the back is a Latin-music lover's paradise, complete with stage and makeshift dance floor. There, you'll be compelled to find a partner and squeeze yourself in—especially on Wednesdays, when Johnny Almendra and Los Jóvenes del Barrio hit you with a blast of Cuban *charanga.*

Latin Quarter

2551 Broadway at 96th St (212-864-7600). Subway: 1, 2, 3, 9 to 96th St. $10–$20. MC, V.

On the Latin-music scale, the Latin Quarter is to the cognoscenti what the Copacabana is to everybody else. Connoisseurs by the hundreds mob the place on weekends, making the giant dance floor seem like a cozy corner. The dancers come for salsa (Tito Nieves, Conjunto Clásico, Jose "El Canario" Alberto), merengue (Oro Sólido) and hot Latin freestyle.

S.O.B.'s

See page 311 for listings.

Zinc Bar

90 Houston St between La Guardia Pl and Thompson St (212-477-8337). Subway: A, C, E, B, D, F, Q to W 4th St. $15, plus $5 minimum. Cash only.

Located in the subnook situated where Noho meets Soho, Zinc Bar is the place to catch up with the most die-hard night owls. The after-hours feel starts well before daybreak, and the atmosphere is enhanced by the cool mix of jazz (Ron Affif), Latin (Juan Carlos Formell), samba (Cidinho Texiera's Brazilian Showfest), African (Leo Traversa) and flamenco bands.

Blues, Folk & Country

Blarney Star

43 Murray St between Church St and West Broadway (212-732-2873). Subway: A, C, 1, 2, 3, 9 to Chambers St. $10. Cash only.

This nice Irish pub hosts authentic music every Friday, often with award-winning musicians coming all the way from the old country. Look for great fiddlers and pipe players regularly.

Chicago B.L.U.E.S.

73 Eighth Ave between 13th and 14th Sts (212-924-9755). Subway: A, C, E to 14th St; L to Eighth Ave. Free–$20. AmEx, MC, V.

When Otis Rush or some other blues titan comes to town, he often settles in at this snug West Village club. The opening acts can be startlingly bad, but the chance of seeing the likes of Johnnie Johnson at close range makes this a must-visit. The Monday-night open jam is also noteworthy.

Find your groove

If you like...	Go to...
Beck	Sidewalk (page 311), Irving Plaza (page 307), the Supper Club (page 311), Knitting Factory (page 307) and Mercury Lounge (page 309)
Blur	Bowery Ballroom (page 306), Irving Plaza (page 307) and Knitting Factory (page 307)
Fatboy Slim	Hammerstein Ballroom at the Manhattan Center (page 307), Twilo (*see chapter* **Clubs**), Shine (page 310) and Bowery Ballroom (page 306)
Macy Gray	Bowery Ballroom (page 306), S.O.B.'s (page 311), Hammerstein Ballroom at the Manhattan Center (page 307) and the Supper Club (page 311)
Jay-Z	Irving Plaza (page 307), Madison Square Garden (page 303) and Nassau Veterans Memorial Coliseum (page 303)
Tito Puente	Copacabana (page 314), Latin Quarter (page 314), S.O.B.'s (page 311) and Zinc Bar (page 314)
The Ramones	Continental (page 306), CBGB (page 306) and Manitoba's (page 308)
Sonic Youth	The Cooler (page 306), Maxwell's (page 308), Mercury Lounge (page 309), Brownies (page 306), Tonic (page 311) and Knitting Factory (page 307)
Sonny Rollins	Village Vanguard (page 314), Sweet Basil (page 314), Iridium (page 313), Fez (page 307) and Blue Note (page 313)
The Roots	Bowery Ballroom (page 306), Wetlands Preserve (page 312), Irving Plaza (page 307) and Hammerstein Ballroom at the Manhattan Center (page 307)
Lucinda Williams	Lakeside Lounge (above), Rodeo Bar (page 316), Irving Plaza (page 307) and Hogs & Heifers Uptown (page 121)
John Zorn	Tonic (page 311), Makor (page 308), Knitting Factory (page 307), Roulette (page 313) and Merkin Concert Hall (page 318)

Kate Kearney's

251 E 50th St between Second and Third Aves (212-935-2045). Subway: E, F to Lexington Ave; 6 to 51st St. Free. Cash only at bar.

This authentic, cozy Irish pub gets a good crowd for its events: Thursdays you can see an informal *seisiún* with Patrick Ourceau and Don Meade, while other nights feature a variety of Irish-flavored country and folk.

Lakeside Lounge

162 Ave B between 10th and 11th Sts (212-529-8463; www.lakeside.com). Subway: L to First Ave; N, R, 4, 5, 6 to 14th St–Union Sq. Free. Cash only at bar.

While nouveau electronic music bars and yuppie hangouts have sprung up around it, the Lakeside remains a great downscale hangout with a killer jukebox, photo booth and rockabilly- and roots-loving types. Shows are free, so you can spend more at the bar as you get soaked to Mary Lee's Corvette or the bluegrass sound of Jim & Jennie & the Pine Barons.

Paddy Reilly's Music Bar

519 Second Ave at 29th St (212-686-1210; www.paddyreillys.com). Subway: 6 to 28th St. $5–$10. AmEx.

The premier local bar for Irish rock hosts nightly music from the likes of the Prodigals and Pierce Turner, with *seisiúns* thrown in.

Rodeo Bar

375 Third Ave at 27th St (212-683-6500). Subway: 6 to 28th St. Free. AmEx, MC, V.

Rodeo Bar looks like any other midtown joint—and half of it is, actually. But the sawdust-strewn northern half books local roots outfits like Hangdogs and Laura Cantrell and occasional visiting country phenomenons, like Hank Williams III (yes, he's Hank's grandson) and BR5-49.

Terra Blues

149 Bleecker St at Thompson St (212-777-7776; www.nytoday.com/terrablues). Subway: A, C, E, B, D, F, Q to W 4th St. Free–$15. AmEx, MC, V.

You'll hear a wide range of blues-based artists at this otherwise ordinary Bleecker Street bar—anyone from Chicago guitar pickers to NYC duo Satan and Adam.

Tribeca Blues

16 Warren St between Broadway and Church St (212-766-1070). Subway: A, C to Chambers St; N, R to City Hall. $5–$20. AmEx, MC, V.

Opened in 1999, Tribeca Blues is still developing its house vibe. You can see local blues acts and the occasional big name.

Summer venues

The Anchorage

Cadman Plaza West between Hicks and Old Fulton Sts, Dumbo, Brooklyn (212-206-6674; www.creativetime.org). Subway: 2, 3 to Clark St; A, C to High St. $7–$20. Cash only.

There isn't a more evocative place to catch an avant-rock or DJ event (think: John Zorn, Sonic Youth, Giant Step) than this arty cavern inside the base ("anchorage") of the Brooklyn Bridge; it's so roomy, you'll think you're outside. The nonprofit public-art presenter Creative Time puts on the events.

Bryant Park

Sixth Ave between 41st and 42nd Sts (212-983-4142). Subway: B, D, F, Q to 42nd St; 7 to Fifth Ave. Free.

Directly behind the New York Public Library, Bryant Park is a serene and distinctly European-style park with a substantial free summer concert series.

Castle Clinton

Battery Park, Battery Pl at State St (212-835-2789). Subway: E to World Trade Ctr; N, R, 1, 9 to Cortlandt St; 2, 3 to Park Pl; 4, 5 to Bowling Green. Free.

Space is limited at this historic fort in the heart of Battery Park, where lucky summer-music hounds get an unobstructed view of classic performers like Frank Sinatra Jr., John Mayall's Bluesbreakers and John Zorn's Masada.

Central Park SummerStage

Rumsey Playfield, enter Central Park at 72nd St at Fifth Ave (212-360-2777). Subway: B, C to 72nd St; N, R to Fifth Ave; 6 to 68th St–Hunter College. Free, benefit concerts $15–$25. Cash only.

On a humid summer weekend, SummerStage is one of New York's great treasures. Although there are always two or three pricey shows, most concerts at this amphitheater are free. Think about it: Solomon Burke or Stereolab, Junior or James Brown, under blue skies, for free, with beer!

Downing Stadium

Randall's Island (212-830-7715, tickets sold through Ticketmaster 212-307-7171). Travel: 4, 5, 6 to 125th St, then M35 bus to Stadium. $25–$40.

This former soccer stadium and adjoining field on an East River island host such megaevents as Lollapalooza, the Vans Warped Tour, the Tibetan Freedom Concert and Reggae Sunsplash. It is by no means lovely; it is by all means convenient.

Giants Stadium

East Rutherford, NJ (201-935-3900; tickets sold through Ticketmaster 212-307-7171). Travel: NJ Transit bus from Port Authority Bus Terminal, Eighth Ave at 42nd St, $3.25 each way (212-564-8484). $20–$75. AmEx, MC, V.

At Giants Stadium, you can catch biggies like U2 and the Rolling Stones, while overhead airliners fly to and from Newark Airport. Band members look like ants, and you'll wait a long, long time for beer, but the hot dogs aren't that bad. And because it's outdoors, it's the last venue in the Meadowlands complex where you can actually smoke.

Jones Beach

Jones Beach, Long Island (516-221-1000). Travel: LIRR from Penn Station to Freeport, then Jones Beach bus. $18–$45. Cash only.

From July to September, a diverse bunch of performers—perhaps Diana Ross, Oasis, Barry White, Blues Traveler and PJ Harvey—sing under the setting sun at this beachside amphitheater.

Lincoln Center Plaza

65th St at Columbus Ave (212-875-5400). Subway: 1, 9 to 66th St–Lincoln Ctr. Free.

The home of Lincoln Center's summer Out-of-Doors and Midsummer Night Swing festivals, the Lincoln Center Plaza hosts many of New York City's sundry cultural communities. In one week, it's possible to hear the world's hottest Latin and African bands and a concert by tenor-saxophone god Sonny Rollins.

Prospect Park Bandshell

Prospect Park, enter at 9th St at Prospect Park West, Park Slope, Brooklyn (718-965-8969). Subway: F to Seventh Ave; 2, 3 to Grand Army Plaza. Free.

Prospect Park Bandshell is to Brooklynites what Central Park SummerStage is to Manhattan residents: the place to hear great music in the great outdoors. The shows mirror the borough's great melting pot, so you're just as likely to hear Afropop or Caribbean music as jazz and blues.

World Financial Center

See page 320 for listing.

Classical & Opera

A glance through the listings for a typical week in NYC will reveal more than a dozen classical-music events occurring each day. Carnegie Hall is still the place to play for visiting orchestras and soloists, and Lincoln Center (the largest performing-arts center in the world) on a busy night might simultaneously host operas, an orchestral concert and a couple of recitals. The number of performances in the city's churches, schools, cultural centers and other spaces is also staggering. The performers or commentators will often offer preconcert lectures or panel discussions for free or for a small fee.

▶ For information on concerts, times and locations, see ***Time Out New York***'s classical-music listings.

▶ The Theater Development Fund (*see chapter* **Theater & Dance**) also provides information on all music events via its **NYC/On Stage** service.

Tickets

You can buy tickets directly from most venues either in person or online. You can also purchase tickets over the phone for some venues, though the surcharge can be steep. See chapter **Directory, Tickets.**

CarnegieCharge

212-247-7800. 8am–8pm. AmEx, DC, Disc, MC, V. Surcharge $4.75 per ticket.

Centercharge

212-721-6500. Mon–Sat 10am–8pm; Sun noon–8pm. AmEx, Disc, MC, V. Surcharge $5.50.

Centercharge sells tickets for events at Alice Tully Hall, Avery Fisher Hall and the Lincoln Center Festival, which takes place in July (*see chapter* **New York by Season**).

New York Philharmonic Ticket Club

212-875-5656. Mon–Fri 10am–5pm; Sat noon–5pm. AmEx, DC, MC, V. Surcharge $5.

You can buy discounted tickets for most performances.

Ticketmaster

212-307-4100. 6:45am–11pm. AmEx, Disc, Disc, MC, V. Surcharges vary by venue.

You can buy tickets for performances at New York State Theater, Town Hall and BAM.

TKTS

See chapter **Directory, Tickets** *for listings.*

TKTS offers 25 or 50 percent discounts on many Lincoln Center performances, including those by the New York Philharmonic, New York City Opera, the Chamber Music Society and Juilliard School musicians (though not the Metropolitan Opera).

Backstage passes

It's possible to go behind the scenes at several of the city's major concert venues. Backstage at the **Met** (*212-769-7020*) takes you around the famous house during opera season (generally September through May); **Lincoln Center Tours** (*212-875-5350*) escorts you inside Avery Fisher and Alice Tully Halls and the New York State Theater; **Carnegie Hall** (*212-247-7800*) shepherds you through what is perhaps the world's most famous concert hall. It's also possible to sit in on rehearsals of the **New York Philharmonic,** usually held on the Thursday before a concert, for a small fee.

Concert halls

Brooklyn Academy of Music

30 Lafayette Ave between Flatbush Ave and Fulton St, Brooklyn (718-636-4100; www.bam.org). Subway: G to Fulton St; D, Q, 2, 3, 4, 5 to Atlantic Ave; B, N, R to Pacific St. $17–$95. AmEx, MC, V.

BAM's opera house is America's oldest academy for the performing arts. The programming is more East Village than Upper West Side: BAM helped launch the likes of Philip Glass (who still performs there regularly) and John Zorn. Current music director Robert Spano has made the resident Brooklyn Philharmonic Orchestra play together and sound good, though the group doesn't get the monetary support its Manhattan counterparts do. Every fall and winter, the Next Wave Festival provides an overview of established avant-garde music and theater, while the spring BAM Opera season brings innovative European productions to downtown Brooklyn. (*See page 303 and chapter* **Theater & Dance.**)

Carnegie Hall

154 W 57th St at Seventh Ave (212-247-7800; www.carnegiehall.org). Subway: A, C, B, D, 1, 9 to 59th St–Columbus Circle; N, R to 57th St. $20–$70. AmEx, DC, Disc, MC, V.

You don't have to practice, practice, practice to get there; you can take the subway to the best of the city's visiting-artist concert venues. A varied roster of American and international stars regularly appears in the two auditoriums: Carnegie Hall itself and the lovely, smaller Weill Recital Hall. This venue is undergoing a massive renovation that includes the addition of a big subterranean performance space, slated to open in spring 2002.

Colden Center for the Performing Arts

LeFrak Concert Hall, Queens College, 65-30 Kissena Blvd at 65th Ave, Flushing, Queens (718-793-8080; www.coldencenter.org). Travel: F to Parsons Blvd, then Q25 or Q34 bus to campus. $10–$30. AmEx, Disc, MC, V.

The home of the Queens Philharmonic, this multipurpose hall also stages concerts by international artists who are in town for Manhattan performances. Due to the Colden Center's remote location, tickets are often half the price of those in Manhattan.

Florence Gould Hall at the Alliance Française

55 E 59th St between Madison and Park Aves (212-355-6160; www.fiaf.org). Subway: N, R to Fifth Ave; 4, 5, 6 to 59th St. $15–$35. AmEx, MC, V.

You don't *have* to brush up on your French to attend the recitals and chamber works performed at this intimate space, but the programming does have a decidedly French accent, both in artists and repertoire.

Merkin Concert Hall

129 W 67th St between Broadway and Amsterdam Ave (212-501-3330; www.elainekaufmancenter.org). Subway: 1, 9 to 66th St–Lincoln Ctr. $10–$25. AmEx, MC, V (for advance purchases only).

This unattractive theater with rather dry acoustics is tucked away on a side street in the shadow of Lincoln Center. But its mix of early music and avant-garde programming (heavy on recitals and chamber concerts) can make it a rewarding stop. Merkin also houses the Lucy Moses School for Music and Dance and the Special Music School of America.

Hall mark You know they've made it when they're playing Carnegie Hall.

New Jersey Performing Arts Center

1 Center St at the waterfront, Newark, NJ (888-466-5722; www.njpac.org). Travel: PATH train to Newark, then take Loop shuttle bus two stops to center. $12–$100. AmEx, DC, MC, V.

Designed by Los Angeles–based architect Barton Myers, the NJPAC complex is impressive, featuring the oval-shaped, wooden 2,750-seat Prudential Hall and the more institutional-looking 514-seat Victoria Theater. It may sound far away, but, in fact, it takes only about 15 minutes to get to NJPAC from midtown. It's a good place to catch big-name acts that may be sold out at stodgy Manhattan venues.

92nd Street Y

1395 Lexington Ave at 92nd St (212-415-5440; www.92ndsty.org). Subway: 4, 5, 6 to 86th St. $15–$40. AmEx, MC, V.

The Y emphasizes traditional orchestral, solo and chamber masterworks, but also foments the careers of young musicians.

Town Hall

123 W 43rd St between Sixth and Seventh Aves (212-840-2824; www.the-townhall-nyc.org). Subway: B, D, F, Q to 42nd St; N, R, S, 1, 2, 3, 9, 7 to 42nd St–Times Sq. Prices vary. AmEx, MC, V. $2.50 surcharge for credit-card orders.

This recently renovated hall has a wonderful, intimate stage and excellent acoustics. Classical music often shares the programming lineup with New Age speakers, pop concerts and movie screenings.

Lincoln Center

This massive arts complex, built in the 1960s, is ground zero for classical music in Manhattan. In addition to the main halls—**Alice Tully, Avery Fisher, Metropolitan Opera House, New York State Theater** (*see below*)—Lincoln Center also hosts lectures and symposia in the **Rose Building.** Also on the premises are the **Juilliard School of Music** (*see page 322*) and the **Fiorello La Guardia High School of the Performing Arts** (yes, the *Fame* one, but in a new location), which also occasionally hosts professional performances. The Mostly Mozart festival (at Avery Fisher Hall) used to be the big summer event, but lately it has been upstaged by the larger, multidisciplinary Lincoln Center Festival. The big guys (Yo-Yo Ma, Daniel Barenboim, Anne-Sophie Mutter) perform here, but the Center has been venturing into more adventurous programming in recent years.

Lincoln Center

65th St at Columbus Ave (212-875-5400, programs and information 800-LINCOLN; www.lincoln center.org). Subway: 1, 9 to 66th St–Lincoln Ctr. AmEx, MC, V.

Alice Tully Hall

212-875-5050. Free–$75.

Built to house the Chamber Music Society of Lincoln Center (*212-875-5788*), Alice Tully Hall somehow makes its 1,000 seats feel intimate. It has no central aisle; the rows have extra leg room to compensate. The hall accommodates both music and spoken text well; its vocal recital series is one of the most extensive in town.

Avery Fisher Hall

212-875-5030. $19–$86.

Originally called Philharmonic Hall, this 2,700-seat auditorium used to have unbearable acoustics; it took the largesse of electronics millionaire Avery Fisher, and several major renovations, to improve the sound quality. The venue is now handsome *and* comfortable. This is the headquarters of the New York Philharmonic (*212-875-5656*), the country's oldest orchestra (founded in 1842) and one of the world's finest, now under the direction of Kurt Masur. Its evangelical philosophy has given rise to free concerts and regular open rehearsals. The hall also hosts concerts by top international ensembles as part of the Great Performers series. Every summer, the famous Mostly Mozart series is held here.

Metropolitan Opera House

212-362-6000. $12–$225.

Marc Chagall's enormous mystical paintings hanging inside its five geometric arches: The Met is the grandest of the Lincoln Center buildings, a spectacular place to see and hear opera. It's home to the Metropolitan Opera, and it's also where major visiting companies are most likely to appear. Met productions are lavish (though not always tasteful), and cast lists are an international who's who of current stars. Under the baton of artistic director James Levine, the orchestra has become a true symphonic force. Although the audiences are knowledgeable and fiercely partisan—subscriptions stay in families for generations—the Met has been trying to be more inclusive in recent years, and English-language subtitles on the backs of seats now allow operagoers to laugh in all the right places. Tickets are expensive, and unless you can afford good seats, the view won't be great. Standing-room-only tickets start at $12, though you have to wait in line on Saturday mornings to buy them. The Met has commissioned productions by the likes of Robert Wilson—to mixed reception from conservative Met audiences. (Wilson was booed at the 1998 premiere of his production of *Lohengrin*.) Other recent daring programming includes Schoenberg's *Moses und Aron* and the world premiere of John Harbison's *The Great Gatsby*. But over-the-top Franco Zeffirelli productions of the classics remain the Met's bread and butter.

New York State Theater

212-870-5570. $25–$98.

NYST houses the New York City Opera, which has tried to upgrade its second-best reputation by being defiantly popular and ambitious. That means hiring only American singers, performing many works in English, bringing American musicals into opera houses, giving a more theatrical spin to old favorites and developing supertitles for foreign-language productions. City Opera has championed modern opera—mixing Tan Dun's *Ghost Opera* with *Madama Butterfly*—resulting in a few great successes and some noble failures. City Opera is ultimately much cooler than its stodgier neighbor—tickets are about half the price. In 1999, City Opera shocked purists by using a sound-enhancement system in the New York State Theater, but frankly, the acoustics sucked before and are better now.

Walter Reade Theater

212-875-5601. $4.50–$9 for regular events.

Lincoln Center's newest concert hall is a glorified movie house: This is the home for the Film Society of Lincoln Center, and its acoustics are the driest in the complex, yet uniformly perfect sight lines make up for it. The Chamber Music Society uses the space for its Music of Our Time series, and the postminimalist Bang on a Can festival houses its resident ensemble here. A Sunday-morning concert series is fueled by pastries and hot drinks in the lobby.

Other venues

Bargemusic

Fulton Ferry Landing, next to the Brooklyn Bridge, Brooklyn (718-624-4061; www.bargemusic.com). Subway: A, C to High St. $15–$23. Cash only.

This former coffee barge, with a spectacular view of the Manhattan skyline, offers four chamber concerts a week. It's a magical experience, but dress warmly in winter. When the weather's nice, enjoy a drink on the upper deck during intermission.

CAMI Hall

165 W 57th St between Sixth and Seventh Aves (212-397-6900). Subway: B, Q, N, R to 57th St. Prices vary. Cash only.

Located across the street from Carnegie Hall, this 200-seat recital hall is rented out for individual events, mostly by classical artists.

Continental Center

180 Maiden Ln at Front St (212-799-5000, ext 313). Subway: A, C to Broadway–Nassau St; 2, 3, 4, 5 to Wall St. Free.

The Juilliard Artists in Concert series offers free lunchtime student recitals here on Tuesdays; the schedule expands during the summer.

Kaye Playhouse

Hunter College, 68th St between Park and Lexington Aves (212-772-4448). Subway: 6 to 68th St–Hunter College. $20–$45. AmEx, MC, V.

This refurbished theater, named after comedian Danny Kaye and his wife, offers an eclectic program of professional music and dance.

The Kitchen

512 W 19th St between Tenth and Eleventh Aves (212-255-5793; www.thekitchen.org). Subway: C, E to 23rd St. Free–$25. AmEx, Disc, MC, V.

Occupying a 19th-century icehouse, the Kitchen has been a meeting place for the avant-garde in music, dance and theater for almost 30 years.

Kosciuszko Foundation House

15 E 65th St at Fifth Ave (212-734-2130; www.kosciuszkofoundation.org). Subway: B, Q to Lexington Ave; 6 to 68th St–Hunter College. $15–$35. MC, V.

This East Side townhouse hosts a chamber-music series with a twist: Each program must feature at least one work by a Polish composer. That makes for a lot of Chopin, but there are some unexpected offerings.

Metropolitan Museum of Art

See chapter **Museums** *for listings.*

This is one of the city's best chamber-music venues, so concerts usually sell out quickly.

Miller Theatre at Columbia University

Broadway at 116th St (212-854-7799; www.millertheater.com). Subway: 1, 9 to 116th St. AmEx, MC, V. Prices vary.

The new director of Columbia's acoustically excellent space has been shaking up programming with innovative, multidisciplinary events. (When was the last time you saw a staged version of Jacques Offenbach's "A Trip to the Moon"?)

New York Public Library for the Performing Arts

40 Lincoln Center Plaza (212-870-1630). Subway: 1, 9 to 66th St–Lincoln Ctr. Free.

Bruno Walter Auditorium, which usually hosts recitals, solo performances and lectures, is undergoing renovation until February 2001. In the meantime, most events are being held in Cooper Union's Great Hall (*7th St at Third Ave, 212-642-0142*).

Roulette

228 West Broadway at White St (212-219-8242; www.roulette.org). Subway: A, C, E to Canal St; 1, 9 to Franklin St. $10. Cash only.

Roulette is the place to go to hear all sorts of experimental music in a Tribeca loft—very downtown (*see page 313*).

Theodore Roosevelt Birthplace

28 E 20th St between Broadway and Park Ave South (212-260-1616). Subway: N, R, 6 to 23rd St. $2. Cash only.

Shortly after Teddy's death, New Yorkers pitched in to rebuild the childhood home of the only U.S. president born in Manhattan. On Saturday afternoons, there's a concert series in the house's small upstairs auditorium. For $2, you can see a concert and get a tour. Often, the same person will take your money, escort you upstairs in the elevator, turn the pianist's pages and show you around. Now *that's* service.

Symphony Space

2537 Broadway at 95th St (212-864-5400). Subway: 1, 2, 3, 9 to 96th St. Free–$40. AmEx, MC, V.

The programming here is eclectic; best bets are the annual Wall to Wall marathons, which offer a full day of music featuring a given composer or theme.

John L. Tishman Auditorium

The New School, 66 W 12th St at Sixth Ave (212-229-5689). Subway: F, 1, 2, 3, 9 to 14th St; L to Sixth Ave. $10. AmEx, MC, V.

The New School's modestly priced Schneider concerts, a chamber-music series, run from April to October and feature up-and-coming young musicians, as well as more established artists, who play here for a fraction of the price charged elsewhere.

World Financial Center Winter Garden

West St between Liberty and Vesey Sts (212-945-0505; www.worldfinancialcenter.com). Subway: N, R, 1, 9 to Cortlandt St. Free.

Logan's Run meets *Blade Runner* at the glassed-in Winter Garden (palm trees spring straight from the marble floor, and you can see the bright lights of the World Financial Center and the World Trade Center). Free concerts (timed to fit the schedule of the working day and usually amplified) range from chamber and choral music to Eno-esque installations for public spaces.

Churches

An enticing variety of music—sacred and secular—is performed in New York's churches. Many resident choirs are excellent, while superb acoustics and serene surroundings make churches particularly attractive venues. A bonus: Some concerts are free or very cheap. The Gotham Early Music Foundation sponsors a terrific annual early-music series at churches around the city. For tickets, call 516-329-6166.

Cathedral of St. John the Divine

1047 Amsterdam Ave at 112th St (212-662-2133; www.stjohndivine.org). Subway: 1, 9 to 110th St.

The 3,000-seat interior is an acoustical blackhole, but the stunning Gothic surroundings provide a comfortable atmosphere for the church's own heavenly choir and such groups as the Ensemble for Early Music. (*See chapter* **Uptown**).

Christ and St. Stephen's Church

120 W 69th St between Columbus Ave and Broadway (212-787-2755). Subway: 1, 2, 3, 9 to 72nd St.

This West Side church offers one of the most diverse concert rosters in the city.

Church of the Ascension

12 W 11th St (212-254-8553). Subway: N, R to 8th St–NYU.

This little Village church's professional choir periodically goes uptown to give concerts at Lincoln Center, but their home turf is much more aesthetically pleasing.

Church of the Heavenly Rest

2 E 90th St at Fifth Ave (212-289-3400; www.heavenlyrest.org). Subway: 4, 5, 6 to 86th St.

Heavenly Rest is home to the Canterbury Choral Society and the New York Pro Arte Chamber Orchestra.

Church of St. Ignatius Loyola

980 Park Ave at 84th St (212-288-2520). Subway: 4, 5, 6 to 86th St.

This church's Sacred Music in a Sacred Space series is a high point of Upper East Side musical life.

Corpus Christi Church

529 W 121st Street between Amsterdam Ave and Broadway (212-666-9350). Subway: 1, 9 to 116th St.

Early music fans can get their fix from Music Before 1800 (*212-666-9266*), a series that presents innovative international musical groups as well as a resident ensemble.

Good Shepherd Presbyterian Church

152 W 66th St between Broadway and Amsterdam Ave (212-799-1259). Subway: 1, 9 to 66th St–Lincoln Ctr.

Musically, Good Shepherd is best known for Jupiter Symphony's twice-weekly recitals, but you can also see other classical-music events here.

Riverside Church

490 Riverside Dr at 120th St (212-870-6700; www.theriversidechurchny.org). Subway: 1, 9 to 116th St.

Riverside plays a large part in the city's musical life. It has a fine choir and organ, and hosts visiting guests such as the Orpheus Chamber, among others. The church's famous carillon is alone worth the trip.

St. Ann's Church

157 Montague St at Clinton St, Brooklyn Heights (718-875-6960). Subway: 2, 3, 4, 5 to Borough Hall.

This Brooklyn Heights Episcopal church doesn't restrict itself to Grandma's sacred music. You can also expect avant-garde opera by the likes of dark-humor cartoonist Art Spiegelman, creator of *Maus*.

St. Bartholomew's Church

109 E 50th St between Park and Lexington Aves (212-378-0248; www.stbarts.org). Subway: E, F to Lexington Ave; 6 to 51st St.

Large-scale choral music and occasional chapel recitals fill the magnificent dome behind the church's facade, designed by Stanford White.

St. Francis of Assisi

135 W 31st St between Sixth and Seventh Aves (212-736-8500). Subway: B, D, F, Q, N, R to 34th St–Herald Sq; 1, 9 to 28th St.

Hear a weekly Thursday concert series.

St. Paul's Chapel/Trinity Church

Broadway at Wall St (212-602-0747; www.trinitywallstreet.org). Subway: N, R, 1, 9 to Rector St; 2, 3, 4, 5 to Wall St.

Historic Trinity, in the heart of the Financial District, schedules individual concerts and the Noonday Concerts series, which are held Mondays at St. Paul's Chapel (Broadway at Fulton St) and Thursday at 1pm at Trinity Church.

St. Thomas Church Fifth Avenue

1 W 53rd St at Fifth Ave (212-757-7013; www.saintthomaschurch.org). Subway: B, D, F, Q to 47–50th Sts–Rockefeller Ctr; E, F to Fifth Ave.

Some of the finest choral music in the city can be heard here, performed by the only fully accredited choir school for boys in the country. The church's annual *Messiah* is a must-see.

Schools

Juilliard, Mannes and the Manhattan School of Music are renowned for their students, their faculty and their artists-in-residence, all of whom regularly perform for free or for minimal admission fees. Noteworthy music and innovative programming can be found at several other colleges and schools in the city.

Brooklyn Center for the Performing Arts at Brooklyn College

Campus Rd at Hillel Pl, one block west of the junction of Flatbush and Nostrand Aves, Brooklyn (718-951-4543; www.brooklyncenter.com). Subway: 2, 5 to Flatbush Ave–Brooklyn College. $20–$50. AmEx, MC, V.

While it mostly hosts concerts by mass-appeal pop performers, this hall, smack in the middle of Flatbush, is also a destination for traveling opera troupes and soloists of international acclaim.

Juilliard School of Music

60 Lincoln Center Plaza, Broadway at 65th St (212-769-7406; www.juilliard.edu). Subway: 1, 9 to 66th St–Lincoln Ctr. Mostly free.

New York's premier conservatory stages weekly concerts by student soloists, orchestras and chamber ensembles, as well as student opera productions.

Manhattan School of Music

120 Claremont Ave at 122nd St (212-749-2802; www.msmnyc.edu). Subway: 1, 9 to 125th St. Mostly free.

MSM offers master classes, recitals and off-site concerts by its students, faculty and visiting pros. The opera program is very adventurous.

Mannes College of Music

150 W 85th St between Columbus and Amsterdam Aves (212-496-8524; www.newschool.edu/academic/mannes.htm). Subway: B, C, 1, 9 to 86th St. Free.

Long considered a weak link in the city's conservatory triumvirate (with Juilliard and Manhattan), this New School affiliate has been raising its profile of late. Concerts are by a mix of student, faculty and pro ensembles-in-residence. See the Orion String Quartet at Lincoln Center for big bucks, or here for free.

Opera

The Metropolitan Opera and the New York City Opera may be the big guys, but they're hardly the only arias in town. The following companies perform a varied repertory—both warhorses and works-in-progress—from Verdi's *Aïda* to Wargo's *Chekhov Trilogy*. Call the individual organizations for ticket prices, schedules and venue details. The music schools (*see above*) all have opera programs, too.

Amato Opera Theatre

319 Bowery at 2nd St (212-228-8200; www.amato.org). Subway: B, D, Q to Broadway–Lafayette St; F to Second Ave; 6 to Bleecker St. $25. MC, V.

Presented in a theater only 20 feet wide, Anthony and Sally Amato's charming, fully staged productions are like watching an opera in a living room. Many well-known singers have sung here, but casting can be inconsistent.

American Opera Projects

463 Broome St between Greene and Mercer Sts (212-431-8102). Subway: J, M, Z, N, R, 6 to Canal St.

AOP is not so much an opera company as a living, breathing workshop for the art form. Productions are often a way to follow a work-in-progress.

Bronx Opera Company

718-365-4209. Performances take place at different locations in Manhattan and the Bronx.

This 32-year-old company, a training ground for up-and-coming singers, provides a low-key opera alternative. BOC performs lesser-known English-language works along with classics.

Dicapo Opera Theater

184 E 76th St between Lexington and Third Aves (212-288-9438; www.dicapo.com). Subway: 6 to 77th St.

This top-notch chamber-opera troupe benefits from City Opera–quality singers performing on intelligently designed small-scale sets in the basement of St. Jean Baptiste Church. A real treat.

New York Gilbert & Sullivan Players

See **Symphony Space,** *page 320.*

Victorian camp's your vice? This troupe presents a rotating schedule of the Big Three (*HMS Pinafore, The Mikado* and *The Pirates of Penzance*), plus lesser-known G&S work.

Opera Orchestra of New York

154 W 57th St at Seventh Ave (212-799-1982). Subway: A, C, B, D, 1, 9 to 59th St–Columbus Circle; N, R to 57th St.

The program organizers unearth forgotten operatic gems and showcase great new talent in semi-staged concert performances at Carnegie Hall.

Operaworks

Raw Space Theater, 529 W 42nd St between Tenth and Eleventh Aves (for ticket info, call 212-873-9531). Subway: A, C, E to 42nd St–Port Authority.

This theater-oriented company accompanies its modestly staged performances of obscure works with synthesizer music.

Regina Opera Company

Regina Hall, Twelfth Ave at 65th St, Bay Ridge, Brooklyn (718-232-3555). Subway: B, M to 62nd St; N to Ft. Hamilton Pkwy.

The only year-round opera company in Brooklyn, Regina offers complete orchestras and fully staged productions.

Sports & Fitness

If the action of Times Square doesn't send your pulse racing, then try watching a Knicks game or biking around Central Park

When it comes to spectator sports, particularly the big four (baseball, basketball, football and hockey), New Yorkers believe they hold a special monopoly on wisdom. This is a place where every third person you meet is convinced that, given enough time and money, he or she could run the local team better than whoever is calling the plays now. New Yorkers read the tabloids back to front, and arguments over half-remembered sports trivia can be far more heated than disputes about politics, sex or religion.

The New York metropolitan area has more professional teams than any other city in America: three basketball, three hockey, two baseball and two football, not to mention myriad pro and amateur soccer, lacrosse and rugby leagues. New Yorkers are passionately devoted to their local heroes; they may grouse about players and condemn owners, but when the home team is in contention for a championship, the city practically grinds to a halt during games. If the team wins, it's ticker-tape parades and pandemonium in the streets.

But when it comes to sports, the city isn't just for those who like to watch. The place is filled with action junkies who get their fix right in town and nearby surrounding areas. Nationally ranked cyclists spin their wheels in Central Park (and take off over the George Washington Bridge on weekends), and swimmers go the distance in the annual Manhattan Marathon Swim in June. Besides satisfying a need to sweat, outdoor activities such as walking, cycling, horseback riding, in-line skating and even kayaking are great ways to see the city.

Spectator Sports

All the daily papers (except the *Wall Street Journal*) carry massive amounts of sports analysis and give listings of the day's events and TV coverage—concentrating on the big four professional leagues. *The New York Times* may have the most literate reporting, but the tabloids—the *Daily News* and the *New York Post*—are best for hyperdetailed information and blunt, insistent opinions. Local cable and broadcast television is likewise inundated with sports—the Fox Sports and Madison Square Garden networks (channels 26 and 27 in Manhattan) provide 24-hour events and news coverage.

▶ ***Time Out New York*** lists upcoming games played by area teams.
▶ For details on big sporting events, contact **NYC & Company–the Convention & Visitors Bureau** (212-484-1222; www.nycvisit.com).
▶ Visit **www.nysports.net** for the latest news on all professional sports in the city.
▶ See chapter **Directory** for ticketing information on New York events.

The Camby-man can New York Knick forward Marcus Camby lays one in at the Garden.

Entertainment

Baseball

Baseball is very much a product of the five boroughs. The basic rules of the game were drawn up by New York amateur player Alexander Cartwright in 1845, and the first professional leagues originated in the city during the 1870s. Babe Ruth and the Yankees' "Murderers' Row" of the 1920s cemented the game's hold on the popular imagination. Joe DiMaggio reinforced it in the 1930s. Today the American League Yankees are known as "the team of the century" after clinching the World Series an incredible 25 times in the 20th century, including back-to-back wins in 1998 and 1999. And the National League Mets are coming on strong in their own right. Tickets are available at the stadiums for most regular-season games (played from April to early October), but they're almost impossible to get for the postseason championship games.

New York Mets

Shea Stadium, 123-01 Roosevelt Ave at 126th St, Flushing, Queens (718-507-8499; www.mets.com). Subway: 7 to Willets Point–Shea Stadium. Information and tickets available Mon–Fri 9am–5:30pm. $12–$30. AmEx, Disc, MC, V.

New York Yankees

Yankee Stadium, River Ave at 161st St, Bronx (718-293-4300, ticket office 718-293-6000). Subway: B, D, 4 to 161st St–Yankee Stadium. Information and tickets available Mon–Fri 9am–5pm; Sat and during games 10am–3pm. $15–$55. AmEx, Disc, MC, V.

Basketball

The local basketball scene is dominated by two NBA teams, the New York Knicks and the New Jersey Nets, with the Knicks reigning supreme in most New Yorkers' hearts. Tickets range from expensive to unobtainable. The hottest seat in town is courtside for Knicks games at Madison Square Garden, where scene-makers, corporate types and hard-core fans rub shoulders with (equally rabid) celebrity fixtures like Spike Lee and Woody Allen. What draws them is an on-court mix of pure athleticism, intuition, improvisation and individual expression not

Photo finish Lemon Drop Kid (left) wins the Belmont Stakes by a nose in 1999.

found in any other sport—and the perennial hope of a championship.

Exciting court action is also on display at the WNBA's New York Liberty's games and at the local colleges (St. John's University in Queens is a top-tier team), or for free by watching hustlers play pickup games on street courts (*see page 329*).

New York Knickerbockers (Knicks)

Madison Square Garden, Seventh Ave at 32nd St (212-465-6741; www.nyknicks.com). Subway: A, C, E, 1, 2, 3, 9 to 34th St–Penn Station. Ticket office Mon–Sat noon–6pm. $22–$60 (the $220 courtside seats are long gone). AmEx, DC, Disc, MC, V.
Official prices are meaningless—ticket information is usually restricted to, "This game is sold out."

New Jersey Nets

Continental Airlines Arena, East Rutherford, NJ (201-935-8888, tickets 201-935-3900). Travel: NJ Transit bus from Port Authority Bus Terminal, Eighth Ave at 42nd St, $3.25 each way (212-564-8484). Ticket office Mon–Fri 9am–6pm; Sat 10am–6pm; Sun noon–5pm. $30–$75. AmEx, MC, V.

New York Liberty

Madison Square Garden, Seventh Ave at 32nd St (212-465-6741; www.wnba.com/liberty). Subway: A, C, E, 1, 2, 3, 9 to 34th St–Penn Station. Ticket office Mon–Fri 9am–6pm; Sat 10am–3pm. $8–$57.50. AmEx, DC, Disc, MC, V.
The WNBA, launched in 1997, is producing its own Amazonian stars. The Liberty has established itself as one of the top women's teams, and the games are a lot of fun to watch. The season runs from June to August.

St. John's University Red Storm

Madison Square Garden. Seventh Ave at 32nd St (212-465-6741). Subway: A, C, E, 1, 2, 3, 9 to 34th St–Penn Station. $18–$31.
Season runs from November to March.

Boxing

Madison Square Garden

Seventh Ave at 32nd St (212-465-6741; www.thegarden.com). Subway: A, C, E, 1, 2, 3, 9 to 34th St–Penn Station.
After several decades of the biggest bouts being fought in Atlantic City or Las Vegas, boxing has punched its way back to the Garden, once considered a mecca for the sport. There are usually a few major fights here over the course of a year.

Golden Gloves Boxing Championships

The Theater at Madison Square Garden, Seventh Ave at 32nd St (212-465-6741). Subway: A, C, E, 1, 2, 3, 9 to 34th St–Penn Station.
The Golden Gloves, a long-running New York tradition and amateur boxing's most prestigious competition, takes place every April.

Church Street Boxing Gym

25 Park Pl between Church St and Broadway (212-571-1333; www.nyboxinggym.com). Subway 4, 5, 6 to Brooklyn Bridge–City Hall; 2, 3 to Park Pl.
Church Street is a workout gym and venue. Amateur fights (including women's bouts) are staged throughout the year, as well as professional kickboxing. Evander Holyfield, Mike Tyson, Felix Trinidad and other heavy hitters practice punches here when in town.

Cricket

The hilarity of hearing an American attempt to explain cricket is rivaled only by a European doing the same for baseball. Nonetheless, thanks to its large populations of Indians, Pakistanis and West Indians, not to mention Britons, New York has about 145 cricket teams and at least two parks where the sound of leather on willow can be heard. The season runs from May to September.

Van Cortlandt Park

Van Cortlandt Park South at Bailey Ave, Bronx. Subway: 1, 9 to 242nd St–Van Cortlandt Park. There are 11 pitches here.
The Commonwealth Cricket League (*718-601-6704*), the largest league in the nation, plays here on weekends. The New York Cricket League (*201-343-4544*) also arranges weekend matches.

Walker Park

50 Bard Ave at Delafield Court, Staten Island. Travel: Staten Island Ferry, then S61 or S74 bus to Bard Ave.
The Staten Island Cricket Club (*718-447-5442*) plays here most weekends during the season.

Football

New York is the only city in the country that currently supports two professional teams. Of course, they both play in Giants Stadium, which is in New Jersey, but that's a technicality. From August to December every year—and longer if the playoffs are involved, which they increasingly are—New York is as fanatical a football town as any.

The Giants have a 10-year waiting list for season tickets, so the only way to see a game is to know someone with season tickets or pay blood money to a broker. The Jets situation is no better; there are 13,000 people on the waiting list. When you call for tickets, the recording explains that tickets have been "sold out since 1979."

New York Giants

Giants Stadium, East Rutherford, NJ (201-935-8222). Travel: NJ Transit bus from Port Authority

Bus Terminal, Eighth Ave at 42nd St, $3.25 each way (212-564-8484).

New York Jets

1000 Fulton Ave, Hempstead, NY (516-560-8200). The Jets play home games at Giants Stadium—for directions, see above.

Hockey

A game of speed and skill with the perpetual promise of spectacular violence—it's no wonder hockey is popular in New York. In recent years, the New Jersey Devils have surpassed their competitors, the New York Islanders and Rangers, but the Rangers remain the hometown favorites. While hard to get, tickets are available; they go on sale at the beginning of the season, which runs from October to April.

New Jersey Devils

Continental Airlines Arena, East Rutherford, NJ (Devils information 201-935-6050; www.newjersey devils.com). Travel: bus from Port Authority Bus Terminal, Eighth Ave at 42nd St, $3.25 each way. (212-564-8484). Ticket office 9am–5pm and during games. $20–$74. AmEx, MC, V.

New York Islanders

Nassau Veterans Memorial Coliseum, 1255 Hempstead Turnpike, Uniondale, Long Island (516-794-4100; www.newyorkislanders.com). Travel: Long Island Railroad (718-217-5477) from Penn Station, Seventh Ave at 32nd St, to Hempstead, then N70, N71 or N72 bus. Ticket office 9am–7pm and during games. $15–$70. AmEx, MC, V.

New York Rangers

Madison Square Garden, Seventh Ave at 32nd St (212-465-6741; www.newyorkrangers.com). Subway: A, C, E, 1, 2, 3, 9 to 34th St–Penn Station. $25–$65. AmEx, DC, Disc, MC, V.

Horse racing

There are four major racetracks just outside Manhattan: Belmont, Aqueduct, the Meadowlands and Yonkers. If you don't want to trek out to Long Island or New Jersey, head for an Off-Track Betting (OTB) outpost to catch the action and (reliably seedy) atmosphere.

Aqueduct Racetrack

110th St at Rockaway Blvd, Ozone Park, Queens (718-641-4700). Subway: A to Aqueduct Racetrack.

Be a spokes person

Use pedal power for an intimate look at NYC (and a good workout)

One of the best ways to tour New York is by bicycle. It's faster than going on foot—and sometimes cab and subway, too—which is why about 100,000 New Yorkers rely on bikes for their daily transportation (at least when the weather is good). And biking is more liberating than a tour bus—you set your own pace and itinerary.

About 120 miles of bike paths lead riders from the bottom to the top of the island. The popular 6.1-mile (9.8km) loop around Central Park is closed to traffic on weekdays from 10am to 3pm and all day on weekends, when the asphalt teems with cyclists. Visitors can take a DIY trip using rental bikes and path maps, or go on organized rides.

A word of caution: Unless you stick to Central Park, cycling in the city is serious business. Riders must stay alert and abide by traffic laws—drivers and pedestrians often don't. In 1999, 35 cyclists died in road accidents. This isn't Amsterdam: New York drivers and pedestrians generally treat cyclists as pests. But keep your ears and eyes open (*see* **Bike riding safety tips,** *page 328*), and you'll have an adrenaline-pumping joyride.

Bike rentals

Gotham Bikes

112 West Broadway between Duane and Reade Sts (212-732-2453). Subway: A, C, 1, 2, 3, 9 to Chambers St. Mon–Fri 9am–6:30pm; Sat 10am–6:30pm; Sun 10:30am–5pm. In summer, open until 7:30pm Wed, Fri. $5 per hour, $25 per day (helmets $2 per day). AmEx, DC, MC, V.

Rent a hybrid or rigid mountain bike from this shop and ride a short way to the Hudson River Esplanade, which runs from Battery Park to 23rd Street.

Loeb Boathouse

Central Park, enter at Central Park West at 72nd St (212-517-2233). Subway: B, C to 72nd St. Apr–Nov Mon–Sun 9am–6:30pm (weather permitting). $8–$12 per hour, children $4 per hour. AmEx, MC, V.

This is the most convenient place to rent a bike for a park cruise. Although the Boathouse has 100 bikes (hybrid 3- and 18-speeds and tandems), reservations are recommended for large groups in summer.

Oct–May. Thoroughbred races are held five days a week (Wed–Sun) during the season. Clubhouse $3, grandstand $1. Cash only.
The Wood Memorial, held each April, is a test run for promising two-year-olds headed for the Kentucky Derby.

Belmont Park

2150 Hempstead Turnpike at Plainfield Ave, Elmont, Long Island (718-641-4700). Travel: Pony Express or Belmont Special from Penn Station to Belmont Park. May–Oct. Thoroughbred races are held Wed–Sun during the season. Clubhouse $4, grandstand $2. Cash only.
The 1.5-mile Belmont Stakes, the third leg of the Triple Crown, is usually held on the second Saturday in June. In October the year's best horses run in the $1 million Jockey Gold Cup.

Meadowlands Racetrack

East Rutherford, NJ (201-935-8500). Travel: bus from Port Authority Bus Terminal, Eighth Ave at 42nd St, $3.25 each way (212-564-8484). Jan–Aug harness, Sept–Dec Thoroughbred. Feb–Apr Wed–Sun. May–Aug Tue–Sat. Sept–Dec Wed–Sat. Clubhouse $3, grandstand $1, Pegasus Restaurant $5. Cash only.
Top trotters race for more than $1 million in the prestigious Hambletonion, held the first Saturday in August.

Yonkers Raceway

Central Park Ave, Yonkers, NY (914-968-4200). Travel: 4 to Woodlawn, then #20 bus to the track. Mon, Tue, Thu–Sat 7:40–11:30pm. Evening tickets $3.25, daytime free. Cash only.
Harness racing isn't as glamorous as Thoroughbred racing, but you can lose your money here all the same.

Soccer

Soccer is popular in New York, especially in the outer boroughs, where you can catch matches every summer weekend in parks in the Polish, Italian and Latin-American neighborhoods. For major-league action, catch a New York/New Jersey MetroStars game at Giants Stadium in New Jersey. The team draws an international crowd and has attracted a devoted following. The season runs from March to September.

New York/New Jersey MetroStars

Giants Stadium, East Rutherford, NJ (888-4-METRO-TIX; www.metrostars.com). Travel: take NJ Transit

Mr C's Cycles

4622 Seventh Ave between 46th and 47th Sts, Sunset Park, Brooklyn (718-857-8557). Subway: N, R to 45th St. Mon–Fri 10am–7pm. Sat, Sun 10am–6pm. $15 per 4 hrs, $25 per 8 hrs (helmet $5 per day).
Prospect Park's 3.4-mile loop is a lot less crowded than Central Park's. The shop is about 20 blocks from the park and rents hybrids and mountain bikes.

TOGA Bike Shop

110 West End Ave at 64th St (212-799-9625). Subway: 1, 9 to 66th St–Lincoln Ctr. Mon–Fri 11am–7pm; Sat 10am–6pm; Sun 11am–5pm. $25–$50 for 24 hrs (includes helmet).
Serious cyclists frequent TOGA. Locals rent dual-suspension mountain bikes to take out of town, since there are no legal off-road trails within the city.

Bike-path maps

Transportation Alternatives

115 W 30th St between Sixth and Seventh Aves, suite 1207 (212-629-8080; www.transalt.org). Subway: B, D, F, Q, N, R to 34th St–Herald Sq; 1, 2, 3, 9 to 34th St–Penn Station.
This nonprofit citizens' group lobbies for more bike-friendly streets. You can pop into the office to get free bike-path maps, or you can download them from their website.

Department of City Planning Bookstore

22 Reade St between Broadway and Centre St (212-720-3667). Subway: N, R to City Hall; J, M, Z to Chambers St; 4, 5, 6 to Brooklyn Bridge–City Hall. Mon–Fri 10am–1pm, 2–4pm.
The Department of City Planning oversees the bike-path system. The Bicycle Master Plan has an ambitious 909 miles of bike lanes. Only 789 to go!

Organized bike rides

Fast and Fabulous

212-567-7160.
This "queer and queer-friendly" riding group leads tours of various lengths throughout the year, usually meeting in Central Park and heading out of the city.

Five-Borough Bicycle Club

Hosteling International, 891 Amsterdam Ave at 103rd St (212-932-2300, ext 115). Subway: 1, 9 to 103rd St.
The club organizes day and weekend bike

bus 351 from Port Authority Bus Terminal, Eighth Ave at 42nd St (212-564-8484). $3.25 each way. $15–$35. Present your bus ticket when you purchase your ticket to get a $2 discount. AmEx, MC, V.

Tennis

U.S. Open

USTA National Tennis Center, Flushing, Queens (718-760-6200, tickets 888-673-6849; www.usopen.org). Subway: 7 to Willets Point–Shea Stadium. Late Aug–early Sept. $33–$69 day tickets. AmEx, DC, Disc, MC, V.
Tickets go on sale in early June for this Grand Slam thriller, though seats tend to be snapped up by corporate sponsors. As you would expect, the biggest names in tennis hit the hard courts for some of the fastest forehands and blistering backhands of the year.

Chase Championships

Madison Square Garden, Seventh Avenue at 32nd St (212-465-6500). Subway: A, C, E, 1, 2, 3, 9 to 34th St–Penn Station. Second and third weeks of Nov. $15–$75. AmEx, DC, Disc, MC, V.
The top 16 women's singles players and top 16 doubles teams compete for megabucks in this premier indoor tournament. Tickets go on sale at the beginning of April.

Active Sports

New York offers plenty for those who define "sports" as something to do, not watch. Central Park is an oasis for everybody from skaters to cricket players (*see chapter* **Uptown**). Gyms have practically replaced bars as hip pick-up spots (*see* **Gyms**, *page 331*), and massive complexes such as Chelsea Piers have brought suburban-style space to the big city.

Department of Parks & Recreation

Call 888-NY-PARKS for a list of scheduled events.

New York Sports Online

www.nysol.com
Visit this site for a comprehensive roundup of recreational sport options in the city.

Basketball

They don't call basketball "the city game" for nothing. The sport's minimal demand for

Entertainment

Be a spokes person (continued)

rides, as well as the annual Montauk Century Ride in May (a 100-mile trip to the end of Long Island). It also offers bicycle-repair classes.

Bicycle Habitat

244 Lafayette St between Spring and Prince Sts (212-431-3315; www.bicyclehabitat.com). Subway: N, R to Prince St; 6 to Spring St. Mon–Thu 10am–7pm; Fri 10am–6:30pm; Sat, Sun 10am–6pm. AmEx, MC, V.
This excellent source for bike gear also has informal mountain-bike excursions to such places as Blue Mountain Park in upstate New York. Ask for staffer Patrick Dougherty.

Time's Up!

212-802-8222; www.times-up.org.
This alternative-transportation advocacy group sponsors rides throughout the year, including "Critical Mass," in which hundreds of cyclists and skaters meet on the steps of Union Square Park at 7pm on the last Friday of every month, then go tearing through Greenwich Village.

Bike riding safety tips

- Always wear a helmet.
- Bicycles are vehicles and must obey traffic laws—heed red lights, never ride against traffic, etc.
- Keep an eye out for potholes, metal plates, broken glass and other ground-level hazards.
- Watch for reckless motorists and jaywalking pedestrians.
- Avoid car doors—stay at least four feet from the nearest parked car. Getting "doored" is the leading cause of bicycle crashes in New York City.
- Always yield to pedestrians (they have the right of way) and stay off sidewalks (it's illegal to ride on them).
- Never leave your bike unlocked. In fact, don't even leave it locked on the street, if you can avoid it.

space and equipment makes it ideal for an urban environment, and the level of play on today's street courts is good enough to draw the pros during the off-season. If you have the skills to shoot with the best, check out these public courts. Visit www.ci.nyc.ny.us/html/dpr/html/athbasketball.html for a complete listing of courts.

West Fourth Street

Sixth Ave between 3rd and 4th Sts. Subway: A, C, E, B, D, F, Q to W 4th St.

Asphalt Green

East End Ave at 90th St. Subway: 4, 5, 6 to 86th St.

The Battlegrounds (Carmensville Playground)

Amsterdam Ave at 151st St. Subway: 1, 9 to 145th St.

Marcus Garvey Park

Madison Ave at 121st St. Subway: 4, 5, 6 to 125th St.

Billiards

Chelsea Bar & Billiards

54 W 21st St between Fifth and Sixth Aves (212-989-0096). Subway: F, N, R to 23rd St. 11am–4am. Mon–Thu 11am–5pm $5 per hour for first player, $10 for two players, $3 per additional person per hour; 5pm–4am $12 per hour for two players, $3 for each additional player. Fri–Sun 11am–5pm $12 per hour for two players, $3 for each additional player; 5pm–4am $14 per hour for two players, $3 for each additional player. AmEx, MC, V.

Cue up in this comfortable and welcoming pool hall (there are 32 pool tables and 3 full-size snooker tables). Beer and snacks are available, or you can sit down at the new Mediterranean restaurant.

Amsterdam Billiard Club

344 Amsterdam Ave at 77th St (212-496-8180). Subway: 1, 9 to 79th St. Sun–Thu 11am–3am; Fri, Sat 11am–4am. $4–$7 per player per hour. Group lessons $8 per person, private $35–$50 per hour.

Owned by comedian David Brenner, Amsterdam was named No. 1 billiard club in the country by *Billiards Digest*. The swanky club features a full bar—and a fireplace.

Other location: *210 E 86th St between Second and Third Aves (212-570-4545).*

Bowling

AMF Chelsea Bowl

Chelsea Piers, between piers 59 and 60, 23rd St at West Side Hwy (212-835-BOWL). Subway: C, E to 23rd St. Sun–Thu 9am–2am; Fri, Sat 9am–4am. $6.25 per person per game, $4 shoe rental.

This megacomplex features 40 lanes, a huge arcade and bar and glow-in-the-dark "disco" bowling every night.

Social climber Belay the day away at ExtraVertical Climbing Center.

Bowlmor Lanes

110 University Pl between 12th and 13th Sts (212-255-8188). Subway: L, N, R, 4, 5, 6 to 14th St–Union Sq. Tue, Wed, Sun 10am–1am; Thu 10am–2am; Mon, Fri, Sat 10am–4am. $4.95 per person per game before 5pm; after 5pm $5.95; weekends $6.45; $3 shoe rental. AmEx, MC, V.

Renovation turned this seedy historic Greenwich Village alley (Richard Nixon bowled here!) into the bowling equivalent of a hip downtown nightclub.

Leisure Time Recreation

625 Eighth Ave at 40th St, in the Port Authority Bus Terminal, second level (212-268-6909). Subway: A, C, E to 42nd St–Port Authority. Sun–Thu 10am–11pm; Fri, Sat 10am–4am. $4.25 per person per

The in-line crowd Bladers and roller skaters of all skill levels traverse Central Park.

game before 5pm; after 5pm $5.25; $3.50 shoe rental. MC, V.
Let fly a few strikes down one of 30 lanes while you're waiting for your bus. Or sink some shots at the bar.

Climbing

ExtraVertical Climbing Center

Harmony Atrium, 61 W 62nd St, entrance on Broadway between 62nd and 63rd Sts (212-586-5382; www.extravertical.com). Subway: A, C, B, D, 1, 9 to 59th St–Columbus Circle. Mon–Fri 1–10pm, Sat 10am–10pm, Sun noon–8pm. Call for winter hours. Day pass $16. Lessons $55–$110. Equipment rental available.
When local rock rats can't get to the Shawangunk Mountains, they keep limber at this public climbing gym inside the atrium of an office building. Play Spiderman on 3,000 square feet of wall, which includes a 50-foot outdoor lead wall (taken from a past X-Games). There's no heating, so it's chilly in winter.

Chelsea Piers Field House

Pier 62, 23rd St at West Side Hwy (212-336-6500; www.chelseapiers.com). Subway: C, E to 23rd St. Gym and climbing wall $17 per person, ages 4 and older. Batting cages $1 per 10 pitches. Basketball and playing fields $7 for one hour per person. Toddler gym $8 per session. Mon–Fri 9am–10pm; Sat, Sun 9am–9pm.
Besides a rock-climbing wall, the 80,000-square-foot Field House includes a gymnastics training center, basketball courts, turf fields, batting cages, a toddler gym, dance studios and locker rooms. Call for information on rock climbing classes.

Golf

Chelsea Piers Golf Club

Pier 59, 23rd St at West Side Hwy (212-336-6400; www.chelseapiers.com). Subway: C, E to 23rd St. Apr–Sept 5am–midnight; Oct–Mar 6am–midnight. Peak hours Mon–Fri 6–10pm; Sat 9am–10pm; Sun 9am–8pm, $15 minimum (65 balls). All other times $15 minimum (94 balls). Golf Academy (212-336-6444). Mon–Fri 9am–10pm; Sat, Sun 8am–8pm.
The Golf Club has 52 weather-protected and heated driving stalls (stacked four stories high), a 1,000-square-foot practice putting green, an automatic ball transport system and a 200-yard artificial-turf fairway that extends along the pier. The academy offers clinics and lessons.

Kissena Park Golf Course

164-15 Booth Memorial Ave at 164th St, Flushing, Queens (718-939-4594). Travel: 7 to Main St–Flushing, then Q65 bus. Dawn–dusk. Green fees Mon–Fri before 3pm $19; Sat $21.50; Mon–Sun $11 after 3pm. Club rental $15 per round. Cash only.
The short "executive" course has great views of the Manhattan skyline. Pro lessons cost $35 for 30 minutes. Par 64.

Richard Metz Golf Studio

425 Madison Ave at 49th St, third floor (212-759-6940). Subway: E, F to Lexington Ave; 6 to 51st St. Mon–Fri 9am–7pm; Sat 10am–6pm; Sun 11am–5pm. 30-minute lesson $60, five lessons $250, ten lessons $400. AmEx, DC, Disc, JCB, MC, V.
PGA pros give lessons that include instant video replay of your swing for movement analysis. There are three nets, several putting areas and a golf shop.

Silver Lake Golf Course

915 Victory Blvd between Clove Rd and Forest Ave, Staten Island (718-447-5686). Travel: Staten Island Ferry, then S67 bus. Dawn–dusk. Green fees Mon–Fri $19 (after 1pm $17.50, twilight round $10); Sat, Sun $21.50; booking fee $2. AmEx, DC, MC, V.
Narrow fairways and tough hills make Silver Lake a difficult course to negotiate. Console yourself with nature when your ball ends up in the woods once again—it's a very picturesque setting. Par 69.

Van Cortlandt Park Golf Course

Van Cortlandt Park South at Bailey Ave, Bronx (718-543-4595). Travel: 1, 9 to 242nd St; BXM3 bus from Madison Square Park to Van Cortlandt Park South. 30 minutes before sunrise–30 minutes after sunset. Green fees Mon–Fri $25; Sat, Sun $27.50; club rental from $25 per round. AmEx, MC, V.

Created in 1895, this is the oldest public course in the country, rich in history and easily the most "New York" of the city's 13 public courses. It's quite short but challenging—narrow, tree-filled and hilly. There's also a newly renovated and expanded pro shop. Par 70.

Gyms

For travelers who just don't feel right without their regular workout, these megagyms offer single-day memberships (some form of photo ID is usually required). Most have more than one branch: Call for more details about classes and facilities. Towel and locker rentals are usually available.

Asphalt Green

555 E 90th St between York and East End Aves (212-369-8890). Subway: 4, 5, 6 to 86th St. Pool Mon–Fri 5:30am–3:30pm, 8–10pm; Sat, Sun 8am–8pm. Fitness center Mon–Fri 5:30am–10pm; Sat, Sun 8am–8pm. Day membership $15.

The fee gets you access to either the Olympic-size pool or the fitness center. An additional $10 is required to use both; sauna access is included with the pool.

Duomo

11 E 26th St between Madison and Fifth Aves, fourth floor (212-689-9121). Subway: 6 to 28th St. Mon–Fri 6am–11pm; Sat, Sun 8am–9pm. Day membership $26.

Owned by former Mr. America Rich Barretta, Duomo is a mix of gym and clubhouse. The 23,000-square-foot space has state-of-the-art machines, fitness classes and 20 personal trainers, and there's also a pool table and a vintage jukebox that plays Sinatra. Sweat along with Swedish models and young investment bankers.

New York Sports Club

151 E 86th St between Lexington and Third Aves (212-860-8630). Subway: 4, 5, 6 to 86th St. Mon–Thu 5:30am–11pm; Fri 5:30am–10:30pm; Sat, Sun 8am–9pm. Day membership $25.

A day membership at New York Sports Club includes access to the weight room, aerobics classes, squash courts, cardio machines, studios, steam room and sauna. For a little extra, you can also get a massage. Call for other gym locations.

Sports Center at Chelsea Piers

Pier 60, 23rd St at West Side Hwy (212-336-6000; www.chelseapiers.com). Travel: C, E, to 23rd St. Mon–Fri 6am–11pm; Sat, Sun 8am–8pm. Day membership $40. 16 and older with ID.

The Sports Center comprises a quarter-mile indoor track, a 25-yard-long swimming pool, basketball courts, hard and sand volleyball courts, weight room and cardio machines, two studios of fitness classes, steam room, sauna, an indoor climbing wall and the Origins Feel-Good Spa.

World Gym of Greenwich Village

232 Mercer St between Bleecker and 3rd Sts (212-780-7407). Subway: B, D, F, Q to Broadway–Lafayette St; 6 to Bleecker St. Mon–Thu 5am–midnight; Fri 5am–11pm; Sat 6am–10pm; Sun 7am–10pm. Day membership $20.

All the amenities of regular membership (except personal training) are available, including a weight room, aerobics classes and machines, a boxing gym and steam rooms in the men's and women's locker rooms. **Other locations:** *1926 Broadway at 64th St (212-874-0942); 65-75 Woodhaven Blvd, between 65th and 66th Sts, Rego Park, Queens (718-459-3248).*

Horseback riding

Claremont Riding Academy

175 W 89th St between Amsterdam and Columbus Aves (212-724-5100). Subway: 1, 9 to 86th St. Mon–Fri 6:30am–10pm; Sat, Sun 6:30am–5pm. Rental $40 per hour; lessons $45 per 30 minutes; introductory package for first 3.5 hours $110. MC, V.

The academy, in an Upper West Side townhouse, teaches English-style (as opposed to Western-style) riding. Beginners use an indoor arena; experienced riders can go for an invigorating canter along the six miles (9.6km) of trails in Central Park. It's fun to watch the horses being led down the ramp from their upstairs "apartments."

Kensington Stables

51 Caton Pl, Windsor Terrace, Brooklyn (718-972-4588). Subway: F to Fort Hamilton Pkwy. 10am–sundown. Guided trail ride $20 per hour; lessons $40 per hour. AmEx, MC, V.

The paddock is small, but there are miles of lovely trails in nearby Prospect Park, which was designed to be seen by horseback (*see chapter* **The Outer Boroughs**).

Ice skating

Rockefeller Center Ice Rink

1 Rockefeller Plaza, between Fifth and Sixth Aves and 49th and 50th Sts (recorded information 212-332-7654). Subway: B, D, F, Q to 47–50th St–Rockefeller Ctr. Oct–Apr Mon–Thu 9am–1pm, 1:30–5:30pm, 6–10:30pm; Fri, Sat 8:30–11am, 11:30am–2pm, 2:30–5pm, 5:30–8pm, 8:30pm–midnight; Sun 8:30–11am, 11:30am–2pm, 2:30–5pm, 5:30–10pm. Mon–Thu $7.50, children under 12 $6; Fri–Sun $10, children under 12 $6.75; skate rental $5. Figure skates only in sizes baby 7 to men's 14. Cash only.

Rockefeller Center's famous outdoor rink, under the giant statue of Prometheus, is perfect for atmosphere but bad for elbow room. It's not to be missed, however, when the towering Christmas tree is lit.

Sky Rink at Chelsea Piers

Pier 61, 23rd St at West Side Hwy (212-336-6100; www.chelseapiers.com). Travel: C, E, to 23rd St. $11, children and seniors $8; skate rental $5; helmet rental $3. Call rink for hours.

This Manhattan's only year-round indoor ice-skating rink. There are several general skating, figure skating and ice hockey programs, including lessons and performances. It often closes for a few hours in the early evening for ice maintenance.

Wollman Memorial Rink

Central Park, enter at Fifth or Sixth Ave at 59th St (212-396-1010). Subway: B, Q to 57th St; N, R to Fifth Ave. Mon, Tue 10am–3pm; Wed, Thu 10am–9:30pm; Fri, Sat 10am–11pm; Sun 10am–9pm. $7, children and seniors $3.50; skate rental $3.50; lockers $6.75. Open mid-Oct–Mar 31.

Join the crowds of kids skating to Mariah Carey blasting from the speakers. Some practice twirls and others spray you with ice shards from their hockey skid stops. The outdoor setting is gorgeous in snowy winters.

In-line skating

With an estimated 500,000 in-line skaters in the city, that quiet *skish-skish* is a familiar sound on New York streets. It's not unusual to see the more insane-on-wheels hurtling toward oncoming traffic at 30 miles per hour. A slightly tamer crowd can be found whirling around Central Park, either on the Park Drive loop (closed to traffic 10am to 3pm during the week and all day on weekends) or near the bandshell at 72nd Street. The "coneheads," or slalomers, strut their stuff near Central Park West at 67th Street, across from Tavern on the Green.

To give it a try yourself, visit Wollman Memorial Rink. If you don't want to be restricted to the rink, rent skates there for $15 a day (plus a $100 deposit). Or try one of many shops close to the park, such as **Blades, Board and Skate** (*120 W 72nd St, 212-787-3911*).

Group skates—some mellow and social, others wild blitzkriegs on wheels—are a popular city pastime. Bring skates, a helmet and a sense of adventure to such events as the Empire Skate Club's Thursday Evening Roll.

Your safest bet is to stick with the pack and go with the flow of traffic. On weekends from mid-April to mid-October, volunteer skate patrollers (in red T-shirts with white crosses) run free "stopping" clinics for beginners. You'll find them on Saturdays and Sundays from noon to 6pm at the 72nd Street entrances on the east and west sides of the park.

Roller Rinks at Chelsea Piers

Pier 62, 23rd St at West Side Hwy (212-336-6200). Travel: C, E, to 23rd St. General skating 10am–5pm (weather permitting). $5, children $4. Skate Park 10am–10pm. Mon–Fri $8.50; Sat, Sun $8.50 per session. Equipment rental (including protective gear) $13.50, children $8.

There are two regulation-size outdoor roller-skating rinks at Chelsea Piers. The Skate Park features an 11½-foot vertical ramp, a six-foot mini vert ramp, a mini vert ramp with spine and a four-way fun box for in-line skating.

Wollman Memorial Rink

Central Park, enter at Fifth or Sixth Ave at 59th St (212-396-1010). Subway: B, Q to 57th St; N, R to Fifth Ave. Thu, Fri 11am–6pm; Sat, Sun 11am–8pm. $4, children and seniors $3; skate rental $6; pad and helmet rental $3. April–mid-Oct.

In warm weather, the ice rink turns into a roller rink.

Empire Skate Club of New York

P.O. Box 20070, London Terrace Station, New York, NY 10011 (212-774-1774; www.empireskate.org).

This club organizes frequent in-line and rollerskating events throughout the city, including island-hopping tours and moonlight rides such as the year-round Thursday Evening Roll. Skaters meet at Columbus Circle (the southwest corner of Central Park, 59th Street at Broadway) at 6:45pm.

Time's Up!

212-802-8222; www.times-up.org

See **Be a spokes person,** page 326.

Kayaking

Access to the Hudson River continues to improve with the ongoing development of the Hudson River Park—a five-mile-long, 550-acre shoreline play zone running from Battery Park to 72nd Street. The project, slated for completion in 2003, aims to reconnect people with the water, and, believe it or not, people are diving in—environmental officials say the city's waters are the cleanest they've been in the last century (just don't swallow).

The best way to explore New York Harbor and the Hudson River—and get a waterbird's-eye view of Manhattan—is by kayak. Between sometimes hairy river traffic, tricky currents and the tide, navigating the city's waters can be demanding. For this reason, no outfitters rent out kayaks. But you can go on an organized excursion or take a class.

Manhattan Kayak Company

Pier 63 Maritime, 23rd St at West Side Hwy (212-924-1788; www.manhattankayak.com). Subway: C, E to 23rd St.

Run by seasoned kayaker Eric Stiller, who once paddled halfway around Australia, Manhattan Kayak Company offers beginner to advanced classes and tours. Paddle tours range from a 90-minute "Paddle & Pub" for $45 to the eight-hour circumnavigation of Manhattan for $175.

NYC Downtown Boathouse

Pier 26, North Moore St at West Side Hwy. Subway: 1, 9 to Franklin St. Mar–Nov.

This nonprofit, all-volunteer-run organization provides free kayaks to the public on a first-come, first-served basis. Get your sea legs by paddling around the pier. You can have a snack at the BBQ/hot dog stand next door on Pier 25. Don't miss the homemade lemonade.

New York Kayak

601 W 26th St between Eleventh Ave and West Side Hwy (212-924-1327). Subway: C, E to 23rd St. Mon–Thu 10am–6pm; Fri, Sat 10am–5pm. Call for prices.

Manhattan's only shop devoted exclusively to kayaking offers beginner to advanced classes and short tours along the Hudson River from mid-May to October. Excursions to destinations such as the Statue of Liberty and Governors Island depend on the day's tides. All instructors are certified by the British Canoe Union. In fact, business has been so brisk, owner Randy Henriksen imports instructors from the U.K. during the summer.

Running

Join the joggers in Central and Riverside parks or around Washington Square in the early morning or early evening. It's best—for women especially—to avoid jogging alone. And don't carry or wear anything that's obviously valuable.

New York Road Runners Club

9 E 89th St between Fifth and Madison Aves (212-860-4455). Subway: 4, 5, 6 to 86th St. Mon–Fri 10am–8pm; Sat 10am–5pm; Sun 10am–3pm. Membership from $30. AmEx, Disc, MC, V.

Hardly a weekend goes by without some sort of run or race sponsored by the NYRRC; it's the largest running club in the U.S. with almost 34,000 members. Most races take place in Central Park and are open to the public. The club also offers classes and clinics and can help you find a running partner.

Squash

New York Sports Clubs

151 E 86th St at Lexington Ave (212-860-8630). Subway: 4, 5, 6 to 86th St. Mon–Thu 6am–11pm; Fri 6am–10pm; Sat, Sun 8am–9pm. Nonmember fee $25.

This uptown branch of the NYSC chain has four newly renovated regulation international courts and is the epicenter of the New York squash world (as far as public courts go). Its well-rounded coaching staff gives evening and weekend clinics and caters to all levels of play. The club also hosts tournaments and training weekends. It's the best place to see the stars in action and even join them on the court. Two regulation squash courts are also at NYSC's branch on 62nd Street at Broadway.

The Printing House Racquet and Fitness Club

421 Hudson St between Leroy and Clarkson Sts (212-243-7600). Subway: 1, 9 to Houston St. Round-robin for nonmembers $18 Mon 8–10pm, Thu 7–8:30am, Fri 6–8pm; $27 Sun noon–6pm.

Although its five courts are just shy of regulation width, the Printing House offers the coolest game of squash in the city. Even if you aren't a member of the spectacular panoramic penthouse fitness facility, you can play in the happy-hour round-robin on Mondays and Fridays. Chris Widney, the squash director and author of *Keep Eye on Ball, Is Most Important One Thing I Tell You,* attracts a steady flow of international players.

Swimming

Municipal Pools

For more information, call New York Parks & Recreation (800-201-PARK; www.ci.nyc.ny.us/html/dpr/html/swimming.html).

An annual membership fee of $25, payable by money order at any recreation center, entitles you to use all of New York's municipal indoor pools for a year. You need proof of your name, an address in the New York City area and a passport-size photograph to register. Outdoor pools are free to all, and are open from July to September.

Some of the best and most beautifully maintained city-run pools are: **Carmine Street Recreation Center** (*Clarkson St at Seventh Ave South, 212-242-5228*); **Asser Levy Pool** (*23rd St between First Ave and FDR Dr, 212-447-2020*); **East 54th Street Pool** (*348 E 54th St at First Ave, 212-397-3154*); **West 59th Street Pool** (*59th St between Tenth and Eleventh Aves, 212-397-3159*).

Sheraton Manhattan Hotel

790 Seventh Ave at 51st St (212-581-3300). Subway: B, D, E to Seventh Ave; N, R to 49th St; 1, 9 to 50th St. Open to nonguests Mon–Fri 6am–9:45pm; Sat, Sun 8am–7:45pm. $20 for nonguests. AmEx, DC, Disc, MC, V.

Pricier than the municipal pools but much less crowded, this 50-footer is the place to come if you want to swim in peace. Pay for your pass across the street at the health club in the lower lobby of the Sheraton New York.

Tennis

The city maintains excellent municipal courts throughout Manhattan. Permits are available from the Department of Parks (*212-360-8131*), cost $50 ($20 for senior citizens, $10 for those under 18) and are valid for the season (April to November); single-play tickets are $5. For a list of city courts, visit www.ci.nyc.ny.us/html/dpr/html/athtennis.html.

HRC Tennis

Pier 13 and 14 on the East River (212-422-9300). Subway: J, M, Z to Broad St; 2, 3, 4, 5 to Wall St. 6am–midnight. Court fees $50–$120 per hour. AmEx, MC, V.

This part of the New York Health & Racquet Club is open to nonmembers. There are eight Har-Tru courts under bubbles on twin piers in the river. Ten tennis pros are on hand to give lessons ($28 per hour plus court fees). This facility may lose its lease to a proposed Guggenheim Museum satellite designed by Frank Gehry, but it could be a long, drawn-out real-estate battle. To be on the safe side, call to confirm.

Manhattan Plaza Racquet Club

450 W 43rd St between Ninth and Tenth Aves (212-594-0554). Subway: A, C, E to 42nd St–Port Authority. 6am–midnight. $32–$50 per court per hour Mar–Apr; $28–$38 per court per hour, plus nonmember $20 guest fee May–Sept. AmEx, MC, V.

This is primarily a private club, so call for nonmember hours. Nonmembers are welcome to play in the singles leagues on Saturday and Sunday nights. The hard-surface outdoor courts are enclosed by a bubble come winter. There's also a gym, pool and two climbing walls. Rates vary according to the time of day.

Midtown Tennis Club

341 Eighth Ave at 27th St (212-989-8572). Subway: 1, 9 to 28th St; C, E to 23rd St. Mon–Thu 7am–11pm; Fri 7am–10pm; Sat, Sun 8am–8pm. Court fees $37–$72 per hour. AmEx, MC, V.

This club offers eight indoor Har-Tru courts and four outdoor ones when weather permits.

YMCAs

There are Ys throughout the five boroughs, all with a wide range of facilities. Three of the Manhattan sites offer day rates for visitors. Y membership in another country may get you discounts, and if you're already paying for accommodations, the sports facilities are free. (*See chapter* **Accommodations**).

Harlem YMCA

180 W 135th St at Seventh Ave (212-281-4100). Subway: B, C, 2, 3 to 135th St. Mon–Fri 6am–10pm; Sat 6am–6pm. $10 per day. AmEx, MC, V.

The main attractions here are a four-lane swimming pool, a basketball court, a full gym and sauna.

Vanderbilt YMCA

224 E 47th St between Second and Third Aves (212-756-9600). Subway: S, 4, 5, 7 to 42nd St–Grand Central; 6 to 51st St. Mon–Fri 5am–11pm; Sat, Sun 7am–7pm. $25 per day. AmEx, MC, V.

The day membership includes use of the two swimming pools, a running track, a sauna and a gym with basketball, handball and volleyball—plus you can participate in any of the yoga and aerobics classes.

West Side Branch YMCA

5 W 63rd St between Central Park West and Broadway (212-875-4100). Subway: A, C, B, D, 1, 9 to 59th St–Columbus Circle. Mon–Fri 8am–9pm; Sat, Sun 8am–8pm. $15 per day. MC, V.

This Y has two pools and three gyms with all the equipment you could imagine, plus an indoor track, squash courts and facilities for basketball, volleyball, handball, racquetball, boxing, aerobics and yoga. There is also a full range of classes. The day rate includes access to everything.

Yoga

Yoga is an increasingly popular way to remain lucid and limber in New York City. Many gyms now mix yoga classes in with aerobics and step sessions (*see* **Gyms,** *page 331*), and yoga centers are popping up all over the city. The following are three of the best.

Integral Yoga Institute

227 W 13th St between Seventh and Eighth Aves (212-929-0585; www.integralyogaofnewyork.org). Subway: A, C, E, 1, 2, 3, 9 to 14th St; L to Eighth Ave. Mon–Fri 10am–8:30pm; Sat 8am–6pm; Sun 10am–2pm. $10, Hatha III classes $12.

Integral Yoga Institute offers classes for beginners and advanced students. The schedule is flexible, so there's no need to book ahead, but do arrive 15 minutes before class begins.

Other location: *200 W 72nd St at Broadway, fourth floor (212-721-4000).*

Jivamukti Yoga Center

404 Lafayette St between 4th St and Astor Pl (212-353-0214; www.jivamuktiyoga.com). Subway: 6 to Astor Pl. Mon–Fri 7am–11pm; Sat 8am–8pm; Sun 7am–8pm. $15.

Classes (1 hour 35 minutes) are vigorous Hatha yoga in the Jivamukti style, with an emphasis on ancient yogic teachings and chanting. The place has developed a glamorous following (past patrons include Christy Turlington and Willem Dafoe). Class packages are offered at discount prices.

Yoga Zone

138 Fifth Ave between 18th and 19th Sts, fourth floor (212-647-YOGA; www.yogazone.com). Subway: L, N, R, 4, 5, 6 to 14th St–Union Sq. Mon–Thu 7:30am–9pm; Fri 7:30am–7:30pm; Sat 9am–6:15pm; Sun 9am–5pm. $20 per class, introductory offer of three classes for $40. Hours vary.

You'll practically trip over all the models and actors, but that's beside the point. Classes here emphasize the less strenuous side of yoga and last at least an hour. Ample time is devoted to breathing, posture and stretching.

Other location: *160 E 56th St between Lexington and Third Aves, 12th floor (212-935-YOGA).*

Theater & Dance

New York's stages will fulfill all of your performance preferences, whether you're into method acting or arabesques

Theater

The Big Apple is the big cheese when it comes to live theater. There are myriad venues throughout Manhattan—and more in the outer boroughs. New York's long tradition as an artist's proving ground still prevails: This is the only city in the U.S. where superstars regularly tread the boards eight times a week. Big-name players who have recently stuck their necks out on the sometimes unforgiving NYC stages include Matthew Broderick, Philip Seymour Hoffman, Christopher Walken and even Elton John, who wrote the music for Disney's latest big-budget musical, *Aïda*. The stakes are high, but the gamble remains ever alluring.

Audiences eager to experience this ephemeral art form pack the city's performance spaces, which range from the landmark palaces of the glittering "Great White Way" of Broadway, to more intimate houses along 42nd Street's Theater Row (technically Off Broadway) and the nooks and crannies of Off-Off Broadway. The performer-fan relationship is more up-close-and-personal in the New York theater world than in Hollywood. Not only can you watch your favorite actors perform just a few feet away from you, you can also grab autographs at the stage door, and maybe even dine at the same restaurant afterward. Whatever your dramatic wishes may be, New York theater can, and undoubtedly will, satisfy you.

▶ To find out what is playing, see the listings and reviews in ***Time Out New York.***
▶ For plot synopses, show times and ticket info, call **NYC/On Stage** (212-768-1818), a service of the Theater Development Fund (see page 337). You'll get info about shows on Broadway, Off Broadway and Off-Off Broadway (as well as classical music, dance and opera).
▶ If you already know what you want to see, try the **Broadway Line** (212-302-4111, outside New York 888-411-BWAY), which is limited to Broadway and Off Broadway shows.

A head for theater BAM hosts shows like the Robert Wilson–Lou Reed piece *Time Rocker.*

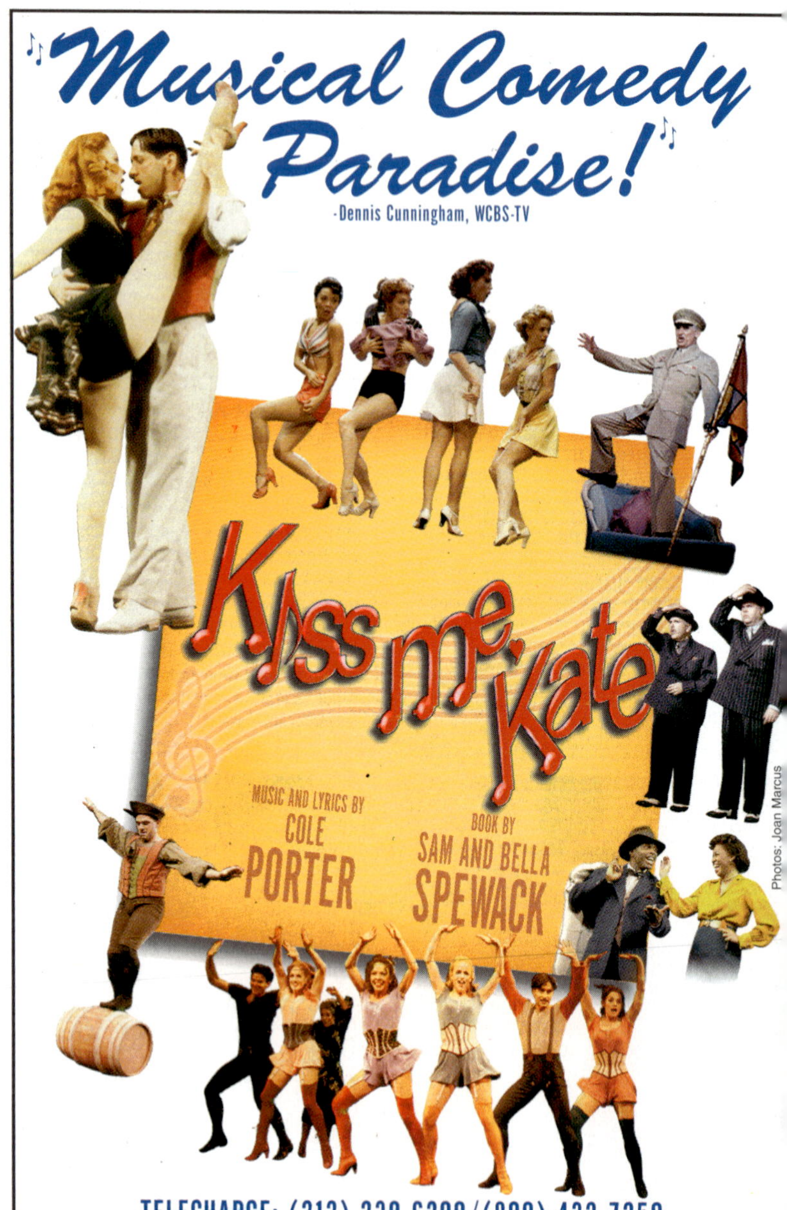
"Musical Comedy Paradise!"
-Dennis Cunningham, WCBS-TV
Kiss me, Kate
MUSIC AND LYRICS BY
COLE PORTER
BOOK BY
SAM AND BELLA SPEWACK
Photos: Joan Marcus
TELECHARGE: (212) 239-6200/(800) 432-7250
MARTIN BECK THEATRE, 302 W. 45 ST. www.kissmekateonbroadway.com

Suspended animation You'll be hanging on De La Guarda's every movement.

BUYING TICKETS

Provided you have a major credit card, buying Broadway tickets requires little more than picking up a telephone. Almost all Broadway and Off Broadway shows are served by one of the city's 24-hour booking agencies. Theater information lines will refer you to ticket agents, often on the same call. (*See chapter* **Directory**).

The cheapest full-price tickets on Broadway are rush tickets (tickets purchased the day of a show at the theater's box-office), which cost about $20, though not all theaters offer these. If a show is sold out, it's worth trying for standby tickets just before show time. Tickets are slightly cheaper for matinees and previews, and for students or groups of 20 or more. Keep an eye out for twofers—vouchers that allow you to buy two tickets for slightly more than the price of one. These generally promote long-running Broadway shows, and occasionally the larger Off Broadway ones. Some sold-out shows offer good seats at reduced rates (usually $20) after 6pm on the day of performance; those in the know line up hours beforehand.

The best way to obtain discount tickets, however, is to go to **TKTS** (*see chapter* **Directory, Tickets**), where you can get as much as 75 percent off the face value of some tickets. Arrive early to avoid the line, or go around 7pm, an hour before most shows are about to start. You can also buy matinee tickets the day before a show at TKTS in the World Trade Center. (One caveat: Avoid scam artists selling tickets to those waiting in line. Often, the tickets are fake.) If you are interested in seeing more than one Off-Off Broadway theater, music or dance event, then consider purchasing the Theater Development Fund's book of vouchers.

Theater Development Fund

1501 Broadway between 43rd and 44th Sts (212-221-0013; www.tdf.org). Subway: N, R, S, 1, 2, 3, 9, 7 to 42nd St–Times Sq. Cash only.

TDF offers a book of four vouchers for $28, which can be purchased at the TDF offices by visitors who bring their passport or out-of-state driver's license. Each voucher is good for one admission at Off-Off Broadway music, theater and dance events, at venues such as the Joyce, the Kitchen, Dance Theater Workshop and P.S. 122. TDF also provides information by phone on all theater, dance and music events in town with its NYC/On Stage service (*212-768-1818*).

NEW YORK SHAKESPEARE FESTIVAL

The **Delacorte Theater** in Central Park is the fair-weather sister of the Public Theater (see page 341). When not producing Shakespeare under its roof, the Public offers the best of the Bard outdoors for free during the New York Shakespeare Festival (June to September). If you're in the city during the summer, you won't want to miss these innovative alfresco productions. In 2000, *The Winter's Tale* and *Julius Caesar* were presented. Tickets are free (two per person), and are distributed at 1pm on the day of the performance at the Delacorte and the Public. Normally, 11:30am is a safe time to line up, but when shows feature box-office giants, the line starts as early as 7am.

Delacorte Theater

A few minutes' walk inside Central Park. Enter the park from either Central Park West at 81st St or Fifth Ave at 79th St; then follow the signs in the park. (212-539-8750; www.publictheater.org). Subway: B, C to 81st St; 6 to 77th St.

Broadway

Broadway is booming. In recent years, box-office receipts for newly opened shows have repeatedly broken records, and, by putting movie stars in leading roles, Broadway now competes directly with Hollywood for its audiences. And Times Square's extensive cleanup hasn't hurt.

"Broadway," in theatrical terms, is the district around Times Square on either side of Broadway (the street), generally between 41st and 53rd Streets. This is where you'll find the grand theaters, most built in the first 30 years of the 20th century; several are newly renovated. Officially, 38 of them are designated as being "Broadway," for which full-price tickets cost up to $100. The big shows are hard to ignore; newer blockbusters like *Cabaret, The Lion King* and *Saturday Night Fever* join long-running shows such as *Phantom of the Opera, Les Misérables* and *Rent,* all of which declare

themselves on vast billboards. (After 18 years, *Cats* finally closed in June 2000.) Still, there's more to Broadway than cartoon-based musicals and flashy Andrew Lloyd Webber spectacles. In recent years, provocative new dramas by such playwrights as David Mamet, Elaine May, Terrence McNally and Claudia Shear have been resounding successes, as have many revived classics and British imports.

One venue worth a visit is the irrepressible **Roundabout Theater,** the critically acclaimed home of classics played by all-star casts (and the force behind *Cabaret*'s latest incarnation). Its deluxe new Broadway space (*the Selwyn Theatre, 227 W 42nd St, 212-719-1300*) opened in 2000. You may subscribe to the Roundabout's full season or buy single tickets, if available.

Broadway District

Subways: A, C, E to 42nd St–Port Authority; B, D, F, Q to 42nd St; N, R to 49th St; N, R, S, 1, 2, 3, 9, 7 to 42nd St–Times Sq; 1, 9 to 50th St.

Off Broadway

Off Broadway theaters usually have fewer than 500 seats; earlier in the century, most were in Greenwich Village. These days, Off Broadway theaters can be found on the Upper West Side or Upper East Side and in midtown.

As Broadway increasingly becomes a place of spectacle sans substance, playwrights who would once have been granted a Broadway production now find themselves in the more audacious (and less financially demanding) Off Broadway houses, where they find audiences who want plays with something to say.

So if it's brain food and adventure you're after, head Off or Off-Off Broadway—but be prepared for considerable variations in quality. Listed below are some of the most reliable theaters and repertory companies. Tickets cost about $15 to $50.

Atlantic Theater Company

336 W 20th St between Eighth and Ninth Aves (212-645-1242). Subway: C, E to 23rd St. AmEx, MC, V.

Created in 1985 as an offshoot of acting workshops taught by David Mamet and William H. Macy, this dynamic little theater (in a former church sanctuary on a lovely Chelsea street) has presented more than 85 plays. Productions have included Mamet's *American Buffalo* (with Macy), the premieres of Jez Butterworth's *Mojo* and Peter Parnell's *The Cider House Rules,* and the American premiere of Martin McDonagh's *The Beauty Queen of Leenane.*

Bouwerie Lane Theatre

330 Bowery at Bond St (212-677-0060). Subway: B, D, Q to Broadway–Lafayette St; F to Second Ave; 6 to Bleecker St. AmEx, MC, V.

Housed in the old cast-iron German Exchange Bank, this is the home theater of the Jean Cocteau Repertory Company, which is devoted to producing the classics in rep. Recent works include Bertolt Brecht's *Edward II,* Samuel Beckett's *Happy Days* and Tom Stoppard's *On the Razzle.*

Brooklyn Academy of Music

30 Lafayette Ave between Flatbush Ave and Fulton St, Fort Greene, Brooklyn (718-636-4100; www.bam.org). Subway: B, M, N, R to Pacific St; D, Q, 2, 3, 4, 5 to Atlantic Ave. AmEx, MC, V.

Brooklyn's grand old opera house—along with the Harvey Theater, one block away at 651 Fulton St—stages the famous multidisciplinary Next Wave Festival during the last three months of each year. The festival's recent theatrical ventures have included Robert Lepage's *Geometry of Miracles* and the Robert Wilson–Lou Reed collaboration *Time Rocker.* (*See page 345, and chapter* **Music.**)

Classic Stage Company

136 E 13th St between Third and Fourth Aves (212-677-4210). Subway: L, N, R, 4, 5, 6 to 14th St–Union Sq. AmEx, MC, V.

Under the leadership of artistic director Barry Edelstein, the Classic Stage Company has become the best place in town to see movie and TV stars performing the classics. Recent productions have featured John Turturro and Christopher Lloyd in Beckett's *Waiting for Godot,* Mira Sorvino in Pirandello's *Naked* and Uma Thurman in Molière's *The Misanthrope.*

Irish Repertory Theatre

132 W 22nd St between Sixth and Seventh Aves (212-727-2737). Subway: F, 1, 9 to 23rd St. AmEx, MC, V.

Dedicated to performing works by veteran and contemporary Irish playwrights, this company in Chelsea has produced some interesting sold-out shows. Notable are the productions of Frank McCourt's *The Irish and How They Got That Way* and Sean O'Casey's *Shadow of a Gunman.*

Lincoln Center

65th St at Columbus Ave (212-362-7600, tickets 212-239-6277). Subway: 1, 9 to 66th St–Lincoln Ctr. AmEx, MC, V.

The Lincoln Center complex houses two amphitheater-shaped drama venues: the 1,040-seat Vivian Beaumont Theater (considered a Broadway house) and the 290-seat Mitzi E. Newhouse Theater (considered Off Broadway). Expect polished productions of new and classic plays, with many a well-known actor. Recent successes include Susan Stroman's dance-play *Contact* and A.R. Gurney's *Ancestral Voices.* (*See chapters* **Uptown, Upper West Side; New York by Season; Music: Classical & Opera.**)

Manhattan Theatre Club

City Center, 130 W 55th St between Sixth and Seventh Aves (212-581-1212). Subway: B, D, E to Seventh Ave. AmEx, MC, V.

Manhattan Theatre Club has a reputation for sending young playwrights on to Broadway. The club's two theaters, in the basement of City Center, are the 299-seat Mainstage Theater, which offers four plays each year by both new and established playwrights, and the Stage II Theater, an outlet for works-in-progress, workshops and staged readings. One of the Club's highlights is its Writers in Performance series. Guest speakers have included Isabel Allende, Eric Bogosian and Toni Morrison.

The New Victory Theater

209 W 42nd St between Seventh and Eighth Aves (212-239-6200). Subway: A, C, E to 42nd St–Port Authority; N, R, S, 1, 2, 3, 9, 7 to 42nd St–Times Sq. AmEx, MC, V.

No theater symbolizes the new family-friendly Times Square more than the New Victory. Built in 1900 by Oscar Hammerstein, Manhattan's oldest theater became home to a striptease show and XXX cinema in the 1970s and '80s. Renovated by the city in 1995, the beautiful building now features a full season of plays geared toward kids and families, including Julie Taymor's *The Green Bird* and Mabou Mines's *Peter and Wendy*. The New Victory is also a great place to see international shows, like Australia's *Flying Fruit Fly Circus* or the British junk opera *Shockheaded Peter*.

New York Theatre Workshop

79 E 4th St between Bowery and Second Ave (212-460-5475). Subway: F to Second Ave; 6 to Astor Pl. AmEx, DC, MC, V.

Founded in 1979, the New York Theatre Workshop produces new plays using young directors eager to harness challenging works. Besides initiating works by the likes of Claudia Shear (*Dirty Blonde*) and Tony Kushner (*Slavs!*), this Off Broadway company is most noted for the premiere of *Rent*, Jonathan Larson's Pulitzer Prize–winning musical, which still packs 'em in on Broadway. The Workshop also offers a home to upstart performance artists through its O Solo Mio festival.

Pearl Theatre Company

80 St. Marks Pl between First and Second Aves (212-505-3401). Subway: N, R to 8th St–NYU; 6 to Astor Pl. AmEx, MC, V. $4 service charge per phone order.

Housed on the East Village's punk promenade, this troupe of resident players relies primarily on its actors' ability to present the classics clearly. Besides Shakespeare and the Greeks, Pearl has successfully produced the works of Ionesco, Molière and Shaw, plus lesser-known playwrights like Ostrofsky and Otway—all on a small, minimally dressed stage, with actors in the simplest of costumes.

Playwrights Horizons

416 W 42nd St between Ninth and Tenth Aves (Ticket Central 212-279-4200). Subway: A, C, E to 42nd St–Port Authority. AmEx, MC, V. $4 service charge per phone order.

This power-packed company boasts more than 300 premieres of important contemporary plays, including dramatic offerings like *Goodnight Children Everywhere, Driving Miss Daisy* and *The Heidi Chronicles*, and musicals such as *James Joyce's The Dead* and *Sunday in the Park with George*. More recently, the works of newcomers Adam Guettel (*Floyd Collins*) and Kira Obolensky (*Lobster Alice*), and the brilliant Christopher Durang (*Betty's Summer Vacation*), have been staged.

Action-packed

Downtown's plotless, wordless explosions of movement and music are the new theatrical thrill rides

It's no secret that Broadway's importance as a showcase for new straight plays has faded in recent years. Since 1994, five of the Pulitzer Prizes for Drama—***Dinner with Friends, Wit, How I Learned to Drive, Rent*** and ***Three Tall Women***—were produced in downtown Manhattan theaters. What is perhaps more surprising is the changing face of spectacle as theater entertainment. Big-budget Broadway musicals like Disney's ***Aïda*** remain popular, but the most fantastic jaw-dropping attacks on the senses—***De La Guarda, Stomp*** and ***Blue Man Group***—have emerged downtown. These wildly popular shows transport audiences to bizarre, unforgettable worlds, and they're fast becoming theatrical institutions. Not quite musicals, and certainly not plays, these theatrical thrill rides exhibit a bold, experimental spirit and a grand cinematic sweep. Loud, intense music (especially percussion) provides the steady soundtrack.

The biggest adrenaline rush comes from *De La Guarda*, an Argentine band of flying acrobats who exude enough violent sexual energy in their performance to keep audiences buzzing for days. Hooked into

The Public Theater

425 Lafayette St between 4th St and Astor Pl (212-539-8500). Subway: N, R to 8th St–NYU; 6 to Astor Pl. AmEx, MC, V.

This Astor Place landmark is one of the most consistently interesting theaters in the city. Founded by Joseph Papp (who bought the building from the city for $1), and dedicated to the work of new American playwrights and performers, the Public also presents new explorations of Shakespeare and the classics (*see* **New York Shakespeare Festival,** *page 337*). The building houses five stages and a new coffee bar, plus the cabaret space Joe's Pub (*see chapters* **Cabaret & Comedy, Music: Popular music**). The Public is now under the aegis of George C. Wolfe, who directed *The Wild Party* on Broadway and the New York premiere of Tony Kushner's *Angels in America.*

Second Stage Theatre

307 W 43rd St at Eighth Ave (212-246-4422). Subway: A, C, E to 42nd St–Port Authority; N, R, S, 1, 2, 3, 9, 7 to 42nd St–Times Sq. MC, V.

Created as a venue for American plays that didn't get the critical reception some thought they deserved, Second Stage now also produces the works of new American playwrights. It staged the New York premieres of Tina Howe's *Painting Churches* and *Coastal Disturbances* and August Wilson's *Jitney.* In 1999, the company moved into a beautiful new Rem Koolhaas–designed space, just off Times Square.

Signature Theatre Company

555 W 42nd St between Tenth and Eleventh Aves (212-244-7529). Subway: A, C, E to 42nd St–Port Authority. AmEx, MC, V.

Each season, this unique award-winning company focuses on the works of a single playwright in residence. (The 2000 scribe is Maria Irene Fornes.) Signature has in the past delved into the oeuvres of John Guare, Arthur Miller and Horton Foote, whose *The Young Man from Atlanta* originated here, and went on to win the Pulitzer Prize.

The Vineyard Theatre

108 E 15th St at Union Sq East (212-353-3366; www.vineyardtheatre.org). Subway: L, N, R, 4, 5, 6 to 14th St–Union Sq. MC, V.

This consistently excellent subscription theater near Union Square produces new plays and musicals, and also attempts to revive works that have failed in other arenas. The Vineyard has recently been on a streak of successes, including Paula Vogel's *How I Learned to Drive* and Edward Albee's *Three Tall Women.* The Vineyard is also home to such playwrights as Craig Lucas and caustic wit Nicky Silver.

Off-Off Broadway

The technical definition of Off-Off Broadway is a show created by artists who may not be card-carrying pros, presented at a theater with fewer than 100 seats. It's where the most innovative and daring writers and performers get to experiment. Pieces often meld various media, including music, dance, mime, film, video and performance monologue—sometimes resulting in an all-too-indulgent combo of theater and psychotherapy.

But Off-Off Broadway is not restricted to experimental work. You can also see classical works and more traditional contemporary plays staged by companies such as the Jean Cocteau Repertory Company (*see* **Bouwerie Lane Theatre,** *page 339*), and at venues like the **Second Stage Theater** (*see above*). Tickets at Off-Off Broadway venues usually cost $10 to $25.

mountain-climbing cables, the pumped-up performers speed furiously through the air, hovering inches above the crowd. Audience participation is almost mandatory: Even if you don't want to dance to the pounding beat or join the flying circus, you can expect to get doused with water or, perhaps, kissed by one of the gorgeous performers.

Stomp and ***Blue Man Group*** also break down the fourth wall. You might get wrapped in toilet paper, yanked onstage or splattered with paint. And if you're running late, be prepared to get publicly humiliated upon arrival.

Blue Man Group is an almost-impossible-to-describe multimedia head scratcher cooked up by three bald, blue deadpan characters: The group's most memorable shtick involves flying gum balls and tossed paint. Sure, *Blue Man* critiques art-world pretensions, but you'll remember it for its visual creativity, intense music and the most showstopping finale in New York theater.

A few blocks east from *Blue Man Group* is the noisy percussion sensation, *Stomp.* Using everyday items like buckets, brooms, garbage-can lids and sticks, the talented musicians make beautifully unconventional, unconventionally beautiful music. The performers bang, tap, smash, click, snap, cough and stomp in perfectly choreographed routines. It's by far the best headache in town.

Just one intelligible sentence is spoken in any of these shows: In *Stomp,* when one of the characters asks, "Can you feel it?" the answer is a most emphatic *yes!*

Adobe Theater Company

453 W 16th St between Ninth and Tenth Aves (212-352-0441). Subway: A, C, E to 14th St; L to Eighth Ave. Cash only.

Keep your eyes peeled for new work by this spry nonprofit company, which has mounted 24 shows in the past seven years. Its wacky works appeal to young, hip audiences that can appreciate a theatrical stew filled with pop-culture references. Recent productions have included *Notions in Motion,* a juicy update of Pirandello, and *Poona the Fuckdog and Other Plays for Children,* a modern fable.

The Flea Theatre

41 White Street between Broadway and Church St (212-226-0051; www.thebat.com). Subway: A, C, E to Canal St; 1, 9 to Franklin St. Cash only.

This small Tribeca space is home to the Bat Theater Company, the brainchild of Jim Simpson, Mac Wellman and Kyle Chepulis. The company produces an inventive assortment of work—and took home its first Obie in 1996 for the bizarre *Benten Kozo,* which somehow melded Kabuki with WWF wrestling.

The Kitchen

512 W 19th St between Tenth and Eleventh Aves (212-255-5793). Subway: A, C, E to 14th St; L to Eighth Ave. AmEx, MC, V.

This small, experimental theater—with a season running from September to May—recently celebrated its 25th anniversary. A reputable place to see edgy New York experimentation, the Kitchen presents an eclectic repertoire of theater, music, dance, video and performance art. Laurie Anderson, David Byrne and Cindy Sherman all got a start here.

La MaMa E.T.C.

74A E 4th St between Bowery and Second Ave (212-475-7710). Subway: F to Second Ave; 6 to Astor Pl. AmEx, V.

Off Broadway began at this little gem. When acclaimed producer Ellen Stewart ("Mama" is her nickname) opened La MaMa in 1962, it was New York's best-kept theater secret. (Did you know, for example, that Harvey Fierstein's *Torch Song Trilogy* started here?) Now, with more than 50 Obie (Off Broadway) Awards to its name, it's a fixture in the city's dramatic life. If you're looking for traditional theater, skip La MaMa. New ground is routinely broken here, and some of it is rather muddy.

Performance Space 122

150 First Ave at 9th St (212-477-5288). Subway: L to First Ave; N, R to 8th St–NYU; 6 to Astor Pl. AmEx, MC, V.

One of New York's most exciting venues, P.S. 122 (as it's casually known) is housed in a former school in the East Village. It's a nonprofit arts center for experimental works, with two theaters presenting dance, performance, music, film and video. Artists develop, practice and present their projects here; P.S. 122 has provided a platform for Eric Bogosian, Danny Hoch, John Leguizamo and Whoopi Goldberg.

The Performing Garage

33 Wooster St between Broome and Grand Sts (212-966-3651). Subway: A, C, E, J, M, Z, N, R, 1, 9, 6 to Canal St. Cash only.

The Performing Garage features the works of the Wooster Group, whose members include Richard Foreman, Willem Dafoe, Elizabeth LeCompte and Spalding Gray. This is where Gray developed his well-known monologues, such as *Swimming to Cambodia.* Dafoe once played the lead in Eugene O'Neill's *The Hairy Ape* and appeared in a daring blackface version of *The Emperor Jones.* In addition to presenting deconstructed versions of theater classics, the company hosts a visiting artists series, dance performances and monthly readings.

Dance

Dance in New York has never gotten the generous government subsidies European companies receive. And it's true that the ranks of choreographers have diminished since the 1980s. Yet no other city in the world boasts such a high caliber of established companies and emerging choreographers. Of the two major seasons—October to December and March to June—the spring stretch is decidedly richer. Not only does Paul Taylor regularly present his marvelous troupe each March, but local ballet companies—American Ballet Theatre and the New York City Ballet—are both onstage in full force. There are usually a couple of dance films and lectures presented each week, and if watching those beautiful bodies onstage makes you depressed, don't fret—enroll in a class. New York is jam-packed with wonderful dance schools and teachers. Choose an aggressive rhythm tap class, a retro swing session or a modern dance class—from improvisation to the Martha Graham technique—or drop by a ballet studio for some serious barre work. Call ahead for schedules, but walk-ins are more than welcome at most schools (*see page 349*).

▶ The Theater Development Fund's **NYC/On Stage** service (see page 337) offers information on all theater, dance and music events in town.

▶ For information on weekly performances, see ***Time Out New York,*** which covers all types of dance, previews selected shows and lists dance classes.

▶ ***Dance Magazine*** ($3.95, monthly) is a good way to find out about a performance well ahead of time.

Entertainment

You might as well jump The Paul Taylor Dance Company makes precision moves.

Venues

Brooklyn Academy of Music

30 Lafayette Ave between Flatbush Ave and Fulton St, Fort Greene, Brooklyn (718-636-4100; www.bam.org). Subway: B, M, N, R to Pacific St; D, Q, 2, 3, 4, 5 to Atlantic Ave. $15–$60. AmEx, MC, V.

BAM, as it's called, showcases superb modern and out-of-town companies. The Howard Gilman Opera House, with its Federal-style columns and carved marble, is one of the most beautiful stages for dance in the city. (When in town, Mark Morris, always loyal to his roots, usually performs here.) The 1904 Harvey Theater (*651 Fulton St between Ashland and Rockwell Pls*), named after BAM founder Harvey Lichtenstein, has hosted modern choreographers Ralph Lemon and Susan Marshall. Each fall, the Next Wave Festival showcases experimental and established dance groups; in the spring, short festivals focus on ballet, tap, hip-hop and modern dance (*see page 339 and chapter* **Music**).

City Center Theater

131 W 55th St between Sixth and Seventh Aves (212-581-7907). Subway: B, D, E to Seventh Ave. $25–$50. AmEx, MC, V.

Before the creation of Lincoln Center changed the cultural geography of New York, this was the home of the New York City Ballet (originally known as the Ballet Society), the Joffrey Ballet and American Ballet Theatre. The lavish decor is all golden. So are the established companies that pass through—they tend to be on the mature side, such as the Paul Taylor Dance Company and the Alvin Ailey American Dance Theater.

Joyce Theater

175 Eighth Ave at 19th St (212-242-0800; www.joyce.org). Subway: A, C, E to 23rd St; 1, 9 to 18th St. $17–$35. AmEx, DC, Disc, MC, V.

The Joyce, once a movie house, is one of the finest theaters in town. It's intimate, but not too small—and of the 472 seats, there's not a bad one in the house. Performances by Bill T. Jones and Martha Graham dance companies and works by choreographers Doug Elkins and David Dorfman have recently appeared here. In residence is Eliot Feld's Ballet Tech. Feld, who began his performing career in George Balanchine's *The Nutcracker* and Jerome Robbins's *West Side Story,* presents his company in two monthlong seasons (March and July). The Joyce also hosts out-of-town ensembles, as well as the local Pilobolus Dance Theatre in June and the Altogether Different Festival in January. In summer, when many theaters are dark, the Joyce schedule may include almost a dozen companies. The Joyce Soho offers rehearsal space for choreographers and also showcases work on weekends (*$10–$15, cash only*).

NEW YORK CITY BALLET
For information call 212-870-5570
or order online at www.nycballet.com
New York State Theater
Lincoln Center, Broadway and 63rd St.

get carried away…
…with a Time Out New York messenger bag.
messenger bags
Replace your old bag with a brand new Time Out New York messenger bag.
To order, mail your name, address and phone number with a check for $30 ($25 + $5 shipping and handling) to:
Emily P., Time Out New York
627 Broadway, seventh floor
New York, NY 10012
Questions? Call 212-358-2343
Time Out New York

Hard corps At the New York City Ballet, founded by Balanchine, choreography matters.

Other location: *Joyce Soho, 155 Mercer St between Houston and Prince Sts (212-431-9233).*

Metropolitan Opera House

65th St at Columbus Ave (212-362-6000; www.metopera.org). Subway: 1, 9 to 66th St–Lincoln Ctr. $24–$145. AmEx, MC, V.

The Met hosts a range of top international companies, from the Paris Opéra Ballet to the Kirov Ballet. Each spring, the majestic theater hosts American Ballet Theatre, which presents full-length story classics. The acoustics are wonderful, but the theater is vast, so sit as close as you can afford.

New York State Theater

65th St at Columbus Ave (212-870-5570; www.nycballet.com). Subway: 1, 9 to 66th St–Lincoln Ctr. $10–$82. AmEx, MC, V (telephone sales only; $1 surcharge).

Both the neoclassical New York City Ballet and the New York City Opera headline at this opulent theater, which Philip Johnson designed to resemble a jewel box. NYCB hosts two seasons: Winter begins just before Thanksgiving, features more than a month of *Nutcracker* performances, and runs until the beginning of March; the spring season usually begins in April and lasts eight weeks. Even from the inexpensive fourth-ring seats, the view is unobstructed, but the best seats in the house are in the first ring, where the sound is tops, and one can enjoy the dazzling patterns of the corps de ballet. The stage, 89 by 58 feet, was made to George Balanchine's specifications.

Alternative venues

Aaron Davis Hall

City College, 135th St at Convent Ave (212-650-7148). Subway: 1, 9 to 137th St–City College. $15–$100. Cash only.

It's a trek, but it's worth it. Troupes here often celebrate African-American life and culture. Among the companies that have appeared here are the Bill T. Jones/Arnie Zane Dance Company and the Alvin Ailey Repertory Ensemble.

Brooklyn Arts Exchange

421 Fifth Ave at 8th St, Park Slope, Brooklyn (718-832-0018). Subway: F to Seventh Ave. $8–$12. Disc, MC, V.

Brooklyn Arts Exchange (formerly Gowanus Arts Exchange), located in a lovely section of the borough, presents a variety of dance concerts by emerging choreographers. There are also performances just for children.

Merce Cunningham Studio

55 Bethune St between Washington and West Sts, 11th floor (212-691-9751; www.merce.org). Subway: A, C, E to 14th St; L to Eighth Ave. $10–$30. Cash only.

Located in the Westbeth complex on the edge of Greenwich Village (no matter which subway you take, be prepared for a good, wind-blown walk), the Cunningham Studio is rented by individual choreographers who don't feel like waiting to be asked to join Dance Theater Workshop's lineup. As can be

imagined, the quality of performances ranges from horrid to wonderful. Since the stage and the seating area are in Cunningham's large studio, be prepared to take off your shoes. Arrive early, too, or you'll have to sit on the floor. For more details, contact the Cunningham Dance Foundation (*212-255-8240*).

Dance Theater Workshop

Bessie Schönberg Theater, 219 W 19th St between Seventh and Eighth Aves (212-691-6500, box office 212-924-0077; www.dtw.org). Subway: C, E to 23rd St; 1, 9 to 18th St. $15. AmEx, MC, V.

Pointe shoes are generally looked down upon at this haven for experimental dance and theater. During popular shows, cushions are tossed on the floor for those without a seat (but reservations are taken). The theater is one of the best organized and most user-friendly of the downtown venues, and a must stop if you're interested in exploring the full range of New York dance. You probably won't see performances by anyone now famous—but someday they might be. DTW has launched the careers of dozens of acclaimed artists, including Bill T. Jones, Mark Morris and, believe it or not, Whoopi Goldberg. Since there are plans to build a new theater in 2000/2001, you might want to call first.

Danspace Project

St. Mark's Church in-the-Bowery, Second Ave at 10th St (212-674-8194). Subway: L to Third Ave; 6 to Astor Pl. $12–$20. Cash only.

This is a gorgeous, high-ceilinged sanctuary for downtown dance, and it's even more otherworldly when the music is live. Downtown choreographers are selected by the director, Laurie Uprichard, whose standards are, thankfully, high. Regular programs include Global Exchange/Danza Libre, which features international artists and collaborations between choreographers; and City/Dans and Lone Stars which focus on New York choreographers.

The Kitchen

512 W 19th St between Tenth and Eleventh Aves (212-255-5793; www.thekitchen.org). Subway: A, C, E to 14th St; L to Eighth Ave. $8–$25. AmEx, MC, V.

Best known as an avant-garde theater space, the Kitchen also features experimental choreographers from New York and elsewhere, occasionally including a multimedia element.

Martha @ Mother

432 W 14th St at Washington St (212-642-5005). Subway: A, C, E to 14th St; L to Eighth Ave. $15, $30. Cash only.

Richard Move and Janet Stapleton present their hilarious award-winning series the first Wednesday of each month, portraying Martha Graham, the mother of modern dance. Move hosts the evening, joined by an ensemble of "Graham Crackers." He introduces the evening's guest artists with short dance "herstory" lectures. Brilliant choreographers like Merce Cunningham, Doug Varone and Jennifer Monson have presented their work in the past. But no one can top Move. Innovative, fresh and highly recommended—and you can often catch a glimpse of Mikhail Baryshnikov in the audience.

Movement Research at Judson Church

55 Washington Sq South at Thompson St (212-477-6635; www.movementresearch.com). Subway: A, C, E, B, D, F, Q to W 4th St. Free.

Director Catherine Levine carries on the tradition of free Monday-night performances at the Judson Church, a custom started in the 1960s by avant-garde choreographers Yvonne Rainer, Steve Paxton and Trisha Brown. At least two choreographers'

Morris code Performers in the Mark Morris Dance Group use a special dialect of dance.

works are shown each night, and the series runs from September to June. MR also offers a vast selection of classes and workshops, which are held at Context Studio and Danspace Project. Lectures are held from time to time.

New Jersey Performing Arts Center

1 Center St between Ronald H. Brown St and Park Pl at the waterfront, Newark, NJ (973-642-8989, box office 888-466-5722; www.njpac.org). Travel: Call for directions. $12–$64. AmEx, Disc, MC, V.

The New Jersey Performing Arts Center serves as home base for the New Jersey Symphony Orchestra, and has hosted the Alvin Ailey American Dance Theater and the Miami City Ballet. Large, open theaters make NJPAC a choice venue for dance.

New Victory Theater

209 W 42nd St between Seventh and Eighth Aves (212-382-4000; www.newvictory.org). Subway: N, R, S, 1, 2, 3, 9, 7 to 42nd St–Times Sq. $10–$25. AmEx, MC, V.

The New Victory, in a busy section of Times Square, was the first theater on the block to be renovated. Ever since its opening in 1995, the intimate, comfortable venue has offered exceptional dance programming. What it doesn't present in quantity, it makes up for in quality—among the past artists to present dance seasons here are Suzanne Farrell, Mark Morris, David Parsons and Mikhail Baryshnikov.

Performance Space 122

150 First Ave at 9th St (212-477-5288; www.ps122.org). Subway: L to First Ave; 6 to Astor Pl. $9–$15. AmEx, MC, V.

Once a public school—and the movie set for *Fame*—P.S. 122 (as it's known) is now the site for all kinds of performance. A great alternative to DTW, it presents up-and-coming choreographers (and the occasional established talent) in new and unconventional works. (*See page 343 and chapter* **Music**.)

Playhouse 91

316 E 91st St between First and Second Aves (212-996-1100). Subway: 4, 5, 6 to 86th St. $15. AmEx, MC, V.

The annual monthlong 92nd Street Y Harkness Dance Project is presented uptown, at Playhouse 91. Participants in 2000 included the dance companies of the late Erick Hawkins, Keely Garfield and Janis Brenner. The festival is held in early spring.

Symphony Space

2537 Broadway at 95th St (212-864-1414; www.symphonyspace.org). Subway 1, 2, 3, 9 to 96th St. $10–$20. AmEx, MC, V.

Located on upper Broadway, this is a center for all the performing arts. The World Music Institute presents many international dance troupes here. (*See chapter* **Music**.)

Summer performances

Central Park SummerStage

Rumsey Playfield, enter Central Park at 72nd St at Fifth Ave (212-360-2777; www.summerstage.org). Subway: B, C to 72nd St; 6 to 68th St–Hunter College. Free.

This outdoor dance series runs on Fridays in July and the first couple weeks in August. Temperatures can get steamy, but at least you're outside. The caliber of choreographers is always improving; in 1999, the series featured work by Mark Dendy and Headlong Dance Theater. (*See chapter* **Music: Popular Music, Outdoor summer venues**.)

Dances for Wave Hill

675 W 252nd St at Independence Ave, Bronx (718-549-3200; www.wavehill.org). Travel: 1, 9 to 231st St, then Bx7, Bx10 or Bx24 bus to 252nd St. $4. Cash only.

This is a lovely setting for outdoor dance. The series, sponsored by Dancing in the Streets, runs in July.

Dance shopping

The New York City Ballet and American Ballet Theatre both have gift shops, open during intermission, selling everything from autographed pointe shoes to ballet-themed T-shirts, night-lights and jewelry.

Capezio Dance-Theater Shop

1650 Broadway at 51st St, second floor (212-245-2130). Subway: C, E, 1, 9 to 50th St; N, R to 49th St. Mon–Fri 9:30am–7pm; Sat 9:30am–6:30pm; Sun 11:30am–5pm. AmEx, MC, V.

Capezio carries an excellent stock of professional-quality shoes and practice-and-performance gear, as well as dance duds that can actually be worn on the street.

Other locations: *136 E 61st St between Lexington and Park Aves (212-758-8833); 1776 Broadway at 57th St (212-586-5140).*

KD Dance

339 Lafayette St at Bleecker St (212-533-1037). Subway: B, D, F, Q to Broadway–Lafayette St; 6 to Bleecker St. Mon–Sat noon–8pm; Sun 1–5pm. AmEx, MC, V.

This shop, owned by Tricia Kaye, former principal dancer and ballet mistress of the Oakland Ballet, and dancer David Lee, features the softest, prettiest dance knits around. Check the bins for sale items.

Dance schools

Most major companies have their own schools. Amateurs are welcome at the following (classes for beginners start at $10 per session).

The Ailey School

211 W 61st St between Amsterdam and West End Aves, third floor (212-767-0940; www.alvinailey.org).

Subway: A, C, B, D, 1, 9 to 59th St–Columbus Circle.
The school of the Alvin Ailey American Dance Theater has a full schedule of classes in modern dance, tap, ballet and even yoga.

American Ballet Theatre

890 Broadway at 19th St, third floor (212-477-3030; www.abt.org). Subway: L, N, R, 4, 5, 6 to 14th St–Union Sq.
ABT Company Class teacher Diana Carter (a former Joffrey Ballet principal dancer) leads advanced beginner classical ballet classes.

Broadway Dance Center

221 W 57th St at Broadway, fifth floor (212-582-9304; www.bwydance.com). Subway: A, C, B, D, 1, 9 to 59th St–Columbus Circle; N, R to 57th St.
The center offers daily classes in ballet, modern, jazz and tap.

Merce Cunningham Studio

55 Bethune St at Washington St (212-691-9751; www.merce.org). Subway: A, C, E to 14th St; L to Eighth Ave.
You can learn how to "discipline your energy" at Merce Cunningham technique classes.

Dance Space Inc.

451 Broadway between Howard and Grand Sts, second floor (212-625-8369; www.dancespace.com). Subway: N, R, J, M, Z, 6 to Canal St.
Beginners through advanced dancers can take classes in Simonson jazz, yoga, modern dance, modern jazz, ballet, stretch, capoeira and yoga.

DanceSport

1845 Broadway at 60th St (212-307-1111; www.dancesport.com). Subway: A, C, B, D, 1, 9 to 59th St–Columbus Circle.
At DanceSport you can learn ballroom and Latin—which includes tango, merengue, salsa, samba and "Cuban motion."

Martha Graham School

440 Lafayette St at Astor Pl (212-838-5886). Subway: 6 to Astor Pl.
Learn the moves that spearheaded modern dance in Martha Graham–technique classes.

Limón Institute

611 Broadway between Houston and Bleecker Sts, ninth floor (212-777-3353; www.limon.org). Subway: B, D, F, Q to Broadway–Lafayette St; 6 to Bleecker St.
Former company members teach classes in the José Limón and Doris Humphrey technique.

Paul Taylor School

552 Broadway between Prince and Spring Sts, second floor (212-431-5562; www.paultaylor.org). Subway: B, D, F, Q to Broadway–Lafayette St; N, R to Prince St; 6 to Bleecker St.
This classic company's school offers daily modern technique class.

Steps

2121 Broadway at 74th St (212-874-2410; www.stepsnyc.com). Subway: 1, 2, 3, 9 to 72nd St.
Steps holds daily classes in various skill levels of ballet, modern, jazz and tap.

Mod about you

New and old schools of modern dance fill the city's stages

Modern dance, a deeply respected art form here, has flourished for nearly a century. Perhaps what's most invigorating about the contemporary scene in New York is its variety—along with annual opportunities to see both the **Paul Taylor Dance Company** and the **Merce Cunningham Dance Company,** there are the troupes of late greats such as **Martha Graham** and **José Limón,** which perform regularly at the Joyce Theater. The **Alvin Ailey American Dance Theater** performs to sell-out crowds each December at City Center; it's a wonderful chance to see the work of Ailey, the late choreographer, whose piece *Revelations* is an American classic.

Emerging and established young choreographers mount their work nearly every night of the week. Although these performances are on a smaller scale, they still fill houses. The **White Oak Dance Project,** Mikhail Baryshnikov's company, performs in New York nearly every year and is known for presenting works by such well-known modern choreographers as **Trisha Brown, Bill T. Jones** and **Mark Morris,** as well as their younger counterparts—**Lucy Guerin** and **John Jasperse,** among them. Experimental downtown venues, including P.S. 122, Movement Research at the Judson Church, Danspace Project at St. Mark's Church in-the-Bowery and Dance Theater Workshop, are excellent spaces to view the unexpected. Tickets at these venues are never more than $15—and though the choreographers are taken quite seriously, the crowds are, refreshingly, without airs.

Trips Out of Town

Crossing paths There are a dozen ways to get out of Manhattan—one is over the Triborough Bridge.

Trips Out of Town

From adventure traveling to mild-mannered history touring, New York's easy-access beaches, mountains and presidential manors cover it all

Notice the traffic heading for the bridges and tunnels on Friday afternoons? New Yorkers will defend their city to the death—but come week's end, they're lining up to get out. All kinds of getaways, from frenetic beaches to tranquil historical regions, are within a few hours' reach. Looking for thrills? You can scratch that itch with one of the many nearby roller coasters. And if the hassle of subway navigating and cab hailing has made you more tense than when you got to New York, there's a slew of spas and spiritual centers a stone's throw away. Just remember, wherever you go, one fact remains the same: On Fridays and Sundays, the traffic is crazy. Take advantage of your visitor status and plan your retreat midweek or during off-peak times.

GENERAL INFORMATION

NYC & Company–the New York Visitors and Convention Bureau (*810 Seventh Ave at 53rd St, 212-484-1222*) has many brochures on upstate excursions. Look for special packages if you're planning to spend a few days away. *The New York Times* publishes a travel section every Sunday that carries advertisements for resorts and guest houses. *Time Out New York*'s Travel section and annual Summer Getaways issue (published in late May) can also help point you in the right direction.

GETTING THERE

For all the places listed, we've included information on how to get there from New York City. Metro-North and the Long Island Rail Road are the two main commuter rail systems. Both offer theme tours in the summer. Call the Port Authority Bus Terminal for information on all bus transportation from the city. Car-rental rates in New York are exorbitant; you can save up to 50 percent by renting a car somewhere outside the city, even if it's from the same company. For more information on airports, trains, buses and car rentals, *see chapter* **Directory**.

Long Island Rail Road

718-217-LIRR, 516-822-LIRR; www.lirr.org

Trains run from Penn Station and from Flatbush Avenue in Brooklyn; connections and transfers take place at the hub in Jamaica, Queens.

Metro-North

212-532-4900, 800-METRO-INFO; www.mta.nyc.ny.us.

Metro-North runs lines from Grand Central Terminal to upstate New York (on the east side of the Hudson River).

Port Authority Bus Terminal

212-564-8484.

Many different bus lines depart from Port Authority.

On the Beach

You've heard it before: Manhattan is surrounded by water, but there's nowhere to swim. Luckily, nearby beachfront towns have no shortage of cool Atlantic water and fine sand. Of course, it is possible to get to the coast without leaving the city limits—the candy-coated frenzy of Coney Island and Brighton Beach will make you feel as though you're back in Times Square. But many urban natives prefer the isolated and serene beaches of Long Island. From Memorial Day (late May) to Labor Day (early September), New Yorkers scramble to get out to their summer rentals in the Hamptons and Fire Island.

Nearby

When the city heats up, shore relief doesn't have to mean a long drive. Just 33 miles from Manhattan is **Jones Beach** (*631-785-1600*). Good for picnicking or sunbathing, this spot attracts day-tripping city dwellers and is also the site of big summer music concerts (*see chapters* **New York by Season** *and* **Music**).

Robert Moses State Park (*631-669-0449; www.liglobal.com/highlights/stateparks*), on the western tip of Fire Island, feels wild and isolated, but is only an hour and a half from Penn Station by train and bus. A long stretch of white sand fronts the island's grassy dunes. If you walk far enough toward the lighthouse, you can strip down on a well-known nude beach. A snack bar and public toilets and showers take care of the basic human needs. The park also allows cars.

GETTING THERE

Jones Beach: Take the Babylon Line of the LIRR

Shore is swell New Yorkers flock to the Hamptons' wide, white-sand beaches.

to Freeport (one way $7, children and seniors $3.50), then the JB24 bus (one way $1.50, June–early Sept). $7 entrance fee

Robert Moses State Park: Take the Babylon line of the LIRR to Babylon (one way $5.75–$8.50, children and seniors $3–$4.25), then Suffolk Buses (*631-852-5200; www.sct-bus.org; late Jun–early Sept $1.50 each way, exact fare only*).

Fire Island

Running parallel to the southern coast of Long Island, Fire Island is a pencil-thin, 30-mile-long strip of land that separates the Great South Bay on one side from the Atlantic Ocean on the other. Traffic-weary, rejoice: Cars are banned from most of Fire Island. But expect to walk a lot and get sand in your shoes. The season runs from May to October, when the whole place pretty much shuts down.

Most short-term visitors to the island find themselves in or around the major towns of **Ocean Beach** and the **Pines.** If you really don't feel like walking, water taxis can be found at every public dock.

Ocean Beach is a sanctuary for sunbathing, Frisbee-throwing, volleyball-playing families and postcollegiates. The town has neither the frills nor the conveniences of the Hamptons, but nothing will stop an Ocean Beacher from enjoying a day in the sand. Burgers and bar food are served at Albatross (*Bay Walk, 631-583-5697*), and anyone with a taste for butter cream–frosted cakes and gooey brownies sooner or later ends up at Rachel's Bakery (*325 Bay Walk, 631-583-9552*). Sunset cocktails at the Fair Harbor dock on Saturday evening are a tradition; throw a bottle of wine or a six-pack in your beach bag and follow the sand path known as the Burma Road to Fair Harbor, five towns and a 20-minute walk to the west. City slickers in Ocean Beach tend to share summer rentals with friends or other families, cramming 26 people into a four-bedroom house. For roomier digs, try Clegg's Hotel or Jerry's Accommodations (*both 631-583-5399*).

A mecca for the Chelsea boys and other members of New York's affluent gay male community, the Pines is a world—and a half-hour water-taxi ride—away from Ocean Beach. Elaborate modern wood-and-glass houses with up to ten bedrooms line this community's carless streets. Pines residents keep a very tight social schedule: sunning in the morning, working out in the afternoon and napping before cocktails at sunset. At 8pm, it's the "tea dance" (which involves neither tea nor dancing) outside the world-famous Pavilion (*631-597-6131*), followed by dinner at home (never before ten). Then it's back to the Pavilion at 2am for partying until dawn. Guest rooms are available at Botel (*631-597-6500*), an unattractive concrete structure that houses the Pines' heavily used gym, and at the more quaint Pines Place (*631-597-6131*). Wherever you stay, make sure to get an invite for cocktails and dinner at one of the fabulous beach houses.

GETTING THERE

Ocean Beach: Take the Babylon line of the LIRR to Bay Shore (*$6.50–$9.50*), then walk or take a cab to the ferry station. Tommy's Taxi (*631-665-4800; Mon–Sat $16, Sun and holidays $19*) runs regular van service from various locations in Manhattan. By car, take the Long Island Expwy to Sagtikos Pkwy. Then take the Southern State Pkwy eastbound to Exit 42 south (*Fifth Ave in Bay Shore*); follow the signs for the ferry. From Bay Shore, take the Fire Island Ferry (*99 Maple Ave, Bay Shore,*

631-665-3600; www.fireislandferries.com; round-trip $11.50, children $5.50).

The Pines: Take the Montauk branch of the LIRR to Sayville (*$6.50–$9.50*), then walk or take a taxi to the ferry station. From May to October, Islander's Horizon Buses (*212-477-0094, 631-654-2622; www.islanderstravel.com*) run between Manhattan and the Sayville ferry station, Friday and Saturday departure, return Sunday and Monday ($20 one way). By car, take the Long Island Expwy to Exit 59 south, then turn right onto Ocean Ave and continue for 6.5 miles. Turn left on Main St and follow the green-and-white signs to the ferry. From Sayville, take the Sayville Ferry (*41 River Rd, 631-589-0810; round-trip $11, children under 12 $5*) across the bay.

The Hamptons

The Hamptons, a series of small towns along the South Fork of eastern Long Island, are the ultimate retreat for New York's rich and famous. Socialites, artists and hangers-on drift from benefit bash to benefit bash throughout the summer season. For sightseers, it's tough to choose between the sun-drenched beachfront and the superstar estates. (Steven Spielberg's palace in East Hampton and Alec Baldwin and Kim Basinger's massive homestead in Amagansett—the site of a fund-raising benefit for Bill Clinton in '98—are but two examples.) For an up-to-date social calendar, pick up the free local rags *Dan's Papers, Hamptons Magazine* or *Country Magazine;* all are available at various retail stores.

After Memorial Day, the beautiful beaches of **East Hampton** attract celebs looking for some rest and relaxation. Still, as you walk on the sand, don't be surprised by the pervasive presence of cell phones and laptops. **Two-Mile Hollow Beach** is where you might spot Calvin Klein sunning himself.

When it comes to eating, the trends change more quickly than the winds on the beach, but Della Femina Restaurant (*99 N Main St, 631-329-6666*) and Nick and Toni's (*136 N Main St, 631-324-3550*) are old standbys that promise sophisticated contemporary food and at least one celebrity sighting per night. Keep your eyes peeled for Billy Joel enjoying a doughnut at Dreesen's Excelsior Market *(33 Newtown Ln, 631-324-0465)* or a baseball-capped Jerry Seinfeld (who bought Joel's $40 million estate in early 2000) strolling along the town's tree-lined streets. The Mill House Inn (*31 N Main St, 631-324-9766; www.millhouseinn.com)* is a comfortable bed-and-breakfast in town.

Over the years, many great painters, including Roy Lichtenstein, have kept studios in **Southampton.** Today the former artist sanctuary is known for its antique shops, galleries…and nightclubs. If you're looking to spend money, wander down Jobs Lane. If you're looking to shake your booty, the Tavern (*125 Tuckahoe Ln, 631-287-2125)* and Jet East (*North Sea Rd, 631-283-0808)* are beach-town versions of Manhattan's club scene, with VIP lounges, crowded dance floors, and lots of pretty faces.

While technically not part of the Hamptons—locals bristle at the suggestion—distant and remote **Montauk** is nontheless a worthy and relatively uncommercial destination for East End visitors. The **Montauk Point Lighthouse** is New York State's oldest (erected in 1795), and historical memorabilia is on display inside. The town is simple and unpretentious: The best dinner consists of a three-pound lobster at Gosman's Dock *(West Lake Dr, 631-668-5330)*. Despite the down-market fishing village feel, rental cottages and hotels can still empty your wallet in the summer season. For the best rates, look for pre- and postseason deals. The Royal Atlantic Beach Resort *(South Edgemere St, 631-668-5103)* has family-style cottages set on the water.

East Hampton Chamber of Commerce

79A Main St, East Hampton, NY 11937 (631-324-0362; www.easthamptonchamber.com).

Montauk Chamber of Commerce

P.O. Box 5029, Montauk, NY 11954 (631-668-2428; www.montaukchamber.com).

Southampton Chamber of Commerce

76 Main St, Southampton, NY 11968 (631-283-0402; www.southamptonchamber.com).

www.ihamptons.com

A project by Hamptons maven Steven Gaines (who wrote the infamous "tell-all" Hamptons book *Philistines at the Hedgerow*), this website has real-estate sales and rental listings, the iHamptons Emporium, which sells locally made products (including homemade chicken pot pie from the Sag General Store), services such as yard care and food deliveries, and a live-cam on the Main Street of every Hamptons community.

Montauk Point Lighthouse

Montauk Pt, Rte 27, 516-668-2544.

GETTING THERE

Take the Montauk line of the LIRR to East Hampton, Southampton or Montauk (*$10.25–$15.25*). The Hampton Jitney (*212-936-0440, 631-283-4600, 800-936-0440; $22, Tue–Thu children and seniors $17*) runs regular bus service between Manhattan and the Hamptons, and provides complimentary newspapers and orange juice on morning trips. By car, take the Long Island Expwy (I-495) east to Exit 70 (County Rd 111) south. Continue for three miles to Sunrise Highway (Rte 27) eastbound.

Snow Days

The Catskills, part of the Appalachian Mountain system located just 90 miles from midtown, is the city's nearest major forest and park area. Farther north—about a five-hour trip—are the Adirondacks, the largest area of relatively untouched beauty in the state. If you're jonesing for some slopeside action, you can make one-day getaways to Ski Windham and Hunter Mountain in the Catskills. Both are about a two-hour drive from New York City. They're hills compared to the Rockies or Alps, but are good for some fun runs. Sports stores arrange all-inclusive trips by bus during the winter season.

Blades, Board & Skate

659 Broadway at Bleecker St (212-477-7350, 888-55BLADES; www.blades.com). Subway: B, D, F, Q to Broadway–Lafayette St; 6 to Bleecker St. Mon–Sat 11am–9pm; Sun 11am–7pm. AmEx, MC, V.
Blades draws a big snowboarding crowd; its trips usually consist of noisy busloads of young shredders. The $55 Hunter Mountain package includes lift ticket and transportation (and movies and bagels on the bus). Snowboard rentals (no skis!) are available for an extra $20. You need to book in person at least two days in advance—buses fill up quickly.

Paragon Sports

867 Broadway at 18th St (212-255-8036). Subway: L, N, R, 4, 5, 6 to 14th St–Union Sq. Mon–Sat 10am–8pm; Sun 11am–6:30pm. AmEx, Disc, MC, V.
Paragon's $58 trips (including Hunter lift ticket and transportation) are slightly more adult than Blades', with an even blend of skiers and boarders. Ski and snowboard rentals are available.

Hunter Mountain

518-263-4223; lodging 800-775-4641; weather conditions 800-FOR-SNOW; www.huntermtn.com. Full-day lift tickets $37–$45, students 13–18 $33–$39, children under 12 and seniors $22–$28.
Hunter has a vertical drop of 1,600 feet, 11 lifts and a terrain park.

Ski Windham

*518-734-4300, 800-SKI-WINDHAM; for ski conditions 518-734-4SNO; www.skiwindham.com. Full-day lift tickets $34–$43, children 7–12 $30–$35.*Ski Windham has a vertical drop of 1,600 feet, five lifts and a terrain park and pipe.

GETTING THERE

Use one of the bus packages above. Adirondack Trailways (*800-858-8555*) also offers bus service from Port Authority Bus Terminal (*Hunter Mountain $53.20 round-trip; Ski Windham $58.90 round-trip*). To Hunter from New York City by car, take the NY Thruway (I-87) north to Exit 20 (Saugerties). Take Rte 32 north to Rte 32A west to Rte 23A west. To Windham, take the same route, but from I-87, take Exit 21 to Rte 23 west directly to Windham.

Method man Shred the halfpipe at Hunter Mountain, just a two-hour drive from NYC.

Estate of grace The Rockefellers' Kykuit is one of a string of Hudson Valley mansions.

History Lessons

If you're keen on history or just enjoy scenery, the **Hudson Valley** in upstate New York will satisfy you. The breathtaking former summer residences of such famous New Yorkers as John D. Rockefeller Jr. and Franklin Roosevelt dot the Hudson River. Most of the region's historic sites are maintained by the **Historic Hudson Valley** society and are open to the public for much of the year. The trip to and from the Hudson Valley can be made in a day, but if you have the time, linger a while at a cozy inn and enjoy the area's restaurants that use the valley's fresh bounty. Metro-North frequently offers discounted rates to the area, and New York Waterway, in conjunction with Historic Hudson Valley, runs cruises from Manhattan and New Jersey to several of the historic houses.

Putnam County

Any time of the year, **Cold Spring** is a haven of peace and quiet, and the stunning view from the banks of the Hudson takes in the Shawangunk Mountains across the river. The town is only 50 miles (80km) from Manhattan, but light-years away culturally. The best place to crash is the 1832 Hudson House *(2 Main St, 845-265-9355; www.hudsonhouseinn.com)*, a peaceful, convenient inn with an excellent contemporary American restaurant. From the inn, follow Main Street into the heart of town, where a number of narrow-frame houses with airy porches and shutters sit alongside the four-story commercial buildings. The tiny town is chock-full of antiques shops, and the Main Street Cafe *(129 Main St, 845-265-4548)* sells fresh-baked goods and home-cooking staples such as chicken pot pie.

Just a mile away is the town of **Garrison,** where you'll find the **Boscobel Restoration,** a Federal-style mansion built in 1804 by States Morris Dyckman, a wealthy British loyalist.

Boscobel Restoration

1601 Rte 9D, Garrison, NY (845-265-3638; www.boscobel.org). Apr–Oct Mon, Wed–Sun 9:30am–5pm; Nov, Dec Wed–Sun 9:30am–4pm. $8, seniors $7, children 6–14 $5, children under six free. Disc, MC, V.

Putnam Visitors Bureau, Cold Spring

110 Old Route 6, building 3, Carmel, NY 10512 (845-225-0381, 800-470-4854; www.visitputnam.org).

Dutchess County

About 15 miles north of Garrison is the definitive Hudson Valley estate: **Springwood,** Franklin Roosevelt's boyhood home, in **Hyde Park.** The great New Dealer and his iconoclast wife, Eleanor, moved back to Springwood in his later years. The house is just as Roosevelt left it when he died in 1945, filled with family photos and the former president's collections, including one of nautical instruments. In the nearby FDR Library

Trips Out of Town

and Museum, you can see presidential documents and even FDR's pony cart. Also in Hyde Park is the **Culinary Institute of America,** whose illustrious alumni includes Manhattan celebrity chef and Hudson Valley forager Larry Forgione (An American Place). CIA's chefs-in-training prepare French, Italian and American regional and American contemporary cuisine in four different dining rooms. New at the school is the Apple Pie Bakery Café, which is stocked with baked goods made by pastry majors.

Like many of the valley's towns, Hyde Park has several antiques shops—the Village Antiques Center *(597 Albany Post Rd, 845-229-6600)* and the Hyde Park Antique Center *(544 Albany Post Rd, 845-229-8200)* represent 75 dealers between them. A good place to rest after all these activities is Fala House, a private one-bedroom guest house with a pool—call ahead for reservations *(East Market St, 845-229-5937)*.

Another 10 miles north, beyond the reach of Metro-North, is the town of **Rhinebeck,** cherished by history buffs. **Wilderstein,** an 1852 Italianate villa, was rebuilt in Queen Anne style in 1888. The town also boasts the nation's oldest hotel, the **Beekman Arms** *(6387 Mill St, 845-876-7077, 800-361-6517; www.beekmanarms.com)*, which dates back as far as 1700. The Beekman may be historic, but the kitchen is nothing if not cutting-edge. Chef Larry Forgione took over the inn's Beekman 1766 Tavern *(4 Mill St, 845-871-1766)* in 1991, updating the menu with such innovative dishes as apple-marinated pork tenderloin (*$20.95*) and roasted Adirondack duck (*$21.95*). When you're done eating, check out the Beekman Arms Antique Market and Gallery *(6387 Mill St, 845-876-3477)*, in a converted barn just steps away. The Old **Rhinebeck Aerodrome,** which has three hangars' worth of aviation history, hosts weekly air shows on Saturdays and Sundays from 2 to 4pm. You can also ride in a biplane.

Dutchess County Tourism, Rhinebeck and Hyde Park

3 Neptune Rd, Poughkeepsie, NY 12601 (845-463-4000).

Historic Hudson Valley

150 White Plains Rd, Tarrytown, NY 10591 (845-631-8200; www.hudsonvalley.org).
This historical society maintains several mansions in the area, including John D. Rockefeller Jr.'s **Kykuit,** pronounced "KAI-kut" *(845-631-9491. Apr–Nov. $20, seniors $19, children $17)* and **Washington Irving's Sunnyside** *(845-591-8763. Mar–Dec. $8, seniors $7, children 6–17 $4)*, as well as **Philipsburg Manor** *(845-631-3992. Mar–Dec. $8, seniors $7, children 5–17 $4)*, **Van Cortlandt Manor** *(845-271-8981. Apr–Dec. $8, seniors $7, children 6–17 $4)* and **Montgomery Place** *(845-758-5461. Apr–Dec. $6, seniors $5, children 6–17 $3)*.

Culinary Institute of America

433 Albany Post Rd, Hyde Park, NY (845-471-6608; www.ciachef.edu). AmEx, DC, Disc, MC, V.
Reservations and appropriate attire required.

Hudson River Heritage

P.O. Box 287, Rhinebeck, NY 12572 (845-876-2474).

Old Rhinebeck Aerodrome

At Stone Church and Norton Rds, off Rte 9, Rhinebeck, NY (845-758-8610; www.oldrhinebeck.org). Jun–Oct. $10, children 6–10 $5. MC, V.

Springwood

U.S. 9, Hyde Park, NY (845-229-2501; www.nps.gov/hofr). 9am–5pm. $10, children under 17 free. MC, V.

Wilderstein

330 Morton Rd, Rhinebeck, NY (845-876-4818). May–Oct Thu–Sun noon–4pm; Thanksgiving weekend Fri–Sun 1–4pm; Dec Fri, Sat, Sun 1–4pm. $5.

GETTING THERE

Ask about special package rates from New York Waterway (*800-53FERRY*). Metro-North runs many trains daily to the Hudson Valley (*$7.75–$10.25*). Unfortunately, the Metro-North train line ends at Poughkeepsie, a 20-minute taxi ride from Rhinebeck. Short Line Buses (*212-736-4700, 800-631-8405; www.shortlinebus.com; $25.75 round-trip*) also runs regular bus service to Rhinebeck and Hyde Park. By car, take the Saw Mill River Pkwy to the Taconic Pkwy north to I-84 west. For Cold Spring, take Rte 9 south to Rte 301 west. For Rhinebeck and Hyde Park, take Rte 9 north.

Play Time

Roller coaster fans might want to head to one of these nearby theme parks.

Mountain Creek

Vernon, NJ, on Rte 94, 47 miles (72km) from Manhattan (973-827-2000; www.mountaincreek.com). Travel: By car, take I-80 west to Rte 23 north, then Rte 515 north and go one mile on Rte 94 south. Groups should call ext 319 for transportation discounts. Early June Sat, Sun 10am–7pm; mid-June–early Sept Mon–Sun 10am–7pm; call for fall schedule. Adults $24.99, children under four feet tall $15, three years and younger free. Group discounts available. AmEx, MC, V.
An immense water park in the summer, Mountain Creek (formerly Action Park) caters to fun-loving families looking to splash away the heat. The area plays up its rural mountain setting; it's located amid 200 acres of woods and hills. Bring your swimming gear and enjoy high-action rides like Bombs Away (a faux cavern through which you drop into a pool of water)

or the more kid-friendly Lost Island. There's also a 10,000-square-foot skate park, 30 miles of mountain-biking trails and a BMX park. Since the 1998 season, Mountain Creek has also offered 47 trails for skiing and snowboarding in the colder months. Winter activities begin mid-December; call for more information.

Playland

Rye, NY (845-925-2701). Travel: By train, take Metro-North (New Haven line) from Grand Central Terminal to Rye, then connecting bus #76. By car, take I-95 north to Exit 19 and follow the signs to the park. Summer Tue–Thu, Sun noon–11pm; Fri, Sat noon–midnight; call for winter hours. Closed mid-Oct–mid-May. Admission to park free, rides cost 3–6 tickets (24 tickets $15, 36 tickets $19). MC, V.

An old-fashioned amusement park set on the shore of Long Island Sound, this 73-year-old facility is popular both for its nostalgic attractions and its modern rides, which include the new Double Shot (a stomach-churning vertical drop), Dragon Coaster, Chaos and the virtual-reality extravaganza Morphis. Kiddyland offers Arctic Flume, Demolition Derby and even Slime Buckets for the little tykes. Other attractions include video arcades, miniature golf, picnic grounds, a pool and a beach on the Sound. Ice-skating rinks and other frosty facilities are open in the winter months *(call 845-925-2761 for information)*. A fireworks show is held on the Fourth of July, as well as every Wednesday and Friday night in July and August.

Six Flags Great Adventure & Wild Safari

Jackson, NJ, on Rte 537, 50 miles (80km) from Manhattan (732-928-1821; www.six.flags.com/greatadventure/general). Travel: By bus, NJ Transit (973-762-5100) from Port Authority Bus Terminal ($42 round-trip, incl. admission). By car, take Exit 7A off the New Jersey Tpke, proceed on I-195 east to Exit 16A, then go one mile west on Rte 537 to Six Flags. Or Exit 98 off the Garden State Pkwy to I-195, Exit 16. May–Sept 10am–10pm (closing time variable). Theme park and safari $42.99, theme park only $39.99, children under four feet tall half-price. AmEx, Disc, MC, V.

Six Flags entices Manhattanites with the slogan "Bigger than Disneyland and a whole lot closer." The park features a gargantuan drive-through safari park with 1,200 land animals, a mammoth offering of gut-churning rides and the obligatory fast-food chains. Don't miss Six Flags' signature rides, the Great American Scream Machine, Batman and Robin, and the Chiller, where you can experience 0–70 mph acceleration forward and backward in four seconds. The newest ride is the Medusa, a floorless roller coaster in which riders are strapped to a flying chair.

Body & Soul

If bustling New York City has you stressed out, these relaxing retreats in the Catskill Mountains can help revive you.

New Age Health Spa

Rte 55, Neversink, NY 12765 (845-985-7600, 800-682-4378; www.newagehealthspa). Travel: Minivans are available between Manhattan and the spa for $40 one-way (800-682-4368). Call for directions by car.

Surrounded by 160 acres of wilderness, the New Age Health Spa is low-key and low-intensity. Participants rise at 6am daily and rejuvenate their minds and bodies by engaging in weight-training, water aerobics and tai chi. The standard single rate ($208–$248 per night) includes all meals and activities, consultation with staff nutritionists and a rustic, but private, room. Thriftier vacationers can share a room with friends or be assigned roommates (the nightly rate in triple rooms can be as low as $123). Treatments include Hydro Colon Therapy (yes, it's what you think, $60) and Ayurvedic Botanical Detoxification ($80). For less touchy-feely types, there are tennis courts and a pool.

The Siddha Yoga Meditation Ashram

371 Brickman Rd, South Fallsburg, NY 12779-0600 (845-434-2000; www.siddhayoga.org). Mon–Fri 9:30–11:30am, 2:30–5pm; Sat 10am–2pm.

Siddha Yoga is a Hindu spiritual center, led by Swami Chidvilasananda (also known as Gurumayi), who follows the teachings of ancient Indian sages. Guests (including some Hollywood stars) follow a rigorous regimen of chanting, meditation, selfless work and spiritual study. Interested in learning the wisdom of the ages? Special weekend packages are available, but the ashram does not advertise or publish rates. Siddha Yoga is not a Motel 6—drop-ins are not allowed. Call two weeks in advance, say you'd like to come for the weekend, and you will be quoted a price.

Zen Mountain Monastery

P.O. Box 197, South Plank Rd, Mt. Tremper, NY 12457 (845-688-2228; www.zen-mtn.org/zmm). Travel: By bus, take Adirondack Trailways (800-858-8555) from Port Authority Bus Terminal to Mt. Tremper. Call for directions by car.

The ZMM headquarters, at the base of Tremper Mountain, is located in a century-old building that was intricately constructed from white oak. Burned-out travelers can expect to find inner peace at Zen Mountain Monastery, but it's no walk in the park. Enrollees have to rise during the predawn hours and work through the "eight stages of Zen" daily. The monastery encourages three-month stays, but weekend retreats are available for the more time-pressed. The Introduction to Zen Training Weekend ($195) is recommended for beginners, teaching zazen (a form of meditation), liturgy, art and body practice. This is way beyond the lotus position—Abbott John Daido Loori and his staff offer training in psychotherapy, wilderness skills and ikebana (Japanese-style flower-arranging), among a lot of other things. Lodging is dorm-style, and all meals are vegetarian.

Directory

News to you The Sunday *New York Times* weighs about five pounds.

Directory

These indispensable tips will help you conquer the Naked City

Getting to and from NYC

By air

There are three major airports servicing the New York City area; see page 362 for details. Here are some sources for purchasing airline tickets.

Internet

A few sites to investigate for low fares are **www.airfare.com, www.cheaptickets.com, www.travelocity.com** and **www.airlinereservations.net.**

Newspapers

The best place to get an idea of available fares is the travel section of your local paper. If that's no help, get a Sunday ***New York Times*** or the weekly ***Village Voice.*** Both have advertisements for discounted fares.

Satellite Airlines Terminal

125 Park Ave between 41st and 42nd Sts. Subway: S, 4, 5, 6, 7 to 42nd St–Grand Central. Mon–Fri 8am–7pm; Sat 9am–5pm.
Satellite is a veritable one-stop department store catering to the needs of travelers. Major international airlines have ticket counters here. You can shop for the best deal, exchange frequent flyer mileage, process passports, birth certificates and driver's licenses and arrange for transportation and city tours. There is no direct telephone number to any of the centers, so you must call the carriers individually to reach them by phone.
Other locations: *1 World Trade Center, West St between Liberty and Vesey Sts; 1 E 59th St at Fifth Ave; 166 W 32nd St between Sixth and Seventh Aves; 555 Seventh Ave between 39th and 40th Sts.*

Travel agents

Agents are highly specialized, so find one who suits your needs. Do you want adventure? Budget? Consolidator? Business? Luxury? Round the world? Student? (If so, *see* **Student travel,** *page 375*). Find an agent through word-of-mouth, newspapers, the Yellow Pages or the Internet. Knowledgeable travel agents can help you with far more than air tickets, and a good relationship with an agent can be invaluable, especially if you don't like to deal with sometimes tedious travel details.

By bus

Buses are an inexpensive (though sometimes uncomfortable) means of getting to and from New York City. They are particularly useful if you want to leave in a hurry, since many bus companies don't require reservations. Most out-of-town buses come and go from the Port Authority Bus Terminal.

Bus lines

Greyhound Trailways

800-231-2222 (7am–1am); www.greyhound.com. Buses depart 24 hours. AmEx, Disc, MC, V.
Greyhound offers long-distance bus travel to destinations across North America.

New Jersey Transit

973-762-5100 (6am–midnight); www.njtransit.state.nj.us. Buses depart 24 hours. AmEx, MC, V.
NJT provides bus service to most everywhere in the Garden State.

Peter Pan

800-343-9999 (6am–midnight); www.peterpanbus.com. Buses depart 24 hours. MC, V.
Peter Pan runs extensive service to cities across the Northeast.

Bus stations

George Washington Bridge Bus Station

178th St between Broadway and Fort Washington Ave (bus information 212-564-1114). Subway: A to 175th St; A, 1, 9 to 181st St.
A few bus lines serving New Jersey and Rockland County, New York, use this station from around 5am to 1am.

Port Authority Bus Terminal

40th–42nd Sts between Eighth and Ninth Aves (212-564-8484). Subway: A, C, E to 42nd St–Port Authority.
Be warned: The area around the terminal is notoriously seedy—although, like the rest of Times Square, it is becoming less so. Many transportation companies serve New York City's commuter and long-distance bus travelers. Call for additional information.

By car

Driving to and from the city can be scenic and fun. The obstacles arise once you're here, or almost here. Don't forget that Manhattan is an island and you'll have to take a bridge or tunnel to get in or out of the city. Traffic can cause delays of 10 to 50 minutes—plenty of time to get your money out for the toll (they average $4). Note that street parking is very restricted, especially in the summer (*see* **Parking,** *page 361*).

Car rental

If you are interested in heading out of town by auto, car rental is much cheaper on the city's outskirts and in New Jersey and Connecticut; reserve ahead for weekends. If you're coming from the U.K., most New York authorities will let you drive on a U.K. license for a limited time, though an international one is better. All car-rental companies listed below add sales tax. Companies located outside of New York State offer a "loss damage waiver" (LDW). This is expensive—almost as much as the rental itself—but without it you are responsible for the cost of repairing even the slightest damage. If you pay with an AmEx card or a gold Visa or MasterCard, the LDW may be covered by the credit-card company; it might also be covered by a reciprocal agreement with an automotive organization. Personal liability insurance is optional though recommended (but see if your travel insurance or home policy already covers it). Rental companies in New York are required by law to insure their own cars, so the LDW is not a factor. Instead, the renter is responsible for the first $100 in damage to the vehicle, and the company is accountable for anything beyond that. You will need a credit card (or a large cash deposit) to rent a car, and usually have to be over age 25. If you know you want to rent a car before you travel, ask your travel agent or airline if they can offer any good deals.

Avis

800-331-1212; www.avis.com. 24 hours. Rates from $50 a day, unlimited mileage. AmEx, DC, Disc, MC, V.

Budget Rent-a-Car

212-807-8700; www.drivebudget.com. In the city, call for hours; at the airports 5am–2am. Rates from $70 a day, unlimited mileage. AmEx, DC, Disc, JCB, MC, V.

Enterprise

800-325-8007; www.enterprise.com. Mon–Fri 7am–7pm; Sat 8am–2pm; Sun 9am–9pm. Rates from $35 a day outside New York City; around $50 a day in New York City; unlimited mileage restricted to New York, New Jersey and Connecticut. AmEx, DC, Disc, MC, V.

The cheapest way to rent a car is to leave the city. We highly recommend this cheap and reliable service, which has easily accessible branches from Manhattan. Try either the Hoboken, NJ, location (*take the PATH train from 33rd St*), or Greenwich, CT (*Metro-North from Grand Central*). Agents will pick you up at the station. Call for locations within the five boroughs.

Parking

If you drive to NYC, find a garage, park your car and leave it there. Parking on the street is subject to byzantine restrictions (for information on alternate-side-of-the-street parking, call 212-225-5368), ticketing is rampant and car theft is common. Parking in the outer boroughs is a bit easier, though many restrictions still apply, so if you can't understand the parking signs, find another spot. Garages are plentiful but expensive. If you want to park for less than $15 a day, try a garage outside Manhattan and take public transportation in. Listed below are the best deals in Manhattan. For other options—and there are many—try the Yellow Pages.

GMC Park Plaza

407 E 61st St between First and York Aves (212-838-4158; main office 212-888-7400).

GMC has more than 50 locations in the city; at $18 overnight, including tax, this location is the cheapest.

Kinney System Inc.

212-502-5490.

The city's largest parking company is accessible and reliable, though not the cheapest in town. Rates vary, so call for prices at your location of choice.

Mayor Parking

Pier 40, West St at Houston St (800-494-7007). 24 hours.

Mayor Parking offers indoor and outdoor parking. Call for information.

By train

Thanks to Americans' love affair with the automobile, passenger trains are not as common here as in other parts of the world; American rails are used primarily for cargo, and passenger trains from New York are used mostly by commuters. For longer hauls, call Amtrak. *See also chapter* **Trips Out of Town.**

Train service

Amtrak

800-872-7245; www.amtrak.com.

Amtrak provides all long-distance train service throughout America. Train travel is more comfortable than bus service, but it's also more expensive (a sleeper can cost more than flying) and less flexible. All trains depart from Penn Station.

Weather or not

Rain or shine, New York City is mighty fine

Here is the average temperature and rain/snowfall for NYC by month—but remember, there's *always* something to do indoors when it's too nasty to wander around outside.

	Temperature		Precipitation	
	°F	°C	inches	cm
Jan	32.0	0.0	3.2	8.1
Feb	33.4	0.8	3.1	7.9
Mar	41.3	5.2	4.2	10.7
Apr	52.0	11.2	3.8	9.7
May	62.6	17.0	3.8	9.7
Jun	71.0	21.9	3.2	8.1
Jul	77.0	25.0	3.8	9.7
Aug	75.2	24.0	4.0	10.2
Sept	70.0	21.0	3.7	9.4
Oct	57.5	14.2	3.4	8.6
Nov	47.0	8.3	3.9	10.4
Dec	36.5	2.6	3.8	9.7

Long Island Rail Road

718-217-5477; www.mta.nyc.ny.us/lirr/index.html.
LIRR provides rail service to Long Island from Penn Station and Brooklyn.

Metro-North

212-532-4900, 800-638-7646; www.mta.nyc.ny.us/mnr/index.html.
Trains leave from Grand Central and service cities and towns north of Manhattan.

New Jersey Transit

973-762-5100; www.njtransit.state.nj.us.
Trains based at Penn Station service New Jersey commuters.

PATH Trains

800-234-7284; www.nj.com/njtransit/path.html.
PATH (Port Authority Trans Hudson) trains run from five stations in Manhattan to various places across the Hudson River in New Jersey, including Hoboken, Jersey City and Newark. The system is fully automated and costs $1 per trip. You need change or a crisp dollar bill for the ticket machines. Trains run 24 hours a day, but you can face a very long wait during rush hours. Manhattan PATH stations are marked on the subway map, pages 409–411.

Train stations

Grand Central Terminal

42nd–44th Sts between Vanderbilt and Lexington Aves. Subway: S, 4, 5, 6, 7 to 42nd St–Grand Central.
Grand Central is home to Metro-North, which runs trains to more than 100 stations throughout New York State and Connecticut. *See chapter* **Midtown.**

Penn Station

31st–33rd Sts between Seventh and Eighth Aves. Subway: A, C, E, 1, 2, 3, 9 to 34th St–Penn Station.
Long Island Rail Road, New Jersey Transit and Amtrak (long-distance) trains depart from this terminal.

Getting Around

Despite its reputation to the contrary, New York City is actually quite easy to navigate. What public transportation lacks in cleanliness it makes up for in reach and reasonable efficiency. The Metropolitan Transportation Authority (*MTA; 718-330-1234; www.mta.nyc.ny.us*) runs the subways and buses, as well as a number of the commuter services to points outside Manhattan. Otherwise, hail a cab.

To and from the airport

For a full list of transportation services between New York City and its three airports, call **800-AIR-RIDE** (*800-247-7433*), a touch-tone menu of recorded information provided by the Port Authority. Public transportation is the cheapest method, but the routes are indirect and can be frustrating and time-consuming. Private bus services are usually the best budget option. Medallion (city-licensed) cabs from the New York airports line up at designated locations. Although it is illegal, many car-service drivers and nonlicensed "gypsy cabs" solicit riders around the baggage-claim areas—avoid them.

Airports

John F. Kennedy International Airport

718-244-4444; www.panynj.gov/aviation/jfkframe.HTM.
There's a subway link from JFK (extremely cheap at $1.50), but it takes almost two hours to get to Manhattan. Wait for a yellow shuttle bus to the Howard Beach station and take the **A train** to Manhattan. A private **bus service** is a more pleasant option (*see listings below*). A **medallion yellow cab** from JFK to Manhattan is a flat $30 fare, plus toll and tip. There is no set fare to JFK from Manhattan; depending on traffic, it can be as high as $45. Or try a **car service** for around $32 (*see* **Taxis and car services,** *page 364*).

La Guardia Airport

718-476-5000; www.panynj.gov/aviation/lgaframe.HTM.
Seasoned New Yorkers take the **M60 bus** ($1.50), which runs between the airport and 106th Street at Broadway. The ride takes 20 to 40 minutes (depending on traffic). The route crosses Manhattan on 125th Street in Harlem; you can get off at the Lexington Avenue subway station for the 4, 5 and 6 trains or at Lenox Avenue for the 2 and 3. You can also disembark on Broadway at the 116th Street–Columbia University subway station for the 1 or 9 train. Other options: Private **bus services** cost around $14; **taxis** or **car services** charge about $25 plus toll and tip (*see* **Taxis and car services,** *page 364*).

Newark Airport

973-961-6000; www.panynj.gov/aviation/ewrframe.HTM.
Though it's a bit far afield, Newark isn't difficult to get to or from. The best option is a **bus service** (*see listings below*). A **car service** will run about $32 and a **taxi** around $40, plus tolls and tip (*see* **Taxis and car services,** *page 364*).

Bus services

Gray Line

212-757-6840; 800-451-0455.
A minibus service runs from each of the three area airports to any address in midtown (*between 23rd and 63rd Sts*) from 7am to 11pm; the wait at the airport is never more than 20 minutes. On the outbound journey, Gray Line picks up at several hotels (you must book in advance).

New York Airport Service

212-875-8200; www.nyairportservice.com.
This service operates to and from JFK and La Guardia airports between 6am and 11pm, with stops near Grand Central Terminal (*on the east side of Park Ave between 41st and 42nd Sts*), inside the Port Authority terminal (*see* **Bus stations,** *page 360*) and outside a number of midtown hotels.

Olympia Trails

212-964-6233.
Olympia operates between Newark Airport and outside Penn Station,

Grand Central Terminal, the World Trade Center and inside Port Authority; the fare is $11 and buses leave every 15–20 minutes. Call for exact drop-off and pick-up locations.

SuperShuttle

212-258-3826

Blue SuperShuttle vans offer 24-hour door-to-door service between NYC and the three airports. You need to allow extra time when catching a flight, as vans will be picking up other passengers. The fare is $19.50.

Buses

MTA buses are fine if you aren't in a hurry. Or, if your feet hurt from walking around, a bus is a good way to continue your street-level sightseeing. They're white and blue with a route number and a digital destination sign. The fare is $1.50, payable either with a token or MetroCard (*see* **Subways,** *below*) or in exact change (silver coins only, no bills accepted). Express buses operate on some routes; these cost $3. If you're traveling uptown or downtown and want to catch a crosstown bus (or vice versa) ask the driver for a transfer when you get on—you'll be given a ticket for use on the second leg of your journey. MetroCards allow automatic transfers from bus to bus and between buses and subways. You can rely on other passengers for advice, but bus maps are posted on most buses, at all subway stations and are available from **NYC & Company–the Convention and Visitors Bureau** (*see* **Tourist information,** *page 379*). The Manhattan Bus Map is reprinted on page 407. Buses make only designated stops (about every two or three blocks going north or south and every block east or west), but between 10pm and 5am you can ask the driver to stop anywhere along the route. All buses are equipped with wheelchair lifts. Contact the MTA (*718-330-1234; www.mta.nyc.ny.us*) for further information.

Driving

Manhattan drivers are fearless, and taking to the streets is not for the faint of heart. Don't bother renting a car unless you are planning a trip out of town (*see* **Getting to and from NYC,** *page 360*). If you're going to be wheeling around the city, restrict your driving to evening hours, when traffic is less heavy and on-street parking a bit more plentiful. Even then, keep your eyes on the road, and be prepared for anything.

Breakdowns

Citywide Towing

61–67 Ninth Ave at 15th St (212-924-8104). 24 hours. Cash only.

All types of repairs are done on foreign and domestic autos.

Parking

Don't ever park within 15 feet (5 meters) of a fire hydrant, and make sure you read the parking signs. Unless there is metered parking, most streets have "alternate-side-of-the-street parking"—i.e., each side is off limits for certain hours every other day. The **New York City Department of Transportation** (*212-442-7080*) provides information on daily changes to parking regulations. If precautions fail, call 718-422-7800 for car towing/car impound information. See **Getting to and from NYC,** page 360.

24-hour gas stations

Amoco

610 Broadway at Houston St (212-473-5924). AmEx, DC, Disc, JCB, MC, V. No repairs.

Hess

502 W 45th St at Tenth Ave (212-245-6594). AmEx, Disc, MC, V. No Repairs.

Shell

2420 Amsterdam Ave at 181st St (212-928-3100). AmEx, Disc, MC, V. Repairs.

Subways

Subways are easily the fastest way to get around town during the day, and despite their dangerous, dirty reputation, they're now cleaner and safer than they've been in 20 years. Trains run around the clock, but with sparse service and fewer riders at night, so it's advisable (and usually quicker) to take a cab after 10pm. Entry to the system requires a MetroCard or a token costing $1.50 (both also work on buses), which you can buy from a booth inside the station entrance. Many stations come equipped with brightly colored vending machines that dispense MetroCards. These machines accept either cash or credit cards (AmEx, Disc, MC, V); they're easy to use and a time-saver when there is a line at the booth.

Once through the turnstile, you can travel anywhere in the system. If you're planning to use the subway a lot, it's worth buying a MetroCard, which is also available at some stores and hotels. Free transfers between subways and buses are available only with the MetroCard. There are two types: pay-per-use cards and unlimited ride cards. Any number of passengers can use the pay-per-use cards, which start at $3 for two trips and run as high as $80. A $15 card offers 11 trips for the price of 10. The unlimited ride MetroCard—an incredible value if you plan to ride the subway frequently—is available in three denominations: a 1-day Fun Pass ($4, available at station vending machines but *not* at booths), a 7-day pass ($17) and a 30-day pass ($63). These are good for unlimited rides on the subway or buses but can only be used once every 18 minutes (so only one person can use them at a time). Contact the MTA (*718-330-1234; www.mta.nyc.ny.us*) for further information.

Trains are known by letters or numbers and are color-coded according to the line on which they run. Stations are named after the street at which they're located. Entrances are marked with a green globe (a red globe marks an entrance that is not always open). Many stations (and most of the local stops) have separate entrances to the uptown and downtown platforms—look before you pay. "Express" trains run between major stops; "local" trains stop at every station. Check on a subway map (posted in all stations and reprinted on pages 409–411) before you board.

To ensure safety, don't stand too close to the edge of the platform and board the train from the off-peak waiting area, marked at the center of every platform (this area is monitored by cameras; it's also where the conductor's car often stops). More advice: Hold your bag with the opening facing you, and don't wear any flashy jewelry.

Taxis and car services

Once you start using cabs in New York, you'll begin to wish they were this cheap everywhere in the world. Yellow cabs are hardly ever in short supply, except in the rain and at around 4 or 5pm, when rush hour gets going and when many cabbies—annoyingly—change shifts. If the center light on top of the cab is lit, it means the cab is available and should stop if you stick your arm out. Jump in first and *then* tell the driver where you're going (New Yorkers give cross streets, not building numbers). Cabs carry up to four people for the same price: $2, plus 30¢ per fifth of a mile, with an extra 50¢ charge after 8pm. This makes the average fare for a three-mile (4.5km) ride $5 to $7, depending on traffic and time of day.

Cabbies almost always enforce the law of not allowing more than four passengers in a cab, although it may be worth an attempt. Smoking in cabs is prohibited; but some cabbies won't object.

Since some cabbies' knowledge of the city is lamentably meager, it helps if you know where you're going—and speak up. By law, taxis cannot refuse to take you anywhere, so don't be duped by a cabbie who is too lazy to drive you to Brooklyn or the airport. In general, tip 15 percent. The cab number and driver's number are posted on the partition if you have a problem. Or ask for a receipt—there's a meter number on it. If you want to complain or trace lost property, call the **Taxi and Limousine Commission** (*212-221-8294, Mon–Fri 9am–5pm*).

Late at night, cabbies stick to fast-flowing routes and reliably lucrative areas. Try the avenues and the key streets (Canal, Houston, 14th, 23rd, 42nd, 59th, 86th). Bridge and tunnel exits are also good for a steady flow from the airports, and passengerless cabbies will usually head for nightclubs and big hotels. Otherwise, try the following:

Chinatown

Chatham Square, where Mott St meets the Bowery, is an unofficial taxi stand; or hail a cab exiting the Manhattan Bridge at Bowery and Canal St.

Financial District

Try the Marriott World Trade Center or 1 World Trade Center; there may be a line, but there'll certainly be a cab.

Lincoln Center

The crowd heads toward Columbus Circle for a cab; those in the know go west to Amsterdam Ave.

Lower East Side

Katz's Deli (*Houston St at Ludlow St*) is a cabbies' hangout; otherwise, try Delancey St, where cabs come in over the Williamsburg Bridge.

Midtown

Penn Station and Grand Central Terminal attract cabs through the night, as does Port Authority Bus Terminal (*Eighth Ave between 40th and 42nd Sts*) and Times Square.

Soho

If you're west, try Sixth Ave; east, the gas station on Houston St at Broadway.

Tribeca

Cabs here (many arriving from the Holland Tunnel) head up Hudson St. Canal St is also a good bet.

Car services

The following companies will pick you up anywhere in the city, at any time of day or night, for a prearranged fare.

Bell Radio Taxi

212-206-1700

Sabra

212-777-7171

Tel Aviv

212-777-7777

Resources A to Z

Directory

Computers

There are hundreds of computer dealers in Manhattan (*see chapter* **Shopping & Services, Objects of Desire,** *for some stores*). You might want to buy out of state to avoid the hefty sales tax. Many out-of-state dealers advertise in New York papers and magazines. Here are reliable places if you're just looking to rent.

Kinko's

24 E 12th St between University Pl and Fifth Ave (212-924-0802; main number 800-2-KINKOS). Subway: L, N, R, 4, 5, 6 to 14th St–Union Sq. 24 hours. AmEx, Disc, MC, V.

This is a very efficient and friendly

place to use computers and copiers. Most branches have IBM and Macintosh workstations and design stations, plus all the major software. Color output is available, as is laptop hookup and internet connections ($12 per hour, 49¢ per printed page). Check the phone book for other locations.

Fitch Graphics

130 Cedar St at Liberty St (212-619-3800). Subway: N, R, 1, 9 to Cortlandt St. Mon–Fri 8am–11pm (some services until 5pm only). AmEx, MC, V.
Fitch is a full-service desktop-publishing outfit, with color-laser output and prepress facilities. Fitch works on Mac and IBM platforms and has a bulletin board so customers can reach the shop online.
Other location: *25 W 45th St between Fifth and Sixth Aves (212-840-3091).*

USRental.com

212-594-2222; www.usrental.com. Mon–Fri 9am–5pm. Call for appointment. AmEx, MC, V.
Rent by the day, week, month or year. A range of computers, systems and networks, including IBM, Compaq, Macintosh and Hewlett-Packard, is on hand. One-hour delivery service is also available.

Consulates

Check the phone book for a complete list of consulates and embassies.

Australia

212-351-6500

Canada

212-596-1700

Great Britain

212-745-0200

Ireland

212-319-2555

New Zealand

212-832-4038

Consumer information

Better Business Bureau

212-533-6200; www.bbb.org. Mon–Fri 9am–5pm.
The BBB offers advice on consumer-related complaints: shopping, services, etc. Each inquiry costs $4.30 (including New York City tax).

New York City Department of Consumer Affairs

212-487-4444. Mon–Fri 9:30am–4:30pm.
Here's where you go to file complaints on consumer-related matters.

Customs and immigration

When planning your trip, check with a U.S. embassy or consulate to see if you need a visa to enter the country (*see* **Visas,** *page 379*). Standard immigration regulations apply to all visitors arriving from outside the United States, which means you may have to wait up to an hour when you arrive. During your flight, you will be handed an immigration form and a customs declaration form to be presented to an official when you land.

You may be expected to explain your visit, so be polite and be prepared. You will usually be granted an entry permit to cover the length of your stay. Work permits are hard to get, and you are not permitted to work without one (*see* **Students,** *page 375*).

U.S. Customs allows foreigners to bring in $100 worth of gifts ($400 for Americans) before paying duty. One carton of 200 cigarettes (or 50 cigars) and one liter of liquor (spirits) are allowed. No plants, fruit, meat or fresh produce can be brought into the country. If you carry more than $10,000 in currency, you will have to fill out a report.

If you must bring prescription drugs to the U.S., make sure the container is clearly marked and that you bring your doctor's statement or a prescription. Of course, marijuana, cocaine and most opiate derivatives and other chemicals are not permitted, and possession of them is punishable by stiff fines and/or imprisonment. Check with the U.S. Customs Service (*800-697-3662, 212-637-7914; www.customs.gov*) before you arrive if you have any questions about what you can bring. If you lose or need to renew your passport once in the U.S., contact your country's embassy (*see* **Consulates,** *above*).

Student immigration

Upon entering the U.S. as a student, you will need to show a passport, a special visa and proof of your plans to leave (such as a return airline ticket). Even if you have a student visa, you may be asked to show means of support during your stay (cash, credit cards, traveler's checks, etc.).

Before they can apply for a visa, nonnationals who want to study in the U.S. must obtain an I-20 Certificate of Eligibility from the school or university they plan to attend. If you are enrolling in an authorized exchange-visitor program, including a summer course or program, wait until you have been accepted by the course or program before worrying about immigration. You will be guided through the process by the school.

You are admitted as a student for the length of your course, in addition to a limited period for any associated (and approved) practical training, plus a 60-day grace period. When your time's up, you must leave the country or apply to change or extend your immigration status. Requests to extend a visa must be submitted 15 to 60 days before the initial departure date. The rules are strict, and you risk deportation if you break them.

Information on these and all other immigration matters is available from the **U.S. Immigration and Naturalization Service**

(INS). The agency's 24-hour hotline (*800-375-5283*) is a vast menu of recorded information in English and Spanish; advisers are available from 8am to 6pm Monday through Friday. You can visit the INS at its New York office located in the **Jacob Javits Federal Building** (*26 Federal Plaza, on Broadway between Duane and Worth Sts*). The office is open 7:30am to 3:30pm Monday through Friday and cannot be reached directly by telephone.

The **U.S. Embassy** also offers guidance on obtaining student visas (*visa information in the U.S. 202-663-1225; in the U.K. (0)207-499-9000; travel.state.gov/visa_services.html*) . Or, you can write to the Visa Branch of the Embassy of the United States of America, 5 Upper Grosvenor Street, London W1A 2J.

When you apply for your student visa, you'll be expected to prove your ability to support yourself financially (including the payment of school fees), without working, for at least the first nine months of your course. After those nine months, you may be eligible to work part-time, but you must have specific permission to do so.

If you are a British student who wants to spend a summer vacation working in the States, contact **BUNAC** for help in arranging a temporary job and the requisite visa (*16 Bowling Green Lane, London EC1R 0QH; (0)20-7251-3472; bunac@easynet.co.uk*).

Disabled

Under New York city law, all facilities constructed after 1987 must provide complete access to the disabled—restrooms and entrances/exits included. In 1990, the Americans with Disabilities Act made the same requirements federal law. In the wake of this legislation, many owners of older buildings have voluntarily added disabled-access features. Due to widespread compliance with the law, we have not specifically noted the availability of disabled facilities in our listings. However, it's a good idea to call ahead and check.

Despite its best efforts, New York can be a challenging city for a disabled visitor, but there is support and guidance close by. One useful resource is the **Hospital Audiences, Inc.** (*212-575-7660*) guide to New York's cultural institutions, *Access for All* ($5). The book tells how accessible each place really is, and includes information on the height of telephones and water fountains, hearing- and visual aids, passenger-loading zones and alternative entrances. HAI also has a service for the visually impaired that provides audio descriptions of theater performances.

All Broadway theaters are equipped with devices for the hearing impaired; call **Sound Associates** (*212-582-7678*) for more information. There are a number of other stage-related resources for the disabled. Call Telecharge (*212-239-6200*) to reserve tickets for wheelchair seating in Broadway and Off Broadway venues. **Theater Development Fund's Theater Access Project** (TAP) arranges sign language interpretation for Broadway shows (*212-221-1103, 212-719-4537*). **Hands On** (*212-822-8550*) does the same for Broadway and Off Broadway performances.

In addition, the organization **Big Apple Greeter** (*see chapter* **Tour New York**) will help any person with disabilities enjoy New York City.

The Society for the Advancement of Travel for the Handicapped

347 Fifth Ave, suite 610, New York, NY 10016 (212-447-7284; fax 212-725-8253).

This nonprofit group, based in New York City, was founded in 1976 to educate people about travel facilities for the disabled. The society promotes travel for the disabled worldwide. Membership is $45 a year ($30 for students and senior citizens) and includes access to an information service and a quarterly travel magazine.

Lighthouse International

111 E 59th St between Park and Lexington Aves (212-821-9200; 800-334-5497). Subway: N, R to Lexington Ave; 4, 5, 6 to 59th St. Mon–Fri 9am–5pm; Sat 10am–5pm; Sun noon–5pm.

In addition to running a store that sells handy items for sight-impaired people, this organization provides the blind with help and info to deal with life—or a holiday—in New York City.

Mayor's Office for People with Disabilities

100 Gold St between Spruce and Frankfort Sts, second floor (212-788-2830). Subway: J, M, Z to Chambers St; 4, 5, 6 to Brooklyn Bridge–City Hall. Mon–Fri 9am–5pm.

This city office provides services for disabled people.

New York Society for the Deaf

817 Broadway at 12th St (212-777-3900). Subway: L, N, R, 4, 5, 6, to 14th St–Union Sq. Mon–Thu 9am–5pm; Fri 9am–4:30pm.

The deaf and hearing-impaired come here for information and services.

Electricity

The U.S. uses 110–120V, 60-cycle AC current, rather than the 220–240V, 50-cycle AC used in Europe and elsewhere. Except for dual-voltage, flat-pin plug shavers, you'll need an adapter to run any foreign-bought appliance. They're available at airport shops and some pharmacies and department stores.

Emergencies

Ambulances

In an emergency, dial **911** for an ambulance or call the operator (dial 0). To complain about slow service or poor treatment, call the **Fire Dept. Complaint Hotline** (*718-999-2646*).

Fire

In an emergency, dial **911.**

Police

In an emergency, dial **911.** For the location of the nearest police precinct, or for general information about police services, call **212-374-5000.**

Health and medical facilities

The public health-care system is practically nonexistent in the United States and costs of private health care are exorbitant, so if at all possible make sure you have comprehensive medical insurance when you travel to New York.

Clinics

Walk-in clinics offer treatment for minor ailments. Most require immediate payment, although some will send their bill directly to your insurance company. You will have to file a claim to recover the cost of prescription medication.

D•O•C•S

55 E 34th St between Madison and Park Aves (212-252-6000). Subway: 6 to 33rd St. Walk-in: Mon–Thu 8am–8pm; Fri 8am–7pm; Sat 9am–3pm; Sun 9am–2pm. Extended hours by appointment. Basic fee: $75–$150. AmEx, MC, V.

These excellent primary-care facilities, affiliated with Beth Israel Medical Center, offer by-appointment and walk-in services. If you need X-rays or lab tests, go as early as possible—no later than 4pm Monday through Friday.

Other locations: *1555 Third Ave at 88th St (212-828-2300); 202 W 23rd St at Seventh Ave (212-352-2600).*

Dentists

NYU College of Dentistry

345 E 24th St between First and Second Aves (212-998-9800, emergency health care in off-hours 212-998-9828). Subway: 6 to 23rd St. Mon–Thu 8:30am–6:30pm; Fri 8:30am–4pm. Base fee $85. Disc, MC, V.

If you need your teeth fixed on a budget, you can become a guinea pig for final-year students. They're slow but proficient, and an experienced dentist is always on hand to supervise. Go before 2pm to ensure a same-day visit.

Emergency rooms

You will be billed for emergency treatment. Call your travel insurance company's emergency number before seeking treatment to find out which hospitals accept your insurance. Emergency rooms are always open at:

Bellevue Hospital

462 First Ave at 27th St (212-562-4141). Subway: 6 to 28th St.

Cabrini Medical Center

227 E 19th St between Second and Third Aves (212-995-6120). Subway: L, N, R, 4, 5, 6 to 14th St–Union Sq.

Mount Sinai Hospital

Madison Ave at 101st St (212-241-7171). Subway: 4, 5, 6 to 96th St.

Roosevelt Hospital

428 W 59th St at Ninth Ave (212-523-4000). Subway: A, C, B, D, 1, 9, to 59th St–Columbus Circle.

St. Vincent's Hospital

153 W 11th St at Seventh Ave (212-604-7998). Subway: L to Sixth Ave; 1, 2, 3, 9 to 14th St.

Gay and lesbian health

See chapter **Gay & Lesbian.**

House calls

NY Hotel Urgent Medical Services

3 E 74th St between Fifth and Madison Aves (212-737-1212; www.travelmd.com). 24 hours. Hotel visit fee: $200; office visit fee: $135. Rates increase at night and on weekends.

Dr. Ronald Primus and his partners provide medical attention right in your Manhattan hotel room or private residence. Whether you need a simple prescription or an internal examination, this service can provide a specialist. In-office appointments are also available.

Pharmacies

See also chapter **Shopping & Services.**

Duane Reade

224 W 57th St at Broadway (212-541-9708). Subway: N, R, to 57th St. AmEx, MC, V.

This chain operates all over the city, and some stores offer 24-hour service. Check phone book for additional locations.

Other 24-hour locations: *2465 Broadway at 91st St (212-799-3172); 1279 Third Ave at 74th St (212-744-2668); 378 Sixth Ave at Waverly Pl (212-674-5357).*

Rite Aid

303 W 50th St at Eighth Ave (212-247-8736; www.riteaid.com). Subway: C, E to 50th St. AmEx, Disc, MC, V.

Select locations have 24-hour pharmacies. Call 800-RITE-AID for a complete listing.

Other 24-hour locations: *2833 Broadway at 110th St (212-663-8252); 144 E 86th St between Lexington and Third Aves (212-876-0600); 210 Amsterdam Ave between 69th and 70th Sts (212-873-7965); 542 Second Ave at 31st St (212-873-7965).*

Women's health

Eastern Women's Center

44 E 30th St between Madison Ave and Park Ave South (212-686-6066). Subway: 6 to 33rd St. Tue–Sat 9am–5pm. AmEx, MC, V.

Pregnancy tests cost $20; counseling is also available.

Maternal, Infant & Reproductive Health Program

2 Lafayette St at Reade St, 18th floor (212-442-1740). Subway: N, R to City Hall. Mon–Fri 8am–5pm.

You can pick up leaflets and advice here; call for an appointment. The **Women's Health Line** (*212-230-1111*), on the 21st floor of the same building, gives over-the-phone contraceptive advice.

Planned Parenthood
Margaret Sanger Center, 26 Bleecker St at Mott St (212-274-7200). Subway: B, D, F, Q to Broadway–Lafayette St; 6 to Bleecker St. Mon–Fri 8am–8pm; Sat 8am–4pm.
This is the main branch—newly relocated to a state-of-the-art facility—of the best-known, most reasonably priced network of family planning clinics in the U.S. Counseling and treatment are available for a full range of gynecological needs, including abortion, treatment of STDs, HIV testing and contraception. Phone for an appointment and for more information about services. No walk-ins.

Helplines

AIDS and HIV

CDC National HIV & AIDS Hotline
800-342-2437. 24 hours.

Alcohol and drug abuse

Alcoholics Anonymous
212-647-1680. 24 hours.

Cocaine Anonymous
212-262-2463. 24-hour recorded info.

Drug Abuse Information Line
800-522-5353. 24 hours.
This program refers callers to recovery programs around the state.

Pills Anonymous
212-874-0700. 24-hour recorded info.
You'll find information on drug-recovery programs for users of marijuana, cocaine, alcohol and other addictive substances, as well as referrals to Narcotics Anonymous meetings. You can also leave a message, if you wish to have a counselor speak to you directly.

Child abuse

Childhelp's National Child Abuse Hotline
800-422-4453. 24 hours.
Counselors provide general crisis consultation, and can help in an emergency. Callers include abused children, runaways and parents having problems with children.

Gay and lesbian health

See chapter **Gay & Lesbian.**

Psychological services

Center for Inner Resource Development
212-734-5876. 24 hours.
Therapists will talk to you day or night, and are trained to deal with all kinds of emotional problems, including those resulting from rape.

Help Line
212-532-2400. 9am–10pm.
Trained volunteers will talk to anyone contemplating suicide, and can also help with other personal problems.

The Samaritans
212-673-3000. 24 hours.
People thinking of committing suicide, or suffering from depression, grief, sexual anxiety or alcoholism, can call this organization for advice.

Rape and sex crimes

St. Luke's/Roosevelt Hospital Rape Crisis Center
212-523-4728. Mon–Fri 9am–5pm, recorded referral message at other times.
The Rape Crisis Center provides a trained volunteer who will accompany you through all aspects of reporting a rape and getting emergency treatment.

Sex Crimes Report Line of the New York Police Department
212-267-7273. 24 hours.
Reports of sex crimes are handled by a female detective. She will inform the appropriate precinct, send an ambulance if requested and provide counseling and medical referrals. The detectives will make house calls. Other issues handled: violence against gays and lesbians, child victimization and referrals for the families and friends of crime victims.

Victim Services Agency
212-577-7777. 24 hours.
VSA offers telephone and one-on-one counseling for any victim of domestic violence, rape or other crimes, as well as practical help with court processes, compensation and legal aid.

Holidays

For a list of public holidays observed in the United States, see **U.S. Holidays,** *page 218.* Banks and government offices are closed on these days (and sometimes others). Public transportation still operates on all holidays, though usually on a reduced schedule. Many stores and restaurants remain open on all holidays except Christmas—and even then a few stay open for Santa.

Insurance

If you are not an American, it's advisable to take out comprehensive insurance before arriving here; it's almost impossible to arrange in the U.S. Make sure you have adequate health coverage, since medical costs are high. For a list of New York urgent-care facilities, *see* **Emergency rooms,** *page 367.*

Internet & e-mail

Cyber Café
273 Lafayette St at Prince St (212-334-5140; www.cyber-cafe.com). Subway: B, D, F, Q to Broadway–Lafayette St; N, R to Prince St; 6 to Spring St. Mon–Fri 8:30am–10pm; Sat, Sun 11am–10pm. $12.80 per hour, 50¢ per printed page.
This is your standard Internet-connected café, though at least this one serves great coffee.
Other location: *250 W 49th St between Broadway and Eighth Ave (212-333-4109).*

Internet Café
82 E 3rd St between First and Second Aves (212-614-0747). Subway: F to Second Ave. Mon–Sat 11am–2am; Sun 11am–midnight. $10 per hour, 25 cents per printed page.
E-mail your loved ones from the

Directory

basement café to the sounds of nightly live jazz.

Kinko's

See **Computers,** page 364.

New York Public Library

188 Madison Ave between 34th and 35th Sts (212-592-7000; www.nypl.org/branch). Subway: 6 to 33rd St. Mon, Fri 10am–6pm; Tue, Thu 11am–8pm; Wed 11am–7pm; Sat noon–6pm. Free.

The 83 branch libraries scattered throughout the five boroughs are a great place to e-mail and surf the net for free. A select number of computer stations may make for a long wait, and, once on, your user time may be limited. Check the Yellow Pages for the branch nearest you. Several branches are listed in chapter **Museums.**

Other location: *455 Fifth Ave at 40th St, fourth floor (212-340-0863).*

Legal assistance

If you are arrested for a minor violation (disorderly conduct, harassment, loitering, rowdy partying, etc.) and you're very polite to the officer during the arrest, you'll probably get fingerprinted and photographed at the station and be given a desk-appearance ticket with a date to show up at criminal court. Then you get to go home.

Arguing with a police officer or engaging in something more serious (possession of a weapon, drunken driving, gambling or prostitution, for example) might get you processed. In that case, expect to embark on a 24- to 30-hour journey through the system.

If the courts are backed up (and they usually are), you'll be held temporarily at a precinct pen. You can make a phone call after you've been fingerprinted. When you get through central booking, you'll arrive at 100 Centre Street. Arraignment occurs in one of two AR (arraignment courtroom) units, where a judge decides whether you should be released on bail and then sets a court date. If you can't post bail, you'll be held at Rikers Island. Unless a major crime has been committed, a bail bondsman is unnecessary. The bottom line: Try not to get arrested, and if you are, don't act foolishly.

Legal Aid Society

212-577-3300. Mon–Fri 9am–5pm.

Legal Aid gives free advice and referrals on legal matters.

Legal Services for New York City

212-431-7200. Mon–Fri 9am–5pm.

This is a nonprofit referral service that offers assistance to people with any kind of legal problem.

Sandback, Birnbaum & Michelen Criminal Law

212-517-3200; 800-766-5800. 24 hours.

These are the numbers to have in your head when the cops read you your rights in the middle of the night.

Libraries

Several branches are listed in chapter **Museums.** See **Internet & e-mail,** page 368.

Locksmiths

The following emergency locksmiths are open 24 hours. Both require proof of residency or car ownership plus ID.

Champion Locksmiths

16 locations in Manhattan (212-362-7000). $15 service charge day or night, plus minimum of $35 to fit a lock. AmEx, MC, V.

Elite Locksmiths

470 Third Ave between 32nd and 33rd Sts (212-685-1472). $45 during the day; $75–$90 at night. Cash only.

Lost property

For property lost in the street, contact the police. For lost credit cards or traveler's checks, see **Money,** page 370.

Buses and subways

New York City Transit Authority, 34th St–Penn Station, near the A train platform (212-712-4500). Mon–Wed, Fri 8am–noon; Thu 11am–6:30pm.

Grand Central Terminal

212-340-2555. Mon–Fri 7am–11pm; Sat, Sun 10am–11pm.

Call if you've left something on a Metro-North train.

JFK Airport

718-244-4444, or contact your airline.

La Guardia Airport

718-476-5115, or contact your airline.

Newark Airport

973-961-6230, or contact your airline.

Penn Station

212-630-7389. Call for items left on Amtrak, New Jersey Transit and the Long Island Rail Road.

Taxis

212-221-8294. Call this number if you leave anything in a cab.

Luggage lockers

For security reasons, luggage lockers are increasingly a thing of the past. However, there are baggage rooms at Penn Station, Grand Central Terminal and the Port Authority Bus Terminal.

Messenger services

A to Z Couriers

105 Rivington St between Ludlow and Essex Sts (212-253-6500). Subway: F to Delancey St; J, M, Z to Essex St. AmEx, MC, V.

These cheerful couriers will deliver to anywhere in the city (and Long Island, too).

Breakaway

43 Walker St between Church St and Broadway (212-219-8500). Subway: A, C, E to Canal St. Mon–Fri 7am–9pm; by arrangement Sat, Sun. AmEx, MC, V.

Breakaway is a highly recommended citywide delivery service that promises to pick up and deliver within the hour. With 25 messengers, you can take them at their word.

Jefron Messenger Service

141 Duane St between West Broadway and Church St (212-964-8441). Subway: 1, 2, 3, 9 to Chambers St. Mon–Fri 7am–6pm. Cash only.

Jefron specializes in transporting import/export documents.

Money

Over the past few years, a lot of American currency has undergone a subtle facelift—partly as national celebration and partly to deter increasingly adept counterfeiters. However, the "old" money is in circulation and still as good as the new. The U.S. dollar ($) equals 100 cents (¢). Coins range from copper pennies (1¢) to silver nickels (5¢), dimes (10¢), quarters (25¢) and less common half-dollars (50¢).

In 1999, the U.S. Mint began issuing commemorative "state quarters." George Washington's profile still graces the front, but the reverse (or "tails") side is dedicated to 1 of 50 states, each fitted with a corresponding design symbolizing its history and achievements. These quarters are being issued in segments of five states per year in the order of state entry into the Union—by 2009 all 50 will be in circulation.

The year 2000 marked the introduction of the "golden dollar" coin. This coin is about one inch in diameter and features a portrait of Sacagawea (the Native-American woman who helped guide explorers Lewis and Clark on their journey across America). The new gold coin replaces the older Susan B. Anthony silver dollar, and fulfills a growing need for dollar coins in vending and mass transit machines. You might still get a Susan B. on occasion—they're increasingly rare and worth holding on to. For more information on U.S. coins call 800-USA-MINT or check the website www.usmint.gov.

Paper money is all the same size and color, so make sure you fork over the right bill. It comes in denominations of $1, $2, $5, $10, $20, $50 and $100. All denominations, except for the $1 and $2 bill, have recently been updated by the U.S. Treasury, which elected for a larger portrait placed off-center with extra security features; the new bills also have a large numeral on the back to help the visually impaired identify the denomination. The $2 bills are quite rare and make a smart souvenir. Small shops will rarely break a $50 or $100 bill, so it is best to carry smaller denominations (and cab drivers aren't required to change bills larger than $20). For more information on paper currency, refer to the U.S. Treasury website at www.ustreas.com.

ATMs

New York City is full of automated teller machines (ATMs). Most accept Visa, MasterCard or American Express, among other cards, if they have been registered with a PIN number. There is a usage fee, although the convenience (and the superior exchange rate) often make ATMs worth the extra charge.

Call the following for ATM locations: **Cirrus** (800-424-7787); **Wells Fargo** (800-869-3557); **Plus Systems** (800-843-7587). Also, look for branch banks or delis, which often have mini ATMs by the front counter. If you've lost your number or have somehow demagnetized your card, most banks will give cash to card holders, with proper ID.

Banks and currency exchange

Banks are generally open from 9am to 3pm Monday through Friday, though some have longer hours. You need photo identification, such as a passport, to cash traveler's checks. Many banks will not exchange foreign currency, and the *bureaux de changes,* limited to tourist-trap areas, close around 6 or 7pm. It's best to arrive with some dollars in cash but to pay mostly with credit cards or traveler's checks (accepted in most restaurants and larger stores—but ask first, and be prepared to show ID). In an emergency, most big hotels offer 24-hour exchange facilities; the catch is that they charge high commissions and give atrocious rates.

American Express Travel Service

65 Broadway between Rector St and Exchange Pl (212-493-6500). Subway: N, R, 1, 9 to Rector St. Mon–Fri 8:30am–5:30pm.
AmEx will change money and traveler's checks, and offers other services, such as poste restante. Call for other branch locations.

Chequepoint USA

22 Central Park South between Fifth and Sixth Aves (212-750-2400). Subway: N, R to 59th St. 8am–8pm.
Foreign currency, traveler's checks and bank drafts are available here.
Other location: *1568 Broadway at 47th St (212-869–6281).*

People's Foreign Exchange

575 Fifth Ave at 47th St, third floor (212-883-0550). Subway: E, F to Fifth Ave. Mon–Fri 9am–6pm; Sat, Sun 10am–5pm.
People's provides free foreign exchange on banknotes and traveler's checks.

Thomas Cook Currency Services

29 Broadway at Morris St (212-363-6206). Subway: 4, 5 to Bowling Green. Mon–Fri 8:30am–4:30pm.
A complete foreign exchange service is offered.
Other locations: *9am–7pm daily. 1590 Broadway at 48th St (212-265-6063); 511 Madison Ave at 53rd St (212-753-2595). (Call 800-287-7362 for other locations).*

Credit cards

Bring plastic if you have it, or be prepared for a logistical nightmare. It's essential for things like renting cars and booking hotels, and handy for buying tickets over the phone. The six major credit cards accepted in the U.S. are American Express, Diners Club, Discover, JCB, MasterCard and Visa. If cards are lost or stolen, contact:

American Express
800-528-2122

Diners Club
800-234-6377

Discover
800-347-2683

JCB
800-366-4522

MasterCard
800-826-2181

Visa
800-336-8472

Traveler's checks

Before your trip, it is wise to buy checks in U.S. currency from a widely recognized company. Traveler's checks are routinely accepted at banks, stores and restaurants throughout the city. Bring your driver's license or passport along for identification. If checks are lost or stolen, contact:

American Express
800-221-7282

Thomas Cook
800-223-7373

Visa
800-336-8472

Wire services

If you run out of cash, don't expect your embassy or consulate to lend you money—they won't, although they may be persuaded to repatriate you. In an emergency, you can have money wired.

Western Union
800-325-6000

MoneyGram
800-926-9400

Newspapers and magazines

Daily newspapers

Daily News

The *News* has drifted politically from the Neanderthal right to a moderate but tough-minded stance under the ownership of real-estate mogul Mort Zuckerman. Labor-friendly Latino pundit Juan Gonzalez has great street sense (not to mention a Pulitzer), and in 2000, the paper appointed former *Newsweek* head Edward Kosner as editor-in-chief.

New York Post

Founded in 1801 by Alexander Hamilton, the *Post* is the city's oldest surviving daily newspaper. After many decades as a standard-bearer for political liberalism, the *Post* has swerved sharply to the right under current owner Rupert Murdoch. The paper appointed its first female editor, Xana Antunes, in 2000. The *Post* has more column-inches of gossip than any other local paper, and its headlines are usually the ones to beat. Many New Yorkers read the *News* and the *Post* from back (where the sport pages are) to front.

The New York Times

Olympian as ever after almost 150 years, the *Times* remains the city's (and the nation's) paper of record. It has the broadest and deepest coverage of world and national events—as the masthead proclaims, it delivers "all the news that's fit to print." The mammoth Sunday *Times* weighs in at a full five pounds of newsprint, including magazine, book review, sports, arts, finance, real estate and other sections.

Other dailies

One of the nation's oldest black newspapers, ***Amsterdam News,*** offers a left-of-center, Afrocentric view. New York also supports two Spanish-language dailies, ***El Diario*** and ***Noticias del Mundo. Newsday*** is the Long Island–based daily with a tabloid format but a sober tone. ***USA Today,*** also known as McPaper, specializes in polls and surveys, skin-deep news capsules and a magazinelike treatment of world events.

Weekly magazines

New York

This magazine is part newsweekly, part lifestyle report and part listings. Founded 30 years ago by Clay Felker, *New York* was a pioneer of New Journalism, showcasing such talents as Aaron Latham, Gloria Steinem and Tom Wolfe.

The New Yorker

Since the 1920s, *The New Yorker* has been known for its fine wit, elegant prose and sophisticated cartoons. In the postwar era, it established itself as a venue for serious, long-form journalism. It usually makes for a lively, intelligent read.

Time Out New York

Of course, the best place to find out what's going on in town is *Time Out New York,* launched in 1995. Based on the tried-and-trusted format of its London parent, *TONY* is an indispensable guide to the life of the city (if we do say so ourselves).

Weekly papers

Downtown journalism is a battlefield, pitting the scabrous neo-cons of the ***New York Press*** against the unreconstructed hippies of ***The Village Voice.*** The *Press* uses an all-column format; it's full of youthful energy and irreverence as well as cynicism and self-absorption. *The Voice* is sometimes passionate and ironic, but just as often strident and predictable. Both papers are free. In contrast, ***The New York Observer*** focuses on the doings of the "overclass," its term for the upper echelons of business, finance, media and politics. This salmon-colored paper is famous for its knowing observations of New York's power elite. ***Our Town*** and ***Manhattan Spirit*** are on the sidelines; these sister publications feature neighborhood news and local political gossip, and can be found in a squadron of street-corner bins.

Magazines

Black Book

Since its start in 1996, this quarterly covers New York high fashion and culture with intelligent bravado. The mix of models, pretension and politics makes *Black Book* an increasingly popular downtown rag.

Paper

Paper covers the city's trend-conscious set with plenty of insider buzz on bars, clubs, downtown boutiques and the people you'll find in them.

Photocopying and printing

Dependable Printing

10 E 22nd St at Broadway (212-533-7560). Subway: N, R to 23rd St. Mon–Fri 8:30am–7pm; Sat 10am–4pm. AmEx, MC, V.
Dependable provides offset and color printing, large-size Xerox copies, color laser printing, binding, rubber stamps, typing, forms, labels, brochures, flyers, newsletters, manuscripts, fax service, transparencies and more.
Other location: *245 Fifth Ave between 27th and 28th Sts (212-689-2217).*

Fitch Graphics

See **Computers,** page 364.

Kinko's

See **Computers,** page 364.

Performa Print Graphics

280 Madison Ave between 39th and 40th Sts (212-213-6700). Subway: S, 4, 5, 6, 7 to 42nd St–Grand Central. Mon–Fri 9am–5pm. Cash and checks only.
Performa Print Graphics specializes in assisting international firms and offers foreign-language typesetting and printing, as well as graphic design, brochures and reports, and more.

Servco

130 Cedar St between West and Washington Sts (212-285-9245). Subway: E to World Trade Ctr; N, R, 1, 9 to Cortlandt St. Mon–Fri 8:30am–5pm.
Photocopying, offset printing, blueprints and binding services are available here.
Other location: *56 W 45th St between Fifth and Sixth Aves (212-575-0991).*

Directory

Postal services

U.S. Postal Service

Stamps are available at all post offices and from drugstore vending machines. It costs 33¢ to send a one-ounce letter within the U.S. Each additional ounce costs 22¢. Postcards mailed within the U.S. need 20¢ in postage; international postcards require 55¢. Airmail letters to anywhere overseas cost 60¢ for the first half ounce (14g) and 40¢ for each additional half ounce.

General Post Office

421 Eighth Ave at 33rd St (212-967-8585; 24-hour postal information 800-725-2161). Subway: A, C, E to 34th St–Penn Station. Open 24 hours; midnight–6pm for money orders and registered mail.
This is the city's main post office; call for the branch nearest you. There are 62 full-service post offices in Manhattan alone; lines are long, but stamps are also available from self-service vending machines. Branches are usually open 9am to 5pm, Monday through Friday; Saturday hours vary from office to office. *See chapter* **Midtown.**

Express Mail

Information: 212-967-8585.
You need to use special envelopes and fill out a form, which can be done either at a post office or by arranging a pickup. You are guaranteed mail delivery within 24 hours to major U.S. cities. International delivery takes two to three days, with no guarantee. Call for more information on various time deadlines.

General Delivery

390 Ninth Ave at 30th St (212-330-3099). Subway: A, C, E to 34th St–Penn Station. Mon–Sat 10am–1pm.
U.S. visitors without local addresses can receive their mail here; it should be addressed to recipient's name, General Delivery, New York, NY 10001. You will need to show some form of identification—a passport or ID card—when picking up letters.

Poste Restante

421 Eighth Ave at 33rd St, window 29 (212-330-2912). Subway: A, C, E to 34th St–Penn Station. Mon–Sat 8am–6pm.
Foreign visitors without U.S. addresses can receive mail here; mail should be addressed to Poste Restante, New York, NY 10199. Be sure to bring some form of identification to claim your letters.

Couriers

DHL Worldwide Express

2 World Trade Center, Liberty St between West and Church Sts (800-225-5345). Subway: E to World Trade Ctr. 8:30am–8:30pm. AmEx, DC, Disc, MC, V.
DHL will send a courier to pick up packages at any address in New York City, or you can deliver packages to its offices and drop-off points in person. No cash transactions.

Federal Express

Various locations throughout the city; call and give your zip code to find the office nearest you, or get pickup at your door (800-247-4747). 24 hours. AmEx, DC, Disc, MC, V.
Federal Express rates (like those of its main competitor, United Parcel Service) are based on the distance shipped. An overnight letter to London costs about $26.25. You save $3 per package if you bring it to a Federal Express office. Packages headed overseas should be dropped off by 6pm for overnight delivery (depending on destination); packages for most destinations in the U.S., by 9pm (some locations have a later time; call to check).

United Parcel Service

Various locations throughout the city; free pickup at your door (800-742-5877 for 24-hour service). Hours vary by office; call for location and times. AmEx, DC, MC, V.
Like DHL and FedEx, UPS will send a courier to pick up parcels at any address in New York City, or you can deliver packages to its offices and drop-off points in person. UPS offers domestic and international service.

Private mail services

Mail Boxes Etc. USA

1173A Second Ave between 61st and 62nd Sts (212-832-1390). Subway: N, R to Lexington Ave; 4, 5, 6 to 59th St. Mon–Fri 9am–7pm; Sat 10am–5pm. AmEx, MC, V.
Mailbox rental, mail forwarding, overnight delivery, packaging and shipping are available. There's also a phone-message service, photocopying and faxing, typing service and business printing. There are more than 30 branches in Manhattan, many

offering 24-hour access to mailboxes; check phone book for locations.

Telegrams

Western Union Telegrams

800-325-6000. 24 hours.
Telegrams to addresses are taken over the phone at any time of day or night, and charges are added to your phone bill. Service is not available from pay phones.

Radio

There are nearly 100 stations in the New York area, offering a huge range of sounds and styles. On the AM dial, you can find intriguing talk radio and phone-in shows that attract everyone from priests to nutcases. There's plenty of news and sports as well. Although the Federal Communications Commission's recent deregulation of ownership rules has allowed such broadcast giants as Chancellor Media to buy up some of New York's most prominent commercial radio stations, many independent stations still thrive, offering everything from underground sounds to Celtic tunes. Radio highlights are printed weekly in *Time Out New York,* and daily in the *Daily News.*

News and talk

WINS-AM 1010, WABC-AM 770 and **WCBS-AM 880** offer news throughout the day, plus traffic and weather reports. Commercial-free public radio stations **WNYC-FM 93.9/AM 820** and **WBAI-FM 99.5** provide excellent news and current-affairs shows, including WNYC-AM's immensely popular *All Things Considered* (weekdays AM: 4–6pm, 7:30–8pm; FM: 5–6:30pm, 7–8pm), and guest-driven talk shows, notably WNYC-AM's *New York and Company* (weekdays noon–2pm) and WNYC-FM's *Fresh Air* (weekdays 4–5pm). WNYC also airs Garrison Keillor's godawful *A Prairie Home Companion* and Ira Glass's quirky *This American Life.* WBAI is one of the very few electronic media platforms for left-wing politics anywhere in the States.

The AM phone-in shows will take you from one extreme to the other. **WLIB-AM 1190** is the voice of black New York, with news and talk from an Afrocentric perspective, interspersed with Caribbean music. David Dinkins, former mayor of New York, has a lunchtime-dialogue show from 11am–noon on Wednesdays. Neofascist Rush Limbaugh airs his scarily popular views on **WABC-AM** (noon–3pm), where you can also get some therapy from the oh-so-conservative Dr. Laura Schlessinger (weekdays 9–11:45am) and, in the evening, the heavily street-accented demagoguery of Guardian Angels founder Curtis Sliwa (weekdays 10pm–1am).

WQXR-FM 96.3 and **WNYC-FM 93.9** serve a varied diet of classical music, WNYC being slightly more progressive.

WNEW-FM 102.7 has shifted from a rock station to primarily talk with an emphasis on the wacky and humorous. The station still dabbles in music, however, when Vin Scelsa offers his brilliant free-form rock tribute *Idiot's Delight* on Sundays from 8pm to 2am.

Jazz

WBGO-FM 88.3 "Jazz 88" plays phenomenal classic jazz. Here, Branford Marsalis broadcasts his weekly *JazzSet* program, which features many legendary artists. And there are special shows devoted to such categories as piano jazz and the blues. **WQCD-FM 101.9** is a soft-jazz station and **WCWP-FM 88.1** plays jazz as well as hip-hop, gospel and world music.

WKCR-FM 89.9, the student-run radio station of Columbia University, is where you'll hear legendary jazz DJ Phil Schaap.

Dance and pop

American commercial radio is rigidly formatted, which makes most pop stations extremely tedious and repetitive during daylight hours. However, in the evenings and on weekends, you'll find more interesting programs. **WQHT-FM 97.1** "Hot 97" is New York's commercial hip-hop station, with Steph Lova and former *Yo! MTV Raps* cohost Ed Lover cooking up a breakfast show for the homies; there's rap and R&B throughout the day. On Fridays, the station hosts *Ladies Night,* which showcases women in hip-hop. **WKTU-FM 103.5** is the city's premier dance-music station.

WBLS-FM 107.5 is an "urban [meaning black] adult" station, playing classic and contemporary funk, soul and R&B. Highlights include Chuck Mitchell's house and R&B mix on Saturday mornings, plus *Hal Jackson's Sunday Classics* (blues and soul). **WWRL-AM 1600** switched from its gospel format to R&B oldies in 1997. **WRKS-FM 98.7** ("Kiss FM") has an adult-contemporary format, which translates as unremarkable American pop. The only legacy of its more soulful days is the Sunday-morning gospel show (6–9am; 10am–noon).

WCBS-FM 101.1 is strictly oldies, while **WTJM-FM 105.1** ("Jammin' Oldies") plays a mix drawn from the '60s, '70s and '80s. **WPLJ-FM 95.5** and **WHTZ-FM 100.3** are Top 40 stations. **WLTW-FM 106.7** ("Lite FM") plays the kind of background music you hear in elevators.

Rock

WAXQ-FM 104.3 and **WXRK-FM 92.3** ("K-Rock") offer a digest of classic and alternative rock. K-Rock also attracts the city's largest group of morning listeners, thanks to Howard Stern's 6–10am weekday talk sleezefest. **WLIR-FM 92.7** plays "alternative" (indie and Gothic) sounds with a British bias. **WSOU-FM 89.5** is a college station devoted to heavy metal. At **WFMU-FM 91.1,** the term *free-form radio* still has some meaning: An eclectic mix of music and oddities, like Joe Frank's eerie stream-of-consciousness monologues (Thu at 7pm), characterizes this Jersey-based station.

Other music

WQEW-AM 1560 ("Radio Disney") has kids' programming. **WYNY-FM 107.1** plays country music. **WEVD-AM 1050** broadcasts wacky talk shows, sports games and music.

College radio

College radio is innovative and free of commercials. However, smaller transmitters mean that reception is often compromised by Manhattan's high-rise topography. Try New York University's **WNYU-FM 89.1** and Columbia's **WKCR-FM 89.9** (*see* **Jazz,** *above*) for varied programming across the musical spectrum. Fordham University's **WFUV-FM 90.7** is mostly a folk/Irish station, but also airs a variety of shows, including good old-fashioned radio drama on *Classic Radio* every Saturday night and Sunday evening.

Sports

WFAN-AM 660 covers games live. In the mornings, NYC talk-radio fixture Don Imus offers his take on sports and just about everything else going on in the world. **WWRU-AM**

1660 ("Radio Unica") covers the MetroStars soccer games.

Religion

Here are just a few of the many places of worship in New York. Check the Yellow Pages for a more detailed listing.

Baptist

Abyssinian Baptist Church

See page 75.

Catholic

St. Francis of Assisi

135 W 31st St between Sixth and Seventh Aves (212-736-8500; www.st.francis.org). Subway: B, D, F, Q, N, R to 34th St–Herald Sq; 1, 2, 3, 9 to 34th St–Penn Station. Services: Mon–Fri 6, 6:30, 7, 7:30, 8, 8:30, 10, 11, 11:45am, 12:15, 1:15, 4:30, 5:30pm; Sat 7:30, 9, 10:30, 11:15am, noon, 4, 5:15, 6:15pm; Sun 7, 8, 9:30, 10 (Korean), 11am, 12:30, 5:15, 6:15pm.

St. Patrick's Cathedral

See page 60.

Episcopal

Cathedral of St. John the Divine

See page 72.

Jewish

UJA-Federation Resource Line

212-753-2288; www.youngleadership.org. 9am–5pm. 24-hour voice mail.
This hotline provides referrals to other organizations, groups, temples and synagogues as well as advice on kosher foods and restaurants.

Methodist

St. Paul and St. Andrew United Methodist Church

263 W 86th St between Broadway and West End Ave (212-362-3179). Subway: 1, 9 to 86th St. Services: Sun 11am.

Salem United Methodist Church

2190 Adam Clayton Powell Jr. Blvd at 129th St (212-678-2700). Subway: A, C, B, D, 2, 3 to 125th St. Services: Sept–Jun Sun 11am. Jul, Aug Sun 10am.

Muslim

Islamic Cultural Center of New York

1711 Third Ave between 96th and 97th Sts (212-722-5234). Subway: 6 to 96th St. 9am–5pm and for all prayers.

Presbyterian

Fifth Avenue Presbyterian Church

7 W 55th St at Fifth Ave (212-247-0490; www.fapc.org). Services: Sun 11am.

Restrooms

Visitors to New York—like New Yorkers themselves—are always on the go. But in between all that go, go go, sometimes you've really got to…go. Contrary to popular belief (and the unpopular smell, especially in summer), the street is no place to drop trou. The real challenge lies in finding a (legal) public place to take care of your business.

Though they don't exactly have an open-door policy, the numerous **McDonald's** restaurants, **Starbucks** coffee shops and **Barnes & Noble** bookstores all contain (usually clean) restrooms. If the restroom door is locked, you may have to ask a cashier for the key. Don't announce that you're not a paying customer, and you should be all right. The same applies to most other fast-food joints (**Au Bon Pain, Wendy's,** etc.), hotels and bars that don't have a host or maître d' at the door. Here are some other options around town that can offer sweet relief (although you may have to hold your breath).

Downtown

Kmart

770 Broadway, Lafayette St at Astor Pl. Mon–Fri 9am–10pm; Sat 10am–9pm; Sun 10am–8pm.

Tompkins Square Park

Ave A at 9th St. 7am–7pm.

Washington Square Park

Thompson St at Washington Sq South. 7am–9pm.

Midtown

Bryant Park

42nd St between Fifth and Sixth Aves. Mon–Sat 7am–7pm.

Penn Station

Seventh Ave between 30th and 32nd Sts. 24 hours.

Port Authority

Eighth Ave at 41st St. 6am–1am.

St. Clement's Church

423 W 46th St between Ninth and Tenth Aves. Mon–Fri 10am–6pm; Sat, Sun 9–11am.

School of Visual Arts

209 E 23rd St between Second and Third Aves. Mon–Fri 8am–10pm.

United Nations

First Ave between 44th and 45th Sts. Mon–Sat 9am–5pm.

Uptown

Barneys New York

660 Madison Ave at 61st St. Mon–Fri 10am–8pm; Sat 10am–7pm; Sun 11am–6pm.

Central Park

Mid-park at 81st St. 8am–sundown.

Avery Fisher Hall at Lincoln Center

Amsterdam Ave at 65th St. Mon–Sat 10am–6pm; Sun noon–6pm.

Safety

Statistics on New York's crime rate, particularly violent crime, have nose-dived in the past few years, though bad things still happen to good people. More than ever, most of it stays within specific ethnic groups, and occurs late at night in low-income neighborhoods. Don't arrive thinking you need an armed guard to accompany you wherever you go; it is unlikely that you will ever be bothered.

Still, a bit of common sense won't hurt. If you look comfortable rather than lost, you should deter troublemakers. Do not flaunt your money and valuables. Avoid desolate and poorly lit streets, and if necessary, walk facing the traffic so no one can drive up alongside you. On deserted sidewalks, walk close to the street; muggers prefer to hang back in doorways and shadows. If the worst happens and you find yourself threatened, hand over your wallet or camera at once (your attacker will likely be as anxious to get it over with as you are), then dial **911** as soon as you can (it's a free call).

Be extra-alert to pickpockets and street hustlers—especially in busy tourist areas like Times Square—and don't be seduced by cardsharps or other tricksters you may come across. A shrink-wrapped camcorder for 50 bucks could turn out to be a load of bricks when you open the box.

New York women are used to the brazenness with which they are stared at by men and usually develop a hardened or dismissive attitude toward it. If your unwelcome admirers ever get verbal or start following you, ignoring them is better than responding—unless you are confident about your acid-tongued retorts. Walking into the nearest shop is your best bet to get rid of really persistent offenders. If you've been seriously victimized, see **Helplines,** page 368, for assistance.

Smoking

New Yorkers are the target of some of the strictest antismoking laws on the planet (well, except for California). The 1995 NYC Smoke-Free Air Act makes it illegal to smoke in virtually all public places, including subways, movie theaters and most restaurants—even if a no-smoking sign is not displayed. Bars and restaurants with fewer than 35 indoor seats are the exceptions, although large restaurants can have separate smoking areas. Fines start at $100, so be sure to ask before you light up. Now could be the time to quit.

Students

Student life in NYC is unlike anywhere else in the world. An endless extracurricular education exists right outside the dorm room—the city is both teacher and playground. For further guidance, check the ***Time Out New York Student Guide,*** available free on campuses in August.

Student identification

Foreign students should get themselves an International Student Identity Card (ISIC) as proof of student status and to secure discounts. These can be bought from your local student travel agent (ask at your students' union). If you buy the card in New York, you will also get basic accident insurance—a bargain. The New York branch of the **Council on International Educational Exchange** can supply one on the spot. It's at 205 East 42nd Street between Second and Third Avenues (*212-822-2700; see* **Student travel,** *below*). Note that a student identity card may not always be accepted as proof of age for drinking (you must be 21).

Student travel

Most agents offer discount fares for those under 26; specialists in student deals include:

Council Travel

205 E 42nd St between Second and Third Aves (212-822-2700; www.counciltravel.com). Mon, Tue, Thu, Fri 10am–6pm; Wed 11am–6pm; Sat 11am–5pm.
Call 800-226-8624 for other locations.

STA Travel

10 Downing St at Sixth Ave (212-627-3111; www.statravelgroup.com). Mon–Fri 9am–9pm; Sat 10am–6pm; Sun 10am–5pm.
Call 800-777-0112 for other locations.

Tax and tipping

New York is no more expensive than most would-be capitals of the Western world, but you will still have to account for a few extras. While sales tax (8.25 percent) is added to the price of most purchases, a recent fortuitous law exempts this tax on clothing items and footwear that costs less than $110. This is a good reason—as if you need one—to buy a whole new outfit and matching shoes.

There is still a lot of tipping to do, and Europeans and other out-of-towners have an especially bad reputation in this area. Don't confirm the stereotype. Waitstaff get 15 to 20 percent (as a rough guide, double the sales tax on your bill), and cabbies get 15 percent (many New Yorkers round up to an even dollar amount on small fares). But don't forget to tip bartenders ($1 a drink), hairdressers (10 to 15 percent), hotel doormen ($1 for hailing a cab), porters ($1 per bag) and maid service ($2 per day). And remember that the person who delivers your Chinese food probably receives no salary at all ($2 is considered a good tip).

Telephones

New York, like most of the world's busy cities, is awash in telephones, cellular phones, pagers and faxes. This increasing dependence on a dial tone accounts for the city's abundance of area codes. As a rule, you must dial 1 + area code before a number if the phone you are using is in a different area code. The area codes for Manhattan are 212 and 646; Brooklyn, Queens, Staten Island and the Bronx are 718 and 347; generally (but not always) 917 is reserved for cellular phones and pagers. The Long Island area codes are 516 and 631, and the codes for New Jersey are 201, 732, 973, 609, 908 and 856. Numbers preceded by 800, 877 and 888 are free of charge when dialed from anywhere in the United States. When numbers are listed as letters (e.g. 800-AIR-RIDE) for easy recall, dial the corresponding numbers on the telephone keypad.

Remember, if you carry a cellular phone, make sure you turn it off inside restaurants, plays, movies and museums. New Yorkers are quick to show their annoyance at an ill-timed ring. Some establishments even post signs designating "cellular-free zones."

General information

The Yellow Pages and White Pages have a wealth of useful information in the front, including theater-seating diagrams and maps; the blue pages in the center of the White Pages list all governmental numbers and addresses. Hotels will have copies; otherwise, try libraries or Bell Atlantic (the local phone company) payment centers.

Collect calls or credit card calls

Collect calls are also known as reverse charges. Dial 0 followed by the area code and number, or dial AT&T's 800-CALL-ATT, MCI's 800-COLLECT, Sprint's 800-ONE-DIME; for calls to the U.K., dial 800-445-5667.

Directory assistance

Dial 411 (free from pay phones). For long-distance directory assistance, dial 1 + area code + 555-1212 (long-distance charges apply). Bell Atlantic also offers national 411 directory assistance, but the charges can be high.

Emergency

Dial 911. All calls are free (including those made on pay and cell phones).

International calls

Dial 011 + country code (U.K. 44; New Zealand 64; Australia 61).

Operator assistance

Dial 0.

Toll-free directory

Dial 1 + 800 + 555-1212 (no charge).

Pagers & cellular phones

InTouch USA

212-391-8323; 800-872-7626. Mon–Fri 9am–5pm. AmEx, DC, Disc, MC, V.

InTouch, the city's largest cellular phone rental company, rents out equipment by the day, week or month.

Public pay phones

Public pay phones are easy to find. Some of them even work. Bell Atlantic's phones are the most dependable (those from other phone companies tend to be poorly maintained). If someone's left the receiver dangling, it's a sign that something's wrong. Phones take any combination of silver coins: Local calls usually cost 25¢ for three minutes. If you're not used to American phones, know that the ringing tone is long; the "engaged" tone, or busy signal, is short and higher pitched.

If you want to call long distance or make an international call from a pay phone, you need to use one of the long-distance companies. Most pay phones in New York automatically use AT&T, but phones in and around transportation hubs usually use other long-distance carriers, whose charges can be outrageous. Look in the Yellow Pages under Telephone Companies. Sprint and MCI are respected brand names (*see* **Collect calls or credit card calls,** *above*).

Make the call either by dialing 0 for an operator or by dialing direct (the latter is cheaper). To find out how much a call will cost, dial the number and a computer voice will tell you how much money to deposit.You can pay for calls with your credit card. The best way to make calls, however, is with a phone card, available in various denominations from any post office branch or from chain stores like **Duane Reade** or **Rite Aid** (*see page 367*). Delis and kiosks sell phone cards, including the New York Exclusive, which has incredible international rates. Dialing instructions are on the card.

Recorded information

For the exact time and temperature, plus lottery numbers and the New York City weather forecast, call 212-976-2828—a free call 24-hours a day. Other helpful 24-hour information lines, which add extra costs to your phone bill, are listed below. An opening message should tell you how much per minute you are paying.

Horoscope

900-438-7337

Sports scores

900-976-1313

Telephone-answering service

Messages Plus

1317 Third Ave between 75th and 76th Sts (212-879-4144). Subway: 6 to 77th St. 24 hours. AmEx, MC, V.
Messages Plus provides telephone-answering services, with specialized (medical, bilingual, etc.) receptionists if required, and plenty of ways to deliver your messages. It also offers telemarketing, voice mail and interactive website services.

Television

A visit to New York often includes at least a small dose of cathode radiation and, particularly for British visitors, American TV can inflict culture shock. Each moment of network programming is constructed to instill fatalistic curiosity for the next, with commercial breaks coming thick and fast.

The TV day is scheduled down to the second, beginning with news and gossipy breakfast magazine programs and segueing into a lobotomizing cycle of soap operas, vintage reruns and game shows—it remains unbroken until around 3pm. Then *Oprah* and *Jerry Springer* take over, broadcasting peoples' not-so-private problems, with subjects along the lines of "I married my mother's lesbian lover" and "Mad Cow Disease ruined my family."

At 5pm, there's showbiz chat and local news, followed by national and international news at 6:30pm. Early evening is the domain of popular reruns (*The Simpsons*, *Friends*, *Frasier*) and syndicated game shows like *Jeopardy!* and *Wheel of Fortune*. Huge audiences tune in at prime time, when action series, dramas, sports, movies, game shows and sitcoms battle for ratings. Finally, as sedate viewers go to bed, out come the neon personalities of the various late-night talk shows.

The only broadcast alternative to consumerist programming is public television. Public stations receive little money from traditional advertising and rely heavily on "membership" donations garnered during on-air fund drives. Public television has its own nightly news and a few local productions; its *Frontline* and *P.O.V.* documentaries are often incisive.

And then there's cable—that is, the 50 or so channels of basic cable, plus premium channels offering uninterrupted movies and sports coverage. Pay-per-view channels provide a menu of recent films, exclusive concerts and sports events at around $5 a pop. Cable also features paid "infomercials" and public-access channels, an eclectic array of weirdos, activists, scenesters and soft-core pornographers.

If you're feeling nostalgic, the Museum of Television & Radio has a huge collection of classic and hard-to-find TV shows. (*See chapter* **Museums.**)

Time Out New York offers a rundown of weekly TV highlights. For full TV schedules, including broadcast and cable television, save the Sunday *New York Times* TV section or buy a daily paper; they all have comprehensive listings.

The networks

Six major networks broadcast nationwide. All offer ratings-led variations on a theme. **CBS** (Channel 2 in NYC) has the top investigative show, *60 Minutes*, on Sundays, and its programming overall is geared to a middle-aged demographic (*Diagnosis Murder*, *Touched by an Angel*). But check out *Everybody Loves Raymond* (Mondays at 9pm) and *The Late Show with David Letterman* (weeknights at 11:30pm) for some solid humor. The most popular network, **NBC** (4), is the home of the long-running sketch-comedy series *Saturday Night Live* (Sat at 11:30pm) and some hugely popular sitcoms, such as *Friends*, *Frasier* and *Will & Grace*. **ABC** (7) is the king of daytime soaps, working-class sitcoms (*The Norm Show*, *The Drew Carey Show*) and now, primetime game shows (thanks to the remarkable success of *Who Wants to Be a Millionaire*). **Fox-WNYW** (5) is popular with younger audiences for hip shows like *Malcolm in the Middle*, *King of the Hill* and *The X-Files*.

Among the other networks, **UPN-WWOR** (9) and **WB-WPIX** (11), don't attract as huge of an audience but have some offbeat programming including *Buffy the Vampire Slayer*, *Dawson's Creek*, *Felicity*, *The Beat* and *Star Trek: Voyager*. There are also two Spanish language channels, **WXTV** (41) and **WNJU** (47). Offering Mexican dramas and titillating game shows, these are also your best bet for soccer.

Public TV

You'll find public TV on channels 13, 21 and 25. Documentaries, arts shows and science series alternate with *Masterpiece Theatre* and reruns of British shows like *Inspector Morse* and *Poirot* (in *Mystery!*). Channel 21 broadcasts *ITN World News* daily at 7pm and 11pm.

Cable

(Note: All channel numbers listed are for Time Warner Cable in Manhattan. In other locations, or for other cable systems—such as RCN and Cablevision—check listings.) For music videos, there is the old standby **MTV** (Channel 20) and its more conservative sibling **VH1** (19). The latter airs the popular *Behind the Music* series, which delves into the lives of artists like Vanilla Ice and the Partridge Family. Sports fans have **ESPN** (28), **ESPN2** (29), **MSG** (Madison Square Garden, 27) and **Fox Sports** (26). **CNN** (10), **MSNBC** (43), **Fox News Channel** (46) and **NY1** (1) offer news all day, the last with a local focus. **C-SPAN** (38) broadcasts the floor proceedings of the U.S. House of Representatives and an array of scintillating public-affairs seminars.

Comedy Central (45) is your stop for 24-hour laughs, with hits like the raunchy cartoon *South Park* (Wednesdays at 10pm), plus a glut of stand-up and nightly reruns of classic *Saturday Night Live* shows, starring the young Eddie Murphy, Mike Myers, et al. **TNT** (3), **TBS** (8), and **USA Network** (23) offer a potpourri of quality reruns (*ER*) and feature films. **E!** (24) is "Entertainment Television," a mix of celebrity and movie news. This is where you'll find New York icon Howard Stern conducting hilariously intrusive interviews and such tabloid TV as *E! News Daily* and the unmissable *E! True Hollywood Story*, which profiles the likes of Mr. T and the Brat Pack.

Bravo (64) shows the kind of arts programs public TV would air if it could afford them, including *Inside the Actors Studio*, a good number of quality art-house films, and repeats of classic series like *Moonlighting* and *Twin Peaks*. **A&E** (16) airs the shallow but popular *Biography* documentary series, and **Lifetime** (12) is "television for women." The **Discovery Channel** (18) and the **Learning Channel** (52) feature science and nature programs, and show gruesome surgeries, while **Nickelodeon** (6) presents programming more suitable for kids and nostalgic fans of shows like *The Brady Bunch* and *Happy Days*. **Court TV** (51) scores big ratings when there's a hot trial going on. **The History Channel** (17), the **Weather Channel** (36) and **Sci-Fi Channel** (44) are self-explanatory.

Public Access TV is on channels 16, 34, 56 and 57—surefire sources of bizarre camcorder amusement. Late-night on **Channel 35** is where you'll find the *Robin Byrd Show*, a forum for porn stars that's also riddled with ads for escort services and sex lines. Premium channels, often available for a fee in hotels, include **HBO, Showtime, Cinemax, The Movie Channel** and **Disney Channel,** all of which show uninterrupted feature films and exclusive specials.

Tickets

It's always showtime somewhere in New York. And depending on what you're after—music, sports, theater—scoring tickets can be a real hassle. Smaller productions usually have their own in-house box office, which should be contacted directly for seats. Larger venues like Madison Square Garden and Yankee Stadium have a number of ticket agencies—and an equal number of devoted spectators. You may have to try more than one approach to get into a popular or sold-out show.

Box-office tickets

Moviefone

212-777-FILM; www.moviefone.com. 24 hours. AmEx, MC, V. $1.50 per ticket surcharge.
Use this service to purchase advance movie tickets by credit card over the phone and pick them up at an automated teller located in the theater lobby.

Telecharge

212-239-6200; www.telecharge.com. 24 hours. AmEx, DC, Disc, MC, V. $5.75 surcharge per Broadway ticket; $4.75 surcharge per Off-Broadway ticket.
Broadway and Off-Broadway shows are the ticket here.

Ticket Central

416 W 42nd St between Ninth and Tenth Aves (212-279-4200; www.ticketcentral.org). Subway: N, R, S, 1, 2, 3, 9, 7 to 42nd St–Times Sq. 1–8pm. AmEx, MC, V. $4 surcharge.
Off- and Off–Off Broadway tickets are available at the office or over the phone.

Ticketmaster

212-307-7171; www.ticketmaster.com. Call 212-307-4100 for Broadway productions; call 212-307-4747 for Disney productions. 9am–9pm. AmEx, DC, Disc, MC, V.
This reliable service sells tickets to a variety of large-scale attractions: rock concerts, Broadway, sports events and everything in between. A service charge (usually $3 to $8) is added onto each ticket price. You can buy tickets by phone, online or at outlets throughout the city—Tower Records, the Wiz, HMV, J&R Music World and Filene's, to name a few.

TKTS

Duffy Square, 47th St at Broadway (212-221-0013; www.tdf.org). Subway: N, R, S, 1, 2, 3, 9, 7 to 42nd St–Times Sq. Mon–Sat 3–8pm; Sun 11am–7pm. Wed, Sat 10am–2pm and Sun 11am–2pm for matinee tickets. $2 surcharge. Cash or traveler's checks only.
TKTS has become a New York tradition. Broadway and Off-Broadway tickets are sold at a discount of 25 and 50 percent (plus a small service charge); tickets to other highbrow events are also offered. The line can be long, but it's often worth the wait. The TKTS building in Duffy Square is getting a major overhaul (the dates haven't been set), but will remain open during construction.

Other location: *2 World Trade Center mezzanine between Church, Vesey, West and Liberty Sts. Subway: E to World Trade Ctr; 1, 9 to Cortlandt St. Mon–Fri 11am–5:30pm; Sat 11am–3:30pm. Next-day matinee tickets only.*

Scalpers and standby tickets

You needn't give up all hope when a show sells out. There's always the slightly risky scalper option. If you choose to scalp tickets, you won't be able to get your money back if you're scammed—but if you're careful, this can be a reliable way to get into a show. Before you part with any cash, check that the ticket has the correct details. Sometimes scalpers will overestimate demand and, as showtime nears, try to unload their tickets at bargain prices. The police have been cracking down on scalpers in recent years—particularly outside of Madison Square Garden—so be discreet.

Some venues also offer standby tickets right before show time, while others give reduced rates for tickets purchased on the same day as the performance. Those in the know start lining up hours beforehand.

Ticket brokers

Ticket brokers offer much the same service as scalpers, although their activities are much more regulated. It's illegal in New York State to sell a ticket for more than its face value plus a service charge, so these companies operate by phone from other states. They can almost guarantee tickets for sold-out events, and tend to deal only in better seats. Not surprisingly, this is a service you pay for (good seats to the basketball playoffs run close to $1,000). Look under "Ticket Sales" in the Yellow Pages for brokers. Listed below are three of the more established outfits.

Apex Tours

800-CITY-TIX; www.tixx.com. Mon–Fri 9am–5pm; Sat 10am–1pm. AmEx, MC, V.

Prestige Entertainment

800-2GET-TIX; www.prestige entertainment.com. Mon–Fri 9am–6pm; Sat 9am–2pm. AmEx, MC, V.

Sold Out

800-SOLD-OUT; www.soldout.com. Mon–Fri 8am–8pm; Sat 9am–5pm; Sun 10am–3pm. AmEx, MC, V.

Time and date

New York is on Eastern Standard Time, which extends from the Atlantic coast to the eastern shore of Lake Michigan and south to the Gulf of Mexico. This is five hours behind Greenwich Mean Time. Clocks are set forward one hour in early April and back one hour at the end of October. Going from east to west, Eastern Time is one hour ahead of Central Time, two hours ahead of Mountain Time and three hours ahead of Pacific Time. Call 212-976-2828 for the exact time of day.

When writing down a date in the U.S., the order is month, day, year; so 2/5/02 is February 5th, 2002.

Tourist information

Hotels are usually full of maps, leaflets and free tourist magazines that give advice about entertainment and events. But be aware: The advice is not always impartial. Plenty of local magazines (including *Time Out New York*) offer opinionated info.

New York City's Official Visitor Information Center

810 Seventh Ave at 53rd St (212-484-1222; www.nycvisit.com). Subway: B, D, E to Seventh Ave; N, R to 49th St; 1, 9 to 50th St. Mon–Fri 8:30am–6pm; Sat, Sun 9am–5pm.
Leaflets on tours, attractions, etc., plus free advice on accommodations and entertainment, discount coupons and free maps are available at this center run by NYC & Company–the Convention and Visitors Bureau.

Times Square Visitors Center

1560 Broadway between 46th and 47th Sts (212-768-1560). Subway: N, R, S, 1, 2, 3, 9, 7 to 42nd St–Times Sq. 8am–8pm.
Housed in a landmarked movie theater, this comprehensive center offers information, brochures, discount coupons for Broadway tickets, MetroCards, an Internet station and all the usual tourist paraphernalia.

Translation and language services

All Language Services

545 Fifth Ave at 45th St (212-986-1688; fax 212-986-3396). Subway: S, 4, 5, 6, 7 to 42nd St–Grand Central. 24 hours. AmEx, MC, V.
ALS will type or translate documents in any of 59 languages and provide interpreters.

Visas

Under the Visa Waiver Program, citizens of Andorra, Argentina, Australia, Austria, Belgium, Brunei, Denmark, Finland, France, Germany, Iceland, Ireland, Italy, Japan, Liechtenstein, Luxembourg, Monaco, the Netherlands, New Zealand, Norway, Portugal, San Marino, Singapore, Slovenia, Spain, Sweden, Switzerland, the United Kingdom and Uruguay do not need a visa for stays shorter than 90 days (business or pleasure), as long as they have a passport that is valid for the full 90-day period and a return ticket. An open standby ticket is acceptable.

Canadians and Mexicans don't need visas but must have legal proof of their residency. All other travelers must have visas. Full information and application forms can be obtained from your nearest U.S. embassy or consulate. In general, send in your application at least three weeks before you plan to travel. To apply for a visa on shorter notice, contact the travel agent booking your ticket.

For information on student visas, *see* **Customs and immigration,** *page 365.*

U.S. Embassy Visa Information

In the U.S. 202-663-1225; in the U.K. 09061-500-590; travel.state.gov/ visa_services.html.

Websites

Websites come and go with unpredictable frequency. But here are a few old reliables.

www.timeout.com
www.timeoutny.com

For info on all the city has to offer, see the *Time Out New York* site.

eatdrink.timeoutny.com

This *TONY* website is essential for navigating the wilderness of New York restaurants.

www.ci.nyc.ny.us

The "Official New York Web Site" is produced by the folks at City Hall.

www.clubnyc.com

The latest news and grooves on the city's nocturnal scene.

www.ny1.com

New York 1 News's site covers local news, weather and events.

www.nytoday.com

A substantial compilation of news, entertainment, weather and all things New York, courtesy of *The New York Times.*

www.nynetwork.com

A useful list of New York websites.

www.citysearch.com

Up-to-the-minute information on events and entertainment.

www.villagevoice.com

Listings and features from the *Village Voice.*

www.whitehouse.gov

Your connection to the high and mighty in U.S. government.

Further Reading

In-depth guides

Eleanor Berman: *Away for the Weekend: New York.* Trips within a 200-mile radius of New York City.
Eleanor Berman: *New York Neighborhoods.* Ethnic enclaves abound in this food lover's guide.
Arthur S. Brown: *Vegetarian Dining in New York City.* Includes vegan places.
Eve Claxton: *New York's 100 Best Little Places to Shop.*
William Corbett: *New York Literary Lights.* An encyclopedic collection of info about NYC's literary past.
Sam Freund and Elizabeth Carpenter: *Kids Eat New York.* A guide to child-friendly restaurants.
Alfred Gingold and Helen Rogan: *The New Ultra Cool Parents Guide to All of New York.*
Hagstrom: *New York City 5 Borough Pocket Atlas.* You won't get lost with this thorough street map.
Chuck Katz: *Manhattan on Film.* A must for movie buffs who want to take the city by foot.
Ruth Leon: *Applause: New York's Guide to the Performing Arts.* Detailed directory of performance venues.
Sexy New York City 2000: Hot stuff.
Lyn Skreczko and Virginia Bell: *The Manhattan Health Pages.* Everything from aerobics to Zen.
Earl Steinbicker: *Daytrips from New York.*
Time Out New York: *Eating & Drinking 2001.* A comprehensive guide to more than 2,000 places to eat and drink in the five boroughs. Written by food critics.
Where to Wear 2000: A fix for shopoholics.
Zagat: *New York City Restaurants.* The popular opinion guide.

Architecture

Margot Gayle: *Cast Iron Architecture in New York.*
Karl Sabbagh: *Skyscraper.* How the tall ones are built.
Robert A.M. Stern: *New York 1930.* A massive coffee-table slab with stunning pictures.
Robert A.M. Stern: *New York 1960.* Another.
Elliot Willensky and Norval White: *American Institute of Architects Guide to New York City.* A comprehensive directory of important buildings.
Gerard R. Wolfe: *A Guide to the Metropolis.* Historical and architectural walking tours.

Culture and recollections

Candace Bushnell: *Sex and the City.* Smart woman, superficial New York.
George Chauncey: *Gay New York.* New York gay life from the 1890s on.
William Cole (ed): *Quotable New York.*
Martha Cooper and Henry Chalfant: *Subway Art.*
Josh Alan Friedman: *Tales of Times Square.* Sleaze, scum, filth and depredation in Times Square.
Nelson George: *Hip-Hop America.* The history of hip-hop, from the Bronx to Puffy.
Pat Hackett: *The Andy Warhol Diaries.*
A.J. Liebling: *Back Where I Came From.* Personal recollections from the famous *New Yorker* columnist.
Legs McNeil: *Please Kill Me.* Oral history of the city's punk scene in the 1970s.
Joseph Mitchell: *Up in the Old Hotel.* An anthology of the late journalist's most colorful reporting.
Frank O'Hara: *The Collected Poems of Frank O'Hara.* The great NYC poet found inspiration in his hometown.
Andrea Wyatt Sexton (ed): *The Brooklyn Reader.*
Andrés Torres: *Between Melting Pot and Mosaic.* African-American and Puerto Rican life in the city.

Fiction

Paul Auster: *The New York Trilogy.* A search for the madness behind the method of Manhattan's grid.
Kevin Baker: *Dreamland* A poetic novel about Coney Island's glory days.
James Baldwin: *Another Country.* Racism under the bohemian veneer of the 1960s.
Caleb Carr: *The Alienist.* Hunting a serial killer in New York's turn-of-the-century demimonde.
E.L. Doctorow: *The Waterworks.* A tale inspired by Edgar Allan Poe and set in late 19th-century New York.
Bret Easton Ellis: *American Psycho.* A serial killer is loose among the young and fabulous in 1980s Manhattan.
Ralph Ellison: *Invisible Man.* Coming of age as a black man in 1950s New York.
F. Scott Fitzgerald: *The Beautiful and Damned.* A New York City couple squanders their fortune during the Jazz Age.
Larry Kramer: *Faggots.* Hilarious gay New York.
Jonathan Lethem: *Motherless Brooklyn.* An orphan-cum-detective discovers the intricacies of Brooklyn.
Phillip Lopate: *Writing New York.* An excellent eclectic anthology of short stories, essays and poems set in New York.
Toni Morrison: *Jazz.* Music and glamour of 1920s Harlem.
Hubert Selby Jr.: *Last Exit to Brooklyn.* Brooklyn dockland degradation, circa the 1960s.
Betty Smith: *A Tree Grows in Brooklyn.* An Irish girl in 1930s Brooklyn.
Edith Wharton: *Old New York.* Four novellas of 19th-century New York, by the author of *The Age of Innocence.*
Tom Wolfe: *The Bonfire of the Vanities.* Rich/poor, black/white. An unmatched slice of 1980s New York.

History

Irving Lewis Allen: *The City in Slang.* How New York living has spawned hundreds of new words and phrases.
Robert A. Caro: *The Power Broker.* A biography of Robert Moses, the early and mid-20th century master builder in New York, and his political practices.
Federal Writers' Project: *The WPA Guide to New York City.* A wonderful snapshot of 1930s New York by writers employed under FDR's New Deal.
Clifton Hood: *722 Miles: The Building of the Subways and How They Transformed New York.*
Kenneth T. Jackson: *The Encyclopedia of New York City.* The authoritative reference work.
Rem Koolhaas: *Delirious New York.* New York as a terminal city. Urbanism and the culture of congestion.
David Levering Lewis: *When Harlem Was in Vogue.* A study of the 1920s Harlem Renaissance.
Shaun O'Connell: *Remarkable, Unspeakable New York.* The history of New York as literary inspiration.
Jacob Riis: *How the Other Half Lives.* A pioneering photojournalistic record of gruesome tenement life.
Roy Rosenzweig and Elizabeth Blackmar: *The Park and the People.* A lengthy history of Central Park.
Luc Sante: *Low Life.* Opium dens, brothels, tenements and suicide salons in 1840–1920s New York.
Bayrd Still: *Mirror for Gotham.* New York as seen by its inhabitants, from Dutch days to the present.
Mike Wallace and Edwin G. Burrows: *Gotham: A History of New York City to 1898.* The first volume in a planned mammoth history of NYC.

Index

Numbers in **bold** indicate key information on a topic; *italics* indicate photographs.

b

d

Index

Advertisers' Index

Please refer to the relevant pages for addresses and telephone numbers.

Necessities

Entertainment

Maps

Going your way The subway is usually the quickest way to get to your next stop.

O P 86575 TIME OUT GUIDES NEW YORK F 5 SIG 18

Street Index

MANHATTAN

BROOKLYN

QUEENS

Manhattan
Hudson River
TRIBECA
CHINATOWN
BATTERY PARK CITY
BROOKLYN
WEST ST
WEST BROADWAY
CHURCH ST
BROADWAY
CENTRE ST
PARK ROW
VESEY ST
WALL ST
STATE ST
WHITEHALL ST
SOUTH ST
FRANKLIN D ROOSEVELT DR
BROOKLYN BRIDGE
MANHATTAN BRIDGE
THE BOWE
CANAL ST
LISPENARD ST
WALKER ST
WHITE ST
LEONARD ST
WORTH ST
THOMAS ST
DUANE ST
READE ST
CHAMBERS ST
WARREN ST
PARK PL W
MURRAY ST
PARK PL
BARCLAY ST
DEY ST
CORTLANDT ST
LIBERTY ST
CEDAR ST
ALBANY ST
THAMES ST
RECTOR PL
CARLISLE ST
W THAMES ST
THIRD PL
SECOND PL
FIRST PL
MORRIS ST
BATTERY PL
NORTH END AVE
S END AVE
RIVER TERR
VESEY PL
PUBLIC PL
LAIGHT ST
HUBERT ST
BEACH ST
NORTH MOORE ST
FRANKLIN ST
HARRISON ST
STAPLE ST
JAY ST
GREENWICH ST
WASHINGTON ST
BENSON ST
CORTLANDT ALLEY
LAFAYETTE ST
BAXTER ST
MOTT ST
BAYARD ST
PELL ST
PARK ST
HAMILL PL
CARDINAL HAYES PL
FOLEY SQ
ST ANDREWS PLAZA
AVE OF THE FINEST
PEARL ST
ST JAMES PL
OLIVER ST
CATHERINE ST
HENRY ST
MONROE ST
MARKET ST
MADISON ST
PIKE ST
RUTGERS ST
CHERRY ST
FORSYTH ST
DIVISION ST
WATER ST
WAGNER PL
FRANKFORT ST
SPRUCE ST
BEEKMAN ST
ANN ST
FULTON ST
GOLD ST
DOVER ST
PECK SLIP
JOHN ST
BURLING GAP
PLATT ST
MAIDEN LANE
FLETCHER ST
NASSAU ST
PINE ST
FRONT ST
DEPEYSTER ST
HANOVER ST
EXCHANGE PL
BEAVER ST
HANOVER SQ
GOUVERNEUR LA
OLD SLIP
CUYLER'S
COENTIES SLIP
WILLIAM ST
BROAD ST
NEW ST
MARKETFIELD ST
STONE ST
BRIDGE ST
MOORE ST
City Hall Park
City Hall
Foley Square
Confucius Plaza
Eldridge St. Synagogue
Rutgers Park
Woolworth Building
World Trade Center
World Financial Center
Trinity Church
NY Stock Exchange
Bowling Green
Museum of the American Indian
Museum of Jewish Heritage
Castle Clinton
Battery Park
Ferry to Statue of Liberty
Staten Island Ferry Terminal
BROOKLYN-BATTERY TUNNEL
Fraunces Tavern
18 South Street Seaport
19
17
16
15
14
13
11
9
A,C
1,9
A,C,E
N,R
2,3
E
J,M,Z, 4,5,6
J,M,Z, 2,3,4,5
4,5
F
1 2 3 4 5 6
A B C D E F G H J K L M N O P Q R S T U
S
T
U
3
4
5
6
LEGEND
Place of Interest ....
Railroad Station ....
Parks ....
Subway Station ....
Subway Lines .... A,C,E
Area Name .... SOHO
0.4 mile
600 m
© Copyright Time Out Group 2000

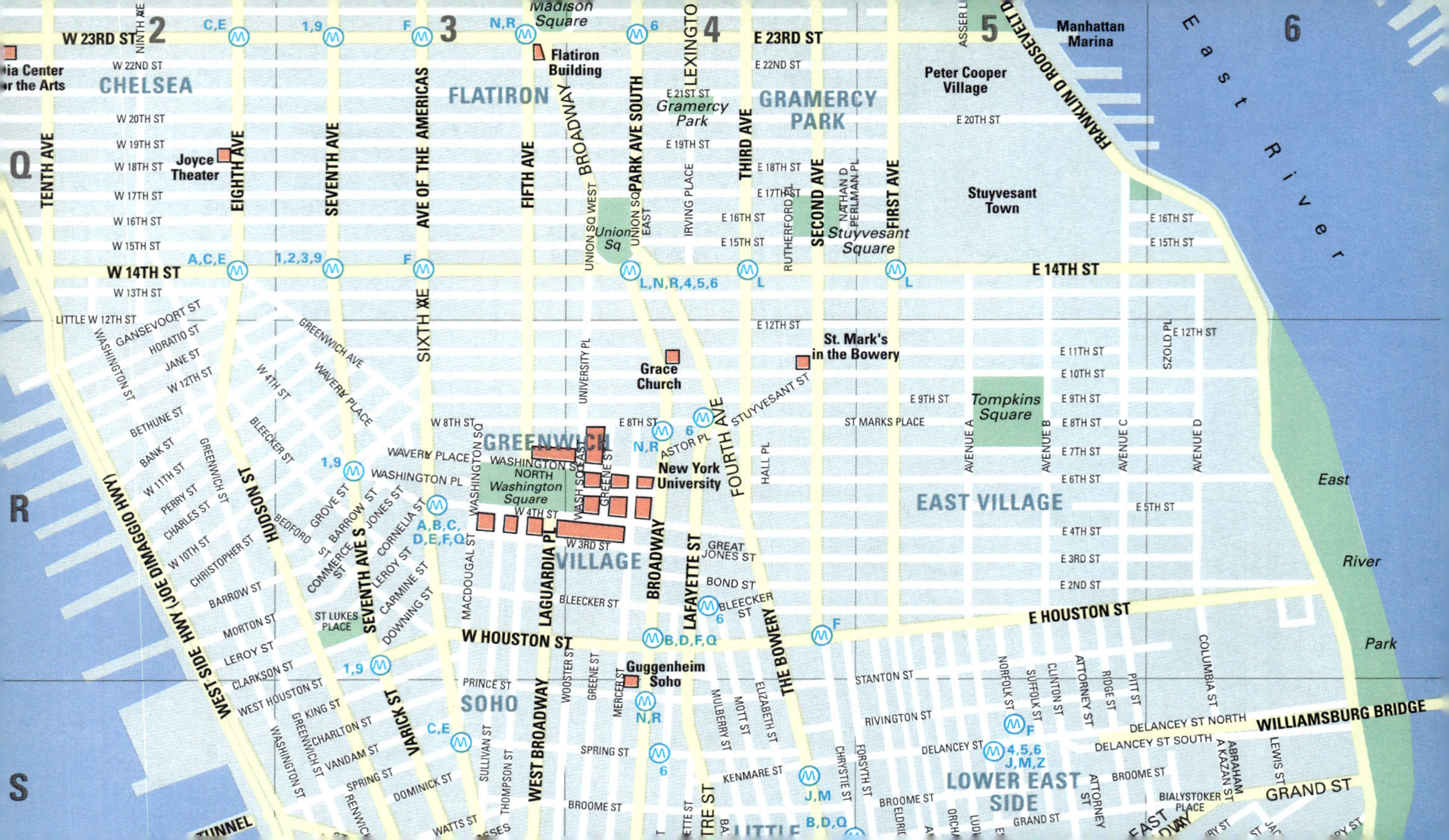

2
3
4
5
6
Q
R
S
CHELSEA
FLATIRON
GRAMERCY PARK
GREENWICH VILLAGE
SOHO
EAST VILLAGE
LOWER EAST SIDE
W 23RD ST
E 23RD ST
NINTH AVE
Madison Square
Flatiron Building
ia Center r the Arts
Manhattan Marina
East River
Peter Cooper Village
Stuyvesant Town
ASSER L
FRANKLIN D ROOSEVELT D
W 22ND ST
E 22ND ST
W 20TH ST
E 20TH ST
W 19TH ST
E 19TH ST
W 18TH ST
E 18TH ST
W 17TH ST
E 17TH ST
W 16TH ST
E 16TH ST
W 15TH ST
E 15TH ST
E 21ST ST
Gramercy Park
Joyce Theater
TENTH AVE
EIGHTH AVE
SEVENTH AVE
AVE OF THE AMERICAS
FIFTH AVE
BROADWAY
PARK AVE SOUTH
LEXINGTO
THIRD AVE
SECOND AVE
FIRST AVE
IRVING PLACE
RUTHERFORD PL
NATHAN D PERLMAN PL
Stuyvesant Square
UNION SQ WEST
UNION SQ EAST
Union Sq
W 14TH ST
E 14TH ST
W 13TH ST
LITTLE W 12TH ST
E 12TH ST
WASHINGTON ST
GANSEVOORT ST
HORATIO ST
JANE ST
W 12TH ST
BETHUNE ST
BANK ST
W 11TH ST
PERRY ST
CHARLES ST
W 10TH ST
CHRISTOPHER ST
BARROW ST
MORTON ST
LEROY ST
CLARKSON ST
WEST HOUSTON ST
KING ST
CHARLTON ST
VANDAM ST
SPRING ST
DOMINICK ST
WATTS ST
GREENWICH ST
WASHINGTON ST
WEST SIDE HWY (JOE DIMAGGIO HWY)
TUNNEL
HUDSON ST
BLEECKER ST
W 4TH ST
GREENWICH AVE
WAVERLY PLACE
SIXTH AVE
W 8TH ST
E 8TH ST
UNIVERSITY PL
Grace Church
St. Mark's in the Bowery
STUYVESANT ST
E 11TH ST
E 10TH ST
E 9TH ST
E 7TH ST
E 6TH ST
E 5TH ST
E 4TH ST
E 3RD ST
E 2ND ST
ST MARKS PLACE
SZOLD PL
Tompkins Square
AVENUE A
AVENUE B
AVENUE C
AVENUE D
East River Park
BEDFORD
GROVE ST
COMMERCE ST
BARROW ST
JONES ST
CORNELIA ST
LEROY ST
CARMINE ST
DOWNING ST
SEVENTH AVE S
ST LUKES PLACE
WASHINGTON PL
WASHINGTON SQ
NORTH Washington Square
WASH SQ EAST
GREENE ST
W 4TH ST
W 3RD ST
MACDOUGAL ST
LAGUARDIA PL
New York University
ASTOR PL
FOURTH AVE
HALL PL
GREAT JONES ST
BOND ST
BLEECKER ST
LAFAYETTE ST
THE BOWERY
W HOUSTON ST
E HOUSTON ST
Guggenheim Soho
PRINCE ST
WOOSTER ST
GREENE ST
MERCER ST
WEST BROADWAY
SULLIVAN ST
THOMPSON ST
VARICK ST
STANTON ST
RIVINGTON ST
MULBERRY ST
MOTT ST
ELIZABETH ST
KENMARE ST
CHRYSTIE ST
FORSYTH ST
BROOME ST
NORFOLK ST
SUFFOLK ST
CLINTON ST
ATTORNEY ST
RIDGE ST
PITT ST
COLUMBIA ST
DELANCEY ST
DELANCEY ST NORTH
DELANCEY ST SOUTH
WILLIAMSBURG BRIDGE
ABRAHAM A KAZAN ST
LEWIS ST
BIALYSTOKER PLACE
GRAND ST
EAST DWY
C,E
1,9
F
N,R
6
A,C,E
1,2,3,9
L,N,R,4,5,6
L
A,B,C, D,E,F,Q
B,D,F,Q
J,M
B,D,Q
4,5,6 J,M,Z

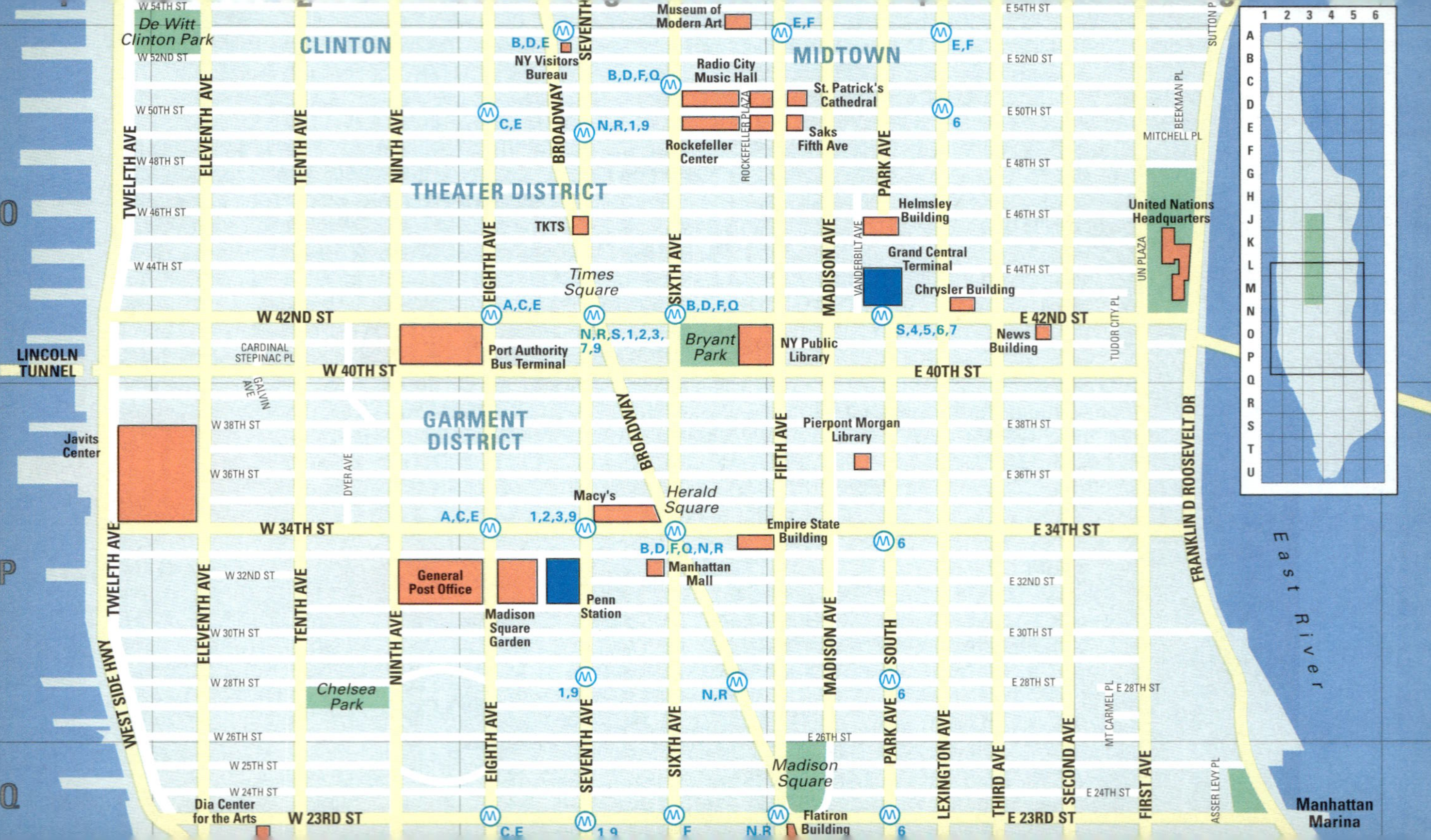

De Witt Clinton Park
W 54TH ST
W 52ND ST
W 50TH ST
W 48TH ST
W 46TH ST
W 44TH ST
CLINTON
B,D,E
NY Visitors Bureau
SEVENTH
Museum of Modern Art
E,F
MIDTOWN
E,F
E 54TH ST
E 52ND ST
E 50TH ST
E 48TH ST
E 46TH ST
E 44TH ST
SUTTON P
B,D,F,Q
Radio City Music Hall
St. Patrick's Cathedral
C,E
N,R,1,9
6
BEEKMAN PL
MITCHELL PL
TWELFTH AVE
ELEVENTH AVE
TENTH AVE
NINTH AVE
BROADWAY
Rockefeller Center
ROCKEFELLER PLAZA
Saks Fifth Ave
PARK AVE
THEATER DISTRICT
Helmsley Building
United Nations Headquarters
TKTS
EIGHTH AVE
SIXTH AVE
MADISON AVE
VANDERBILT AVE
Grand Central Terminal
UN PLAZA
Times Square
Chrysler Building
A,C,E
B,D,F,Q
W 42ND ST
E 42ND ST
TUDOR CITY PL
N,R,S,1,2,3,7,9
S,4,5,6,7
News Building
CARDINAL STEPINAC PL
Port Authority Bus Terminal
Bryant Park
NY Public Library
LINCOLN TUNNEL
W 40TH ST
E 40TH ST
GALVIN AVE
GARMENT DISTRICT
BROADWAY
FIFTH AVE
Pierpont Morgan Library
W 38TH ST
E 38TH ST
FRANKLIN D ROOSEVELT DR
Javits Center
W 36TH ST
E 36TH ST
DYER AVE
Macy's
Herald Square
A,C,E
1,2,3,9
W 34TH ST
Empire State Building
E 34TH ST
6
East River
B,D,F,Q,N,R
TWELFTH AVE
W 32ND ST
General Post Office
Manhattan Mall
E 32ND ST
ELEVENTH AVE
TENTH AVE
Penn Station
Madison Square Garden
MADISON AVE
W 30TH ST
E 30TH ST
NINTH AVE
SOUTH
W 28TH ST
E 28TH ST
1,9
N,R
6
Chelsea Park
MT CARMEL PL
E 28TH ST
WEST SIDE HWY
EIGHTH AVE
SEVENTH AVE
SIXTH AVE
E 26TH ST
PARK AVE
LEXINGTON AVE
THIRD AVE
SECOND AVE
FIRST AVE
W 26TH ST
W 25TH ST
Madison Square
E 24TH ST
ASSER LEVY PL
W 24TH ST
Dia Center for the Arts
W 23RD ST
E 23RD ST
Flatiron Building
Manhattan Marina
C,E
1,9
F
N,R
6
O
P
Q
1 2 3 4 5 6
A B C D E F G H J K L M N O P Q R S T U

1
2
3
4
5
L
M
N
Central Park
UPPER EAST SIDE
HENRY HUDSON PKWY
RIVERSIDE DR
WESTSIDE HWY
FREEDOM PL
WEST END AVE
AMSTERDAM AVE
BROADWAY
COLUMBUS AVE
CENTRAL PARK WEST
CENTRAL PARK SOUTH
FIFTH AVE
MADISON AVE
PARK AVE
LEXINGTON AVE
THIRD AVE
SECOND AVE
FIRST AVE
YORK AVE
EAST END AVE
FRANKLIN D ROOSEVELT DR
QUEENSBORO BRIDGE (59TH ST)
TRAMWAY
W 84TH ST
W 82ND ST
W 80TH ST
W 79TH ST
W 78TH ST
W 76TH ST
W 74TH ST
W 72ND ST
W 70TH ST
W 68TH ST
W 66TH ST
W 64TH ST
W 62ND ST
W 60TH ST
W 59TH ST
W 58TH ST
W 57TH ST
W 56TH ST
E 84TH ST
E 82ND ST
E 80TH ST
E 79TH ST
E 78TH ST
E 76TH ST
E 74TH ST
E 72ND ST
E 70TH ST
E 68TH ST
E 66TH ST
E 64TH ST
E 62ND ST
E 60TH ST
E 58TH ST
W 57TH ST
E 56TH ST
79TH ST TRANSVERSE RD
65TH ST TRANSVERSE RD
WEST DRIVE
EAST DRIVE
Great Lawn
Delacorte Theater
Belvedere Castle
Rose Center
American Museum of Natural History
The Ramble
Loeb Boathouse
The Lake
Bow Bridge
Conservatory Water
The Dakota
Strawberry Fields
Bethesda Terrace
Naumburg Bandshell
Sheep Meadow
Tavern on the Green
Heckscher Playground
The Dairy
Zoo
Wollman Memorial Rink
Lincoln Center
Columbus Circle
Grand Army Plaza
Carnegie Hall
Trump Tower
Goethe House
Metropolitan Museum of Art
Whitney Museum of American Art
Frick Collection
Temple Emanu-El
Bloomingdales
CHEROKEE PLACE
John Jay Park
Schurz Park
GRACIE SQ
GRACIE TERR
Rockefeller University
SUTTON PLACE
Roosevelt Island
1,9
1,2,3,9
B,C
A,B,C,D 1,9
N,R
4,5,6
6
0.3 mile
400 m

J
K
L
of St. John the Divine
Cathedral Close
Park
W 111TH ST
CATHEDRAL PARKWAY
CENTRAL PARK NORTH
1,9
B,C
2,3
6
Riverside
W 109TH ST
Harlem Meer
SPANISH HARLEM
W 107TH ST
Verdi Square
DUKE ELLINGTON BLVD
WEST DRIVE
Park
W 105TH ST
El Museo del Barrio
Conservatory Gardens
Museum of the City of NY
W 103RD ST
W 102ND ST
RIVERSIDE DR
The Pool
EAST DRIVE
COLUMBUS AVE
MANHATTAN AVE
FIFTH AVE
MADISON AVE
PARK AVE
W 100TH ST
W 98TH ST
E 98TH ST
97TH ST TRANSVERSE RD
W 96TH ST
E 96TH ST
Symphony Space
1,2,3,9
Central Park
HENRY HUDSON PKWY
W 94TH ST
WEST END AVE
BROADWAY
AMSTERDAM AVE
CENTRAL PARK WEST
LEXINGTON AVE
THIRD AVE
SECOND AVE
FIRST AVE
FRANKLIN D ROOSEVELT DR
W 92ND ST
Jewish Museum
Cooper-Hewitt National Design Museum
W 90TH ST
HENRY J BROWNE BLVD
The Reservoir
Guggenheim Museum
Soldiers' & Sailors' Monument
W 88TH ST
UPPER WEST SIDE
YORKVILLE
Gracie Mansion
EAST END AVE
W 86TH ST
86TH ST TRANSVERSE RD
E 86TH ST
4,5,6
HENDERSON PLACE
Carl Schurz Park
Great Lawn
W 84TH ST
Metropolitan Museum of Art
Goethe House
W 82ND ST
E 111TH ST
E 109TH ST
E 107TH ST
E 105TH ST
E 103RD ST
E 102ND ST
E 100TH ST
E 94TH ST
E 92ND ST
E 90TH ST
E 88TH ST
E 84TH ST
E 82ND ST
GRACIE SQ
GRACIE TERR
0.3 mile
400 m
© Copyright Time Out Group 2000

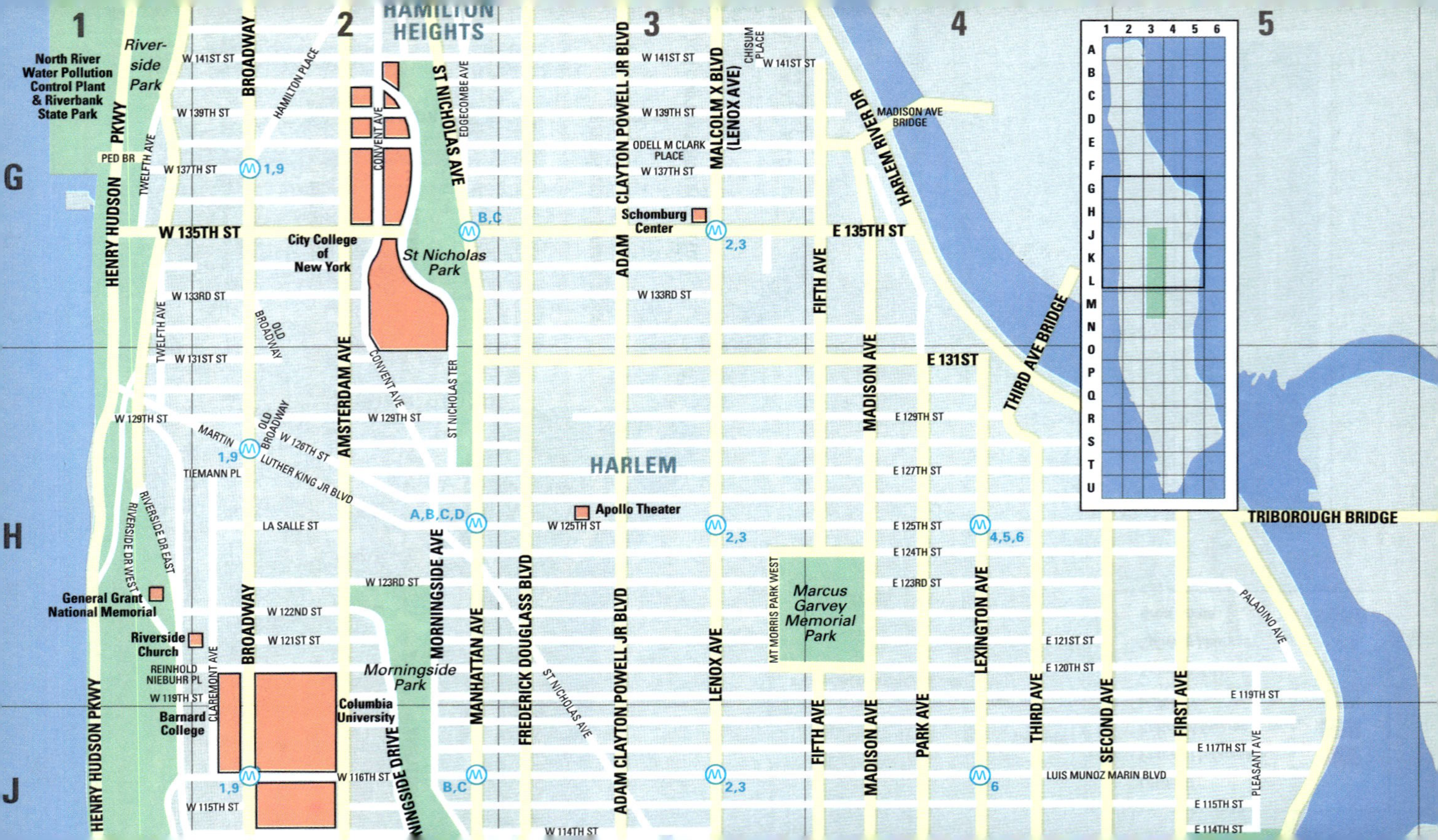

1
2
3
4
5
G
H
J
HAMILTON HEIGHTS
North River Water Pollution Control Plant & Riverbank State Park
River-side Park
HENRY HUDSON PKWY
PED BR
TWELFTH AVE
W 141ST ST
W 139TH ST
W 137TH ST
W 135TH ST
W 133RD ST
W 131ST ST
W 129TH ST
BROADWAY
HAMILTON PLACE
OLD BROADWAY
1,9
CONVENT AVE
City College of New York
St Nicholas Park
ST NICHOLAS AVE
EDGECOMBE AVE
ST NICHOLAS TER
B,C
AMSTERDAM AVE
ADAM CLAYTON POWELL JR BLVD
MALCOLM X BLVD (LENOX AVE)
CHISUM PLACE
ODELL M CLARK PLACE
Schomburg Center
2,3
E 135TH ST
FIFTH AVE
HARLEM RIVER DR
MADISON AVE BRIDGE
MADISON AVE
E 131ST
THIRD AVE BRIDGE
E 129TH ST
E 127TH ST
E 125TH ST
E 124TH ST
E 123RD ST
MARTIN LUTHER KING JR BLVD
W 126TH ST
TIEMANN PL
HARLEM
LA SALLE ST
A,B,C,D
Apollo Theater
W 125TH ST
4,5,6
TRIBOROUGH BRIDGE
RIVERSIDE DR WEST
RIVERSIDE DR EAST
General Grant National Memorial
W 123RD ST
W 122ND ST
W 121ST ST
Riverside Church
REINHOLD NIEBUHR PL
CLAREMONT AVE
W 119TH ST
Barnard College
W 116TH ST
W 115TH ST
W 114TH ST
Columbia University
Morningside Park
MORNINGSIDE AVE
MORNINGSIDE DRIVE
MANHATTAN AVE
FREDERICK DOUGLASS BLVD
ST NICHOLAS AVE
LENOX AVE
MT MORRIS PARK WEST
Marcus Garvey Memorial Park
PARK AVE
LEXINGTON AVE
THIRD AVE
SECOND AVE
FIRST AVE
PALADINO AVE
E 121ST ST
E 120TH ST
E 119TH ST
E 117TH ST
LUIS MUNOZ MARIN BLVD
E 115TH ST
E 114TH ST
PLEASANT AVE
6
A
B
C
D
E
F
G
H
J
K
L
M
N
O
P
Q
R
S
T
U
1
2
3
4
5
6

APOLLO
Manhattan'
Newes
Landmar
HMV: Harlem's first music superst
hip hop • gospel • salsa • blues • rock &
merengue • bachata • reggae • com
2 floors • 15,000 sq. ft. • over 200,000 ti
video • dvd • accessories • ticketmaster • and m
hmv record stores at harlem
125th st between frederick douglass + st. nich
APOLLO
PRESENT
AMATEUR NITE